A Modern Economic History of Africa
Volume 1 : The Nineteenth Century

Paul Tiyambe Zeleza

WITHDRAWN

CODESRIA BOOK SERIES

A Modern Economic History of Africa
Volume 1 : The Nineteenth Century

First published in 1993 by CODESRIA

Copyright © CODESRIA

*HC
800
.245
1993
v. 1*

CODESRIA is the Council for the Development of Social Science Research
in Africa head-quartered in Senegal. It is an independent organisation whose
principal objectives are facilitating research, promoting research-based
publishing and creating multiple fora geared towards the exchange of views
and information among African scholars. Its correspondence address is:
B.P. 3304, Dakar, Senegal.

ISBN   2-86978-026-5 (Cased back)
          2-86978-027-3 (Soft back)

Cover designed by Simon Acquah
Typeset by Marie Therese Coron, CODESRIA
Printed by Antony Rowe
Distributors: ABC, 27 Park End Street, Oxford OX1, IHV

CODESRIA would like to express its gratitude to the Swedish Agency for
Research Cooperation (SAREC), the International Development Research
Centre (IDRC), the Ford Foundation, the Norwegian Ministry of Foreign
Affairs and the Danish Agency for International Development (DANIDA)
for support of its research and publication activities.

Contents

List of Maps

These maps were adapted and drawn by Steve Gardiner, Geography Department, Trent University, Canada; from J F Ade Ajayi and Michael Crowder, *Historical Atlas of Africa*, Longman, Burnt Hill, Harlow 1985. CODESRIA acknowledges with thanks Longman for its permission to use the maps.

Weights and Measures

The following weights and measures are encountered in the text. They are approximations for they tended to vary from place to place and changed over time.

1 frasila = 35 pounds (lbs).
1 legger (leaguers) = 582 litres.
1 ardabb = 180 litres.
1 feddan = 1.038 acres.
1 cantar = 44.928 kg.

Currencies

Maria Theresa Dollars (MT$): For most of the nineteenth century, the MT$ was equivalent to US$1 and 2.125 rupees. Its value against the pound sterling was MT$4.75 until the 1870s, falling to MT$6-6.50 in the early 1890s.

Preface

This study attempts to provide a synthesis of African economic history in the nineteenth century (volume two will examine the twentieth century). Writing a synthesis is an exercise fraught with pitfalls, more so in an era like ours which puts scholarly premium on narrow specialization. Syntheses are suspect as indulgences of naive or retiring scholars, purveyors of simplistic models or grand theories. Many would regard an attempt at providing a synthesis of the economic history of the entire African continent an act of hopeless temerity, for so much remains to be done to fill the gaping holes in our knowledge. Moreover, such an exercise requires linguistic, methodological and analytical skills unlikely to be possessed by any one individual, especially one who is a relatively young scholar.

Notwithstanding these problems, the importance of syntheses cannot be overemphasized. They are a means of taking stock of the academic capital accumulated at various moments in the development of scholarship. Ideally, they provide signposts of where a subject is, and possible directions for future research. As overviews, syntheses place micro-studies in a broader context, and help integrate their findings into a wider body of scholarship. Ignorance of the research results and trends in areas or disciplines outside one's own field of specialization often breeds fatuous generalizations and futile re-inventions of the wheel. Syntheses capture the interconnectedness of social processes and realities often obscured in micro-studies. A synthesis is like a forest that gives shape to the distinctive trees of knowledge. It is not a substitute, but an indispensable complement, of primary and micro-research.

The case for a new synthesis of African economic history is overwhelming. In the last two decades or so a substantial body of literature on the subject has been produced. A lot of this material is hidden in journals, dissertations, monographs, conference papers, and even books that are often inaccessible in African universities, especially since the onset of the 'book famine' from the early 1980s. This study was partly inspired by the need to fill this void, to bring into wider circulation and discourse some of the most enlightening recent studies on various aspects of the African economic past. Second, over the last few years it became increasingly apparent to me that this literature has not been adequately synthesized. As demonstrated in the introduction, the existing syntheses suffer from various degrees of inadequacy. The third motivation for undertaking this study was to counter the excessive preoccupation with micro-studies which, while they have furnished us with innumerable 'facts' essential for historical reconstruction, they have also tended to promote untenable or untestable generalizations because of the disregard for intercontinental comparisons.

Given the enormity of the literature, my reading was necessarily selective. Only the literature in English was consulted. That leaves out very important studies in many other languages, especially French, Arabic and other European and African languages. Needless to say, even of the studies in English I only looked at a relatively small proportion. Consequently, some topics and regions are far better covered than others. Specialists on the areas that have been inadequately dealt with may find that disconcerting, and confirm their conviction that academic athleticism is a treacherous pursuit. But my aim was not to be comprehensive, but to indicate to those unfamiliar with African economic history, non-specialists and students the great advances that have been made in the last two decades in the study of the subject.

Writings on African economic history tend to oscillate between the slippery poles of excessive empiricism and grand generalization. Sometimes the two dovetail into each other, as generalizations are based on one or two case studies. This study seeks to critique both past interpretations and current orthodoxies about the nature and development of African societies and economies in the nineteenth century. It will be demonstrated that these economies were far more complex and diverse than is generally recognized. Unravelling generalizations, myths and stereotypes is an indispensable first step towards a better understanding of our world. The real world is far more complex and fascinating than it often appears through the lenses of abstract theories and models. This is not to suggest that theoretical constructions should be dispensed with. That would leave us with banal empiricism. It is merely to underline the need to constantly engage theories with empirical data, to judge the validity of theoretical paradigms by their power to explain concrete historical processes. This study makes an attempt to do that. It is an exercise in historical reconstruction. It aspires to explain how Africans in the nineteenth century produced and reproduced their material lives. As historians we must try, to paraphrase Soyinka, to 'escape the abstract tyranny of grand theory, so leaving real people now dead some room to dance' (Lonsdale, 1989a:130).

Acknowledgements

I wish to thank the Rockefeller Foundation for funding this study (under the Reflections on Development Fellowship programme grant RF 88075 #43) and the Council for the Development of Economic and Social Science Research in Africa (CODESRIA), through whom the programme in Africa is coordinated, for selecting my proposal on which this work is based. I would also like to thank the two organizations for arranging two conferences, one in Kampala, Uganda, to critically discuss each fellow's original proposal, and the other in Bellagio, Italy, at the Rockefeller Conference and Study Centre, where all the 1990 African and Asian fellows met for two weeks to assess and deliberate on the preliminary findings of their respective research projects.

A special note of thanks goes to the other fellows for their friendship, critical comments and invaluable suggestions. I also benefited from the critiques on the first five chapters of this study offered by a panel of experts brought by the Rockefeller Foundation and CODESRIA to the Bellagio meeting, especially Thandika Mkandawire, Mahmood Mamdani, Micere Mugo, Kodjo Ewusi, Kernial Sandhu, Chai-Anan Samudavanija, Robert Bates, James C Scott, Joyce Moock and David Court.

This study would probably not have been undertaken without the encouragement of friends and colleagues at Kenyatta University, especially Professors B A Ogot, W R Ochieng, M B K Darkoh and Alamin Mazrui. We spent long, happy hours discussing African history, societies and development. We often expressed concern about the fact that African scholars tend to concentrate on primary research and leave the writing of syntheses to Western Africanists. I will always remain grateful for the faith they expressed in my ability to undertake a synthesis of African economic history, a subject I had been teaching for many years. All I can hope for is that they will not be too disappointed by my tentative efforts in this volume to synthesize Africa's economic history in the nineteenth century, and in the next volume on the twentieth century.

In the course of working on this study since October 1989, I have become indebted to numerous librarians and individuals in various countries, universities and institutions. Initial work was conducted at the libraries of Kenyatta University, the University of Nairobi and the United Nations Environmental Programme. In January 1990 I was privileged to spend time working at the excellent library of the United Nations Economic Commission for Africa in Addis Ababa, Ethiopia. The researchers and officials I met in the various divisions of the ECA went out of their way to assist in locating information and discussing various issues with me. In particular, I would like to thank Dr Peter N Mwanza, Director of the Natural Resources Division, for the inordinate amount of time he took facilitating my work at the ECA, Mr Ben Kasamale, Chief of the General Services Section, for arranging the despatch of loads of material that I had collected, and Dr Nancy J Hafkin, the Officer-in-Charge of the Pan African Documentation and Information System (PADIS), for her assistance in locating some important studies and documents.

After Addis Ababa, I spent the next five months at Dalhousie University, N S, Canada, my old Alma Mater. I would like to thank the President of the university and the Head of the History Department for my appointment as a research fellow, and John E Flint for his customary kindness and the use of his office. While at Dalhousie, the Killam Library was the base of my operations.

It was while at Dalhousie that I got my present appointment at Trent University. Since joining the History Department at Trent in July, 1990 I have benefitted from the encouragement of several colleagues, especially Doug McCalla, who took time from his busy schedule as Chair of the History Department and work on Canadian economic history to read and offer incisive comments on parts of the draft. Being so close to Toronto, I took full advantage of the great libraries of the University of Toronto and York University.

To all the librarians and the people who assisted me in one way or another in Nairobi, at the ECA, Dalhousie, Trent, and Toronto, I express my sincerest thanks. I cannot envisage how I would have typed this study without a computer, so I would like to extend my thanks to the Computer Services Department, Trent University, which arranged for the purchase of it.

As always, I feel indebted in a way I cannot express to my wife, Pauline, and daughter, Thasha, for their patience that allowed me to do less than my fair share of the domestic obligations, and for tolerating me when I occasionally seemed more preoccupied with the frustrations of historical writing than the joys of family life.

When I look back, the real inspiration for writing this book came from the students I taught at the University of Malawi, the University of the West Indies, and Kenyatta University. I sensed their frustration at not being able to find a single text that satisfactorily dealt with the economic history of the entire African continent in modern times. Their questions, comments, and essays, did much to focus my thinking, constantly evaluate my interpretations, and deepen my understanding of the African economic past. They will recognize many of my lectures and our tutorial discussions. I hope I have belatedly answered some of their questions and addressed many of their concerns which I was then unable to deal with adequately. And it is my fond hope that they would have found, and may still find, this synthesis useful. It is to these students that this book is dedicated.

Paul Tiyambe Zeleza
February 12, 1992
Peterborough, Ontario

Introduction: Rethinking African Economic History

In the last two decades African economic history has come of age. One only needs to compare the tentative and anaemic reviews on the subject written in the early 1970s (Austen, 1971; Klein, 1972; Alpers, 1973) with the self-assured and comprehensive surveys of the 1980s to see this (Hopkins, 1980, 1988, 1989; Cooper, 1981; Lonsdale, 1981; Freund, 1984a; Berry, 1984; Austen, 1985; Manning, 1989; Isaacman, 1990). In the space of two decades, African economic history has become a vast international enterprise, 'dominated by no single national or methodological tradition' (Hopkins, 1980:154). While this 'heterogeneity has the drawback of permitting a wide range of scholarly standards, ... it also guarantees an openness to new ideas and it acts as a protection against the dominance of a single orthodoxy' (Hopkins, 1980:154). This has made economic historians of Africa 'much more interdisciplinary than other economic historians' (Manning, 1989:53).

Two decades ago African economic history was the poor relation of political history. Now it has become an equal, if not a more privileged, relation. This is partly due to the dominance of the developmentalist discourse in African studies and public policy, and partly because of the unravelling of nationalist historiography (Fyfe, 1976; Gutkind and Waterman, 1977; Bernstein and Depelchin, 1978, 1979; Temu and Swai, 1981; Zeleza, 1983, 1989; Young, 1986; Wamba-dia-Wamba, 1986, 1987; Jewsiecki and Newbury, 1986). Yet, there has not been much communication between economic historians and development economists, policy makers and practitioners, because of their different languages, methodologies, and focus. 'Policy makers (mostly economists by training) work on the period after 1960, while economic historians (mostly historians by training) work on the period before 1960, and neither relies on the work of the other' (Manning, 1989:52). The former tend to see history as antithetical to their effectiveness because of the historians' propensity for 'debunking conventional wisdoms...and undermining the simple faiths and pious illusions that governments require for effective policy making' (Roe, 1987:46). For their part, historians, fearful of compromising their eternal quest for 'objectivity', seek to keep their hands clean of the historicist dirt of development prescriptions.

This chequered relationship between economic historians and development economists has helped neither group. History almost sinks into antiquarianism, while development studies and policies become blind forays into an incomprehensible present. Economic history has much to offer development economics, and certainly it can assist in reducing the incredible naivety that informs much development policies advanced by the development experts, both domestic and foreign, including those sequestered in the ubiquitous international development agencies. As Hopkins (1988) has shown in a perceptive paper on African entrepreneurship, its history is hardly recognized or known within the development community. Consequently, programmes designed to promote entrepreneurship are often based on wrong assumptions and tend to fail. Hopkins (1988:23) concludes that 'a historian is not equipped to recommend solutions to present-day problems, but he can help to ensure that the questions are properly posed... Those who do not know the past may indeed be condemned to relive it; that is their tragedy. But if they also wish the results of unhistorical reconstructions of the past on others, then the innocent suffer too'.

This does not mean all is well with African economic history itself, despite the considerable advances made in the last two decades. This study is, in fact, inspired by a sense of dissatisfaction with the current state of knowledge, especially as reproduced in standard texts and syntheses. All too often, grand generalizations are made about African economic history based on data that is rather narrowly focused geographically, thematically, and historically. The Africa usually analyzed is 'sub-Saharan', 'Tropical' or 'Black' Africa (Munro, 1976; Konczacki, 1977; Freund, 1984, Austen, 1987). Of the major works only Wickins (1981), looks at Africa as a whole. Unfortunately, cocooned in South Africa, he does not seem to have been fully aware of current researches on the subject.

The correlation of Africa with 'sub-Saharan' Africa is based on a racist construct intended to divorce North Africa from the mainstream of African history. As Bernal (1987, 1991) has convincingly demonstrated, this construct was invented in the nineteenth century, an era of unbridled European imperialist arrogance and racism. In this respect, the existing syntheses on African economic history are behind the general histories, such as the UNESCO and Cambridge series, and the works by Curtin, et.al. (1978) and July (1992), which treat Africa as one, albeit a highly differentiated, historical unit. In this study, Africa is taken to refer to the entire continent. Generalizations that purport to be referring to 'Africa' must be abstracted from a reading of Africa history as a whole, rather than partial accounts of regions segmented according to rather dubious geographical or racial considerations.

Thematically, in most of the literature, there is undue emphasis on trade and exchange systems, especially external trade, rather than on the history of production, which would tell us far more about the dynamics of economic, social and political change. The problem can be seen even in works that consciously seek to examine the development of both production and exchange. For example, Hopkins (1973) discusses production in precolonial West Africa in terms of static structure and function. Historical movement only seems to appear with the coming of colonialism. This shortcoming is even more pronounced in Zwanenberg and King's study of Kenya and Uganda (1975). In Austen's (1987) long anticipated, but disappointing, monograph, trade generates a 'developmental impact' first in 'commercial organization' and then brings 'changes in production.' The bias toward trade over production is particularly pronounced among dependency writers, although their conclusion, contrary to that of writers using neo-classical approaches, is that trade had an 'underdevelopmental' impact (Rodney, 1982; Gutkind and Wallerstein, 1976).

Many of the general works also lack historical depth. The precolonial period is often seen as the 'traditional' backdrop to changes introduced by colonialism, despite the ritual attacks historians make against the term 'traditional'. For example, peasants and hired labour are seen as creations of 'colonial capitalism'. No wonder Klein's (1980) collection on peasants in Africa, elegantly subtitled 'Historical and Contemporary Perspectives', has virtually nothing to say about the precolonial period. The same is true of the studies on labour history (Sandbrook and Cohen, 1975; Gutkind, Cohen and Copans, 1978; Stichter, 1985; Freund, 1988).

Much of the writing on socio-economic change in Africa is bedeviled by dichotomous models, in which change is often depicted as the abrupt substitution of one ideal type by its opposite. These dualisms come in all manner of convoluted forms: 'traditional-modern' societies, 'subsistence-market' economies, 'formal-informal' sectors, just to mention some of the most common ones. These dichotomies have a long pedigree in the dualistic conceptualizations of colonial anthropology and development economics (Mafeje, 1976; Streeten, 1984). The persistence of these dichotomous models, and the simplistic generalizations they give rise to, is quite striking.

African economic history has been dominated by three main approaches: neo-classical, dependence and Marxist. Each of these offers partial, and sometimes misleading, analyses of the process and content of economic change and development in Africa in the precolonial era. In fact, the first two paradigms have little to say about precolonial economic history, apart from offering myths and stereotypes, because their concepts are derived from, and are intended to analyze, the operations of capitalism, or relations between advanced capitalist and dependent capitalist formations.

The neo-classical paradigm, with its deductive abstract models, is inherently ahistorical. Neo-classical economists avoided examining the question of growth and development which used to preoccupy the classical economists, and concentrated on the marginalist analysis of market processes and the problems of resource allocation. They constructed universal economic laws, which were independent of time and place. This gave neo-classical concepts an aura of scientific objectivity and ideological neutrality. In reality, these concepts were abstractions from, and rationalizations, if not legitimations, of the capitalist system. Faced with non-capitalist economies, neo-classical concepts had no explanatory power, except to create the false dichotomies mentioned above (Kay, 1975; Dean, 1978; Usoro, 1978; Onimode, 1985).

The dependency approach was born out of dissatisfaction with prevailing neo-classical descriptions, analyses and prescriptions for Third World development, and was inspired by moral indignation against the West and deep pessimism about the development prospects of countries in Latin America, Africa and Asia. But its concepts of 'incorporation', 'unequal exchange', 'development of underdevelopment', and 'centre-periphery', emphasized external economic linkages and tended to ignore internal processes. In fact, like its nemesis, the neo-classical approach, the dependency approach had far more to say about exchange relations than production processes. Also, studies written from the dependency perspective offered little economic history before Africa's, or any society's, 'incorporation' into the world capitalist system, apart from idealized images of 'auto-centric' and 'self-sustaining' development. From the moment of Africa's incorporation, dated to the sixteenth century with the onset of the Atlantic slave trade, African history, like the history of other so-called Third World regions, is often frozen into an unrelenting saga of deepening underdevelopment (Amin, 1974, 1976; Wallerstein, 1974, 1976, 1979, 1980, 1983; Legassick, 1976; Brenner, 1977; Palma, 1978; Warren, 1980; Cooper, 1981; Zeleza, 1983; Harris, 1986; Blomstrom and Hettne, 1988).

Marxist scholars attacked both neo-classical and dependency writers for their theoretical inadequacies, empirical shortcomings, and ideological biases. Specifically, they criticized the two approaches for giving primacy to exchange rather than production relations, their reductionism, and for ignoring class struggles. The Marxists sought to employ their concepts of dialectical and historical materialism, which seek to examine how specific systems originate, develop, function and change in given historical epochs, to unravel Africa's historical realities. But the results have been less than inspiring. It proved difficult to fit Africa into the Marxian modes, whether 'primitive communism', 'slavery', 'feudalism', or the 'Asiatic mode of production'. Similarly problematic were constructions of 'African', 'tributary', and 'lineage' modes of production, all of which have pronounced biases towards mechanisms of surplus appropriation, but are weak on the analysis of the actual organization and control of the labour process, and especially, the mobilization and use of the productive resources themselves. By the mid-1980s the debate on modes of production had become exhausted (Terray, 1972; Hindess and Hirst, 1975, 1977; Asad and Wolpe, 1976; Zwanenberg, 1976; Coquery-Vidrovitch, 1977, 1978; Seddon, 1978; Foster-Carter, 1978; Law, 1978, 1981; Jewsiewicki and Letorneau, 1985; Guy, 1987; Hall, 1987; Suret-Canale, 1988).

Thus, each of the three approaches has its own shortcomings, as well as strengths. Part of the problem has been the eagerness with which scholars construct models and theories, which they then glibly impose over the diverse and complex historical reality that is Africa. Greater care needs to be taken to wed theories to facts, link structures and processes, production and exchange, integrate the relations and forces of production, society and nature, decipher the dialectic between internal and external forces, short-term and long-term trends, and capture the similarities and differences in the patterns of economic change between and within regions in Africa.

This study offers no grand theory or interpretation. Its aims are far more modest. It is informed by the conviction that economic history cannot be reduced to the markets of neo-classical theorists, the world system of the dependency writers, or the modes of production of the Marxists. Economic history is about people, how they produce and reproduce their daily lives in their households, communities, societies, states, regions, and within the continent as a whole. The material and social conditions of production and reproduction are moulded by a complex interplay of nature and society, men and women, rulers and ruled, locals and foreigners, the past and the present.

This study begins with an examination of Africa's environment and demography in the nineteenth century. This seeks not only to reconstruct the patterns of environmental and demographic change and assess their impact on economic transformation and development in various parts of the continent, but also to unravel and critique the methodologies which historians and other social scientists have used in analyzing these processes. African historians have tended to treat the natural environment merely as 'background' upon which historical action developed (Howard, 1976; Ogot, 1979; Sindiga, 1985). They have not taken the environment more seriously because many of them have been wary of environmental and technological determinism. It was not a very long time ago when imperialist historians used to see Africa as a natural wilderness occupied by a people who were as untamed as their environment. Reinforcing the historians' bias against the role of the environment have been Marxist analyses stemming from the Althusserian definition of a mode of production, in which causal primacy is assigned to relations of production rather than the productive forces (Mandala, 1990:8-10).

The two chapters in Part I look at the patterns of climatic change, the ways in which various societies handled these changes, the ecology of disease, population growth, the impact of the slave trade, the processes of migration and immigration, and settlement patterns, especially urbanization. The literature on each of these subjects is now quite vast. However, many of these issues have yet to be fully incorporated into the corpus of African economic history.

Part II contains three chapters on agricultural development, one on the systems of land use, the second on the agrarian relations of production, and the third on the beginnings of colonial agriculture in the Portuguese colonial enclaves of Angola and Mozambique, South Africa and Algeria.

African agricultural history continues to suffer from over-broad generalizations, imprecise comparisons, unwarranted evolutionism, and unsubstantiated assertions (Richards, 1983:24). Entire societies have been, and still are, labelled as 'shifting cultivators', 'hunter-gatherers', or 'pastoralists'. Goody's (1971, 1976) grand but spurious comparisons between Africa's supposedly hoe, land-rich but labour-poor, and Eurasia's plough, land poor but labour-rich, farming systems still attract adherents (Iliffe, 1987:3-14; Hogendorn and Gemery, 1990-91). African agriculture is still described as 'shifting' and African economies characterized as 'subsistence' by many authors (Moran, 1979; Sutton, 1984; Austen, 1987; Coquery-Vidrovitch, 1988), despite persuasive critiques of these concepts by others (McLoughlin, 1970; Hopkins, 1973; Richards, 1983; Hart, 1982 and Richards, 1985). The notion that precolonial Africa was distinctive for its labour-shortage and land-abundance is too simplistic, for as Thornton, (1990-91a:51) points out: 'in the seventeenth century there were large areas of Africa that had high population densities by the standards of the non-Chinese world, and particularly compared to Europe'.

Indeed, this is a notion that tells us 'nothing whatsoever about labour supply and demand in micro terms', of the different labour regimes of poorer and richer households; it is myth created by 'colonial governments and expatriate firms [who] found it so difficult to recruit labour in the early days' (Hill, 1978:128). 'Shifting cultivation', it is implied or categorically stated, was 'backward' compared to the supposedly intensive agriculture of Europe, which is placed on top of the evolutionary ladder of agricultural progress. Not only does this misrepresent and oversimplify the development of agriculture in both Africa and Europe, it also fails to place the highly diversified patterns of land use, and the agricultural techniques and technologies used in each continent, in their ecological and socio-economic context.

In the development literature assertions are common that 'traditional' African agriculture was, and is, unproductive, without clearly specifying the measures of productivity used (Phillips, 1966:75-79). A recent debate amply bears this out. In a major revision of current historiography, Thornton (1990-91b:7-8) has argued that available data clearly suggests 'that African agriculture, even without the plow, was more efficient than that of early modern Europe'. Instead of assessing the evidence presented, Thornton's critics fall back on standard assumptions, clothed in neo-classical theoretical formulations on productivity and efficiency, that this could not have been possible. They argue, quite ahistorically, that since colonial and more contemporary data shows that African agricultural productivity whether in labour, land or other inputs, is lower than in Europe, African agricultural productivity could not have been high in precolonial times (Austen, 1990-91:22; Hogendorn and Gemery, 1990-91:32-33). The latter conclude that 'not enough is known about labour's physical productivity in precolonial Africa to support that it was high relative to other areas such as Europe' (Hogendorn and Gemery, 1990-91:35). Yet, in the same breath they believe they know enough to assert that it 'was lower than elsewhere'. Their case rests on age-old racist stereotypes about Africa. They invoke 'tropical heat and humidity [which] sap human strength', Africa's 'debilitating disease environment, the widespread existence of slavery and slave raiding, the lack of complementary transport and credit facilities, and the shortage of physical capital' (Hogendorn and Gemery, 1990-91:33,35). For Austen (1990-91:24) and Manning (1990-91:28-29) the best demonstration that African agricultural productivity was low was the Atlantic slave trade. Africa had nothing better to export than its people. This is a pathetic apologia of the slave trade.

It can be seen that technology, especially ploughs, environmental conditions, labour-land ratios, and the slave trade, have been used as proxy measures or explanations of the alleged low levels of agricultural productivity in precolonial Africa. These arguments tell us little about the actual dynamics and development of African agriculture. This debate and the comparisons between African and European agriculture has three problems.

First, the comparisons are imprecise. Different periods are compared: precolonial African agriculture is compared to modern European agriculture, rather than European agriculture of the same period. The result is to 'both understate the strength of the African economy and overstate the modernity and productivity of the European economy' (Thornton, 1990-91a:50). These comparisons emphasize the environmental and other difficulties which African agriculture faced, forgetting that at this time European peasants also faced environmental problems, vicious diseases, low life expectancy and high levels of infant mortality, savage exploitation, and the fact that many were too poor to use plows (van Bath, 1963; Kerridge, 1968; Abel, 1980).

Second, the comparisons are meaningless in so far as African and European peasants worked in extremely varied environments and contexts. What was at issue for African peasants 'was production relative to their own needs and resources, not to those of Europe. And since it is the human decision-making process in historical context that we are seeking to understand, it is African producers' assessments of their success in achieving desirable, «efficient» production that are relevant' (McDougall, 1990-91:38). This points to the third problem that has bedeviled African studies since their inception, namely, a false universalism, constructed from idealized European conditions, against which Africa is constantly compared, and which forces African scholars, to 'waste time tilting at windmills to find out why we deviate from these patterns instead of finding out what our own patterns and realities are' (Mama and Imam, 1990:20-21; Zeleza, 1992).

It is remarkable how racist and imperialist conceptions of African economies and societies constructed during the slave trade era and the colonial period persist, repackaged and re-labelled to fit currently fashionable discourses. For example, most so-called radical analysts of the 1970s and 1980s, including those of Marxist persuasion, despite their customary invocations on the importance of understanding the dynamics of precolonial economies or pre-capitalist social formations on their own terms, rested on a bedrock of old interpretations principally drawn from anthropological orthodoxies (Chanock, 1977; Cameroff, 1982). Many of them used the notional baseline of 'subsistence' economy, and agrarian change was perceived as movement away from this 'natural' economy to either a modern 'cash economy' or into the clutches of underdevelopment. So agrarian change, even the creation of the peasantry itself, is seen as the product of the introduction of colonial markets, in the language of neo-classical economic historiography, or of Africa's incorporation into the world capitalist economy, in the terminology of dependence and world systems approaches.

Many writers have resisted calling African farmers 'peasants', preferring to label them 'husbandsmen', 'protopeasants', 'traditional peasants', 'traditional agriculturalists', 'subsistence cultivators', 'emergent farmers', or simply 'tribesmen', cultivators, or herdsmen, because they do not seem to conform to the European model where peasants had landlords, to whom they paid rent, and they produced for the market (Reining, 1970; Post, 1972;

Welch, 1977; Silberfein, 1977; Bernstein, 1979; Klein, 1980; Hesselberg, 1985). Never mind that peasants in northern Africa, along the Nile valley, Ethiopia, the interlacustrine regions of eastern Africa and the emirates of northern Nigeria, just to mention the most obvious cases, did all these things. The problem is that African peasants entered intellectual discourse through the discipline of colonial anthropology, with its ahistorical methodologies and eternal fascination with 'exotic', 'closed', and small-scale societies. In anthropological constructions, or invented traditions, to borrow Ranger's (1989) term, African farmers looked like 'primitive' cultivators living in self-sufficient, kin-based communities impervious to change. The myths of 'traditional' society and 'subsistence' economy were born.

It was said that as 'subsistence' cultivators, African farmers could not be considered peasants, for peasants produce primarily for the market (Dalton, 1967). Others were prepared to upgrade those African farmers who partly produced for the market to the hallowed league of peasants (Middleton, 1966). Producing for the external market became the definitional key (Wolff, 1966). The radical scholars of the 1970s and 1980s, in spite of their fulminations against colonial anthropological orthodoxies, based their elegant paradigms on the same orthodoxies. All they did was to coin new words to describe the same old wine. The external market was substituted with capitalism. History was brought in, but it was the truncated history of dependency theory. African peasantries, it was claimed, developed as a result of Africa's incorporation into the world capitalist system (Saul and Woods, 1979). Since capitalism was implanted during the colonial period, it followed that the African peasantry was created, or at least bred, by colonial capitalism. The search was on for the rise, and in the case of the settler colonies such as South Africa, Zimbabwe and Kenya, the eventual fall, of the peasantry (Bundy, 1979; Palmer, 1977; Atieno-Odhiambo, 1974). The term 'peasantization' was coined to describe the process.

Forgotten in all these grand constructions was the simple fact that peasantries elsewhere, for example in Europe and Asia, antedated capitalism, the modern world system or colonialism. Some conceded that historically, peasant agriculture was a precapitalist mode of production even though it continued to exist in capitalist formations (Boesen, 1979). But the argument was soon turned on its head. The peasant mode of production, Hyden (1980, 1983) discovered, has an 'economy of affection', which is inherently antagonistic to market relations, pressures or incentives. He postulated that Africa's contemporary agrarian crisis is rooted in 'the hold that the economy of affection has over African society' (Hyden, 1983:25). This paradigm is not only too holistic and reductionist to capture the diversity of peasant social solidarities and relations, it is also static and lacks analytic precision (Mamdani, 1985; Lemarchand, 1989). It ignores the fact that manifestations of the so-called moral economy or economy of affection in present-day Africa may not really be relics from the 'traditional' past, but could represent the contemporary forms of capitalist production and reproduction (Watts, 1983; Zeleza, 1986). Counterpoised to Hyden's moral economy model is the equally simplistic rational choice model advocated by Bates (1983, 1986, 1988).

With Hyden's formulation there was danger that the clock would be set full circle back to the anthropological simplicities of 'traditional', 'subsistence' Africa. As the debate on the peasantry got bogged down in sophistry and circumlocutions, Cooper (1980:312) was driven to call for 'a long moratorium on the use of the words «peasantization»... Not only is the use of such words an act of violence against language, but they pose a danger to thought processes as well.' Cooper's call may have been heeded, for in the 1980s new studies emerged showing the immense diversity in African peasant production systems due to variations in environmental conditions, state formations and processes of commodity production (Kea, 1982; Richards, 1983; Thornton, 1983). Researchers also became increasingly receptive to peasant voices and supplemented their archival findings with oral data to begin reconstructing a rich tapestry of peasant experiences (Bradford, 1987; White, 1987; Keegan, 1988; Cohen and Atieno-Odhiambo, 1989, van Onselen, 1990). As they saw peasants up close, rather than from the exalted position of grand theory, researchers discovered that peasants were not inertly conservative. They were not only capable of generating scientific and technological innovation (Berry, 1974; Martin, 1984; Richards, 1985), but they also struggled against predatory external forces that sought to exploit them (Crummey, 1986a). Rural struggles were not confined to the episodic eruptions of peasant rebellions during times of crisis but were woven into the texture of everyday life as peasant communities, households, and members of households, struggled over the control of and access to critical resources and the appropriation of the surplus product (Isaacman, 1976, 1977; Scott, 1985; Ranger, 1986; Beinart and Bundy, 1987; Watts, 1988).

Despite many of their insights, most of these studies have not paid enough attention to peasant labour processes and gender relations (Isaacman, 1990:23-30). Labour studies have tended to concentrate excessively on slavery, partly based on the untenable assumption that 'slaves rather than peasants were the primary source of surplus and the most important form of investment in those societies more involved in market relations' (Klein, 1980:13). The vast majority of Africa's peoples in the nineteenth century did not reproduce themselves through the use of slave labour, so any talk of slave modes of production is hollow. It is encouraging to note, however, that some recent work has begun to correct these deficiencies (Mandala, 1990).

Chapter 4 examines the changing relations of production in nineteenth century African agriculture, where the question of the sexual division of labour in agriculture is also discussed. Gender analysis is in fact incorporated throughout the study, for gender roles played a central role in the organization of production. The literature on women in Africa has grown enormously in the last two decades (Pellow, 1977; Walker, 1987; Geiger, 1987; Wipper, 1988; Hay, 1988). There have been important shifts in emphasis, from a preoccupation with what Hay (1988) calls the heroines, the queens of politics and commerce, to the victims, the prostitutes, domestic workers and slaves, and more recently on women as producers, especially as peasants. Unfortunately, these studies practice the same academic apartheid of dividing North Africa from their beloved sub-Saharan Africa (Johnson-Odim and Strobel, 1988).

Moreover, much of this work covers the colonial and post-colonial periods. When the precolonial period is examined, the objective is often to contrast it positively or negatively with the colonial period. At one time, it was believed that colonialism liberated African women from the shackles of 'traditional' oppression (Klingshirn, 1971). Now, the consensus is that colonialism undermined women's position and power. In Qunta's (1987: chapter 1) exposition, with colonial conquest African women fell from the grace of matriarchal egalitarianism into the patriarchal clutches of imperialist, racist, class and sex oppression. Both interpretations oversimplify the social processes of gender construction in African history. We are still very far from getting a full picture of the historical experiences of African women producers during the precolonial era. For example, most of the papers in the collections by Hafkin and Bay (1976), Bay (1982), Hay and Stichter (1984), Robertson and Berger (1986), Stichter and Parpart (1988), Parpart and Staudt (1989) have little to say about the precolonial era, except to offer the obligatory genuflections on women's roles in 'traditional' Africa. It is as if gender roles in precolonial Africa remained static until the coming of colonial rule.

This often results in untenable generalizations. In her analysis of women in the rural economy, Henn (1984:1-2), for example, tells us that 'food farming systems in pre-colonial Africa was almost everywhere a system of shifting hoe culture' and proceeds to divide the continent into regions of 'women's farming systems', 'men's farming systems' and 'mixed farming' systems. This not only misrepresents the nature of African agriculture, it also oversimplifies and freezes what were dynamic processes of gender differentiation in the agricultural labour process. Equally simplistic and over-schematic is White's (1984:55) assertion that 'people who practised intensive hoe agriculture tended to be matrilineal'. The evidence suggests that 'intensive' agriculture cut across a wide range of family forms. Robertson's (1984:14) contention that the 'hierarchical organization of labour recruitment and control prevailed in much of sub-Saharan Africa in various forms and can be offered as one explanation for the technological lag whereby neither the plough nor the wheel were adopted, even though some African societies had early contact with other societies which used them', betrays a lack of understanding of the relationship between agricultural technology and environmental conditions. Her concept of the 'corporate kin mode of production' is a poor attempt at theorizing.

Inadequate theories in fact mar the few works that do discuss gender relations in precolonial societies in some detail. Many of the theories are often based on highly stylized anthropological 'facts' on the nature of kinship and households. Kinship is often taken as a given, rather than explained, or rather problematised (Bernstein and Depelchin, 1979:34). Early evolutionary models contrasted the 'backward' extended family systems of Africa and the 'advanced' nuclear conjugal units of Europe, forgetting that the latter was itself a relatively late historical development (Stone, 1979). Indeed, the wide range of family structures in both Africa and Europe made a mockery of the typological and unilineal view. In short, the classificatory labels could not withstand the glare of empirical scrutiny and historical research (Netting, et.al, 1984).

Households are complex social units, whose forms and functions, divisions of labour and struggles, size and composition vary enormously cross-culturally and intra-culturally, and change over time, so that attempts to offer universalistic definitions of households in terms of such factors as coresidence, commensality, joint ownership, pooling of income, and shared companionship is not very useful (Oppong, 1981). Household morphology, practices and ideology change or adapt to changing economic, political, or ecological circumstances (Smith, 1984, et.al., 1984; Mafeje, 1991). Patterns of intra-household relations also vary greatly within and between social classes, cultural groups, and social formations and change over time (Moock, 1986). In short, the nature of households should not be established a priori, but concretely investigated, because households constitute complex aggregations of interacting productive and reproductive processes, residential patterns and ideological practices. 'All the evidence suggests', Guyer (1981:104) maintains, that terms like household 'indicate problems to be explored and not analytical concepts to be applied in a rigid fashion'.

Part III looks at mining and manufacturing, and examines the technologies and techniques employed, as well as the relations of production. The history of mining and manufacturing in Africa has been haunted by diffusionist models, whereby attempts are made to trace the external origins of certain technologies and their eventual adoption or lack of it in Africa. The hindrances to technology transfer have been blamed variously on ecological variables or the continent's (read sub-Saharan) 'isolation'. Austen and Headrick (1983:172) find these explanations wanting, but offer alternative explanations drawn from colonial racial anthropology and psychology. They attribute Africa's alleged 'technological conservatism' to 'economic strategies favouring risk aversion over profit maximization; broader world views which suppress innovation; lack of literacy; preference for political and military rather than economic solutions to social problems; and patterns in the sexual division of labour and child-rearing practices.' The banality of their argument is thrown into sharp relief when they examine African child-rearing practices, which they obviously know nothing about. They argue that in Africa 'child-rearing is human-energy-intensive and anti-materialistic. For the growing child, the results are a high degree of interpersonal relations but less experience in manipulating the physical world than one finds among European children' (Austen and Headrick, 1983:174). This is racist clap-trap.

While many historians do not sink this low, it is widely assumed that African mining and manufacturing technologies were 'backward' (Goody, 1971; Johnson, 1978a:15; Miller, 1988:78-81). This position is also advanced by the dependency writers who, however, attribute the underdevelopment of African manufacturing industries to the Atlantic slave trade (Rodney, 1982:chapter 4; Inikori, 1982, 1983). In contrast, Gemery and Hogendorn (1978) celebrate the technological innovations brought by the slave trade, especially the widespread adoption of firearms which improved 'slave gathering'.

Thornton's (1990-91a, 1990-91b) intervention provides a useful correction against these prevalent views. He argues, using the reports of contemporary European travellers in Africa and the findings of archaeologists, that African metallurgy and textile manufacturing were far more advanced than has been recognized. Large quantities of metals and textiles were produced. Indeed, by the standards of the seventeenth or eighteenth century world, he concludes, African metalworkers and textile manufacturers were producing their goods at the same or higher levels of productivity as their European counterparts. For example, Leiden, one of the leading European centres of textile production which had almost the same population as Momboares in the eastern Congo, produced about 100,000 metres of cloth per year in the early seventeenth century, as compared to 300-400,000 metres in Momboares (Thornton, 1990-91b:12-14). Not only were these products traded widely within the continent by African merchants, as well as European merchants along the West African coast, African textiles were exported to the Caribbean and South America (Johnson, 1978a:263; Thornton, 1990-91a:53).

The question of whether or not African mining and manufacturing industries declined in the nineteenth century in the face of external, especially European, competition needs to be more carefully assessed. Chapters 6 and 7 argue that the contention of both neo-classical and dependency writers that the local industries could not compete is too simplistic. Growing levels of imports from Europe, on which the contention of African uncompetitiveness is based, did not automatically imply that local production was declining. African societies were neither autarchic, nor were African consumers content with mere subsistence. Imports of textiles, for example, had a lot to do with expansion of the market and changes in fashion. Recent studies have demonstrated that African mining and manufacturing industries proved far more resilient than has been generally recognized (Johnson, 1978a; Goucher, 1981; Pole, 1982; Thornton, 1990, 1990-91b). The balance between decline and survival varied according to the intensity of foreign competition and the organization of local production. The last section of Chapter 7 examines attempts by African societies to industrialize and examines the familiar case of Egypt and the less familiar one of Madagascar. Chapter 8 focuses on the beginnings of colonial industrialization in Southern and West Africa.

The greater part of this study, unlike most previous syntheses, examines the development of productive forces and production processes and relations. The last two sections, Part IV and Part V, analyze trade and the question of Africa's incorporation into the world system. Part IV has four chapters on the development of domestic and regional trade in all the major regions of the continent. The subject of trade was once dominated by the subtantivist-formalist debate, in which the substantivists interpreted 'primitive' economic behaviour in terms of the non-economic norms of reciprocity and redistribution, while the formalists focused on the overriding importance of market forces in regulating economic behaviour (Gislain, 1987). The controversy, as Curtin (1984:14) has noted, was not 'especially enlightening', for it needs to be recognized 'that both market and other forms of exchange have a role to play. The problem is to measure the influence of each in specific situations'.

In spite of these admonitions, and the considerable advances that have been made in the study of African exchange systems, the substantivist ghosts of economic anthropology have not been entirely banished. African trade, markets and currencies are still tainted with the brush of exotica. Some continue to portray them as pale imitations of the 'real' trade, markets, and currencies of western Europe. As late as the 1980s Wickins (1981:116) and Austen (1987:20-21) could still argue that internal exchange in Africa was limited because of the predominance of poor production methods, transport bottlenecks and low population densities. Exchange was largely confined to exchanges between communities occupying different ecological zones, and reflected social rather than market relations. This 'subsistence trade', as Gray and Birmingham (1970) once called it, was only transformed into 'marketed-oriented trade' with Africa's integration into international trade networks.

Discussing trade solely in terms of ecological zones is as simplistic as analyzing it in terms of ethnic groups, for neither constitutes a production unit, but refers to spatial entities and ideological constructs. African societies and communities were fluid aggregates of households which were rarely self-sufficient. Austen's distinction between social and economic values is too contrived, as Hopkins (1973:52-53) observed almost two decades ago.

The substantivist argument that social rather than economic motives, redistribution and reciprocity rather than trade and commerce characterized precolonial African exchange systems was popularized by the Bohannans (1955, 1968, 1969) and Bohannan and Dalton (1965), who distinguished between societies that have either market place or market principle, or one of the two, or neither. They concluded that most African societies had market places but did not operate on market principles, an argument repeated as recently as 1988 (Bohannan and Curtin, 1988:169-89; also see Dalton, 1978). In the 1970s, historians of Tiv society, on which the model was built, queried the methodology the Bohannans had used. For example, Latham (1971:600-1) showed convincingly that their analysis of the Tiv copper rod currency as a 'primitive rationing system', rather than a 'general purpose currency' was based on information 'gathered after the rod had ceased to be used widely in exchange'. Doward (1976:589) developed the argument further by noting that 'in their preoccupation for the subsistence aspect of the Tiv economy, the Bohannans failed to grasp the significance of' production for sale because, 'they never observed the «traditional» Tiv economy, did not have access to or were unaware of the relevant documentation'. Hopkins (1973:52-53) concluded that the distinction between market place and market principle is based on ideal types rather than historical realities, and proceeded to demonstrate Goody's (1971:23-24) argument that 'the concept of non-monetary economics is hardly applicable to precolonial Africa'. Recent monetary studies have amply borne this out (Webb, 1982; Hogendorn and Johnson, 1986). However, Hopkins' (1973) distinction between local and long-distance trade was problematic. The key differentiation was based on the distance a trader could travel in a day to and from the market. The organizational differences between local and long-distance trade remained rather fuzzy. Certainly there was little evidence that local trade was restricted to local products.

In this study, a distinction is made between domestic and foreign trade. Admittedly, this framework can be more usefully applied to state societies where some kind of national economic space was constructed. Chapters 9 to 12 clearly demonstrate that the patterns of trade organization varied and changed considerably in the course of the nineteenth century, and underscores the inadequacies of many of the generalizations that are often made about African precolonial economies. Apart from examining the conventional issues of markets and money, the chapters incorporate some of the recent work on the formation of merchant classes and the development of groups of transport workers, who played such a vital role in the expansion of commercial networks.

Finally, Part V dwells on Africa's international trade and imperialism. It is shown that there was an enormous expansion in the volume of trade between Africa and Europe, although there were considerable differences between the various regions. The commodities traded varied, notwithstanding the fact that each region increasingly exported a narrow range of raw materials and largely imported manufactured goods. The impact of the imports on the local economies also varied depending on each region's domestic socio-economic and political structures. In short, the patterns and processes of incorporation into the world capitalist system differed significantly from one region to another. Perhaps the most deeply integrated regions by the mid-nineteenth were North and West Africa, which are therefore examined in separate chapters. The incorporation of Central, Southern and Eastern Africa accelerated during the second half of the century. The differentiated processes of incorporation were also reflected in the varied patterns of colonization, which conditioned the subsequent development of colonial capitalism.

By 1870, the vast part of Africa was still free of foreign control. There was little to indicate that this was about to change. Indeed, according to Boahen (1987a:23), the continent, recently freed from the scourge of the slave trade and the revolutionary wars of the first half of the century, 'was in a mood of change and revolution, accepting new challenges, showing ability at adaptation and modification, fighting back against racist doctrines, and above all changing its economy and politics to suit the socioeconomic realities of the day.' The Scramble came, with sudden, unpredictable, and merciless fury. By 1914 the entire continent, except Ethiopia, which salvaged its independence from the teeth of Italian defeat, and Liberia, an American dependency, had been partitioned and fallen into the clutches of European colonial rule (Boahen, 1987b). What happened, why, and what were the consequences? These questions have preoccupied African historians and intellectuals ever since. The questions have remained as simple as ever, but the answers have proved more elusive.

The partition of Africa is normally discussed in connection with the 'new imperialism'. The temporal and structural linkages between the two appear obvious at first sight. The only problem is that neither term, the partition nor imperialism, lends itself easily to definition, for both describe complex processes. The term imperialism is particularly vexatious. Like beauty, its meaning is in the eye of the beholder. It has mutated beyond recognition since the time it first entered the English language 'as a gloss on [Napoleon's] regime which had been established in France' (Koebner and Schmidt, 1964:1).

To Hobson, whose book Imperialism: A Study did much to popularize the term 'imperialism', the 'new imperialism' referred to the colonization of tropical and sub-tropical lands. He believed that the 'new imperialism' was bad for Britain as a whole, but profitable to certain trades and classes, especially the financiers, for whom colonies offered profitable outlets for surplus capital, that is capital that could not be profitably invested at home, thanks to the underconsumption of the workers. It followed that if underconsumption could be removed the tap-root of imperialism could be removed.

For Lenin, who acknowledged his indebtedness to Hobson in his monograph Imperialism: The Highest Stage of Capitalism, this line of reasoning represented liberal reformism. Imperialism, in his view, marked an actual stage in the evolution of capitalism, the highest stage, the monopoly stage that would eventually give way to socialism. So for Lenin, colonialism was simply one characteristic of imperialism. The other features included the rise of monopolies, the emergence of finance capital, the export of capital and the division of the world among capitalist associations.

Thus two traditions emerged in the historiography of imperialism. Following Hobson's footsteps the liberal tradition tended to equate imperialism with colonialism, and the Marxist tradition came to see imperialism as the global expansion of capitalism. For the latter it became an article of faith that imperialism was essentially driven by economic forces, while for the former the importance of economics receded the further removed the writers were from Hobson and the more they debated the Marxists.

The demotion of economic forces in the liberal tradition as explanatory factors was assured once underconsumption, the linchpin of Hobson's thesis, could be disproved empirically or theoretically. Schumpeter argued in his influential essay, Imperialism and Social Classes, that there was nothing 'new' about the 'new imperialism'. Imperialism was as old as human society, a product of persistent tendencies toward war and conquest, of attitudes which are deeply encrusted in the mentality of the warrior classes. The 'new imperialism' had nothing to do with capitalism. Indeed, capitalism is antithetical to imperialism, for it thrives best with peace and free trade. The revival of imperialism represented the resurgence of atavistic instincts and interests, made possible by a peculiar and an 'unnatural alliance' between a declining but still powerful 'war-oriented' nobility and a rising, but not yet dominant, bourgeoisie. He located this 'unnatural alliance' in Central Europe, thereby removing the Western European powers, including Britain and France, and those across the Atlantic, the United States, from the scourge of imperialism.

After Schumpeter the scramble was on for non-economic explanations. Some reduced imperialism to diplomatic squabbles among the great powers. The partition of Africa was reduced to a diversionary diplomatic game orchestrated by Bismarck. Not only did Bismarck want a place in the sun for his newly unified state, but he also encouraged France to seek colonies in Africa to divert her attention from the loss of Alsace-Lorraine and embroil her in conflicts with other European powers (Taylor, 1938). Others attributed the creation of the colonial empires to the rise of nationalism in Europe. It was the nationalistic masses, it was said, hungering for national prestige and glory, who forced their 'reluctant' governments to conquer colonies. The imagination of the masses had been fired by the enormous publicity given to the travels and activities of missionaries, explorers and adventurers (Hayes, 1941).

More recently, some historians have discovered the primacy of technological, ecological, sociobiological, and sexual factors. For some, steamers and quinine and other nineteenth century technologies offer the best 'model of causality' for European expansion (Headrick, 1981:3-12, 1988:3-48). Others believe, in the words of Crosby (1989:5), that behind what he calls the 'Neo-European adventures were factors perhaps best described as biogeographical'. Sociobiological explanations attribute imperialism to the innate violence of the human species (Reynolds, 1981:chapter 5). And then there are those, like Hyam (1976, 1986) who believe that imperialism was motivated by the need to export, not surplus capital, but surplus sexual energy, accumulated in repressive Victorian England.

These theories offer tantalizing speculations. It cannot be disputed that technology facilitated colonization, but it is an exaggeration to argue that it was its major 'cause' (Law, 1982). For one thing, Headrick exaggerates the impact of the technological breakthroughs in tropical medicine, for they mostly occurred in the 1930s and 1940s rather than in the 1870s and 1880s, long after the partition of Africa (Arnold, 1988:10). Colonization was of course promoted by and, in turn, generated, complex ecological changes. It was also advanced by extreme aggression and violence, and entailed sexual encounters between the colonizers and the colonized. But elevating these factors to the level of 'causalities' behind imperialism is not convincing. The sociobiological thesis with its simple reductionism, is inherently non-explanatory, for it 'merely transfers the problem of explanation from one context to another' (Reynolds, 1981:230). The ecological and sexual explanations often read like apologias or celebrations of European imperialism. European expansion is portrayed as nothing more than a mission to spread and reinforce Europe's biological stock (Crosby, 1988), or diffuse repressed collective libidos. Hyam, for example, talks of 'sexual opportunity' and 'sexual interaction', but not the sexual exploitation and rape of colonial women (Berger, 1988; Hyam, 1988).

Few of the old writers on imperialism, and many of the contemporary ones, had pretensions to being historians of Africa, for until the 1950s African history was not taught in the metropolitan or colonial universities. By 1960 the situation was beginning to change. Independence had arrived in Africa, and with it African historical studies began to bloom. In 1961, Robinson and Gallagher published their famous work, Africa and the Victorians, which sought to reinterpret the partition, to tell the story, as was popular in those days of fervent nationalism, from the perspective of the periphery, not the centre. They argued that the partition of Africa was triggered by strategic considerations, not economic reasons. Britain, the leading colonial power, had little or no commercial interest in Africa before 1880 and there was certainly no public clamour in Britain for colonies. Rather, Britain was forced to abandon its preferred 'informal empire' because nationalist agitation in Egypt and South Africa threatened its sea route to India.

This argument had elegant simplicity and, as befitting historians, was copious in details and archival references. The British occupation of Egypt in 1882, and interventions in the recalcitrant South African Boer Republics triggered the partition of the rest of the continent, as other powers sought not to be left behind. The thesis dominated the historical debate in the following two decades (Louis, 1976; Hopkins, 1978a, 1986). This so-called 'peripheral' theory of imperialism was further developed by Fieldhouse (1967, 1973), who dismissed the thesis of 'capitalist imperialism' and argued that faced with local disturbances, spawned by the cumulative pressures of European influence, European interests had to choose between either annexation or complete withdrawal. However, unlike Robinson and Gallagher, Fieldhouse was willing to concede that there was 'imperialism of trade'.

Robinson and Gallagher's thesis is unsustainable on methodological and empirical grounds. Their strict separation of economic, political and

strategic factors is too contrived. Also, as Hopkins (1986:370) has perceptively noted, 'the methodology underpinning Africa and the Victorians
derives from the formal distinction between reasons and causes of actions.
The authors make it clear that their main concern is with 'subjective' motives
rather than with 'historic cause', and that their purpose is to reconstruct the
'contemporary perception of events in Africa', as recorded by the 'official
mind' of imperialism'. Close studies of the official documents in the last
three decades have in fact shown that commercial considerations, rather than
strategic ones, were central to the 'official mind' and determined policy
(Uzoigwe, 1974; Parsons, 1976; Scholch, 1981; Owen, 1981; Johns, 1982).
Besides, attempts by France and other European powers, such as Portugal
and Germany, to create colonial empires in Africa antedated the Egyptian
crisis.

Hopkins (1973) himself advanced the persuasive argument, further
elaborated on in Chapter 14, that the partition of West Africa was a product
of commercial rivalries. Wrigley (1978:27-28) added the point that the
European governments acceded to their merchants' requests for formal
colonization not for reasons of 'protectionism, nor even the quest for
mercantile profit, but the policy of provision', that is, the need to secure
industrial raw materials and consumer commodities. He even tried to elevate
'provision' into the determining feature of 'advanced industrialism'. More
recently Cain and Hopkins (1986, 1987) have argued that British imperialism was not predominantly determined by the forces of industrial
capitalism, but by the changing fortunes of 'gentlemanly capitalism', that is,
up to 1850 landed interests, and from 1850 to 1914 financial and commercial
magnates. They argue that the activities of the gentlemanly capitalists were
not only far more important than has been recognized, but it was they who
ruled Britain. This formulation appears to marry elements of the Hobsonian
thesis on the role of financiers, the Schumpetarian notion that the 'new
imperialism' was hardly new, and the Marxian argument on the centrality
of economic factors behind imperialism, although the authors claim they are
trying to stay clear of these contending historiographical traditions.

While liberal historians, with the notable exception of writers like Hopkins,
generally abandoned economic explanations for the partition, Marxist and
dependence writers emphasized them. They saw the partition as a moment,
a conjuncture, in the global expansion of capitalism (Kiernan, 1974; Brown,
1978). Imperialism was, as Luxembourg (1941:446) put it, 'the political
expression of the accumulation of capital in its competitive struggle for what
remains still open of the non-capitalist environment'. To Marxists, the
economic foundations of imperialism were so self-evident that there was no
need for further verification. The partition was attributed to the need by the

advanced capitalist countries to find outlets for investment, markets for their manufactured goods and sources of raw materials.

But important elements of the Marxist theory of imperialism have come under sustained criticism. The earlier Marxists believed that capitalism had a 'double mission', that it was both exploitative and emancipatory. The concept of colonies as outlets of surplus capital captured the contradictoriness of the capitalist mission. However, this did not seem to fit the historical record. The colonies, certainly in Africa, with a few notable exceptions, were never inundated with surplus capital from the metropoles. Indeed, instead of metropolitan investment, the colonies were expected to pay for themselves from their own resources. The dependence writers turned the reverse flow of resources from the colonies to the metropoles into the pivot around which imperialism spun (Frank, 1967, 1969, 1978a, 1978b, 1980, 1981; Emmanuel, 1974; Amin, 1974, 1976, 1977, 1978, 1980; Wallerstein, 1974, 1979, 1980, 1983, 1984; Rodney, 1982).

Warren (1973, 1980) dismissed surplus capital as a cause behind imperialism by pointing out that 'a number of challenging imperialist powers were themselves net capital importers between 1870 and 1914; the fact that capital export was always a significant feature of industrial capitalism, [and] showed no sudden acceleration in the late nineteenth century' (Warren, 1980:67). Indeed, for Warren far from being a product of a senile, decaying capitalism, imperialism was the product of young, vigorous economies; it was the 'pioneer of capitalism'. His celebration of imperialism's progressive role in the Third World has been strongly attacked (Michael, Petras and Rhodes, 1974; Hansen and Schulz, 1981; Polychroniou, 1991). Other Marxist scholars have queried Lenin's definition of advanced capitalism as imperialism and have urged its abandonment (Brewer, 1980; Arrighi, 1983; Willoughby, 1986). Willoughby (1986:7), for example, finds the definition both too general because 'it leads us away from studying the specific phenomena of territorial domination/exploitation and nation-state conflict which most consider central to understanding imperialism today' and 'too specific because far too many historically-situated aspects of early twentieth century international capitalism are seen as fundamental to a general theory of capitalist imperialism'.

The dependence and Marxist writers have had a lot to say about the economics of imperialism. Ironically, despite their fetishization of the 'economic facts' of dependence, or imperialist exploitation, these writers have done little to advance our understanding of the actual economic dynamics of the partition. This is because the partition was not problematised in their grand theoretical constructs. Failure to do so has obfuscated the highly differentiated processes and patterns of colonization and colonial and post-colonial capitalist development in Africa. The failure to recognize the fact that the partition was a heterogeneous experience is perhaps the most glaring weakness of early Marxist and dependence theories of imperialism. Thus, the partition of Africa has not been adequately accounted for by either the liberal or Marxist and dependence writers. The former tend to focus on local events and the policies of individual governments, and thus fail to see the larger picture, while the latter adopt a global approach, without paying enough attention to the mediating 'facts on the ground'.

Scholars do not agree on the meaning of the concepts they use, so that they often talk past each other, explaining different phenomena, as some seek long-term causes, and others search for the trigger mechanism that set off the explosion that was the partition of Africa (Penrose, 1974; Ratcliffe, 1981). Attempts to explain the partition, colonization, or incorporation of Africa in exclusive categories, the economic versus the political, metropolitan versus peripheral, capitalist versus mercantilist, Afro-centric versus Euro-centric, oversimplify what were very complex processes.

This study takes the view, argued in detail in Part V, that economic factors indeed played the decisive role in engendering the forces of colonization. Needless to say, these factors did not act in splendid isolation, but were articulated in complex ways with political, ideological, technological and military factors. The partition was too messy and complex a process to be attributed to single causes and triggers. Thus, it will be argued that even with regards to the economic factors different 'economics' operated in the different regions. In North Africa, the colonization was conditioned by the economic and political crises brought about by rising indebtedness, while in West Africa colonization emerged in the context of intensifying trade rivalries. Central Africa attracted speculative capital, while Southern Africa became a haven for mining capital. East Africa, the last region to be incorporated into the European-dominated world capitalist system, fell victim to preemptive colonization. This is not to argue, as some do, that imperialism was 'caused' by crises in the periphery. As Boahen (1987a:29) has recently reminded us, 'the nature of the internal conditions of Africa...could not and did not precipitate the Scramble, which was in fact a worldwide phenomenon. I believe that the causes of this phenomenon can be found, not in Africa, or Southeast Asia, but rather in the congruence of the economic as well as the political and social forces operating in Europe during the last two or three decades of the nineteenth century'. However, it is important to understand the differentiated processes of colonization in Africa in order to explain the different patterns and forms of colonial state construction, development and underdevelopment, class formation, and popular struggles in the twentieth century.

Part I

Environmental and Demographic Change

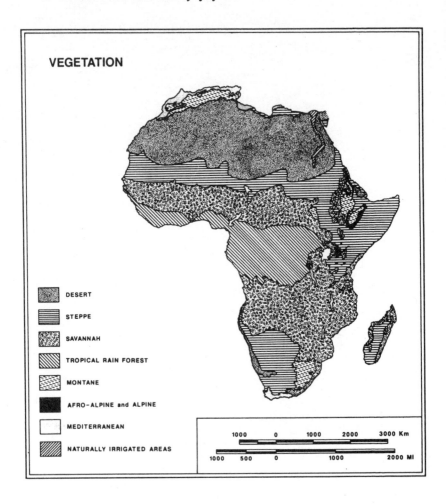

1. Environmental Change

Climate and History

Environmental studies have amply demonstrated that the natural environment is neither an irrelevant backdrop to, nor an unchanging determinant of, human activities. Human action and the natural environment have continually interacted in complex ways, altering in the process both society and the environment. The human past can in fact be regarded as a record of the continuous interaction between history and geography, humans and habitat, society and nature, time and space. Both natural and social scientists have increasingly come to recognize the interactions of climates, ecosystems, and societies over a wide range of temporal and spatial scales (Clark, 1985; Glantz, 1987a; Lewis and Berry, 1988; Worster, 1988).

Until recently, climate was taken as constant, regardless of year-to-year fluctuations. This conclusion was based on the first long records of weather observations made with standard meteorological instruments in the world's leading cities. 'Many of these records had covered a hundred years by about the end of the nineteenth century, and so it happened that between 1875 and 1895 the temperatures prevailing in Europe and North America had reverted to values quite similar to those of just a century earlier' (Lamb, 1982:10). This illustrates some of methodological problems involved in historical climate reconstruction. It is difficult to get useful meteorological data, especially for earlier periods, and to determine the causes of climate change.

In reconstructing past climate three types of evidence are used by historians and climatologists. First, there are instrumental measurements of meteorological phenomena. This data is limited to a few places and goes no further than the late seventeenth century even for the oldest meteorological stations in Western Europe. Also, readings from old instruments are not always comparable to those from modern instruments in standard exposures. Second, there are written sources, such as weather diaries and descriptive accounts of the weather. Such information is often relative and subjective, difficult to measure and quantify.

Finally, there is 'proxy data', based on physical and biological data, which provide 'fossil' evidence of the effects of past climate. Geological, archaeological and botanical evidence offer a rich source of information about climatic sequences. In the case of botanical data, for example, the oldest evidence can be gleaned from spores, leaves, stems and petrified wood fossilized in rocks, while more recent evidence can be inferred from pollen, seeds, needles, woods and phytoplankton preserved in ocean and lake sediments, and the most recent evidence can be deduced from analyzing tree rings. Needless to say, interpreting 'proxy data' is fraught with its own complications. It must not be forgotten that a biological system may exhibit remarkable resilience towards a change in the climate, and the impact of human actions may decrease our ability to detect the effects of climatic events on the biological system (Lamb, 1977, 1982; Rotberg and Rabb, 1981).

The factors behind climatic fluctuations and changes are extremely complex. For the sake of clarity they 'can be put into three interlocking categories: those arising from events outside the earth; those generated within the terrestrial system; and those caused by man himself' (Tickwell, 1977:17). Some of these changes are slow and gradual, others are sharp and marked by abrupt events. The most critical extraterrestrial influence on climate is the sun. Variations in the energy output of the sun, caused by different types of solar disturbances, such as sunspot cycles, can lead to variations in global temperature levels. Variations in the earth's orbit, which affect the amount of solar radiation reaching the earth, also affect climate. The transparency of the atmosphere to either incoming solar radiation or the outgoing earth radiation may be significantly altered by volcanic dust in the atmosphere following massive volcanic eruptions. Such eruptions often produce significant cooling and related effects on climate lasting several years or decades. It is also known that variations of the circulation and heat distribution in the atmosphere and oceans help in changing climate temporarily or permanently.

Human activities, particularly farming, industrialization and urbanization, have significantly altered the terrestrial environment, which has affected climate, certainly at local and regional levels. The clearing of forest cover from vast tracts of land for agriculture and settlement has affected local patterns of rainfall and, to a lesser extent, temperature. Modification of climate on a local scale has also resulted from the building of cities, the creation of artificial lakes and extended areas of irrigation and the diversion of river systems. Since the beginning of the industrial revolution the human capacity to alter or substantially affect the climate of the world as a whole has increased. The combustion of fossil fuels, such as coal, oil and gas, has led to a steady rise in the quantity of carbon dioxide in the atmosphere.

The quantity of man-made aerosol particles has also risen. Rising concentrations of carbon dioxide and other greenhouse gases are expected to lead to an unprecedented global warming, which will change temperature and precipitation patterns with serious implications for agriculture and natural ecosystems. Depletion of the earth's protective ozone layer by chlorofluorocarbons, which are used as a propellant in spray and aerosol cans and as a refrigerant in cooling devices, would allow more harmful radiation to reach the earth's surface, thereby harming both human health and delicately balanced natural systems (World Resources Institute, 1988).

Clearly, human actions have had, and will continue to have, an impact on climate. The converse is also true: climate has had a far-reaching impact on human affairs and human history. Climatic fluctuations and changes affect water supply, temperatures, wind patterns, and levels of sunshine, humidity and clouds. They impinge upon many human activities, including agriculture and forestry, the spread of insects and other pests, the state of health and diseases for plants, animals and humans, the development of weather-sensitive manufacturing and construction industries, the ebbs and flows of trade and prices, the modes of travel and communication, the patterns of population movements and settlement, the nature of diseases and social upheavals, the arrangements for and costs of insurance and relief measures, the dynamics of national expansion and disintegration, and the forms of art and architecture. The effects of changes in the climatic regime may be direct or indirect, short-term or long-term, superficial or substantial (Lamb, 1982:271-309).

It is often difficult to measure the influence of climatic change on historical change. Many of the studies that deal with the human consequences of climatic fluctuations focus on brief periods of climatic crisis, in which they set out to uncover the misfortunes that befell the contemporaries to the crisis. Some writers have even posited that climatic cycles are guarantors of economic cycles, indeed, that they are the cause behind the rise and fall of civilizations (Lopez, 1966; Post, 1977). Such an approach smacks of environmental determinism. Focusing on dramatic moments of climatic crisis obscures the fact that 'the consequences of climatic change do not flow only, probably not primarily, from differences in level; they also flow from differences in variance' (De Vries, 1981:46). Moreover, looking exclusively at the 'harm done' forces researchers to study short-term crises at the exclusion of processes of adaptation.

Patterns of Climatic Change

There are only a few places in Africa where meteorological instrument records extend back a century or more. As a result African historical climate reconstruction has relied heavily on observations and descriptions of climate contained in historical and geographical records and oral traditions. Information on climatic fluctuations and changes has also been obtained from or corroborated through dendroclimatology and studying lake sediments and river levels (Nicholson, 1979). The Nile River, Africa's and the world's longest river, in particular has been studied extensively. Attempts have been made to correlate Nilometer readings, rainfall events around the Upper Nile headwaters, and oral traditions in an effort to date droughts and famines, migrations and state formation in the interlacustrine region (Webster, 1979).

Many writers have tried to distinguish long-term trends or regular periodicities in the climate lasting thousands of years, from minor changes lasting hundreds of years, and from variations or trends which are experienced for ten to 50 years. 'The shorter period variations are superimposed on the longer period fluctuations, and we must recognize that as we attempt to penetrate further into the past, so our ability to distinguish minor oscillations diminishes and only the major changes can be detected' (Grove, 1977:55).

Long-term reconstructions going back to millions of years ago show that Africa has undergone amazing patterns of geomorphic evolution and climatic change. In the last 20,000 years or so, which is the most important period in terms of the current environment, climatic regimes have alternated between aridity and humidity. According to Nicholson and Flohn (1980), the last 20,00 years have been characterized by five periods. First, the period 20,000-12,000 BP which was characterized by aridity in most parts of the continent, except the north which was predominantly wet. The second period, a lacustrine phase, peaked between 10,000 and 8,000 BP, again with the exception of parts of North Africa which experienced aridity. A brief arid episode returned toward 7,000 BP. Another lacustrine phase reappeared from about 6,500 to about 4,500 BP. Finally, about 4,000 years ago the trend towards the present aridity began.

During the first phase the Sahara advanced considerably southwards. The discharges of rivers, such as the Senegal and the Blue and White Nile, were reduced. Lake Chad probably dried up, and the lakes of East Africa, including Mobutu Sese Seko (Albert) , Magadi, Nakuru, Turkana, Naivasha and Victoria were low. The latter even fell below its Nile outlet. The tropical rainforest in Central Africa retreated, while the evergreen forest of Uganda virtually disappeared (Kendall, 1969; Burke and Durutoye, 1971; Butzer et.al., 1972; Harvey, 1976; Street and Grove, 1976; Livingstone, 1979). The lacustrine phase which followed saw the levels of lakes in West and East Africa rise tremendously and numerous lakes formed in the basins and depressions of Niger, Mauritania, the Sudan and Ethiopia. Lake Chad, for example, was 160 metres deep and its area expanded to about 350,000 square kilometres, about the size of the Caspian Sea. Rivers also deepened and became more expansive. The Sahara Desert contracted considerably and the present Sahelian belt was covered with dense vegetation (Kutzbach, 1980; Maley, 1977; Lewis and Berry, 1988). These conditions were temporarily reversed during the brief arid phase that occurred toward 7,000 BP, and then returned until 4,500 BP, when the slide toward the present aridity began. The

Sahara, a sensitive indicator of climatic change in Africa, began to expand once again.

The factors behind these changes are too complex to be adequately covered in this chapter. Suffice it to say that they reflected changes in atmospheric circulation patterns spawned by changing thermal conditions in the northern and southern hemispheres (Nicholson and Flohn, 1980:331-45). For example, the subtropical and tropical aridity of the period 20,000-12,000 was affected by the presence of ice masses in the northern hemisphere and the increased upwelling and lower ocean temperatures. It is quite unlikely that human activities had any impact on climate before the neolithic revolution some 6-8,000 years ago when the anthropogenic reduction of vegetation began. The impact of human exploitation of the environment on climate is not as easy to establish as popular environmental discourses imply. The interaction between land surface processes and atmospheric circulation are very complex (Sud and Fennessey, 1984).

It can be seen from the preceding analysis that the Sahara Desert is not a man-made dustbowl. The African deserts 'are to be ascribed primarily to the continent's geographic position' (Grove, 1977:54). This has led Darkoh (1989:15) to argue that the term desertification, bandied about by some environmentalists to call attention to the expansion of the deserts in Africa, 'in many respects is misleading. The popular image of «sand dune encroachment» or «spreading desert» is only a minor part of the problem'. And the Sahel is not simply the shadow of an advancing Sahara, another human-inspired dustbowl in the making. As Rasmusson (1987:18) puts it, there is 'yet no proof that man-induced environmental degradation (deforestation and desertification) is leading to climatic deterioration in this region'.

Historical information for climatic reconstruction becomes increasingly plentiful from about the sixteenth century. Studies by Nicholson (1978, 1979, 1980, 1981) have established that conditions more humid or wetter than those of today prevailed in many parts of West, East and North Africa in the sixteenth and seventeenth centuries and part of the eighteenth century. She suggests that the Sahara Desert may have contracted. Nicholson bases her conclusions on lake and river levels which were higher than present ones, geographical descriptions, vegetation and geological evidence, tree-ring studies and architectural styles. Severe drought episodes erupted periodically from after 1680. The Sahel was devastated by drought in the 1680s, then between 1710 and 1730 drought engulfed most of the continent, except South Africa. Another series of droughts occurred in different parts of the continent between 1738 and 1756, and in the 1770s and 1790s. The drought of the 1790s ravaged Chad, Bornu, and Kano in northern Nigeria.

The trend towards aridity accelerated at the turn of the century. Thus Africa entered the nineteenth century in the midst of a dry spell. The driest spell was experienced until 1840. There was a continual decline in rainfall and progressive desiccation of lakes, rivers and springs throughout the continent. The levels of such lakes as Malawi, Tanganyika and probably Victoria were very low, while Lake Chad shrunk in size, and Lake Ngami dried up. Then from 1870 to 1895 wetter conditions returned to much of the continent, as rainfall increased. In fact, the levels of many lakes and rivers exceeded twentieth century levels. The situation changed again dramatically from 1895, when drier conditions returned, lasting until 1920.

There was of course considerable regional variability. For example, the North African coast, the Guinea coast and southeastern South Africa escaped the desiccation of the early nineteenth century, while poor rain was reported from the Moroccan coast and West-Central Africa during the lacustrine period late in the century (Miller, 1982). Rainfall over much of South Africa began to increase and there was a period of notably high rainfall from 1855 to 1895, reaching a peak about 1890. The period 1897-1907 was dry over South Africa, Lesotho and Swaziland (Grove, 1977; Tyson, 1980:367; Ballard, 1986; Newitt, 1988).

In eastern Africa rainfall became high in the 1870s, slightly later than in southern Africa, at least judging from the level of Lake Victoria which was 2.4 metres higher in 1880 than in 1868. The lake's level fell between 1880 and 1890, then recovered and rose to a higher level from 1892 to 1895, and then fell steadily by 0.76 metres in the seven years to 1902. Many other East African lakes appear to have been higher at the end of the nineteenth century than they have been since (Dalby, et.al., 1977; Webster, 1979, 1980). While many parts of East Africa were generally wet, in 1888-92 Ethiopia suffered its worst drought of the nineteenth century. Altogether Ethiopia experienced eight droughts during the century (Pankhurst, 1966; Wood, 1977; Degefu, 1987).

The Sahel was more prone to drought than any other region in nineteenth century Africa. In the period 1800 to 1900 droughts occurred at least every 20 years, with concentrations in 1800-1, 1811-14, 1825-27, 1864-65, 1869-70, 1875-76 and 1884-85 (Schove, 1977:46; Curtin, 1975). In North Africa, Morocco experienced about 40 years of drought between 1795 and 1895, the worst one in 1878-9 (Schroeter, 1988:197-200). Algeria enjoyed a period of high rainfall from 1884 to 1896. These rains extended to the northern Sahara, Tripoli and Benghazi in Libya and Alexandria in Egypt. While many parts of the continent were becoming drier rainfall in north-eastern Africa increased slightly from 1896 until the end of the century when a pronounced decline set in (Grove, 1977:58).

These regional variations can be attributed to the fact that 'Africa spans a variety of temperate and tropical climatic zones, and the meteorological situation associated with precipitation events is quite different in different parts of the continent' (Rasmusson, 1987:5). The factors affecting the patterns of rainfall in the different regions include the topographical features and latitudes of each region, its hemispheric position and the impact of the oceanic tradewind systems and the cross-equatorial monsoon circulations (Schove, 1977; Shukla, 1984). Generally the equatorial zones experience two rainfall maxima, while there is a single summer rainy season in the subtropics and a single winter-time rainfall maximum in the northern temperate latitudes (Nicholson, 1980; Nicholson and Entekhabi, 1986). The Sahel's shorter and more unpredictable rainy season can be attributed to the region's 'position between the major circulation systems of the southern and northern hemispheres' (Nicholson, 1978:17).

The rainfall patterns and climatic regimes of nineteenth century Africa were not simply products of some arcane meteorological circumstances. Lamb (1982:236) has suggested that 'a good case can be made out for attributing many (or most) of the reverses of the climatic recovery in the eighteenth and nineteenth centuries to the extraordinary frequency of explosive volcanic eruptions, which maintained dust veils high up in the atmosphere between 1752 and the 1840s' (Lamb, 1982:236). There were, for example, major eruptions in 1812 on St. Vincent Island in the Caribbean and in 1814 in the Philippines, and the enormous eruption of 1815 in Tamboro, Indonesia, all of which spewed dust veils into the atmosphere that subsequently blanketed the earth, thereby reducing the penetration of the sun's rays, cooling much of the northern hemisphere and distorting the pattern of global wind circulation.

Climatic change in Africa should, therefore, be considered as part of a much larger pattern of world-wide climatic variation. Many of the droughts that Africa experienced in the eighteenth and nineteenth centuries afflicted much of the southern hemisphere. Climatic research of wind circulation patterns shows that the southern oscillation, a pressure sea-saw between the Atlantic and Indian Oceans, plays an important role in triggering wetter or drier periods in the southern hemisphere. The climatic regimes of the southern and northern hemispheres are linked in quite complex ways (Pittock, et.al., 1978). When Africa was in the midst of a dry spell in the early nineteenth century, Europe was colder and wetter than normal. But the 1860s were dry in both Africa and Europe, while the 1870s were generally wetter in both continents.

Environmental Change and Society

The impact of the climatic changes outlined above on African societies in the nineteenth century was far-reaching. The literature on the subject can be divided into two groups. First, some writers emphasize the great stress and suffering, often culminating in famine, warfare and migration, that was caused by drought (Ogot, 1979; Webster, 1979). Second, there are those who portray the precolonial era as the golden age of harmonious relations between humans and nature and blame colonialism and underdevelopment for environmental degradation in Africa (Kjekshus, 1977a; Vail, 1977). Neither approach satisfactorily explains the different ways in which African societies dealt with environmental change and stress. The problems of assessing the impact of drought on African societies cannot be overemphasized.

Part of the problem lies with the sources themselves, which are often impressionistic and imprecise. The written sources often talk of drought and famine using superlatives. These records, especially those produced by European travellers and adventurers in the nineteenth century, an era of unbridled European racial arrogance and imperialist zeal, have not always been taken with the caution they deserve. For example, the statistical basis of Degefu's (1987:30) statement that about one-third of the Ethiopian population perished during the great drought of 1888-92 is unclear. Who did the counting? What was Ethiopia's total population before and after the famine? Writing on the great Moroccan drought and famine of 1878-9, Shroeter (1988:198) notes that 'some estimates say that one-fourth to one-third of Morocco's population perished'. He believes that 'these sources may well be exaggerated', although he has 'little doubt that the country was ravaged by famine'. Again, it is a conclusion that lacks any statistical certainty.

If the mortality toll of recent famines in Africa have been hard enough to ascertain accurately, it may be futile to try to do so for the nineteenth century given the greater paucity of data (Bell, 1987:85). Oral traditions do not fare any better in offering concrete evidence on the impact of environmental changes. It is well to remember that the designations 'famine' and 'drought', common refrains in the oral traditions concerning migrations, warfare and political turmoil, may not always be literal references to climate and dearth, but metaphors of internal economic crisis and loss of political legitimacy (Richards, 1983:45).

To some historians drought has become the *deus ex machina* of African history, a blanket explanation of all the revolutions, ills and traumas that African peoples experienced in the nineteenth century. It has, for example, been offered as the explanation for the rise of the Zulu state. Guy (1980:103) has argued that by the end of the eighteenth century Zululand was confronted with an ecological crisis, an 'imbalance had risen between population density and resources of the region and... this contributed to the radical social changes which took place'. These changes included the reorganization of production, reproduction and the state. The Zulu state emerged out of the intense competition for scarce resources among powerful African chiefdoms in the region. This thesis has been further elaborated by Ballard (1986) and Gump (1989). Ballard believes the drought of 1800-1806/7 not only gave rise to the reorganization of society, economy and politics in the region embodied in the formation of the Zulu state under Shaka, but that the Shakan revolution inflicted its own hardships which compounded the effects of the disastrous drought of 1820-1823, which facilitated the British colonization of Natal 'as starving African refugees submitted willingly to white rule in exchange for food and security' (Ballard, 1986:378). Gump (1989) stresses the regional unevenness of the ecological disequilibrium. Competition for resources forced the Zulu to strengthen the age-set system in order to better protect their pasture lands coveted by their northern neighbours whose lands had been ravaged by drought. Out of this emerged the Zulu state.

These explanations are tantalizing, but ultimately unconvincing. Ballard's alleged African 'willingness' to accept European rule does not accord well with the history of fierce conflict between the Zulus and the settlers, while Gump's age-set thesis is not persuasive. In a compelling revision of 'mfecane' historiography, Cobbing (1988, 1991) has demonstrated that the 'mfecane' purported to mean 'the crushing' of peoples, was invented by liberal historians as an alibi for European colonization and later apartheid. The term 'mfecane' itself was coined by a historian in 1928, and 'has no root in any African language, but it crudely conveyed the myth of a cataclysmic period of black-on-black destruction in the era of Shaka (roughly 1810-1830)' (Cobbing, 1988:487). This self-serving racist myth, first constructed by European invaders in the nineteenth century, and later refined by liberal historians and propagated by the apartheid state, became a dominant paradigm seized on by even 'respectable' historians, including those with an Afrocentric perspective who were anxious to show African 'initiative'.

The formation of the Zulu state and other states in the region, Cobbing has convincingly argued, had little to do with ecological crisis, overpopulation, or Shaka's genius and brutality. It was a reactive process in which Africans in the region sought to defend themselves against the expansion of the Cape colonial frontiers from the west and the Portuguese slave trading empire in the east. Both the Cape colonists and the Portuguese desperately wanted African labour, the former for their own use, and the latter for slave exports. It was the two onslaughts, rather than some imaginary 'mfecane' or any internal revolutionary process within African societies, that generated the unprecedented violence in the subcontinent.

Even less convincing are the attempts that some historians have made to attribute the growth of the slave trade to drought. Writing on West-Central Africa , Miller (1982:29) argues that drought not only significantly conditioned the political history of the region and generated conflict and warfare over resources, concretized in the emergence of the Imbangala or 'Jaga' raiding bands, it 'must also have increased the number of enslaved refugees that lured European slavers away from their usual haunts on the West African coast'. Curtin (1983:380-1) agrees that 'the correlation between high levels of slave shipments and prolonged drought is very clear, especially in Senegambia and Angola'. Webster (1983:11) has gone so far as to characterize the entire period from 1725 to 1840 as the 'century of drought and slavery'. He believes that the droughts of this period swelled 'the supply of slaves and the supply curve moved up in each successive drought until the historic peak of slave exports'. This is 'voodoo' supply-side economics, to borrow a term from the 1980 American presidential elections, an inept attempt to 'blame' the slave trade on nature and the victims themselves.

If Miller, Curtin and Webster blame drought for the growth of the slave trade, Newitt (1988) invokes drought as the cause for the disintegration of the economy of Mozambique , including the prazos, and absolves the slave trade. 'Before the slave trade could have such dire effects', he tells us, 'the great drought [of 1823-1831] had began to wreak havoc on the society and the testimony of contemporaries is overwhelmingly to the effect that the calamities they were experiencing were the direct result of famine' (Newitt, 1988:31). The author states quite clearly that 'the purpose of this paper is to shift the emphasis in the interpretation of the nineteenth century history of Mozambique' from the role played by the Portuguese slave trade to that of 'internal' factors, principally natural disasters. Thus it was capricious nature, and the Mozambicans inability to tame it, that lay behind the social and economic dislocations the country experienced in the nineteenth century. It could be argued, on the contrary, that the slave trade exacerbated the impact of drought because it helped alter the labour and social relationships within groups, and forced many people to move away from more productive environments into more marginal ones (Lewis and Berry, 1988:60).

Newitt's analysis of the impact of drought in Mozambique in the first half of the nineteenth century reads much like recent neo-classical apologias that ascribe the African famines of the 1980s to nature and other 'internalist' factors (Zeleza, 1986; Mkandawire and Bourenane, 1987; Glantz, 1987a). It is quite revealing that the 'contemporaries' Newitt summons were all Portuguese traders and government officials, many of whom were deeply involved in the slave trade. They could not be expected to censure their own activities any more than the functionaries of the state and international capital in contemporary Africa can be expected to. This is to suggest that environmental discourses cannot be divorced from the material interests and ideological preoccupations of the protagonists involved (Anderson and Grove, 1987).

Droughts and other forms of environmental stress did not start in the nineteenth century. Over the centuries African societies had developed adaptive strategies to minimize their impact. There is need for more research by historians on how African societies coped or failed to cope with the problems brought by environmental problems, such as drought. It stands to reason that the coping mechanisms changed as a result of changes in the organization of society. Too many simplistic associations are often made between drought and famine. Whenever the word drought is mentioned it is almost invariably followed by the word famine (Webster, 1979; Ogot, 1979; Degefu, 1987; Shroeter, 1988). It is as if every drought inevitably led to famine, and every famine was caused by drought. Famine is not simply a curse of nature; it is a product of complex interactions between nature and society.

The nature of drought is often poorly understood. It is difficult to define the term 'drought' itself, for 'drought conditions in one region may be considered normal conditions in a more arid region, or during a more arid epoch' (Rasmusson, 1987:8). There are, in fact, different types of drought, including meteorological, agricultural and hydrologic droughts, just to mention the most important ones (Wilhite and Glantz, 1985). A meteorological drought can be defined as 'a 25% reduction of the long-term average rainfall in a given region', while an agricultural drought occurs when there is not enough moisture available at the right time for the growth and development of crops', and a hydrologic drought refers to a situation 'in which streamflow falls below some predetermined level' (Glantz, 1987b:45-46). What causes an agricultural drought is not necessarily inadequate total rainfall, but the pattern of its distribution during the growing season. In fact, in so far as different crops require different amounts of moisture, drought for one crop need not necessarily spell disaster for all the crops. This is why it is important to understand the crop regime of a particular society before concluding that drought led to crop failure, and by extrapolation, famine.

The literature on strategies developed by African societies to cope with drought and food shortages has grown, most of it inspired by the Sahel and Ethiopian crises of the early 1970s and mid-1980s (Campbell, 1977; Watts, 1984; Dyson-Hudson and McCabe, 1985; Mortimer, 1988; Johnson and Anderson, 1988; Shipton, 1990). This literature shows that African societies use a wide variety of strategies to prevent, adjust to, and recover from food shortages and famines. The preventive strategies include the diversification of cultivation and herding fields, the rotation of fields, crops and pastures, intercropping and the planting of drought-resistant crops, lending out livestock, grazing herds in different locations and keeping them larger than needed for sustenance in good times, and building social networks. Adjustment to actual food shortages also takes various forms, such as increasing trade, substituting staple foods with irregular and gathered foods, reducing sizes of communities, households, and herds, fostering out children, mobilizing kinship, friendship and patronage ties, recalling loans or incurring debts and borrowing goods, selling property, and migration. For recovery, the split communities, households and herds are reassembled and resettled, pledges redeemed or loans incurred in order to repossess or repurchase lost land, tools, and livestock, and work is intensified.

In short, the coping mechanisms are not only varied, encompassing the manipulation of production practices, social networks, and ecological reserves, but are often staggered to meet different types or stages of a subsistence crisis. A few of these studies show the nature of the coping strategies, the way in which they changed in the course of the nineteenth century, and the effects of those changes on subsequent developments. Let us focus on three examples: the Hausa in Northern Nigeria, the Basotho in Southern Africa and the Zigua in northeastern Tanzania.

Among the Hausa the organization of the extended household, both as a production and consumption unit of food and other commodities, reduced the vulnerability of individuals and component nuclear family units to food shortages caused by climatic fluctuations. Patterns of redistributive and reciprocal gifts between households, in turn, reinforced the society's ability to withstand a crisis of food shortage. The social insurance measures also extended to the level of food storage and consumption strategies. Elaborate techniques of storage permitted grain to be stored for relatively long periods. Seeds for planting and grains for subsistence were carefully separated. Rituals often guided when granaries could be opened at each point in the agricultural cycle. The tributary appropriation of agricultural surplus further provided a collective insurance against the possibility of drought-induced famine. The graduated patron-client relations culminated with the state which used the grain tax stored in central granaries for organized redistribution in times of famine. The systems of agriculture were adapted to the precarious conditions of the environment. Patterns of intercropping, the selection of drought-resistant strains, and the use of crop combinations which varied with yearly environmental fluctuations minimized the risk of crop failure due to unfavourable climatic conditions, such as drought.

Finally, 'unused' land was kept as a hunting and gathering reserve (Shenton and Watts, 1979).

The case of Lesotho demonstrates the complex interaction between drought and famine, and how politics and the economy determined the social impact of drought. As in much of Southern Africa, Lesotho experienced a severe drought in 1802-3. There was an absolute and severe regional shortage of food. The result was famine. But not everybody was equally affected. Those with large herds of livestock avoided starvation. Within families women and children suffered disproportionately; it is reported that polygamists got rid of their wives since they could not feed them! 'In subsequent decades', writes Eldredge (1987:71), 'the links between drought and famine were indirect: famine occurred in the aftermath of drought only when wars broke out, production and trade were disrupted, and entitlements were reduced by depredations. In these circumstances the causes of famine were political rather than ecological'.

Following the drought of 1802-3 the Basotho tried to diversify their arable and pastoral production. They expanded the production of drought resistant sorghum and adopted new grain crops at the same time, first maize and later wheat. They energetically bought and built large herds of livestock. In addition, hunting techniques were improved and more wild roots and vegetables were identified for food gathering. Thanks to these measures, they were able to survive the drought of 1812 and 1834. They were not so lucky with the droughts of 1818-18 and 1826-28. During these droughts there were conflicts among the Basotho and between them and their neighbours over pasture lands, which led to migrations and wars. Famine ensued directly out of these migrations and wars, rather than the actual droughts, although of course the droughts had triggered the conflicts in the first place.

From the 1830s the Basotho found themselves pitted against the expansionist Boer pastoral farmers. Wars with the Boers and the subsequent confiscation of over one-half of their arable land and large herds of livestock by the Boers significantly curtailed Basotho productive capacity. Population growth only made matters worse and led to the progressive erosion and depletion of the soils. Moreover, 'the disappearance of wild game depleted a traditional source of famine relief [and] the increasing commercialization of Basotho agriculture depleted grain reserves and increased Basotho dependency on a volatile market' (Eldridge, 1987:75). All this made the Basotho more vulnerable to the droughts of 1858-9, 1860-3, 1865, 1883-5, and 1895-8, all of which turned into famine.

The Zigua also found their social insurance mechanisms against drought-induced food shortages weaken, but for different reasons. Giblin (1986:86) has argued that there is 'no evidence to suggest that the precolonial Zigua experienced a prolonged subsistence crisis comparable to the repeated disasters of 1880-1940 ... the threat of scarcity only materialized as widespread famine in rare, extraordinary circumstances'. The Zigua succeeded in warding off famine despite living in a harsh environment because they expected drought, although its timing was not predictable, and planned for it. Their settlements were located in well-watered valleys and seasonal watercourses and separated from one another by uninhabited woodlands. Their cropping practices were also designed to minimize the effects of drought. The staples were supplemented with livestock that were kept in tsetse-free zones. Moreover, the extensive trade conducted among the Zigua, and between them and their neighbours and faraway communities provided access to food reserves during periods of localized drought or crop failure. The social organization of kinship and clientage allowed poorer members of the society to be incorporated into networks that provided for their subsistence in times of hardships.

But these drought management strategies and famine insurance mechanisms were undermined from the 1840s with the growth of the caravan and slave trade to the coast. As the caravan trade expanded, food stocks were sold and patrons, upon whom poorer people depended in times of food scarcity, began transferring food out of the redistributive networks into markets. Slave raiding generated violence and disrupted the social fabric and political order. Both the caravan trade and slave dealing reached a peak in the 1870s and early 1880s as plantations expanded on the island of Pemba and along the lower Pangani river. When drought occurred in 1884-5 famine struck at the poor who had lost their entitlement to reserves. Many were forced to pawn themselves or members of their households to wealthy individuals, including chiefs, who had become the interlocutors of the caravan trade. To the 'wealthy patrons the famine was an opportunity to achieve increased power', for not only did they 'attract more dependents', but they also 'acquired a greater degree of dominance over them' (Giblin, 1986:97).

It can be seen that drought did not inevitably lead to famine. Conversely, the absence of drought did not ensure enough food supply. Famine is a complex phenomenon. As Sen (1981) has forcefully argued, famines have not always been caused by an absolute shortage of food. Rather, famines have occurred when certain segments of the population have lost their entitlement to the food that is available. And in times of actual severe food scarcity the distribution of entitlements determines who survives in a famine. The link between drought and famine, and the social impact of famine, are articulated in complex ways by the political economy of food distribution, access to resources, and the effectiveness of social networks (Raikes, 1988).

The three cases examined above demonstrate some of the ecological practices developed by African societies to overcome the pressures and constraints of their environment. The history of African ecological ideas has yet to be fully investigated. For example, none of the recent major publications on environmental change in Africa say much on the subject (Anderson and Grove, 1987; Glantz, 1987; Lewis and Berry, 1988; Journal of Southern African Studies, 1989). As is so common in African studies, environmental historians have so far concentrated on the ecological ideas of the colonizers. Since most of Africa was not colonized until the late nineteenth century, that has meant working on southern Africa, principally South Africa.

It is becoming quite clear from this work that the droughts of the nineteenth century provoked the emergence of colonial conservation ideologies whose implementation led to the gradual erosion of African control over natural resources, especially land. The intense competition between the settler and African communities over natural resources 'ensured that any state attempt to regulate the environment became a deeply politicized issue' (Beinart, 1989:147). Settler and state concern about the environment was triggered by the droughts of 1821-3, 1845-7, 1862-3. The decline in rainfall and occurrence of droughts was attributed by the colonial scientists to the removal of vegetation. Before the 1820s 'it had been recognized that European agricultural methods were specifically responsible for deterioration in soils and pastures and the destruction of forests', but from the 1820s the blame for 'desiccation' was increasingly put on the Africans (Grove, 1989:165).

This led to the development of what Grove (1989:184) has called 'discriminatory environmentalism'. State environmental intervention in the Cape Colony began in earnest in the 1850s. Officially protected 'forest reserves', from which Africans were removed, were set up. These 'were effectively the first «state» game reserves in Africa' (Grove, 1987:27). Africans found themselves being denied not only of land for cultivation, but also seasonal grazing and hunting. In fact, hunting gave way to 'the Hunt', a pursuit divorced from the mundanity of commercial and nutritional utility and increasingly restricted to the settler elite and imperial adventurers and playboys seeking sporting pleasure, from which the Africans, now defined as poachers, were to be excluded (Mackenzie, 1987; Carruthers, 1989; Mutwira, 1989).

Thus ideas about forest reserves and hunting, justified in the name of conservation, demarcated the new lines of power and privilege in colonial society, and reinforced the imperial construction of Africa as a natural wilderness. The idea of forest reserves soon gave way to that of 'native reserves', which provided both the means and justification for settler seizure of African lands. In this way the virtuous language of conservation was used to rationalize the progressive removal of Africans from their land, and their confinement to marginal land.

The Ecology of Disease

Environmental changes and transformations in the political, social and economic order provided the framework within which patterns of disease and health emerged in nineteenth century Africa. The state of disease and health, in turn, had a far-reaching impact on society. Severe epidemics have been known to disrupt existing political, social, and economic systems and demographic regimes (Briggs, 1961). For example, the bubonic, pneumonic and septicemic plague that afflicted Europe and Asia between 1347 and 1351 and led to the death of about 75 million people, the worst pandemic in human history, had an incalculable impact on the history of the two regions. The activities of fleas had a lot to do with the plague. Thus fleas alone, and insects as a whole, have had a profound impact on human history (Cloudsley-Thompson, 1976; McNeil, 1976). As Lehane (1969:18) colourfully puts it, 'the combined effects of Nero and Kubla Khan, of Napoleon and Hitler, all the Popes, all the Pharaohs, and all the incumbents of the Ottoman throne, are as a puff of smoke against the typhoon blast of fleas' ravages through the ages'.

The link between climate, disease and history is, a close, but complicated one. The literature on African medical history is now quite impressive and wide ranging, although the precolonial period is not as well covered as the twentieth century (Patterson, 1974, 1978, 1979; Feiermann, 1979, 1985). There are three approaches to the ecology of disease in Africa. The first is that Africa has always been unhealthy, hence the continent's relative underpopulation. Not only is 'the intrinsic unhealthiness argument ... untestable [since] measuring levels of medical hazardness in tropical Africa, compared to say, western Europe, over the last 1000 years raises insoluble data problems' (Richards, 1983:15), but it is also based on an assumption that since the early Europeans in Africa, an alien disease environment, suffered greatly, then Africa had always been unhealthy place to live for its inhabitants (Turshen, 1984:9).

Native Americans or Africans visiting Europe would have reached a similar conclusion about Europe's disease environment. Some scholars believe that until the last quarter of the nineteenth century, when European medicine acquired 'scientific foundations, which gave it a technical advantage over some aspects of African medical practice', health conditions, as well as medical technology in Africa and Europe were quite comparable (Turshen, 1984:10; Dubos, 1959, 1968).

The construction of Africa, as well as Asia, as an unhealthy tropical cesspool, which could only be cleaned up by the superior knowledge and skill of European medicine, was an essential part of imperialist ideology. In the words of Arnold (1988:7), 'as Europe began to free itself from its own epidemiological past, it was forgotten that diseases like cholera, malaria, smallpox and plague, though increasingly banished to the tropics, were part of Europe's recent experience. Disease became part of the wider condemnation of African and Asian «backwardness» just as medicine became a hallmark of the racial pride and technological assurance that underpinned the «new imperialism» of the late nineteenth century'. Indeed, imperialist intervention was increasingly justified in the name of spreading the benefits of western medicine. Dr. Livingstone, the Scottish medical missionary and explorer, became the archetypal hero of a benevolent imperialism that was bringing spiritual light and good health to a blighted continent. This ignored the fact that the most significant advances in tropical medicine only came in the 1940s on the eve of decolonization, and not in the 1850s (Bruce-Chwat, 1980). Also forgotten was the Europeans' role in transmitting alien and previously localized diseases in Africa. The advent of colonialism in Africa marked, in Ford's (1971:489) withering condemnation, 'an outbreak of biological warfare on a vast scale'.

The second approach, then, states that Africa's disease environment deteriorated as a result of intensified contact with the rest of the world, particularly Europe from the period of the slave trade. Major epidemic diseases, such as smallpox, venereal diseases, influenza and cholera, were introduced through ports and spread into the interior along the major trade routes. This process was intensified by colonialism. Thus colonialism, in Arnold's (1988:4) damning phrase, was itself 'a major health hazard for indigenous peoples. The «successes» of Western medicine, if apparent at all', either 'arrived late in the colonial era' , or benefitted 'only a fraction of the total population'. There is, indeed, abundant evidence to show that African health standards declined sharply during the late nineteenth century and early twentieth century, as a result of the introduction of non-African epidemic diseases. In the words of Hartwig and Patterson (1978:4), 'the unhealthiest period in all African history was undoubtedly between 1890 and 1930'. It was Africa's equivalent of the Black Death, the cataclysmic pandemic that ravaged Europe in the fourteenth century.

The third approach, in some ways, a refinement of the second, emphasizes the dynamic interactions between environments, peoples and pathogens. According to this view, epidemics occur when a society's biological and cultural adaptation to the disease environment has been broken by intrusion of a new disease, or by population disruptions caused by war or famine, adoption of new productive activities, and intensified contacts with foreigners. The foreigners may bring with them new diseases or because of their lack of immunity to local endemic diseases they fall victim to a disease, and if their numbers are large enough the traditional therapeutic systems are overstretched and the endemic disease suddenly erupts into an epidemic (Richards, 1983:19-22).

It appears that during the nineteenth century North and West Africa did not suffer from epidemics on the same scale as in the other parts of the continent. By the beginning of the century many societies in North and West Africa had adjusted to European diseases, for they had been in relatively close contact with Europe for a long time. Moreover, movement within and between these regions was comparatively more intense through trade, urbanization and state formation, so that people 'had many generations to build up defenses to cope with their more complex disease environment, though such defenses were, of course, only partial' (Hartwig and Patterson, 1978:8). In contrast, in many parts of eastern, central and southern Africa contacts with alien disease environments as well as regional communications did not become intensive until the nineteenth century.

East Africa was one of the regions that suffered catastrophic epidemics in the nineteenth century, particularly towards the end of the century. Through long distance trade alien diseases penetrated the interior where they usually erupted into epidemics since the people lacked immunity against the disease. The trade caravans also served as an effective mechanism for transmitting indigenous diseases (Hartwig, 1975:63, 68). The most lethal among the new or newly reappearing epidemics in East Africa were cholera and smallpox. Cholera was recorded for the first time in East Africa in 1821. Three severe cholera epidemics struck Zanzibar and the mainland in 1836-7, 1858-9 and 1869-70. The last epidemic apparently penetrated deep into the interior. The epidemics arrived in East Africa via Arabia, by land through Ethiopia, and by sea through the coastal ports (Koponen, 1988:661). Their impact on the region was as devastating as anywhere else, although figures are hard to come by. The epidemic of 1869-70 is estimated to have claimed the lives of some 20,000 people in Zanzibar alone.

All these cholera epidemics were offshoots of wider pandemics, originating in India, and engulfing the rest of Asia, Europe and Africa. Cholera advances in the Mediterranean led to outbreaks of cholera epidemics in Morocco in 1835, 1848, 1855, 1865, 1868 and 1878-9 in which thousands of people perished. Egypt was first struck by a cholera epidemic in 1831, and there were six more outbreaks between 1850 and 1902, which claimed tens of thousands of victims (Panzac, 1987:74-75).

Smallpox was another dreaded disease. In Morocco, 'smallpox epidemics constantly took a heavy toll of lives, especially those of children, despite a programme of vaccination which had been initiated in the 1870s' (Shroeter,

1988:199-200). In Egypt there were periodic outbreaks of smallpox epidemics which affected little children the most, killing 50,000-60,000 of them annually (Panzac, 1987:17-18). Plague was another terror in North Africa. Between 1799 and 1848 outbreaks of plague in Egypt were recorded for 30 out of the 50 years. The most deadly years were 1801, 1813, 1816, and 1835. 'According to various authors, the country as a whole lost between 150,000 and 500,000 to the plague' (Panzac, 1987:19). In Tunisia, there were outbreaks of plague from 1794 to 1800, and again in 1818-20 (Valensi, 1985:183).

Smallpox was dreaded in East Africa. In the Sudan the turbulent Maddiyyah period proved fortuitous for smallpox epidemics, with major outbreaks in 1885, 1891 and 1895, and less severe ones in 1898 and 1900. According to Hartwig (1981:9), 'the army in the Sudan frequently provided a reservoir of non-immune people that fostered epidemics'. Ethiopia was wrecked by six major smallpox epidemics in the nineteenth century, that is, almost one every 16 years (Pankhurst, 1965). In Tanzania, where the disease was probably new, a smallpox epidemic erupted in 1809 in which 5,000-15,000 people are believed to have died in Zanzibar and the northeastern coast. There were recurrent epidemics, at intervals of a few years of decades, with major recorded outbreaks in 1858, 1868, the early 1880s, and throughout the 1890s (Kjekshus, 1977a:132-4).

The worst outbreaks of smallpox epidemics in South Africa occurred in the eighteenth century. The country was afflicted by a virulent strain of smallpox which was brought by ships coming from India. Three major epidemics broke out in 1713, 1755 and 1767, which decimated the Khoisan people who had no immunity, and seriously disrupted Cape colonial society (Elphick, 1989; Ross, 1989; Elphick and Giliomee, 1989). Further north in Angola smallpox epidemics broke out at periodic five to ten-year intervals in the nineteenth century, where they 'were provoked especially by Portuguese troop movements during campaigns of conquest' (Dias, 1981:359). The relatively well-documented Angolan smallpox epidemic of 1864, which came from the north as part of a wider epidemic sweeping southwards across the continent, claimed about 40,000 lives.

Historical research on such important diseases as malaria is surprisingly few and far between. Malaria's dubious claim to fame rests on the suffering and death it inflicted upon European adventurers and conquerors rather than on its impact on Africans. Over generations Africans in malaria-infested areas had developed genetic defenses, such as sickle cell trait, which provided some protection against malaria, and cultural responses, which allowed conditions of relative balance between the people and the disease. But the immunity was often to the local strain of malaria parasites which was bound to prove ineffective when one moved to an area with a different strain. Thus movement undermined immunity and adverse circumstances broke the balance between people and the disease, with resulting rises in morbidity and mortality rates from malaria. The disruptive forces increased in the nineteenth century, so that as with other diseases, the incidence of malaria appears to have been on the increase, as was the case in Angola (Dias, 1981:357-8). The disruptions induced by colonialism in Uganda, Davies (1979:4) has noted, led to the spread of strains of malaria from one part of the country to another. In Tanzania, malaria also spread from the turn of the century to many places that were previously malaria-free, including the highlands and some coastal areas (Koponen, 1988:657-8). One of the worst recorded malaria attacks occurred in Mauritius between 1865 and 1870. The disease 'recently introduced from India, took the lives of 78,000 people' (Padayachee and Morrell, 1991:74). Relapsing fever, a tick-borne parasitic disease, which may have long been prevalent in endemic foci in areas of eastern, central and southern Africa, was activated and spread in these regions 'during the age of exploration and early colonial administration' (Good, 1978:60).

One endemic disease that has recently attracted historians' research interest is leprosy. Illife (1987:214) claims, rather extravagantly, that 'leprosy brings into high relief the scale and tenacity of African poverty'. Leprosy was prevalent mostly in hot and humid areas, especially the equatorial regions such as Zaire. But it was less virulent in these places than in the higher altitudes where it was less common. The disease itself is rarely fatal but it weakens resistance to other diseases. Leprosy victims are noticeable by their deformities which are not caused by the disease itself but result from ulcers and injuries suffered by the patient because of the inability to feel pain. It is not clear from Iliffe's account whether or not the disease was on the increase in the nineteenth century. Another disease also identifiable by the physical deformities that develop in its sufferers is jiggers, caused by the jigger-flea or sand-flea which burrows into the toes. The jigger-flea was apparently first brought to Africa by a British ship coming from Rio de Janeiro when it docked at an Angolan port in 1872. The flea quickly spread and ravaged communities from Angola and Zaire to the East African coast, undermining its victims' mobility and work (Kjekshus, 1977a:134-6).

The outbreak of epidemics in the nineteenth century has often been linked to drought, war, and famine because of the striking temporal connections between them: the epidemic years were usually also major war and famine years. However, the dynamics of diseases, drought, war and famine were more complex than appears at first. Some diseases, such as typhoid fever and dysentery, which spread when sanitation is poor and drinking water is contaminated with human waste, may have been more common during periods of drought when water was scarce. For example, these diseases took a toll of human life during the Moroccan drought and famine of 1878-9 (Shroeter, 1988:198).

The relationship between the other disease epidemics and droughtis more difficult to establish. As we noted earlier, the major cholera epidemics were local offshoots of global pandemics imported from outside. The case of smallpox is quite complex, for by the nineteenth century the disease was no longer alien in many African societies. Some writers have suggested that its spread was aided by famine. In Hartwig's (1981:9) words, 'a physically weakened population was vulnerable to any number of diseases, not least of which was smallpox'. But this is disputed by others who argue that while famine can weaken the resistance of the body to the effects of disease, 'one's immunity to smallpox is determined solely through a previous infection or artificial vaccination' (Koponen, 1988:671).

This is part of a more general problem. Since 'present-day epidemiological knowledge has not resolved every aspect of the interaction of nutrition and infection, historical investigations of pre-industrial epidemics may not always provide definitive answers' (Post, 1985:18). Medical specialists do not agree on the link between famine and malnutrition and the rate of morbidity and mortality of diseases. Some see a synergistic relationship between nutritional deficiency and infection, while others emphasize the ecological and social consequences of famine in triggering epidemics. In the case of smallpox in nineteenth century Africa, the argument has been made that epidemics were not caused by famines as such. Rather, during severe food shortages people were sometimes forced to move and congregate in a few places which became centres for the transmission of smallpox and other diseases (Dawson, 1979; Dias, 1981). Similarly, warfare encouraged mobility and dense settlements in a few strategically located areas in which people were much more vulnerable to invading infectious diseases.

Apart from the human epidemics, livestock, especially cattle, also suffered from periodic outbreaks of fatal diseases. As in the case of human diseases, the cattle epidemics were both alien and indigenous in their origins, and were triggered by changes in the disease environment. Among the old diseases was East Coast fever, or theilerioisis, which was probably indigenous to eastern and southern Africa. But East Coast fever did not show its full wrath until the turn of the twentieth century. It came hard on the heels of the great rinderpest epidemic. Rinderpest was a new disease in most of Africa. Prior to 1864, according to Davies (1979:12), 'rinderpest seems never to have entered trans-Saharan Africa from its home in the Russian steppes. In the early 1860s, however, it reached Egypt through cattle imported from the

Crimea and in 1865 spread to Western Sudan and West Africa'. This epizootic died before it could affect eastern and southern Africa. Then in the mid-1880s, infected cattle were imported from South Russia and India to feed British and Italian troops attempting to conquer the Sudan and Ethiopia, respectively. 'In 1889 rinderpest broke out in Somaliland and rapidly extended to Ethiopia, the Sudan and East Africa. The virulence of the virus had increased substantially and afflicted cattle and other animals which, with no previous exposure, lacked immunity' (Davies, 1979:13). By the mid-1890s the disease had spread to southern Africa.

Livestock herds were decimated. Sometimes up to 80 or 90% of the cattle in an area perished, as was the case in Ethiopia (Degefu, 1987:30), among the Maasai in East Africa (Kjekshus, 1977a:126-32), in parts of Angola (Dias, 1981:374), and in the Transkei in South Africa (Bundy, 1980:119-22), and Nigeria (Davies, 1979:14). 'Almost overnight,' Davies (1979:14) notes grimly, 'the greater part of the wealth of tropical Africa was swept away'. Thus it would seem that with regard to cattle, as on the human side, the greatest havoc in the nineteenth century was caused by new diseases that invaded the continent, rather than by old-established diseases. Another alien disease, but one whose impact was milder than rinderpest, was contagious bovine pleuro-pneumonia, or lungsickness, which was apparently introduced in South Africa in 1853, and was recorded in Chad in 1870 and observed among East African cattle in the 1880s (Koponen, 1988:667).

The rinderpest epidemic also facilitated the spread of tsetse flies, which afflict both human beings and animals and cause sleeping sickness or nagana. This disease is caused by parasitic protozoa called trypanosome which are transmitted from one host to another by species of tsetsefly of the genus Glossina. According to Ford (1971:494), one of the leading authorities on trypanosomiasis in Africa, sleeping sickness epidemics sprang from specific ecological imbalances in the 'relationship of three of the five populations involved - man, his domestic livestock and the wild fauna - and the effects of these changes upon the remaining two populations, the trypanosome and the tsetses'. Tsetse fly belts appear to have expanded from the mid-nineteenth century in many parts of Africa.

In Sierra Leone, we are told, until 1865 horses were an integral part of administrative and social life. Then suddenly they started dying from a mysterious disease which wiped out the existing equine population and made re-establishment of horses impossible. This disease has been identified as trypanosomiasis. It was apparently brought about by deforestation in the hinterlands of Freetown as a result of the rapid expansion of the timber trade. 'The large scale removal of forest must have led to a decline in the population of rain forest mammals and their replacement with savanna types such as bushbuck which itself is a favourite victim of G. longipalpis and is also known frequently to be host of G. brucei' (Dorward and Payne, 1975:254).

With the large-scale decimation of cattle as a result of the rinderpest epidemics, short-cropped grass previously used by cattle as pasture was replaced by scrub and shady thorn thickets, favourite haunts of the tsetse, and bush pigs, one of the favourite food animals of the tsetse. It has been shown that the devastations of the rinderpest epidemic, combined with declining population densities, led to the expansion of the tsetse fly belt in the Sahel in the 1890s. Rinderpest sharply reduced the need for transhumance, while population decline, attributed by Ford (1971) to the cumulative effects of the slave trade, drought and the spread of smallpox, curtailed agricultural activities. 'Less transhumance, and a retreat from the agricultural frontier as a result of falling population densities, led to a diminution in resistance to trypanosome infection in human and cattle populations through lack of periodic, immunity-inducing, contact with Glossina species' (Richards, 1983:21).

Sleeping sickness also appears to have spread in parts of southern Africa in the latter part of the nineteenth century. In Angola the disease first attracted official attention in 1870. A series of epidemics erupted in the 1870s, 1880s and 1890s. The spread of sleeping sickness in Angola at this time was probably related to changes in the regional disease environment through forest clearance to establish coffee plantations, the shooting out of game, and the rapid growth and expanded volume of caravan trade traffic. The sudden influx of population, both Portuguese planters and Angolan labourers, to the newly established plantations possibly made conditions even more favourable for the spread of sleeping sickness (Dias, 1981:371-3).

In Zambia the disruption of the fragile ecological balance that kept trypanosomiasis at bay began from the mid-nineteenth century, first through the Ngoni invasions and later European colonial conquest. The Ngoni lived in compact settlements. Their Chewa neighbours were forced to crowd themselves in stockaded villages to defend themselves. The result was that bush regenerated in areas that had once been inhabited. Then the colonial invaders came and pillaged people's cattle, seized their land, forced the amalgamation of villages, made laws prohibiting hunting and set up games reserves and instituted male labour migration. These government decisions gave 'trypanosomiasis a headstart by perpetuating and deepening the imbalance between man and the wild animals and bush that had begun in Ngoni days, and the diseases made rapid headway under this protection' (Vail, 1977:142; also see Vail, 1983:228-9).

Similar processes were at work in central and eastern Africa where the spread of sleeping sickness 'was furthered during the 1880s and 90s by the

Madhist movement in the Sudan, by the caravans of men like Tippu-Tib, a Zanzibari ivory trader, and by Belgian and Arab traders' (Azevedo, 1978:122). More important, perhaps, were colonial policies introduced at the turn of the twentieth century. The creation of vast and exclusive game reserves, which altered pastoral patterns of transhumance, coupled with ill-conceived colonial settlement schemes, land alienation programmes and enforcement of labour migration, tipped the ecological scales and mild endemicity in the nineteenth century turned into devastating epidemics in the early twentieth century (Kjekshus, 1977a:165-79).

McCracken (1987) has tried to reassess the Vail-Kjekshus thesis. He argues, using Malawi as a case study, that 'the impact of colonial administration has been oversimplified in accounts of the spread of tsetse, so too have been the effects of the emergence of the capitalist economy'. McCracken's contention that the colonial state was too weak to impose policies that facilitated the spread of tsetse and that capitalist penetration was tentative does not invalidate the Vail-Kjekshus thesis. The formation and exercise of colonial state power and the penetration of capital were not events, but processes. Both the colonial state and capital progressively altered the ecological situation and facilitated the spread of tsetse belts in colonial Malawi. Indeed, he acknowledges that in the 1890s, before colonization, tsetse was confined to a few areas. 'From the early years of the twentieth century, however, Malawi, in common with her neighbours, suffered a dramatic expansion in tsetse fly belts' (McCracken 1987:65-66).

The ecological and epidemiological disasters, individually and collectively, had a far-reaching impact on African societies and economies. Their effects of course varied from one society to another depending on the nature of the disease, its manner of transmission, and the society's biological, therapeutic and cultural defenses against it. New diseases were more dangerous because the affected population was less likely to have developed defenses against them. Also, new diseases were less discriminatory in their effects unlike famine or warfare whose victims were often specific in terms of social status, age and gender. The varied effects of the different diseases can be seen in the case of cholera and smallpox in Tanzania where 'it was observed that cholera carried off mainly the poor, whereas smallpox struck all social strata' (Koponen, 1988:673).

Over the centuries African societies had developed preventive and curative measures against various diseases that confronted them. The medical practices of African societies are often seen in terms of mysterious rituals. Recent studies have began to correct this. Davies (1979:10) for example, discusses the complex surgical techniques used in Bunyoro-Kitara in the nineteenth century. The methods they employed in making Caesarian sections 'betokens a high degree of medical and intellectual sophistication... The Caesarian section was, indeed not the only field in which their surgery was advanced. They amputated, operated on the chest and head, and sutured abdominal wounds as well as intestinal lesions. Nor were their medical advances purely surgical, for they variolated against smallpox and, much more remarkably, inoculated against syphilis and were much criticized for so doing' by the first western medical practitioners to visit the region, and 'we know they experimented'. Imperato's (1977) study examines the multifarious therapeutic processes and pharmacopoeias of the Bambara peoples of West Africa, who were able to deal with a wide range of diseases from problems of infertility and childhood diseases, to communicable and chronic diseases. Dentistry and surgery were also practised. Variolation was used against smallpox.

Inoculation against smallpox appears to have been widely practised throughout the continent as Herbert's (1975) study has shown, although the inoculation techniques varied in terms of the material used and the site of inoculation. The effectiveness of inoculation depended on the techniques used. Herbert (1975:559 believes that inoculation 'clearly provided some defenses against smallpox in spite of the risks involved', a conclusion echoed by Hartwig (1981). In Egypt inoculation was gradually abandoned in favour of vaccination which was promoted by Muhammad Ali's government from the 1820s. The vaccinations were performed by specially trained barbers. By the mid-nineteenth century smallpox had been brought under control. New born infants were vaccinated; between 1870 and 1872 the proportion of vaccinated infants reached 85% in Cairo and 74% in Alexandria (Panzac, 1987:20, 24). Quarantine strategies were adopted to prevent the spread of epidemics.

Preventive and curative measures were also taken with regards to animal diseases and sleeping sickness which attacked both animals and human beings. The pastoral Fulani of northern Nigeria inoculated their cattle as a means of protection against bovine pleuro-pneumonia (St. Croix, 1947). In the case of sleeping sickness people often knew the epidemic foci which they tried to avoid. If they had to pass through tsetse infested areas herdsmen in East Africa either moved during the night, or they smeared their cattle with such repellents as lion's fat. Smoking the cattle also acted as a temporary repellant against tsetse fly. In addition, there were herbal cures of infected cattle (Kjekshus, 1977a:52-6).

The organization of healing varied from society to society and changed over time as well (Feierman, 1985:116-8). In some societies the roles of healer, ruler and ritual specialist overlapped, while in others they were loosely connected. There were also differences in the ways in which health care was institutionalized. Access to health care was differentiated by the idioms of social power: age, gender, and class. The patterns of public and domestic hygiene were conditioned by the forms of settlement, nature of the productive activities, and popular perceptions of disease etiology.

The preventive and curative measures did not always work. For example, some of the measures taken in Morocco to contain cholera epidemics may have proved counterproductive. The incarceration of pilgrims from the East simply led to their death 'from privation rather than epidemic. Sewage canals which were installed in the 1860s due to foreign [European] pressures may have worsened conditions of hygiene in the towns' (Shroeter, 1988:197). Improvements in sanitation in the coastal towns were often counteracted by the influx of rural migrants, which led to squalor and overcrowding, propitious breeding grounds for cholera and other diseases.

The virulence of the epidemics of the last quarter of the nineteenth century was a telling commentary on the limits of the existing therapeutic systems in African societies. The acute social tensions that this engendered found expression in some societies, such as the Karebe of Tanzania, in increased incidence of sorcery and witchcraft (Hartwig, 1978). In other societies a sense of collective solidarity may have been strengthened, especially as was the case in parts of eastern and southern Africa, the epidemics were blamed on European colonial invaders. For example, the rinderpest epidemics formed the political backdrop to the 1896-7 Shona-Ndebele uprising in Zimbabwe (Ranger, 1967), and other less well known revolts and protests in South Africa (van Onselen, 1972).

The epidemics had a profound effect on social structure. During the great rinderpest epidemics of the 1890s in East Africa existing social differences were accentuated in many areas. This was the case, for example, 'among the Wahehe where the surviving cattle became concentrated in the hands of chiefs and headmen only' (Kjekshus, 1977a:131). In some places there was an increase in 'servitude' or 'domestic slavery' as powerful societies, lineages and households incorporated poorer people in order to replenish their demographic losses or to extend patronage networks (Hartwig, 1978).

In South Africa's emerging racial capitalism the ecological disasters accelerated the processes of social and structural differentiation. The rinderpest epidemic, which came head on the heels of other cattle diseases, increased social differentiation among and between African and European farmers. Africans sustained much higher losses than the settler farmers for a number of reasons, including the fact that inoculation was reserved for the latter, 'emergency laws prevented notably black-owned cattle from being moved, thus making it very difficult to isolate infected from still healthy cattle once rinderpest had broken out; and finally white farmers were granted access to compulsory black labour to help eradicate locusts on their land - thus depleting labour on African farms, which were as seriously affected by locust plagues' (Campbell, 1990-91:113). The result was that in Natal, for example, African-owned cattle fell by 77% in 1897, compared to 48% for European-owned cattle. In the next two years settler-owned cattle increased, while 'African-owned decreased by a further 34%: Thus whereas Africans in Natal possessed 494,402 cattle in 1896, just over double the total white owned stock, by 1898 their cattle stock had plummeted to 75,842, or just under half the number of cattle owned by whites' (Campbell, 1990-91:113).

A second epidemic of rinderpest, closely followed by an outbreak of East Coast fever, hit South Africa at the beginning of the twentieth century, and reinforced the growing structural differentiation between African and European farming in the country. The state abetted this process. For example, when aerial spraying proved effective against locusts, the Natal government used it almost exclusively to help settler farmers and not the Africans (Ballard, 1983). The impoverishment caused by these disasters contributed to the growing proletarianization of Africans and the development of the system of labour migration.

Few would dispute the fact that the ecological and epidemiological disasters of the late nineteenth century coincided with, and facilitated, colonial conquest. They weakened the capacities of many African societies to resist the European colonial invaders. Lugard, the British conqueror, wrote that rinderpest in East Africa 'has favoured our enterprise. Powerful and warlike as the pastoral tribes are, their pride has been humbled and our progress facilitated by this awful visitation' (quoted in Davies, 1979:17). He was writing about the Maasai of Kenya. The Maasai were, of course, not the only people in Kenya 'humbled' by these disasters. Their effects on the Kikuyu of Central Kenya are also well documented. At the same time that the colonial forces were invading, the Kikuyu were struck by a devastating mixture of drought, a rinderpest epizootic, a smallpox epidemic, locust swarms, jiggers and pleuro-pneumonia. The results were catastrophic. The worst famine in memory began. It lasted from 1897 to 1900. Dawson (1981) suggests that more than half the Kikuyu population may have been wiped out by the famine and epidemics. Whatever the true figure, this made colonial conquest so much easier. And it also made it simpler to justify the European seizure of Kikuyu lands, in the name of 'victory' and the 'emptiness' of the lands.

The pestilences not only facilitated conquest, they also played an important role in the construction of the ideologies of both European imperialism and African resistance. To the invading Europeans the devastations, for which they did not recognize any responsibility, were proof of the inherent 'bar-

baric misery' of Africa, from which Africans could be only saved by Europe's magnanimous civilizing mission. To the Africans, on the other hand, these miseries coincided with the coming of the Europeans, and so they held the latter responsible for them. 'Mutual understanding,' Ford states, 'was almost total'. Out of this incomprehension emerged the contradictory ideologies of imperial arrogance and anti-colonial resistance.

Conclusion

It can be seen that in the nineteenth century Africa underwent important environmental and ecological changes which defy simplistic notions of a 'static' or 'traditional' past that was either 'merrie' or 'primitive'. From the research that has been conducted to date a clearer picture is beginning to emerge of the patterns of climatic change in Africa, especially since the sixteenth century. The available evidence suggests that climatic regimes in Africa have alternated between aridity and humidity since time immemorial. This pattern persisted in the nineteenth century and has continued in this century. There were, of course, important regional variations.

The impact of climatic changes on African societies is in serious dispute. This chapter has been critical of the tendency among many historians to see drought as the key causal factor behind nineteenth century revolutions, migrations, and the growth of the slave trade. Part of the problem is that the nature of drought is poorly understood. Drought did not invariably cause famines, and inversely, the absence of drought did not always mean that there was enough food for everybody. The dialectic between food shortages and environmental distress was very complex. Many strategies were developed to prevent, adjust to, and recover from natural disasters and climatic changes. Needless to say, the capacities to deal with these challenges varied between and within societies and changed over time. In the process, the patterns of development, social class formation, and gender differentiation were altered. Moreover, ecological ideologies were transformed, as has been demonstrated in the case of nineteenth century South Africa. More work still needs to be done on the history of African ecological ideas.

In examining the links between climate, disease and society in nineteenth century Africa, the dominant approaches in the study of African medical history have been summarized and critiqued. Many regions experienced an epidemiological disaster in the last quarter of the nineteenth century, which coincided with, and facilitated, colonial conquest. It can be argued, moreover, that the combined epidemiological and ecological disasters played an important role in the construction of the ideologies of European imperialism and African resistance.

Clearly, climatic and ecological crises in Africa are not only a twentieth century phenomena. African societies had to deal with climatic and ecological changes and problems in the nineteenth century with varying degrees of creativity and success. But the nature and management of these problems was profoundly transformed from the late nineteenth century with the imposition of colonialism. The connection between these crises and colonization was not simply a temporal one. Rather, it was structural and fundamental. Colonial conquest altered the ways in which African societies had met, managed, and contained similar crises in the past. In other words, as will be demonstrated in volume two in this series, imperialism and colonialism in Africa were not simply confined to the reorganization of economies and polities, they also transformed the environment itself and the ways it was managed or mismanaged.

The environmental and ecological changes outlined in this chapter affected, and in turn, were affected by, the patterns of demographic change in the continent.

2. Demographic Change

Historical Demography

Historical demography developed as a discipline after the Second World War (Glass and Eversley, 1965; Hollingsworth, 1969; Glass and Revelle, 1972). Its methods were developed using a very unique set of data found in European parish registers and, when available, census rolls. The main preoccupation of historical demography became the measurement of demographic events, mainly births, deaths and marriages. No adequate theory was developed to analyze demographic processes in their entirety, let alone to explain the demographic regimes of societies without the conventional sources. When studying such societies demographers, inspired by Malthusian fears of population explosion, concentrated their research on fertility, often studying it in isolation from other demographic parameters and socio-economic processes and their historical development (Pool, 1977; Cordell and Gregory, 1980, 1989; Gregory et.al, 1984; Cordell et.al, 1987).

One of the main challenges that has faced students of African demographic history has been the need to collect both conventional and non-conventional sources of demographic data, and to extend the disciplinary boundaries of the subject itself, by blurring the distinction between historical demography and demographic history, and emphasizing the importance of both quantitative and qualitative information in answering questions about the historical processes of population change (Moss and Rathbone, 1975; Fyfe and Mc-Master, 1977, 1981; Wrigley, 1979; Miller, 1984).

The conventional sources of formal historical demography include censuses, vital registration, parish registers and demographic surveys (Ajaegbu, 1977; Cordell and Gregory, 1980, 1989). A wide variety of censuses exist for African societies, a few going back to the nineteenth century. Earlier censuses were often partial, irregular enumerations and for most of Africa censuses in the modern sense started in the middle of this century. Used with care they can yield useful demographic information. Vital registration is still incomplete in many African countries, but a lot may be buried in archives.

Parish registers exist in some places where Christian missions were established. However, few have been collected for a long time and are not demographically representative of the general population. Thornton (1977a, 1977b) has tried to use parish registers to reconstruct the demographic history of the Congo kingdom from the mid-sixteenth century. Benoit and Lacombe (1977, 1981) have also tried to use parish registers for more recent times. Demographic surveys have only been used widely in Africa since the

1950s. The demographic information culled from all these conventional sources is still insufficient for any definitive study of African populations and their development in the nineteenth century.

The non-conventional sources are numerous. They include archaeological findings, historical linguistics, oral tradition, travellers' accounts, economic and ecological data, administrative records, tax data and military lists. Administrative records, including those of colonial governments, religious groups and others, tax data, with all their inherent tendency to underestimate the taxable population as a result of tax evasion, and military lists, have mainly been used as sources of information on population during the colonial period. The other sources have been found useful for the demographic history of the nineteenth century and before.

Archaeologists have attempted to reconstruct African demographic patterns during prehistoric times (Gabel, 1977; Shaw, 1977, 1977, 1981; Onyango-Abuje and Wandibba, 1979; Phillipson, 1977a, 1981; Derricourt, 1977) and historic times (Sutton, 1981; Brothwell, 1981), by analyzing material culture, settlement and skeletal remains. Given the nature of their evidence, archaeologists have been reluctant to suggest numbers, preferring instead to outline broad demographic trends. Historical linguistics has also been used to bridge the archaeological and historical records. According to Ehret (1981:154): 'Past demographic relations leave linguistic artifacts behind, in the shape of either ... modifications in a language attributable to contacts with other languages (or other dialects of the same language) or... the replacement in common use of one language by another (or of one dialect of a language by another)'.

Historical linguistics has been particularly useful in mapping out broad demographic changes, such as migration. One of the most famous migrations in African history reconstructed with the aid of historical linguistics is the so-called Bantu migration. But it does not always follow that linguistic changes reflect demographic changes, and vice-versa (Hair, 1975; Curtin et.al., 1978:26-27).

Oral traditions and travellers' accounts have provided major sources of demographic data. While oral traditions are weak on quantitative information and tend to relate to limited geographical areas and demographic groups, if carefully used they are a rich source of data for such demographic events as migrations, wars, famines, epidemics, droughts and settlement patterns.

Many historians and demographers question the reliability of the quantitative data produced by travellers or European residents in Africa, on the grounds that the data is often impressionistic, partial and anecdotal. However, Heywood and Thornton (1988) have challenged such scepticism. They believe that: 'Some of the travellers may have been informed by African statistical sources which, while not written down and preserved for posterity, were nevertheless an integral part of an ongoing administration, and answered to the needs of any administration, in order to function efficiently' (Heywood and Thornton, 1988:213).

Demographic trends can also be gleaned from information on socio-economic and ecological change. Estimates of food consumption and production and analysis of weather patterns, soils, ecological and epidemiological disasters, have been used to infer population size, structure and distribution. Faced with the lack of statistical data for East Africa in the nineteenth century historians have based their demographic reconstructions on readings of prevailing economic and political conditions. Needless to say, they have reached contradictory conclusions, as we shall see shortly (Kjekshus, 1977a, 1977b; Zwanenberg and King, 1975; Hartwig, 1979; Iliffe, 1979; Turshen, 1984; Koponen, 1988).

Population Growth

While population statistics do not exist for many African countries and regions in the nineteenth century, it is still possible to provide estimates and educated guesses about magnitudes and trends. Like so much else in African economic history, it is reasonable to assume that there were considerable regional variations in the patterns of population growth, given the fact that the separate regions were affected quite differently by the Malthusian checks of pestilence, famine and war, and the demographic calamities of the slave trade and colonial conquest. In some regions population grew slowly, while in others it stagnated or declined. Taking Africa as a whole, it will be demonstrated that the continent experienced sustained population decline up to at least the mid-nineteenth century. The primary cause for this was the slave trade.

Among the few countries for whom population statistics exist in the nineteenth century in the forms of censuses are South Africa, Egypt and Algeria. They all show trends of population growth, although there was a period when Egypt experienced stagnation and Algeria faced actual decline. The three countries offer insights into the different dynamics behind population growth and change in nineteenth century Africa. Let us begin with South Africa.

The enumeration of the population of the Cape Colony, the first colonial settlement in present-day South Africa, goes back to 1670. The Khoikhoi in the colony were not enumerated until 1798. In that year the total population of the Cape came to about 62,000, of whom a third were European freeburghers, two-fifths the burgher's slaves, and the rest 'Free Blacks' and Khoikhoi. By 1840 the colony's population had risen to over 150,000, divided almost equally between the European settlers, on the one hand, and the ex-slaves and the Khoikhoi on the other (Elphick and Giliomee, 1989:524). These figures tell us very little about South Africa's population, for they only refer to the population within the colonial frontiers, which had yet to encompass the whole of modern South Africa. By 1840 the vast majority of South Africa's peoples still lived in independent African states and communities. Their numbers can only be guessed.

Colonial ideologues in nineteenth century South Africa tended to underestimate the size of the indigenous population in order to justify European settlement, while their twentieth century counterparts have been inclined to emphasize the threat of the 'Black Peril' as a rationalization for African population control and the promotion of the settler population both absolutely and relatively (Brown, 1987). In the accounts of the nineteenth century writers, Africans were perennially afflicted by the scourges of 'inter-tribal' warfare, epidemics, drought and famine (Bryant, 1965; Delegorgue, 1990). Many modern historians writing on the so-called 'mfecane' have reinforced this image of perpetual warfare and population decline (Omer-Cooper, 1978; Guy, 1979; Denoon and Nyeko, 1982). But as Cobbing (1991:27) has forcefully argued, while there was violence in southern Africa in these years, the 'mfecane', which he believes is a false construct, is untenable 'as an explanatory system for understanding that violence'.

Unlike the censuses of nineteenth century colonial South Africa which did not report on large sections of present-day South Africa, those of Egypt dealt with the country as it is currently constituted. Egypt's census records go back to the early nineteenth century, although the 1897 census is taken as the first real census. This census showed that Egypt's population was 9.7 million. Debate has centred around the size of Egypt's population in 1800, upon which the country's rate of population growth in the nineteenth century can be deduced. Estimates vary from 2.5 million to 3.9 million and 4.5 million (McCarthy, 1976; Panzac, 1987).

Panzac suggests the latter figure on the grounds that if the population in 1800 was 2.5 million it would entail a growth rate that was higher than the 1.2-1.4% experienced by Egypt in the four decades after the 1897 census. 'There is no reason to believe', he argues, 'that at the end of the nineteenth century the situation should have been different' (Panzac, 1987:12). He estimates that in the nineteenth century the population grew at the slightly lower rate of 1.0-1.2% because of epidemic diseases. For example, population stagnated at 5 million between 1830 and 1840 because of the epidemics of cholera in 1831 and plague in 1835 in which tens of thousands of people perished. By 1900 Egypt had an estimated population of 10.2 million (Issawi, 1982:94).

Algeria had its first census in 1856 which showed a population of 2,487,373, including the European settlers. It had declined from an estimated three million in 1830, the year France colonized Algeria. This sharp decline has been attributed to the brutality of the French conquest and the ruthlessness of primitive colonial accumulation which made it difficult for Algeria's population to reproduce itself demographically. Algeria's 'population did not reach its 1830 level again until 1886, when a census revealed the existence of 3,287,000 persons' (Bennoune, 1988:42). From then on, as colonial conditions stabilized and demand for labour both in the peasant household economy and in the colonial sector increased, the population began to grow, reaching 4.7 million in 1900 (Issawi, 1982:94; Bennoune, 1988:53). The steady growth of the indigenous population, at an annual rate of nearly 1%, apparently 'surprised the colonial racial supremacists, who asserted that «history is here to prove that the inferior races have always been either absorbed or destroyed by the superior races» (Bennoune, 1988:54).

Elsewhere the first comprehensive censuses were only conducted in the twentieth century. But this did not stop governments and other interested parties from making estimates and guesses, nor has it deterred historians from discussing the trends of population growth in these regions and countries. The estimates deserve to be treated with extreme caution. Some of the most detailed estimates come from the Maghreb. The first censuses in Libya, Tunisia and Morocco were conducted in 1911, 1921 and 1931, respectively. Data culled from several sources suggests that Libya's population may have been 0.5 million in 1800 and 0.7 million in 1914. It fell sharply during the Italian wars of conquest in the period 1911-15 and 1921-32 (Evans-Pritchard, 1949:39; Issawi, 1982:94).

Tunisia's population was estimated at two million in 1914, having risen from approximately 1.1 million in 1860 and one million in 1800 (Brown, 1974:375-8; Valensi, 1985:183-90). Widely divergent estimates have been made for Morocco's population. According to Shroeter (1988:230), 'foreign estimates of Morocco's population from the 1770s to the end of the nineteenth century range from 2-25 million'. Issawi (1982:94) suggests a possible figure of three million in 1800 and four million by 1914. It has been posited that Morocco's rate of population growth declined during the famine and epidemics of 1878-81.

The difficulties inherent in many early population estimates can be seen in the case of the Sudan. As Daly (1986) has observed, the estimates made before and after the Anglo-Egyptian Condominium was imposed in 1898 were either fanciful, or they reflected the political biases of their originators. The new regime was keen to portray the Madhist state, which it had replaced, 'as one of the bloodiest regimes in history, marked by massacres, epidemics, and other depopulating curses: it was the moral duty of Britain to save those who had survived... Statistics showing a huge decline in population went unchallenged because they confirmed the worst' (Daly, 1986:18-19).

Widely divergent, and mostly fictitious, estimates were made for the various provinces. In 1903 the Sudan Almanac put the country's total population at 3,500,000, 'while the annual report for the same year put the total at 1,870,500. The 1904 Sudan Almanac then fell into line unblinkingly informing its readers that «the general population of the Sudan may, very approximately, be taken at about 1,500,000 to 2,000,000», without any explanation of how or why the estimate (or the population) had decreased by 50 per cent since the year before' (Daly, 1986:20). The best that can be said is that the Sudan was relatively underpopulated in 1900.

Such estimates do not even exist for some regions. They have had to be produced by the historians themselves. One creative attempt to do so is the one made by Thornton (1977a, 1977b), and Thornton and Heywood (1988). Thornton concludes from an examination of parish registers that Congo's population at the beginning of the eighteenth century was 'far lower than the two million suggested by the literary estimates, with an overall slight growth rate, despite the civil wars and expansion of the slave trade' (1977a:525). And after examining the notes of the Hungarian traveller Lazlo Magyar, Heywood and Thornton (1988:227) resolve that his data 'is reliable and can be used to show population trends from 1800 to 1900. Population appears to have increased rapidly in the central highland [of Angola] during this period, probably because of the importation of slaves, while it decreased dramatically after 1850 in the lands of the Lunda empire to the east'.

Faced with the lack of statistical data and the unreliability of the existing documentary sources, Kjekshus (1977a, 1977b) decided to base his reconstruction of Tanzania's demographic trends in the nineteenth century on a reading of economic and political conditions. He examined the two major factors that are held to have contributed most to population disruption, namely, internecine warfare and slave raiding. He demonstrates that the scale and impact of both has been exaggerated. Given this and the evidence of economic expansion, Kjekshus proposes a new demographic hypothesis which asserts 'that the population of Tanganyika was either stable or showed slight tendencies to expansion throughout the nineteenth century until its last decade' (Kjekshus, 1977a:9-10). Using similar methods Zwanenberg and King (1975) and Koponen (1988) reach the same conclusion.

Turshen (1984:28) questions the validity of extrapolating from a few groups, as Kjekshus does, which 'probably represented less than one-seventh of the Tanzanian population'. Hartwig (1979) recounts the impact of famine and alien epidemic diseases, particularly smallpox and cholera, but he does not state whether East Africa's population fell as a result of this. He contends, however, that the region began to experience a serious and sustained decline from the 1890s until the mid-1920s. Iliffe (1979:6-13), who underestimates the capacity of people in precolonial Tanzania to control their environment almost in the same measure that Kjekshus overestimates it, asserts that famine and disease were the main reasons for Tanzania's underpopulation in 1800. Any population in the nineteenth century was due to migration. He does not specify who these migrants were, nor why they would be better able to manage the environment. An alternative explanation might be that slow population growth was augmented by the flow of slaves from the interior to the East Africa coast where demand for slaves was growing. Some of these slaves were retained in Tanzania.

All the available global estimates seem to agree that between 1750 and 1850 Africa's population declined or stagnated (Monsted and Walji, 1978:19-20). In 1750 Africa's population stood at either 95 million (Carr-Saunders, 1936), 100 million (Wilcox, 1931), or 106 million (Durand, 1967). If the latter figure is taken, then in 1750 Africa constituted about 13% of the world's population. In 1800 it ranged from 90 million (Carr-Saunders, 1936), to 100 million (Wilcox, 1931), and 107 million (United Nations, 1973). Durand (1967) posits a high of 142 million, a low of 69 million, and a median of 107 million.

By 1900 Africa's population had increased to between 120 million (Carr-Saunders, 1936) and 141 million (Wilcox, 1931), or a high of 154 million, a low of 115 million and median of 133 million (Durand, 1967). Needless to say, the average rate of African population growth, as well as Africa's share of total world population, depends on which estimate is used. The United Nations (1973:32) estimates that Africa's average annual population growth rate was a mere 0.1% between 1880 and 1850, and 0.4% from 1850 to 1900. The population of the rest of the world grew slightly faster, so that Africa's share of world population declined from 11% in 1800 to 8% in 1900.

The Slave Trade

The figures mentioned above may not be accurate, but the trend they show most probably is, given the fact that vast areas of the continent were ravaged by the slave trade, which is probably the best documented aspect of African historical demography up to 1900 (Pool, 1977:58). Perhaps no other subject has generated as much heated debate in African historiography. A trading system in which the commodities were human beings raises troubling moral questions. The controversies centre on several issues, five of which stand out. First, the total number of Africans exported. Second, the demographic impact of the trade on Africa. Third, the economic impact. Fourth, its effects on the growth of slavery within African societies themselves and finally, its role in the development of industrial capitalism in Britain and the West generally.

Our main focus in this chapter is on the demographic impact of the slave trade, but the other questions cannot be entirely avoided, so they will be addressed briefly. Two approaches can be identified in the debates. On the one hand, there are some who tend to minimize the adverse impact that the slave trade had on Africa, and on the other, those who emphasize the damage. Scholars of European descent tend to be proponents of the first approach and those of African descent of the second, although there are considerable overlaps. This should not be surprising. The slave trade remains the ultimate moral measure of the relationship between Africa and Europe, although all too often many historians hide their motives and biases behind sophisticated methodologies. It is sometimes not sufficiently recognized that many of the disputes are as old as the slave trade itself.

The general outlines of the Atlantic slave trade are too well-known to be recounted here in detail (Davidson, 1961; Mannix and Cowley, 1962; Rodney, 1982; Rice, 1975; Rawley, 1981). This trade began slowly in the fifteenth century, then grew dramatically in the subsequent centuries, reaching a peak in the eighteenth and nineteenth centuries. The trade was first dominated by the Portuguese, then by the Dutch in the seventeenth, the British in the eighteenth, and the Europeans settled in the Americas in the nineteenth century.

The slave trade was triggered by the demand for cheap and productive labour in the Americas. Attempts to use the indigenous peoples of the Americas floundered because many of them were killed by unfamiliar European diseases. As it was not possible to bring labourers from Europe in the quantities required, attention was then turned to Africa. To begin with, Africans were experienced farmers and miners, activities for which labour was demanded in the Americas. Also, unlike the indigenous peoples of the Americas, they were more resistant to European diseases since the disease environments of the Old World overlapped. Moreover, Africa was relatively close to the Americas. All these factors, and the fact that the slaves were captured, that is, they were stolen, made African slave labour relatively cheap.

African merchants and ruling classes sold slaves, not because their societies had surplus population or underutilized labour, as some have maintained (Fage, 1975:20; Gemery and Hogendorn, 1974:237-9; Le Veen, 1977:128), but for profit. The notion that they did not know what they were doing, that they were 'bamboozled' by the European merchants is just untenable as the view that they monopolized the trade (Rodney, 1982:79). The slave market, as immoral as it was, was a competitive one (Bean, 1974;

Bean and Thomas 1979). It was ultimately controlled and organized by Europeans, however, for after all, it was the European merchants who came to buy the slaves, transported them in their ships to the Americas, and sold them to European settlers who used them to work on mines and plantations, and to build the economic infrastructure of the New World. As Manning (1990:172) has reminded us: 'It was only with the end of the slave trade that European immigrants, whose descendants now predominate in New World populations, came to outnumber African immigrants to the Americas'.

Like modern corrupt ruling classes in Africa, the African slave traders benefited from trading a commodity they had not 'produced', except the cost of transport to the coast. Despite some fluctuations slave prices generally maintained an upward trend until the 1790s when they began to fall (Eltis, 1989; Manning, 1990:92-99). To assume that African merchants did not profit because their societies paid a heavy price is just as ahistorical as to equate their gains with those of their societies. The calculus of profit is usually individual and corporate, rarely societal. In other words, African slave traders pursued narrow interests and short-term economic calculations to the long-term detriment of their societies. It can be argued that they had little way of knowing that their activities were under-populating and under-developing 'Africa', a configuration that hardly existed in their consciousness or entered into their reckoning, so it is rather specious to argue that the slave trade did not lead to depopulation because, as Fage (1989:106) contends, 'it seems unlikely that African rulers and merchants would have provided slaves for sale to the Europeans, and on the scale they did, if they had thought that this would lead to demographic catastrophe'.

The slaves were acquired in two main ways, through violence and by judicial and administrative means. The use of force, in the form of warfare, raids and kidnapping, was the most important. The judicial and administrative means involved enslaving people accused of violating the rules of society and witchcraft, or the payment of tribute and taxation in the form of slaves. Far less important was the incidence of voluntary enslavement in which individuals sold themselves or were sold by their families in times of hardship, such as famine.

Thus enslavement was essentially a violent robbery of human beings. The families of the slaves got nothing for the loss of their relatives. All the gains were shared by the slave dealers, from the local merchants and rulers in Africa to the European merchants and slave owners in the Americas. Unlike European emigrants to the New World, the African slaves could not even send remittances to their families back home.

There is no agreement on the global estimates of the Atlantic slave trade. Curtin (1969) estimated that 9,566,100 African slaves were imported into the Americas between 1451 and 1870. Curtin's estimates, with slight upward adjustments, have generally been accepted by most Western historians (Fage, 1969, 1975, 1978, 1980, 1989; Hopkins, 1973; Thornton, 1980, 1983; Wrigley, 1981; Miller, 1988). Lovejoy's periodic re-assessments amply bear this out. In a 1982 article he attacked the counting methods of Curtin's critics, and maintained that 'Curtin's initial tabulation was remarkably accurate', and estimated that 11,698,000 slaves were exported from Africa, of whom 9.8-9.9 million made it to the Americas; the rest perished during the Middle Passage (Lovejoy, 1982:501). More recently, Lovejoy (1989), following the discovery of new material by Richardson (1989a, 1989b) and others, has revised his estimates slightly upwards without abandoning his fidelity to Curtin's original estimates. He proposes 'an estimate of 11,863,000 slaves exported from Africa, allowing for losses at sea of 10-20%, [which] would mean that 9.6-10.8 million slaves have been imported into the Americas, which is well within Curtin's limits' (Lovejoy, 1989:373).

Some African historians have been critical of these estimates. In his controversial monograph Rodney (1982:chapter 4) implied that the numbers exported were much larger, although he did not give a specific figure. The most sustained attack has come from Inikori (1976, 1981, 1982, 1983), who has consistently questioned Curtin's methods of computation and the quality of the data employed, particularly the underestimation of the imports of slaves to Spanish, Portuguese and French America. He has suggested a 40% upward adjustment of Curtin's figures which brings the Atlantic slave exports to a total of 15.4 million, of whom about 8.5 million were from West Africa (Inikori, 1981:302).

The exact number of African slaves exported to the Americas may never be known. As Henige (1986) has observed, trying to provide an accurate global estimate of the volume of the Atlantic slave trade might be 'measuring the immeasurable', for there may be extant sources not yet known to historians or others that have been lost. Moreover, it is difficult to establish the number of slaves who arrived through the clandestine or 'illegal' trade, and those who died between the time of embarkation and arrival in the New World in both the 'legitimate' and clandestine trade. Even harder to discern is the number of captives who died during transit to, or while at, the coast awaiting embarkation, and of those who were killed during slave wars and raids. Ironically, after enumerating all these hurdles, he argues against the higher estimates. He concludes by urging historians to abandon broad analyses of the impact of the slave trade on Africa and focus on micro-studies, a call that has been echoed by Cordell and Gregory (1989:21-22), who recommend a 'temporary moratorium' on speculation about global figures. This is a summons to pedantic empiricism.

The 'numbers game', to use Curtin's phrase, is really less about statistical exactitude than the degree of moral censure. It is as if by raising or lowering the numbers the impact of the trade on the societies from which the slaves came and on the slaves themselves can be increased and decreased accordingly. The language and methods often used unveil the underlying ideological biases. There is a long tradition in Western scholarship of minimizing the demographic impact of the slave trade on Africa. It began with the pro-slavery propagandists during the time of the slave trade itself. The tradition lives on. There are those, as was mentioned earlier, who have argued that Africa had 'surplus' population or 'underutilized' labour.

Others have argued that the introduction of new foods, such as maize and manioc by the Portuguese, more than compensated for any population losses. In the words of Curtin (1969:270), 'it seems possible and even probable that population growth resulting from new food crops exceeded population loss through the slave trade'. More perversely, Gemery and Hogendorn (1978:247) state that 'it is likely that the pool of potential captives for the slave trade was larger because of the spread of American crops'. This argument rests on the dubious assumption that maize and manioc were more nutritious than existing food crops, and ignores the fact these crops were not widely adopted in many parts of Africa until the nineteenth century when the slave trade was coming to an end (Jones, 1959; Miracle, 1966). Certainly Africa did not require the slave trade to receive maize and manioc.

Some have called upon Malthus and nature to come to their aid. Caldwell (1977:14-15) has claimed that 'if one were to accept that there were fixed Malthusian limits set by subsistence at any given time, then the impact [of the slave trade] on total numbers would have been zero'. Miller (1988:156) asserts that 'slaving merely removed people who would otherwise have starved'. For Wrigley (1981:28), the slave trade could not have done the job of underpopulating Africa 'unaided, the argument must revert back to nature'. Alternatively, African women have been hailed for their fertility. Miller (1988:164) believes that slaving did not deplete the population of the Angola in the long run because 'the population containing such large numbers of fertile women possessed enormous abilities to produce children, great enough in fact to replace fully the demographic losses attributable to slaving'.

Similarly, Thornton (1983b:41) insists, on the basis of one census, that Angola did not suffer from depopulation because so many women were left behind. Never mind that his 'model is, of course, an average calculation based on rather crude assumptions'. Crude methodology has also not prevented Fage (1975) from making exaggerated claims. He contends, on the basis of Curtin's figures and the modern population of West Africa that the slave trade did not have a 'crippling' effect on population in West Africa, because the region suffered an average decline of only 1.6 per thousand per year, which was about the same rate of natural growth. Despite conceding that 'this is a very crude result... because of the crudity of the assumptions' (Fage, 1975:18), the conclusion that the slave trade did not lead to depopulation in West Africa is presented by Fage and his followers as if it were a fact.

Another tack has been to inflate the numbers of Africans sent to the 'Muslim World', or the 'Orient', which mainly means North Africa, as if the region is not in Africa. In the imperialist constructions of Orientalism and Africa the two are of course distinct configurations (Said, 1979; Mudimbe, 1987). It was the French historian Mauny who originally suggested that eight million Africans were taken north between 1500 and 1900, then later decided that more slaves went north, just as there were more going south and west, so he set a new figure of 14 million. Austen (1979) comes to the same figure, through a more circuitous, and supposedly thorough, route. Austin's figure includes all those slaves from 'Black' or 'sub-Saharan' Africa to the 'Muslim' world or 'Islamic' markets from 650 to 1900. But his 'direct evidence has accounted for a little more than 25% of the total estimate'. The present demographic configuration of Austen's 'Muslim world' has nowhere near the 100 million descendants of African slaves that are to be found in the Americas. One wonders what happened to all those slaves (Mazrui, 1986).

Austen's ideological objective is quite clear. It is, in his own words, to 'undermine beliefs that the Muslim slave trade was either very much worse (i.e. greater) or very much milder (i.e. smaller) than the European demand for African labour. Invidious comparisons between the two historical trends with sub-Saharan Africa may still be made, but if this chapter has any validity all partisans will have to be more cautious about invoking the support of numbers' (Austen, 1979:66). That is a rather extravagant claim given the fact that Austin's own case is weakly grounded on numbers.

Manning (1990:84) has demonstrated quite convincingly that the 'Oriental' slave trade, as he unfortunately calls it, was far smaller than the 'Occidental' trade. The former drew its slaves largely from the western coast, and the latter mainly from the Savanna and Horn. The eastern coast fed into both trades. Altogether he estimates that some 18 million were exported from tropical Africa from 1500, over three quarters of them in the seventeenth and eighteenth centuries: 11 million from the western coast, five million from the Horn and Savanna, and two million from the eastern coast.

The studies by Manning (1981, 1983, 1987, 1990), Manning and Griffiths (1988), and Inikori (1976, 1981, 1982, 1983) have persuasively demonstrated that the slave trade had a profound impact on the demographic processes of mortality, fertility and migration. The regions affected by the slave trade lost population directly through slave exports and deaths incurred during slave wars and raids. Manning (1990:171) estimates 'the absolute loss through slavery-related mortality as a cumulative total of four million persons'. Indirectly population losses were induced by epidemics caused by increased movements and famines brought about by the disruption of agricultural work, and flight to safer but less fertile lands.

The slave trade also altered the age and sex structures of the remaining populations and the patterns of marriage, all of which served to depress fertility rates. The people who were exported were largely between the ages of 16 and 30, that is, in the prime of their reproductive lives, so that their forced migration depressed future population growth. Moreover they were lost at an age when their parents could not easily replace them owing to declining fertility. The age structure of the population left behind became progressively older, further reinforcing the trend toward lower growth. Thus population losses could not easily be offset by natural increases, certainly not within a generation or two.

The sex ratio, which varied considerably between regions, was generally 60% for men and 40% for women in the Atlantic trade, and 67% female and 33% male in the trans-Saharan trade. This affected marriage structures and fertility patterns. In the areas affected by the Saharan trade, shortage of women reduced absolute fertility levels, while in the areas affected by the Atlantic trade the proportion of polygynous marriage increased, which, since it may have meant less sexual contact for women than in monogamous marriages, probably served to depress fertility as well.

The fertility of the coastal areas was also adversely affected by the spread of venereal diseases. The Mpongwe of Gabon, for instance, were ravaged by syphilis and smallpox, both brought by European slave traders. Smallpox epidemics killed many people, including those at the peak of their reproductive years, which, coupled with the disruption of local marriage customs and the expansion of polygyny, served to reduce fertility (Patterson, 1975).

The demographic impact of the slave trade varied according to region, locality and period. The regional variations were determined by the mechanisms of capture, institutions of enslavement, the distances travelled to the coast, and the ratio of males and females in the slave population. Overall, the western coast from West Africa to Angola suffered the longest and most sustained population decline, especially between 1730 and 1850. The most seriously affected was the Bight of Benin, where the population declined almost uninterrupted from 1690 to 1850. Senegambia and the Upper Guinea Coast underwent a modest population decline in the eighteenth century, while the decline of population in the Bight of Biafra began in the last four decades of the eighteenth century and persisted to the early nineteenth century. Following the collapse of Oyo, the Yoruba became the dominant group among West Africa's slave exports in the nineteenth century, so that their population declined noticeably. The Loango and Angolan regions began to suffer from severe population decline from the late eighteenth century until the 1840s. By then the slave trade had largely ended in West Africa and the region began to experience modest population growth.

In East Africa the trends were contradictory. Slave exports from the Horn, including Somalia and Ethiopia to Arabia and beyond, do not seem to have been large enough to reduce the population, although its growth was slowed. In the Sudan the smallness of the population and intensity of the slave trade may have led to population decline in the first half of the nineteenth century. Further south along the coast from Kenya through Tanzania to Mozambique the slave trade was relatively insignificant before the late eighteenth century. It exploded in the nineteenth century, thereby telescoping developments which elsewhere had unfolded over several centuries into one century. The slaves were mainly exported to the Indian Ocean islands where European and Arab plantation economies had been established, and to Brazil and Cuba. Madagascar both imported slaves from the mainland, and exported slaves to the islands of Mauritius and Reunion, and to South Africa (Campbell, 1981, 1987, 1988a). Mozambique, suffered the most (Isaacman, 1972; Alpers, 1975; Vail and White, 1980; Liesgang, 1983; Campbell, 1989).

The abolition of the slave trade brought to an end the massive exportation of Africans abroad and Africa's demographic decline could now be reversed. The factors behind the abolition have long been debated since Williams (1981) first suggested about 50 years ago that the slave trade ended because it had ceased to be profitable to the new system of industrial capitalism, itself a partial product of slavery. Previously historians had attributed the abolition to the pressure of humanitarians who were opposed to the slave trade on moral grounds (Mathieson, 1926; Coupland, 1933). The two approaches can be reconciled. The ideology of abolitionism did not emerge in a vacuum; it evolved in the context of an evolving industrial capitalism. Thus the two reinforced each other to render the slave trade and eventually slavery morally indefensible and economically archaic (Davis, 1975).

The abolition was a product of complex processes taking place in the Atlantic world, which should not be confined to events transpiring in Britain as is sometimes the case. Abolition was fomented by growing opposition to slavery by the slaves themselves, religious leaders, and human rights advocates. The various trends and tendencies were articulated in the Haitian Revolution which began in 1791 and culminated in the establishment of an independent republic in 1804 (James, 1963). This revolution and others in the Americas spelled the beginning of the end of the slave trade and slavery (Genovese, 1979). Abolitionist movements sprang up in the leading centres of the slave trade, Britain, West Africa, and the United States, out of which came a series of laws abolishing the slave trade and later slavery, as well as the resettlement schemes of Sierra Leone, Liberia and Gabon (Fyfe, 1974; Manning, 1990:149-57).

The timing of the abolition varied from country to country. For example, Denmark abolished its slave trade in 1792, followed by Britain in 1807, the United States in 1808, Brazil 1851, and Cuba 1868, to mention a few. The abolition of slavery itself came much later: 1838 in the British colonies, 1865 in the United States, 1886 in Cuba and 1888 in Brazil.

The end of the slave trade from Africa was, therefore, a protracted process which lasted a century. Thus the trade ended at different times for the various regions (Munro, 1976:40-55). The trade first came to an end in West Africa, for so long the mainstay of the Atlantic slave trade. By the 1830s the slave trade had become a thing of the past in this region. In west-central Africa, the trade continued until the 1850s when it began to slow down. In contrast, by then the slave trade was intensifying in eastern Africa. Thus West Africa was the first region to enjoy demographic solace from the slave trade. By the time of colonial conquest in the 1880s and 1890s it had been enjoying a rising population for a generation or two. West-central Africa enjoyed a much shorter 'baby boom' before colonial conquest brought its own demographic slump. In East Africa colonialism came when the slave trade was still taking its toll on the region's total population. Hence, the greater demographic catastrophe suffered by East Africa than West Africa at the turn of the twentieth century.

It is reasonable to conclude, therefore, that given the demographic impact of the slave trade on various regions in Africa, the continent's total population was probably in decline at least up to the mid-nineteenth century and may have remained stagnant for the rest of the century. Inikori (1982:37) has argued that there would have been '112 million additional population in sub-Saharan Africa had there been no export slave trade'. Manning (1990:85) believes it would have been at least 50 million more. The implications for Africa are enigmatic. Inikori postulates, using Boserup's (1965) model of population growth and development in pre-industrial societies, that population pressure would have provided an effective economic stimulus to technical innovation and development. Manning simply makes the observation that Africa's population was declining at precisely the same time that population elsewhere in the world was growing.

Of course we will never know exactly what would have happened if the slave trade had not occurred. For one thing, we do not know what decisions parents would have made if there had been no slave trade. Demographic processes involve complex interactions of biological and sociological variables. Their configurations as well as their articulation would have been quite different under a different demographic regime. The existing patterns and regulation of fertility would not necessarily have entailed more children (Jewsiewicki, 1987:272; Soejarto et.al., 1978; Farnsworth et.al., 1975). It may be as misleading to assume that underpopulation in precolonial Africa by itself caused underdevelopment as it is to argue that rapid population growth in the last half of the twentieth century is the cause of Africa's continuing crisis of underdevelopment. Economic development or underdevelopment cannot be correlated in any simple way to either population growth, stability, or decline, for population is not an independent variable, but a web that is interwoven in quite intricate ways into the fabric of socio-economic and political change.

This is merely to suggest that the slave trade had other effects, apart from the demographic one, which undermined Africa's economies and societies. One impact, which is sometimes obscured by excessive regionalization of world history, is that during the era of the slave trade, and partly because of the trade itself, Europe and North America became industrialized, and acquired the physical capacity, as well as the economic appetite and the ideological armour of racism to conquer Africa. Thus the colonial conquest of the late nineteenth century was a direct outcome of the slave trade (Rodney, 1982; Wallerstein, 1976, 1989).

The Atlantic slave trade, the largest forced migration in world history, may not have created European racism against Africans but it certainly bred it. As Patterson (1982) has demonstrated in his magisterial study, before it began slavery in the world was not confined to Africans. Indeed, in 1500 Africans were probably a minority of the world's slaves. But by the nineteenth century slavery was almost synonymous with Africans, so that the continent and its peoples carried the historical burden of prejudice and contempt accorded to slaves and despised social classes (Curtin, 1964). The debate started by Williams (1981) on the links between the slave trade and the development of capitalism needs to be widened beyond the narrow scope of whether or not the Caribbean slave trade was 'profitable' for British entrepreneurs (Anstey, 1975; Drescher, 1977, 1987; Solway and Engelman, 1987), and encompass the key contributions made by the slave trade to the constructions of capitalism and racism throughout the triangular world of the slave trade: Africa, Europe and the Americas.

Migrations and Immigration

The slave trade also led to population redistribution within and between regions in Africa. Not all the captives were exported, some were retained locally. This suggests that the Atlantic slave trade was linked to the growth of slavery within Africa. The thesis that slave exports generated an expansion of African slavery was first proposed by Rodney (1966, 1981) who argued that the trade necessitated the creation of unfree Africans who could be sold. He pointed out that the group of servile Africans was larger in the eighteenth century than it had been in the sixteenth. This challenged an older thesis which stated that slavery was already widespread by the time the Atlantic slave trade commenced (Wyndham, 1935:221-2; Fage, 1955:77-79). More recently, Fage (1980:310, 1989:108-9) has argued that slavery existed in West Africa prior to the external slave trade, although the latter led to its enlargement.

Manning (1990:20) and Mandala (1990:32) generally support Rodney's argument that slavery in Africa expanded and became a major institution as a direct result of the external trade. Some historians maintain, following Fage, that internal factors contributed more to the development of slavery in Africa than external factors. But their evidence is drawn from the period after, not before, the Atlantic trade started. For example, in his eagerness to find slavery among the Nguni, the best that Harries (1981:318) can do is to argue that 'domestic forms of slavery probably existed in Gazaland before the 1860s but they were hidden by the export of male slaves and the ease with which women and children were incorporated into the kin group'. Needless to say, by this time the external trade had been in operation for generations. Similarly, Searing (1988:475, 488, 500) believes that slavery in the Wolof states between 1700 and 1850 had little to do with the external trade, and even denies, unconvincingly, that, as many historians have argued, slavery expanded in the nineteenth century following abolition.

The weight of the evidence suggests that in many parts of Africa slavery greatly expanded in the nineteenth century (Miers and Kopytoff, 1977; Lovejoy, 1981, 1983, 1986; Robertson and Klein, 1983; Watson, 1980; Cordell, 1985; Willis, 1985; Manning, 1990; Mandala, 1990). The temporal and structural connections between African slavery and the Atlantic slave trade cannot be denied. As demand and prices for slaves in the Atlantic trade fell, demand for African commodities in Europe increased. It was the interplay of these two factors, and the existence of elaborate institutions developed to service the Atlantic trade, that led to the expansion of African slavery in the nineteenth century. Its abolition was gradual and was not completed well into the colonial period (Igbafe, 1975; Roberts and Klein, 1980; Romero, 1986; Miers and Roberts, 1988). As in the Americas, abolition of African slavery was fostered by slave revolts and the contradictory demands and ideologies of colonial capitalism. Its immediate legacy was not the development of 'free' labour, but of forced labour, which all the colonial powers instituted (Manning, 1990:160-8).

African slavery, which in this discussion includes the trans-Saharan slave trade, was part of the great waves of population migration in nineteenth century Africa. The slave trade from West to North Africa across the Sahara represented migration and population redistribution on an inter-regional scale. Many captives were also retained within West Africa itself as slaves. The Sokoto Caliphate, Asante, and Dahomey, just to mention some of the most well-known cases, imported large numbers of slaves to work on agricultural plantations and in craft industries. It has been estimated that slaves may have accounted for up to 15% of the region's total population (Manning, 1990:72). This figure may be too high, for various forms of servility and dependency which strictly did not connote 'slavery', are included. Whatever the true figure might be, it is quite clear that slavery was an important feature of the demographic structure and economies of the region.

The slave importing communities gained population, while those supplying slaves lost. The coastal areas of western Africa became relatively densely populated in the nineteenth century because of, not despite, the slave trade. The low population densities in eastern Angola and southern Zaire today have been attributed to the fact that these regions lost men and women to slave traders from further west (Thornton, 1980:427). The relative depopulation of the Nigerian Middle Belt has also been attributed to the slave trade (Mason, 1969; Gleave and Prothero, 1971).

It is more difficult to establish whether the population gains of acquiring slaves were reproduced generationally. Available fertility data shows that slave women had low rates of fertility and nuptiality (Meillassoux, 1983; Strobel, 1983; Klein, 1983, 1987). The reasons for the low fertility of slave women are not fully understood. It has been suggested that slave women limited the number of children they had by using various birth control methods (Harms, 1983; Cooper, 1977, 1980). The low fertility of slave women entailed that slave reproduction took place mostly through purchase or capture. This suggests that the tendency for slaves not to reproduce themselves as a class was not simply because African slave owning classes preferred to absorb the offspring of slaves for social reasons, or that they lacked sufficient power to control a self-reproducing slave class outside of the existing lineage structures, as various historians maintain, but was also governed by the dynamics of slave fertility and resistance.

In one sense, slaves resembled migrant workers, for they were mainly taken to centres of, and used for, commodity production. Of course, unlike the latter, they never went back to their respective homes unless they escaped. The expansion of commodity production in the nineteenth century also led to large scale voluntary migrations of farmers and agricultural labourers to regions where cash crop production was expanding, such as the peanut and cocoa growing regions of Senegambia and Ghana, respectively, as will be shown in Chapter 4. In Tunisia, the south and southeast dispersed migrants to the more favoured regions of the north and the Sahel (Valensi, 1985:12-15). In addition to migrant farmers and pastoralists, there were also the migrant transport workers, to be discussed in Part IV, who plied along the long distance trade routes within and between vast regions. In short, the economic transformations of the nineteenth century played a key role in encouraging the migrations of increasing numbers of people within the continent. Thus 'economic' migrations, including, labour migration, were not created by colonial capitalism (Amin, 1974).

The nineteenth century also witnessed the more familiar migrations of 'peoples', those epic movements of putative ethnic groups that historians love to chronicle. Ajayi (1989:3) states that the great migrations, involving extraordinary movements of large numbers of people over wide areas of space and time, had long since ended, for 'by 1800, the main linguistic and cultural divisions of the African population had long been established in their various locations, claiming their own portions of the land mass'. But some spectacular regional migrations and movements did take place in the nineteenth century, such as 'those of the Nguni in Southern Africa and Central Africa, the Chokwe in Central Africa, the Azande in East Africa, the Fang in Equatorial Africa and the Yoruba in West Africa' (Boahen, 1989:40). These movements were triggered by profound political, social and economic revolutions which took place in these regions in the course of the century.

These migrations need to be conceptualized more carefully. The notion that entire ethnic groups were moving is too simplistic, for it ignores the fact that ethnic groups are not objects cast in stone, but social constructions produced and reproduced under quite specific conditions. Often the actual migrants, as in the case of the Ngoni, were relatively few, but the societies constructed as Ngoni out of an integration of the migrants and the more numerous local inhabitants, were much larger. Projecting the migration backwards for the newly constructed 'Ngoni' is ahistorical at best. As it will be demonstrated in subsequent chapters with reference to many famous trading peoples, their ethnic identities were formed out of the constructions of trading diasporas. This is not to deny that large-scale movements of ethnic groups took place. It is simply to underline the need to identify migrations in terms of their causes and patterns, rather than ethnicity.

Three types of internal migration can be distinguished: first, the slave migrations; second, the migrations of voluntary labourers, farmers, and traders; third, the migrations of people displaced by warfare, natural disasters and famine. Slaves were emigrants who rarely returned to their societies, the second group usually engaged in oscillatory migration, and the third group can be considered as refugees, whose migration could either be temporary or permanent. Either status could of course be changed; slaves could escape and become refugees, migrant labourers could be enslaved, and refugees could become migrant labourers. The distinctions are valid only in so far as they distinguish the conditions that generated migration and its duration.

The first two types have been analyzed or referred to above. As for the refugees, little systematic work has been done on them. Most studies of African refugees concentrate on very recent times (Brooks and El-Ayouby, 1976; Kibrieab, 1983; Nindi, 1986; Harrell-Bond, 1986). The flow of refugees probably increased in the nineteenth century as a result of increased climatic pressures, the expansion of the slave trade and slavery, and the wars of colonial conquest. Withdrawal to other territories and maroonage in inaccessible regions were used to resist enslavement, and later the exactions of colonial conquerors. Isaacman (1976) has shown that withdrawal and maroonage increased in Mozambique at the turn of the twentieth century as the Portuguese tried to consolidate a ruthless colonial regime.

European and Asian Immigration

In addition to the internal migrations, there was also immigration of European and Asians into Africa. European immigration in the nineteenth century was concentrated in northern and southern Africa. Algeria, colonized by France in 1830, boasted the largest number of European settlers in North Africa. Their number grew from 7,812 in 1833 to 553,000 in 1901, two-thirds of whom were French citizens. From 1896 the number of Europeans born in Algeria exceeded those of immigrants. More than half of the French settlers in Algeria were rural farmers (Abun-Nasr, 1987:268-9; Bennoune, 1988:53). The European population in Egypt was the next largest. It rose from 6,000 in 1840 to 89,733 in 1882 and 111,270 in 1897, of whom 34% were Greeks, 22% Italian, 18% English, 13% French, and the rest Austro-Hungarians, Germans and others. The British community trebled between 1882, the year of the British occupation, and 1897. Altogether, the European immigrants made up 1.1% of the country's population. Unlike the settlers in Algeria, the Europeans in Egypt were concentrated in the cities and worked as military men, merchants, artisans and technicians (Panzac, 1987:25-28). Tunisia had 71,000 Italians and 24,000 French settlers by 1901

(Abun-Nasr, 1987:294). The European population in Morocco increased from about 130 in 1800 to 1,400 in 1867 and 20,000 in 1913, while in Libya foreigners did not number more than 5,000 in 1908, of whom 3,00 were Maltese and 1,000 Italians (Issawi, 1982:83). Thus at the end of the nineteenth century North Africa as a whole had about three quarters of a million European immigrants.

This was almost the same as the European population of South Africa, which had passed the 200,000 mark in the mid-nineteenth century and surpassed three-quarters of a million in the 1890s. The rapid growth of the European settlers in South Africa during the second half of the century was largely a product of the mineral revolution. Between 1890 and 1913 24,000 immigrants arrived annually from all over Europe, especially Britain, mostly to take up employment in the mining centres (Houghton, 1967:13). The first large batch of British settlers arrived in 1820 when nearly 5,000 of them were brought as indentured labourers (Hunt, 1984; Peires, 1989a). The original settler population, whose forbearers had arrived in the late seventeenth and eighteenth centuries, was largely of Dutch, German, and to a lesser degree, French extraction (Guelke, 1989). They later became known as Boers or Afrikaners and largely remained as farmers until the beginning of the twentieth century.

Outside of North and South Africa, the Portuguese colonial enclaves in present-day Angola and Mozambique were the only other places where there were noticeable numbers of European immigrants. Although the Portuguese had been in these countries since the sixteenth century 'in 1875 they would only have numbered a few hundred in all' (Newitt, 1981:148). The officials among them often returned to Portugal after their tour of duty. The traders and the convicts, the so-called degredados, who were supposed to spearhead Portuguese settlement and civilization in these territories, stayed. But since there were so few European women, they tended to intermarry with the African women, so that in a couple of generations they became indistinguishable from the African population (Bender, 1978). Most of the settlers came from Portugal itself and some were brought from Brazil. From 1880 Boers began arriving in southern Angola from South Africa and by 1900 there were 900 of them (Clarence-Smith, 1979:44). In Zimbabwe there were over 5,000 odd European settlers by the late 1890s (Phimister, 1988).

Taken together, the total number of European settlers in Africa in 1900 were about 1.5-1.7 million, most of whom had arrived in the second half of the nineteenth century. They far outnumbered Asian immigrants. The largest influx of Asians was in South and East Africa where the Asians were brought as indentured labourers largely to work on plantations, as in South Africa, or to build railways as in Kenya. The first Asians to come to South Africa were not, in fact, the indentured labourers, but slaves who were brought to the Cape Colony from India and the East Indies (Worden, 1985; Armstrong and Worden, 1989). Between 1860 and 1866 and 1874 and 1911 152,814 Indian labourers were taken to the Natal sugar plantations (Richardson, 1982:519). 'Besides working on the farms, Indian labourers were employed on the railways and in the coal mines, and even as domestic servants. Some later took to fishing' (Latham, 1978a:118). Some Indians, especially merchants, came on their own (Padayachee and Morrell, 1991).

In Kenya over 20,000 Indians were brought to build the Kenya-Uganda railway (Mangat, 1969; Ghai and Ghai, 1970; Bharat, 1972; Zeleza, 1982; Seidenberg, 1983). Those who remained after the end of their contracts joined the old Indian communities established in the region. Tanzania also had several thousand Indians. Large numbers also came to Mauritius. In addition, Arabs migrated to the East African coast probably in larger numbers than before, lured by the development of the plantation economies in the region. It is probable that altogether not less than 200,000 immigrants from Asia, both Indians and Arabs, arrived in eastern and southern Africa between the beginning of the nineteenth century and the early twentieth century. Adding that to the number of Europeans, Africa received close to two million immigrants.

The European and Asian immigrants engaged in a series of internal migrations of their own. Some of them were quite dramatic, such as the Boer trek in South Africa in which some 15,000 Afrikaners emigrated from the Cape Colony in the 1830s in protest against British hegemony in the colony and in search of a place where they could govern themselves. They first went to Natal, which they left when it became a British possession in 1843, and then moved on to the Orange Free State and the Transvaal, where their rivalries with the British continued (Keppel-Jones, 1975:61-75; Peires, 1989a:499-510). Some Indian merchants who came to South Africa relocated from Mauritius (Padayachee and Morrell, 1991:73-78). Indian merchants also moved from the East African coast into Uganda where there were 2,216 of them by 1911 (Latham, 1978a:118).

Patterns of Urbanization

The vast majority of Africans in the nineteenth century lived in rural communities - an aspect of course not peculiar to Africa. In 1800 only 2.4% of the world's population lived in cities of more than 20,000 (Mobogunje, 1968:19). Students of African urbanization have generally abandoned the old ethnocentric inanities of not calling African urban concentrations cities because they did not fit a particular index, such as literacy and the absence of agriculture (Childe, 1958; Sjoberg, 1960). Urbanization is a complex process that has not historically unfolded according to a pattern predestined in any particular region of the world. It is for the same reason that it is quite meaningless to talk of the 'African City', for there was no such thing. Urbanization in Africa, as elsewhere in the world, was a diverse process (Mabogunje, 1968:33-43; Gugler and Flanagan, 1978:19-22; Peel, 1980; O'Connor, 1983:25-55).

One of the most comprehensive quantitative analyses of the development of cities worldwide in the last 3,000 years has been produced by Chandler and Fox (1974). The study shows that some African cities were among the largest dozen cities in the world between 1360 BC and 1800 AD (Chandler· and Fox, 1974:367). For example, Cairo has consistently remained a large city by world standards since it was founded in the mid-tenth century AD (Abu-Lughod, 1961). The number of African cities with over 20,000 inhabitants or more rose from 15 in 800 to 38 in 1300 and 33 in 1800 (Chandler and Fox, 1974:44-48). This data, if correct, demonstrates that urbanization was not an uninterrupted process: cities rose and fell. By 1800 some of Africa's famous ancient cities, such as Thebes and Rosetta in Egypt, Napata and Meroe in the Sudan, Axum and Adulis in Ethiopia, Kumbi-Saleh, Awdaghust, Timbuktu, Jenne and Gao in West Africa, Mbanza Kongo, Loango, Dongo and Chungo in Central Africa, Zimbabwe and Mapungubwe in Southern Africa, and Kilwa, Gedi and Malindi along the East African coast, had long since declined or had even been abandoned (Hull, 1976; Conah, 1987).

This suggests that the number of urban dwellers in 1800 may not have been higher, in absolute terms, than in 1300 or 1500. For example, the population of both Cairo and Fez, the largest cities in 1500, had dropped almost by half in 1800. Out of the 33 large African cities in 1800, 18 were in West Africa, 12 in North Africa, and three in East Africa. But North Africa had five of the six largest, beginning with Cairo with 263,000, Tunis, 120,000, Meknes 110,000, then Oyo in West Africa with 85,000, and finally Algiers with 73,000 and Fez 60,000. By 1850 Cairo was still in first place but with a reduced population of 256,000, Alexandria had risen to second place with 138,000, Fez had risen into third place with 85,000, Tunis had fallen into fourth place with 90,000, and the last places were taken by the Yoruba cities of Abeokuta and Ilorin, each with 65,000. Altogether, by 1850 there were 25 cities of 40,000 inhabitants or more, 13 in West Africa, eight in North Africa, two in East Africa, and one each Central Africa and the Indian Ocean island of Mauritius (Chandler and Fox, 1974:48,366).

The North African data indicates that at the beginning of the century about 10% of the region's population lived in cities of 10,000 inhabitants or more (Issawi, 1982:100-101; Valensi, 1985:4-11; Bennoune, 1988:27; Shroeter, 1988:230). This ratio was higher than the world average. It was double that of the United States, slightly higher than France's, but far below the 25% for England and the Netherlands. The populations of Cairo, Tunis and Meknes have already been indicated. The other eight cities with populations of 20,000 or over ranged from Asyut, Damietta and Tarudant with 25,000 each, to Algiers with 72,000. During the nineteenth century North Africa's urban population grew steadily. In Egypt, it increased twice as fast as that of the country as a whole. By 1897 17% of the country's people lived in cities, led by Cairo with 570,062, followed by Alexandria with 319,396, and the Suez canal cities of Port Said with 42,328, Suez 17,173, and Ismailia 7,207 (Panzac, 1987:28-31). Morocco's urban population had increased to nearly 12%, led by Fez, after which came cities such as Rabat, Marrakech, Casablanca and Essaouira (Shroeter, 1988:219-21, 230). In Algeria, urban dwellers made up 6.5% of the total population in 1906 (Bennoune, 1988:53). The population of Tunis reached 170,000 in 1900, and that of Tripoli in Libya exceeded 30,000 (Issawi, 1982:101; Panzac, 1987:29). Libya lagged behind. The trend towards urbanization only began to accelerate in the last quarter of the century, so that 'by the early twentieth century Tripoli's population was about 30,000 people, [and] Benghazi's 19,000' (Anderson, 1984:329-330).

West Africa, as shown above, had a large number of the continent's cities. The development of Yoruba towns and cities has been chronicled in detail by several scholars (Mabogunje, 1968; Krapf-Askari, 1969; Law, 1977a). By the 1850s, there were at least 18 Yoruba towns with 15,000 inhabitants or more. The three largest were Ibadan, Ilorin and Abeokuta, each of which had a population of over 55,000. By the end of the century Ibadan, which began in 1829 as an insignificant Egba village, had become the third largest city in Africa with a population of nearly 200,000. Following the establishment of the Sokoto Caliphate in northern Nigeria, old cities, such as Kano, expanded and new ones, like Sokoto, emerged. By 1850 Sokoto had a population of 33,000, while Kano had 50,000-100,000 people at the end of the century (Frishman, 1977:225). The capitals of the costal states of Asante, Benin and Dahomey, namely, Kumasi, Benin city, and Abomey, also experienced remarkable growth (Hull, 1976:6-7, 16-18). Then there were the new towns of Freetown in Sierra Leone and Monrovia in Liberia founded by ex-slaves from Britain, North America and the Caribbean and captives rescued from slave ships off the West African coast.

In eastern Africa, some of the old coastal cities experienced revival and expansion. Malindi, for example, was ransacked by Oromo nomads in the late eighteenth century and by the 1850s was an abandoned ruin. But by the end of the century it had recovered and was a thriving town of several thousand people. Mombasa and Zanzibar expanded as well (Cooper,

1977:chapters 2-3). Port Louis on the Indian Ocean island had a population of 49,000 by 1850. On the mainland, Mengo, located on the northern shores of Lake Victoria and founded in the seventeenth century, remained the largest city with a population of over 40,000 (Chandler and Fox, 1974:55-57). A number of new urban centres also emerged, such as Ujiji on the eastern shore of Lake Tanganyika after 1830, Urambo and Tabora which evolved from clusters of Nyamwezi villages into towns in the 1870s, and Bweyorere and Rubaga, the capitals of Ankole and Buganda (Hull, 1976:8-9; Conah, 1987:214-5, 223).

Ethiopia and the Sudan had numerous towns and cities of various sizes. During the century some declined due to wars, while others expanded or were founded. The old Ethiopian capital of Gondar was devastated by civil wars and its population fell from about 80,000 at the end of the eighteenth century to about 4,000 in 1881. The capital shifted to Ankobar, which in the 1840s had 10,000-15,000 inhabitants, then in the 1880s Menelik settled at Liche, whose population was 15,000. Menelik established another temporary capital at Entoto, comprised of 50,000 people. Addis Ababa was founded in 1887. It grew rapidly, so that by the eve of the First World War it had 100,000 inhabitants. Other major Ethiopian cities included Harar, whose population rose from about 8,000 in the 1850s to 40,000-50,000 by the end of the century. The Eritrean cities of Asmara and Massawa grew steadily (Pankhurst, 1968:689-715). In the early nineteenth century a series of small towns grew in the northern Sudan, such as Shendi, al-Matamma and Kobbei. These towns were soon eclipsed by Khartoum, which grew from a small village to a major city with 30,000-40,000 inhabitants by 1860. There was also rapid growth of al-Masallamiyya on the Blue Nile, Kassala to the east, Dongola in the North and Suakin on the Red Sea coast (Bjorkelo, 1989:114-7).

The pattern and rate of urbanization in the hinterlands of the continent, especially Central Africa, is not as well known. This could either reflect the fact there were relatively few cities in the region, or that insufficient work has been done by historians and archaeologists on the region's urban history. For example, very few of the moving capitals of the interlacustrine states, such as Buganda and Ankole, some of which were described as very large by nineteenth century European explorers, have been investigated by archaeologists. The low 'archaeological visibility' of these sites has been attributed to the very mobility of the capitals and the use of construction materials, such as wood and grass, that left few deposits or structural remains (Conah, 1987:214-6). Recent studies on Central Africa are beginning to show that the region was not entirely left behind in terms of urbanization. By the mid-nineteenth century there were numerous towns scattered all over the Zaire basin and the 'northern savanna woodlands, some with populations over twenty thousand' (Hull, 1976:xvi). Among them were Kinshasa, founded in the early sixteenth century, and Malebo Pool (Vansina, 1973:247-65; Harms, 1981:73-81). The largest was Kasongo, which had over 40,000 inhabitants.

Southern Africa was probably the least urbanized region in Africa for the greater part of the nineteenth century. Following the rise of the Zulu state, a number of Zulu towns emerged, the largest of which was Umgungundhlovu, constructed in 1836, and burned two years later by Boer commandos. Other towns included Lattako, which had an estimated population of 10-15,000 people and was as large as Cape Town in circumference, Kaditshwene with 13-16,000, and Mashaw with approximately 12,000. Moshweshwe, the founder of the Basotho nation, established Thaba Bosiu, and Mzilikazi, father of the Ndebele state, set up Bulawayo, which had an estimated 10,000 people in 1888 (Hull, 1976: xvii, 22-24). Cape Town, the largest colonial town in region, had a population of 26,000 in 1850 (Chandler and Fox, 1974:379). Urbanization in Southern Africa accelerated from the 1870s, following the discovery of minerals. By 1871, within five years of the diamond discoveries, Kimberley had a population of 37,000. The city became the first in Africa to have electric street lighting (Wheatcroft, 1985:102). The growth of Johannesburg was even more spectacular. Gold was discovered in 1885. Ten years later Johannesburg had 100,000 inhabitants, and had become one of the largest cities in the continent (Keppel-Jones, 1975:107).

The diversity of African cities in the nineteenth century cannot be over-emphasized. These cities developed in a wide range of environments, political systems, social structures, cultural traditions and economic conditions. Thus it would be simplistic to posit a single model of urbanization. Characterizing them as 'traditional', 'preindustrial' or 'peripheral' does not explain much. Neither does differentiating them according to the contrived dichotomies of 'indigenous' and 'alien', or prefixing them with a religious badge such as 'Islamic'. It also follows that their development in the nineteenth century was spawned by different factors, especially the growth of trade, manufacturing and mining industries, agriculture, the rise of new states, social dislocations caused by warfare and natural disasters, and migrations.

The nineteenth century, as will be demonstrated in Parts IV and V, witnessed an enormous expansion in all levels of trade, domestic, regional, inter-regional and international throughout the continent. This contributed to the establishment of new cities and the expansion of old ones. In North Africa, for example, port cities grew faster than 'inland' cities due to the development of international trade. An additional factor in some cities, such as Cairo and Kano, was the expansion of manufacturing industries (Chaichian, 1988; Mahadi and Inikori, 1987). The growth of salt mining and production in Borno contributed to the growth of cities in that state (Lovejoy, 1986). Kimberley and Johannesburg in South Africa were products of mineral discoveries.

The revival and growth of some of the East African coastal cities owed a lot to the establishment of plantation agriculture in the region (Cooper, 1977, 1980). So did some of the cities of the Sokoto Caliphate, and Cape Town and Natal in South Africa (Lovejoy, 1978a; Lovejoy and Baier, 1975; Richardson, 1982). Many African cities, it is often forgotten, grew on lands of high productive potential (Conah, 1987:240-2).

The rise of new states was often accompanied by the establishment of new administrative centres which sometimes grew into large cities. The Sokoto Caliphate set up the city of Sokoto, the Ndebele state Bulawayo, the Madhist state Omdurman, and the Ethiopian state Addis Ababa, and the inter-lacustrine states had their moving capitals. Towards the end of the century the newly imposed colonial states turned existing towns and cities, such as Lagos, Khartoum and Cairo into administrative capitals, or established new ones where towns had never existed before, such as Lusaka, Nairobi and Harare. The influx of European administrators, traders and rural immigrants seeking work led to the rapid expansion of some of these old cities. For example, Cairo grew at an average annual rate of 12.5% during the 1882-1897 period, as compared to 1% from 1846 to 1882 (Chaichian, 1988:26). Lagos grew from a population of 18,000 in 1850, a year before the British occupation, to 41,000 in 1901. In the second half of the nineteenth century Lagos became a major trading port along the Nigerian coast and the springboard of British colonialism into Nigeria (Aberibigbe, 1975).

The social dislocations caused by warfare, slave raiding, and the collapse of states sometimes led to the creation of defensively laid out towns and cities, or the inflow of refugees into existing urban centres. The collapse of the Oyo empire, for example, profoundly affected Yoruba urban development and the expansion of cities such as Ibadan (Mabogunje, 1968; Krapf-Askari, 1969). Many towns and cities grew by natural increase, but migration sometimes played an important role as well (O'Connor, 1983:57). The migrations could be temporary or permanent. Ethiopian cities tended to swell in size during important marketing days (Pankhurst, 1968:chapter 15). In urban formations, such as the Yoruba cities, where farmers formed a considerable part of the inhabitants, rural-urban migration was an integral part of city life (Mabogunje, 1968; Krapf-Askari, 1969). In Egypt the rate of rural-urban migration increased with the development of cotton cash crop production and land concentration (Chaichian, 1988:30-32).

European and Asian migration contributed to the growth of some cities. For example, until the 1920s Europeans 'constituted a large minority of the population of such cities as Algiers, Oran, Casablanca, Tunis, Tripoli, Benghazi, ... Alexandria, and Port Said' (Issawi, 1982:102). The Europeans in these cities often lived in separate quarters under the control of their consuls. In Tunis attempts were made to bring them under control through the creation of a municipal council, especially as the number of Europeans 'without means of support increased, [so that] the crime rate, which in all North African cities had been quite low, rose sharply' (Cleveland, 1978:46). In 1897, Europeans made up 6.2% of Cairo's population, 14.4% of Alexandria's, and 21.6% of the Canal Zone cities (Panzac, 1987:31). European immigrants constituted a large proportion of South African cities, including Cape Town, Natal, Kimberley, and Johannesburg. Natal also attracted many Asian immigrants, so did Saint Louis in Mauritius, and the Kenyan cities of Mombasa and later Nairobi.

City Layout

The physical structure of African cities varied enormously. As already noted some were very large, others no better than overgrown villages. The great cities of North and West Africa were often surrounded by walls, interspaced with gates. The walls were constructed for many reasons: for defence, to facilitate economic and population control, and to enhance the political prestige of the rulers. Public walling was absent from some West African cities such as Kumasi, Freetown and Monrovia, as well as in the East African coastal cities and the new colonial cities. In the last quarter of the nineteenth century gates were removed from inside Egyptian cities. This, together with the opening up of enclosed neighbourhoods and the introduction of night lighting, transformed urban and bazaar morphology (Toledano, 1990:166-70).

The organization of space in the cities reflected their economic and administrative functions, the articulation of class, kinship and ideological relations and the configuration of internal struggles, and their relation to both the rural hinterland and the regional systems of power in which they were set (Hull, 1976; Abrams and Wrigley, 1978; Peel, 1980; al-Sayyid-Marsot, 1984; Conah, 1987). In many West African towns and cities dwellings were built 'close to each other, but blocks of buildings were separated by narrow alleys. Many of the larger towns and cities were intersected by avenues, and alleyways not only opened onto these broad thoroughfares but were broken by pleasant community plazas. In politically centralized societies, particularly Asante, Yoruba, Hausa, and Ganda, towns tended to be radial concentric with roads commencing at the royal compound or central marketplace and radiating to the various provincial centres' (Hull, 1976:41).

North African cities were generally divided into two parts, the open 'public city', with its thoroughfares, markets and mosques, royal palaces and government offices, and the relatively secluded 'private city', with its labyrinth of winding streets and narrow alleys where families resided (Hourani and Stern, 1970; Raymond, 1984). The focal points at the core of these cities were the market area or bazaar and the principal mosque.

The large towns and cities were often separated into quarters and wards, themselves usually made up of several compounds of households. For example, Kano held 127 wards, and Kumasi 77. These quarters or wards reflected the divisions and solidarities of class, occupation, age, ethnicity, and religion. In the major cities of West and North Africa, foreign merchants sometimes lived in their own quarters. As it will be argued in Part IV, this was to facilitate control and taxation by the state. In some societies, such as Old Calabar and the Sokoto Caliphate, servile populations lived in segregated quarters (Hogendorn, 1977; Mason, 1981).

It was also common practice for the wealthy and the poor, the rulers and the subjects, to live in separate sections of the cities. For example, in Kukawa, the capital of Bornu, 'the eastern half was reserved for wealthy residents (kings, leading chiefs, and merchants), while the western half, separated by a cleared open space approximately half-mile long, was crowded and poor, with narrow, winding alleys' (Hull, 1976:81). Class distinctions were often marked by the size and type of houses. In Egyptian cities by the mid-nineteenth century 'perhaps the most significant difference between types of dwellings, was the space allocated to gardens. Palaces and elite mansions had gardens', while the poor did not (Toledano, 1990:169). A visitor to Ashanti in 1874 noted that 'an ordinary house has one courtyard; a large house three or four; the King's palace had ten or twelve' (Rutter, 1971:155).

Conclusion

It is evident from this chapter that great efforts have been made in the last two decades to reconstruct Africa's demographic history using a wide range of conventional and non-conventional sources. The popular use of the so-called non-conventional sources in African historical demography has been partly dictated by the paucity of the conventional sources in many parts of the continent, as well as by the historians' interest in unravelling broader demographic processes that go beyond measuring demographic events.

Attempts have been made to estimate Africa's population and its rate of growth in the nineteenth century, but these estimates need to be treated with extreme caution. Trying to get exact figures may be an exercise in futility.

More fruitful are attempts to gauge the general trends. The available estimates seem to indicate that Africa's total population declined or stagnated between 1750 and 1850. It probably rose slightly in the next half century, but by 1900 Africa most likely had a lower share of the world's population than in 1750.

The major factor behind the decline in Africa's total population compared to other continents is the Atlantic slave trade. Obviously this does not mean that all parts of the continent were affected equally by the slave trade. North Africa, for example, was a net importer of slaves. Among the slave-exporting regions the demographic impact of the slave trade was extremely uneven. For one thing, the timing of the abolition varied. Apart from contributing to the global redistribution Africa's population, the Atlantic slave trade also led to population redistribution within and between regions in Africa itself, for not all captives were exported outside the continent. This chapter generally supports the argument that the Atlantic slave trade contributed to the growth of slavery within Africa.

There was, of course, more to African demographic history than the slave trade and slavery. It has been argued that African slavery was part of the great waves of population migration within the continent in the nineteenth century. In addition to the slave migrations, there were the migrations of voluntary labourers, farmers and traders, which grew as a result of economic expansion, especially the production of export commodities as will be demonstrated in the next few chapters. Finally, people who were displaced by warfare, natural disasters and famine also migrated. Besides these internal migrations, it has been estimated that Africa received about two million immigrants from Europe and Asia, who were mostly concentrated in northern and southern Africa.

The diversity of the processes and patterns of urbanization makes a mockery of attempts to encapsulate African cities under any one rubric, such as 'traditional', 'preindustrial', or 'peripheral'. It is quite remarkable how urbanized some parts of the continent were in the precolonial era. However, the fact still remains that the vast majority of Africans, perhaps as much as 95%, lived in rural communities. Unfortunately, little historical research has been done on rural settlement patterns but it would not be far-fetched to assume that there were enormous variations across the continent. For one thing, the systems of agriculture, the mainstay of African economies and societies, differed greatly. In turn, Africa's diverse agrarian systems were, to a considerable extent, spawned by the continent's varied demographic regimes, not to mention environmental conditions.

Part   II

Agricultural Production

3. Systems of Land Use

Methods of Cultivation

Africa is a vast continent with varied ecological and demographic regimes, and different socio-economic and political structures, all of which have affected the development of agriculture in various parts of the continent. In the nineteenth century, the methods of cultivation used in any given area were a product of the complex interactions of physical and human geography, history and political economy. Among the environmental conditions which set the broad parameters of agricultural development were the nature of the climate, especially the patterns of rainfall, the existence and nature of drainage systems, and soil formations. As noted in Chapter 1, climate in Africa is neither uniform nor unchanging. African farmers have to adapt to the climatic variations and the conditions of their soils. Many of the broad generalizations about African agricultural practices do not take into account the wide range of environmental settings within the continent and are often extrapolated from a single specific case to represent the whole continent.

Africa can be divided into eight climatic regions: the hot deserts, comprising the Sahara and Kalahari deserts; the semi-arid, on the fringe of the desert areas; the tropical wet-and-dry, covering most of the savanna belt; the equatorial found in the rainforest regions of Central Africa; the Mediterranean on the northern and southern extremities of the continent; the humid subtropical marine of the southeast coast of southern Africa; the warm temperate upland of the Highveld of southern Africa; and the mountain climatic region encompassing the high mountain areas of Ethiopia and the lake region of East Africa. The major drainage basins include those of the Nile, the Niger, the Congo, the Zambezi, the Orange rivers, and of Lake Chad. The soil types in Africa can be divided into about five broad categories: desert soils, the chestnut brown soils of the semiarid regions, chernozem-like and black soils, red tropical soils and laterites, and Mediterranean soils (D'Hoote, 1964; Moss, 1968; Thomas and Whittington, 1969; Hance, 1975; Thompson, 1975; Lewis and Berry, 1988).

The human environments of the nineteenth century were no less diverse than the physical ones. Population densities and settlement patterns differed from one society and region to another (Stevenson, 1968). Agricultural development was also affected by each society's political and economic structures, including the rules governing land tenure, the revenue base of the state, divisions of labour, the development of markets and the society's incorporation into regional and international trading networks. In addition to these factors, the methods of cultivation were influenced by the range and nature of the crops grown.

There was a continuum of land use, ranging from discontinuous and extensive forms to continuous and intensive forms of cultivation. The specific form used in a particular area at a particular time depended on a combination of the various factors identified above. Continuous and intensive land use tended to be found where and when some or all of the following conditions prevailed: a high level of management of the soil's physical properties had been attained, population settlement was relatively dense, rainfall was regular or other water resources were available for irrigation, the crops were wide in range, perennial in nature, or ecologically restricted, and state intervention was pronounced. Discontinuous and extensive forms were found where and when the opposite prevailed. It is difficult to label the subdivisions in the continuum of land use in precolonial Africa, and certainly it is fatuous to try to rank them in lineal progression from 'backward' to 'advanced' (Hopkins, 1973:36; Richards, 1985).

By the beginning of the nineteenth century, farmers in various parts of Africa had long learned how to manipulate and exploit their respective ecosystems, each of which demanded different forms of land management. The need for careful management was particularly acute in the tropical heartlands of the continent. It has been established that in tropical soils it is easier to restore nutrients to exhausted soils than to repair soils that have physically 'collapsed' (Ahn, 1970; Greenland and Lal, 1977; Lal and Greenland, 1979). Soil moisture conservation and supplementation and erosion control are important in the drier extremes of the tropical zones, while in the equatorial zone maximizing the use of available sunlight and coping with excess soil moisture, apart from erosion control, are the most important land management issues. All these issues assume significance in the intermediate zone of wetter savannas, though at different times during the cultivation cycle. It was here that the widest range of cultivation techniques were developed, including limited tillage, heaping, ridging and terracing, crop and land cultivation, mulching, the application of soil conditioners, and inter-cropping.

Space does not allow us to discuss the wide range of agricultural systems developed or used in nineteenth century Africa. It will suffice to consider seven methods and techniques of cultivation and soil management: shifting cultivation, intercropping, agro-forestry, terracing, wet land and irrigated farming, and mixed farming. Shifting cultivation has had a bad name among many scholars. It has been portrayed as a backward and wasteful method of farming (Boserup, 1965; McLoughlin, 1970; Anthony, et.al, 1979; Erskine, 1987). Others have pointed out that shifting cultivation does not belong to an early rung on the evolutionary ladder of agricultural development, but constitutes an integrated farming system suited to tropical ecology (Ahn, 1970; Hopkins, 1974; Ruthenberg, 1980). For example, the importance of bush burning in shifting cultivation can only be appreciated when it is realized that phosphorous is the only major plant nutritional element that is 'frequently deficient in both the forest and savanna zones of Africa' (Ahn, 1970:167). Burning releases phosphorous from the vegetation to the soil.

The two approaches above, despite their different characterizations of shifting cultivation, have one thing in common: they see it as a single system. In reality, the term refers to a wide variety of land management procedures. Miracle (1967), for example, has identified no less than 12 types of shifting cultivation in the Congo basin alone. This has led some to abandon the use of the term and talk of 'land fallowing systems'. Richards (1985:54) has suggested that far from being a relic of tradition, shifting cultivation may, in fact, have expanded in the late nineteenth century as communities ravaged by the slave trade sought to reclaim previously long-settled areas, or as they tried to respond 'rapidly to new demands of food production created by colonial conditions. On this reckoning, then, the extent of shifting cultivation in the early colonial period, rather than signalling the intrinsic «backwardness» of African agriculture, might be better interpreted as evidence of its innovativeness and responsiveness to changing economic circumstances'.

Perhaps the most widespread method of cultivation and soil conservation was intercropping. Intercropping involves planting different species, and different varieties of the same species on the same farm. Related to intercropping were sequential cropping, and 'relay cropping', in which crop sequences in an agricultural year did not and did overlap (Steiner, 1982). Among the Swazi, Crush (1987:16) informs us, 'intercropping of the grain crops with pumpkins, gourds, melons, cowpeas, beans, and sweet potatoes was common'. Among the Mang'anja of southern Malawi, Mandala (1990:58) states, maize 'was intercropped with beans, pumpkins, tobacco, sugarcane, and many kinds of vegetables and legumes'. Miracle's (1967) study provides fascinating details of the intricate systems of crop combination and sequences among the peoples of the Congo basin. Intercropping was once viewed by the self-righteous but ignorant colonial officials as a sign of Africa's agricultural backwardness. Now agronomists have discovered the advantages of intercropping (Igbozurike, 1977; Belshaw, 1979; Okigbo and Greenland, 1977; Steiner, 1982).

The advantages of intercropping were many. First, the mixture of crops on one plot of land provides a cover of plants for the soil, thereby protecting it from erosion due to excessive rainfall and winds. Second, the available soil moisture and plant nutrients are fully used because different plants have different and complementary requirements and root at different depths. Third, the spread of pests and diseases is lessened because neighbouring plants are less likely to be of the same species. Fourth, the growth of weeds is lessened, which helps reduce the amount of labour required for weeding in the later stages of the crops' growth. Fifth, the use of available sunlight is maximized because different plants have different growth characteristics and leafing patterns. Sixth, yields tend to be better and higher than under sole cropping systems because crop combinations have beneficial effects on soil-temperatures and the micro-climate. Finally, the risks of crop failure due to, for example, drought are lessened, because the different crop varieties and species grow and mature at different speeds and they have different moisture requirements. 'Intercropping', Richards (1983:27) enthuses, 'is one of the great glories of African science. It is to African agriculture as poly-rhythmic drumming is to African music and carving to African art'.

Agro-forestry, or the planting of trees in cultivated fields, was a notable feature of farming in some parts of Africa, such as Zimbabwe. The trees not only helped maintain soil fertility and provided shade and shelter during work and cloudbursts, they also provided fruits in the case of fruit trees, timber, firewood and fibre. The types, diversity and density of trees grown in the sandy soils differed from those in the red clay soils. In the sandveld the diversity and density of trees was greater than in the clayveld. Also, the sandveld trees produced large quantities of slowly decomposing leaf litter, which helped improve the soil 'by releasing nutrients collected below the rooting depths of cereals', while in the clayveld where water was a more limiting factor for plant growth than nutrients, farmers used trees that 'improve infiltration of rainfall into the soil and reduce evaporation losses' (Wilson, 1989:376-7). So integrated were trees in the farming system that there were taboos against cutting them in the fields. Thus prevailing environmental ideology or 'religion', as Wilson calls it, imbued field trees with a protective sacredness.

Terracing has been reported from many places and was used to manage loose soils on slopes, which would otherwise erode badly. The terraces were usually constructed with stones cleared from the field during hoeing or ploughing. Some people chose to live in hilly places not only for security reasons, but also because despite the dangers of erosion, hills 'tended to bear a more varied vegetation and richer natural resources, and to attract the rain which so often passes over the surrounding plains' (Sutton, 1984:32). This is what attracted the Kamba and Taita of Kenya, for example, to settle around the Mbooni and Taita hills, respectively, where they built terraces and occasionally irrigation ditches, which enabled them to practice intensive agriculture (Sheriff, 1985).

Extensive terraced fields also existed in Inyanga in eastern Zimbabwe along with miles of irrigation channels. It is believed that the Inyanga terraces were abandoned in the eighteenth or early nineteenth century for reasons that are not very clear (Sutton, 1984). Among the Wasambaa of Tanzania it is said stones were piled in walls and ridges which were reinforced by planted hedges (Kjekshus, 1977:33). The Wahehe and Pare of Tanzania also constructed impressive terraces against erosion. Terracing was a particularly important aspect of soil conservation in the hilly countries of Burundi and Rwanda (Miracle, 1967:174).

Various forms of wet-land, flood retreat and valley farming systems were developed along rivers in various parts of the continent. It has been argued that wet land ridge farming on vlei lands or dambos was the dominant agricultural system in southern Zimbabwe in the nineteenth century. The dambos were rich and fertile. Dambo cultivation provided 'great stability in production in the face of rainfall variability' (Wilson, 1989:371). The Mang'anja of southern Malawi also cultivated in dambos besides using the dry lands. The dambo fields were known as dimba, while those on the dry land were called munda (plural minda). The dimba were located on the plains surrounding the Tchiri and other rivers. Contrary to the contemporary situation in the region in which munda cultivation predominates, 'during the nineteenth and early twentieth centuries... dimba farming contributed as much to the food economy as, if not more than, the alternate munda system' (Mandala, 1990:56). This system was intensive, highly productive, and an effective insurance against drought.

In West Africa wet-land agriculture was also widespread. In the late nineteenth century the Temme of Sierra Leone created extensive estuarine rice polders on the lower Scarcies to meet the demand of the growing market for rice in Freetown (Richards, 1985:26). In fact, swamp rice cultivation with varying degrees of water control was quite widespread throughout the West African rice zone. Dry season flood retreat cultivation was also practised. Richards (1985:73) has argued that the various forms of wet-land cultivation constituted irrigation agriculture, if irrigation is understood to mean 'any process, other than natural precipitation, which supplies water to crops' (Stern, 1980:3).

Small-scale irrigation techniques were developed in several parts of Southern and Central Africa (Vansina, 1973; Palmer and Parsons, 1977; Birmingham and Martin, 1983). In West Africa there was irrigation in parts of the savanna, for example, near Katagun in northern Nigeria where there were irrigated wheat fields (Wickins, 1981:41), and along the south-west where swamp rice was grown, and on the flood-plains of the Niger and Senegal rivers, where millet, maize and rice were cultivated (Hopkins, 1973:34). But there were some valley environments in West Africa which were agriculturally unsuitable for irrigation because of river blindness (Richards, 1983:28-29).

Large, labour-intensive irrigation systems also existed in some parts of the continent. One of the oldest and most extensive systems of irrigation farming was found in Egypt, a desert country that has survived since Pharaonic times by the skin of the Nile. Since ancient times Egypt used 'basin' or 'flood' irrigation. The flood needed relatively little land preparation, but a great deal of labour was required to raise water to fields growing crops in the dry pre-flood months by means of the saqiya and shaduf. The periodic floods not only allowed the basin lands to lay fallow for a considerable time, enabling the soil to be regenerated, but the annual 'washing' of these lands and the higher fields also prevented the accumulation of salts in the soil (Richards, 1981:47-:47-48).

Egypt's irrigation system was radically transformed in the nineteenth century. After taking power in 1805, Muhammad Ali's regime set out to repair and extend the old system and then, from the 1820s, to introduce perennial irrigation through the construction of dikes, dams and canals in order to raise the water level in the river and in the canals during the dry, pre-flood summer months. By 1833 some 400 kilometres of canals had been dug. Ali's successor, Ishmail (1863-79), added another 13,500 kilometres at a cost of some 12.6 million. The expansion programme continued when the British seized the country in 1882 (Issawi, 1982:129-30). The development of perennial irrigation made possible the dramatic growth in the cultivated and cropped areas. The cultivated area increased from 3,053,000 feddans in 1821 to 4,943,000 feddans in 1897, while the cropped area increased from 3,053,000 feddans to 6,725,000 feddans during the same period (Waterbury, 1979:36 - See note on weights and measures on p.iv).

But population grew at an even faster rate, so that by 1897 there were 0.52 cultivated feddans per person, down from 0.62 feddans in 1821 (Parvin and Putterman, 1980:84). And perennial irrigation had its costs. The use of dikes to prevent the flooding of land while the summer crops were still in the ground meant that the land devoted to summer cultivation no longer received the benefits of periodic washing by the Nile floodwater, so that salination increased and reduced the productivity of the land. Moreover, the shutting off of the canals at flood time to safeguard summer crops resulted in much of the water carrying the rich Nile mud being lost to the sea. Far more labour was required than before to build the works, operate the greatly increased number of saqiyas, of which there were 52,836 by 1844, and shadufs, keep up the dikes, and clean the canals and drains. Most importantly, the substitution of basin irrigation by perennial irrigation led to the spread of bilharzia (Rivlin, 1961:213-49).

Egypt's irrigation system was by far the largest in the continent. But it was by no means the only one. In the subdesert zones of Tunisia an indigenous system was developed whereby foggara, or underground conduits, were constructed which 'carried water from the foothills to the irrigable land. There, as in other oases, it was less a question of digging for water than of assuring its equitable and regular distribution during the period of scarcity' (Valensi, 1985:124). The distribution and control of the water was carefully managed. In some regions the water was private property, with each farmer having a fixed share of water. In Algeria seven small dams were built by the French colonial government at a cost of 6.3 million francs in the second half of the century.

In north-eastern Africa irrigation was considerably extended in the northern Sudan. The saqiya irrigated lands were highly valued and struggle over them intensified in the course of the century as a result of population growth and increased commodity production (Spaulding, 1982). In Ethiopia 'irrigation was fairly widely practised in many areas, including Tigre and Semen, Yeju, Awsa, the Alamaya area, and Konso. The usual practice in Tigre... [was] that small channels would be dug from the higher parts of a stream to conduct the water across a plain which would be criss-crossed with small ditches' (Pankhurst, 1968:187).

In Kenya elaborate irrigation systems developed in lower Marakwet in the Kerio rift, 'especially in the Endo section with its long furrows spectacularly engineered from high up the rivers and along the escarpment face, eventually to feed the fields laid out on the valley floor' (Sutton, 1984:37). In Tanzania irrigation was practised by the Wasambaa, in the Usagaras, and most importantly among the Chagga where 'detailed irrigation systems... were cut from the mountain streams often several miles above the settled areas and the water conducted in skilfully constructed troughs and tunnels along the mountainside to reach the individual settlements by way of innumerable branches and rivulets' (Kjekshus, 1977:35). Elaborate rights and privileges were attached to the irrigation system which allowed a third cropping season beyond the normal two. Irrigation provided the basis of agriculture among the Sonjo as well who lived in a relatively dry area (Gray, 1963).

Large scale irrigation works were built in Madagascar in the nineteenth century. It has been suggested that the transition from swidden agriculture to irrigated riziculture began in Imerina in the late seventeenth century. Rice had been cultivated on the east coast of Madagascar for centuries from where it spread to Imerina through the southern plateau. Irrigated riziculture in

Imerina apparently began as forests disappeared due to swidden cultivation. By the nineteenth century two irrigation systems had developed. The first depended on mountain run-off in which the water was distributed to numerous terraces down the mountain slopes. Dikes were built to control the amount of water let into each terrace and paddy. The second irrigation system derived its water from dammed lowland rivers. The water was collected in reservoirs and delivered to surrounding fields through canals. Both systems expanded and by the end of the nineteenth century irrigated riziculture had become the basis of the agricultural economy of Imerina (Berg, 1981).

Irrigation systems did not always survive the vagaries of population movements, exhaustion, or climatic change. The abandoned Inyanga terraces and irrigation channels testify to that, as does the irrigation system of Engaruka in the northern Tanzanian rift valley, perhaps the most sophisticated of its time in the region. Engaruka 'was an essentially isolated and self-sufficient settlement in dry country, absolutely dependent on its exquisite irrigation devices. Eventually this community expired, as its soil was exhausted and its water supplies declined' (Sutton, 1984:41). This apparently happened in the seventeenth or eighteenth century.

Farming Tools

Generations of farming experience produced the agricultural tools most suited to the soil in various parts of the continent. Thus tools were adapted to environmental conditions and also reflected the crops being cultivated. The tools, in turn, affected the system of cultivation. Wilson (1989:371-2) has made the tantalizing suggestion that in Zimbabwe 'in the early twentieth century there was a general trend towards the greater adoption of shifting cultivation [partly due to] the wider availability of axes, [and] the introduction of ploughs...'. This underscores the fatuity of evolutionary agricultural models that posit a unilineal development from shifting and extensive to permanent and intensive farming.

Broadly speaking, there were two main types of tools for cultivation, ploughs and hoes. Ploughs have been used in parts of north and north-eastern Africa since time immemorial. The ploughs varied from region to region even within the same country, depending on the soil conditions. In Tunisia, for example, there were three types of ploughs - the tooth plough, the swing plough, and the frame-handle plough, each of which had its own variations. The ploughs tended to be larger and heavier in the north with its relatively heavier soils than in the south. Self-righteous European observers considered the Tunisian ploughs 'inferior to the heavier implements used in northern Europe that could plough more deeply. Now that natural conservation is as much a concern as increased production, there is no question that the

[Tunisian] plough was less harmful to the soil, that it slowed erosion, and prevented a too deep evaporation of soil moisture. Requiring only light draft animals, easy to construct, and inexpensive to replace, it was clearly the implement best suited to the household economy of precolonial Tunisia' (Valensi, 1985:138-9).

Egyptian peasants also used a wide range of wooden ploughs with iron tips, which were best suited to their respective soils, a fact recognized by Muhammad Ali, the ambitious modernizer. Ali and his cohorts 'resisted the temptation to introduce European tools' because they realized 'that with all its faults the Egyptian plough worked the land better than the European ones, which made the furrows too wide and deep. Various experiments by the government with European devices demonstrated their unsuitability and no attempt was made to provide fellahin with them. As late as 1916 it was confirmed that not as single plough with which experiments had been made had proved superior to the indigenous one, mechanically, agriculturally, and economically, at one and the same time' (Rivlin, 1961:168-9).

But there were places where European ploughs spread in the nineteenth century. One was Algeria, with its large European settler population, and the other was South Africa, also a country with a large settler population. African peasants in South Africa, according to Bundy (1979), quickly took to the use of ploughs and other European implements, which not only increased their productivity, but also changed the gender division of labour in agriculture. The upkeep of livestock had traditionally been a male preserve, and tillage a female domain. The use of ox-drawn ploughs ensured that men would become more active in tillage. The adoption of the plough had other social ramifications. For example, 'the economic basis of polygamy - the need of the head of a large household to have more than one (food-producing) wife - was greatly diminished' (Bundy, 1979:95). Indeed, according to a contemporary observer, by the 1890s few girls would 'consent to marry a man who does not possess a plough, knowing that if her husband is without one, her life must be one of severe toil' (Bundy, 1979:95).

It has been argued, however, that ploughs did not become as widespread among the peasants as Bundy contends, so that the changes that Bundy attributes to the adoption of ploughs were probably caused by other factors (Lewis, 1984). Bundy's account, which was intended to celebrate the peasants' capacity for innovation, is inadvertently Eurocentric. European ploughs are placed, as in Goody's (1971) model, on the pedestal of agricultural technological development. The adverse environmental effects of these ploughs is left unacknowledged. Showers' (1989) recent study on soil erosion in Lesotho has demonstrated that the adoption of European ploughs in the country from the mid-nineteenth century contributed significantly to the process of accelerated soil erosion.

'The adoption of ploughs', Showers (1989:276) argues:

> *not only reduced the absolute amount of grazing land, but also affected the quality of land available for grazing... As agriculture displaced grazing on the best soils, livestock was increasingly relegated to [the] more marginal lands.*

The increase in livestock herds only made matters worse. The problems of soil erosion were compounded by the activities of missionaries who indiscriminately cut trees for carpentry, harvested shrubs for fuel, and tilled grassland for farming, as well as the introduction of ill-planned roads. The result was that: 'gully erosion [which] was essentially unknown in the 1830s... had developed along the roads and on some mission stations by the early 1880s... [and] was apparent on government reserves by the mid 1890s' (Showers, 1989:268).

It would of course be too simplistic to extrapolate from the case of Lesotho and conclude that European agricultural technology introduced accelerated erosion in Africa. It was mentioned above that swidden agriculture led to environmental degradation in precolonial Madagascar, in response to which irrigation farming developed. In Ethiopia the problems of soil erosion caused by deforestation worsened in the course of the nineteenth century. Not only did the people fell large numbers of trees without method or replanting, the 'country's trees were slow growing, and, when cut down took many years to grow' (Pankhurst, 1968:244). Under Menelik's rule efforts were made to restore the problem. The king:

> *gave orders forbidding the cutting or burning of trees without permission... More important, he gave his support to the project of introducing the new types of trees, above all the eucalyptus tree... [which] was fast growing, required little attention and when cut grew up again from the roots; it could be harvested every ten years. The tree proved successful from the outset* (Pankhurst, 1968:246).

Ethiopia bridged the plough and hoe-based farming systems of Africa, for both tools were used. Ploughs were mostly used in the northern provinces, where they were supplemented with hoes. In the southern region the peasants 'used a trident-shaped tool, about eight feet long, made of hard wood, the three prongs being sometimes shod with iron' (Pankhurst, 1968:187). In the vast expanse of tropical and savanna Africa, farmers used hoes of varying lengths and shapes. Writing about the Congo basin, Miracle (1967:286), for example, notes that hoes varied among communities:

from very small ones with short handles to large ones with long handles;
the blade may be of any numerous shapes from rectangular to heart-
shaped and may form various angles with the handle from 90 degrees to
less than 45 degrees.

The predominance of hoe cultivation in these regions has been attributed to
the fact that hoes were more suitable than ploughs for working the shallow
and fragile soils to avoid over-exposing the soil and causing erosion (Hopkins, 1973:36-37; Wickins, 1942).

The hoes were made of either wood or iron, or both as, for example, a hoe
with an iron blade and a wooden handle. Many communities produced their
own hoes, or they purchased them from other communities, especially in the
case of iron hoes. The Luo and Kikuyu of Kenya, for example, mainly used
wooden implements because of the shortage of iron in their areas until
sometime in the nineteenth century when trade in iron products increased
(Sheriff, 1985:20). As might be expected, iron hoes were more expensive
than wooden ones, so that they tended to be concentrated among the
relatively well off peasants, as was the case among the Mang'anja (Mandala,
1990:47). In addition to ploughs and hoes, other agricultural tools included
axes, machetes, digging poles, and sickles for harvesting, to mention the
most important ones.

Crop Patterns

By the beginning of the nineteenth century a wide range of crops, both
indigenous and immigrant cultigens, were cultivated in Africa. It is now
commonly accepted that different parts of Africa domesticated crops ranging
from cereals, oil seeds, root crops to vegetables, fibres, fruits, beverages and
stimulants, and that the continent played a major role in the history of
agriculture (Clark, 1976; Shaw, 1976; Smith, 1976). The idea that there was
a single centre of origin, the so-called 'Near East' or south-western Asia,
where an 'agricultural revolution' occurred, and from where agriculture
spread to the rest of the world has long been abandoned (Harlan, et.al, 1976).
Recent evidence on the existence and use of wild barley and einkorn wheat
in Egypt in very early times has even cast doubt on the idea that 'cultivated
wheat, barley and flax were all introduced into Africa from the Near East'
(Phillipson, 1985:113-4). It now appears, contrary to earlier assertions that
Africa received most of its crops from outside (Athony, et.al., 1979:135-6),
that with a few exceptions, 'most of the crops which are or have been
cultivated in Africa are species that are indigenous to that continent' (Phillipson, 1985:113-4).

North Africa

The geographical distribution of the crops was conditioned by environmental and socioeconomic factors. In North Africa, most of the cultivated land, since time immemorial, had been used for cereals. In Roman times Egypt and later the Magh.eb used to be known as the 'granary of Rome' (Kehoe, 1988). In the nineteenth century cereals still predominated, led by wheat, followed by millet, sorghum and barley, which was grown in marginal areas with less rainfall. Rice was grown in the Egyptian wetlands of the northern Delta. The output of these cereals was mostly consumed locally, although a considerable amount was sent to the towns in payment of taxes or rent and sometimes, in good years, exported. There were also crops grown primarily for the market, mostly fibres and tree crops, such as flax in Egypt and olives in Tunisia (Issawi, 1982).

In the nineteenth century there was a general expansion in agricultural production, involving both old and new crops. In Egypt the traditional cereals, wheat, millet, sorghum and barley came to be supplemented by maize. Maize was known in the seventeenth or eighteenth century, but its cultivation was restricted until the advent of perennial irrigation in the nineteenth century (Hamdan, 1961; Waterbury, 1979). Maize became a major staple of the peasants, replacing millet and sorghum. It has even been suggested that 'the diffusion of maize played a role in the dramatic growth of Egyptian population during the century. Increasing reliance upon it also underlay the spread of pellagra, first treated in 1893' (Richards, 1981:51). By 1844 maize output was second only to barley. In that year 3.1 million ardabbs of barley were produced compared to 2.6 million ardabbs of maize, 2.5 million ardabbs of wheat, and 0.5 ardabbs of rice (Rivlin, 1961:261). Some rice was also grown.

In addition to the cereals, large quantities of vegetables, including beans, peas, safflower, sesame, groundnuts, lentils and lupins, were produced. In 1844 the output of beans was 2.2 ardabbs and lentils 163,000 ardabbs. These crops were increasingly grown on land previously planted with grains. In Upper Egypt, wheat regions were converted to sugarcane as well (Lawson, 1981:143). Egypt had been producing sugar for centuries. Its expansion in the nineteenth century was due to the introduction of perennial irrigation and the growth of both internal and external markets. Consumption of sugar per capita within the country rose considerably in the second half of the nineteenth century. By 1887 41,000 tons of sugar were being produced (Hansen, 1979:38-41). The production of tobacco increased as well, although there is little information about the extent of its cultivation, either by acreage or output. The peasants grew it mainly for their own use, though some was exported. The cultivation of tobacco was forbidden in 1890 partly for fiscal reasons and partly in order to stamp out hashish, which was grown in tobacco fields. Fiscally the government made more from taxing cigarette imports than promoting local production (Issawi, 1982:120).

The real king of Egyptian agriculture in the nineteenth century was cotton. Cotton had been grown in the country for centuries. The 'cotton revolution' of the nineteenth century was based on three main factors. First, there was the discovery and widespread adoption of long-staple cotton in the 1820s. Second, Muhammad Ali's regime was determined to encourage export-led modernization. Third, the introduction of perennial irrigation made large-scale cotton production possible. Cotton not only supplied the raw material needed by the textile factories within the country, but it also became the leading export and the main source of government revenue.

The volume of cotton exports rose from an annual average of 65,160 cantars in 1822-4 to 473,737 cantars in 1850-4 (See note on weights and measures on p.iv). The American civil war gave a boost to the Egyptian cotton economy. Cotton exports reached an average 943,829 cantars during the period 1860-64 and 1,706,480 in 1865-9. In the period 1865-9 cotton exports fetched an average 9,073,655 per annum, while the value of cereal exports was 1,037,046 and sugar 82,130 (Owen, 1969:166, 171). By 1895-9 Egypt was exporting an average 5,765,000 cantars of cotton per annum (Owen, 1969:161, 198). Cotton was Egypt's 'white gold'. The acreage devoted to cotton increased to 871,847 feddans in 1874 and reached 1,230,319 feddans in 1899-1900, of which 93% was in lower Egypt, and the rest in Upper Egypt. Altogether, between 1899-1900 and 1903-4 cotton took about 23% of the land devoted to the major crops, only surpassed by maize with 30%, and followed by wheat with 22%, beans 11%, barley 9%, rice 3%, sugar 1%, and fruit and vegetables 0.3% (Owen, 1969:130, 186, 247).

The trend towards export production gathered momentum in the other North African countries as well. Farmers in the Maghreb had traditionally concentrated on wheat, barley and dates, apart from a wide variety of fruits and vegetables. In Libya these crops were cultivated in the high rainfall areas of the coastal plain and Jabal, and in the irrigated oases of the interior, principally in Fezzan and Ghadmes. The oases were particularly famous for their dates, of which there were many varieties. From the early nineteenth century three agricultural products became important exports. One was olive oil, in demand by the growing industries of southern France. The big coastal farmers converted some of their land to olive plantations. The other two products were barilla, used for making soda ash, and madder for dyeing cloth. The two plants had not been produced in Libya in large quantities before. Their production grew to meet the demand of French textile industries. Barilla exports continued until the 1820s when a new industrial process for making soda from salt came into widespread commercial use. The production and export of olive oil continued to rise. In fact, olive oil became one of Libya's leading exports in the nineteenth century (Dyer, 1984). Export crop production in Libya was encouraged by the Ottoman administration, which reoccupied Libya in 1835. The new administration also promulgated laws which encouraged private land ownership and registration (Anderson, 1984:332).

Olive oil became the primary export of Tunisia in the nineteenth century. By 1881, on the eve of the French occupation, there were some eight million olive trees in the county, spread throughout the country from the well-groomed groves of the north with its regular rainfall, to the irrigated fields of the Sahel region in the south, the olive-growing region par excellence. The olive tree, like the date palm, provided not only food but several by-products which had many uses in the domestic economy. By the mid-nineteenth century there were over a million date palms in the oases of Tunisia. All kinds of fruit trees flourished, many of which were grown in multiple varieties. For example, there were four kinds of plums and apples, two kinds of apricots and pears, not to mention grapes, limes and lemons, and oranges. Virtually every village produced a wide variety of vegetables, from carrots and turnips, to cabbages, leeks, peppers and okra. As in Libya, dye-producing plants, as well as cotton, became increasingly important as the century progressed. After colonization the exports of Tunisian wheat and wine to France grew rapidly (Valensi, 1985:110-27).

Algeria, colonized by France in 1830, was one of the first countries in Africa to feel the full blast of European colonial conquest. The French were keen to promote export production. They tried unsuccessfully to turn Algeria into a vast tropical farm producing sugarcane, coffee and tea. They enjoyed slightly more success with silk, cotton, flax and tobacco. In the end, they settled on wheat and vines, grown for centuries in Algeria and also the mainstays of the French agricultural economy itself. Export production of these crops became a virtual monopoly of French settlers. Algerian wheat exports to France were exempted from duties in 1851, and wine exports in 1867. Wine making and exports soon came to dominate Algerian agriculture.

The area devoted to wheat cultivation had reached 158,607 hectares by 1872, producing 1.36 million quintals, and in the 1880s it extended over 232,129 hectares, producing close to two million quintals (Bennoune, 1988:63). The acreage for vineyards expanded from 18,000 hectares in 1878 to 103,000 hectares in 1888, while output increased from 338,000 hectolitres to 2.5 million hectolitres (Issawi, 1982:126). By 1888 the vineyards were almost wholly owned by European settlers. In 1900 wine contributed one-third of Algeria's exports. Viticulture did not become significant in the other North African countries until the twentieth century.

West Africa

The crop regime of West Africa was even more diverse than that of North Africa. West Africa is generally divided into two broad ecological zones, the savanna and the forest belt. The dividing lines between the two zones are not sharp; the transition from savanna to forest is protracted and gradual, so that there is considerable overlap in crop regimes in several parts of the region where the two zones interact. Generally, since time immemorial, cereals have been produced in the savanna belt, and root crops and tree plants in the forest zone. The most important cereals were millets, sorghums, West African rice, and maize. The first three were indigenous domesticates, each of which had several varieties, probably ten for millet, six for sorghum and three for rice. Each variety was suited to particular conditions. Rice was grown mostly along the banks of the Niger, Benue, and the Senegal and Gambia rivers. Maize was first introduced to West Africa by the Portuguese in the sixteenth century. It spread slowly. Barley, bread and durum wheat were also grown (Miracle, 1966; Irvine, 1969:125-50; Curtin, 1975:13-18; Purseglove, 1976:302-7; Harris, 1976:329-33).

In addition to cereals, the savanna belt was suitable for growing legumes, especially groundnuts. Two varieties of groundnut, the Hausa and Bambara groundnuts, were indigenous, but the common groundnut variety, Arachis hypogea, known to Americans as the peanut, to the French as arachides, and to the Hausa as gyada, was most probably introduced into West Africa from the Americas by the Portuguese, 'although specific knowledge of the introduction is lacking' (Hogendorn, 1978:36). Peanut production for export to European markets increased from the 1830s. In 1835 Gambia exported 47 tons, rising to 11,095 tons in 1851 (Brooks, 1975:34). In Senegal, peanut exports averaged 29,000 a year in the period 1886-90 (Hopkins, 1973:128). In Portuguese Guinea, peanut exports peaked in 1878 when 1,120,828 bushels were exported, then began to decline, falling to 16,455 bushels in 1897. This decline has been attributed to dwindling markets and prices due to the European recessions of 1873-96 and the competition offered by cheap oil seeds from the United States and India which began to enter the market after the American civil war in 1865 and the opening of the Suez Canal in 1869. This exacerbated conflicts in the peanut growing regions which further undermined production (Bowman, 1987:100-6). Other legumes included cowpeas, pigeon peas, and a variety of beans (Irvine, 1969:1993-210; Harris, 1976:329-33).

A number of non-food crops and plants were also grown in the savanna region, including cotton, indigo and tobacco. There were at least six different species of cotton, suitable for a variety of environmental conditions (Curtin, 1975:211). There is evidence to show that cotton production increased considerably in the nineteenth century as the local textile industry expanded in such places as Kano. In the Sokoto Caliphate cotton became a major cash crop and cotton plantations were established in several areas. Kano supplemented the cotton produced in its immediate vicinity with imports from other parts of the caliphates, which in 1904 amounted to about 500 tons. The large scale of indigo production can be gauged from the fact that by the end of the century there were an estimated 15,000-20,000 dye pits in the Caliphate (Lovejoy, 1978a:356; Mahadi and Inikori, 1987:64-70). Many Senegambian farmers successfully integrated tobacco into their agricultural system (Curtin, 1975:15). Finally, a number of tree crops were cultivated in the savanna, including the shea butter tree, from which shea butter was made, the locust bean, the tamarind, lime, and lemon. Other crops included watermelon, black beniseed, a West African domesticate, and beniseed or sesame, onion, shallot, chilies and sweet pepper (Irvine, 1969:71-85; Harris, 1976:329-33).

The most important root crops cultivated in the forest zone were yams, of which there were about six indigenous domesticates (Coursey, 1976). Also grown was cocoyam or taro, originally from South East Asia, cassava and sweet potatoes, both introduced by the Portuguese (Irvine, 1969:153-86; Harris, 1976:329-33). Before 1800 cassava in West Africa spread slower than maize or sweet potatoes and in comparison to its spread in Central Africa. Its importance increased in the nineteenth century, perhaps because of the frequency of drought in the region, for cassava tends to be drought-resistant and labour-efficient (Johnston, 1963:106-12; Jones, 1959:72-80). The forest belt was also known for its fruits, principally bananas and plantains, whose cultivation was concentrated in the humid coastal areas between Côte d'Ivoire and Cameroon. In addition, mangoes, pawpaws, pineapples, and citrus fruits were grown (Irvine, 1969:79-102).

The tree crops included indigenous cultigens, such as the oil palm, kola, liberica coffee and akee, and immigrant cultigens, such as cocoa, coconut, sugarcane, and plantain. From the oil palm, of which there were numerous varieties, came oil which was used for cooking, soap making, and many other tasks. The kernels could be tapped for palm wine and the fronds were a source of fibre for roofing and matting (Hart, 1982:57). Palm products were widely traded within West Africa. In the nineteenth century there was a massive expansion of palm oil exports from West Africa to Europe, as will be demonstrated in Chapter 13. In some areas, such as Krobo and Kwapim in Ghana, palm trees were cultivated, while in other areas such as Fante palm production was an extractive activity (Sanders, 1982:62).

The nuts from the shea tree were used to make oil and butter. Kola nut comprised a major item of trade between the forest and savanna zones. The spread of Islam in the nineteenth century in the western Sudan boosted the demand for kola nuts, for they were the only readily available stimulant which Islam did not condemn. There were at least 40 varieties. The major species were cola acuminata and cola nitida. The latter was the most widely traded (Agiri, 1977; Lovejoy, 1980:1-5).

Apart from liberica coffee, West Africa also cultivated the other two African coffees, robusta and arabica. Coffee production increased in the nineteenth century and had become a major export from Ghana by the middle of the century. Ghana also became a major producer of cocoa, an American crop, first introduced into the region by a Ghanaian, Tetteh Quarshie, in 1879, on his return from Fernando Po, where the plant had been brought by a West Indian-Sierra Leonean, William Pratt (Hill, 1963:112; Crowder, 1981:8). In the following year, cocoa was introduced to southern Nigeria by J P L Davies, a Lagos merchant, who also got the seeds from Fernando Po. Many Lagos merchants turned to cocoa production because British colonialism was circumscribing their opportunities for commercial accumulation and the prices of existing staples were plummeting on the world markets (Berry, 1975; Hopkins, 1978b).

Cocoa takes many years to bear fruit, so that not much cocoa was produced in the closing decades of the nineteenth century. In 1891 cocoa exports from Ghana, the country that was poised to be the leading cocoa producer in the world in the first half of the twentieth century, were a paltry 80 lbs (Crowder, 1981:282). The spectacular growth of cocoa production and exports lay in the next century. In 1908 Ghana exported 12,800 tonnes of cocoa, rising to 173,000 tonnes in 1919 (Hill, 1956:103-104). In the twentieth century cocoa became for southern Ghana and southern Nigeria what palm oil was in the nineteenth. Coconut and sugarcane did not become major export crops. They were grown largely for local consumption (Irvine, 1969:39, 62).

Farmers in the forest zone also produced other crops, such as okra, egg plant, gourds, roselle, and a wide range of vegetables (Irvine, 1969:105-120; Harris, 1976:329-33). In the last quarter of the nineteenth century West Africa became a major supplier of rubber to Europe. Demand for raw rubber in new industrial uses began growing steadily from the 1840s. Production was initially dominated by Brazil but West Africa entered the scene in the 1880s as demand increased with the invention of vulcanization and British brokers sought new sources to break the Brazilian monopoly. West African merchants and producers quickly rose to the challenge. A spectacular but short-lived boom ensued. Ghana was the leading rubber producer in West Africa. Indeed, from 1890 to 1905 the country was the leading producer of wild rubber in the world. Its rubber exports rose from a mere 1,200 lbs in 1880 to 1.5 million lbs in 1885 and nearly five million lbs in 1897. The industry declined at the beginning of the twentieth century because of over-exploitation, competition from other areas, particularly the burgeoning rubber plantations of south-east Asia, and labour shortages (Dumett, 1971).

Central Africa

The crop regime in Central Africa largely consisted of variations on the West African pattern. This vast region domesticated a wide range of important crops, from the cowpea, pigeon pea, gourd, watermelon, melon, robusta coffee, diploid cotton and kenaf, to okra, fruits like baobab, desert date and jujube, and such crops as indigo, fan palm and raffia palm. The region was the conduit through which the continent received such American crops as pineapple, guava, pawpaw, avocado and upland cotton (Purseglove, 1976:302-8).

Central Africa also had its own different ecological layers composed of forest and savanna belts, with many transitional zones between them. By the beginning of the nineteenth century, well-developed systems of forest vegeculture, savanna cereal farming and fishing had been in operation for centuries (Birmingham, 1983). It was not uncommon for farmers to grow between a dozen and five dozen different crops, in order to maximize the productive potential of their soils and environment. For example, at the turn of the twentieth century the Medje in the Kinshasa region cultivated 27 varieties of bananas-plantains, 32 of yams and related crops, seven of cassava, seven of maize, four of sweet potatoes, and three of taro; the Lele and Mamvu had 18 varieties of bananas-plantains, 16 of yams, seven of sweet potatoes, six of cassava, six of maize, and four of sugarcane; and the northern Mongo had 53 varieties of bananas-plantains, five of cassava, four of yams, five of sugarcane, and 'several' of sweet potatoes, rice, maize, peanuts, and oil palms (Miracle, 1967:44, 49, 53). The Zande had one of the most diversified range of crops in Central Africa (Schlippe, 1956:chapter 5).

Overall, ten major staple foodstuffs or food groups were cultivated in the Congo basin alone: millets, sorghums, maize, cassava, bananas-plantains, pulses, rice, yams, taro, and sweet potatoes. In addition, there were a wide range of vegetables, including many varieties of beans, spinach and egg plants, as well as sugarcane, groundnuts and tobacco. These crops were both African cultigens and imports from outside the continent. Of the latter, the most important were bananas-plantains, cassava, and maize. Banana and plantains were of south-east Asian origin and were the first to be introduced. They became a staple among some forest communities in the north-eastern regions of the Congo basin. Cassava and maize were introduced in the sixteenth century 'either by the Portuguese or by Africans sent to Portugal during this period' (Miracle, 1967:232). Maize was adopted gradually and incorporated into local food systems at different rates. For example:

> by the 1860s the Mangbetu had maize but it was not the staple and the plant was not known to their north and east. Maize was the staple of the Pomo in the forest (Central Africa/Congo) but not of their neighbour in the forest, only of their neighbours in the northern savanna' (Vansina, 1979:13).

By the end of the nineteenth century maize and cassava, despite their various disadvantages, rivalled or had supplanted the older staples of yams, millets, sorghums and bananas in many regions of Central Africa. In parts of the forest belt 'farmers came to prefer maize to sorghum because of its better adaptation to high humidity' (Vansina, 1983:108), while the less nutritious cassava replaced the more nutritious yam because its yield was not only so much greater than yams, but it could also be left in the ground for up to four years and was thus a better hedge against short-term climatic disaster and famine (Jones, 1959:60-72). Moreover, specially prepared cassava 'bread' could be preserved for up to six months, which made cassava an ideal food for expanding regional long-distance trade. In north-central Africa cassava spread because of its qualities as an insurance crop, for it 'helped societies to survive the violence of incorporation into the Muslim economy' which was expanding into the region in the second half of the nineteenth century from the Sudan (Cordell, 1983:70).

Commodity production of cassava emerged along the major trade routes. For example, cassava plantations were established in Alima, Ikelemba and Lulonga. There were also other cash crops which were produced in the region in the nineteenth century. Nzabi country exported groundnuts, while Malebo Pool and its northern plateau exported tobacco (Vansina, 1983:109). The lower Congo produced palm oil although in much less quantities than West Africa. Also, as in West Africa, there was a short-lived rubber boom from the 1870s, dominated by the Chokwe and Ovimbundu. By 1886 rubber was the leading export from Angola. The rubber boom reached its peak in 1899 and began to decline sharply thereafter. The foraging methods used meant that rubber production could not last for long. Moreover, the Portuguese wars of conquest which intensified at the turn of the century disrupted production. Falling prices on the world market took their toll as well (Vansina, 1975:188, 201; Miller, 1970; Heywood, 1987).

From the early nineteenth century the Portuguese sought to encourage large scale production of cotton, coffee, wheat, sugar, vines and tobacco, especially after the loss of Brazil in 1820. The cotton experiment failed despite strong encouragement from the state. By the 1870s over 600,000 hectares of land devoted to cotton in Angola and 500,000 hectares in Mozambique had been abandoned. The volume of Angolan cotton exports was 86.5 metric tons in the 1890s, down from 417.8 tons in the 1870s (Pitcher, 1991:46, 67). Coffee in Angola achieved more modest success. Coffee exports grew unsteadily from three tons in 1844 to about 11,000 tons in the 1890s (Birmingham, 1978:523). The coffee was mainly produced in Cazengo by both African and European farmers. The fortunes of the coffee industry in Angola were tied to the capricious fluctuations on the world market.

To the north of Angola, Leopold sought to turn the vast Congo basin into a private personal estate. He instituted one of the most ruthless processes of 'primitive colonial accumulation'. In 1888 the Congo Free State exported 4,000 metric tons of palm oil, rising to over 6,000 tons in 1900. It also exported large quantities of rubber, increasing from 7,000 tons in 1895 to over 12,000 tons in 1900. In addition large quantities of copal were exported, amounting to about 12,500 tons in 1903. In the same year 13,000 tons of other products were also exported (Miracle, 1967:239).

Southern Africa

Agriculture in southern Africa has exhibited trends towards regional specialization, innovation and expansion, as in North and West Africa. Cereal production has predominated in this largely savanna region with the traditional cereals consisting of several varieties of millet and sorghum. The Shona of Zimbabwe have depended mainly on bulrush and finger millet. Millet was grown in the drier areas. In addition, they grew at least two varieties of groundnuts, as well as a variety of beans and a very wide range of vegetables. They did not adopt maize, which had appeared in the Zambezi valley in the eighteenth century, as a staple until the twentieth century (Beach, 1977, 1983).

Maize became a staple in some parts of the region in the nineteenth century, such as southern Mozambique and eastern Zambia. It supplanted millet and sorghum in southern Mozambique as male labour migration to South Africa increased. Maize had the advantage that its yield per work hour was higher and it also had fewer labour peaks than millet and sorghum, which usually required constant watch to keep birds away. The replacement of millet and sorghum by maize 'was further speeded up by the fact that sorghum was harvested only by men' (Berg, 1987:379). In southern Malawi, large-grained maize had become the principal dimba or wetland crop by the mid-nineteenth century. The Mang'anja peasants also grew millet and sorghum, as well as pumpkins, groundnuts, peas, cucumbers, two varieties of cotton, and other minor crops (Mandala, 1990:50-65).

One of the most diversified crop regimes in the region was in the flood plains of Barotseland in western Zambia. Early staples included finger millet, sorghum and several varieties of root crops, which were supplemented in the eighteenth century by flint maize and sweet potatoes. By the mid-nineteenth century sugarcane, Egyptian arum, two types of cassava, pumpkins, watermelons, beans, and groundnuts were also being produced. 'This growth in the variety of crops was paralleled by an increase in the types of gardens being prepared' (Horn, 1977:145-6). The adoption of new crops involved changing not only the methods of cultivation, but also social conventions.

The case of tobacco growing among the Thlaping of South Africa clearly illustrates this point. Up to the early nineteenth century, Thlaping agriculture was mainly based on the cultivation of two varieties of sorghum which was suited to their dry farming method and was intercropped with about four varieties of cooking melon, watermelon, a small species of 'kidney' beans, and varieties of pumpkin. They avoided tobacco growing because of insufficient rainfall in their area and a disinclination to upset their trade relations with the Hurutshe from whom they bought tobacco. The switch to tobacco growing was made following the introduction of irrigation and a new tobacco variety by the missionaries and the establishment of new trading relations with Kgalagadi hunters who exchanged their skins for Thlaping tobacco (Okihiro, 1984).

South Africa experienced remarkable agricultural growth as a result of the expansion of both internal and external markets, a process accelerated by the mineral revolution of the 1870s and 1880s. Both Africans and the European settlers participated in this process, and competed vigorously against each other, until the conjunction of political, economic and ecological factors conspired to marginalize the Africans. Apart from new agricultural techniques, African farmers in the colonial territories also adopted new crops. By the beginning of the nineteenth century the Cape Nguni cultivated sorghum, maize, cocoyam, pumpkins, gourds, calabashes, melons, peas and several varieties of beans, tobacco, and many types of fruits and vegetables. The richness and variety of the 'traditional' diet can be seen in the case of the Pedi, who consumed 48 varieties of cereal meal porridges, 13 varieties of whole grain stews, over 40 varieties of fruits and vegetables, and 12 varieties of beverages (Webster, 1986:450). Maize production grew the fastest during the century and became the staple food for the ever increasing numbers of people, replacing sorghum. The most important of the new crops was wheat (Bundy, 1979; Marks and Atmore, 1980; Okihiro, 1984).

The Mfengu, one of the most celebrated peasant communities in South African historiography, increased its grain sales steadily until the 1890s when the process of peasant underdevelopment intensified. Bundy (1979) uses grain sales as one of the indices of Mfengu surplus production and prosperity in the nineteenth century. Lewis (1984), however, believes that for the majority of Mfengu households increased grain marketing was less a reflection of the availability of grain surplus above 'subsistence needs' than it was the result of their deepening integration into the colonial economy with its constant cash demands. This qualification is important, but it does not necessarily contradict the fact that Mfengu commodity production increased. Until the 1880s, African peasants in Natal produced most of the colony's grain, comprised of the 'traditional' cereals, maize, millets and sorghum, far outstripping the settlers, and paid a large share of the taxes (Harries, 1987:374-5, 382-3).

The Basotho became large-scale producers of the new cereal, wheat. Since 'little grain was cultivated by the Boers... the Eastern Cape was heavily dependent on Basotho grain supplies, and during the frontier wars of the late 1840s and early 1850s, «enormous quantities» of wheat were imported from Basotholand' (Keegan, 1986a:198). As late as 1893, after the Basotho had lost some of their most fertile land to the Boers and other settlers, Lesotho was still able to export more than 11,600 metric tons of wheat and 6,000 metric tons of maize, in addition to other products such as wool,(Morojole, 1963:iv-8). The situation later changed dramatically as the Boers intensified their opposition to Basotho competition and entrepreneurship, and new trading concerns emerged that were less tied to peasant production for their accumulation, all of which was compounded by market fluctuations and ecological disasters. The result was that 'from the 1920s, Basotholand became irrevocably and perennially a net importer of grain products for internal consumption' (Keegan, 1986a:214). Labour migration from Lesotho to South Africa became less of a discretionary move and more of a necessity for increasing numbers of Basotho households.

The only commodity over which the settlers enjoyed dominance in the early nineteenth was wine growing. The production of wine was greatly encouraged by the reduction of the British custom duty on Cape wines in 1813 (Freund, 1989:330). Output rose from 5,528 leggers (nearly 3.25 million litres) in 1775, and 9,643 leggers (over 5.5 million) in 1806, to 19,250 leggers (11.2 million) in 1924 (Newton-King, 1980:173; Ross, 1989:248-9).

What was wine for the Cape colony in the first half of the century sugar became for Natal in the second half. The settlers of Natal had tried in vain to develop commercial agriculture based on cotton and other tropical crops. In the late 1840s and early 1850s they began to experiment with the cultivation of sugarcane. They had discovered their 'white gold'. Between 1854 and 1866 the acreage under cane increased from 338 to 12,781 acres.

The Natal sugar industry developed rapidly 'as a result of a combination of favourable prices, reasonably low wages and a protective tariff structure. To these advantages were added subsequently a partially-controlled labour market and the short-lived benefits of financial speculation' (Richardson, 1982:518).

The sugar industry was monopolized by the settlers, although Africans in the region had been growing sugarcane from at least the seventeenth century. In the 1860s some Africans tried to join the sugar bonanza, encouraged by missionaries. A few plantations were established by the kholwa, as the African Christians were called, but several factors conspired against them. The growers lacked access to both freehold land and capital (Etherington, 1978:4). The scope for African production was further limited by 'attractiveness of crops such as maize and the possibilities presented by stock rearing for African squatters on absentee lands in the European sector' (Richardson, 1982:521). The settlers consolidated the sugar industry amidst market fluctuations and changes in production processes and ownership structure. In the 1880s sugar interests began clamouring for more African lands along the coast and in the interior into the Zulu heartland.

Eastern Africa

Sugar also became king on the Indian Ocean islands of Mauritius and Reunion, off the East African coast. Sugarcane was introduced to Mauritius, the larger of the two islands, by the Dutch in the mid-seventeenth century. The French, who succeeded the Dutch as the island's colonial masters at the end of the century, encouraged large scale sugar production. The British replaced the French at the beginning of the nineteenth century and they expanded sugar production even further. By the end of the century Mauritius had become one of the largest sugar producers and exporters in the world, a truly sugar island, dependent on the sugar industry for the bulk of its national income, export revenues and employment (Zeleza, 1988:2).

Along the East African coast numerous plantations were also established. In Zanzibar they concentrated on cloves, which were introduced in the 1820s, and the long-established coconuts. Clove exports increased sharply from 9,000 frasilas (nearly 143,000 kgs) in 1839-40 to an average 415,398 frasilas (6.6 million kgs) during the period 1854-65 (Sheriff, 1987:62-63). Outside the plantations various fruits were grown including mangoes, bananas, lemons, oranges, jack fruit and bread fruit, as well as grains, particularly rice and millet, and cassava which was the staple food of the slave population.

Malindi, an abandoned ruin at the beginning of the century, saw its fortunes rise with the expansion of grain plantations. It reached the height of its prosperity in the 1880s. Its exports peaked in 1887: millet 500,000 frasilas

(7.9 million kgs), sesame 250,000 frasilas (close to 4 million kgs), and beans 200,000 frasilas (3.2 million kgs) (Cooper, 1977:85). The more urbanized, trade-oriented and land-short Mombasa witnessed a less dramatic expansion in its plantation agriculture. In 1884 it exported 100,000 frasilas (1.6 million kgs) of millet, 200,000 frasilas of maize, 20,000 frasillas (about 318,000 kgs) of sesame, and 100,000 nuts of coconuts, among other items (Cooper, 1977:101).

The East African coast played a major role in the dispersion of Asian crops into the African interior. Among the earliest Asian crops to be introduced were bananas, which reached Buganda by no later than the fourteenth century. By the nineteenth century Buganda had become a major centre of banana diversification and dispersion. At least 31 varieties had been developed, divided into four groups: cooking, roasting, beer, and dessert bananas (McMaster, 1977:15). Other crops introduced through the East African coast included sugarcane, coconut, mango, egg plant, orange, lemon, Asian rice, ginger, tea, soya bean, and greater yam (Purseglove, 1976:305-6). And from the Americas came maize, sweet potatoes and tobacco.

Most of these crops were known at the coast and parts of the interior by 1800. Others spread from the coast into the interior in the nineteenth century, assisted by the caravan trade. Among them were cassava, rice, peanuts and haricot beans (Jones, 1959:80-84; Ehret, 1985). The new crops supplemented the long established millets, sorghums, fruits and vegetables, and facilitated the expansion of the agricultural frontier in Kenya, Tanzania and Uganda (Kjekshus, 1977; Sheriff, 1985).

Many of the African cultigens used in the three countries were first domesticated in Ethiopia and the Sudan, through which some Asian domesticates were also dispersed. Ethiopia domesticated teff, Arabica coffee, bulrush millet, ensete and noog, while the Sudan was part of the savanna and Sahelian complex in which sorghum and finger millet was domesticated (Purseglove, 1976:302-5; Phillipson, 1985:114). In Ethiopia, great efforts were undertaken by Menelik's government to expand agriculture. Coffee production, once frowned upon by the church, was encouraged to supplement the state's dwindling revenues from the declining ivory trade. Previously coffee had been produced in the Harar region of eastern Ethiopia. The government sought to expand its production in this region and elsewhere in the country. Tens of thousands of coffee trees were planted. At the turn of the century coffee production was boosted by the completion of the rail link from French Somaliland to Dire Dawa near Harar in 1902 and growing world demand for the beverage. Coffee was on its way to becoming the shallow bedrock of the Ethiopian export economy (McClellan, 1980).

The other cash crops which received growing attention from the second half of the nineteenth century were tobacco, also once vigorously opposed by the church, cotton, which had been extensively cultivated since ancient times, and rubber and sisal. Needless to say, peasants gave priority to food crops. Ethiopia produced most of the major cereals, vegetables and fruits cultivated in various parts of the continent. The cereals included wheat, barley, millet, sorghum, as well as teff, while the fruits ranged from oranges, lemons, limes, pomegranates, to peaches, bananas and pawpaws. Pumpkins, sugarcane and vines were also grown (Pankhurst, 1968:184-208).

Sudanese peasants also cultivated numerous crops, but the main staples were sorghums, of which there were at least a dozen varieties, millets, vegetables and leguminous plants, and tree plants, including coffee, cotton, shea butter tree and fruit trees (Lado, 1986:17-25; Bjorkelo, 1989:64-68). From 1821 the Turco-Egyptian colonial conquerors sought to transform northern Sudanese agriculture by encouraging large-scale commercial production. They not only pressurized peasants to grow cash crops, but they also tried to set up plantations. Emphasis was put on four crops: rice, sugar, indigo and cotton, but almost from the beginning, rice was not a success, neither was sugar. Indigo also soon showed signs of decline, because peasants resisted growing it for 'it tended to exhaust the soil quickly and required much and continuous watering and labour' (Bjorkelo, 1989:71). Cotton was a more established crop, but 'as with indigo, the peasants were reluctant to devote more time and energy to cotton lest it should affect their ability to grow food, particularly when the prices paid to them were not worth it' (Bjorkelo, 1989:72). Large scale cotton production was not attempted again until after British colonization. In 1900 experimental cotton planting began on the Gezira plain, the future site of the giant Gezira cotton irrigation scheme (Holy and Daly, 1979:127).

Animal Husbandry

Animal husbandry was an important activity in many African economies - one that is as old as crop farming. However, it would appear that Africa domesticated far fewer animals than crops. 'Sheep and goats have no African prototypes... Cattle present more difficulties, and could be descended from wild forms in North Africa and/or the Near East' (Phillipson, 1985:114). The three comprised the most important stock animals. By the nineteenth century, there were, of course, numerous varieties of sheep, goats and cattle, each adapted to specific micro-environments and agrarian structures.

Animal husbandry is often associated with pastoralism, which, in turn, is conflated with nomadism. At best, pastoralism has tended to be seen by scholars, including historians, and modern governments and development agencies, which are keen to sedentarise pastoralists, as a poor cousin of arable farming, or at worst as the instigator of environmental degradation. In the anti-nomadic discourse, pastoralists are accused of suffering from an irrational 'cattle complex', overgrazing, and endemic wanderlust (Herskovits, 1926; Murdock, 1959; Lomax and Arensberg, 1977; Lamprey, 1983). Current patterns of pastoral marginalization and environmental degradation are mistaken for relics of the 'natural economy' of pastoralism, when they are in fact products of specific historical processes, especially colonial capitalism and ill-considered post-colonial development strategies (Hedlund, 1979; Watts, 1987; Homewood and Rodgers, 1987; Timberlake, 1988).

Like arable farming, there were several systems of animal husbandry of which three can be identified. First, mixed farming, which combined crop farming and stock raising. Second, transhumance, which involved a regular, annual trek within a definite orbit of transhumance. Third, nomadism proper, in which herds and households moved from place to place in search of pasture. Nomadism was quite rare in nineteenth century Africa. There is certainly little evidence that it was practised in either West or East Africa (Hopkins, 1973:41-42; Waller, 1985). Thus the two major systems of animal husbandry were mixed farming and transhumance.

The distinction between the 'pastoralists' and the 'mixed farmers' was not as sharp as is sometimes imagined. Many of the so-called pastoral societies cultivated crops, although specialization was quite common, whereby different sections or sexes within the same society, or different communities in an articulated agro-pastoral region, specialized in either crop farming or livestock rearing (Galaty, 1981; Schneider, 1981; Bonte, 1981; Brandstrom, 1979:22-23). This was obscured by the tendency among researchers to ignore women, who remained behind cultivating crops and running the household economy, and to put pastoralists in imaginary worlds of splendid isolation.

Under the system of mixed farming the livestock provided much needed manure for crop cultivation. In West Africa the Serer employed 'mixed farming as their principal system of production' (Hopkins, 1973:34). They did not practise transhumance. Instead they penned their cattle in the fields soon to be cultivated. The pens were integrated with the Acacia albida tree which sheds its leaves just before the rains begin. The cattle and the tree provided manure and humus which enabled the Serer 'to use the land more intensively than their neighbours and therefore to have denser patterns of settlement' (Curtin, 1975:28).

Mixed farming was quite widespread and of considerable antiquity in Southern Africa. Garlake's (1978:486) archaeological excavations of the zimbabwe (stone enclosure) at Manekweni, in southern coastal Mozambi-

que, 'suggests strongly that Manekweni benefited primarily from an intensive pastoral economy, producing a steady surplus of prime beef; that this
was based on seasonal transhumance; and that the demands of this system
were an important determinant in the siting of the stone enclosure'. He
believes that crop cultivation and animal husbandry characterized the other
centres of the Zimbabwe culture in present-day Zimbabwe and Mozambique. This enabled them to achieve high densities of population and per-
manency of settlement in a savanna environment which could not have been
achieved by crop farming alone. Thus mixed farming was at the base of the
Zimbabwe economy, rather than simply gold production and foreign trade,
as is commonly assumed (Mudenge, 1988:162-6).

In nineteenth century Southern Africa mixed farming was also practised
among the Nguni and Sotho (Omer-Cooper, 1978:11, 14) and the Swazi
(Crush, 1987:17-18). Mixed farming has been reported from many parts of
eastern Africa, such as central Kenya (Muriuki, 1986:107), and among the
Ngoni and other peoples of Tanzania (Kjekshus, 1977a:51-68). Although
the economies of central Kenya were all 'based on a combination of
cultivation and pastoralism, substantial differences in the configurations of
crop and livestock production distinguished central Kenya's myriad communities one from the other' (Ambler, 1985:203). Mixed farming was also
widespread in Ethiopia (Pankhurst, 1968:209-13). In northern Africa, many
Tunisian and Egyptian agricultural peasants also combined crop cultivation
with livestock rearing (Valensi, 1985:148-52; Ayrout, 1963:chapter 4).

Livestock was valued as an important source of manure, draft power and
accumulation. In the northern Sudan, for instance, tens of thousands of cattle
were required as bulls to operate the saqiyas, for breeding, and as a capital
asset. It is because cattle were so central to the economy that Egyptian
schemes to export large numbers of Sudanese cattle to provide animal motive
power for Egypt's industrial and agricultural development in the 1830s
nearly destroyed the riverine economy of the northern Sudan (Bjorkelo,
1989:77).

While cattle predominated in northern Sudan, sheep dominated Tunisia.
'There were several varieties, distinguished by the colour of the coat and the
quality of the wool. The fatty excrescence of the tail increased as one moved
from north to south' (Valensi, 1985:145). Next in number came goats. The
little goat was most prevalent in the villages of the deep south. Then came
cattle which held first place only in the plains of Mateur. The animals were
valued for their meat, milk, wool and skins, which were made into many
products, such as butter, tents, blankets and coats. Almost every house or
tent had a donkey, which was used for transport. For the long haul, camels,
horses and mules were used. The animals were rarely provided with shelter

and no forage was stored. They ate whatever they found in their wanderings. The patterns of transhumance followed the seasons. 'The direction of collective migrations fell to the chief shepherd, called by his constituents quaid al 'azib. He supervised the order of transhumance, settled arguments, and saw to good relations with the inhabitants of the regions traversed' (Valensi, 1985:151).

Livestock statistics hardly exist for most societies that practised animal husbandry and the available estimates must be treated with caution. Writing on Ethiopia, Pankhurst (1968:209), states that 'livestock in normal times was exceedingly plentiful, the country being inhabited by millions of cattle, donkeys, mules, goats, sheep, camels, horses and chickens'. He quotes one estimate which indicates that in the 1890s over 747,000 oxen, 315,000 cows, nearly 171,000 goats, about 162,500 sheep, and close to 700,000 chickens were sold annually (Pankhurst, 1968:210). Livestock prices were relatively low, reflecting the abundance. The cattle were almost entirely grass fed. The first modern commercial cattle farms were established in the 1890s. Cattle products played an important role in the economy. They included meat and milk, from which butter, a major trade item, was made, and hides which provided leather products, for which Ethiopia became renowned. In addition, there were sheep, valued for their meat and wool. Horses and mules provided much needed transport.

Perhaps the most well known pastoralists of East Africa were the Maasai. The Maasai are, indeed, seen as the quintessential pastoralists, which ignores the fact that Maasai women cultivated crops, and that 'the Maasai economy itself interlocked with, and was dependent upon, other local economies' (Waller, 1985:84). Some have tried to go behind these messy facts by distinguishing the Maasai into the 'pure', 'semi' or 'mixed' pastoralists. The Maasai kept cattle, their most valued asset, and sheep and goats. Each family also owned a few donkeys mainly for transport, although they were milked in extremity. The Maasai kept large herds not because they suffered from the 'cattle complex' of anthropological folklore, but because cattle played so many different roles. Not only did livestock serve as a means of subsistence and the society's main stock of capital, cattle also acted as media of exchange and store of value. Moreover, livestock was important as prestige goods and objects of mystification, articulated with the social and ideological system. Livestock was slaughtered or given as gifts at births, initiations, in marriage transactions, and other occasions (Hedlund, 1979:16-17).

The equivalent of the Maasai in West Africa were the Fulbe, who over a millennia had spread from their putative homeland in Senegambia across the Western Sudan, during which their collective identity was reconstituted through the processes of ethnic and religious segmentation, sedentarisation, and class and state formation. Some of the strongest pressures for Fulbe sedentarisation came in the nineteenth century, following the establishment of new Islamic states. In Massina, 'Shehu Ahmadu engaged in a large-scale forced sedentarisation of the pastoral Fulbe population, claiming that Islam was the religion of villages' (Azarya, 1979:180). More to the point, 'sedentarisation simplified the provision of religious and educational services; it also made administration, conscription, and taxation much easier' (Johnson, 1976a:494).

The sedentarised Fulbe now had to entrust a large part of their cattle to professional herdsmen for the transhumance voyages. The rest were kept in the vicinity either to provide the household with the necessary subsistence products or because they were too young for the voyages. The state decided on the transhumance route to be followed and also provided armed escorts for protection. The herds were usually organized in caravans led by the official herdsman in charge of state cattle. He had authority:

> *to give orders relating to privately owned herds, as to the movement of the herds, control of diseases, etc. Cattle owners were required to pay grazing dues to ruling authorities across whose land the cattle passed, or to the state if the transhumance trek crossed state grazing land* (Azarya, 1979:182).

This level of state intervention in livestock production was rather rare. Fulbe pastoralists in many parts of West Africa were able to control their stock rearing. In addition to cattle and goats, the West African savanna countries and societies also kept large numbers of horses and camels for cavalry and transport. Animal husbandry in the forest region was restricted by the disease trypanosomiasis.

If Islamic state formation transformed Fulbe pastoralism in West Africa, in South Africa it was European colonization. The marginalization of Khoisan pastoralists, which had began in the mid-seventeenth century, was finally completed in the nineteenth. Those Khoisan who had managed to survive the deadly onslaught of colonization were turned either into a cheap proletariat, or pushed into unproductive wastelands where they were forced to eke out the existence of hunter-gatherers (Elphick, 1977; Elphick and Malherbe, 1989). In the meantime, settler pastoral agriculture continued to expand. By the 1820s, it is estimated, the colonial livestock herd in the Cape had risen to 1.75 million sheep and over 300,000 cattle, up from about 1.25 million sheep and 250,000 cattle in the 1770s. By 1840 the number of colonial sheep had risen to nearly 1.9 million. This growth 'was of course the result of the steady trekboer expansion into the Cape's interior, which was conquered from the Khoisan and later the Xhosa' (Ross, 1989:253), and one could add, the Basotho and Zulu. In short, the settlers expanded their herds through commando raids and confiscation of livestock from conquered African societies, a method of 'primitive accumulation' that was later adopted by other European settlers in Africa, especially in Algeria, Zimbabwe and Kenya.

It was not until the 1840s that settler pastoral farming in South Africa was put on firmer footing, thanks to the introduction of the high-yielding merino sheep. Wool production became the mainstay of the colonial export economy until the advent of the mineral revolution in the 1860s and 1880s. The Cape Colony 'became a source of wool for Britain second only to Australia' (Munro, 1976:59). Some African farmers also took to sheep rearing, but it is difficult to know the total size of their herds. The figures reported in magistrates reports which show that in 1895 a total of 24,000 peasants in Herschel district possessed 89,000 sheep and 44,000 cattle, and in Fingoland 25,000 peasants owned over 40,000 sheep (Bundy, 1979:96, 155) may be questionable, but what seems certain is the fact that African peasants increasingly offered stiff competition to settler sheep farmers. Among the Thlaping a sign of expanding cattle herds was the emergence of the cattle post system. 'The system involved keeping a few cattle and goats within the town while placing the major portion of the herd at an outpost miles away tended by clients or junior branches of the clan' (Okihiro, 1984:72).

For some groups the days of pastoral prosperity were already beginning to draw to a close by the mid-nineteenth century. The most outlandish case is that of the Xhosa. In the cattle killing of 1856-7 the Xhosa lost over 400,000 cattle. The Xhosa themselves blamed the cattle-killing on the machinations of the colonial government, while the latter accused the chiefs and the prophets who told people to kill their 'diseased' cattle as a precondition for the rise of wonderful new cattle. Peires (1989b) believes the lungsickness epidemic of 1855, which decimated a lot of Xhosa cattle, triggered the cattle-killing. The prophecy tapped into Xhosa religious beliefs about the nature of sickness, evil, death and purification, and was born out of Xhosa frustration with colonial conquest and domination. It appealed to people in chiefdoms that had been afflicted by lungsickness and to those who opposed colonial rule and were committed to the old economic and social structure. Also, 'women, who performed the toilsome and socially unrewarding labour of cultivating the soil, were liable to be responsive to a message which promised them a future free of agricultural work' (Peires, 1989b:315).

The colonial state abetted the disaster. After the cattle-killing was over, the Cape government did its best 'to turn this human tragedy to the political and economic profit of the Cape Colony. Instead of making food freely available to the hungry, [it] utilized the desperate starvation of the people to engineer their mass exodus via the colonial labour market, while filling their former lands with white settlers' (Peires, 1989b:317). The result was that:

> *the Xhosa population of British Kaffraria dropped by two thirds between January and December 1857, from 105,000 to 37,000, and then again by another third to reach a low point of 25,916 by the end of 1858. How many of these actually died is hard to say* (Peires, 1989b:319).

The Xhosa cattle-killing brings into sharp relief the complex interplay between agriculture, disease, ideology, class, demography and colonization.

Conclusion

This chapter has tried to capture the immense diversity and complexity of the systems of land use in nineteenth century Africa, which should put to rest many of the standard depictions which characterize African agriculture as uniform, simple or backward. An attempt has been made to examine the nature of so-called shifting cultivation, outline the advantages of intercropping, delineate the development of agro-forestry, terracing, wet land and irrigated farming, and examine the growth of mixed farming.

The development of these and other methods of cultivation was conditioned by complex interactions of physical and human geography, technology and political economy. Like arable farming, there were several systems of animal husbandry. In fact, the distinction between 'pastoral' and 'farming' societies appears far less sharp once women and their activities are included. African pastoralists were not the quintessential 'traditionalists' of anthropological folklore, for, as the analysis makes clear, livestock rearing practices changed in response to changing environmental, economic and socio-political conditions.

The question of agricultural technology has been explored not only with a view to depicting the kinds of tools that were used in different parts of the continent, but also to challenge the widespread evolutionistic view which puts European tools, especially ploughs, on the pedestal of agricultural advancement. Some studies have shown that the indigenous ploughs used in parts of North Africa, Ethiopia and the Sudan, were far superior to the European ones mechanically, agriculturally, economically and environmentally. In appraising the 'efficiency' of agricultural tools and techniques, historians have often not incorporated into the equation the environmental impact of the tools and techniques concerned. For example, in Lesotho where European ploughs were widely adopted, short-term increases in production were followed by long-term decline in soil productivity through accelerated soil erosion.

One of the most striking features of African agriculture in the nineteenth century was the extraordinary range of crops that were grown and cultivated. It can be argued that many African societies witnessed a kind of 'agricultural revolution' in the nineteenth century: new food and cash crops were widely adopted, and old indigenous cultigens spread within and across regions. Moreover, the available statistics, mostly on cash crops exported to Europe, show that there were phenomenal increases in production. This agricultural revolution had a darker side, however. In some countries, as the case of Egypt patently shows, cash crop production increasingly outstripped food production. The more integrated into the world economy these countries became, the more vulnerable they were to the unpredictable price fluctuations on the world market.

It could also be argued that cash crop production gradually led to the diminution in the range and variety of crops grown. The impact of this has yet to be fully explored by historians, who have tended to celebrate the nineteenth century expansion of agricultural commodity production as a vindication of the innovativeness and initiative of African farmers. This may be so. But the cash crop revolution, reinforced by the establishment of colonial capitalism towards the end of the century, had far-reaching implications for twentieth century Africa in terms of the diversity of food crops available and susceptibility to hunger. Certainly, the diets of many people in present-day African societies are not as rich and varied as those of their nineteenth century ancestors. The increasing monoculturization of agriculture also engendered important changes in cultivation practices and production relations.

4. Agrarian Relations of Production

Peasants and the State

From the preceding chapters, it is quite clear that African farmers lived in a wide range of environments and social formations. It stands to reason, therefore, that their relations of production varied enormously. In some societies the state played an important role in peasant agriculture through its organization of the land tenure system, and appropriation of peasant surpluses. Needless to say, the mechanisms of appropriation differed considerably. The diversity and complexity of African state formations and land tenure systems cannot be overemphasized (Lonsdale, 1981; Conah, 1987).

Trying to fit African land systems into the 'individual-communal' dichotomy is an exercise in futility. As Bohannan and Curtin (1988:137) have observed, the 'concept called «communal ownership» is silly, for it is based on erroneous notions of the basis of grouping in African societies. African land tenure systems were complex articulations of settlement patterns, systems of land use, distributive networks, kinship and community structures, state forms and ideologies.

Agriculture formed the economic basis of most African societies in the nineteenth century. Thus states largely depended on surpluses extracted from agriculture. Mkandawire (1989), referring to twentieth century African economies, classifies states which obtained their revenue from agriculture as 'merchant states'. The vast majority of states in nineteenth century Africa would fit this characterization. But their methods of surplus appropriation and control of agrarian production differed quite considerably as the cases of Egypt, the northern Sudan, Ethiopia, the Sokoto Caliphate, Barotseland and Swaziland will demonstrate.

Egypt

The Egyptian peasantry was one of the oldest and most exploited in Africa. At the beginning of the nineteenth century, the iltizam or tax farming system operated. Under this system the fellahin or peasants paid taxes to the multazims, who held the land in return for the payment of a set land tax to the state. The multazims were allowed to retain any amount over this tax that they could extract from the peasants. They could also extract corvee labour from the peasants. The new government of Muhammad Ali, established in 1805, sought, as part of its modernization programme and efforts to undermine the material base of the old ruling class, to change the system by removing the multazims, which would allow the state to maximize the surpluses it could appropriate directly from the peasants. By 1812 all multazim lands had been confiscated by the state. Four years later a new taxation system was introduced by which land was registered in the name of a village community, and the latter became responsible for the payment of taxes directly to the state (Rivlin, 1961; Baer, 1962, 1969; O'Brien, 1966; Owen, 1969; Cuno, 1980; Richards, 1982).

Muhammad Ali's drive for centralization made peasant life more onerous than before. Peasants were now obliged to turn over their crops to the government at low prices. To add salt to injury, they were not paid immediately in cash but received promissory notes, known as assignations, which sometimes were not honoured. In 1826, for example, the government refused to accept the assignations from the peasants in payment of taxes. The peasants were also expected to pay the costs of transporting their crops to the central depot. And the government could seize the crops by force, whenever it wanted, as it did in 1812, which led to a serious shortage of food. Peasants caught diverting even a small part of their harvest for sale on the open market, where prices were higher, were punished. In 1816, the government even went so far as to forbid the population eating beans and other crops aimed for export. And when peasants were late paying taxes their animals and other assets were sometimes seized.

All these exactions, as well as the military conscriptions, were bitterly resented by the peasants. In 1812 several uprisings broke out in Upper Egypt against the tax collectors and the troops that had accompanied them. The government brutally suppressed the uprisings by burning villages and massacring their inhabitants. In 1816 there were renewed protests over the prohibitions against the local consumption of beans and other export crops.

The most prolonged unrest occurred in the 1820s in Qina Province, where the discontented peasants were joined by disgruntled artisans, both of whom were dissatisfied with the government's control and exploitation, and their sharply declining fortunes. The artisans objected to the flood of European cloth on the local market. The textile industry in the province was on the verge of collapse. Many workers lost their jobs. The peasants and artisans joined forces and erupted into a series of rebellions from 1820 to 1824 (Lawson, 1981). The peasants also protested in more covert ways, through desertion, refusal to pay taxes, and self-maiming to avoid conscription. Migration to Cairo was another method of avoiding conscription, for residents of the city were exempted from it (Toledano, 1990:181-8).

By the 1830s state policy and peasant resistance were coming home to roost: the rural areas were impoverished and gripped by food shortages, and state revenues had declined sharply. In response, the state relaxed some of its policies and in 1831 peasants were allowed to cultivate food crops without restriction. Moreover, the system of agricultural administration was decentralized in order to improve and maximize tax collection. This led to the development of a new rural landlord class which came to mediate state appropriation of peasant surpluses. Free grants of large tracts of uncultivated land were given to high state bureaucrats, military cadres and others in order to retain their loyalty. They were exempted from paying taxes on condition that they cultivated these lands, called ibadiyya. Members of the royal family received land known as jifliks. The village shaykhs, upon whom the administrative system rested, received tax-free land, called masmuh, in lieu of salaries. At first, the recipients of ibadiyya lands did not own the land, they only had usufructuary rights. From 1836 the eldest sons of the recipients could inherit the land, and by 1842 the recipients acquired full rights of ownership.

Indeed, by then the old iltizam system had been revived in a new form. A decree of 1840 allowed high government officials, military officers and members of the royal family to take over responsibility for bankrupt villages, pay their tax arrears, provide working capital to the peasants, supervise their cultivation, and collect taxes from them on behalf of the central government. The apparent return of the old system reflected the rising power of the ruling class which the state itself had helped create, as well as the growing weaknesses of the state itself, following Egypt's military defeat in Syria in 1840. This defeat curtailed opportunities for external pillage upon which the state had partly relied to reward its functionaries. Members of the ruling class, like others before them, discovered the land was their anchor. They sought to consolidate their position as landlords, especially now that the value attached to land was increasing, thanks to the irrigation works and the adoption of lucrative 'king' cotton.

The big landowners, including members of the royal family, produced a larger and larger proportion of the cotton. Muhammad Ali himself acquired a lot of land, up to 239,426 feddans (over 248,500 acres) between 1838 and 1846. His successors acquired more land and completed the drive to private landownership. From 1846 the peasants were allowed to pledge their land against loans, and in 1855 to inherit it. The Bedouin pastoralists were given land on condition that they cultivated it, but they preferred to sublet it to tenants. Government efforts to stop this practice and tax their land provoked Bedouin revolt and migration. In subsequent decades the peasants acquired full rights of ownership.

By 1891 virtually all landowners possessed full ownership rights, but the pattern of land distribution was grossly unequal. In 1897 the number of large landowners, that is, those with more than 50 feddans, amounted to 12,184, or 1.5% of all land owners, yet they held 2.2 million feddans (nearly 2.3 million acres), or 44% of the total agricultural land area. At the other end, the small proprietors, those with less than five feddans, represented 80.4% of the landowners, but held only 20.2% of the land (Mabro and Radwan, 1976:24-25). The landed classes in Egypt became more powerful and enduring than their predecessors in the previous century (Cuno, 1980).

Northern Sudan

As noted earlier, the northern Sudan fell under Turco-Egyptian rule between 1821 and 1885. During this period profound changes took place in the systems of land tenure and appropriation of peasant surpluses. The new rulers continued the policy of their Funj predecessors of giving some people titles to land or the right to collect for themselves land dues from its occupants. The landlord class, which consisted of chiefs, religious leaders, and settlers from Egypt and elsewhere, expanded rapidly (Awad, 1971:218-21). The new state divided the land into two, freehold land, milk, and government land, miri. The former referred to regularly cultivated land, while the latter encompassed land that was cultivated only when natural irrigation made it possible. Thus the state came to own and control large tracts of land (Bjorkelo, 1989:58-59).

Not only did large private estates develop, but existing land tenure arrangements also changed. With the spread of private landed property, irrigated land, known as saqiya land, which traditionally had been regarded as the common property of the household or households that worked it and who received from the produce according to their shares and labour input, increasingly became 'divided into discreet plots of land with individual owners; thus right to the first fruits of the land gave way to rights to the land itself' (Spaulding, 1982:4). Plots and boundaries were carefully demarcated. Unlike before, it became more common for different people to own the saqiya land and the lands below, known as salluka (Bjorkelo, 1989:60-62).

Private land ownership and the application of the Islamic laws of inheritance resulted in widespread fragmentation of land. One orphan girl reportedly inherited 1/10,500 share in a saqiya land (Spaulding, 1982:5)! But when 'a family holding had reached this stage of sub-division, or probably long before then, the owners reverted to the old system of roka [joint cultivation] again' (Bjorkelo, 1989:63). Also, the process of fragmentation was slowed by emigration as some people fled the exactions of the Turco-Egyptian state. The old system of transferring land through parental gifts or bridewealth increasingly gave way to land sales and other forms of land transfer, which was facilitated by the new land-tax policy, whereby tax-delinquent land could be appropriated by anyone who paid the arrears, regardless of the value of the land itself. This enabled merchants to turn themselves into landlords by channelling part of their commercial capital into acquiring such land and lending money to peasants.

The Turco-Egyptian state also introduced a new and more onerous system of taxation . Peasant communities were collectively responsible for paying ever increasing taxes regardless of fluctuations in production and prices of their produce. In fact, the fact that prices were fixed and kept low, while the prices of consumer goods and taxes followed the currency fluctuations, reinforced the tax burden and ensured that the peasants became progressively worse off. Corrupt officials often collected over and above the stipulated tax rates and pocketed the difference. The taxes were based principally on the size of the saqiya lands. The methods of tax collection resembled military campaigns.

Peasants responded to all this in various ways. Many abandoned the registered riverain lands and took up cultivation in the rainfed areas. Indeed, desertions and emigration became widespread. Others resorted to borrowing from merchants, or they turned to part-time trade or wage labour. Tax collectors were sometimes ambushed and killed. Revolts also erupted throughout the period of Turco-Egyptian rule, beginning with those of 1823. Several attempts to reform the system and make it more 'fair' and efficient proved unsuccessful. The taxation system succeeded in disrupting and decreasing agricultural production in the northern Sudan, which not only reduced state revenues, but ultimately facilitated the overthrow of the regime by the Mahdist movement in 1885 and the creation of the Madhiyya (Bjorkelo, 1989:82-103).

Ethiopia

Ethiopia also had a long suffering peasantry. At the beginning of the nineteenth century Ethiopian rule was confined to the north of the country where the nobility was engaged in perpetual struggle amongst its members for supremacy and control of the monarchy, which became weakened in the process (Crummey, 1975, 1979). The nobility survived on the backs of the peasantry, although the latter enjoyed the right to use land and transmit it by inheritance. This was known as rist. But rist did not confer rights to a specific piece of land, but to land 'held corporately by the descendants, through any combination of male and female ancestors' (Hoben, 1973:12). Thus the tenure of actual fields was subject to constant revision and relocation.

The system of ambilineal descent among the northern peoples, including the Amhara, meant individuals belonged to several cognatic descent groups and could have land claims in several areas. This encouraged land fragmentation and conflict, which undermined the peasants' solidarity and their ability to meet the machinations of the predatory nobility. In fact, it enhanced the latter's role as arbiters in land conflict. In parts of Eritrea and Tigray a system developed whereby rist was based on residence, not descent. This system was perhaps developed in order to correct the fragmentation of plots. All those who held rist rights were known as *ristegnas*.

There was also another set of land rights, known as gult or gwilt, which were given to members of the ruling elite as a reward for loyal service to their lord, and to churches and monasteries as endowment. The gult holder had the right to collect taxes on behalf of the state from those who farmed the land, and exercise judicial and administrative authority over them. There were few controls over the amount of taxes that could be exacted. The gult system was, therefore, a part of the administrative system. Those who held gult could also have rist rights, and when this was hereditary, it became rist gult. 'Virtually all arable land was held by someone or some institution as gwilt' (Hoben, 1973:5).

The ristegnas were in theory not tenants, but in practice the nobility exacted dues from them, which took the form of corvee labour, a percentage of the production, usually 10%, tributes of cattle or honey, or services for the maintenance of the local church, and so on. In addition, peasants were sometimes forcibly conscripted into the army and their food requisitioned by passing armies. The predatory soldiers were, in fact, used regularly 'to supervise and directly benefit from the collection of taxes and use of labour services due from already cultivated land' (Caulk, 1978:467). Some of them were given recoverable grants of gult, called maderiya, for their support. Altogether, Crummey (1981a:232) believes, 'the cumulative levels of surplus extraction from the Abyssinian peasants during the eighteenth and nineteenth centuries ran around 30%'.

This pattern of peasant production and exploitation was perfected in the south, which was conquered and incorporated into Ethiopia from the mid-nineteenth century under the reigns of Emperor Tewodoros II (1855-1868), Yohannes II (1872-1889) and Menelik II (1889-1913). It was under the three monarchs that Ethiopia's imperial institutions were reconstructed and consolidated, and the Ethiopian state entered one of its most expansive phases, buoyed by military success in wars against foreign invaders, including the Italians at Adowa in 1896. The central government systematically appropriated and redistributed the conquered lands to both the indigenous ruling class and immigrant settlers, who became the new overlords.

In this way, private landownership was created. The south provided a wonderful opportunity for members of the Ethiopian nobility to acquire private land holdings and for the government to reward soldiers, civil servants, church officials, and local collaborators. The conquered peoples, regardless of their system of land tenure, became tenants to those whom the conquered land was assigned. Some nomadic peoples were even 'converted by this process into farmers because of their need to generate tribute for the grantees of their clan lands' (Cohen and Weintraub, 1975:36).

The position of the southern tenants was much worse than that of the northern ristegnas. They became more like feudal serfs. In addition to paying rent to the landlord and taxes to the state, the tenants were also required to perform such services as ploughing or weeding land held by the landlord, maintaining his homestead, repairing his fences, herding his animals, or carrying his produce to the market. On holidays the tenants were expected to give gifts to the landlord as well! Military conscription, plunder and billeting were also more pronounced in the south than in the north. Furthermore, local labour was used to build the fortified towns, known as ketemas, which came to dot the landscape, and to build roads linking them. Additional labour in the south 'was derived from slaves, sometimes purchased, but more frequently received by the settlers as booty. Menelik himself was Ethiopia's «greatest slave entrepreneur», expropriating 10% of all captives taken' (McClellan, 1980:71). The slaves were mainly used by the settlers in domestic service, or they were exported to Egypt, Arabia or the East African coast.

The peasants responded to this exploitation and oppression in several ways. The most common forms of resistance were flight, evasion, outright refusal, revolt, and armed struggle. Against plundering the peasants adopted various strategies, including locating their villages in obscure and easily defensible positions, storing grain in secret underground pits, and using churches to hide their grain and cattle. In the face of looming battles they would gather at strategic points in the vicinity to prey on the losers, whom they killed or held for ransom. Peasant resistance stiffened in the 1850s and 1860s as the nobility robber bandits, known as shefta, intensified their activities. Peasant revolts and armed struggles broke out periodically not only against the shefta, but also against the king himself.

In 1853, for instance, the peasants of Gajjam ambushed Tewodoros' soldiers, killing many of them, although the peasants were later routed. In January 1866, the peasants of Begamder rebelled against government demands for higher taxes. The rebellion was fuelled when the king turned to plundering. It lasted until October 1867 when Tewodoros finally left the province, to meet a British expeditionary force of whose landing he had just learned (Crummey, 1986b). It was a mark of continued peasant disaffection that Italian survivors of Adowa 'were given hospitality in the neighbourhood of Debre Damo monastery east of the battlefield. Villagers there roundly abused the emperor although the able-bodied had obediently gone off... to besiege the Italian fort at Adigrat' (Caulk, 1978:473).

The Sokoto Caliphate

There were not many societies in nineteenth century Africa where the position of the peasantry approached the grimness of the situation in Ethiopia, the Sudan and Egypt. But the practice of paying land taxes or rent became increasingly common as states expanded and became more interventionist in the economy. This was the case in the Sokoto Caliphate, which was established early in the century following the jihad movement led by Uthman dan Fodio. The Caliphate became the largest and most populous state in West Africa. It developed a complex agrarian formation based on peasant and plantation production. Peasant production was clearly dominant and was the basis upon which the country's political economy revolved.

Peasant surpluses sustained the huge state apparatus. As in the countries already examined, the state extracted two principal forms of surplus from the peasantry, first, labour, largely drawn as corvee labour for public works and work on the farms and estates of the officeholders, and, second, taxation . There were different types of taxes, including the canonical zakkat, the taxes on households, and the taxes on crafts. The zakkat comprised a ten percent levy on grain production, levies on non-grain commodities, and the cattle tax raised on pastoralists (Johnson, 1976a:486-8; Watts, 1983:69-71). The revenue systems varied greatly between and within the emirates. The individual magnitude and relative importance of each tax also fluctuated throughout the century. Corvee labour and the taxes represented rents from the peasantry to the state in whom the land was ultimately vested. This system was ideologically legitimated through the idioms of religion and tradition, and sustained by the instruments of state coercion.

The land tenure system was a complex amalgam of Islamic and customary laws. The peasants cultivated land that was inherited from their parents or obtained by occupation of bush sanctioned, in theory, by an agent of the state, or land that they had been granted by the ruler. The peasants enjoyed considerable security of tenure for they could pledge, loan, inherit and give land as a gift. In many parts of the caliphate, especially in the densely populated areas, 'the distinction between possession and freehold was increasingly chimerical' (Watts, 1983:74).

Barotseland

In Barotseland land was ultimately vested in the King, which gave him power to demand allegiance from those who wanted to settle it. The King could also distribute unallocated land, claim any abandoned land, expropriate land for public services, subject to giving the holder other land, and to pass laws about the holding and use of land. The king was obliged, in turn, to give every subject land to live on and to cultivate, and allow the subjects free access to the use of forest land for hunting and gathering and public waters for fishing. The land rights were delegated from the King to the village headmen, and from the latter to the heads of households who finally distributed it to members of the household for actual use. Thus the use of land as a unit of production was vested in individuals (Gluckman, 1977). But the land could not be sold, leased, pledged or mortgaged, while cattle and fishing sites could be rented out on a sharecropping basis.

The land was unequally distributed. The King owned by far the most land, and his relatives and the councillors had the next largest holdings. These people constituted the landholding class. The ordinary peasants were expected to pay rent and tribute to the King which was mainly redistributed among members of the landholding class. In addition, the peasants were called upon to provide corvee or forced labour in the flood plain to reclaim fertile marshy soils for cultivation and to improve communications by water (Clarence-Smith, 1979a). Farming plots were normally divided between those in the plain and those outside. Peasants had small plots both in the plain and outside, which entailed time-consuming travel. In order 'to rationalize production it became more common for a household to maintain two sets of dwellings, but this too required extra labour' (Horn, 1977:146).

Swaziland

The centralization of land control by the monarchy in Swaziland was largely a product of the consolidation of the Swazi state in the mid-nineteenth century. This process was began by Mswati, the renowned Swazi monarch who from the late 1830s embarked on a programme of strengthening the Swazi state against the twin threats posed by the expansionist Boer and British colonists and the Zulus. Mswati's reforms affected agriculture in several ways. First, he acquired vast tracts of land to be used for cultivation, grazing and settlement by members of the royal household, his personal followers, and his appointed chiefs. Indeed, he extended nominal control over all the country's land, and 'exerted absolute rights over natural resources, such as timber and reeds, which he often called upon local chiefdoms to supply' (Crush, 1987:20). The country was divided into numerous more chiefdoms, more than one hundred by the 1890s.

For administrative convenience and to preserve local relations of domination, the allocation of land to commoners remained in the hands of the chiefs... [who] allocated land for building, cultivation, and communal grazing to commoners who offered allegiance and tribute in return (Crush, 1987:20).

The consolidation of state power was accompanied by the strengthening of the age regiment system and the construction of new rituals of kingship, all of which altered the patterns and structures of agricultural organization. The regiments not only served as military units for the defence of the state, they were also vehicles of socializing young men from recently incorporated chiefdoms, and thus played an important role in the construction of Swazi nationhood. In addition, the regimental system, 'gave the aristocracy direct control over a vast reservoir of labour for military and agricultural purposes as well as providing them with a virtual internal monopoly of coercive power' (Crush, 1987:24).

Apart from working in the royal fields, the soldiers, or imbutfo, performed numerous domestic tasks for the aristocracy, and were deployed in hunting as well during the winter months. The surplus product from the royal fields was mostly used to sustain the regiments themselves and the large royal villages. The appropriation of so much male labour power from the homesteads, altered the sexual division of labour, and led to the intensification of female labour time in the home-stead economy. Mswati instituted a number of new rituals of kingship, including the incwala, a first fruits ceremony, in which the bounties of nature and kingly supremacy and supernatural powers were celebrated. 'The ritual was also one element in the assertion of central control over agricultural production in Swazi society [for] as a «first fruits» ceremony no Swazi could partake of the new harvest until after it was celebrated. Earlier in the agricultural cycle, Mswati instituted a ceremony known as neza ilikuba where no homestead was allowed to break the soil for planting until the king had publicly doctored an agricultural implement' (Crush, 1987:22).

Peasant Labour Processes

Not all African peasantries lived under centralized and interventionist states. Many lived in independent village communities, or in highly decentralized states. But even the highly centralized states did not always succeed in controlling the organization of peasant production and in managing every aspect of their lives. Indeed, these states were generally less interested in regulating production itself than in maximizing their appropriation of what was produced. Thus peasant farming communities enjoyed varying degrees of autonomy from external pressures and sanctions. The organization of peasant labour processes transcended differences in the patterns and forms of state organization.

Peasant farmers used different forms of labour, the most important of which was that provided by the peasant household itself. Household labour was sometimes supplemented by inter-household labour pools, sharecropping, slave, indentured and wage labour. Households varied widely in terms of size, composition, and internal divisions of labour. As Hopkins (1973:21) has observed, with reference to West Africa, the household 'was quite capable of adapting its size and skills to meet changing circumstances and to create new opportunities. Each household approximated to the optimum size for the conditions in which it operated'. He notes, for example, that 'small households predominated among the Kofyar of Central Nigeria because they were best suited to the system of intensive agriculture which prevailed in the area,' while in the Cameroons, 'the demand for extra labour was a principal cause of the existence and growth of polygynous families' (Hopkins, 1973:21).

In Ethiopia, peasant households varied considerably in size, composition, and resources. The Ethiopian household was more fluid than in most African societies because of the family descent structure. Households contracted and expanded as grown-up children left to found new households and non-kins were incorporated. Generally, the households of the poor ristegnas were smaller than those of the richer ones, for the latter had more resources for incorporation. The households of the gult holders tended to be among the largest. Also, the latter could work in more than one altitude zone in order to diversify their crops (Hoben, 1973; Cohen and Weintraub, 1975).

In many African societies, it was quite common for several households to pool their labour resources together during peak periods in the agricultural cycle, such as field clearing, planting and harvesting. Among the Hausa, where the household was known as gida, and included in its attenuated form the family clients and slaves (Smith, 1954), individual farmers could call on four main types of work groups, called gayya. First, there were work parties organized for bride service by a daughter's fiance; second, those sponsored by a client for his patron; third, those organized by wealthy men; and fourth, the compulsory gayya for office holders (Watts, 1983:127).

In the northern Sudan , work parties called nafir or faza'a, were mostly used for tasks such as cutting and threshing. The participating households 'were treated with food and beer' (Bjorkelo, 1989:65). In Lesotho, the ability to mobilize collaborative inter-household labour gave Basotho farmers an edge over their Boer counterparts. Keegan (1983:217) quotes one settler who complained that:

> *a native gives notice that he is about to reap and will kill a sheep and supply unlimited Kaffir beer. It is astonishing to see the crowd that collects in no time, and the ease with which his crops come off. But the poor [white] farmer when he gets up finds his boys missing, off to the beer drink. They turn up the next day, muddled and useless.*

Labour from the peasant household was the backbone of agricultural production not only on the peasant plot itself, but also on the large estates, as was the case in Egypt , where these estates increasingly relied on corvee or forced labour drawn from peasant households. 'Unlike conscription forced labour was imposed on the whole of the rural population' (Toledano, 1990:188). The irrigation works were maintained by corvee labour. Forced labour for public works was as old as the irrigation system itself, but with the enormous expansion of the system in the nineteenth century, the demand for maintenance labour increased sharply. Muhammad Ali's regime introduced a new system whereby, unlike before, corvee labourers could be moved away from their locality to any part of Egypt as required. This meant that the peasants who were moved could not take care of their own land and livestock. Often the entire peasant household went. Their work consisted of clearing canals and repairing dikes. The average amount of time contributed by each peasant was 60 days, later reduced to 45 days. Usually the peasants furnished their own tools and food. They were paid a piaster a day.

Share Cropping

The importance of sharecropping in African agriculture in the nineteenth century has not been fully appreciated. There is evidence that it was more widespread than is commonly realized. Sharecropping has not enjoyed a good name among some scholars. From the vantage point of neo-classical economics, it has been dismissed as 'inefficient' and 'irrational' (Johnson, 1950; Sen, 1966; Warriner, 1969; Jacoby, 1971). To Marxists, it is seen as an iniquitous, 'pre-capitalist', 'semi-feudal' system (Dumont, 1957; Bhaduri, 1973; Bell, 1977; Pearce, 1983). These indictments tend to oversimplify the issue. As Robertson (1987:2) has observed, sharecropping is not 'an inflexible and immutable relationship.' It is a highly flexible, diverse and complex system, that historically has hindered as much as it has promoted capitalist accumulation, conserved as well as transformed class exploitation.

As for its productivity, Robertson (1987:4) notes that 'empirical evidence has confirmed the view that yields under sharecropping may be as high as, if not higher than, yields under owner-cultivation or the more «progressive' land-labour arrangements'. Moreover, there is evidence that contradicts the assertion that sharecropping invariably inhibits innovation (Hsiao, 1975; Braverman and Srinivasan, 1981; Nabi, 1984). The cash crop 'revolution' that Senegambia and southern Ghana experienced from the late nineteenth century was in fact facilitated by the development of sharecropping arrangements.

As noted earlier, cocoa production in southern Ghana began in the last quarter of the nineteenth century. Almost from the beginning household labour in the cocoa growing areas was supplemented by hired labour and sharecropping. Unlike palm oil production, cocoa farming was less compatible with slave labour because 'most of the investment in cocoa farming in the first areas to grow it was in land... Investing in both land and slaves for cocoa farming would have put an unbearable strain on most farmers' (Sutton, 1983:496). Moreover, producing cocoa was less labour-intensive than palm oil. The migrant cocoa farmers of southern Ghana bought land either as a family group or through companies formed by non-kinsmen, and then subdivided the land for individual use. The family form of organization was associated with the matrilineal Akan, while the company form was identified with the patrilineal peoples (Hill, 1963).

The system of employing sharecroppers was known as abusa. Before the beginning of cocoa farming, abusa was commonly used in the form of tribute for land with usufruct rights, in which a chief could expect one-third share of what came out of the land cultivated by foreigners for whom the land was not free. This system expanded as cocoa farming developed and 'stranger farmers' flocked to the cocoa growing areas. The chief of the area granted land to the abusa in exchange for a two-thirds share of the cocoa farm 'when it came to full bearing; up to this stage he might pay the latter in food, but within a very short time by today's standards the latter became the proprietor of one-third of the farm, which he was entitled to sell, bequeath or entrust to a caretaker' (Robertson, 1987:75). Thus, in the early days of cocoa farming, 'abusa was a kind of hire-purchase' arrangement, allowing a fairly rapid transformation of an investment in labour into land rights. What distinguishes abusa at this stage from its successors is that its principal function was to transact a share of the farm - the developed land - rather than of the produce (Robertson, 1987:75). Increasingly, the abusa were hired either when new farms were being established or afterwards to look after an existing farm. They usually brought their families with them. Their tasks included picking, drying and fermenting the cocoa. The advantages of the system for the owners of the farms just being developed was that they did not have to pay for labour before the cocoa farm started bearing. In the meantime, the abusa labourer was given a piece of land to grow food, which he could also sell. Those who carried the additional tasks of carrying the cocoa to the market and sometimes weeding were paid extra. They were known as nkotokuano (Sutton, 1983:473). Robertson's conclusion that abusa facilitated the rapid expansion of cocoa production in southern Ghana cannot be disputed, but his contention that the system has led to the 'de-classing' of rural society, and prevented 'the consolidation of clearly defined class categories' is debatable (Robertson, 1987:79).

The cash crop revolution that occurred in groundnuts production in the Senegambia region from 1830 was based on migrant farmers. These farmers, variously called sama manila in Mandinka, or serawoolies, tillibunkas, or Strange Farmers, came from the Upper Senegal and Niger Valleys in search of land best suited, ecologically and commercially, for the cultivation of lucrative cash crops, especially groundnuts. The migrants followed the trails of the long-distance traders. They were mostly young men, who stayed for two to three years farming peanuts before returning back home with various goods that they had acquired. The origins of the sama manila is in dispute. Some impute that they were of slave origins (Klein, 1977:355). Others contend that they were voluntary migrants (Jeng (1978:108; Robertson, 1987:256-7). The weight of the evidence would seem to support the latter position, despite the fact that some sama manila may originally have been ex-slaves and despite any apparent similarities in the organization of slave and sama manila labour (Swindell, 1980:101-2).

Thus the sama manila were essentially free agricultural entrepreneurs. Their migrations were organized by merchants or chiefs in the interior, especially from people who were already familiar with the cultivation of an indigenous groundnut variety. For their part, the Gambian peasants involved in peanut production lacked sufficient labour, especially after the abolition of domestic slavery by the British. The migrants were offered land to work, seed, and sometimes food by the landowner, in exchange for labour services (Swindell, 1980:94-97). These contracts could be renegotiated several times and endure over a period of years, during which time the migrant could graduate into an independent producer (Robertson, 1987:205). Thus the migrants played a dual role, as migrant farmers and as farm labourers.

By the end of the century the system in the Gambia had changed from one 'based on the «renting» of land from local chiefs, which was closely associated with the activities of long-distance traders... towards a system based on labour-sharing with individual host farmers' (Swindell, 1981:93). The change reflected the new realities in the groundnut growing regions. Increasingly, the strangers made deals with individual landholders, rather than chiefs. This process was further assisted by the imposition of '«custom» in the form of fixed rents, to be divided between chiefs and government, and then the transformation of this rent into a tax' (Robertson, 1987:255).

Migrant farmers also played a vital role in the development of groundnut production in Guinea-Bissau, where groundnuts were grown on establishments called feitorias, which were owned by African and European traders, and functioned both as agricultural properties and as commercial posts. By the late 1850s there were 30 feitorias, two-thirds of whose labour came from the interior. The feitoria owners provided the migrants with transport and furnished them with food on their trip south. When they arrived they were given a certain amount of land to cultivate, as well as seeds, utensils and provisions, for which they paid at the end of the harvest season. This system of credit worked against them, and many ended up staying longer than they had anticipated (Bowman, 1987). Sharecropping was not restricted to commodity production for the world market. Deep in the interior of West Africa, a sharecropping system appears to have developed in parts of the Sokoto Caliphate, whereby 'a new farmer in search of land could go into partnership with the owner, in effect paying rent by sharing the produce' (Last, 1977:104).

Cases of sharecropping and tenancy have also been reported from northern, eastern and southern Africa. In Egypt, for example, sharecropping was quite common. The owner of the land paid the taxes, the irrigation dues, and furnished the implements, beasts, seed and fertilizer, while the sharecropper and his household provided all labour for the crops, from ploughing to harvest, for which he received a fifth or a quarter of the yield. He could receive half of the crop if he bore half the expenses. In many cases, the sharecroppers were already indebted to the landowners by the time of harvest, so that they often received nothing, and if a balance remained they were obliged to pledge their work for the following year. A variant of sharecropping was tenant farming, in which a fellah would rent a field for the agricultural year. The owner paid the taxes and received a fixed income from the tenant (Ayrout, 1963:55-56).

In the Sudan, sharecropping was integrated into the saqiya land system. The system spread as the new landed classes created by the Turco-Egyptian state sought to exploit their newly acquired lands. In the Blue Nile province, for example, many of the new landlords preferred to use agents, called *wakils*:

> to manage their estates for them for a commission while they remained at Sannar, forming a new class of wealthy absentee landlords. The farmers were in fact tenants-at-will, working on a cropsharing basis in the plots assigned to them by the landlord or his agent (Awad, 1971:220).

The rentals and land dues were heavy. The share of the landowner varied from one-tenth of the crop in the rainlands to one-fifth in the riverain lands. In addition, there were extra charges if the plot required no clearing or if it included the slope of a river bank, and whenever the tenant constructed a house on the plot or grew sesame. The tenant was also sometimes required to spend a morning working on his landlord's private plot without pay. Bjorkelo (1989:80) has argued that the gradual disintegration of the saqiya system under the Turco-Egyptian administration increasingly narrowed the opportunities for incorporating land-hungry and landless peasants and labourers into the production process through sharecropping arrangements. The importance of sharecropping in the Sudanese agricultural economy increased following the establishment of the giant Gezira scheme at the beginning of the twentieth century which relied heavily on sharecropping (Robertson, 1987:chapter 4).

One of the most fascinating tenancy systems in eastern Africa developed among the Kikuyu. Unlike the northern Sudan and many of the societies considered above, the Kikuyu lived in numerous autonomous communities scattered all over the central highlands of present-day Kenya. The frontiers of Kikuyu settlement expanded as their agriculture developed in the nineteenth century. Land was acquired by the act of first clearance, or through purchase, the forging of alliances and partnerships with the original owners, and through the use of force, chicanery, and the practices of adoption and absorption (Muriuki, 1974; Murmann, 1974:60-61). Land ownership rights were vested in the founder or head of the mbari, a lineage grouping reckoned through the male line that combined land owning with the regulation of marriage. The mbari was headed by a muramati who controlled the allocation of the land, called githaka, although he did not enjoy more rights than the other members. The right to use the land could be sold, but only after the right holder had won the approval of the whole mbari.

By the second half of the nineteenth century, the Kikuyu had cleared and occupied most of the highlands. That, coupled with population growth, led to the emergence of groups of people who had little or no land. This led to the development of land tenancy. There were three types of tenants, all of whom paid some form of rent. First, there was the muguri, who were given access to the use of land against a loan of stock. Second, there was the muhoi, who were granted temporary cultivation rights, but were not allowed to plant permanent crops. The muhoi paid an annual tribute of first fruits and beer and helped on the frontier with the arduous task of clearing the forest, building houses or cattle pens and in providing defence against external attack. Finally, there was the muthami, who were like the muhoi, except that they were given the additional right to erect buildings on the plot.

These tenants provided additional labour for Kikuyu peasants. The majority, as already pointed out, had little or no land in their own mbari. Tenancy could also be based on status ties, for example, a father giving land to a landless son-in-law; or a begetter of a widow's children bestowing upon the offspring land rights. The tenants could be evicted, in the case of the muguri on the redemption of his stock and their natural increase, and for the muhoi after reaping his crops, and for the muthami upon the removal of his house. These land tenancy arrangements were not mediated or reproduced by an overarching despotic state apparatus. That came with British colonization at the end of the century, which extended and transformed them.

The development of sharecropping in Lesotho was conditioned by the expansion of crop cultivation and animal husbandry, on the one hand, and the encroachment of European settlers on Basotho lands, on the other. These two processes contributed to the growth of land concentration and landlessness. Thus some people had more land than labour, while others had more labour than land. In the early days of sharecropping, the system was based on the share of produce between the landholder and the tenant. Later it was supplemented by fixed land rents and wage labour. In addition to working for other Basotho, Basotho sharecroppers also increasingly worked for European settler farmers in the neighbouring Orange Free State (Matsetela, 1982; Keegan, 1983).

The sharecroppers sometimes organized work parties, called matsema (Matsetela, 1982:221). Many of them thrived and they certainly became 'more prosperous than the poor white sharecropping bijowners [which] only provoked white indignation' (Robertson, 1987:191). This indignation, combined with the expansion and consolidation of settler capitalist agriculture, put pressures on the sharecropping system: increasingly contracts were shortened, evictions became more common, the shares were reduced, and the labour demands were raised. Some Basotho sharecroppers became proletarianized, others returned to Lesotho, where the sharecropping system was also undergoing significant changes as well. It was becoming less flexible and more commercialized.

The cases of these sharecroppers should go some way to explode the myth that African peasants were inertly conservative and did not develop additional forms of labour to supplement household labour, or that they lived in egalitarian communities which knew neither exploitation nor differentiation. They also demonstrate that labour migration in the continent did not start with colonialism. The migrant farmers of West Africa are remarkable in that they straddled different communities, and did not reproduce themselves solely through the spatial confines of their own societies. It is quite clear that sharecropping developed in response to the expansion of commodity production and growing inequalities among peasants. Also, different forms of sharecropping emerged, and changed over time.

The Use of Slaves

The use of slaves in peasant agriculture also appears to have increased. The literature on slavery in Africa is now quite vast. It demonstrates the great diversity of African slave systems, and the hazards of making generalizations. Some have found the variety of forms too great to warrant their encapsulation under a single term called 'slavery' (Kopytoff and Miers, 1977). Not surprisingly, many authors hesitate to give a definition of slavery, yet they proceed to discuss it 'as though we all know what it is' (Harms, 1978:328). The debate has often centred on determining whether slavery was primarily a social or an economic phenomenon, as if the two were, and can be, separated.

Those who emphasize the social dimension of slavery concentrate on the role of enslavement in the incorporation or absorption of people into society, especially into kinship groups, and seek to demonstrate the way this was done, without explaining why, except in deterministic cultural and ahistorical terms. They tend to highlight the 'rights' the slaves did and did not have (Grace, 1975:1-20; Igbafe, 1975:410-2; Kopytoff and Miers, 1977; Falola, 1987; O'Sullivan, 1980; Bohannan and Curtin, 1988:287). Others have argued, in the words of Hopkins (1973:26), that 'there was a long-established labour market in Africa. The fact that this market took the form of slave labour rather than wage labour was the result of a deliberate choice based on elementary, but broadly accurate, cost-benefit analysis'. In other words, slaves were acquired because slave labour was cheaper and more efficient than wage labour (also see Northrup, 1979:3-5; Manchuelle, 1989:115).

Neither approach is satisfactory. As Cooper (1979:104) has argued, the latter 'reifies the market as much as the absorptionist thesis reifies kinship. Neither provides an adequate framework to analyze the fundamental differences in the ways labour was controlled and surplus value extracted or to understand the consequences that the ability of particular groups to control and use slaves had for social organization, cultural values, and ideology'. The absorptionist thesis ignores the fact that slaves were not acquired by some amorphous 'lineage', 'society' or 'ethnic' group, but by specific individuals and households. Whether or not they were incorporated into these households, treated well or poorly, they had, like other members of the household, to work in order to reproduce themselves and the entire household. For its part the market thesis assumes, quite incorrectly, that the choice facing employers was confined to slave or wage labour. This overlooks sharecropping. Moreover, as will be demonstrated later, wage labour was not entirely absent.

Slavery should not be conflated with every form of servile and dependent relationship or confused with all types of bonded labour. Pawns, indentured labourers, and clients, for example, have to be differentiated from slaves (Igbafe, 1975:414-6; Oroge, 1985). Definitions that seek to distil the essence of 'African slavery' from the gourds of social, economic, or political roles not only disregard the fact that there were different slave systems in Africa, but that each had social, economic and political dimensions, though the mix varied from case to case, and changed over time. Slavery was not an autonomous and timeless institution, but a process articulated with changing productive systems, kinship systems, and systems of dominance (Harms, 1978:329). The roles of slaves were neither cultural givens, nor products of abstract economic principles, but reflections of concrete historical processes, fashioned in part by the slaves themselves. Thus with regard to absorption, the issue no longer becomes one of seeing it as an inherent quality of some mystical 'African slavery', but one of determining how the various processes of absorption took place (Cooper, 1979:121-5).

The links between slavery and other forms of labour were quite complex. In Madagascar, agricultural slavery partly expanded in response to the extraction of male corvee labour, called fanompoana, from peasant households. This left women, children and slaves to do most of the work on the farms (Campbell, 1988a:474-5). Among the Soninke of the Western Sudan, slavery appears to have grown partly in response to Soninke labour migration. The more the Soninke participated in temporary migration to the groundnut fields of the Senegambia, 'the more slaves they were able to buy. And, conversely, the more slaves they bought, the more family members were freed from agricultural obligations to devote themselves to trade on a more or less permanent basis' (Manchuelle, 1989:109). Labour migration to South Africa from the 1870s also facilitate the growth of agricultural slavery among the Gaza Nguni of southern Mozambique (Harries, 1981:320).

In many of these societies slave labour was confined to the rich peasants, wealthy landlords and the elite. The processes that brought this about of course varied from one society to another. In Madagascar, the concentration of slaves among the wealthy began in the 1830s. By this time the supply of both fanompoana and slaves could no longer meet the demand. The resulting labour shortages and the high cost of slaves led to the growing impoverishment of many peasants, who found it more difficult to purchase and retain slaves. Slaves passed increasingly into the hands of the court elite, to the extent that by 1869 it is estimated that at least one-third of the 'free' Merina population owned no slaves at all, with the result that 'agricultural production reverted from slave to peasant labour, a situation which was not reversed until about 1870' (Campbell, 1988a:475-6).

In the Sudan before the nineteenth century, slaves mainly served bureaucratic and military functions and as concubines for noblemen. After 1800 the slave trade and agricultural slavery rose sharply. In Dar Fur, the ruling elite depended almost entirely on slaves to work their estates (O'-Fahey, 1973). Slaves were also widely used among the rich peasants. By the end of the century, an estimated 20 to 30% of the inhabitants were slaves (Warburg, 1978:221). The need for slave labour was brought about partly by the expansion of agricultural production, and partly by the growth of labour-intensive practices in agriculture encouraged by the government's policy of taxing each waterwheel at a fixed rate. Landlords had a choice either to exploit their tenants more thoroughly or to import additional labour. They often did both (Spaulding, 1982:13-16).

In Barotseland the landlord class also increasingly resorted to slave labour to meet their labour requirements. The use of agricultural slave labour increased from the 1880s as the state expanded and its subject population increased and as the regional markets for agricultural produce expanded with the encroachment of colonial capitalism. The work of the slaves involved agricultural tasks, as well as building houses and canoes, acting as paddlers and porters, and so on. The life of slaves was often harsh and brutal. And the slaves responded through flight, working slowly and poorly, and occasionally there were slave insurrections, as in 1893 and 1897 (Clarence-Smith, 1979a:231). By then Barotseland was under British colonial rule in a country called Northern Rhodesia, later renamed Zambia.

The incidence and use of slavery could vary within the same economic region or country, depending on the slaves' economic activities. For example, in the three neighbouring zones of northeastern Nigeria, slavery became important for the economies of the coastal belt and the savanna belt, but not for the oil palm belt, where labour was transferred from food production. Along the coast slave labour was used mostly for canoeing, while in the savanna they were used to produce grain. Differences emerged 'between the rapid assimilating system at the coast and the sharply stratified system in the food exporting zone' (Northrup, 1979:16).

Agricultural slaves were often differentiated from other slaves, such as military slaves, administrative and trading slaves, and in most societies they were at the bottom of the slave class. In the Wolof states 'they were drawn almost exclusively from those who had been recently enslaved and purchased, and performed the most arduous and difficult tasks' (Searing, 1981:477; Falola, 1987:97-101). The first generation slaves laboured directly under their masters on the master's fields, while second- and third-generation slaves were usually settled in separate villages where they divided their time between working on their master's and their own plots, and finally, 'some slaves were allowed to pay their masters tribute or rent that was considered comparable to the labour owed' (Searing, 1988:480-1). Thus agricultural slaves were themselves differentiated according to generational status and labour regimes.

Searing (1988:482) believes that it is 'likely that many household slaves gradually merged with the free peasantry over the course of several generations, either directly through manumission, or by becoming tenants attached to aristocratic households as clients'. This reflected the inability of the aristocracy to reproduce slaves as a social class, partly borne out the resistance of the peasants against their marginalization and the slaves for peasantization. The transition from slavery to peasantization has been noted for the Sokoto Caliphate by Lovejoy (1978a:367-8) and Watts (1983:78), where second generation slaves were often absorbed into the kin solidarities of the rent-paying peasantry.

The transformation from slavery to other labour systems, including indentured and wage labour, was probably an ongoing process, but intensified towards the end of the century as domestic slavery went into terminal decline. In some places, such as the Bida emirate of central Nigeria, former slaves stayed on as labour tenants of their former masters (Mason, 1973: 470-1). Among the Yoruba, indentured labour, known as iwofa, an old and relatively restricted pawning institution, grew rapidly in the 1890s and became 'almost the only extra-familial source of recruiting labour, as the majority of the slaves forcibly liberated or induced to desert by the British did not become wage-labourers' (Oroge, 1985:93). It survived well into the 1920s.

There is growing evidence that agricultural wage labour also expanded in some places, especially in the late nineteenth century. In the Sudan, wage labour initially developed as a supplement to slave labour, then it began to compete with it towards the end of Turco-Egyptian rule as prices of slaves rose sharply (Spaulding, 1982:16; Bjorkelo, 1989:80). Rising slave prices also account for the spread of hired labour among the Soninke (Manchuelle, 1989:114-6). In the Sokoto Caliphate, wage labour, known as kwadogo, developed as well, particularly in the Kebbi valley for dry-season rice cultivation, and among migrant cotton workers in southern Katsina (Watts, 1983). In southern Ghana, cocoa farmers supplemented abusa labour with annual labourers, hired for a one-year term at a fixed wage, and daily labourers employed at specific times of the year or to do a specific job (Sutton, 1983:474-5). Wealthy Yoruba cash-crop farmers also resorted to increased use of wage labour (Oroge, 1985:94).

These labour systems were not confined to cultivators. For example, share contract systems were also used by pastoral communities. In Rwanda, where the Hutu farmers and Tutsi pastoralists lived under the same state, the latter practised an elaborate system of stock sharing. Before the reign of Mwami Yuhi Gahindiro in the second half of the nineteenth century all livestock breeders had free access to pastures. Then gradually, possibly as a result of increased human and livestock populations, private rights of pasture were established over certain lands granted by the mwami or his representatives, known as ibi-kingi, in exchange for rent in the form of cattle. This cattle was used to support the expanding state bureaucracy. The ibi-kingi tenant not only had the right to graze the livestock of his household on his pasture land, but he could also sublet it. The sub-tenant paid rent in advance and paid extra when his cows had calves. The cows of the tenant and sub-tenant grazed together. In this way the original tenants acquired extra labour and income. The ibi-kingi was not divided up even after the tenant died. It was inherited by the tenant's male descendants who became co-tenants (Maquet and Naigiziki, 1977).

The Maasai agro-pastoral economy was based on the exploitation of three resources: grazing land, livestock, and labour. Maasailand was divided into territorial units, ranging from section, to localities, and cattle camps, in which several households lived. Territoriality and coresidence, rather than kinship, constituted one of the main organizing principles of Maasai society. Needless to say, the territorial units varied in size and they expanded and contracted depending on ecological conditions, size of the herds, and relations with neighbouring communities. Each section normally contained both dry season reserves, mostly higher areas with sufficient rainfall, where pasture and water could be found throughout the year, and lower-lying areas that were rich in minerals and salt licks, where grazing was seasonal. The sections generally kept within their own boundaries, in which they practised transhumance. Conflict over pasture and water did arise periodically between and within sections, particularly during times of severe drought, and as sections or localities expanded.

The survival of the household largely depended on the amount of stock it owned, which, in turn, was conditioned by the labour force available to manage it, apart from the carrying capacity of the land. Livestock was owned by the household unit and controlled by its head 'who allocated sufficient milking herd to each of his wives' (Waller, 1985:104). The divisions of labour within the household were articulated with the age set system, the second organizing principle in Maasai society, which complemented, and to some extent, cut across, the spatial divisions. The age set system was a rigid hierarchy of the male population. Each age group had a strictly defined set of responsibility, functions and authority. At the bottom were the shepherds who herded their household's livestock with other boys. As the shepherds grew older, they were successively promoted to the junior warrior, then to senior warriors, junior elders, and finally senior elders (Hedlund, 1979). Each of these grades, particularly the lower ones, played an important role in the pastoral economy.

There was considerable social differentiation in Maasai society which was based on an unequal distribution of resources. Some households owned more livestock than other. The wealthy stockowners were in a better position to survive misfortunes of prolonged drought and disease than the poorer ones because of their greater resources and wider network to draw on for support. But they did not always have sufficient labour, while the poor households sometimes had more labour than stock. This gave rise to the development of patron-client transactions, in which the former distributed their herds among the latter. This arrangement enabled the rich to get extra labour for their livestock, and the poor to improve their subsistence, for they could consume some of the products from the latter's stock. It also helped counteract local overgrazing and drought and reduce the effects of localized disease.

Another practice that developed and became fairly widespread, especially towards the end of the century, was the employment of herders from poor households by wealthy households. The herder was incorporated into the employer's household and given the use of some milking cattle. Sometimes if he had a benevolent employer he might acquire stock and eventually become an independent stockowner. Only a few made this transition. Indeed, the position of herders worsened in the last decades of the century as a result of increased supply of labour and decreased demand due to the contraction of herds and the increase in the numbers of stockless families brought about by the outbreak of cattle epidemics.

These arrangements facilitated the redistribution of both labour and income between rich and poor households among the Maasai. The redistribution of income was also effected by ceremonies to which wealthy households contributed considerably more livestock than their less fortunate compatriots. This served the ideological function of bestowing power and prestige upon the wealthy, while at the same time masking inequality and promoting a pastoral ideology of egalitarianism.

The Maasai also tried to satisfy their demand for labour by incorporating outsiders as voluntary herders or as captives, and through formal adoption and marriage. Outsiders came to Maasailand for purposes of trade, or to acquire a new livelihood. Many of those who came from the surrounding peoples, such as the Kikuyu and Kamba, were boys and young men, who worked as herders, and usually returned to their own communities with a few sheep and goats that they had been given by their employers. Some outsiders were formally incorporated into Maasai clans and households. This often required a long period of residence and service in the home of the elder sponsoring the immigrant. Once adopted, the immigrant was given a nucleus herd to establish himself. He became independent after getting married.

Generally, the Maasai preferred adopting children because as potential brides or herders they helped in the growth and consolidation of the household as a stock holding unit. The children were either acquired as foster-children and debt-pawns from poor people in the neighbouring communities, or as captives during war. The Maasai also placed great value on acquiring foreign women as wives because they 'were «cheaper» than

Maasai wives' (Waller, 1985:112). In short, the Maasai became adept at incorporating outsiders in order to meet their labour needs. Moreover the latter played a useful role as cultivators. It has been suggested that the enclaves of agriculturalists in Maasailand served as 'a transitional stage for those wishing to accumulate stock and contacts necessary to join the Maasai' (Waller, 1985:113).

Plantation Systems

There is considerable disagreement on how to define plantations in general, and whether to characterize large estates in Africa as plantations. Plantations have normally been defined in the context of agricultural organization in the Americas. Accordingly plantations are seen as capitalist enterprises characterized by export-production and foreign or metropolitan ownership, (Beckford, 1972; Mintz, 1977). To deny that large-scale units of agricultural production in Africa can be called plantations because they were organized and managed differently from New World plantations, as Searing (1988:478-9) has recently argued, assumes, erroneously, that plantation agriculture can be reduced to one historical form. This ignores the fact that locally-owned plantations organized on non-capitalist lines and producing for the local rather than the world market have been known to exist (Bernstein and Pitt, 1974; Graves and Richardson, 1980).

In West Africa, plantation agriculture became an important feature of the economy of the Sokoto Caliphate. The plantations first developed in the Sokoto-Rima river basin, where the twin capitals of Gwandu and Sokoto were established. They grew from the defensive centres, known as ribats, that had been built during the course of the *jihads*. The ribats attracted a steady flow of war captives and people seeking security who were soon put to work on the burgeoning plantations. By the 1820s plantations had become firmly established in Gwandu and Sokoto, and soon appeared in other parts of the Caliphate as economic and political conditions stabilized. They varied in terms of size and organization. The largest plantations were owned by the aristocracy and merchant class. By the end of the century government officials controlled a smaller proportion of the plantation sector than the other groups (Lovejoy, 1978a, 1979, 1981; Lovejoy and Baier, 1975).

The life cycle of individual plantations was relatively short. In fact, there appears to have been a marked tendency towards fragmentation of plantations and plantation holdings. Plantations were frequently subdivided among the children of the founding entrepreneurs upon the latter's death. Many wealthy planters preferred to have scattered, smaller estates, as an insurance against bad harvests or trade, rather than consolidate their holdings in one place. In the specific case of Nupe it has been suggested that there may have been a deliberate 'official' policy to prevent the consolidation of holdings in a single area in order to encourage the development of 'a state free from sectional rivalries' (Mason, 1973:467).

The plantations relied on various forms of labour, including household, corvee labour levied from ordinary peasants, and slave labour (Mason, 1981:214). Thus the plantations did not rely exclusively on slave labour as it is so often assumed (Lovejoy, 1978a; Klein and Lovejoy, 1979). It is more than likely that the relative importance of household, corvee and slave labour varied from place to place and changed over the course of the nineteenth century. Slavery became increasingly important as a source of labour as the plantation economy expanded in the second half of the nineteenth century. The Sokoto Caliphate in fact became a major slave trading centre in the region (Tambo, 1976; Smaldone, 1977). The number of slaves on a plantation depended on the plantation's size and the resources available to the owner. They ranged from a handful to thousands. For example, 'one emir of Zaria, Muhammad Sani, reputedly owned 9,000 slaves, which he amassed between 1846-60. While some of these were retained for his harem, court retinue, and other non-agricultural activities, there can be little doubt that most were engaged in agriculture' (Lovejoy, 1978a:359).

The organization of work for slaves varied from one place to another. Mason (1981:214) informs us, for instance, that in Nupe 'slaves did not work together with their lineages as they did, for example, in Zaria to the north'. Hogendorn (1977) has described the conditions under which slaves worked in two communities in Zaria. Their work followed a regular routine, alternating between working on their own plots of land and on the master's estate. The work groups were supervised by an overseer called sarkin gandu, who was himself a slave. His efforts were rewarded 'with food and favoured treatment in the choice of a wife' (Hogendorn, 1977:374). The sarkin gandu enforced discipline. The nature of punishment depended on the severity of the offence. Lateness was punished by extra work which lessened the amount of time the offender could spend on his own plot. Disobeying instruction or running away was punished by beating. The sarkin gandu was also responsible for selling the estate's produce at the market, after which he distributed a small amount of money to each slave to enable them to buy something for themselves. The slaves were free to sell crafts that they had produced. They were sometimes manumitted or allowed to redeem themselves through payment.

The slaves did not of course submit to their oppression and exploitation without resistance. The dialectics of slavery in the Caliphate involved both accommodation and resistance. The lot of slaves could be eased by cooperation, or they could be emancipated through death-bed proclamations of their masters, self-purchase and the ransom of third parties. Resistance was the flip side of accommodation. The concern with discipline is in itself an indication that slaves tried to set the limits of their exploitation. Resistance could take various forms, covert and overt, occur daily or episodically. Slaves were often accused of laziness, meaning not working as hard as the masters wanted them to. Sometimes they resorted to sabotage and theft, or even attacked their masters physically. More daring ones fled and escaped to other plantations or to places where they could not be easily traced. Occasionally, there were mass escapes and revolts, as in Wase in the 1850s or 1860s, and near Bauchi in 1870, when hundreds of slaves rebelled. Slave resistance was often expressed in the religious terms of the need to purge Islam of oppression and corruption (Lovejoy, 1986a, 1986b).

Plantation agriculture also developed in the other newly established Islamic states, such as Massina, where plantations were run by state-appointed officials and worked by slave labour (Azarya, 1979). The state also established government ranches of herds accumulated from booty and taxes (Johnson, 1976a). In Segu Bambara, grain and cotton plantations had been set up among the Maraka by the late eighteenth century. The slaves who worked the plantations lived in fairly stable family units in slave villages of between 50 and 500 people, where work was regimented and supervised by slave overseers. Through slave resistance and the spread of Islam, following the establishment of the Umarian state in 1861, Roberts (1987:chapter 3) has argued, the plantation system gradually became less rigid and harsh. Many planters visited their plantations only once or twice a year, which allowed the slaves greater control over their lives, and increased their sense of corporate identity. The Maraka plantation economy began to decline as the Umarian state shifted the centre of productive and commercial activity from the banks of the Niger to the desert edge.

Plantations in West Africa were not confined to the Islamic states. In Dahomey, plantation agriculture assumed greater importance as the slave trade declined. Slaves who previously would have been exported were diverted to the plantations, mostly producing palm oil. According to Law (1977a:573), 'at least initially, private traders were... the main, if not the sole, proprietors of large-scale oil plantations in Dahomey'. It was only from the mid-nineteenth century that the aristocracy became more involved in the plantation sector, and slavery became more rigid and harsh (Webster and Boahen, 1974:107-20).

Slavery was not the basis of plantation agriculture everywhere in West Africa. In Liberia, planters relied on hired labour. To be sure, they never seemed to have enough of it. Liberia's 'plantation agriculture was encouraged by the government to strengthen its economy as well as extend control over the hinterland' (Saha, 1988:233). By the mid-nineteenth century, there were, in all, 224 plantations in the country, producing a variety of cash crops, including cotton. However, shortages of labour as well as capital plagued and eventually undermined the plantation economy.

In North Africa, plantations were established all along the fertile coastal belt, either by indigenous planters, as in the case of Libya (Dyer, 1984), or European colonists, as in the case of Algeria (Bennoune, 1988). Egyptian plantations relied on both forced and voluntary labour. Corvee labour, as already indicated, was very unpopular. Once on the plantations, the forced labourers sometimes resorted to desertions, theft, sabotage of crops, animals and machinery, and occasionally outright revolt. Corvee labour was finally abolished in the early 1890s, except for fighting locusts, strengthening dikes, and so on. There were of course some peasants who came to work on the plantations voluntarily either because they were landless, or because the amount of land available to their households was insufficient to meet the subsistence requirements of all the household members. By the end of the century there were an estimated one to two million landless people in Egypt (Baer, 1969:215).

Some of the largest plantations in nineteenth century Africa were developed in eastern Africa, both on the Indian Ocean islands and along the coastal mainland. Plantations grew rapidly on the island of Madagascar, particularly following the adoption of autarkist policies by the Merina state in the 1820s (Campbell, 1987). These plantations relied on corvee, or fanompoana, labour, according to which every male was supposed to provide unremunerated labour to the state for a total of 24 days a year. Fanompoana was used for recruitment into the military and administration. Above all, it became indispensable for the construction and maintenance of irrigation works and as the main source of labour on rice plantations in the interior and sugar plantations along the east coast.

The plantations in the interior were owned by members of the ruling class, while those on the coast were set up by a select group of foreigners 'in conjunction with the crown, the former supplying capital, equipment and skill, and the latter land and labour... To fulfil the labour requirements of the plantations and associated industries, the crown was obliged either forcibly to import entire communities from other communities of the island, notably the populous south-east, or to supply slaves, for the plantations were heavily labour-intensive' (Campbell, 1988a:480). It can be seen that slavery supplemented fanompoana labour, but it was not the mainstay either of the plantation sector or the Merina economy as a whole, as it is commonly believed (Bloch, 1980; Lovejoy, 1983:234, 238-9).

The dependence of the state and the economy on fanompoana labour increased 'from the late 1870s due to the financial exigencies of the Franco-

Merina War of 1882-5, and the commercial depression of the 1880s and early 1890s' (Campbell, 1988b:56). The state, whose monarchy had converted to Christianity in 1869, used the mission school system as an instrument for the recruitment of fanompoana for agriculture, the army, industry, and the construction of mission stations. Not surprisingly, opposition to fanompoana became articulated with anti-missionary and anti-Christian sentiment. In November 1895, less than two months after the French occupation, the discontent erupted into revolt. The Menalamba revolt, as it is called, was not effectively suppressed until June 1897. Hundreds of churches were destroyed and many church leaders, government officials and thousands of civilians lost their lives (Campbell, 1988b).

The plantations along the East African coast were part of the Oman commercial empire, which was initially based on the slave trade. The mercantile classes operating along the coast were gravely affected by the collapse of the slave trade to the south (Sheriff, 1987). They established plantations as a substitute source of exports. Clove plantations were set up in Zanzibar, the centre of the commercial empire, in the 1820s. The Sultan became the largest planter. Before long, other members of the ruling class, farmers and Indian merchants took to clove production. More Arabs immigrated from Oman. As the landed aristocracy consolidated itself, indigenous peasant agriculture became marginalized, which undermined the island's self-sufficiency in foodstuffs.

The clove plantations demanded an ever-increasing supply of labour. The traditional fortnightly tributary labour from the indigenous population was clearly not enough. The planters turned to the importation of slave labour. In the 1840s and 1850s about 10,000 slaves were brought annually into Zanzibar and Pemba (Sheriff, 1987:60). The large landowners owned more than one estate and several thousand slaves. The average landowner, however, owned about 30 slaves. In the 1850s coconut and sugar plantations were established or revived, encouraged partly by the fall in the prices of both cloves and slaves.

In Malindi and Mombasa, unlike Zanzibar where most of the planters were Omani Arabs, the planter class included the local Swahili. Also, the plantations of Malindi and Mombasa produced mainly grain. As in Zanzibar, the rich planters owned more than one plantation and hundreds of slaves. An average plantation in Malindi had 61 acres and employed 10-20 slaves (Cooper, 1977:88-89). The plantations of Mombasa were relatively smaller because of the city's location and the fact that its hinterland was densely populated. In Mombasa, unlike Zanzibar, and to some extent Malindi, the slaves worked alongside, not in place of, their masters.

The labour and labour time of the slaves were closely regulated, although the work rhythms of slave labour on these plantations lacked the intensity of the American and Caribbean plantations. Slaves worked in gangs under the supervision of slave overseers. But they enjoyed considerable control over farming, residence and mobility. They could buy and sell 'their homes and farms, borrowed money, and traded', while at the same time working for their masters (Cooper, 1977:236). Like slaves everywhere, they tried to build their own lives in which accommodation and resistance, dependence and autonomy were locked in perennial struggle. Manumission was apparently common, although it rarely severed ties of dependence immediately or completely. When the situation became unbearable, there was always the option of escape.

The commercial empire upon which the East African coastal plantations was based, was increasingly undermined by its growing subordination to the world capitalist economy, as manifested in the establishment of British overrule in both Oman and Zanzibar. British imperial ambitions were wrapped in anti-slavery rhetoric. The establishment of British hegemony over the Indian merchant class, which financed the plantation system and the caravan trade into the interior, 'permitted British consuls to exercise a powerful influence on the financial administration of the Omani state' and undermined the viability of the plantation economy (Sheriff, 1987:207). The planters had no control over either finance or marketing. The suppression of the slave trade from 1873 and later slavery simply made matters worse for them. Slaves became more difficult and expensive to acquire at the same time that commodity prices were falling. To compound matters, the planters were subjected to increased taxation as the rapidly crumbling Omani state sought to fill its increasingly empty coffers. By the 1890s, therefore, the plantation economy along the East African coast was in decline, although it limped along into the twentieth century. It was subsequently transformed by colonial capitalism (Cooper, 1977:chapter 4; 1980).

Gender Divisions of Labour

Analyses of gender roles in precolonial Africa have tended to suffer from sexist and idealist biases. Women are often seen merely as appendages and victims of men. In the models constructed by Terray (1975), Meillassoux (1978, 1981) and Dupre and Rey (1978), women are reduced to 'goods' whose circulation is controlled by male elders. It is argued that by controlling young men's access to women and matrimonial commodities, such as cattle, the elders regulated both demographic reproduction and relations of production and exchange. These models are static and reduce women to 'objects' primarily acquired and exchanged to satisfy male productive and reproductive needs. The subordination of women is taken as a universal and permanent structural condition rather than problematized as a process that was socially constructed and continually contested. Also built into these models, which Mandala (1990:26-27) has perceptively observed in his study on work and control in the peasant economies of Southern Malawi, 'is a sexist definition of social age that equates seniority with the male section of the population, whereas among the Mang'anja differentiation based on age cut across sex boundaries. Moreover, it was boys rather than girls who were circulated between villages in the Valley, and their circulation did not involve the exchange of matrimonial goods'.

Women actively participated in the economic, political and ideological organization of Mang'anja society. It can neither be described as patriarchal nor matriarchal. 'The most one can infer from the evidence,' Mandala (1990:25) states, 'is that the outcome of the battle between the sexes had not yet been decided - although for [some] observers who had a special interest in religion, women appeared to have won the struggle.' Husbands and wives in the relatively loose and fragile Mang'anja household or banja held some property jointly, such as houses, granaries, foodstuffs, and livestock, while 'other goods, especially the instruments of domestic production, were held separately' (Mandala, 1990:51). In the fields, men and women performed similar tasks, except for the strenuous exercise of opening a new farm, which was done by men. Boys guarded crops against birds and predatory beasts. Mandala (1990:60) concludes that there was a technical equivalence of female and male labour in agriculture, although this:

> did not extend to all forms of household production. Some forms, like the construction of nyumba houses and nkhokwe granaries and the making of mats, were specifically male. Specifically female activities included beer brewing, pot making, and, more significantly, food processing.

The subordination of Mang'anja women began from the 1860s as a result of two processes, first, the expansion of the slave trade, and second, the penetration of merchant capital. The slave raiders 'dismembered entire communities, which had been the basis for female power; they upset the delicate balance between settlement patterns... and they exposed the population to the risks of food shortages and famine' (Mandala, 1984:145). Dislocated women, as well as men, sought the protection of armed Kololo warlords, who soon established a new political order in the Tchiri valley, one that entailed the process of female disenfranchisement. The first to experience marginalization were the previously privileged women. The penetration of European merchant capital from the 1870s also led to the expansion of household commodity production, which temporarily revitalized female autonomy and importance. The establishment of the colonial economy in the 1890s, radically transformed these relations and reinforced the struggles between men and women for control of the labour process.

The role of slavery and merchant capital in accentuating the subordination of women to men and increasing the exploitation of female labour power and reproduction has also been demonstrated for other societies in the nineteenth century, such as Southern Mozambique (Alpers, 1984a), Zanzibar and Mombasa, where women's solidarity, as well as opposition and accommodation to their growing subordination, was articulated through spirit possession cults, dance, improvement, and puberty rites associations (Strobel, 1976, 1979; Alpers, 1984b). Feierman (1990:59) has argued, with reference to Shambaai in Tanzania, that it was gender inequality which facilitated the emergency of slavery in the course of the nineteenth century. Women, like the poor, depended on somebody. Some of the poor slid to the margins of society into pawnship or slavery. Women depended on their husbands or their fathers for a place to live. Once a woman was married and came to live in her husband's village, she was given her own farm, from which she was expected to feed her children. The husband had his own farms. Some agricultural tasks were divided between men and women, while others were shared, more or less. For example, the men were responsible for the initial preparation of the soil, and the women for the harvesting. Some crops were gender-specific. Bananas were male crops, while most of the grain supplies came from women's farms.

In many societies the ties of dependency and female subordination were often reinforced by the growth of commodity production, especially if male control over productive resources, such as land and cattle, was already enshrined institutionally and ideologically. This appears to have been the case, for instance, among the Southern Tswana (Kinsman, 1983; Peters, 1983). Our knowledge of the impact of the commoditization of peasant production on gender roles and struggles in peasant households is still patchy. Researchers have been more preoccupied with celebrating the 'African initiative' of increased commercial production, than in investigating the changes that occurred in the labour processs. But things are beginning to change. Carney and Watts' (1991) study on the impact of groundnut production in Senegambia on gender relations is one case in point.

As we saw in the last chapter, this region experienced very rapid growth in cash crop production in the nineteenth century. As more men and richer households shifted to groundnut production, rice production declined, so that by the 1850s the region, which had previously exported rice, now became dependent on rice imports. A famine in 1857 provided a dramatic illustration of the food crisis. Out of all this emerged attempts to increase rice production. Intensification was both a social and gendered process, for the pressure fell on women and poorer households, who continually contested it. Before the groundnut revolution, the gender division of labour was based on tasks. But there was later a change from 'task- to crop-specific gender roles' (Carney and Watts, 1991:657). Rice now became women's work, while groundnuts became men's work. Also, 'as groundnuts cultivation expanded on upland fields' away from the floodplain and swamps, 'male and female agricultural labour became increasingly spatially separated between upland and lowland zones, giving rise to a much more rigid sexual division of labour by crop' (Carney and Watts, 1991:657).

Although female labour time on rice production increased, women's efforts were not enough to satisfy the growing demand for rice, thanks in part to the rise in the regional population due to the influx of strange farmers. Consequently, food imports continued to grow, and pressures for women to intensify rice production were stepped up. This only served to further strain household conjugal relations. The imposition of colonial rule in 1889 reinforced the pressures and gender struggles, for the colonial state was alarmed by the size of the food import bill and strove to re-establish household food self-sufficiency by initiating its own programmes to improve rice production. These measures included the introduction of improved Asian rice, the clearance of mangrove lands, and the establishment of a series of irrigation schemes. Most of these measures were undertaken from the 1920s, but many of the plans were hatched in the 1890s, the first decade of colonial rule.

It soon became clear that increasing rice acreage and production was one thing, and sustaining it was another. The latter required the transformation of the gender division of labour. Men had to be brought into rice cultivation. But they 'successfully resisted efforts to intensify their labour on the grounds that rice was «a woman's crop»' (Carney and Watts, 1991:661). They rested their case on 'tradition', conveniently ignoring the fact that this 'tradition' had only been invented a half a century earlier. The colonial state sided with the men, to preserve the patriarchal property-labour system, upon which the entire colonial enterprise was based.

These cases do not warrant generalizations that the spread of commodity production and more complex social systems inevitably led to the depression of the rights of women in nineteenth century Africa. Crummey's (1981b) study of women and landed property in Ethiopia clearly shows women held extensive rights in land, contrary to the common assumption that in a 'feudal' society like Ethiopia's, women were more oppressed than in acephalous societies.

In other societies, women's productive roles, economic autonomy, property rights, and household relations were transformed by the adoption of new technologies. As we noted in the last chapter, the adoption of ploughs by South African peasants changed the gender division of labour in agriculture in that men became more involved in tillage. A similar process seems to have occurred in Lesotho. Basotho women played a central role in the agricultural economy. They were responsible for gathering, caring for pigs and poultry, cultivation, bird-scaring, harvesting and threshing. In addition to food production, women also looked after food processing, fetched water and collected fuel for cooking, and made many of the household goods, such baskets and pottery, some of which were traded outside the household.

Despite their pivotal role in economic production, women enjoyed little political power. Following the widespread adoption of ox-drawn ploughs important changes took place in the labour time of both men and women. Contrary to those who have argued that technology innovation lessens women's labour time, Basotho women's workload in farming actually increased, for as 'the number and sizes of the fields under cultivation grew significantly after the introduction of the plough, the work of women in hoeing weeds, bird-scaring, and harvesting using traditional methods and technology increased accordingly. In addition, the annual agricultural labour time for women was no longer evenly distributed over time' (Eldridge, 1991:715). .

The intensification of female labour time in farming was accompanied by a reduction in other aspects of productive work in the household. For example, they gave up such 'activities as weaving, pottery and home building', especially as building in cut stone spread (Eldridge, 1991:723). For their part as 'men began to help women' their labour time was also reallocated. 'It became more common to hold work parties for weeding, harvesting, and threshing, at which married and unmarried men helped with the agricultural tasks that women usually performed' (Eldridge, 1991:723). As men became more involved in agriculture, and the goods that they previously produced in the household, such as blankets, clothing, and wooden and iron tools, weapons and utensils became more readily available in the markets, they gave up on, or spent less time, producing these goods. The reallocation of household labour also affected the young and the old who were given new tasks. For example, 'young boys, who had formerly cared only for small livestock, took over care of cattle as well' (Eldridge, 1991:723). These adjustments were of course not simply consequences of the adoption of new agricultural technology, but also of the growth of male labour migration to the expanding colonial economies South Africa. .

In addition to the impact of commercial capitalist penetration, increased commodity production and technological change, the gender division of labour was sometimes transformed as a result of political processes. It has been shown in the case of Swaziland that the massive appropriation of male homestead labour following the establishment of the regimental system under Mswati's reign led to the intensification of 'the range and tasks demanded of women... As well as being largely responsible for homestead agricultural production, women and girls became involved in the supposedly sacrosanct tasks of handling cattle' (Crush, 1987:18).

Among the Nandi of Kenya a similar process unfolded in the second half of the nineteenth century. The military system was reorganized and expanded to defend against the Maasai, who periodically raided Nandi territory, as well as to expand Nandi territory itself for more pasture land for the rapidly growing livestock herds. The expansion of the military and the pastoral economy led to the progressive removal of male labour from the homesteads, and the intensification of female labour time in household production. Prior to this, 'all family members worked together in all phases of cultivation, except that men cleared virgin fields from the forest' (Gold, 1985:178). Now women did most of the cultivation, but the surplus was appropriated by men, usually used to obtain livestock, which they owned as private property, unlike the land over which they only had usufruct rights. Thus women's subordination increased, a process that was reproduced through physical coercion, and more importantly, ideological controls. The growing subordination of women was connected to, but was distinctive from, the increasing inequality in Nandi society. The women themselves became more differentiated. Wives of wealthy men lived different lives from those of the wives of poor men. Despite that, women as a group suffered 'the particular subordination of their sex, which was permanent exclusion from control of the means of production. While poor men may also have lacked such controls, it was not necessarily a permanent condition, nor did it derive from their gender' (Gold, 1985:199).

Women in pastoral societies have been ignored in the literature perhaps more than any other group, partly because researchers have tended to perceive these societies as representing prototypal patrilineal systems, in which male control of the means of production, livestock, is assumed to have been total (Dupire, 1963). The reality was of course far more complex. Women were in fact fundamental to pastoral production and society (Nelson, 1973, 1974; Talle, 1988).

In most East African pastoral societies women participated not only in pastoral production itself, but were almost exclusively responsible for crop cultivation and the household economy (Murmann, 1974). Among the Maasai, for example, the male-defined tasks included grazing, watering and protecting the herd. Women did a lot more than that. They performed virtually all household chores, cared for the children, tended, milked and slaughtered the animals, and took part in herding animals grazing in the vicinity of the homestead (Talle, 1988:180). In addition, women controlled the processing, distribution and consumption of milk, the main product of the herd. Moreover, they cultivated crops around the homestead. Furthermore, they built and maintained houses which were regarded as their private property (Rigby, 1985:147-153). This allowed women to play an important role as heads of houses, which, in turn, gave them both the responsibility to feed their respective households, and management rights over animals held in trust for their sons (Waller, 1985:104). In other words, livestock property, which was owned by men, was channelled through the institution of the house, controlled by women.

Thus there was a 'patrilineal paradox' in Maasai society, in that women were 'denied formal existence or recognition but at the same time [were] of decisive importance to the survival and reproduction of the group' (Talle, 1988:201). Women's importance in mediating production and reproduction relations in Maasai society extended to trade, in which they equally participated with men, 'in striking contrast to the present trade in live animals which is exclusively controlled by men' (Talle, 1988:64). It has been argued that the subordination of Maasai women intensified with the commercialization of the Maasai pastoral economy 'which was initiated by external forces', principally colonization (Talle, 1988:67). But surely internal factors must also have played a role in this process. This only serves to underscore the need for more historical research on the subject of changes in gender roles, practices and ideology. Attributing them solely to colonialism or the penetration of merchant capital is tempting, but rather simplistic.

Also simplistic are studies of women in the Islamic societies of North Africa based on idealist biases, according to which the status and role of women in these societies is primarily attributed to the ideas and values contained in Islamic religious and juridical texts. A sharp contrast is usually drawn between the 'oppressive' Islamic and 'liberal' Western attitudes towards women. Any indication of women's emancipation in the 'Muslim' world is then attributed to 'westernization' or 'modernization'. All too often, the discourse is reduced to a defence or criticism of whether Islam's impact on woman has been positive or negative (Daumas, 1943; Beck and Keddie, 1978; Keddie, 1979:231-5; Rassam, 1984a, 1984b: Kader, 1987:1-14).

Such a formulation ignores the fact that the formal texts do not tell us much about the changing realities of women's lives in the extremely diverse societies and countries that make up the so-called 'Muslim world.' There has never been an unchanging, homogeneous 'Muslim woman.' In the nineteenth century, as well as in contemporary times, women in different classes and productive units have lived, and continue to live, quite different lives. It also follows that the impact of 'westernization' or 'modernization' cannot be generalized, for it varied according to society, culture and class.

Perhaps the most extensive literature on Muslim women in Africa is on Egypt. In her studies of Egyptian women in the nineteenth century, Tucker (1983, 1985) has suggested a useful framework for analyzing changes in women's roles and status within the household and the large society: first, women's access to resources; second, their position in the family; third, their participation in social production; and fourth, the prevailing ideological definitions of women's roles. In examining women's access to property, a distinction needs to be made between formal rights as embodied in Islamic law and accepted customs, and women's ability to actually use those rights. Women's access to property was mediated through the family, in which the demands of production and reproduction were combined in complex ways. There were different family structures, from the large extended family to the small nuclear family, all governed by patriarchal and patrilocal rules. Role differentiation between husbands and wives and women's autonomy and access to property varied depending on the family structure, its composition and its productive resources.

The nineteenth century witnessed profound changes in the organization of Egyptian agriculture, which altered agrarian gender relations. The changes in the system of land tenure noted earlier had a marked impact on women's access to land. The destruction of the iltizam system affected the women who were multazims or wives of multazims. In 1814 some of these women demonstrated in the streets of Cairo against their dispossession. The majority of peasant women both before and after Muhammad Ali's reforms did not possess land. In fact, the intensification of land concentration not only pauperized the peasantry as a class, but also reduced the access of peasant women to the land. There were of course some women who acquired land either through purchase, inheritance, usually in the absence of male children, or grants from male relatives, especially a father (Tucker, 1985:43-52). Women enjoyed far more rights with regard to movable property, including agricultural tools and livestock.

Peasant Egyptian women have been portrayed in stark terms: as leading active and unfettered egalitarian lives, or overburdened by unmitigated drudgery (Marsot, 1978:261; Lane, 1978:194-6). The reality was far more complex. At the beginning of the nineteenth century, Kader (1987:34) has argued, 'there is little evidence that points to any difference in the amount of male or female labour, although particular tasks may well have been distributed along gender lines. In an agrarian system of intensive cultivation of irrigated land, long hours were required of all workers of the land.' The growth of military conscription and corvee labour under Muhammad Ali's reign led to the removal of large numbers of men from the rural economy and the consequent intensification of female labour time in agricultural production. Later the policy of recruiting entire families was adopted. This reinstated the family as a productive unit both on its plot and on corvee projects. 'By the 1880s, however, as the overall demands of corvee lessened, women and families were less often found in corvee labour' (Tucker, 1985:41).

Towards the end of the nineteenth century the shortage of male labour from the rural areas also became less acute than in the days of Muhammad Ali. This had a number of consequences. As more men were increasingly hired on the large estates, the hiring of women became restricted to the harvest season only. Thus sexual differentiation increased as men 'entered the agricultural market economy, while women continued with their traditional chores of animal husbandry and food and fuel processing' (Kader, 1987:35). Not all households, of course, exported their male labour power. Among those that did not, men tended to work full time on the fields and women and children assisted at the times of peak demand, especially at seeding and harvesting. Women were responsible for the domestic chores, such as fetching water, preparing food, cleaning the house, and so on. They also reared poultry. The children looked after the animals, watched the saqiya and collected dung for fertilizer (Ayrout, 1963:58-59). A similar division of labour prevailed in Morocco (Maher, 1974:113-7).

Thus the position of peasant women in Egypt was complex, contradictory and changing. They generally did not possess land, but were central to agricultural production. This weakened as well as strengthened their position within the family. Contrary to popular stereotypes, peasant women often chose their husbands, polygamy was rare, and divorce was common, 'although women were legally disadvantaged in the sphere of child custody and guardianship' (Tucker, 1985:59). Peasant women, moreover, were generally not secluded or veiled, unlike upper class women. The latter, the harem women, 'constituted perhaps no more than 2% of Egypt's five million female population' (Kader, 1987:17). On the whole, the status and security of peasant and other lower class women declined as a result of the various social changes that took place in the course of the century, including the progressive decline of the extended family as a semi-autonomous unit and the consequent consolidation of family property around men.

It has been argued that the development of 'state capitalism' by Muhammad Ali's regime and its successors had a deleterious effect on middle class women. The marginalization of the merchant classes due to the imposition of state trading monopolies 'had an effect of actually increasing the seclusion of middle class women and restricting them to household management rather

than more active careers in tax-farming and business' (Cole, 1981:390). In
the meantime, the wives of the 'new' urban-based petite-bourgeois professionals were increasingly cut off from their husbands' professional lives and
relegated to the domestic sphere, unlike the women in the old artisan classes,
in which the family itself was the unit and sphere of production.

All these changes provoked debate about the position of women in society.
The feminist discourse was conducted among the intellectuals. Men from
the lower middle class, whose positions were quite insecure, tended to
oppose women's emancipation, while those from the upper middle class
were more supportive. The former had more to lose than the latter from
women's emancipation constructed around more access to education and
participation in the public sphere. The debate became intense in the closing
decades of the nineteenth century in the face of British colonization and the
introduction of a new gender ideology (Cole, 1981:392-405; Canon, 1985:
Kader, 1987:chapter 2). Thus the ideological definitions of women's roles
in society became more contested as the country's political economy, class
structure and labour process changed. The feminist movement was not
confined to Egypt. It eventually spread to other Muslim societies (Saadawi,
1980:chapter 18; Badri, 1986).

Conclusion

The above discussion should have gone some way to demythologize the
nature, and capture some of the dynamics, of agrarian relations of production
in precolonial Africa. African peasants were neither inertly conservative, nor
did they live in egalitarian communities blissfully free from both exploitation and differentiation. The relations between peasants and the state have
been complex and changing. In societies with highly centralized despotic
states, peasant surpluses were appropriated through onerous taxation, corvee
labour, and sometimes confiscation of produce. However, the peasants did
not meekly accept their exploitation and oppression. They resisted in a
variety of ways, both covertly and overtly, passively and militantly, subtly
and dramatically. Peasant resistance and state responses, and vice-versa,
constituted the warp from which the dialectical processes and structures of
agrarian relations in these societies were woven.

The complex and vibrant nature of peasant labour processes has not been
fully appreciated. Peasants, both arable farmers and pastoralists, relied on a
bewildering range of labour forms, from household and inter-household
labour pools, to sharecropping, slave, indentured, and hired wage labour. It
has been demonstrated that sharecropping was far more widespread than it
is commonly assumed. It was not only in West Africa that sharecropping
arrangements played such a vital role in mobilizing labour and other resources for the cash crop revolution. Slave labour also played an important role

in agricultural production in some societies, although many scholars have clearly exaggerated its pervasiveness. There can be no doubt that while slave labour played an important role in African plantation economies, household labour was the backbone of agricultural production in peasant agriculture. And peasant production, rather than plantation production, was the mainstay of African economies. There has been a rather careless tendency among some historians to conflate every form of servile and dependent relationship and all types of bonded labour with slavery. Clientage and indentured labour have often been confused with slavery, for example. Excessive preoccupation with slavery has probably also diverted historians' attention from researching the development of agricultural wage labour.

The question of the gender division of labour has also not received the attention it deserves. An attempt has been made in this chapter to outline, rather broadly, the gender division of labour in the agricultural economies of a number of societies, cutting across a variety of family forms from 'matrilineal' to 'patrilineal', and encompassing different ideological systems, including Islam. If the cases analyzed in this chapter serve any purpose, it is to point out how much work still remains to be done, and also, how vacuous is the polemical debate on whether colonialism improved or worsened the position of African women, as if all women led similar lives in the precolonial and colonial eras. While it may be rash at this stage to hazard any meaningful generalization on the gender division of labour in nineteenth century African agriculture, it seems quite likely that future research may confirm the trend of a progressive intensification of women's labour time in agriculture. The factors accounting for this, of course, varied. What we need to know more about are the patterns of agricultural surplus appropriation between men and women, how they changed, and why. Needless to say, African women enjoyed different capacities to appropriate for themselves the fruits of their labour.

5. Colonial Agriculture

Failed Experiments

The peasant and plantation systems examined in the previous chapter developed in societies that were largely controlled by the Africans themselves. But there were a few societies which, by the mid-nineteenth century, had already fallen under the yoke of European imperialism. These societies, examined in this chapter, included the Portuguese colonial enclaves in Angola and Mozambique, the Boer and British colonies in South Africa, and the French colony of Algeria. Colonial agriculture in the colonies involved continuous struggles between the Africans and European settlers over the productive resources of land and labour as well as political power. While the growth of peasant agriculture and plantations in these settler colonial formations was in some ways markedly different, the precondition for the establishment of colonial agriculture was the forcible dispossession of the African population from the land.

Portugal was the first European nation to try to colonize parts of Africa. The Portuguese became far more interested in slave trading than in agriculture. But their slave trading activities had an impact on the agricultural production of the societies they affected. Moreover, some of the Portuguese settlers in Angola and Mozambique became engaged in agriculture. In fact, in the nineteenth century efforts were made by the colonial governments to promote cash crop production in the colonies. Cotton was earmarked for special attention. In Angola, from as early as 1820, the colonial state 'tried to promote cotton cultivation by promising to buy cotton produced in the colony. Twenty-five years later, it offered to exempt Africans from serving military duty if they produced 150 kilos of cotton... the government [also] dispensed free seeds, established bonuses for the largest production, exempted duties, and even hired a cotton specialist from Brazil's major cotton growing region, Pernambuco, to supervise cultivation' (Pitcher, 1991:44-45).

Despite all these efforts, cotton production in Angola, as well as Mozambique, ultimately failed. There were four main reasons for this. First, the fall in cotton prices discouraged producers and weakened imperial interest in the cotton experiment. Second, inappropriate methods of production were used and no attempts were made to involve the more efficient African peasants. Third, there were shortages of labour due to the ravages of the slave trade and African unwillingness to work for the planters. Most Africans still enjoyed independent access to land and markets, so there was little incentive for them to work for the Portuguese planters. In southern Mozambique from the 1850s many prospective workers preferred to migrate to South Africa where wages and conditions were better. Therefore, the planters in Mozambique and Angola came to rely on slaves, but the working conditions were so harsh that the slaves often fled. Slave resistance also took the form of 'social banditry' and revolts, as happened in Mocamedes province in southern Mozambique in 1879-80. Finally, the cotton growing areas were afflicted with pests and diseases in the 1860s and 1870s, which not only decimated population in these areas but also caused Africans to migrate to avoid the diseases (Clarence-Smith, 1979; Pitcher, 1991:48-60).

As noted earlier, coffee production in Angola fared slightly better. Planters from Portugal and Brazil established coffee plantations in the colonial enclave of Cazengo using profits from retail trading. Attempts to use hired labour did not go very far because the indigenous people of Cazengo were too busy producing their own coffee to work for the settlers. Slavery was therefore seen as the answer. The slaves were mostly captured from nearby districts so escape was a major problem. This, together with the fact that management was poor, meant that the settler coffee economy remained fragile. The ambition of many of the settler coffee planters was not to build up their local investment but to make quick profit and transfer their money to Brazil. That is why 'the trading of African coffee remained important even to settlers who owned their own estates' (Birmingham, 1978:527).

Indeed, it could be argued that coffee survived and the production of other cash crops expanded less because the settlers were successful, but because they traded African grown coffee. To quote Birmingham (1978:538) again: 'Black smallholders responded with greater alacrity to opening crop markets than did plantations, and much conflict arose over the sequestration of peasant plots by credit-holding shop-keepers'. Heywood (1987:356) has made the same observation with reference to Ovimbundu who, she notes, 'initially responded enthusiastically to the increased opportunities for export-oriented agricultural production in the early years of the colonial regime, and their products, especially maize, dominated the region's exports'. These comments have been echoed by others (Clarence-Smith and Moorsom, 1975). The majority of Portuguese farmers and fishermen were desperately poor, illiterate, and deeply indebted. In the pithy comment of Bender (1978:98-99), 'they presented a sorry spectacle in the interior of Angola, many living in total misery. A number were forced to beg for food from neighbouring Africans'.

The situation in Mozambique was not much different. By the beginning of the nineteenth century, the colonial farming system based on crown estates, or prazos de cora, which were first established in the Zambezi valley in the mid-seventeenth century, was floundering. The prazos were established on land acquired either through conquest or the manipulation of local African politics. They contained four distinct social classes: the planter class, known as the prazeros, their slaves, known as achikunda, the free indigenous population, the so-called colonos, and their dependents or slaves, called akapolo. The prazos failed to develop into viable plantation economies because their very existence was often contested by the independent African polities from which they had been carved. Moreover, the prazeros themselves lacked capital, sufficient labour, and adequate agricultural experience and techniques. Not surprisingly, the life span of individual prazos was quite short, usually under ten years (Isaacman, 1972).

By the beginning of the nineteenth century the entire prazo system was already in decline, wrecked by the growth of the slave trade, which exacerbated the labour problems, and the emergence of a class of absentee prazeros. Even the achikunda escaped from being exported. Some found refuge and were assimilated into the interior where their military skills were valued. Others founded 'transfrontier' communities which initially lived by hunting and trading ivory, and later by slave trading (Isaacman and Isaacman, 1975; Isaacman, 1986). The disbanding of the achikunda armies made the prazos very vulnerable. In the 1830s the prazos were devastated by drought and raids from neighbouring African states, which culminated in the Nguni invasions of the 1840s. By the mid-nineteenth century production had been abandoned on many prazos.

In 1854, and again in 1863, attempts were made to reform the prazo system. The 1854 decree abolished the old prazos, and set conditions for the establishment of new ones. Their owners were now required to cultivate the land within five years, pay a 10% tax on profits to the state, the old tributary obligations of the colonos to the prazeros were abolished, and so was slavery. The decree remained a dead letter. The decree of 1863 called for the enforcement of the 1854 decree by increasing military presence in the region. There was hardly any improvement. The problem was that Portugal had neither the financial nor manpower resources to enforce its policies (Vail and White, 1980; Newitt, 1981; Newitt, 1988; Seleti, 1990).

In the meantime, in the Zambezi valley, where most of the prazos were located, an agricultural 'revolution' based on peasant production was taking place. Peasant production of vegetable oils and grains skyrocketed. This led to increased differentiation among the peasant communities and changes in labour organization. Associations of young and married men, called nomi and ndomba respectively, formed to provide agricultural labour, proliferated, and local slavery expanded. Attempts by the state to cash in on the peasants' apparent growing prosperity through the imposition of a head tax and a company to buy peasant produce provoked the Makuta rising of 1878 and the Massingiri rising of 1884. In 1886 the government conceded that the peasants had the right to raise and sell crops without interference. But this was a temporary victory, for in the 1880s the forces of colonization and the partition of Africa were gathering momentum. Indian merchants came to dominate the trade in peasant produce. Not only did this deprive the state of much-needed revenues, it also gave the dangerous impression that Portugal was not in effective occupation of Mozambique.

In the 1890s, a determined but impoverished Portuguese government granted concessions to foreign-owned companies in order to secure 'effective occupation' and to encourage investment. These companies were allowed to tax the inhabitants in their areas, control trade in peasant produce, and to establish plantations, for which the state would ensure adequate labour supply. The prazos in the Zambezi valley were taken over by the Zambezia Company. The other major concession companies included the Mozambique Company and the Niassa Company. These companies established huge plantations of sugar, coconuts, sisal, tobacco, cotton, coffee, and sheep rearing based on a ruthless regime of forced labour that survived in one form or another until decolonization in the early 1970s.

Constructing Racial Capitalism

In South Africa, colonial agriculture began at the Cape. The Khoisan pastoralists were the first to be confronted by the settlers, followed later by the Xhosa and other agricultural peoples deeper in the interior. This process of primitive accumulation was violent, accompanied by wars of conquest and resistance. Conquest did not always entail the end of the conflict over land, but often led to its intensification. Attempts to evict the original African inhabitants from the land were either resisted, or could not be effected totally because the settlers needed African labour and rent tenants.

Cape settler farmers were initially dependent on slave labour acquired from Asia, Madagascar and Mozambique, and the labour of the dispossessed Khoisan. In 1798 there were 25,754 slaves as compared to a free burgher population of 21,746, excluding the Khoikhoi. By 1834 there were 36,169 slaves. Contrary to the commonly held assumption, Cape slavery was not 'mild'; it was as harsh and brutal as slavery in the Americas (Worden, 1985; Armstrong and Worden, 1989). The legal disabilities on the slaves and the Khoisan were removed between 1828 and 1838, although their position did not change significantly. Most of the ex-slaves and Khoisan were simply turned into a lowly paid and oppressed agricultural proletariat (Ross, 1986). Poor and landless whites, whose numbers increased from the 1860s as rural land holding among the settlers became concentrated, became an important part of the agricultural labour force, both as wage workers and labour tenants (Bundy, 1986).

As the colonial frontiers expanded deeper into the eastern Cape, Natal, the Orange Free State and the Transvaal, African tenants, sharecroppers and, to a smaller extent, migrant labourers became the most important sources of labour for the settler farmers. Tenancy and sharecropping arrangements were congenial to both the landlord and tenant households. The former got protection against desertion and the latter against eviction. Moreover, the system allowed the tenants to control their own labour, pace of work, patterns of production and accumulation, while it enabled the landlords to increase production on their lands without having to raise capital for investment, especially since the agricultural technology of the peasants and the landlords was similar. In fact, tenants' oxen were widely used to supplement landlords oxen for ploughing (Keegan, 1982, 1986, 1987; Matsetela, 1982; Beinart, 1986; Trapido, 1986).

This does not mean there were no conflicts between tenants and landlords. The terms of tenancy and sharecropping were contested. African resistance against exploitation was widespread, taking various, often localized, forms. 'Specific action could include refusal to pay rent, delays in supplying labour, refusal to perform certain types of work or holding back skills, reduction in the pace of work, direct damage to fences or hamstringing of cattle' (Beinart and Delius, 1986:45). Also, dissatisfied tenants and sharecroppers responded by moving away to other farms or to the reserve locations. Occasionally they revolted. Sometimes they would pool their resources and purchase their own land. Such collective endeavours, struggles and defences were articulated through the idiom, and facilitated the construction, of ethnicity (Beinart and Delius, 1986:42-49; Keegan, 1986b:234, 245-9; Beinart, 1986:278-85).

For the greater part of the nineteenth century these struggles succeeded in containing settler control over the labour process. In fact, 'surplus appropriation before the late nineteenth century was sporadic and arbitrary. Most of the black population, whether they lived on land which was owned by whites or not, were yet very marginally integrated into new productive relationships under the authority of the colonizers' (Keegan, 1989:675). African peasant agriculture was actually expanding (Bundy, 1979; Beinart, 1980a, 1982). In fact, as late as the early twentieth century the bulk of grain produced on the arable Highveld came from African farmers (Keegan, 1987:51). This raised the spectre of long-term settler economic decline and the prospects of their increasing dependence upon African farmers. The settler farmers were determined to forestall such a future.

The labour process among African peasants was quite complex, for there were different systems of social production, each with its own mechanisms for the appropriation of surplus-labour (Murray, 1989:653). First, there were the labour tenants, who used their household labour to work on their own plot as well as that of the landlord. Far more important in settler areas were the sharecroppers. Sharecropping expanded in the last two decades of the century as settler landowners and lessees, many of them absentee, and displaced and dispossessed Africans sought to take advantage of the rapidly growing economy. It was not always possible for sharecropping households to pool the labour of the entire household, for these households were usually partly dependent on wage employment for their accumulation. Many households entering sharecropping often exploited kinship networks to acquire stock and labour to establish the farm. In addition to this, wealthier sharecroppers were sometimes assisted by labour tenants on the farm, especially during the hoeing, harvesting and threshing seasons (Keegan, 1987:Chapter 3).

Then there was the group of peasants with freehold tenure, which expanded in size in the last few decades of the century. These peasants controlled both their labour and production. The big African landowners often supplemented their household labour with hired labour, tenants and sharecroppers. Finally, there were peasants who enjoyed customary usufructuary tenure. They relied on their household labour and could pool labour from other households on a reciprocal basis. Lewis (1984:4-8) in fact argues that among the Xhosa the productive unit was not the household but the homestead, which was composed of several households, and was usually headed by the head of the household with most cattle. Young men from households without cattle attached themselves to, and worked for, households with a lot of cattle with the aim of acquiring cattle for paying bridewealth, among other things.

The rich African farmers probably reached the zenith of their success between 1870 and 1890 due to the mineral revolution, which, simultaneously, opened windows of opportunity for peasants by dramatically increasing markets for their produce and laid the conditions for their eventual marginalization . It has been argued by Legassick (1977) and Bundy (1979) that an alliance emerged between mining companies and settler farmers, 'gold' and 'maize', to deprive the Africans of land to force them to enter wage employment and, in the case of the settler farmers, to remove them as competitors from the internal markets, especially now that the world market was in a state of recession. The 'gold and maize' alliance became the dominant 'power bloc' in the state apparatus, eclipsing 'the liberal friends of the native', that is, the merchants and other liberal ideologues, whose liberalism had been latched onto the ox-cart of peasant accumulation (Trapido, 1980). The congruity of interests between the settler farmers and the mining industry should not be exaggerated, for there were some conflicts between them, especially over labour (Lacey, 1981; Morris, 1981; Murray, 1987).

The rapid economic growth of the last quarter of the nineteenth century was accompanied by increased differentiation between and among the settler and African farmers. The class of landless Boers, called bywoners, increased due to growing land concentration, excessive land fragmentation, and indebtedness, which was triggered by the boom and bust cycles of the agricultural market. Over half the settler rural families of the Highveld were bywoners (Keegan, 1987:21). The bywoners found it difficult to compete with African producers, including sharecroppers. This fuelled popular Boer antagonism against African sharecroppers, especially those living, unsupervised, on absentee-owned land. Thus, settler society, like African society, became more differentiated.

But these divisions were increasingly blurred as the grievances of the rural settler classes coalesced into an exaggerated sense of collective Afrikaner victimization. The discovery and growth of 'poor whiteism' facilitated the drive towards racial capitalism and the marginalization of the African peasantry (Bundy, 1986:119-23). And for its part, the fact that the cleavage between settler farmers and merchants 'largely corresponded with the ethnic cleavage in the white group it was easy to define farmers' interests as Afrikaner interests' (Giliomee, 1987:58). Thus there was a growing tendency to define Afrikanerhood ideologically, as a movement in opposition both to English merchants and African competitors. Afrikaner ideologues began agitating for state intervention. They demanded the provision of protected markets, easier access to credit, the elimination of African competition and the regular supply of reliable, cheap African labour.

The activities of mining capital helped fuel land speculation, which intensified the pressures for African land dispossession. 'This speculative urge accounted for the fact that by 1900 almost one fifth of the total land area of the SAR [South African Republic] was claimed by land companies or absentee landlords' (Trapido, 1986:337). This had a retrogressive impact on the development of both capitalist and peasant agriculture, for absentee landowners were hardly interested in agricultural production and investment, while the independent peasants increasingly lost their land, and the extraction of labour and tribute from the tenants and sharecroppers greatly intensified.

The tide began turning decisively against African peasants in the 1890s. To begin with, there were the ecological disasters of drought and rinderpest epidemics, and the depredations of the South Africa War of 1899-1902 in which tens of thousands of Africans faced forced removal, had their foodstuffs and stock requisitioned, and saw their homes and fields destroyed.

The terms of trade also turned against the peasants as traders tightened the system of credit and raised interest rates on advances made to them. Moreover, the traders increasingly preferred to pay for the peasants produce in kind, not cash. African tenants on crown land and on commercial settler farms increasingly faced eviction or rises in rents and limitations on the amount of land available and livestock allowed. The distinction between peasants and sharecroppers became increasingly blurred. The settler farmers, Keegan (1987:121-4) believes, wanted a dependent, servile and malleable tenant labour force, rather than a fully proletarianized workforce.

The state played a central role in this process of trying to create a servile tenantry, and later in subsidizing and consolidating settler capitalist farming, by providing cheap credit through the Land Bank, building the transport infrastructure, co-ordinating marketing facilities, and maintaining extension services, to mention the most important forms of assistance. A series of pass and anti-squatting laws were developed from the 1880s. The former sought to control tenants' mobility and standardize low wages and the latter to curb the incidence of sharecropping on absentee-owned land. Other laws, such as the Glen Grey of 1884 which stipulated the universalization of private land holding in African areas and imposed limits on the amount of land that an African farmer could have, were meant to check African accumulation.

The screws were tightened on the African peasantry at the turn of the century. A series of laws were passed between 1903 and 1905 prohibiting the sale of crown lands to Africans, and imposing a number of new levies and fees upon Africans, all of which raised the cost of living for peasants and made it more difficult for them to purchase or hire land or make any improvements on it in order to increase productivity. The final legislative nail in the coffin of peasant marginalization was the Native Lands Act of 1913 which abolished a free market in land between the settlers and the Africans, and divided the country into 'White' South Africa, with 92.5%, later reduced to 87%, of the land, and the African 'reserves' on the rest of the land (Bundy, 1979:chapter 4).

This battery of legislation did not lead to the immediate decline of the African peasantry. 'The struggle to dispossess blacks on alienated land and subjugate them in the interests of capital accumulation was to last a lot longer' (Keegan, 1989:677). Indeed, this period witnessed the intensification of African struggles against dispossession and proletarianization. The rural populations waged day-to-day struggles, as well as the larger, more organized forms of resistance. These struggles ranged from making appeals through delegations, petitions and litigation, to refusal to pay taxes, opposition to rural councils, anti-dipping protests which sometimes led to dipping tanks being blown up, destroyed or picketed, the boycott of stores, and the occasional revolts and disturbances.

The organization and articulation of these struggles varied, for the rural population was divided into different groups, such as the traditional ruling elite, the self-consciously 'progressive' Christianized elite, the rich peasants, and the mass of poor peasants and migrant workers. The protesters channelled their resistance through either chieftaincy movements formed to reclaim or protect land and other 'traditional' resources, independent churches which served as vehicles for asserting cultural autonomy, or associations of migrant workers and trade unions, and expressed their struggle in the idioms of defensive traditionalism, African nationalism, or Christianity. These struggles did not succeed in defeating the thrust of state and capitalist intervention, but they set the terrain for future struggles (Marks, 1986; Beinart and Bundy, 1987; Bradford, 1987).

The development of settler capitalist farming was accompanied by the growth of corporate plantation agriculture. In the second half of the nineteenth century a large sugar plantation industry was established in Natal, following the failure of commercial cotton growing. The Natal sugar plantations grew rapidly between 1855 and 1866, expanding from 862 to 12,746 acres. This growth was the result 'of a combination of favourable prices, reasonably low wages and a protective tariff structure. To these advantages were added subsequently a partially controlled labour market and the short-lived benefits of financial speculation' (Richardson, 1986:133). The creation of a tariff policy favourable to the planters underlines the critical importance played by the state in the development of the plantation system from the very beginning. The planters were allowed, through the 'free import schedules', to import seeds, plants, manures, farming implements and sugar processing machinery, and even livestock free of duty. Moreover, the state intervened in the labour market to ensure that the planters had sufficient labour supply, through the creation of African reserves and the importation of migrant labour, including indentured labour from India.

The total acreage under cane production by plantations in Natal rose from 12,746 in 1866 to 33,033 acres in 1898. The growth was far from steady. The industry experienced cyclical fluctuations in its development in tandem with the country's economy itself. In 14 out of the 24 years between 1867 and 1890-1 the cane acreage was below the 22,182 acres recorded for 1871, and the production peak of 1868 was not surpassed until 1874. In subsequent decades the cyclical pattern continued, although the general level of production rose (Richardson, 1986:149). Until the early 1870s the average size of the estates remained well below 300 acres. Most of the lands were held on freehold tenure, with a few on leasehold tenure. The main market of Natal sugar was the Cape, then the Transvaal, following the development of the mining industry. The domestic market accounted for 15 per cent of total sugar production. Exports onto the world market 'never amounted to more than 6.2 per cent of Natal exports by value' between 1888 and 1908, so that it can be argued, the Natal plantation economy was not 'integrated into a world market in the manner of the West Indies, Fiji or Mauritius' (Graves and Richardson, 1980:222).

The Natal plantations combined two production processes within the same unit. One was agricultural, based on the cultivation and harvesting of the cane, and the other was industrial, involving the processing of the cane in a mill. This partly explains the plantations' heavy demand for labour. Attempts to recruit labour from the Zulus, the most numerous and powerful African group in the region, were frustrated by the fact that the Zulus remained unconquered until 1879, and the colonial state did not have the ability to coerce them through the colonial mechanisms of generating labour: land alienation and taxation. However, some Zulu workers volunteered their labour to the sugar plantations. But the conflicts between them and the plantation owners probably acted as a disincentive for many others.

In a fascinating paper, Atkins (1988) has argued that the planters' failure to attract Zulu labour was rooted in conflicting temporal orientation of the two groups. Disagreements over the computation of time led to labour conflict, and attempts by the planters to enforce their industrial time through summary punishments had the effect of further driving the Zulu from the labour market. The Zulu calendar consisted of the lunar month of 28 days, called inyanga, and the working day fell strictly between sunset and sunrise. So when hired on 'monthly' payment the Zulu expected to be paid every 28 days, not 30 or 31 as the case may be on the Europeans' calendar. Moreover, while in summer there were fourteen hours of day light, in winter, which was the height of the manufacturing process, there were only 10.5 hours of sunlight. Attempts to get the Zulu to work the same number of hours in winter as in summer were resisted. In short, the planters' efforts to impose their temporal system on the Zulu were 'viewed as an attempt to cheat them of their time', and so in order to mollify them, 'the employers had either to submit to indigenous usages or risk the former's precipitate withdrawal from the market' (Atkins, 1988:232). Furthermore, observance of traditional holidays and work schedules on their own farms regularly interrupted the flow of Zulu labour.

Thus, the struggles over the definition of time played a role in the planters' search for alternative sources of regular, reliable and cheap labour. Slavery was of course now out of the question. And so, with state assistance, they turned to migrant labour. Contrary to popular belief, this labour was not entirely composed of indentured Indian workers. The importation of the Indian workers started in 1860, then it was stopped in 1866 due to the collapse of sugar prices, which made it very expensive for the planters and the state to continue the importation programme. Imports of indentured Indian labour was not resumed until 1874. 'Yet over the period 1866-1874, sugar production rose by 51 per cent. In these years, African immigrant workers from outside Natal played an important, if not a preponderant, role in establishing sugar cultivation in the colony' (Harries, 1987:379).

The African migrant labourers were initially drawn from various chiefdoms in the northern and eastern Transvaal. But these sources dried up following the development of the mining industry in the 1870s and 1880s. This led to the importation of workers from Mozambique, called amatonga, and contributed to the resumption of indentured Indian immigration. The foreign importation schemes became less critical following the defeat of the Zulus in the Anglo-Zulu war of 1879. The abolition of the Zulu military system and introduction of colonial taxation and land alienation forced increasing numbers of Zulus into the labour market.

Thus by the 1890s, the Natal plantations had a workforce that was highly differentiated according to race, place of origin and skill. Management was largely the preserve of Europeans. The planters valued the indentured labourers because these workers provided 'reliable' service, and 'reduced the planters' exposure to the fluctuations in the cost and supply of labour, fluctuations that were brought about by the unstable international price of sugar and by competition from new southern African labour markets' (Harries, 1987:394). The amatonga, for example, increasingly flocked to the better-paid jobs of the Transvaal mining centres. Altogether, about 152,814 indentured Indian labourers were brought to Natal between 1860 and 1874, and between 1874 and 1911, the majority to work on the sugar estates on five-year contracts (Richardson, 1982:519). The Indian labourers lived under stiff conditions. They were refused ownership of property and many were forcibly repatriated at the end of their contracts. But some remained and formed the core of South Africa's Indian population (Pachai, 1971).

In the last two decades of the nineteenth century the Natal sugar industry also became increasingly concentrated in 'response to a variety of pressures, such as price instability, fluctuations in the cost and volume of available capital, the price of labour-power, changes in technology, problems of crop disease and marketing changes' (Graves and Richardson, 1980:226). For example, in 1878 yields fell for the first time to below one ton per acre, a performance that was repeated in 1885 and 1890-1, and most disastrously in 1896 when yields were decimated by a combination of soil exhaustion and locus infestation. All these pressures not only facilitated the concentration of capital, but also technological modernization and the intensified exploitation of the labour force 'through increasing the length of the working day' (Richardson, 1982:424-5). The small planters declined in importance. The larger mills and estates increasingly fell under corporate ownership, a process that was buttressed by the inflow of foreign, mainly British, capital, and the rise of a monopolistic ownership structure characterized by inter-locking directorships in the plantation and milling companies. The structure of twentieth century agribusiness in Africa had been laid.

The construction of capitalist agriculture in South Africa was a protracted process. By the end of the nineteenth century it was still far from over. But the basis had been laid. The role of the colonial state in this process cannot be overemphasized. Ultimately, as Denoon (1983:122) has put it, 'the colonists' victory in sugar, maize, wine, wool, beef, and fruit production, were all political victories. Suppression of African rivals, the dispossession of African tenant farmers, the mobilization of a labour force, extension services, credit facilities, and even the guarantee of markets, were ac-complished by the several states in response to the needs of white farmers'. In concrete terms, peasant underdevelopment entailed the ecological decay of the reserves, chronic poverty, and persistent hunger and malnutrition. In the new racial capitalist order that was emerging African entitlement to resources diminished, so that the old productive and social strategies of adapting to food shortages became progressively ineffective without effec-tive new ones taking their place. Thus South Africa presaged the broad outlines of hunger's new and hideous capitalist face that came to stalk Africa in the twentieth century (Webster, 1986; Wylie, 1989).

Reproducing the Metropole

France began its conquest of Algeria in 1830. It was a protracted process, which underwent four phases. The first phase lasted between 1830 and 1839 and was marked by the occupation of the urban centres and their surrounding agricultural regions. The second phase from 1839 to 1847 involved the conquest of the fertile agricultural plains of the Tell in northern Algeria. The third stages extended from 1848 to 1871, and the fourth from 1872 to 1900, during which the Kabylie mountains and deserts were conquered. The French colonization of Algeria was so protracted because of stiff Algerian resistance. The rural populations resisted the occupation of their lands until 1884, although 'the backbone of the rural resistance to colonialism was smashed in 1871' (Bennoune, 1988:40).

Each of the four phases, 'with the exception of the last, which concerned an area of little significance to sedentary European agriculture, was accom-panied by a series of sequestration decrees and actions', which resulted in the dispossession of Algerians of their lands (Ruedy, 1967:38). Land was expropriated either by the state itself through force, or by private interests through purchase. During the nineteenth century the first method was of greater significance than the second. The first to be seized were the public lands of the realm, known as beylik, of which 400,000-500,000 hectares were appropriated between 1830 and 1851. Then followed the seizure of other lands, such as the freehold lands of the Tell, known as milk, the religious lands or habous, the makhzan lands granted by the rulers, the deys and beys, to specific tribes in return for military, police and tax-collecting services, the tribal lands, called the arsh, and the mawat lands of the forests, ravines and mountainsides, through the arbitrary measures of sequestration, confiscation, cantonment, the manipulation of Muslim law, and the promulgation of colonial laws and decrees (Ruedy, 1967).

By 1851 the basic legislative, judicial and administrative structures of land alienation and settler agriculture had been laid. The laws passed before and after 1851 aimed at promoting settler accumulation and the marginalization of the Algerian peasantry. The senatus-consulte law of 1863, for example, specifically sought to bring about 'the disintegration of the tribe' through the cantonment and break-up of the tribal lands and the establishment of private property. As a result of this law hundreds of tribes were delimited and broken up, and Algerian rural communities lost between 1863 and 1870 14% of their best fertile lands and all forests (Hermassi, 1972:22; Bennoune, 1988:44-45).

If the 1863 law sought to uproot the peasantry from collective social organization and 'threw all land held by Muslims upon the open market, and made it available for purchase or seizure by French colonists' (Wolf, 1969:213), the Warnier Law of 1873 tried to foster the systematic fragmentation of familial holdings into unviable plots. This became 'an effective instrument of spoliation in the hands of the speculators. Usurious loans with power of redemption led to the dispossession of innumerable peasants. The speculators used every imaginable means to provoke a legal sale by auction' (Bennoune, 1988:47). Through this mechanism, the settlers appropriated 563,000 hectares of fertile arable land between 1871 and 1896. Altogether, by 1908 the settlers had bought 896,180 hectares of some of the most fertile lands in Algeria. For its part, the state distributed 1,178,099 hectares to the settlers, located in 706 'centres of colonization', between 1841 and 1900. On the whole, by 1900 the settlers controlled 1,912,000 hectares, and the state several millions more (Bennoune, 1988:48-50).

Not only did the Algerian peasants lose some of their most fertile land to the settlers, the state also exacted from them money to cover the costs of implementing these laws. This does not mean that the rural Algerian communities were reduced into a homogenized mass of poor peasants. Old differentiations between the rich and poor remained and new ones were created. In fact, in order to secure allies, the state became increasingly willing to 'reach an accommodation with freeholders, the small and rural bourgeoisie' some of whom had their confiscated land restituted (Ruedy, 1967:66). Indeed, many established families retained some of their lands, and a considerable amount of their local power. Thus, behind the 'drastic and sometimes devastating political, social, and economic change', there was 'remarkable family continuity' for significant segments of the 'indigenous Algerian leadership' (Sivers, 1975:274; 1979).

As Brett (1986:160) has observed, this analysis challenges popular notions of a collectively 'decapitated' society (Hermassi, 1972). There were some Algerians who managed to buy back some land from the settlers. Between 1878 and 1908 the land sold by the settlers to the Algerians amounted to 257,168 hectares. Admittedly, during the same period settlers bought almost 3.3 times as much land from the Algerians. Moreover, the terms of exchange were unequal: the land cost the Algerians almost twice as much as it cost the French to buy (Bennoune, 1988:49).

The settler population was also differentiated. As in South Africa, there were rich and poor rural settlers. The ranks of the latter probably increased from the 1860s as land became more concentrated and efforts were made to develop 'an agrarian capitalism based on large-scale units of production, usually managed by companies, the bulk of which fell under the control of finance capital or banks' (Bennoune, 1988:43). Like their counterparts elsewhere in Africa, during the early period of primitive colonial accumulation the Algerian settlers faced severe shortages of labour. The colonial state in Algeria, too, resorted to land alienation and taxation, as mechanisms through which resources were not only appropriated on behalf of the settlers, but also to generate labour supply.

Algeria was colonized after France had abolished slavery, so slave labour was not a viable option ideologically. Instead forced labour was widely used, especially to construct the public infrastructure. The settler farmers and corporate producers relied on three main sources of labour. The first was wage labour, provided by both poor settlers and dispossessed Algerians. The flow of Algerians into wage employment increased as the conditions of rural production and reproduction deteriorated. They were employed either on daily or monthly basis. In 1851 the daily workers were paid 2-2.5 francs, while those on monthly contracts received 20-30 francs. On the whole the Algerian agricultural workers were paid about a quarter of the settlers' wages. By 1913 the situation had not changed much. The daily agricultural wage was 2.5 francs for Algerians and 6-8 francs for the settlers. By 1901 there were 152,102 agricultural workers (Bennoune, 1988:56-65).

Far more numerous were the sharecroppers, of whom there were 350,715 by 1901, or 2.3 times the number of agricultural wage labourers. Sharecropping was an old Algerian practice, known as khammassat, in which tenants, 'in return for their labour, received, in addition to the other productive elements of land, tools, seed, and animals, supplied by the landlord, one-fifth of the harvest' (Ruedy, 1967:6). Many of the settlers were undercapitalized, so they could neither afford wage labour, nor the full exploitation of their holdings. Sharecropping provided a way out for them and was also preferable to wage employment for many dispossessed Algerians. As in South Africa, several varieties of sharecropping emerged. There were those who worked on occupied lands and others who cultivated absentee-owned lands. In addition to sharecroppers, there were labour tenants. In the literature, the labour tenants tended to be mixed with sharecroppers. They formed a separate category, for what they shared with the landholders was their labour, not their produce. By the 1880s, over one-third of the colonized land was either cultivated by the Algerian sharecroppers or rented out to impoverished peasants.

As in South Africa, the sharecropping and labour tenancy arrangements were regularly contested. The struggles were both covert and overt, individualized and collective, and articulated in the various idioms of religion and Algerian nationalism. Refusal to pay rent and open revolts were not uncommon. In short, underneath the intimidating coercive exterior of settler production lay feet of clay. The periodic restitution of sequestered properties and the purchase of settler lands by Algerians testified to the weaknesses and incompleteness of settler hegemony and the resilience of Algerian resistance. By 1900 settler production concentrated on the same crops cultivated in France, but the social relations of production in the metropole had yet to be reproduced in the colony.

The majority of Algerians remained independent landholders. In 1901 the number of peasant landholders was 620,899. The bulk of them owned less land than their parents and grandparents did in the precolonial period. A large number of rural households could therefore not reproduce themselves entirely on their holdings, so that they had to hire or rent part of their household labour to wealthier farmers or the colonial sector. Thus the peasant household labour process was significantly transformed. The new colonial settler capitalist order spelled impoverishment for the majority of Algerian peasants. The statistics of livestock holdings amply bear this out. In 1867 Algerians had eight million sheep, and in the 1880s 3.7 million goats, and one million cattle. By 1927 the numbers had dropped to 3.3 million, 2.1 million, and 707,000 respectively (Bennoune, 1988:59).

Conclusion

The three cases of the Portuguese colonies, South Africa and Algeria expose some of the broad trends in colonial agriculture which extended into twentieth century Africa. Following their failed agricultural experiments, the Portuguese turned to concession companies, a model adopted by other colonial powers. The European settlers in South Africa and Algeria sought to monopolize commercial farming, an example later followed by European settlers in Zimbabwe and Kenya. The organization of the plantation industry in Natal by the end of the century held a mirror to the future of agribusiness in twentieth century Africa. There were of course remarkable differences between the three cases. By the end of the century Portugal had failed to establish settler agriculture; South Africa was on the road to succeeding; and the French in Algeria had turned parts of the country into a replica of France.

Despite their considerable differences, the three cases share some similarities. First, the colonial state played a critical role in setting the conditions for the establishment and reproduction of settler farming, both by trying to eliminate African competition and by providing the settlers with extensive support. Great efforts were made to dispossess Africans of their land and increase surpluses extracted from them through taxation, rents, and other mechanisms, all of which was meant to reduce their capacity to reproduce themselves through agriculture. For their part, the settlers were provided with cheap labour and credit, discriminatory extension and infrastructural services, and marketing facilities. Without this there is no way that the settlers would have succeeded in overcoming African competition and resistance. In a fundamental sense, therefore, their successes were political, not economic.

However, despite all these over-generous supports, the establishment of a viable settler agricultural economy was a protracted process. One of the main reasons why the process proved so prolonged was African resistance. Not only did Africans wage extended wars and battles against colonial conquest itself (the precondition for building the settler economy) once colonial rule had been imposed they resisted land alienation and labour recruitment, and when they entered settler agricultural employment they struggled against the settlers' cheap and coercive labour control system in innumerable ways. In the case of the Portuguese these struggles helped ensure the failure of the whole enterprise of settler agriculture. In the more successful cases of South Africa and Algeria, it is now quite clear that victory took much longer to achieve than was originally thought. For example, the draconian land laws in South Africa, including the 1913 Native Lands Act, no longer appear as the last chapter in the struggle between Africans and settlers over land, labour, and power, but another hump in the terrain of struggle between the two groups. Indeed, the settler victories were not ironclad, for Africans continued contesting settler hegemony until independence was eventually won. At the same time, there was growing class differentiation and conflict on either side of the deepening divide between settler and African farmers.

Third, the cleavages of class did not simply wear a racial face. It was in fact because the legions of poor settler peasants were so large and expanding and the ranks of prosperous African farmers growing that the various racial capitalisms were constructed in the settler colonies. Racial capitalism helped to mute intra-settler class struggles, and forestall interracial class solidarity among the poor peasants, both of which, if allowed to flourish, threatened to abort the entire project of settler colonialism. But racial capitalism also ensured its own eventual demise for it helped conceal intra-African class struggles and projected them into collective punches of anti-colonialism.

Part III

Mining and Manufacturing

6. Mining and Metallurgy

Iron Production

Iron was one of the most important minerals produced in Africa before and during the nineteenth century. Indeed, historians and archaeologists, some of whom have a tendency towards technological determinism, baptized, with characteristic oversimplification, the era during which iron production developed as the Iron Age (Shinnie, 1971; Oliver and Fagan, 1975; Phillipson, 1977b). In a recent work, Phillipson (1985:5) has concluded that this term and others, like 'Late Stone Age' and 'Neolithic' 'cannot be precisely defined', so they are better avoided. Much ink has been spilled debating the origins of iron production in Africa. Diffusionist generalizations have had a field day.

It was once widely believed that iron technology diffused into Africa from western Asia, first landing in North Africa from where, through Egypt and Carthage, it spread to the rest of the continent. From Egypt, the story went, iron technology diffused along the Nile to Meroe, which became the 'Birmingham of Africa' and the transmission centre of iron technology to East and West Africa. West Africa, it was said, may also have received its iron technology from Carthage via the Sahara or the Atlantic coastal region. Then the Bantu-speaking peoples migrated with the new technology to central and southern Africa. Iron did not reach South Africa until the seventeenth century as the European settlers were arriving (Wickins, 1981:74-83).

The diffusionist trail was constructed on thin evidence and speculation, underpinned by the racist notion that Africa, or more precisely that truncated Africa of western scholarship known as 'Black' or 'sub-Saharan' Africa, was too 'primitive' for independent technological innovation and development. Some archaeologists and historians, such as Diop (1968), Keteku (1975) and Andah (1983), have argued forcefully that iron technology was invented independently in Africa. Others still believe that iron technology, and metallurgy in general, were introduced into Africa from external sources (Posnansky, 1977:293; Herbert, 1984:10; Kense, 1985:22-24). It is as if this technology was an immutable idea, conceived, bred and transmitted whole from the outside world to Africa, rather than as a continuous process of innovation and change spawned by complex interactions between iron production techniques and economic, cultural, social, political and environmental transformations.

There is need for caution. 'It is astonishing', one researcher notes, 'to see how many archaeologists misunderstand the iron smelting remains they find in their excavations' (Noten, 1985:118). Sutton (1985:182) candidly admits that 'we still know very little about the history of iron working in Africa, and not much more about the products'. Neither the ethnographic data nor the archaeological record has been able to go much beyond static descriptions of the material features of the industry. Indeed, Kense (1985:27) acknowledges that: the 'reconstruction of African metallurgical development and diffusion throughout the continent depends upon a level of integration of archaeological, metallurgical, ethnographic and linguistic data that has not yet been achieved'.

What is now known casts doubt on many popular assumptions. For example, the assumption that the Egyptians were introduced to the use of iron by the Assyrians or the Greeks has been challenged (Shinnie and Kense, 1982:19-20). Meroe has been dethroned as the centre of iron diffusion (Trigger, 1969; Shinnie, 1985:28). Available dates for the beginnings of iron smelting from several centres in West, Central and East Africa show that the knowledge of iron working was known in these centres between the tenth century BC and the first century AD, at a time contemporary with, and in some cases even earlier than, Meroe. The West African centres include Taruga in Nigeria (Tylecote, 1975; Fagg, 1970; Sutton, 1982), Do Dimmi in Niger (Calvocoressi and David, 1979), Daboya in Ghana (Kense, 1981), and Jenne-Jeno. For East Africa there is the extraordinary evidence from Kutaruka in Tanzania (Schmidt, 1975, 1978, 1980, 1981; Schmidt and Avery, 1978). Evidence of early iron working has also come from the Zaire basin region in Central Africa (Maret, 1982; Maret and Nsuka, 1977; Maret, Noten and Cohen, 1977; David, 1982). Dates for South Africa have been pushed further back to the third and fourth centuries AD (Maggs, 1977, 1980; Hall and Vogel, 1980; Mason, 1981).

The simplistic correlation between the dispersal of Bantu languages and iron age technology has been questioned on archaeological and linguistic grounds. It has been demonstrated that iron age cultures of East African communities preceded those of communities closer to the putative Bantu homeland (Phillipson, 1977b:210-30). Linguistic studies have shown that stems relating to metallurgy in the various Bantu languages are not all derived from a common proto-Bantu, nor are they always different from those in non-Bantu languages (Maret and Nsuka, 1977). It would seem, in fact, that the expansion of Bantu-speaking peoples from their homeland in south-eastern Nigeria started much earlier than once thought, some 2000-3000 years BC, before the advent of iron working in West, Central or East Africa (Ehret, 1982). Thus the earliest Bantu-speaking communities in these regions did not produce iron (Kense, 1985:25).

By the beginning of the nineteenth century most African societies were able to produce their own iron or obtain it from neighbouring communities through trade. Iron production was a complex, skilled, lengthy and labour-intensive process involving prospecting, mining, smelting and forging. Iron ore was available in virtually all parts of the continent, especially in the lateritic crust that covers much of the savanna regions. Iron ore deposits were found by means of outcrops and was extracted through either alluvial or shallow mining. Smelting was done in furnaces using charcoal fuel, after which the iron was forged in workshops. Many products were made, including tools, utensils and jewellery.

There were many types of smelting furnaces. Several attempts have been made to classify them on the basis of either form and appearance (Cline, 1937; Coghlan, 1956; Williams, 1974:chapters 9 and 10), or function and method of operation (Kense, 1977; Shinnie and Kense, 1982; Kense, 1983). In the first category the furnaces are described variously as domed, shaft, spherical, cylindrical, induced-draught, bowl, tall, high, and so on. In the second category three types of furnaces are distinguished, according to the presence and absence of a smelting chamber and bellows system. The smelting chamber refers to a closed structure for heat retention. The bellows themselves can be divided into the bowl and bag types, with some arguing that the use of bowl bellows preceded that of bag bellows. These classifications fail to take into account historical changes and focus excessively on the shape of the furnace in a production process that involved many other variables. One can only agree with Pole's (1982:147) conclusion that 'there are no clear cut *types* which can be confidently assigned to either geographical areas or cultural groups'. Pole himself suggests 16 'types' based on the present knowledge of the technology, organization and process of iron production.

The furnaces were normally built of clay. In West Africa, the clay was usually mixed with soil from a 'live' termite hill to make the clay water-resistant (Curtin, 1975:207). In Buhaya, Tanzania furnaces were also built of ant-earth as well as slag lumps from previous smelts and cemented with clay (Sutton, 1985:172). The durability of the furnaces varied. Some were built for temporary use in one season, while others were permanent installations which could last decades. The latter were not, as many would assume, necessarily better than the former. Furnaces with solid permanent shafts delayed the recovery of the bloom, for they had to be allowed to cool, while those dismantled after each smelt allowed easier recovery and the cleaning of slag from the pit. Moreover, the permanent furnaces could 'be awkward for charging and uncharging' (Sutton, 1985:172).

The wide range of furnace types is one pointer to the originality and variability of iron technology in Africa. Out of the furnaces came wrought iron or steel. The production of steel was achieved in several ways. In one method, tuyeres were fitted deeply inside the furnace, which allowed the preheating of the air in the tuyere to very high temperatures before it entered the chamber. According to Goucher (1981:180-1), this 'constituted a significant technological innovation unique to African industries, with the smelted product being an intentional steel' - a fact that has led Childs and Schmidt (1985:122) to argue that:

> *the operation of preheated furnaces in Africa likely produced iron in a process altogether distinctive from Europe, and more efficiently... the African technology represents a separate evolutionary branch in iron technology'. Another method, also uniquely African, was to force a natural draft in the furnace sufficiently powerful to increase the combustion temperatures to the level at which carburization of the bloom occurred. Such a draft could be achieved if the input apertures were kept at low enough proportion to the air output and if the shaft itself was tall* (Kense, 1985:21).

In Oyo, Nigeria, smelters developed the technique of using slag from a previous smelt as flux which 'helped to decarbonize the iron and absorb other impurities, thus increasing the quantity and quality of the yield. When this cinder flux was used at low furnace temperatures, for example, it helped to reduce the phosphorous content of the iron. If the same ore had been put through an ordinary European blast furnace of the period, it would have produced pig iron of .06% phosphorous. With the African process, phosphorous was kept at .01% and the finished product after puddling was a good steel of .22% carbon' (Curtin, 1975:209). Goucher (1981:187) has argued that West African smiths were adept at using the techniques of quenching, annealing and cementation to produce steel. Austen and Headrick (1983:167), who are otherwise dismissive of African technological capacities, grudgingly concede that:

> *African smelting was technologically in advance of European, Middle Eastern, or South Asian smelting techniques, although, [they cannot resist adding], it was backward compared to ancient Chinese or early modern European power-driven blast furnaces which produced a molten pig iron.*

In some places, smelting involved more than one furnace. The Fipa of Tanzania used two furnaces in the smelting process. The first was a tall furnace called ilungu, which was well over three metres high and cone-shaped with a base diameter of about 2.5 metres. The bottom was made twice as thick as the top. The furnace had between seven and 11 vents at regular intervals around the base, one of which served as an entrance, while the rest were ventilators. The floor of the furnace was spread with ashes and pieces of bark, then the furnace was loaded with charcoal, followed by the iron ore and then green firewood in alternate layers until it was full. The furnace was fired at the top and left for three to four days to burn. After that the iron was extracted and taken to a blast furnace called kitengwe to undergo a second heating for further purification. The kitengwe was smaller than the ilungu and over it was built a grass-thatched shed. The kitengwe usually had four openings at the base, two containing tuyeres to conduct air from a pair of goatskin bellows, each operated by one person. All this enabled the smelters to carefully control the amount of heat in the furnace. In the process slag trickled out and the pure iron formed into a ball. The balls of iron were later taken to the workshop for forging. The iron was heated over charcoal in a hearth-like depression and when it got red hot, it was taken, with the help of tongs, and put on a stone where it was hammered with heavy stone hammers. The process was repeated until the ball had been flattened and the required product made. The most important tools manufactured were hoes, followed by sickles and razors, knives and daggers, rings and wire circlets, and weapons, such as spears, assegais, arrow-heads and battle-axes (Wembah-Rashid, 1969; Wright, n.d., 1985).

Iron production required large amounts of energy resources and labour. The industry depended on charcoal fuel, as was the case in Europe and North America, before coal was adopted from the mid-eighteenth century. Writing about West Africa, Goucher (1981:181) states that 'coal did not have the same potential... since the deposits there are recent and of poor calorific value'. Not every tree was suitable for the charring process, and the number of species suitable for the smelting and forging of iron was extremely limited. Only four savanna species were suitable for making charcoal. The charcoal-making process was labour intensive. It required the felling of trees and charring during which periodic monitoring was necessary to maintain proper conversion conditions, that is, a constant burning rate (Goucher, 1981:182).

Indeed, the whole process of iron production was labour-intensive, for apart from making charcoal, labour was required to build the furnaces and other pieces of apparatus, obtain and prepare the ore, smelt the iron and forge it into the required tools and objects. It is impossible to quantify the relative share of each of these activities in the total labour input because of poor or inadequate data. The labour process was affected by the availability of resources, the design and durability of furnaces, and the organization of smelting activities. Production centres which were near to abundant resour-

ces of clay used for building furnaces and trees suitable for making charcoal
required less labour to produce these materials than those that were not.

The impact of furnace design on the labour process has been demonstrated
by Pole (1982) using the case of northern and southern Ghana. He shows
that more labour was used operating the smaller furnaces of northern Ghana
than the larger furnaces of the south. The furnaces of Lawra, Tiza and Chiana
in northern Ghana required:

> *frequent additions of ore and charcoal and almost continuous tapping
> of slag, together with pumping the bellows, [which] contributed to
> keeping four or five persons busy throughout the day. In contrast, at
> Akpafu in south-eastern Ghana, where larger furnaces were used, once
> the charge had been burning for some time the operators could leave the
> furnace unattended, except for slag tapping. One person was appointed
> to keep watch over the furnace, to make sure the air inlet tubes did not
> become blocked and that the charge was not burning too fiercely. The
> Akpafu furnaces produced more iron per smelt than those of northern
> Ghana* (Pole, 1982:504).

In southern Ghana more labour was spent in making charcoal, which
constituted about 60% of the total labour input, than in northern Ghana where
the trees suitable for iron-smelting were more readily available. Overall, the
labour cost per kilogram of usable iron in Akpafu was far below that in
Lawra, Tiza and Chiana, which Pole (1982:504) has calculated, in man-
hours, at 8-13, 50, 40 and 93, respectively.

The organization of smelting activities and the relations of production and
distribution also varied. In many places smelting was a part-time activity,
undertaken between the harvesting and planting seasons. But there were
other places, for example in the imperial workshops in the cities of Ethiopia,
where smelting was a full-time activity (Pankhurst, 1968:256, 271-2). In
some societies smelting and smithing were performed by the same group,
while in others the two functions were divided between two different groups.
In parts of Nigeria, for instance, such as Nupe, 'anyone could smelt iron, but
only members of certain families were allowed to become blacksmiths'
(Pole, 1982:506). In 'northern Ghana most villages had blacksmiths'
quarters, the rest of the community knowing nothing of the work' (Pole,
1982:155). Among the Fipa, iron production, which was confined to the
period between the harvesting and planting seasons, involved the labour of
many members of the community as well as specialized craftsmen. The
community participated by collecting the raw material, fuel, building the
furnace, providing food, and so on. There was some specialization of men's
and women's tasks. For example, women prepared the clay for the ilungu,

while only men moulded the tuyeres. The actual smelting was restricted to the craftsmen, known as wasilungu, and their assistants and apprentices. In Darfur, the blacksmiths were men, and were called mir. Their wives were also called mir, although they specialized as potters (Haaland, 1985:56-57).

The Ufipa iron production centres were located some distance away from the villages. The wasilungu came with their spouses and children. They did both smelting and forging. Overseeing the work was a master smelter and blacksmith, called mwami. The wasilungu received some of the finished product, usually hoes, as payment, which they could later sell. Thus payment in kind made the wasilungu both workers and traders. Hoes were also given to the chief as tribute. These hoes were later distributed to those who came to 'beg' for them, usually to pay for bridewealth. The rest of the output was marketed either as iron, which still required to be forged into a particular item, or as finished products (Wembah-Rashid, 1969; Wright, n.d, 1985). It is difficult to assess the size of the Ufipa iron industry. There are various estimates that in the 1880s 150,000 field hoes were sold annually on the market in Tabora, and 30,000 in the 1890s in Uvinza (Kjekshus, 1977a:90). The industry survived until the 1930s when imported iron established its hold over the local market.

The position of iron producers varied considerably among African societies. In some they were held in high esteem, in others they were despised. Sometimes the attitude to smelters and smiths varied where the two functions were performed by separate groups. In such societies it was often the smiths rather than the smelters who were held in high esteem. Smiths enjoyed high status in Mali (Filipowiak, 1985:48), and in many societies in Central Africa where they were admired for their skills, knowledge and power. Indeed, popular mythologies celebrated the symbolic relationship between the blacksmith, the king, and certain iron objects, such as the hammer (Maret, 1985). There were of course societies where iron working was identified with subject peoples or lower classes whose repute was low. Blacksmiths were stigmatized in Dar Fur (Haaland, 1985:56-60), where they were excluded from the rest of society by living separately or in separate quarters of a village, and Ethiopia where they were not permitted to cultivate, own or inherit land and intermarry with others outside their caste (Pankhurst, 1968:271; Todd, 1985:91).

For centuries, most of the iron used in Africa was locally produced. By the beginning of the nineteenth century Africa still satisfied a substantial part of its iron needs from local production. But by the end of the century, imports had become dominant in some parts of the continent. Three explanations have been advanced to account for this.

First, there is the trade-impact model, according to which African iron industries declined because they could not face European competition (Williams, 1974). Indeed, Flint (1974a:387) believes, with reference to West Africa, that:

as early as 1800 the West African mining and smelting industries which the blacksmiths had once had to rely completely for their material, were almost at an end, ruined by competition of cheaper and purer iron bars imported from Europe.

This assertion is based on the wrong assumption that at this time West African metallurgy was backward and inferior to European metallurgy. On the contrary:

far from being «pure», after the eighteenth century much of the European iron had a high sulphur content due to the use of coal as fuel which seriously affected the quality of the smelted product and made it a poor substitute for the carbon-steel or pure iron bloom from some African furnaces (Goucher, 1981:179-80).

This explains why throughout the nineteenth century and the early twentieth century Africans showed a marked preference for locally-produced iron.

An alternative explanation for the alleged steady decline of African production in the nineteenth century emphasizes the role of ecological factors and the production constraints that they brought about. According to this view, the iron industry was increasingly constrained by the shortage of charcoal fuel caused by deforestation, itself a cumulative product of the industry's reliance on trees for making charcoal. To make matters worse, the climatic shift in the nineteenth century towards drier conditions 'severely slowed the natural rate of replacement of species and original forest which had been exploited... Pressures to supply charcoal would have demanded the eventual exploitation of younger species, thus interfering with the replacement of cut trees' (Goucher, 1981:183). In West Africa 'these technological pressures toward deforestation would have been exacerbated by the European exploitation of forests' (Goucher, 1981:184). In the face of growing scarcity of suitable charcoals for smelting, efforts were made to improve fuel conservation and manufacturing efficiency by, for example, increasing furnace height, adapting variations in the number and angle of tuyeres, and developing preheating techniques. But these innovations were apparently not enough. Increasingly African metal workers relied on imported iron bars, as a matter of necessity, and not because they were 'cheaper' or 'purer' (Goucher, 1981:188-9).

African imports of European iron certainly increased in the nineteenth century, although reliable statistics are hard to come by. However, increased imports do not necessarily imply an absolute decline in local production. There were some areas which produced their own iron in competition with the European product as late as the 1890s and beyond. This was particularly true for countries in the interior. For instance, as late as 1904 there were about 1,500 high furnaces in production in Yatenga, the northernmost of the Mossi states, turning out an estimated 540 tons of iron or steel a year, which was probably more than the iron imported in this region in the late nineteenth century (Curtin, 1975:210-11). Thus the rate of decline and the capacity to survive varied from place to place. These variations cannot be adequately explained by the ecological model.

The third approach seeks to explain these variations by examining the role of labour organization and distribution in the iron industry. Indeed, the problem to be explained, according to Pole (9182), is not the eventual decline of indigenous iron production, but rather why it survived for so long following the introduction of imported iron. After all, it survived for over four hundred years.

The trajectory of survival and decline was affected by many factors. Local iron was preferred, both by its producers and users, for qualitative and cultural reasons. It was generally of higher quality than imported iron. Moreover, local iron was often intimately bound up with ritual, religious and other cultural practices. In short, the odds were generally against imported iron. Pole (1982:507-9) has suggested that: 'it was not until imported iron was cheaper by a factor of six that preference for the local product was out-weighed'. In many parts of the continent, especially the interior, imported iron did not achieve this until the twentieth century.

The durability of the local industry was also considerably affected by the organization of labour . The likelihood of substituting local with imported iron tended to be higher in societies where smelting and smithing were done by two different groups than where the two functions were done by the same group. Smiths who got their iron from local smelters could switch more readily to imported iron, as soon as it was profitable for them to do so, than those who smelted their own iron, for whom imported iron did not represent an alternative raw material even if they could afford to buy it, although it could offer a substitute for labour if there was increased pressure on their labour time.

It would appear, then, that indigenous iron production in Africa in the nineteenth century declined in some societies and survived in others. Local iron tended to prevail over a longer period in those societies where the productive resources, particularly charcoal fuel, were relatively abundant, the quality of local iron was demonstrably higher than the imported variety, the iron workers were accorded great respect, and the iron as a symbol and an artifact was well articulated with the society's cultural values and practices. The converse was true for those societies whose iron industries declined precipitously in the course of the nineteenth century. From this analysis, it can be seen why colonialism would eventually lead to the virtual demise of Africa's age-old iron industries. During the colonial period ecological degradation, including deforestation, intensified; the quality of imported iron improved, while its price fell considerably relative to the local product; indigenous iron workers were either sequestered into colonial wage labour or they lost much of their former clout to the new industrial and white collar workers; and many hallowed cultural traditions, with which local iron was articulated, lost much of their relevance and meaning.

Copper Production

As recently as 1983, Austin and Headrick wondered why there was no 'Bronze Age' in Africa. By Africa of course they meant 'sub-Saharan Africa', for it is generally accepted that North Africa had a bronze age. The two authors proceeded to answer themselves. 'One reason', they speculated, 'may be the very existence of iron, which made further experimentation with copper and its alloys economically unattractive' (Austen and Headrick, 1983:108). The study by Herbert (1984) on copper production in pre-colonial Africa shows that both Austin's question and answer were specious. The production and use of copper and its alloys in Africa was widespread. Indeed, in many places it antedated iron (Kense, 1985:14-15; Calvocoressi and David, 1979). This shows the need for caution: African metallurgical history is still in its infancy. Many of the assertions that have been made, on which spurious comparisons are based between Africa and the world, especially Europe, wilt in the face of closer and systematic investigation.

The copper industry in Africa is an ancient one. Indeed, there have hardly been any copper producing areas in twentieth century Africa that were not worked before. It is known that the Egyptians were producing and using copper in pre-dynastic times, that is, before 3000 BC (Lucas and Harris, 1962; Muhly, 1973: Coghlan, 1962). Remarkably early dates are now available for other parts of Africa as well. Copper was being mined and smelted by 2000 BC in Agadez, Niger (Tylecote, 1982), by the fifth century BC at Akjoujt in western Mauritania, and by the second or third century in parts of central and southern Africa (Herbert, 1984:15-28). Thus by the beginning of the nineteenth century Africans had been producing copper and its alloys for centuries. Needless to say, during this long period of development the industry experienced, in different places and at different times, both growth and decline.

The most common copper ores in Africa were the carbonates, malachite and azurite, which have a copper content of 54.7% and 55%, respectively. Much rarer was cuprite with its high copper content of 88.8%. Sulphide ores were mostly found at lower depths and so were more difficult to mine. The richest deposits of copper in Africa were found in central and southern Africa. Less abundant but adequate supplies were found in parts of Niger and Mauritania in West Africa, and Morocco and Algeria in North Africa, the Sinai in Egypt, Hufrat en-Nahas in the Sudan, and Kilembe in Uganda, East Africa.

As in the case of iron, copper deposits were identified by the surface indications. Extraction was done through opencast and underground mining. In opencast mining the ore could be extracted by excavating large holes or by sinking several small shafts into the ground, or by combining the two. Some of the opencast mining operations could be quite substantial. For example, an opencast mine was found in Katanga that was three-quarters of a mile long, and 600 to 1,000 feet wide. At Mindouli in the Congo there were four major mines still actively producing at the end of the nineteenth century in a two square kilometre area along a chain of rocky hills. The largest mine comprised 150 to 200 pits (Herbert, 1984:19-20, 24). Some of the most extensive underground mining operations have been found in Zimbabwe . Shafts were sunk to depths of dozens of feet, sometimes over 100 feet, and underground tunnels were dug to connect the various chambers at the foot of the shafts, and timbering and rock pillars were used to ensure safety. Ventilation was provided through adits. Horizontal galleries were more difficult to ventilate. The practice was to light a fire at the foot of the shaft, and through convection, the rising hot air would draw the foul air from the working site (Summers, 1969).

The African copper miners used both iron and stone tools to dislodge and break up ores. In the case of particularly hard rock the firesetting technique was used and water was applied judiciously to cool and break the rock. In deep mines the ore had to be hauled and hoisted to the surface. In the opencast mines of Katanga , ladders made of fibre were lowered as shafts were dug deeper. Baskets, also made of fibre, were filled with ore and passed on to the surface by men and women stationed on the ladders. Each basket could hold up to 25 kgs of ore. If the block of ore was too heavy for the basket it was raised by fibre ropes to the surface where it was crushed (Herbert, 1984:52). In the case of the underground mines of Zimbabwe the ore was put in small baskets or leather bags and hauled by hand or windlasses (Summers, 1969). In most societies mining and sorting ores was done during the dry season. In contrast, smelting could be conducted any time, indeed, was usually reserved for the rainy months.

As in the case of iron, copper smelting required furnaces. But copper-smelting furnaces were different from iron-smelting furnaces because the two metals have different physical properties. Generally copper furnaces 'were rarely as solid as those used to smelt iron, thanks to the lower temperatures and shorter time required to reduce copper ores. In some regions they were built of ant or termite hills, in others of clay' (Herbert, 1984:69). As might be expected, the copper working furnaces and operations varied quite considerably from region to region and even within the same region, as archaeological excavations from the Agadez region of Niger have revealed (Tylecote, 1982). In the large production centres the furnaces had permanence and solidity lacking elsewhere. The copper ore was smelted either in a single operation or in phases, depending on the quality of the ore and the nature of the furnace used. For the more complex sulphides, different furnaces were used to roast and reduce the ore. Roasting at submelting temperatures enabled the sulphur to be removed, in order to increase the content of copper (Herbert, 1984:69-70). In some places fluxes were used to enhance the efficiency of the smelting (Cline, 1937:72; Trevor, 1930:395; Bower, 1927:146). From the examination of copper samples derived from different parts of the continent it is quite clear that the final product was a metal of high levels of purity (Clark, 1957:16; Friede, 1975:187).

It is virtually impossible to determine the amount of copper produced in Africa in the nineteenth century, or in the previous centuries. However, there has been no shortage of estimates for particular regions. One estimate for the Katanga region, for example, figures that:

in the period immediately preceding Msiri's reign, before 1850, that is, 115,000 kilograms were produced annually in Katanga about 33,000 in Kiembe, and 6,000 in Poyo. During Msiri's reign the total for all three areas fell to about 31,000 kilograms, while after his death, exploitation continued only in the Chefferie Katanga and dwindled... [to] 6,000 kilograms by 1903 (Herbert, 1984:73-74, 179-82).

Copper is a far more versatile metal than iron, so smiths could work it into almost any shape or form. It could be hardened and made brighter and shinier by cold hammering, or it could be softened and darkened by heating. The Luba smiths of Zaire produced their deep red copper by reheating refined copper, then plunging it into water. Some smiths used palm wine or juices from certain plants for the same purpose to obtain a variety of colours. The Lemba smiths of the Transvaal, for example, produced copper wire with a fine yellow through this procedure (Bloomhill, 1963). Colour and the mechanical properties of the copper product could also be fashioned by alloying it with other metals. Smiths in different parts of the continent developed various techniques of wire drawing, casting and alloying. Wire drawing was strenuous work which required skill. On available evidence the craft appears to have been most well-developed in central and southern Africa (Herbert, 1984:78-82).

West Africa is more famous for its casting. A number of casting techniques were used including the relatively simple open casting method and the more complex cire purdue method. The use of the latter method by West African smiths has raised the spectre of diffusionism that always haunts African history whenever anything smacking of 'sophistication' appears. Williams (1974) asserts that the West Africans learnt the technique after 1500 following the arrival of Europeans along the coast. Posnansky (1977) has vigorously dismissed this assertion by pointing out that casting techniques, not only in West Africa but in Africa as a whole, were of considerable antiquity. He goes further to suggest that some possibility exists 'that the cire purdue technique may also have been initiated in West Africa, an area of abundant supply of both beeswax and latex' (Posnansky, 1977:296), the two main modelling agents used in cire purdue casting in Africa.

Most of the castings were done with alloyed copper, especially bronze, that is, alloy of copper and tin, and brass, alloy of copper and zinc. Apart from casting, bronze, like copper, was also worked by being hammered. Bronze was produced in various parts of the continent. The case of Egypt and other parts of North Africa is well-known (Lucas and Harris, 1962:217-223). Evidence of bronze production in West Africa comes from several areas, the most well-known being Igbo Ukwu in Nigeria. In southern Africa bronze was plentiful in various centres of the Zimbabwe cultural complex. It was also made in the Transvaal.

The distribution of brass production was, like bronze, quite uneven. West African brass working is known from the spectacular brass art objects of Ife, Benin, Igbo Ukwu, Tada and other lesser known centres in Nigeria. Far fewer finds of bronze have so far been made in central and southern Africa (Herbert, 1984:100). In Ethiopia 'work in brass was fairly widespread; articles of that metal included incense holders, sistra, small bells, bracelets, chains, harness decorations, and other articles among them jugs and bowls for hand washing' (Pankhurst, 1968:272).

Copper and its alloys were made into a bewildering array of products, which were put to many uses. They were drawn into wire and rods, cast into statues and masks, fashioned into jewellery and ornaments, turned into vessels and utensils, coated on royal insignia and palaces, employed as media of exchange and art, valued as emblems of power and ritual, and traded in local and external markets (Herbert, 1973, 1984:chapters 8-11). In many societies copper was as useful as iron and as precious as gold. According to

Herbert, by the end of the nineteenth century the African copper industry was on the verge of extinction, a victim of the flood of imported metal, ecological constraints, and political turmoil in some of the major copper producing regions. It cannot be overemphasized that the decline of the copper industry was, as in the case of iron, a differentiated process in which there were considerable regional variations and the organization of labour played an important role.

Tin Production

The production of bronze is one indication that tin was mined and smelted in certain parts of Africa. There is evidence that tin was produced in ancient Egypt (Muhly, 1973:259; Lucas and Harris, 1962:253-57). Tin ores occur plentifully in parts of west, central and southern Africa, but it is not known when tin mining in these regions started. The largest prehistoric tin centres have been located in the Bauchi province of Nigeria and in the Rooiberg-Waterberg district of the Transvaal, South Africa. From the size of the ancient workings at Rooiberg, 'it has been calculated that no less than 16,000 tons of ore was taken out, yielding about 1,000 tons of tin' (Steel, 1982).

In the nineteenth century the most important African tin deposits, and among the richest in the world, were located in northern Nigeria, around the Jos Plateau. There is no concrete evidence to explain the origins of Nigerian tin-mining. What is clear is that tin production was an important branch of the local and regional economy in the nineteenth century. Tin prospecting required skills accumulated over generations which made it possible to identify places containing large quantities of tin ore. Alluvial mining apparently predominated, although in the vicinity of Ririwain Kano there was underground mining in which shafts were sunk and galleries driven deep into the tin bearing soils and rocks. The ore was washed to eliminate impurities. The washing operations could be complex, involving the damming of streams, construction of canals, and letting water to race through downward sloping channels, or making artificial sluices when there was no adequate water flow. Simpler washing operations were carried on in specially fashioned calabashes. The resultant 'black tin' was mixed with water and pounded into cakes to prepare for smelting (Freund, 1981:15).

Smelting took place at a few centres, unlike mining and washing which could be done wherever the conditions allowed. The 'black tin', which was up to 70% pure, was smelted in furnaces which were smaller than furnaces used for iron smelting, for tin has a lower melting point than iron. The furnaces were generally up to three feet high, fixed with tuyeres, to which goat-leather bellows were attached. In order to control the heat the furnaces were placed in shelters and the bellows were worked by two men throughout the smelting process. 'The metal, once separated from the slag, run down into a trough and then trickled into the mould... The mould was prepared over a small open charcoal fire with long sticks of grass which, when removed gave the tin the form of straws' (Freund, 1981:17).

The straws could be marketed as they were usually in bundles of one hundred, or they were taken to the tinsmith to be forged into various objects. Smithing, unlike smelting, took place in a variety of locations in Kano, Bauchi, and Bida. The tinsmiths were often distinguished from the black-smiths, and used their own specialized tools. The tinsmiths of Bida were particularly renowned for their skills. Tin was used to make many products, including sheaths, rings, bracelets and horse-gear. It was also widely used for soldering and as a finish for household utensils, such as bowls, jugs, plates and lamps.

The relations of production and distribution in the Nigerian tin-industry were quite complex. The various operations involved in tin production, from prospecting, mining and washing, to smelting and smithing, required a lot of labour. It is reported that slaves were extensively used in prospecting and mining, while women played an important role in processing tin by washing tin ore or the slag after smelting to retrieve any remaining tin. Smelting and smithing involved various forms of labour, all of which were organized around the household, or gida. The smelting crews would consist of ten men putting in 12 hours a day, although not for the whole year. The smelting operations were largely owned by officeholders. These smelter owners appropriated the largest share of the surplus from tin production. The merchants who sold smelted tin to smiths or the manufactured products to the market, also had their share of the surplus. The state extracted its share through taxation.

It is difficult to quantify northern Nigeria's tin production in the nineteenth century. Estimates have been made that one furnace could produce over 20 tons of tin per annum, and that in the 1850s the annual value of the Kano tin trade was about ten million cowries, or £1,200 at the current exchange rate (Freund, 1981:18, 21). Whatever the actual volume, we know that this tin was traded throughout present-day Nigeria and, on smaller scale, beyond. There is no indication that the tin industry, like the iron and copper industries, was in a state of decline at the time of colonial conquest. Nevertheless, it did not escape the clutches of colonial capitalism. The tin industry was taken over and reorganized by capitalist firms from the turn of the twentieth century following the colonization of Nigeria.

Gold Production

Unlike iron, copper and tin, gold had little utilitarian value. It was primarily a metal of ornamentation and prestige. Gold was also relatively easy to work. In the case of alluvial deposits the simple, though laborious, technique of pawning was used, while extraction of gold from ore required hammering the rock into pieces and grinding or pounding it into powder, from which the gold was then washed. It was refined by heating and shaped by hammering and casting.

The origins of gold production in Africa are buried in antiquity. Very old gold workings have been found in Egypt going back to the beginning of the third millennium BC. Some of the mines were worked to a depth of 300 feet. The Egyptians developed to a high level the art of gold refining and smithing. The gold was coloured, soldered and banished, plated on copper and silver, and made into coinage and jewellery, or into sheets and foil for embossing, engraving, gilding and decorating objects and buildings (Lucas and Harris, 1962:224-34). The largest output of gold in ancient times, not only in Africa, but in the world at large, came from the mines of Nubia, which were controlled at various times by the Egyptians and the Kush kingdom at Napata and Meroe. Recent archaeological diggings at Meroe have revealed temples with walls and statues covered by gold dust, and 'it has been computed that during antiquity Kush produced about 1,600,000 kilogrammes of pure gold' (Hakem and Hrbek, 1981:311). Many centuries later, West Africa became a major producer of gold as well. Gold production in Lobi, Bambuku, Boure and Ashanti grew steadily from the first millennium AD. The largest quantities were produced during the European Middle Ages, when West Africa was the principal source of gold for western Europe. Further south, Zimbabwe began producing gold, probably in the eighth century AD.

In Lobi, Bambuku and many other parts of West Africa gold production occurred in societies which lacked overarching centralized polities. Lobi gold mining was controlled by loosely structured lineage groups organized in a complex web linking residential clusters in the semi-autonomous towns to the chiefly towns (Perinbam, 1988). Once located through various methods of prospecting which varied according to culture, terrain and circumstances, the gold was extracted either by collecting the alluvial deposits or through surface or underground mining. Unlike many places where digging mine pits was men's work, in Lobi it was exclusively reserved for women. The women were also primarily responsible for washing the gold ore (Perinbam, 1988:444).

Bambuku gold occurred mainly in alluvial and shallow but scattered ores deposits:

> *The typical excavation was a vertical well, about 75 cm square. As the hole went deeper, it was reinforced with sills at intervals, and at least one side was protected by a grate of horizontal sticks that could serve as a ladder for climbing up and down. Miners usually went to bedrock*

before sending out horizontal tunnels in each direction as far as they dared without risk of a cave-in (Curtin, 1973:628).

Gold mining was done during the dry season after the rains had stopped when there was little demand for agricultural labour.

Land for gold prospecting or mining was allocated by a hereditary village official known as jala nila, whose primary functions were religious. It was the jala nila who chose the site for the season's mining, based on his prospecting knowledge, and performed the necessary rituals, for which he was paid a fee by those who wanted to mine. The mining itself was directed by another hereditary official, known as sanukutigi or duragiti, meaning chief of the works or chief of the goldfield. His responsibility was to assign particular spots to individual digging groups and maintain order, for which he was also paid a fee by the miners. The work was divided between men and women, with the former doing excavation and the latter extracting gold from the ore. Irrespective of the proportion between men and women in a team, the output was shared equally between the two groups, and among the members within each group.

It is virtually impossible to know how much gold was produced in Lobi or Bambuku in the nineteenth century. All that Peribam (1988:445), for example, can say for certain is that 'gold production increased in the late nineteenth and early twentieth centuries'. He dismisses estimates based on Lobi gold sales on coastal markets because most of Lobi's gold was sold in the interior. But that does not stop him from declaring that: 'with low earnings/profit ratios and few opportunities to expand market exchanges, there seemed little need to maximize production, or to develop techniques beyond the most rudimentary' (Peribam, 1988:445).

He echoes Curtin who provides an estimate, which is no better than a guess, that in Bambuku 100 kg of gold was produced annually in the early nineteenth century, up from 60 kg in the eighteenth, but less than the 200 kg of the early twentieth century. Curtin's figures convey a statistical certainty that is grossly exaggerated. On the basis of such a guess, he asserts that per capita production was low, which, he believes, 'helps to explain why the people of Bambuku could treat gold as a free good... The activity was so close to margin that it bore no rent - in Marxian terms, there was no surplus to be expropriated' (Curtin, 1975:205). It would appear, on the contrary, that the jala nila and the sanukutigi or duragiti appropriated rent from the miners, however ideologically camouflaged the process may have been.

Zimbabwe boasted one of the largest gold mining industries in pre-colonial Africa. It developed sophisticated techniques of prospecting, mining and refining. Three main prospecting methods were used. First, alluvial samples along rivers were panned and in the case of positive results the origin of gold was sought upstream until the parent reefs were discovered. Second, they made detailed exploration of auriferous areas by observing soil types and vegetation patterns. In the drier parts of the country the trees normally associated with potentially auriferous soils consisted of acacia karoo, A. rehmanniana and A. benthani, while in the wetter areas it was uapaca kirkiana, or mzhanzhe. Third, selected areas were prospected by sampling termite mounds, which normally contained samples of all the rocks through which the termites had burrowed to get water (Summer, 1969; Phimister, 1974; Mudenge, 1988:166-7).

After finding the deposits, the gold had to be mined. Gold was found either in alluvial form or in reef form. The extraction of alluvial gold involved simple gold washing, while gold-reef mining was more complex. It was done in three ways. The first method was the open cast mining in which the surface outcrop was first cleared and the reef was attacked from both sides. This was possible where the surface rock was relatively soft. Where it was hard the method used was underground stopping. The shafts sank averaged six to 24 metres in depth and one metre in diameter. The reef was worked from every direction until it was exhausted. The third method involved 'driving tunnels or adits into the sides of hills if reasonably flat reefs existed' (Mudenge, 1988:167).

The techniques used for haulage, milling and recovery bore some similarities to those used in copper mining. The tools used for crushing the auriferous rocks were iron or steel hammers, gads and picks. Hard rocks could be broken through the technique of heating the rocks and cracking them by pouring cold water. For haulage, wooden bowls or buckets were passed on from person to person all the way to the surface. Ventilation was provided by natural convection. When underground water was reached, the miners would use bowls to carry the water out, before finally abandoning the mine. Mudenge (1988:169) observes that 'the lack of pumping technology was one of the major constraints on Shona mining activities'. It was this that partly determined that mining would be mostly undertaken during the dry season, rather than the rainy season. Smelting was relatively simple. It involved boiling the auriferous soil or roasting the ore to facilitate its crushing and milling. The gold was then washed repeatedly, in the process of which some of it was lost.

Alluvial mining was largely a household activity, while the underground forms of mining involved the mobilization of the labour of several households in a community and the skills of professionals. The bulk of panning was done by women, although it appears that gold washing techniques were taught by old men. During the gold working season each village ruler commandeered his village to work on his gold washing site or sites where they normally camped for about two months. In the course of the nineteenth century it became increasingly common for enterprising individuals to organize their own gold washing operations, although chiefs remained the largest gold producers by virtue of the fact that they claimed all the larger pieces of gold washed by right or they taxed goldwashing areas. The Mutapa, the ruler, could specifically request that gold be mined for him. He paid the miners in cattle. These miners, unlike the household producers, should be considered as hired workers (Mudenge, 1988:172). Thus the state and its functionaries appropriated a considerable portion of the surplus, through tribute, taxation and other mechanisms, although it would be wrong to conclude that it monopolized the gold industry, as some historians have assumed.

Nobody knows for sure how much gold was produced in Zimbabwe. Mudenge (1988:173) has argued that gold production went into permanent decline from the late seventeenth century, thanks to the break up of the Manyika kingdom from Mutapa, which took away most of the gold producing regions, and the fact that 'with every century the easier deposits were being exhausted and harder ones had to be mined with basically the same technology'. Gold exports from the Mutapa state declined from an average 8,000 kgs in 1500 to 1,500 kgs in the 1670s and about 150 kgs in 1800 and 10 kgs in 1820 (Mudenge, 1988:174-5). Export figures do not, of course, tell the whole story, but they are a good pointer to the scale of surplus production. It has been argued that reef mining declined in the nineteenth century partly because of internal political turmoil in the region culminating in the Nguni invasions, and partly because of market fluctuations and the fact that the mines were becoming worked out. In contrast, alluvial gold working:

> *was better suited to survive in certain areas. It was aided in this by proximity to markets, but more importantly, it was a form of production which could take advantage of the agricultural «slack season» without any of the fixed costs of reef mining, and so was less susceptible to profitability fluctuations* (Phimister, 1974:447).

Summers (1969) has suggested that by the nineteenth century Zimbabwe had produced 34 million ounces of gold, or about ten million kilograms, which, if correct, would mean that the country produced a large proportion of total world production of precious metals. It is estimated that about 10% was used for home consumption, either in the form of jewellery or for ceremonial functions, for example, in the burials of important figures. The rest was passed on to regional and international trade through the Arabs and later Portuguese along the East African coast. Zimbabwe gold, it is widely believed, financed much of the Indian Ocean trading system. By the time the county was colonized in 1890 the Shona had worked out all the payable gold reef. No new gold mines were ever discovered. The European settlers simply reworked the old workings. Indeed, many of them made a fortune excavating the graves of chiefs to recover the gold with which they had been buried!

Gold was also found over much of the island of Madagascar. Not much is known about gold production on the island before the nineteenth century. There is some evidence that:

> *gold alluvial deposits were worked in the south of the island. Moreover, both the Sakalava and Merina monarchs upheld a traditional ban on gold prospecting and exploitation, indicating the likelihood of secretly worked deposits in the centre and west of Madagascar* (Campbell, 1988c:100).

Campbell has argued that the Merina court held back the development of gold deposits 'for fear of exciting European colonial ambitions in the region', but then reversed the policy in 1883 'in the hope that revenue from gold production would stave off bankruptcy and finance a military build-up against the threatened French assault on the island. At the same time the sudden blaze of publicity given the Malagasy gold resources attracted large numbers of white diggers and refuelled French determination to colonize the island' (Campbell, 1988c:102-3). A gold rush ensued, and prospective miners flocked from as far as South Africa, India, China, and Australia. From 1886 foreigners could be granted partnerships with the crown to work gold concessions. There were also private Malagasy gold producers.

The state sought to maximize revenues from the industry by controlling it tightly. The foreign concessionaires were expected to provide all equipment and skilled personnel, give up to 5% of all gold ore produced to the state, and pay 50% of the profits from the sale of the remainder. Private diggers were given short-term licenses, which restricted them to specified areas, and were required to sell their gold to the state at ten dollars an ounce, which was below the market value. These conditions, Campbell believes, discouraged foreign investment and encouraged illicit gold production, so that the state was never able to make as much from gold production as it hoped. 'Clandestine production and smuggling of gold was [also] widespread amongst Malagasy diggers' (Campbell, 1988c:109).

Moreover, the state found it difficult to attract labour, so it resorted to fanompoano, and increasingly child labour as well, which only served to fuel opposition to Merina rule by the exploited workers and subject peoples from whom most of the labour was sequestered. 'As early as 1889', Campbell (1988c:116), writes, 'large numbers of local people living on the gold fields of Vonizongo and Betsileo had fled to join rebel bands rather than be summoned for gold fanompoana'. The gold industry was taken over by the French following their conquest of Imerina in 1895, but the problems facing the industry, such as production bottlenecks, clandestine mining and smuggling, fear of foreign, in this case 'British', competition, labour shortages, and popular opposition and rebellions, persisted.

Salt Production

Salt was one of the most important commodities produced in pre-colonial Africa. Various types of salt were made. They had dietary, medicinal, industrial and other uses. Salt was manufactured in three main ways. First, it was extracted from saliferous springs, lakes and the sea. Second, it was obtained from saliferous plants. Third, it was derived from saliferous soils or mined.

There are salt lakes and salt springs in various parts of Africa, particularly in the Great Rift Valley of eastern Africa, where the local people made salt by taking brine and filling it into holes in the ground and left it there until a sufficient concentration had occurred, after which the brine was boiled in clay jars until the salt was formed. One of the regions where this type of salt was produced on a large scale in the nineteenth century was Uvinza in Tanzania, where it was stimulated by the growth of population, agriculture and the caravan trade (Sutton and Roberts, 1968). The salt could apparently be produced by anybody who wanted to, subject to paying a tax to the local chief. One estimate suggests that up to 500,000 kgs of salt were taken from the salt works annually by the end of the century (Kjekshus, 1977a:97). Considerable amounts of salt were also produced from the brine springs of the Benue trough in West Africa. The brine was scraped from the marshes, washed, and the concentrated solution drained into boiling pots until the pots were full of salt. The salt flats attached to the Benue brine springs were owned or controlled by titled men, while the work was done by women. On the larger holdings most of the labour was provided by slaves (Lovejoy, 1986:50-51, 82-86, 107-10, 159-63).

It has been suggested that not much salt was produced from the sea along the East African coast in the nineteenth century because imported salt from Arabia was readily available. But in West Africa salt from sea water was a major source of regional salt consumption. Extraction of sea salt was favourable where rain averages were good, temperature was high, moisture low, and where natural flats existed close to the shore for evaporation. Along the Ghana coast large amounts of salt were produced at Ada, at the mouth of the Volta River. The Ada specialized in fishing and salt making. Each household reportedly had one or two store houses for salt, each containing

50 Danish tons (Sutton, 1981:47). Salt was extracted from the lagoon, which was quite large, when the lagoon was dry before the rains came.

Extraction was controlled by the chief and the priest and priestess concerned with the fetish of the lagoon. They saw to it that extraction did not begin until the lagoon was completely evaporated. Watchmen were placed on the paths leading to the lagoon. Once extraction was permitted anyone could collect as much salt as they wanted. The collectors were expected to pay a portion of their salt as tax to the priest and priestess and the chief. 'So although everyone had access to the salt in theory, most of the salt wound up in the hands of «big men»' (Sutton, 1981:51). The salt was generally collected by slaves, or women and children. Ada salt production dominated the market for salt in parts of Ghana, particularly the north, well into the 1940s. Along the Senegambian coast salt was extracted from both natural and artificial salt pans. Some of the salt deposits were owned by chiefs. Total Senegambian sea salt production in the late nineteenth century has been estimated at 1,000 to 2,000 tons per year (Curtin, 1975).

Through trial and error various communities came to know the most saline plants in their areas. Such plants were mostly found 'in areas of high rains where little natural concentration of salt would take place in the soil... this type of salt production took place in the southern and western parts of Tanganyika. These areas connect with a wider region of plant-ash salts that covers practically all of Malawi, Zambia, Zaire, Gabon, Cameroon and Chad' (Kjekshus, 1977a:102). Among the plants used for salt production were pistia stratiotes, cypreus alternifolius, or papyrus and bulrusa, and water plants like vallisneria and patamogeton. In the Lake Chad region salt was made from many plants, including Salvadora persica, a bush known in kanuri as babul, three varieties of grass called pagani, kalaslim, and kanido, which were found near the lake, and the bush Capparis aphylla, or tundub in Kanuri (Lovejoy, 1986:71). The bushes or grasses were burnt and the ashes placed in a filter. The resulting brine could be used directly in household cooking or it could be boiled in ovens or pots over a fire until it concentrated in crystalline form.

Extracting salt from saliferous soils, which were largely formed from volcanic rock, extensive grass burning or the decomposition of saliferous plants, was relatively simple. In Uvinza the mud was put in a trough, whose bottom was covered with shreds of bark and under which about half a dozen similar vessels were placed. Hot water was poured into the top trough to dissolve the salt, and as the liquid filtered through the other vessels it became clearer. The final contents in the last vessels were collected, boiled and evaporated, leaving a very good white salt (Kjekshus, 1977a:98-102).

Salt mining was a more complex process. Salt mining in ancient times has been reported from the Sinai and the western desert in Egypt (Lucas and Harris, 1962:208-9) and Dankali, Ethiopia, where 'the salt lay in horizontal beds, and ... was dug up with hatchets into smaller pieces' (Pankhurst, 1968:240). In the nineteenth century successive imperial regimes in Ethiopia tried to break the monopoly over salt production and trade by the Muslim Dankalis. This was partly achieved under Emperor Yohannes. Under Menelik the practice was adopted whereby the Muslims and Christians produced and traded the salt during different times of the year. The salt from Dankali was traded throughout northern Ethiopia, carried in large caravans. One estimate from the 1860s suggests that 30 million bars or amoles were sold in the five main northern markets (Pankhurst, 1968:242). Each amole measured about 25 cm long, 5 cm wide and 5 cm thick.

Some of the largest salt mines in the nineteenth century were located in the Sahara and Sahel. The presence of salt in the Central Sudan was the product of geological and ecological change in the region over thousands of years, involving the depositing of salt by the contracting lakes of the Sahara and the occurrence of efflorescence in the Sahel. The main desert sites were in the depressions of Kawar, Bilma, and Fachi, while the greatest salt concentrations in the Sahel were in areas where efflorescence occurred, such as Mangari, the valleys of Dallol Fogha and Dallal Bosso, and the north-eastern littoral of Lake Chad. The different sources produced a wide variety of salts, whose distinctions were clearly understood by the salt producers of the Central Sudan (Lovejoy, 1986:chapter 3).

In the desert sites the techniques of production were relatively simple, thanks to the high rate of natural evaporation. In Kawar, Bilma and Fachi a series of pits of varying sizes were dug and continually dredged so as to allow salt to form on the surface of the water. Once formed, the salt, called beza, was sometimes packaged, or put in moulds of different shapes and made into cones, the largest of which weighed 15 kgs or more and were called kantu, or flat cakes known as kunkuri. The salt was removed from the moulds when it was dry which took several days. In the Air Massif region salt was produced from shallow decantated basins. Salt production was a seasonal activity, affected by the patterns of rainfall and temperature, and the organization of the agricultural economy.

Two forms of labour were mobilized. The more northerly and remote desert sites were worked mostly by slaves who probably numbered in the thousands, while Kanuri peasants worked in the southern ones. The work units normally consisted of four men and an old woman or child. The desert salines were considered private property, as were agricultural land and date trees, so that they could be bought and sold, inherited, and rented. The northern sites were owned mostly by Tabu pastoralists, while the southern ones were in the hands of prosperous Kanuri families. The Tuareg enjoyed special rights of access and tribute, probably secured towards the end of the eighteenth century. Free women could be proprietors and inherit rights to the salines (Lovejoy, 1978b, 1986:115-20, 139-46, 153-8).

Salt production in the Sahel sites was more scattered and elaborate than in the desert sites. The production techniques depended on the type of salt being produced. The production of manda, a group of salts high in sodium chloride, in Mangari and Muniyo required filtering devices, ovens and furnaces. The filtering devices, known as chagadi:

> *were made of braided straw mats placed on three legs which raised the filter off the ground. Sand was used in the bottom of the filter, and pots were placed underneath to catch the brine...The filters helped separate some of the sodium sulphate out of solution, thereby increasing the concentration of sodium chloride and sodium carbonate* (Lovejoy, 1986:67).

The salt-earth collected after the rainy season was placed in the filters, and the concentrated brine was then placed in ovens, which contained from 40 to 170 moulds. The delicate boiling operation lasted 24 hours and required the skills of an experienced person. In contrast, the production of the different varieties of natron, salts high in sodium carbonate and sometimes sodium sulphate, required no sophisticated apparatus. White natron, farin kanwa in Hausa, was simply scraped from the ground or from edges of ponds and lakes, while red natron, jar kanwa, came from the brine in the depressions (Lovejoy, 1986:63-70, 74-82).

Unlike the desert sites, in Mangari, Muniyo, Dallol Fogha and Dallol Bosso the labour force was predominantly made up of free migrant workers, who came in between the agricultural seasons and lived in temporary settlements, known as tunga. The migrant labour system in Mangari probably began in the early nineteenth century, following the dislocations of the jihad in Borno. The work units consisted of ten to 20 people, working under a supervisor. There was a clear division of labour based on gender.

> *Women gathered the salt-earth and carried water, while the men made the filters, moulds, and ovens, boiled the salt, and gathered firewood... At Bilma the separation of tasks was expressed in the right of women to make small blocks (fochi), which consisted of the same mixture of salt as the large kantu which belonged to the women* (Lovejoy, 1986:148-9).

The hired workers were paid a portion of the salt, normally ninety cones each for a seven-month season. The headman or furnace master received over two and half times that. The rest went to the owner. The salt works were ultimately owned by the state, and authority exercised through titled officials, some of whom held as many as five or six different locations (Lovejoy, 1986:120-33, 148-51, 163-76).

Attempts to estimate the total volume of salt production in the Central Sudan are fraught with difficulties because of inadequate data. Lovejoy's (1978:639, 1986:94-114) estimates, probably the most comprehensive to date, suggest that between 8,000 and 19,200 tons were produced in the late nineteenth century. He believes that the Sahel sites produced more salt than the desert sites. Data on productivity from the early twentieth century seems to indicate that the sahel sites were more productive than the desert sites. For example, the annual productivity rates in 1915 were as follows: manda sites of Muniyo and Mangari 4.5 tons per worker; natron sites of Muniyo and Mangari 2.9 tons; Teguidda n'tesent in the Air Massif 1.3 tons; Bilma and Fachi 0.9 tons. This salt was widely traded throughout West Africa, encouraged by the governments of Borno and Sokoto which derived a lot of revenue for taxing the salt trade (Lovejoy:Chapter 8). Thus salt helped facilitate the process of commercial regional integration in West Africa.

The variety of salts produced in the Central Sudan was astonishing. They included 'sodium chloride, sodium sulphate, sodium carbonate, potassium chloride, calcium carbonate, sodium phosphate, potassium sulphate, and calcium sulphate in various concentrations' (Lovejoy, 1978b:633). Each salt had its own market and uses. The culinary uses of the salts were quite specialized. Some were used to flavour and make various meals. Salt consumption betrayed social class, for the purity of the salt used deteriorated the lower people were down the social ladder, since the higher the purity the higher the price. The medicinal uses were also many. Different salts were used to treat stomach ailments, eye disorders, bruises and infections, venereal diseases, ailments associated with pregnancy, and certain diseases connected with children and the elderly. Some were even valued for their ability to treat dandruff and enhance virility. The industrial uses were equally numerous. Certain salts could be used as a mordant in dyeing textiles, tanning hides and dyeing leather, making soap from shea butter, and smelting copper. In addition, salt was given to livestock as feed and medicine (Lovejoy, 1986:15-32).

It is rather strange that Lovejoy (1986:91) should interpret 'the many and varied - indeed often ingenious - uses of salt [as] a direct consequence of ... retarded technology'. The opposite would in fact seem to be the case. Lovejoy's interpretation rests on a spurious equation of sophistication with salt purity and the latter with sodium chloride, and ultimately on a Eurocentric bias of what 'good' salt should be. West African salt producers were making different salts to satisfy their tastes and the diversified demand of the market, using technologies that were most appropriate ecologically and in terms of labour supply and organization.

Conclusion

The importance of mining in many African economies cannot be overemphasized. This chapter has attempted to examine the technologies and techniques used in the production of some of the most essential minerals and metals in African societies in the nineteenth century and before. In addition, wherever the data has allowed, an effort has been made to outline briefly the relations of production which developed. From this analysis, it would appear that labour processes in the mining industry were no less diverse and complex than in agriculture. The regions analyzed have included both the familiar ones and those that are not as familiar. For example, the section on gold production has focused on the well-known cases of West Africa and Zimbabwe, and the more obscure case of Madagascar. As for salt, the discussion has not been restricted to salt that was mined, but has also examined the production of salt from saliferous springs, lakes, the sea and plants. Three main conclusions can be drawn from this chapter.

First, it is becoming increasingly evident that the diffusionist thesis, according to which major technological advances in Africa are attributed to external sources and are seen to have radiated from one or two receiving centres on the continent, was constructed on thin evidence and excessive speculation. For example, it no longer appears that Meroe was the centre of iron diffusion in so-called sub-Saharan Africa, and the correlation between the dispersal of Bantu languages and iron technology has been seriously questioned. The preoccupation with origins tells us little about the development of the actual production processes, which even in cases of imported technologies could not remain frozen forever in their original patents, oblivious to the tinkering hands of multitudes of people across generations. As it can be seen in the case of iron, not only was there considerable variability in the technology used to produce it, the labour process itself differed from one society to another.

Second, the level of technological sophistication and the scale of production is sometimes not fully appreciated by those unfamiliar with African economic history or trapped by the blinds of Eurocentrism. Some of the African iron-producing techniques, for instance, were among the most advanced in the world during their time. The specialized African metal workers were as skilled as any in the world. As for output, it is well to remember that for centuries West Africa and Zimbabwe produced the bulk of the world's gold supply, which propped up the monetary and commercial systems of western Europe and the Indian ocean trading zone, respectively.

Recent estimates of output from some of the major iron, copper, and salt production sites clearly indicate that the volume of production and productivity rates were comparable to similar sites in other pre-industrial societies.

Finally, the question of the durability and decline of African industries has been reassessed and in particular the argument that African industries collapsed the moment they faced European imports has largely been discredited. The process was far more protracted and indeed, it is remarkable that in many parts of the continent the indigenous industries survived for so long after the introduction of imported products. In the case of iron, the argument has been made, the survival or decline of the local industry in the face of imports from industrial Europe depended on a number of variables, including the availability of the productive resources, especially charcoal fuel, the quality of the local product, and the organization of labour. However, the trajectories of survival and decline not only varied from industry to industry, but also from one society to another, so that it may be rather simplistic to advance a single explanatory model.

7. Handicrafts and Industrialization

Textile Production

The antiquity of textile manufacturing in Africa has been attested to by archaeological, written and oral sources. Woven fabrics made in ancient times have been found in tombs in Egypt (Lucas and Harris, 1962:140-9), the Tellem Caves in Mali (Lamb, 1975:Chapter 2), and the tombs of Ingombe Ilede in Zambia (Davison and Harries, 1980:175-7). Literary sources, mainly in Arabic and European languages, concerning the early history and development of African textiles are particularly plentiful for North and West Africa. Thus by the beginning of the nineteenth century the textile industry in Africa was an old one indeed. Its organization defies simple generalization, for its methods of production varied because different raw materials, machinery and forms of labour were used.

An analysis of textile production must begin with an understanding of the various processes involved in the manufacturing of most fabrics, from the harvesting and collection of fibres, to soaking, drying, softening, cleaning, and spinning them, and their reconstitution and elaboration through weaving, dyeing, bleaching, embroidery, applique, and so on (Schneider and Weiner, 1989:20). Machinery was required for spinning and weaving, and special apparatus for dying, embroidery and tailoring. The manufacturing process demanded skill and was time consuming. The fibres employed in the manufacture of cloth in Africa were bark, bast, raphia, silk, wool and cotton (Picton and Mack, 1979:23-48). The fibres can be divided into those that were spun and those that were not.

Bark, bast and raphia were non-spun fibres, while silk, wool and cotton were spun. Spun and non-spun fibres could sometimes be blended. For example, the Berbers of North Africa made their woven rugs by blending wool and goat hair with esparto grass, dwarf palm and rush (Idiens, 1980:8). Bark was felted. The best-known centres of bark cloth production were in the central parts of the continent. The Baganda alone recognized and used fifty varieties of bark cloth. Bast fibres were obtained by retting the stems of certain dicotyledonous plants. Raphia was peeled from the leaves of the raphia palm, of which there were seven varieties in Africa. Its natural habitat is the marsh or swamp, and it thus grew extensively in, and on the fringes of, the tropical forests of west and central Africa, and on the island of Madagascar.

Silk production was mostly restricted to Nigeria and Madagascar where various species of the moth of the genus Anaphe were found. It was obtained from the larvae of these moths, which bred on tamarind trees. These moths mostly bred in the wild, although in parts of northern Nigeria their breeding was encouraged by the cultivation of the tamarind. In many cases the cocoons containing the silk were collected by chance by farmers or hunters. Silk was also imported from Europe and Asia in the form of cloth. The silk cloths were usually unravelled for thread to be used as inlay in other cloths. Wool was mainly harvested from sheep, and, to a lesser extent, from goats and occasionally from camels, especially in North Africa, the Sudan and the Sahel belt of West Africa. The most widely used yarn in the nineteenth century was cotton which was grown locally in many parts of the continent (see Chapter 3).

Weaving was the heart of the textile manufacturing process. Plain colours, particularly white, were very popular in many Muslim-dominated areas. Natural colours varied between and among fibres. For example, cotton occurred naturally both in white and light-brown colour. The principal means of decorating African textiles was dyeing. Sometimes wool and cotton yarn, raphia and, in Madagascar, bast fibres, were dyed before they were woven although in many cases the cloths were dyed after they had been woven. The manufacture and use of dyes was quite a specialized craft. Dye sources varied according to locality but were usually made by the maceration of barks, woods, roots, fruits, leaves, lichens, and sometimes minerals were also used. The colours produced ranged from black, blue and purple, to red, orange and yellow.

Indigo was by far the most frequently used dye in Africa and preparing it was quite laborious. It was obtained from several plants of the genus indigofera, which occurred in the wild or was cultivated. The preparation of the dye involved:

> breaking up plant structure to facilitate the fermentation process; and preparing the alkaline medium, which, in addition to encouraging the release of indigo-blue, also acts as a mordant serving to fix the dye colour in the yarn or cloth, as the case may be (Picton and Mack, 1979:38).

Details of the preparation process of course varied from place to place. The Yoruba, for example, built furnaces of four feet high or five feet wide, to prepare the potash for the alkaline medium. Dyeing was carried out either in large earthenware pots or pits dug in the ground.

The Hausa city of Kano was famous for its dye pits, of which there were an estimated 2,000 by the mid-nineteenth century (Picton and Mack, 1979:40). Northern Nigeria exported its dyeing techniques to some parts of West Africa. For example, in the middle of the eighteenth century a trader and scholar from Bornu introduced dye pits to the town of Daboya, located on the banks of the White Volta. Daboya became famous for its dyeing in nineteenth century Ghana (Goody, 1982:51-3). In order to produce a pattern the cloth was folded, or raphia was tied and stitched to areas of the cloth for resist dyeing. Designs could be varied by tying seeds, stones and sticks into the cloth, or patterns could be painted on freehand or stencilled with a starch resist. The best known practitioners of indigo resist dyeing in Africa were probably the Yoruba, who called their resist dyed cloths adire. The Bambara people of Mali employed an unusual technique of resist dyeing cloth with mud. The procedure involved using a vegetable dye to colour the cloth yellow, after which the cloth was washed to remove surplus mud and the yellow dye was blocked out using caustic soda. 'Analysis has shown that a chemical reaction takes place between tannic acid in the yellow dye, which acts as a mordant, together with iron oxide in the mud solution' (Idiens, 1980:5).

Dyeing was sometimes accompanied by the decorative techniques of painting, printing, applique, patchwork and embroidery. The range of designs and motifs patterned on cloths was as varied as the societies and producers who made them. The decorations had aesthetic, religious, social and functional value. They distinguished cloths for royalty from those for common people; cloths for ordinary wear from those for solemn occasions, such as funerals. The funerary shrine cloths of the Ibibio of south-east Nigeria, for example, were a combination of applique and patchwork (Salmons, 1980:120). Among the Bakuba of Zaire the embroidered cloth was normally a square, and several squares of embroidered cloth would be sewn together in order to create a length sufficient for a wrap-around skirt. Making these embroidered cloths was a laborious exercise. It could take a month or more to complete even a single cloth of no more than a square metre. No wonder embroidered cloth, representing as it did such an extravagant investment of labour, was, for those who used it, a loud proclamation of their wealth and status, a testament that their households had moved beyond the labour demands of subsistence production (Mack, 1980:163-74).

Weaving, and sometimes tailoring, required some apparatus and equipment, which was generally made from local materials, such as wood, bamboo and palm fibres. A wide variety of looms were manufactured and used. Roth (1950) distinguished seven basic types, namely, the 'vertical mat loom', the 'horizontal fixed heddle loom', the 'vertical cotton loom', the 'horizontal narrow band treadle loom', the 'pit treadle loom', the 'Mediterranean or Asiatic treadle loom', and the 'carton loom'. Lamb and Lamb (1980) have revised Roth's typology of African looms and regrouped them into four types. The first category consists of what they call the North Africa types, which include 'tablet looms', 'Mediterranean treadle looms', and 'nomadic and related ground looms'. The second type is the pit loom. The third type is the horizontal narrow strip treadle loom. The fourth group is termed the 'vertical or raphia looms', the 'Nigerian women's vertical looms', and the 'sub-Saharan ground looms'.

'All these types', Lamb and Lamb (1980:25) argue, 'meet somewhere in the general region which is today called Nigeria'. Each of these categories can further be subdivided. For example, there were several types of pit looms in Africa, used mostly in the Sudan, eastern and north-eastern Africa; and at least three types of horizontal narrow strip treadle looms, concentrated in West Africa, namely the non-frame treadle loom, the frame treadle loom, and the fixed-warp treadle loom, each of which can be divided into several varieties, about four for the frame looms, and eight to twelve for the fixed-warp looms. The classification scheme devised by Lamb and Lamb is exhaustive, but marred by that ever-present spectre of Africanist historiography, the tendency to use the Sahara as the historical dividing line. The different looms produced cloths that varied in width and length and texture.

A great variety of cloths were manufactured depending on the yarn, loom, dye and patterning structure used. The cloths produced ranged from woollen blankets, carpets, funerary shrine, to cloths for ordinary dress and silks for royal dress. In Asante, for example, ordinary people wore cotton cloths, normally blue in colour or with white warp stripes. On the other hand, chiefs, court officials and the monarch wore expensive silk cloths. The royal cloths were known as asasia. Asasia patterns were considered most secret, as they were the private property of the Asantehene, the king (Lamb, 1975). The cloth makers of Mutapa in present-day Zimbabwe, produced expensive textiles by weaving 'threads of imported cloth together with locally-produced cotton so as to produce cloths of rich silk, damask and satin laced with gold' (Mudenge, 1988:187).

Once produced, the cloths could be used right away, or they needed to go for tailoring. Most tailoring was done within the household. For more elaborate wear, there were professional tailors in the main marketing centres and towns. Kano, the 'Manchester' of West Africa, was renowned for its tailors. Each ward was famous for particular garments and styles. For example, Soron D'inki, located in the south section of the city 'was first known as a centre for elaborately embroidered gowns and horse caparisons made by a small number of tailors for dignitaries. The jalala [saddle cloth] for which the ward is now famous became a major product only in the second half of the nineteenth century' (Pokrant, 1982:131). Yalwa, which was located in the western section, became known for making Eastern-style gowns, worn by the aristocratic and business elite. Originally Yalwa had been a major centre for long-distance traders, 'among whose imports were

Eastern-style gowns. The technique of making Eastern-style gowns was first introduced during the nineteenth century, and at first was a carefully guarded secret, spreading outside the family of the original tailor only slowly' (Pokrant, 1982:131).

It is difficult to determine the size of the textile industry in nineteenth century Africa, for it is virtually impossible to get production statistics . Estimates based on trade are available only for a few places and with haphazard dates. In any case, such estimates merely give us the barest indications of the size and productive capacity of the industry, for a large proportion of the textiles never entered the market since they were consumed directly by the people who produced them. To be sure, trade in cloths is said to have been 'large', as Aronson (1980) has demonstrated in the case of the Niger Delta. In Kano, it has been suggested, cloth sales amounted to 300 million cowries, or about £E40,000, annually in the 1850s (Hopkins, 1973:48-9). Johnson (1978a:264) has noted that 'in a bad year in the 1880s, some £E80,000 worth of cloth was left in the hands of Bathurst merchants; at about 1s. per square yard, this represents a lot of cloth.'

In many parts of the continent local textiles were often supplemented with imports from other regions and from overseas. Throughout the nineteenth century the flow of imported textiles into Africa increased. Its impact differed from region to region. In some parts of southeast Africa the local textile industry was unable to compete, so that by the end of the century it had declined sharply. This region was among the first to feel the blast of a predatory colonial capitalism. In the lower Zambezi valley, increasingly dominated by the Portuguese :

> *local production of cloths was in opposition to Portuguese imperial economic policy which centred around the Portuguese profits gained by importing Indian cloth to the area. The Portuguese wished to increase Indian cloth imports to Mozambique because this was an important and profitable royal monopoly. According to official policy, local production was to be relegated to the supply of raw cotton for Indian cloth manufacture* (Davison and Harries, 1980:188-9).

Moreover, as the Portuguese tightened their colonial hold over the region not only was labour transferred from cloth production to forced or migrant labour, but many of the traditional uses of handwoven cloth, for example, as currency and tribute, became obsolete. At the same time, clothing customs changed and European dress was increasingly adopted.

Elsewhere local textile production proved more resilient. For example, the production of 'traditional' textiles has persisted to the present among the Kuba of Zaire (Darish, 1989). The West African 'traditional' textile industry has proved particularly durable, having 'survived competition from imported textiles since the first caravans from North Africa began reaching the markets of the southern Sahara well before the tenth century AD ... It still survives today in the face of competition from cheaper Dutch, Japanese, Indian and African factory-made prints' (Lamb, 1975:157). Hopkins (1973:250) has noted that:

> *as late as 1964, when modern textile factories had been established in West Africa, traditional hand-weavers using hand-spun yarn produced about 9,000 tons of textiles, which was roughly a third of total domestic output* (Hopkins, 1973:250).

The survival of indigenous textile manufacturing in the face of competition from imports and modern factory production can be attributed to a number of factors. As might be expected, some anthropologists have come up with arcane explanations. Darish (1989:118) believes that: 'traditional Kuba textiles persist to the present because textile production and use patterns are linked to Kuba ideas regarding social responsibility, ethnic identity, and religious belief'. Feeley-Harnik (1989:74) postulates that among the Sakalava traditional cloth is a medium through: 'which people apprehend ancestors and communicate with them ... [and] ancestors achieve authority over kin and non-kin'.

The ceremonial role of textiles should not be discounted (Okeke, 1979, 1980), but the survival of indigenous textiles cannot be attributed entirely to the sartorial demands of dead ancestors. There are more mundane explanations. They include the high quality of the local product, the proximity of producers to consumers, the nationalist appeal of traditional apparel, and the adaptability of local producers to new techniques, such as the use of factory-made yarn and sewing machines, which have enabled weavers and tailors to cut their production costs and increase their output (Goody, 1982; Pokrant, 1982; Hopkins, 1973:251; Galleti, et.al, 1965:96). Textile manufacturing enjoyed greater durability in many parts of Africa than metallurgy because it was mostly a household activity, unlike the latter which was an extra-household enterprise, whose organizational structure and labour process was the first to be dissolved by colonialism.

Relations of Production

In many societies textile production was a normal household task, although textiles were also produced in relatively large enterprises in the big towns and cities. The divisions of labour in the household often coincided with gender and age. In other, words, different tasks were often allocated to the youth, men and women. The tasks involved in the production of textiles can be differentiated according to skill, from unskilled, to semi-skilled and highly skilled. In most societies age, rather than gender, corresponded with the skill hierarchy in that children normally performed the unskilled tasks, such as washing new thread, and adolescents did semi-skilled tasks, and adults were responsible for the highly skilled chores (Goody, 1982a:66-77, 1982b:24-28). This is to suggest that in most African societies women played a central role in all stages of cloth production. But the allocation of tasks between men and women showed wide variations, thus underscoring the complexity of gender roles in Africa often obscured by those who make generalizations based on one or two societies.

The long task of beating bark fibre in Buganda was normally carried out by men. Among the Yoruba-speaking Owe people of Kabba women specialized in preparing bast fibres, while in Madagascar this was done by men. The extraction of raphia was done by either men or women or both, although among the Kuba its cultivation was an exclusive male activity. In many African societies sheep shearing was done mostly by men, but the preparation of the wool into yarn and the yarn into cloth was done either by men or women. For example, among the Berbers wool was prepared and woven by women, while among the Fulani this was done by men (Picton and Mack, 1979:24; Idiens, 1980:8). Cotton was generally cultivated, gathered, ginned and processed into yarn by women (Idiens, 1980:10; Picton, 1980:66).

As for weaving, it was done either by women, men or by both. In Berber North Africa and Madagascar weaving was only done by women (Picton and Mack, 1979:19). The same was true among the Igbirra people of southern Nigeria (Picton, 1980:63-88) and in the Zambezi valley (Isaacman, 1972:66). Among the Lele of Central Africa men did all the weaving (Douglas, 1965:197, 1967:107-9). Kuba men were also responsible for weaving. In Tunisia where spinning and weaving were generally women's work, men wove only the huge Bedouin rugs, called ktifa. This was, however, restricted to the Hamama province. The male weavers 'travelled from place to place, working on special order. They were the guests of their clients for the duration of their work' (Valensi, 1985:155). In Ethiopia women spun the thread and men wove it. Interestingly, in Ethiopia spinning was held in higher esteem than weaving. This is perhaps because 'ladies of importance, even princesses, treated spinning as a pastime,' while weaving was 'often carried out by minority groups' (Pankhurst, 1968:258-9).

In societies where both men and women wove, they each used different kinds of looms. This was the case, for example, in Arab North Africa, the Sudan and parts of Nigeria. Among the Yoruba and Hausa, women used the vertical mounted single-heddle loom, while men used the horizontal double-heddle loom (Picton and Mack, 1979:67, 114; Aronson, 1980:100-1). It would appear, in fact, that throughout Africa double-heddle looms were used only by men, except perhaps in Madagascar, while single-heddle looms were used either by men or women according to locality (Idiens, 1980:7). Available evidence from some African societies would seem to indicate that men were mostly responsible for making the looms. As noted earlier, among the Igbirra weaving was done by women, but the husband was expected to provide his wife with the single heddle loom that women used and whatever was necessary for her to weave. The loom became hers (Picton, 1980:68).

In many parts of Africa, dyeing was done by women, although in some areas, such as Hausaland, it was done by men. The patterning and embroidery of cloth was undertaken by either men or women. The well-known adinkira cloths of the Asante of Ghana were printed with geometric designs by men using incisive stamps made from pieces of calabash and bamboo combs. Among the Hausa, men did the embroidery on men's clothing, also using geometric motifs (Idiens, 1980:16-20). In contrast, among the Bakuba of Zaire, all embroidery was the work of women, where it was done both by stitching and through the 'cut pile' technique (Mack, 1980:163). Tailoring was done exclusively by either men or women. In Ethiopia tailoring was traditionally men's work. At the turn of the twentieth century these tailors quickly adopted the use of modern sewing machines (Pankhurst, 1968:261-2).

It can be seen that there was a considerable degree of occupational specialization in textile manufacturing which cut across divisions of gender. What was women's specialization in one locality was men's in another. It is important to emphasize that specialization was a product of determinate historical changes. Among the Ibibio of Nigeria, for example, we are told that men were once involved in weaving. This changed after the decline of slave-trading when the men began travelling:

> *far afield in commercial enterprise, while women stayed at home to weave. Once, when a young man who was unable to engage in any commercial activity took up weaving at home, he was ostracized by the community, and when he later died it was said that he had «desecrated the land». Weaving in Akwete had thus become a female craft, protected from male intervention by taboo* (Nicklin, 1980:156).

It has been observed that where men wove cloth they sometimes worked in groups and specialist associations, while women, who almost invariably combined weaving with other domestic tasks, rarely belonged to such associations and tended to work individually in their homes (Picton and Mack, 1979:21). In the coastal regions of Tunisia:

> *weaving was the occupation of permanent craftsmen who were weavers by profession and no longer worked in the fields. Women might spin the*

wool, but weaving shops were outside the home and occupied a separate place' (Valensi, 1985:56).

In the towns and cities, professional textile manufacturers were able to produce far more than those for whom manufacturing was just one more household chore, especially since given the low level of technology, increases in output could only be achieved by lengthening of the working day, product specialization, more intensive work patterns, and the use of extra labour. For example, the typical weaver in Adowa normally produced only three dresses of fine cloth, each worth perhaps 12 dollars, while the 'Addis Ababa weavers turned out about a dollar's worth of cloth every three or four days and obtained a quarter of a dollar's profit per day' (Pankhurst, 1968:260). Needless to say, the pressure of domestic chores adversely affected women's productivity in household textile manufacturing. In Ethiopia, for example, 'a woman engaged in normal household tasks would take three to four months to spin enough cotton for a shamma' or toga (Pankhurst, 1968:259).

Individual households were rarely self-sufficient in terms of the labour, skills, and capital necessary for textile production. Sometimes they had to use their liquid resources to buy the necessary inputs, particularly raw materials and perhaps labour. Wage labour was too expensive for all but the very rich households. Those who could not afford to acquire additional labour sometimes resorted to the incorporation of dependents and slaves, or through the mechanism of inter-household cooperation and reciprocal labour exchange. Some households also had little or no fixed capital for textile production so they were forced to borrow or rent the necessary means of production.

The organization of household craft production, of which cloth making was one activity, varied from society to society. It could be a part-time or full-time activity, seasonal or perennial. As a general rule, craft production in rural areas tended to be seasonal, mostly carried out during the slack period between harvesting and planting, while urban areas supported more permanent establishments. Thus craft production could be either predominantly rural or urban, and primarily meant for household consumption or for sale. In Tunisia, for instance, the textile industry was largely rural, while pottery making was mainly urban. Many Tunisian households produced textiles for their own use, but in the southern oases production was primarily intended for sale and more specialized (Valensi, 1985:153,155,158). In some societies craft manufactures could be made by any household that had the necessary skills and capital, or it could be restricted to a few. Generally, craft production at the household level was small-scale and scattered. It tended to be relatively larger and more concentrated in the households of rulers and state officials and wealthy merchants. In the Sokoto Caliphate, for example, many wealthy merchants owned private estates where both agricultural produce and craft goods were produced both for local consumption and export (Lovejoy, 1973, Tahir, 1975; Pokrant, 1982).

Industrial concentration tended to occur where raw materials were comparatively rare or where they required large amounts of labour and capital to be processed. Industrial concentrations were also a feature of urban centres with large markets and easy access to raw materials, as was the case with the Kano textile industry. In these centres permanent large numbers of craftsmen were clustered along a specific street or square, or they were concentrated in workshops. They were often organized in guilds (Jagger, 1973; Fika, 1978; Shea, 1975), which were common in many parts of North and West Africa. These guilds exercised control over entry to a craft, methods of production, standards of workmanship and prices. In such societies, 'membership of a craft was usually inherited, though it was sometimes possible for outsiders to join a guild once they had completed the apprenticeship' (Hopkins, 1973:49-50). In the more economically-integrated countries and regions the manufacturing process sometimes spread over different towns, which would then be articulated through the market system. This was the case, for example, with many industries in North Africa where 'there was an elaborate division of labour between towns, each of specializing in one particular process' (Issawi, 1980:470).

Crafts and Construction

In addition to mining and metallurgy and textile manufacturing there were other important economic activities and craft industries, some of which historians have tended to ignore. One of them is the processing of staple food and beverages both for domestic consumption and for sale outside the household. Domestic food preparation was of course a daily chore, mainly undertaken by women. It involved pounding and grinding grain, peeling and preparing tubers, fetching water and firewood, as well as cooking itself. The amount of labour time it consumed depended on the diet, size of the household, and the availability of water and energy resources. The marketing of processed food was quite common, especially in urban centres and along major trade routes.

A wide variety of food preservation techniques were used during the nineteenth century. For example, meat, fish and vegetables could be preserved through drying, smoking, and salting. The Khoikhoi, for instance, used to hang meat up to dry after it had been lightly salted. The meat could be eaten without further preparation. This practice was widely adopted by the European settlers, and the meat came to be called biltong (Elphick and Shell, 1989:228; Delegorgue, 1990:34). The brewing of beverages was also usually done by women. Beer, distilled liquor and wine were made from grains, fruits and from other sources, such as cane and palm sap. The Thonga of South Africa made all three types of alcoholic beverages, while the Chagga, Tiv and Azande mostly brewed beer from grain. The apparatus used for distilling liquor was generally more elaborate than that for brewing beer. The social occasions and ceremonies during which the alcoholic beverages were used of course varied from society to society (Washburne, 1961:3-79).

The major products, apart from textiles, included leather, cordage, basketry, pottery, and furniture. Leather goods were made from hides and skins. In West Africa the production of leather goods was concentrated in the savanna belt where the main centres of animal husbandry lay. 'Many of these products were exported and became known in Europe as «Moroccan» leather, though in fact a proportion of the goods passing under this name originated in West Africa' (Hopkins, 1973:49). In Ethiopia a variety of leather goods were produced, including 'saddles, shields, scabbards, cartridge and other belts, sandals, tents, thongs, straps, bags and pouches, sleeping skins, articles of clothing and parchment. Different places were renowned for various types of leatherwork' (Pankhurst, 1968:267). Leather was also used to make shoes, which, however, were worn by only a small fraction of the population.

Cordage involved the making of ropes, with extensive uses. Basketry and weaving were closely interrelated, for they both involved some kind of weaving. There were three basic techniques of making baskets: coiling, twining and plaiting, each of which had its own distinctive techniques and produced varied decorative motifs. The raw materials used included grasses, leaves and fibres from various plants. The products were as numerous as their uses. They included baskets for general use, food baskets, drinking bowls, lidded containers, milk bottles and buttermilk vessels, carrying baskets, baskets for carrying chickens and small mammals, porters baskets, fish traps, drinking bowls, bags, beds, carpets and tents (Sieber, 1980:212-45). These products were produced either by men or women, and sometimes both. In Tunisia basketry was men's work, while in Ethiopia it was women's work (Valensi, 1985:159; Pankhurst, 1968:270).

Pottery provided cooking utensils, containers for storing liquids and foodstuffs and tiles for roofing. Some items, especially those meant for cooking or containing liquids, tended to be fired, while others, such as those for holding grain were dried in the sun. The final vessels were decorated in many ways. Designs could be 'stamped, impressed, carved, punched, rolled, modeled, scratched, scraped, polished or printed' (Sieber, 1980:246). Pottery manufacture was largely limited to women (David, 1972:23) although there were exceptions. Among the Hausa in Sokoto men were responsible for much of the domestic pottery; in Ife terra-cotta and bronze-casting sculpture was in the hands of men; and in Ashanti men made pots which incorporated anthropomorphic and zoomorphic decoration, while all other pottery was made by women (Fagg and Picton, 1970:9-10). The status of potters varied from one society to another. In Ethiopia pottery work was apparently held in low repute (Pankhurst, 1968:277). Centres of production differed as well. In parts of Tunisia ceramics was mainly an urban industry, while elsewhere in North Africa it was largely a rural industry (Valensi, 1985:158-9).

Woodwork and the manufacture of wood products, including furniture, has not received its due attention from historians. More attention has been focused on the production of household implements, such as iron tools, and containers, such as pottery products, than furniture. Furnishings in most ordinary people's homes may have been relatively slight, but not insignificant, and certainly this was no reflection on the skill and dexterity with which the objects were executed. The most important pieces of household furniture were beds and headrests, stools and chairs. The wooden beds were made in various shapes and sizes and could be carved or constructed. The coastal people of Senegal, for example, constructed very high beds, apparently in order to be sheltered from mosquitoes (Sieber, 1980:100). Beds could also be made out of wood, bamboo, raffia and stain, like the Mangbetu did, or modeled out of clay or mud as was common in parts of Cameroon. Headrests used for sleeping could also double up as stools. Stools of course were used for seating. A wide range were made, some were carved from a single block of wood and would be either broadly cubic or cylindrical in shape, others were constructed out of palm, bamboo, wicker and other materials.

Chairs were also made of the same materials. Elaborate chairs of wood and brass tacks, like those made by the Chokwe of Angola and Ngala of Zaire, were used by the wealthy. In Ashanti there was a prestige chair known as asipim. Another elaborate chair was the akonkromfi, made of wood, leather, brass tacks and finials, which resembled 'a praying mantis [and] was reserved for joyous ceremonial occasions' (Sieber, 1980:160). There were also special stools which were associated with the rulers, such Ashanti's famous Golden Stool. Royal stools have also been reported from Bunyoro, Rwanda, and among the Kuba and Luba (Sieber, 1980:108, 125).

Wood was also used to make other objects, including household utensils and vessels, such as boxes, bowls, bottles, trays, plates, spoons, mortars and pestles. Moreover, wood was an important medium for carving sculpture and ritual objects (Fagg, 1970; Horton, 1965). Finally, wood was used to produce drums, boats and canoes. Pastoralists supplemented wood with calabashes to make items such as milk buckets, buttermilk containers, milk storage bottles and fat containers, as well as cups, jugs, beer jars, flour bowls, and food bowls (Sieber, 1980:170-95). The wood carver was almost invariably male. In many societies wood carving was regarded as a specialized craft. In Benin the wood carvers were organized in a guild called igbesanmwan, which was internally differentiated according to age and seniority. 'Carving was done mainly on commission by the Oba and chiefs, although household objects, such as plates, spoons, and mortars, were sold in the market by women of the guild' (Ben-Amos, 1971:71). The carvers worked in their own homes, individually when the work was light, and with the assistance of sons, relatives or other guild members for large and difficult orders. The most significant work was done at the Oba's palace itself which had workshops (Ben-Amos, 1971:78).

Finally, there was the building and construction industry. This is another subject that has been little studied by historians (Oliver, 1971:7-24). Outside of the great monuments, from the Egyptian pyramids to Great Zimbabwe, and the grand buildings of Islamic Africa and Christian Ethiopia (Smith, 1958; Smith 1968; Michell, 1978), historians have not said much about ordinary dwellings, or what others have called 'folk' or 'vernacular' architecture (Rapoport (1969:2, 1980:285-6), or simply 'shelter' (Oliver, 1987:9-10). African dwellings have often been dismissed as 'huts', better studied as primitive art than genuine architecture. The field has largely been left either to archaeologists or anthropologists. The latter are often more interested in the 'signification and symbolization' of 'vernacular shelter' than in the economic history of the building and construction industry (Oliver, 1975; MacEachern, et.al., 1989). There is also a tendency in anthropological studies to project present 'traditional' architectural forms into a timeless past.

There can be little doubt that the provision of housing was an essential economic activity. Housing construction was a product of many factors, ranging from the physical dynamics of climate and site and the availability of materials, technology and labour, to the socio-cultural forces of religion, family structure, kinship and class (Rapoport, 1965:Chapters 2-4; Levin, 1971)). Given that these factors could be articulated in so many different ways, it is not surprising that there was such great diversity in house types in precolonial Africa, up to maybe 5,000 (Oliver, 1971:20). Variations in architectural forms could be found within a single ecological zone. For example, there were 'six representative forms that might be considered as modal for northern Ghana' despite the region's ecological unity (Prussin, 1969:4; Archer, 1971). In the Algerian oases mud and stone houses, vied with cloth and mat tents (Etherton, 1971; Duly, 1979:30-33). Different styles and sizes of houses often reflected the patterns of social status and differentiation.

Space and the nature of the available evidence do not allow a detailed discussion of the processes of construction in nineteenth century Africa. Suffice it to say that a wide range of materials, technologies and forms of labour organization were used. The materials included mud, bricks, stone, wood, grass, bamboo and tents, which were sometimes combined. For example, the rectangular Ashanti houses, with their spacious courtyards, had walls made of timber anchored upright with bamboo fastened horizontally, and plastered with clay. The upper walls were finished with white clay and the lower walls and floors with red clay and polished. Roofing was done using palm leaves (Rutter, 1971:155).

The use of mud as a building material was widespread, although the structural principles employed in its use were quite diverse, partly because soil types were so varied. In the savannah regions of West Africa mud and sun-dried mud bricks were used to produce houses of all shapes, from roundhouses to rectangular buildings; of different sizes, from humble dwellings to palatial homes for the wealthy and powerful and imposing mosques; and for varied settlement morphologies, the dispersed and nucleate. Apart from constructing the walls, mud was also sometimes used for roofing, in lieu of grass, as was the case among the Hausa (Schwerdtfeger, 1971:67). The prevalence of the mud roundhouse has been explained by the fact that 'as a homogeneous material, mud achieves its maximum comprehensive strength when the structure is circular' (Prussin, 1969:30-31).

Stone was used to construct houses in many parts of the continent. Swahili coastal architecture with its rigid rectangular geometry relied on the use of coral stone, which was common on the coast (Garlake, 1966:15-29). Swahili stone houses, with their plastered walls, decorations and mouldings, and coral tile ceilings supported by squared timber rafters, were 'remarkable for their elaborate plumbing devices, ... drainage' and sophisticated bathrooms (Allen, 1979:22,25). They apparently reached a peak of excellence in construction and design in the late 15th or early 16th century, and again in the late 18th and early 19th centuries. The houses were initially single-storeyed; in later centuries additional floors were added (Lewcock, 1971:83; 1978). The standard house had two bedrooms in addition to the main private room. Houses, together with mosques and tombs constituted the basic forms of Swahili stone architecture (Wilson, 1979:43). In parts of Ethiopia houses for the rich and aristocracy, as well as churches, were also built in stone (Gebremedhin, 1971; Lindahl, 1969).

Outside the sphere of the stone-built houses both in the coastal Swahili towns and Ethiopia, there were houses built of timber and mud. Timber-built houses could also be found in other parts of the continent. In Ganvie, Dahomey, not only were all the houses built of timber, but the entire town was built over water, from which its inhabitants derived their livelihood as fishermen. Canoes were indispensable for fishing and transport. This settlement was probably founded in the middle of the nineteenth century, as the land became increasingly salinised and less capable of supporting agricultural activities. In the meantime, 'the changed biological conditions seemed to have made more intensive fishing possible' (Danby, 1971:40). This remarkable town achieved a fascinating integration between residence and work, architecture and ecology.

Grass was widely used for roof construction. Among the Zulu it was used to construct the entire house. Using only grass, leaves and laths, but no nails, wire, string, or planks, the domed Zulu grass house was a product of exquisite craftsmanship. 'Every detail of its construction', an observer enthuses, 'is both functional and artistic. It is an ingeniously constructed house' (Knuffel, 1973:11). It was developed to a high level of perfection following the Shakan revolution. Not only were the houses round, but they were also carefully arranged in circles (Biermann, 1971). Other materials used to make 'woven' houses were bamboo and raffia palms. Using these materials, various peoples in Cameroon's grasslands and highlands constructed 'grand, even extravagant buildings' (Oliver, 1987:100). The people of Chencha and Sidamo in Ethiopia used bamboo to construct hemispherical houses (Gebremedhin, 1971: 116-22).

Tents formed a significant part of African architecture, for they provided shelter to countless numbers of people in the arid and semi-arid regions of North, West and East Africa where pastoralism was the main economic activity. A wide variety of tents were used to make numerous types of dwellings. As cloths, tents provided a link between textile manufacturing and housing construction. So tent dwellers were often adept weavers. One of the most widely used type of tent was the black tent, normally made out of goat hair, of which there were several varieties (Faegre, 1979:9-41; Verity, 1971; Andrews, 1971)). Mat-skin tents were used south of the black tent zones of northern Africa in a narrow band of territory running from Western Sahara to northern Kenya (Faegre, 1979:62-77). Some of the mat tents, such as those of the Boran of East Africa, were strictly not tents, and could better be described as frame-and-mat dwellings (Oliver, 1987:24). As in other dwellings, the allocation and use of space was carefully organized to reflect gender relations and divisions of labour and age hierarchies. Among the Bedouins the floor on the men's side was covered with carpets and mattresses for guests to sit on. The women's side of the tent 'is bigger. It is the living and working area of the tent and is never seen by men other than the tent owner in accord with the traditional separation of the sexes and seclusion of women' (Faegre, 1979:23).

The construction of houses involved the use of unskilled and skilled labour. Co-operative effort among household members was essential. Women played a critical role in both the construction or production of living space and in its maintenance or reproduction. Among the Zulu the different grasses and plants needed for the construction of the house were gathered by women, who also wove and plaited the grass covering, while the building of the framework was the duty of men (Knuffel, 1973:13,16; Biermann, 1971:100). In Northern Ghana women were responsible for the surfacing and decorative treatment of walls, 'perhaps because the ingredients used [were] those normally falling within the domestic domain' (Prussin, 1969:115). Women's responsibilities for the construction and maintenance of housing was probably greater in pastoral societies. Among the Maasai, for example, each married woman, assisted by her children, was expected to construct her family's house, which was recognized as her own property (Rigby, 1985:147; Oliver, 1987:66-69). Among the Tekna people of southwest Morocco the work of pitching and striking tents was largely women's work (Andrews, 1971:137).

Housing construction often required labour and skills beyond what the household itself could provide. Many building tasks, such as prefabrication of a roof, which would then be transported to the house and hoisted in place, needed co-operative effort. Thus co-operation among households was quite necessary. In the Swahili towns there was a high degree of co-operation in planning and construction. 'All adjoining houses', Garlake (1966:89), has observed, 'invariably share a single common party wall... Moreover, in almost every case, where houses adjoin, the plans interlock rather than simply abut one another, making for compactness of economy and building...[This] entailed complete co-operation and joint planning from the start, followed by simultaneous building'. Public buildings, such as mosques and churches, were usually constructed through the mobilization of various forms of communal and forced labour. It has been argued that some of the great Swahili buildings were clearly designed by architects, rather than simply built by artisans and master builders' (Garlake, 1966:12-13).

Pre-colonial Industrialization Drives

The various industries examined above had taken a long time to develop. The level of industrial development within Africa was quite uneven, and so was that between the continent and parts of the world, especially western Europe. These patterns of uneven development deepened in the course of the nineteenth century as the processes of industrialization unfolded. With a few exceptions, African countries hardly made any attempts to industrialize. The exceptions included Egypt and Madagascar. Both countries' industrialization drives were launched at the same time as in Western Europe and North America. Also, they were inspired by local enterprise and interests and involved large-scale factory machine-based production. Both ultimately failed. Three sets of questions can be raised: why did these countries embark on industrialization, why did they fail, and what were the consequences of failure? Let us begin with the better known case of Egypt.

At the beginning of the nineteenth century Egypt's manufacturing industries, like those of other parts of North Africa, were threatened by European competition. Factories in Western Europe 'were pouring out cheap goods, and peace and increased security in the Mediterranean and improvement in shipping made it possible to land them at low costs. To this should be added the effects of the various commercial treaties which froze import duties at low levels and opened up the region's markets' (Issawi, 1982:151). Muhammad Ali's regime made the first and most vigorous attempt to modernize Egyptian industry by establishing modern factories. But historians are not agreed on the regime's motivations. Some see Muhammad Ali as a modernizer who saw industrialization as a prerequisite for economic development. It is said that he wanted to establish a modern industrial state comparable to those then emerging in Western Europe (Owen, 1969: Chapter 1). Others emphasize that his major objective was military rather than economic development per se. According to this view, Muhammad Ali wanted to have a strong military and he gave special care to industries related to the army and navy (Mabro and Radwan, 1976:10-11).

It is futile to try and single out one or two factors behind Muhammad Ali's industrialization drive. Certainly attempts to attribute it to Muhammad Ali's own personal predilections are unhelpful. The industrialization drive was part of broader transformations occurring in Egyptian society. As Gran (1979) has shown, these transformations were triggered by a conjunction of internal and external factors, including the recomposition of the ruling class and realignment of local class forces, and the integration of Egypt into the world market. From the mid-eighteenth century, the ruling class composed of the Mamluk elite and the rich merchants, most of whom were foreign, faced growing challenges, not least of which was the breakdown of the tributary system, and the growing assertiveness of the indigenous Egyptian lower middle classes, composed of the local merchants, ulama and artisanal elite, and the increasing restiveness of the urban lower classes. The French invasion of 1798 not only accelerated these internal changes, but also concretized Egypt's incorporation into the emerging world capitalist market, a process that had a far-reaching impact on internal developments. Accompanying and reflecting these transformations was the religious and cultural ferment and revival of the late eighteenth and early nineteenth centuries.

Muhammad Ali's regime was brought to power by the Egyptian middle classes, who were tired of corrupt and repressive foreign rule. In order to destroy the power of the old ruling class and establish a new ruling elite, as well as to meet the challenge posed by European competition, Muhammad Ali's regime embarked upon a programme of economic modernization directed by the state. In short, to quote Zaalouk (1989:1), 'when Muhammad Ali came to power, private enterprise could hardly be depended upon. For any economic progress to take place the state would have to take charge of productive activity. This it attempted to do, creating both a landed aristocracy and a bourgeois entrepreneurial class'.

The industrialization drive underwent three stages. The first stage lasted from 1816 to 1818 and was characterized by the imposition of a government monopoly upon a number of existing craft guilds, beginning with the textile industry . The government supplied the artisans with the raw materials and bought the finished products, both at fixed prices. This policy enabled the government to increase revenues, but it was unpopular with both consumers and producers. As a result of either popular opposition or growing government self-confidence the second phase was launched between 1818 and 1830. The government itself set up factories. Machinery and supervisors were brought from abroad. Once the factories were operational, the government banned the existing craftsmen from conducting their trades. This gave it a monopoly which enabled it to sell its products while at the same time securing labour from the now redundant craftsmen although many master craftsmen preferred to retire to the countryside rather than work for a daily wage in the new mills.

The third phase was essentially a period of consolidation during which very few new factories were funded, and 'efforts were devoted to increasing Egyptian participation in industry, at the expense of foreigners who had hitherto been of great importance as technicians and advisers. At the same time the severity of the monopolies enjoyed by the state was relaxed; private citizens were permitted to engage in various crafts in competition with the state factories, upon payment of a substantial monthly tax' (Barbour, 1972:43).

The capital invested in these industries was obtained from the government's monopoly of internal and external trade and from taxation and forced loans (Issawi, 1963:23). Issawi (1980:471, 1982:154) believes that by 1838 an estimated £E12 million had been invested in the industrial establishments. The true figure may never be known. What is certain is that enormous resources were invested in constructing factories and importing machinery.

As Mabro and Radwan (1976:16) put it, 'Muhammad Ali did not attempt to industrialize on the cheap'.

The industries were located throughout the country, with concentrations in Cairo, Alexandria, and Roda island. Attempts at industrial dispersal were made even within individual industries. For example, different centres specialized in the processes of spinning, weaving, dyeing, and indigo processing (Barbour, 1972:38-43). The industries covered a wide range of productive activities, but were mainly devoted to the production of consumer goods, especially textiles and foodstuffs. In addition, there were factories producing iron, weapons, paper and glass, and chemical products. The only attempt to produce modern capital goods was in the textile industry, in which almost all the equipment required was made in Cairo.

There is no reliable data on the number of industrial workers employed. The estimates range from 30,000 (Issawi, 1980:471, 1982:154) to 60,000-70,000 (Mabro and Radwan, 1976:16), and 260,000 (Barbour, 1972:38-39). Whatever the correct estimate, there can be little doubt that the majority of industrial workers were employed in textile factories. Most of the unskilled labour was conscripted and paid low wages, while the technicians were mainly foreigners attracted by high wages. Labour control was coercive and authoritarian. The workers of course reacted and protested. 'Contemporary observers reported many unexplained explosions and other acts of industrial sabotage. And... the urban crime rate rose noticeably' (Gran, 1979:121).

The products of the factories found their market in the armed forces, through import substitution, and by displacing some handicrafts. By the early 1830s, we are told, 'the domestic textile industry had succeeded in eliminating imports of low quality cotton cloth and Indian muslims' (Mabro and Radwan, 1976:16). Some industrial goods were exported, for example, dyes and cotton yarn to Turkey and Europe. Thus, some of the industries produced goods of high quality, and their standards of management were quite high. The best managed and most successful industrial enterprises were reportedly the naval arsenal and the armament factories in Alexandria and Cairo.

Egyptian industries were held back by a number of constraints, which ultimately aborted the industrialization drive. To begin with, the internal market was small because per capita incomes were low. In addition, the market had almost no protection against foreign competition. Egypt, which was then formally under Turkish rule, was bound by Anglo-Turkish treaties and conventions, which upheld free trade and limited duties on British imports to 3%. Moreover, there were shortages of local raw materials, except cotton, as well as energy and capital. Egypt imported most of its coal from Europe at considerable cost. Attempts to use wind and animal power did not go far, while the development of water power, by digging canals and setting up cotton mills beside the first cataract at Aswan, for example, was hindered by the high costs involved. Consequently, the costs of production in Egypt were higher than in Europe.

Most of these constraints by themselves would not have led to the collapse of the industrial experiment. The decline began in the 1840s. 'One after the other', Crouchley (1938:74) has written, 'the factories were abandoned. A few years later, all that remained of the vast industrial structure, which had cost millions to erect, was a quantity of rusting machinery in old, deserted buildings scattered here and there throughout the country. The attempt to make Egypt an industrial country had failed'. The failure is usually attributed to the Anglo-Turkish Treaty of 1838, the latest in a long series of agreements which promoted the interests of European industry in the region (Marsot, 1984). This treaty abolished state monopolies and prohibited any attempt by the state to promote industrialization. The treaty also gave British merchants the right to enter any part of the Turkish dominions and purchase raw materials without restriction. Furthermore, the treaty reduced the size of the Egyptian army which deprived local industry of a vital market. According to Okyar (1980:152), the fatal blow to the experiment came from 'the Ottoman government [which] was interested in attacking the economic and financial bases of Mehemet Ali's military power, and the British government [which was] intent upon imposing free trade throughout the Middle East in order to expand its markets'.

What is often ignored is the possibility that the collapse of Egyptian industrialization reflected a shift in the social forces that originally shaped and sustained the experiment. Some of the very social classes, particularly the indigenous middle classes, that had initially supported industrialization as part of the offensive against the old ruling class, now hindered it, either because they had joined the ruling elite as landlords and big merchants, or they had become alienated from the regime because they had been left behind. In either case, deepening the process of industrialization did not necessarily promote their class interests. Indeed, state monopoly, on which the industrial experiment was based, increasingly came to be seen as an obstacle to their chances for further accumulation in agriculture and commerce, sectors in which the Egyptian bourgeoisie preferred to invest.

The expansion of the agrarian export economy, in fact, reinforced the trend towards deindustrialization. In order to service this economy, as will be demonstrated in Chapter 13, the state was forced to build and expand the transport and communications infrastructure. This cost a lot of money, which the state did not have. So it started borrowing heavily both locally and from abroad. As Egypt's indebtedness mounted, prospects for investment in industry diminished. By 1900 Egypt's public debt was estimated at £E116.6

million, up from £E98.4 million in 1880. Over 30% of the country's export revenues went on debt repayments. Another large chunk was repatriated in the form of profits on foreign investment. Altogether, '5 or 6% of Egypt's national income was taken away and little was left for domestic investment' (Mabro and Radwan, 1976:20).

From the 1840s Egypt entered the road to deindustrialization as the state, which has historically played a critical role in all 'late' industrializing countries, was reduced to an impotent bystander as the creaking industrial locomotive decelerated sharply. Egypt developed a typical dependent economy, primarily agrarian and export-oriented. The remaining small and narrowly-based industrial sector was foreign-owned and geared to the elementary processing of the export crop, king cotton. For example, by 1899 there were 63 companies operating in Egypt. Their combined capital totalled £E17.6 million. Thirty-three of these companies, with capital amounting to £E15.5 million, were wholly or mostly foreign-owned. And 'more than half the locally owned companies in fact belonged either to Jewish bankers or to foreign cotton merchants resident in Cairo or Alexandria' (Barbour, 1972:57).

The British occupation of Egypt in 1882, which was partly an outcome of the country's growing economic and political crisis, itself spawned to some extent by previous British and French activities in Egypt, hammered one additional nail into the coffin of industrial failure. Under British rule the colonial state showed little interest in fostering manufacturing, either through public or private capital. 'On the contrary, the complete absence of protection against foreign competition, together with the imposition of an excise duty of 8% on local products discouraged domestic enterprise' (O'Brien, 1966:42). The Egyptian pattern was to become all too familiar in twentieth century colonial Africa.

The industrial experiment in Madagascar is far less well known. It was attempted by the Merina state between 1820 and 1861. By the beginning of the nineteenth century the base for the industrial experiment existed, 'the intensive agricultural economy was productive, the market system was well developed, and the scale of iron and craft manufacturing was considerable. And the state was determined to pursue a programme of industrialization' (Campbell, 1986, 1987, 1988b, 1991). It has been suggested that 'the Merina crown was pushed into the role of industrial entrepreneur' by the fear of foreign invasion, failure to get foreign investment, the weaknesses of the local merchant class, and the drop in state revenues due to the decline of slave exports, the main export item (Campbell, 1991:531). The state was buoyed by the successes already achieved in agriculture and intended to develop the economy further, and at the same time increase its own revenues,

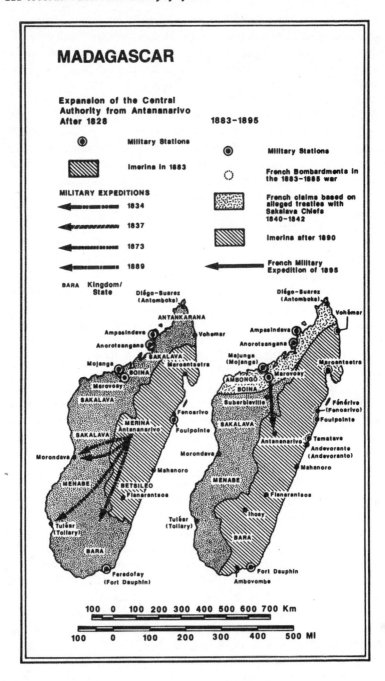

by promoting industrial and commercial growth. The industrialization drive would be based on the mobilization of local resources, principally labour, and the adoption and adaptation of European techniques and technology. Primary emphasis would be placed on the production of textiles and armaments. In order to protect the infant industries tariffs would be raised and foreigners would be restricted to designated coastal ports.

The Merina state was faced with a dilemma, which eventually helped abort the industrial experiment. Given the gross inadequacy of capital, whether local or foreign, the industrialization programme could only be undertaken by investment of human capital. This involved transferring labour from the food agricultural sector to manufacturing and the plantation sector. The latter was expected to produce cash crops for export to finance, and provide raw materials for, manufacturing. Plantations of sugar, coffee, cloves, spices, vanilla, coconuts and mulberry bushes to produce silk were established. Altogether, it has been estimated that about 35% of the Merina work force was transferred 'from agriculture to unremunerated industrial employment' (Campbell, 1991:526). Transferring such a large proportion of the labour force to the industry undermined the agricultural system as a whole, which was the base of the Merina economy, and made it increasingly difficult to sustain the industrial experiment.

This required extreme state coercion. An intensive regime of labour exploitation was established, whereby the state instituted a monopoly on labour, a move that was 'facilitated by the existence of domestic institutions and ideologies designed to create a geographically concentrated and servile workforce', such as fanompoano, or compulsory labour, exacted from 'free subjects', caste based work units, and slavery (Campbell, 1991:532-4). Thus the state had access to the unremunerated or cheap labour of tens of thousands of people. While this cut production costs, it depressed per capita incomes and local purchasing power.

For skilled manpower, the state turned to foreign technical personnel and Malagasy-trained workers at home and abroad, especially Britain and Mauritius. Schools were encouraged and built with fanompoano labour. In 1824 the state took over the three mission schools established two years earlier and established new ones. By 1828 there were one hundred schools. Industrial trade schools were also established. So successful was the education drive that by 1835 the literacy rate in Imerina was 'probably over 7%' (Campbell, 1991:536). The schools did not merely train future workers, they also sought to impart the ideology of loyalty to the state, and docility and discipline. Training did not necessarily translate into adequate remuneration. From 1828 a free skilled craftsman could theoretically be hired at $0.08 a day, double the rate for an unskilled workman. The costs of salaries paid to foreign artisans were defrayed 'not from the treasury but through imposing extraordinary taxes upon the Merina populace' (Campbell, 1991:541). Thus the state tried to minimize the costs of wages, as well as education and skill formation in its industrialization drive.

A number of factories were established to produce a wide range of manufactured goods. The first textile factory was set up in 1824 with '40-50 females from the sewing groups established amongst female students in the Royal Academy' (Campbell, 1991:542). Factory textiles were relatively expensive and it was difficult for them to compete with those produced in households. In order to increase the competitiveness of factory production the state decided to benefit from the economies of scale that could be provided by the establishment of a huge water-powered textile factory that could produce up to 5,000 cotton pieces a year. The idea was abandoned following the French invasion of the north east coast, and an armaments factory was built instead. Factory textile production continued to be small-scale.

Four armaments factories were set up. In subsequent years factories were established to produce soap, paper and leather and other products. By 1850 the largest industrial complex was at Mantasoa, whose five factories and numerous workshops employed 5,000 workers. These factories had 'blast furnaces, which could smelt far larger quantities of iron ore more efficiently than the traditional small scale bellow furnaces... The complex specialized in the manufacture of muskets and cannon, but also produced swords, gunpowder, grape-shot, copper, steel, lightening-conductors, glass, pottery, tiles, silk, a variety of cloths, candles, lime, dye, white soap, paper potassium, processed sugar into sweets and alcohol, and tanned leather' (Campbell, 1991:546-7).

Despite the apparent successes, all was not well with the industrial experiment. Production was not large enough to meet domestic demand, so that both household production and imports were tolerated by the state. The export of manufactures proved an elusive goal. Malagasy products, including sugar, were not competitive in the regional or European markets. The advantage of low labour costs was more than cancelled by high transport costs. The transport system was poorly developed, partly because of insufficient resources, and partly out of strategic considerations. It was feared that transport improvements would aid foreign conquest (Campbell, 1980). Thus while improvements in transport and communications sunk Egypt deeper into debt, which helped derail the industrialization drive, in Madagascar lack of such improvements imposed major restrictions upon the volume and speed of freight carried which undermined the industrial experiment.

More fundamental, perhaps, was the problem of labour. The coercive labour system, upon which both plantation agriculture and manufacturing production were based, institutionalized, first, low wages and, second, desertion as a mode of labour protest. The first depressed, as mentioned earlier, per capita incomes and undermined domestic market demand, so that only the state and a tiny elite provided an effective market for manufactured products. Exports, as already noted, were hampered by relatively high transport costs. The second subverted production and productivity. Desertion and flight were not confined to the manufacturing industries, they also affected the plantations. Artisans abandoned their trades and peasants their land to avoid conscription into fanompoana, to the great detriment of the rural economy, which ultimately foreclosed opportunities to extend and deepen the industrialization process.

Together with high infant mortality, flight from fanompoana contributed to Imerina's population decline, which reduced the labour pool and made coercion more necessary. 'The decline in the population of Imerina is reflected in the fact that the number of Merina males registered for fanompoana fell 86.31 per cent from 400,000 during the 1830s to 54,750 by 1869' (Campbell, 1991:558). Industrial sabotage was another form of protest resorted to by the disgruntled workers. For example, in 1853 two factories were set on fire (Campbell, 1991:555). By the 1860s it was clear that the industrial experiment was doomed to failure.

Conclusion

The history of crafts in Africa has tended to be written by art historians rather than by economic historians. But the production of textiles and other crafts was a major branch of the precolonial economy and requires closer scrutiny and research. This chapter has made some tentative efforts in that direction. It has described the technical processes involved in textile production in various parts of the continent and has briefly looked at the making of such products as leather, cordage, basketry, pottery and furniture. Another subject that has also not received enough attention from economic historians is the construction industry. Historians have been more fascinated by the grandeur of monumental structures than the prosaic and continuous activities of building and providing shelter for ordinary people. This chapter has outlined the wide range of materials and technologies that were used in the construction industry. More research is required to unravel more fully the changes that undoubtedly took place in the production processes of textiles and crafts, as well as the building and construction industry.

An attempt has also been made to sketch the relations of production within households, workshops, and communities. Particular attention has been drawn to the gender division of labour, which underscores, once again, the need to avoid specious generalizations, for what was women's work in one society was men's work in another. Trying to decipher the changes that occurred in these relations is far more difficult and needs further research.

As with mining, it has been shown that in many parts of the continent the textile industry proved more resilient in withstanding foreign competition than has sometimes been recognized. The survival of local textile manufacturing well into the twentieth century was a tribute to the high quality of the local products, their sartorial appeal, and the innovativeness of the producers, among other factors. We need to know more about the fate of the other craft manufactures, not as relics of some eternal tradition fascinating to cultural anthropologists and art historians, but as viable economic activities.

This chapter has gone beyond chronicling the 'traditional' craft industries and tried to examine some of the attempts that were made to initiate industrialization, or to embark on what some scholars have called 'proto-industrialization', a transitional phase between rural-based handicraft manufacturing and modern industrial production (Mendels, 1972; Kriedte, et.al., 1981; Coleman, 1983). The case of Egypt is well-known. The country launched a drive to industrialize from the early nineteenth century. It is now becoming quite clear that Egypt was not the only country that did that. As well as Madagascar, there were a few other attempts. For example, in Ethiopia Menelik spearheaded a 'modernization' drive towards the end of the century. Similarly, the new commercial elite in West Africa, discussed in Chapter 14, tried to 'modernize' their societies and economies. These attempts largely failed or were aborted. The cases of Egypt and Madagascar analyzed in this chapter demonstrate that the reasons for this varied. In the case of Egypt foreign intervention played a critical role, together with the transformations in the class basis of the Egyptian state, and the changing accumulative interests of the bourgeoisie and middle classes. For Madagascar foreign intervention seems to have played a less decisive role than problems associated with labour mobilization and control. The consequences of failure were essentially the same. Both countries were increasingly integrated into the world economy as exporters of primary products and importers of manufactured goods. In the end they were colonized, which further diminished their prospects for industrialization.

8. The Beginnings of Colonial Industrialization

This chapter focuses on three areas where the beginnings of colonial industrialization were set to become entrenched well into the twentieth century. South Africa and West Africa saw mining, particularly of precious stones and other metals, form the basis of industrial development. In Algeria, craft industries and other manufacturing works were run down in favour of control over the country itself. In fact the colonial economy was forced to remain as only a primary product-producing one, where independent industrialization was in some cases actively discouraged.

Mining in South Africa

The colonial mining industry in South Africa began in 1852 when a Cape firm began mining copper in Namaqaland, a remote western part of the Cape Colony (Innes, 1984:21). This venture made little impact. Far more significant was the discovery of diamonds in 1867, followed by gold in the 1870s and 1880s. The mineral discoveries, or the 'mineral revolution' as some historians refer to it, profoundly altered the political economy of the country that eventually became South Africa. It transformed the country from a poor backwater into the leading economy on the subcontinent. As it will be demonstrated in Chapter 15, the mineral revolution led to the extension and consolidation of colonialism in South Africa itself, and the sub-region, and the full incorporation of the country into the world capitalist system. In this chapter our focus will be on the growth of the mining industry itself, and the role played by the colonial state in facilitating its development, and how the industry, in turn, strengthened the state itself, giving it the resources required to conquer the remaining independent African states and to mobilize African labour for the mining industry and settler farming.

The diamonds were discovered in a place that later became known as Kimberley . The diamond industry underwent three phases. The first lasted between 1867 and 1873 and was dominated by small independent capitals. Company production rose to prominence during the second phase from 1874 to 1885. The third period, 1886-1902, saw the emergence of monopoly production and control in the industry. Each of these phases was characterized by different forms of organization and social relations of production. The last two represented temporary resolutions of the struggles and contradictions arising out of each of the preceding phases.

When the diamonds were discovered thousands flocked to Kimberley to dig their fortunes. Each digger worked his claim independently. They would sink pits or cut sloping adits. The broken ground would be lifted to the surface where the rocks were broken up with shovels and then passed through sieves twice and sorted (Wheatcroft, 1985:35-37). The claim holders included both Europeans and Africans. Out of the 757 men and women who owned the four mines that made up the diamond fields in 1875, 120 were African (Turrell, 1982:47).

The main problem facing the diamond producers was labour. Many African communities had not yet been conquered . Those that had were peasantries still with ample access to land and other productive resources, so that their need for wage labour was limited. It was partly for this reason that the white claim holders, many of whom worked as share-workers in the mines, sought to exclude their black counterparts; they wanted to turn them into labourers. Also, the Africans offered stiff competition because their production costs and living expenses were lower than those of the European diggers who came from afar. The former were accused of pilfering and promoting illicit diamond buying.

Many of the diggers did not make money. There were as many as 3,600 at one time. By 1875 the pressures on the European share-workers had become intolerable. They constituted the rank and file of the Diggers Association, which was led by the claim owners. In June 1875 they erupted in the Black Flag Rebellion. Following the rebellion the Association launched a campaign against the African claim owners. Henceforth, they were to be confined to compounds and prohibited from holding claims, while the white workers would be cantoned in a separate suburb (Turrell, 1982:50-57; Innes, 1984:24-25; Wheatcroft, 1985:38-39, 54-60). Thus began the industrial colour bar and the systematic regulation of the black labour force through compounding. It is significant that the first compounds were built simultaneously with those for convict labour brought to work on the mines. It underscored the fact that the compounds were designed and seen as prisons. There was opposition to the compounds from merchants, especially liquor traders and dealers, who feared losing access to the workers as customers. In response to these concerns the compounds were left open. This was later to change (Turrell, 1982:64-67).

Pressures, both technical and financial, soon mounted to force the amalgamation of the diamond-fields. It became increasingly difficult to mine the pits separately at the huge open cast mines as if they were smallholdings. Indeed, as the diggings got deeper the costs of mining increased sharply. Intense competition among diggers simply maximized output and pushed prices downwards. All this forced diggers to form companies in order to cut and spread the costs of production and raise prices. The trend towards capital concentration in the industry was accelerated by the crash of the world diamond market brought about by the global depression of 1873. By the end of 1874 the diamond fields were on the verge of collapse. The large companies and diamond buyers bought out as many claims as they could.

The number of claims on the Kimberley mines was reduced to 71 by 1881 (Innes, 1984:31). Four years later there were only 15 companies and 11 private holdings (Wheatcroft, 1985:94, 104). Consolidation of claims and company formation allowed mechanization of the labour process. This, in turn, increased the need for skilled labour, which was imported from Europe, which 'ensured that gradually the division of labour based on skills became racially demarcated' (Innes, 1984:32). Meanwhile, shortages of local labour continued, with the result that wages went up. The newly formed companies began investigating ways of controlling and disciplining African labour. One device was to increase the use of convict labour. Another was to create stronger companies that could effectively counter labour's demands and struggles. The large companies that emerged raised production to unprecedented levels. Competition among them was fierce. The result was overproduction, which, coupled with the speculative boom that the amalgamations had created, led to the share market crash of 1886.

This debacle intensified the trend towards concentration and centralization of capital in the industry. Soon two giants were left to battle it out. One was the De Beers Company of Cecil Rhodes and the other was the Kimberley Central Diamond Mining Company of Barney Barnato. Rhodes had arrived in Kimberley in 1871, and began digging on his brother's claims, before branching out into other enterprises, including pumping water and selling ice. Barney Barnato came in 1873, also following a brother, and started his business with a little cash and 40 boxes of cheap cigars. The other major Randlord was Alfred Beit who came in 1875 as a diamond buyer. The 1880s were marked by economic war between Rhodes and Barnato for the control of the industry. Rhodes, assisted by the Rothschilds banking group, eventually won, and in 1888 formed De Beers Consolidated Mines Ltd. With this victory not only was the diamond industry firmly integrated into international finance capital, but the stage was also set for the restructuring of production and the labour process.

De Beers became the largest company in South Africa. It dominated the South African and world diamond market, although its hegemony in South Africa was contested in the 1900s, following the discovery of new diamond fields out of its areas of control (Innes, 1984:34-35). De Beers immediately cut production by 40% and diamond prices rose by 50%. Over 3000 workers, 92% of them African, were retrenched. Wages were reduced to between 7s.

6d. to 15s. per week plus food and accommodation. Altogether, production costs were cut by half (Doxey, 1961:19; Kallaway, 1974:12; Simons and Simons, 1969:43). A determined assault on African labour had began. The compound system was strengthened.

In 1886 De Beers began closing the compounds. African workers went on strike, but to no avail. Thus the compounds became overcrowded, unsanitary and enclosed barracks, which ensured almost total isolation of the workers. The possibilities of desertion or theft were reduced. Regimentation allowed the employers to control the workers more effectively, minimize laxity and increase production. Moreover, employers could divide and manipulate the workers and monitor their organization and resistance. The compound stores where the workers purchased extra food and other supplies gave the mineowners sources of extra revenue, and helped to tie the workers into a web of indebtedness (Van Onselen, 1976, 1982a, 1982b). Finally, through compounds the ideology of African subordination and inferiority could be constructed and reproduced on a daily basis (Bozzoli, 1981:72-74).

These conditions did little to attract labour, so that as the industry expanded, the problem of labour shortage became more acute. Labour market intelligence was disseminated through the networks of oscillating migration, through which workers knew which mines to avoid. Desertions continued and persisted well into the 1910s (Jeeves, 1985:165-9). Strikes also occurred from time to time, especially as the workers became more dependent on their jobs as their access to productive resources declined. In April 1887 African miners went on strike against the use of 'the speculum, an instrument for anal examination of workers as they came off shift' (Wheatcroft, 1985:109). Exploitation and managerial control was contested through theft and violence against employers or property, and absenteeism due to self-inflicted injuries or drunkenness. The workers formed various types of associations, based on either ethnic, occupational or residential solidarities or social and recreational interests (Van Onselen, 1982b). In short, they sought to remake the world the mine owners had made for them.

The emergence of De Beers as a monopoly and the restructuring of production that ensued put the diamond industry on firmer foundations. South Africa became the largest diamond producer in the world. By 1901 Kimberley had produced £E100 million worth of diamonds (Lenzen, 1970; Horowitz, 1967; de Kiewet, 1957; Lanning with Mueller, 1979). De Beers, and diamond capital in general, played a key role in the financing and organization of the 'second' mineral revolution, the discovery of gold in the impoverished Boer republic of the Transvaal.

The discovery of gold is conventionally dated to 1886. The process began much earlier, however in 1867, the same year diamonds were discovered. In that year 'old workings were found on the banks of the Tatie river... This rediscovery led to further prospecting and in 1871 gold was struck in the eastern Transvaal' (Wilson, 1972:14). A temporary gold rush ensued. It was not until 1886 that the main reef was found and the South African Rand was born. The quality of the reefs was poor, but their quantities were vast and uniformly distributed over a wide range (Johnstone, 1976:13-20). These geological facts were to have profound consequences for South Africa. They were exploited by the mining companies to promote, quite successfully, the notion that mining in South Africa carried great uncertainty and risk so that it could only be done if costs were low. This was translated into a campaign for low wages and taxes and other privileges (Jeeves, 1985:8).

The truth was far more complicated. The mining companies identified the viability of the industry as a whole with the lowest grade ores. Exploiting such ores required considerable costs in equipment, so to make the venture profitable the cost of the other factor, labour, had to be lowered, especially since the price of gold was fixed which left no room to manipulate market prices. By lowering labour costs, the mining companies intended to lower the pay limit, that is, 'the point at which ore can be mined profitably. The lower the pay limit, the more ore becomes available in the reserves for profitable production and the longer the mine's lifespan; conversely, the higher the pay limit, the less ore is available in reserves and the shorter the life of the mine. Thus if costs are kept low the pay limit will be low and there will be a greater potential for long-term profitability' (Innes, 1984:49). Thus a low cost structure was intended to increase and prolong the profitability of the gold mines, which, in turn, would prove attractive to foreign capital.

By the early 1890s the existing gold mining companies realized that the capital available to them was inadequate to embark on the large-scale development of deep level mining. They needed to attract foreign capital. Deep level mining involved sinking vertical shafts and horizontal tunnels, stopes, and haulages. It was an immensely difficult and technically complicated process (Wilson, 1972:16-20). Separating gold from the quartz required hitherto unused techniques. Both problems were solved in the 1890s by mining engineers. A diamond drill borehole was invented that could sink ever deeper shafts. In 1892 one was sunk 2343 feet, or 714 metres (Innes, 1984:47). The second problem was solved when it was discovered that gold could be separated from pyritic ore by suspending the crushed ore in a cyanide solution (Lanning with Mueller, 1979:45).

The technical breakthroughs and changes in the production process exacted a severe cost in workers' health. The introduction of steam-driven pumping engines, which facilitated deep level mining, and the large scale application of cheap dynamite for blasting operations, as well as the widespread introduction of machine drilling, all 'contributed markedly to the increase in the proportions of dust in the mine air', which led to the increased incidence of phthisis, a form of pneumoconiosis, that often results in the development of pulmonary tuberculosis (Burke and Richardson, 1978:156). By 1909, in the Transvaal, 'deaths from phthisis, including miners' phthisis, accounted for 9.6 [percent] of all deaths recorded that year' (Burke and Richardson, 1978:163).

The high costs of gold production meant that from the very beginning the gold industry was the preserve of big capital. Only companies with sufficient capital could hope to exploit the Rand. The trend towards monopoly was facilitated by the fact that large companies had already emerged at Kimberley. By 1889 four hundred gold companies had been floated with a combined market value of £E100 million. The South African gold industry was revolutionized by the development of mining groups first launched by Alfred Beit who formed Rand Mines Ltd as a holding company, which gave individual mines 'access to more working capital, better engineers and cheaper supplies' than they would have provided for themselves (Lanning with Mueller, 1979:46-47).

Many analysts believe that the group system accelerated the growth of the gold mining industry in South Africa. The fact that gold, as the money-commodity, had almost unlimited demand, and its price was fixed, reduced competition in the industry and facilitated co-operation. Merging several finance houses into groups helped to spread and reduce the risks of mining investment. This made investing in the industry even more attractive and brought much needed capital. Pooling technical and administrative resources also assisted the gold mining companies to achieve greater economies of scale and technical breakthroughs, thereby lowering the industry's costs and extending its lifespan (Wilson, 1972:22-23; Innes, 1984:53-57).

The largest gold mining companies included the Rand Mines, which grew into the largest mining company in the world; Rhodes's Consolidated Gold Fields; Central Mining; Johannesburg Consolidated Investments; General Mining; and Union Corporation. Rhodeshodes, Cecil became the richest and most powerful Randlord (Lockhart, 1963; Flint, 1974b; Wheatcroft, 1985). Huge amounts of capital were invested in the Rand mines. The value of total investment jumped from £E22 million in 1890 to £E75 million by 1899 (van Onselen, 1982a:1). Some of this capital came from reinvested profits. Of the £E200 million invested in the gold mining industry up to 1932 £E80 million represented reinvested profits and other local capital. The rest came from overseas.

Altogether, the mining industry absorbed the bulk of foreign investment in South Africa, and in turn South Africa claimed the lion's share of foreign investment in the continent. According to Frankel (1938:151-70), out of the £E1.2 billion invested in Africa south of the Sahara from 1870 to 1936 over 42.8% went to South Africa, and two-thirds of the private capital invested in South Africa went into the mining industry. Thus the South African economy became firmly integrated into the world economy as an exporter of precious mineral products. By 1910 minerals accounted for 81.1% of South Africa's exports, while agriculture accounted for a mere 18.3%. On the eve of the mineral discoveries wool had accounted for 76% of the exports from the Cape Colony.

The group system enabled the gold mining companies to attract foreign capital and rationalize production in the industry. But their attempts to secure a sufficient supply of cheap labour in order to lower the overall cost structure of the industry were not as successful. Given the technical difficulties of gold mining, highly skilled labour was required, in addition to the masses of unskilled and semi-skilled workers. In the early years the skilled labour was imported from Europe. By 1897 9,530 whites were employed on the Rand. The majority, 83.5% worked underground. This was to change. By 1907 only 7,866 out of 17,328 of the whites, or 45.4%, worked underground (Richardson and Van-Helten, 1982:82-85). This reflected their gradual removal from direct production into the supervisory functions of a labour aristocracy.

It was an expensive aristocracy. In 1898 white workers, who constituted 11% of the total mine workforce, accounted for 28.4 percent of all working costs, compared to 25.1 percent for the African labour force (Richardson and Van-Helten, 1982:82). This meant that white workers earned several times what Africans earned. The average income gap between the Europeans and the Africans rose from a ratio of approximately 7.5:1 in 1889 to approximately 10.5:1 in 1898, and widened further in the twentieth century (Wilson, 1972:45-46). The high wages were also the aristocracy's achilles heel. Indeed, the European workers suffered from what Johnstone (1976:57-64) has called 'extreme structural insecurity'. Unlike many of their African counterparts, who were migrant labourers usually with one foot tied to the land, they were entirely dependent on the wage relation for their reproduction (Davies, 1979:54-59).

As African workers gained industrial experience, the position of the high-cost European workers was undermined. Many of the skilled tasks they had previously performed were increasingly turned to African workers. The deskilling of the European workers accelerated in the first two decades of the twentieth century, and with it these workers 'lost one of their most important bargaining advantages... a factor which mining capital was not slow to recognize' (Davies, 1979:71). Thus the association of black and white with skilled and unskilled labour, respectively, increasingly represented racist discourse rather than reality. The mining companies gradually shed white labour, so that the numbers of whites employed in the industry declined both absolutely and relatively from 1910. It was in response to this that they began to call for job colour bars (Johnstone, 1976:74), demands that were articulated through relentless struggles and militant trade unionism (Simons, 1969:Chapters 2-5; Jeeves, 1985:Chapter 2).

It is one of the supreme ironies of South African economic history that the white mining labour aristocracy was saved from extinction by changes in the agrarian economy and the emergence of 'poor whites'. All sections of the settler ruling class were concerned about the 'poor white' problem because it 'threatened to undermine particular structures through which social control was exerted over the African dominated classes', and detracted 'from the capacity of the power bloc to organize the supportive and allied classes which it needed to maintain its dominance over the social formation' (Davies, 1979:77). The sight of poor whites living in shanty towns with unemployed Africans, and even working for Africans and begging from them, and the prospect of the two groups joining forces against the system, was an unpleasant one. It challenged not only what Bozzoli (1981:63) calls the 'hierarchy of exploitation', but also the racist ideologies and structures upon which South Africa's political economy was constructed. It was in this context that the state intervened to protect white labour. 'Without such support' Denoon (1984:202) has argued, 'it is difficult to imagine that the white working class would have survived'.

The European workers also had the vote. The Africans did not. The political cost of assaults against African workers were, therefore, low. In 1889 the mining companies established the Chamber of Mines in order to reduce the industry's labour costs and standardize wages and working conditions. Soon after its creation the Chamber reduced the African wage rate from 63s. to 44s. a month. This led to an immediate and substantial decline in the size of the African workforce. The Chamber conceded defeat and restored the old wages. It then began seeking a more comprehensive approach to the problems of African labour. In 1893 the Native Labour Department was created. But the NLD was not able to 'systematically organize the native supply', or did it stop the upward spiral of Africa wages.

In the aftermath of the gold share prices crash of 1896, the industry turned to the state to rein in African labour. The colonial state had already played, and was still playing, a fundamental role in creating the conditions to generate and reproduce African labour as cheaply as possible for the mining companies. The conquest of African states and societies was the necessary precondition for African labour mobilization. After that the colonial state used taxation and land dispossession, buttressed by numerous laws, to force Africans into wage employment, either because they needed money to pay taxes, or because they had lost their means of production and could no longer survive otherwise. Taxation was of course a double-edged sword: it encouraged labour supply as much as commodity production. The country was gradually and systematically divided into settler and African areas. (In Chapter 5 we discussed the systematic ways in which African agriculture was undermined).

The mining companies and the state increased their assault on African labour. In the mid-1890s a new pass law was passed ostensibly to curb the 'molestation' of Africans en route to the mines and 'thefts' of labour from one mine by another (Jeeves, 1985:41-43). The pass contained the worker's personal information and employment record. Its real aim was to increase the companies' control over the movement of African workers and to reduce desertions. The pass system became an important pillar of South Africa's racially structured capitalism. Apart from its labour regulatory functions, it served as an instrument of 'influx control' to restrict African urbanization. Emboldened by the crash and the passage of the pass law, in 1896 the Chamber formed the Rand Native Labour Association, which was intended to establish a monopsony over labour recruitment.

In the following year the Chamber decided to cut African wages by 30% overall. The result, as before, was massive withdrawal of African labour. In desperation the Chamber sought to recruit labour from as far as West Africa to no avail. Under this pressure fierce competition for labour emerged among the gold mining companies 'and overall wages began to rise' (Innes, 1984:62). In 1900 the Chamber replaced the RNLA with the Witwatersrand Native Labour Association as the new centralized recruiting agency. Its attempt to reduce wages was met with the same response from African workers: they withdrew in large numbers. The size of the African workforce dropped by 56%, from a peak of 96,704 in 1899 to 42,587 in 1902. This forced wages back up. It was for this reason that it was decided to import over 63,000 indentured Chinese workers (Richardson, 1977; Bozzoli, 1981:93-97; Innes, 1984:66-68).

Thus in the first three decades of its existence the mining industry was faced with severe labour shortages. Part of the problem was that working conditions were harsh and unattractive to most African workers. Underground mining involved long hours of strenuous work in dusty, hot and poorly ventilated mines, six days a week. Accidents were common. Wages were low and the attempts to reduce them did not help. By 1897 the real wages for African mineworkers were about two-thirds of what they had been a decade earlier. The compounds on the gold mines were filthy and congested. Ordinarily several men lived to a room, usually between 20 and 50 (Jeeves, 1985:22). Although they were more open than those on the diamond mines, movement was closely monitored. It has been suggested that the gold companies established the compounds less to reduce thefts and more to cut the costs of housing migrant labourers (Wilson, 1972:6-7).

The compounds were in fact nothing more than manufacturing mills for diseases, especially tuberculosis, an ailment that was relatively rare in South Africa prior to the late nineteenth century (Packard, 1989:31). The spread of tuberculosis in South Africa was promoted by the arrival, from 1843, of consumptive immigrants from western Europe seeking a climatic cure, and of infected eastern European immigrants escaping crushing poverty and persecution. Rapid urbanization following the mineral revolution, especially the mushrooming of congested slums, provided an unprecedented breeding reservoirs for tuberculosis. African mineworkers were particularly suscep- tible. Many recruits arrived at the mines in poor health because they were poorly fed on the way. In the compounds the food rations that they were given were very poor and inadequate. The average Rand diet lacked meat and vegetables, which 'led to serious vitamin deficiencies and, as at Kim- berley, to a high incidence of scurvy' (Packard, 1989:80). The wretched living conditions were aggravated by the deplorable working conditions. Not surprisingly, following the establishment of compounds in Kimberley 'over- all death rates climbed from 80 per 1,000 in 1878 to over 100 per 1,000 ten years later' (Packard, 1989:75).

The failure to establish monopsony in the labour market forced the mining industry to rely heavily on private recruiters, both African and settler. 'For the black recruiters and «runners», working for the labour companies was definitely preferable to working on the mines. For the unemployed miners and other whites «down on their luck» the recruiting industry served as an employer of last resort' (Jeeves, 1985:17). Chiefs and headmen played an important role in labour mobilization. They were also used as extra-super- visory agents through visits to the mines to boost the morale of workers from their areas, in exchange for being allowed to 'raise' funds from them (Jeeves, 1985:161-3). In order to induce labour the recruiters gave wage advances, paid either in cash or sometimes cattle. There was fierce inter-industry competition for labour, which served to push up the wages of the workers and the fees of the recruiters and labour contracting firms.

The failure of the Chamber to eliminate the independent recruiters and control labour supply can be attributed to the endemic divisions and rivalries among the mining companies, which the latter exploited, and the government's unwillingness or inability to clamp down on the independent recruiters (Jeeves, 1985:Chapter 1). It was not until the 1920s that the

Chamber triumphed over the independents, thanks to the greater co-operation among the mining groups, growing state capacity to police the recruiting system more efficiently, and the growth of voluntary African labour supply as conditions for reproduction in the reserves deteriorated (Jeeves, 1985:21, 151-6).

South Africans were generally reluctant to work in the mines. For many of them it was work of last resort. This is one reason why in the 1890s the Chamber turned its attention to neighbouring countries. Its failure to compete with the private recruiters was another factor. In fact, it has been claimed that these recruiters drove the Chamber out of many parts of South Africa. Moreover, the farmers offered some competition. The state actually reserved large areas of South Africa exclusively for them. 'Foreign labour had its own attractions; it came on long contracts and was easier to control' (Jeeves, 1985:57-58, 121-2). Thus the expansion in the geographical area from which mining labour was recruited was not simply a machiavellian capitalist ploy hatched by the mining companies to create an 'artificial' labour reserve army so as to drive down real wages as some maintain, although that was the eventual effect (Legassick and Clercq, 1984:146-8). Between 1889 and 1899 the African labour force increased by over 500%, from 14,000 to 97,000, of whom 70% were from Mozambique (Lanning with Mueller, 1979:54; Jeeves, 1985:187-220).

The world of the mine workers was rough and predominantly male, for there were so few women or families. In 1896, for example, there were only 1,200 African women in Johannesburg (Marks and Rathbone, 1982:12). This male culture was produced and reproduced in the compounds and boarding houses in which the African and European workers lived, respectively. A small number of African workers lived in married quarters in the informal mine 'locations' or townships (Moroney, 1982). The pleasures of working class life generally consisted largely of drinking, gambling and prostitution. Of the 14,000 white women in Johannesburg in 1895, 'at least 1,000 were prostitutes. The town had ninety-seven brothels of various nationalities: thirty-six French, twenty German, five Russian and so on' (Wheatcroft, 1985:4). The 'government and the mine owners - sometimes acting jointly, and sometimes on their own accord - encouraged black workers to consume alcohol, and tolerated the recourse of white workers to prostitutes in order to safeguard the long-term accumulation of capital in the industrializing state' (van Onselen, 1982b:6).

Alcohol and prostitution eased the pangs of proletarianization in the frontier mining towns. But they engendered their own contradictions: drunkenness undermined worker productivity, while prostitution led to the spread of venereal diseases and compromised the image of white women and the sanctity of the emerging racial order, since most of the prostitutes were white. So from the 1890s calls were increasingly made for 'total prohibition' and against the 'social evil' of prostitution. Neither was stamped out, they were merely driven underground or into the segregated compounds and districts where they festered away from the gentrified eyes of the emerging settler middle classes.

The bulk of the African workers who came to work in the mines, whether from within South Africa itself or from the neighbouring countries, were migrant labourers. It has often been argued that migrant labour was functional to capital in that it minimized labour costs. The rural reserves, where the migrants left their families to subsist, subsidized low wages and capital accumulation, for they acted as sponges which absorbed the costs for the maintenance and generational reproduction of the African working class, and as dumping grounds for old, incapacitated and unwanted workers (Wolpe, 1972, 1990; Legassick, 1974, 1977; Johnstone, 1976; Mafeje, 1981). It needs to be emphasized, however, that these were the consequences of migrant labour, not their causes. In other words, the dynamics and costs of migrant labour in the twentieth century should not be conflated with its origins and costs in the nineteenth. In fact, by international standards migrant workers' wages in the nineteenth century were, relatively, not low. Moreover, from the mining companies' point of view, not only were the wages high, but 'the employment of migrant labour called for recurrent recruiting costs, capitation fees and travel costs, as well as heavy losses through desertion' (Harries, 1982:143). Thus in the beginning the mining companies were not necessarily in favour of short-term migrants over more stabilized workers.

Migrant labour emerged out of complex processes involving the nature of the colonial state, the configuration of rural social formations and struggles between African workers and capital. It is important to note that for many peoples in South Africa, such as the Zulu, and in neighbouring countries, such as Mozambique, the destruction of African power only took place towards the end of the century, so that neither the colonial state nor mining capital could dictate the terms of labour mobilization until much later (Harries, 1982; Guy, 1982). Even in areas where colonial conquest had been achieved much earlier and a battery of mechanisms for labour mobilization erected, such as taxation and land alienation, the majority of African peasants did not face an immediate reproduction crisis that would necessitate permanent labour emigration to the mines. In some of the most affected areas, such as the Orange Free State, landless peasants were able to turn to sharecropping, which expanded in the decade after the Anglo-Boer War (Keegan, 1982; Matsetela, 1982).

It was shown earlier that African chiefs played a crucial role in labour mobilization. They did this for their own material interests, as well as to preserve the integrity of their societies. The ruling Koena lineage in Lesotho, for example, sought to retain its country's lands in the face of constant settler threats by acquiring guns through the wages of migrant labourers (Kimble, 1982:121-31). It was not in the interests of the ruling class to encourage permanent labour emigration, for that would result in depopulation, increased vulnerability, and the loss of remittances. In order to encourage the migrants to return, chiefs in southern Mozambique ensured that a migrant's 'property was protected during his migration and that his family had enough land and labour to provide itself with food; it also prohibited any infidelity on the part of the wife' (Harries, 1982:157).

It was not just the traditional ruling classes that sought to safeguard the migrant's ties to his homeland, the latter also needed continued access to land as an insurance in old age and against the low wages and poor conditions on the labour market. The perennial struggles between labour and capital over wages and the steady decline in real wages simply reinforced the workers' need for a rural haven. Besides, life in the early mining towns, with their squalor, diseases, violence and loneliness, compared poorly to the relative warmth, security and tranquility of rural life. To some migrants, therefore, the mining centres, could not be 'home', but temporary hells. This ideology helped reproduce migrant labour in the early days, and later rationalized it after the system had become sanctified by the state and capital as a means of reproducing a low-cost labour force (Mayer, 1980).

The conjunction of interests between the traditional ruling class and the migrants was articulated most concretely through the advance payments system in which the migrant was paid by the recruiter in advance of taking up a job. This system made it easier for the ruling class to appropriate a portion of the workers' wages, enabled the workers' families to control the rest, and 'made it difficult for the worker himself to abscond in town and leave his rural roots behind him [as] he had little cash with him' (Beinart, 1980b:84). The system of course had many strains. Some migrants did not return, others deserted, and many volunteered to go to the mines by themselves to avoid the control of the recruiters, the exactions of the chiefs and the demands of families, and to maximize their options and wages, for voluntary labour received higher wages than recruited labour. Migrant labour remained a contradictory process reflecting a complex articulation of pressures from within African societies and the colonial state and capital. But increasingly, as the twentieth century progressed, all the benefits lay with the latter.

As the migrant labour system developed, its repercussions were felt in all walks of South African life, including health, as Packard (1989) has cogently demonstrated with respect to tuberculosis . The incomplete proletarianization of the African labour force, as entailed by the migrant labour system, affected the epidemiology of tuberculosis in three main ways. First, oscillating labour migration between the rural and urban areas:

> *caused the urban-based TB epidemic to spread into the rural areas of South Africa at a more rapid rate than occurred in Europe or America...* *Second, in contrast to England, labour migrancy may have delayed the development of resistance to TB* (Packard, 1989:11).

In other words, labour migration may 'have retarded the development of a stable balance between African urban populations and the TB bacilli and thus prolonged the TB epidemic... Finally, the fact that African workers were less proletarianized than either their English counterparts or white workers in South Africa, limited the ability of African labour to push for health reforms' (Packard, 1989:12).

Different levels of proletarianization do not, of course, entirely explain why at the turn of the century mortality rates for white workers were uniformly lower than those of African workers. It also reflected the uneasy alliance between white labour, capital and the state, 'which ensured that improvements were instituted in white working and living conditions' (Packard, 1989:13). In the meantime, the rural areas to which the African workers periodically returned were becoming more overcrowded, impoverished, due to land dispossession and ecological crises, and African diets, increasingly based on maize, were becoming less nutritious, all of which aided the spread of tuberculosis.

Mining in West Africa

South Africa was not the only country where Europeans tried to set up mining enterprises. From the late 1870s a number of European mining companies attempted to establish themselves in Ghana. Inspired by stories told by soldiers returning from the Anglo-Asante War of 1873-74 of the 'vast' gold riches to be found in Ghana, a number of European joint-stock companies were hurriedly formed and rushed to the country. Ghana mining shares became the rage on the London and Paris stock exchanges, and 25 companies were founded between 1878 and 1882. European prospectors flocked to the country, where they were often assisted by African entrepreneurs. The trade in land concessions became so frenzied that the colonial government expressed grave concerns about the future of African land rights. But the boom proved short-lived. By 1885 £E1 million had been sunk into Ghana, but the returns were a miserable £E27,000. Many of the companies were unable to start actual mining operations, and of those that did, only one was able to return a dividend to its shareholders in 1897. In the 1890s the European mines exported an average 10,959 ounces of gold, valued at £E36,097, which represented 48.6 and 44.5% of the country's total gold exports in weight and value, respectively (Silver, 1981:511-6; Rosenblum, 1977:149-50).

Clearly by 1900 the European gold mining companies in Ghana were doing badly, indeed they could be conceived of as failures. Their failure has been attributed to several factors, including the lack of infrastructural development in the new colony, which made it difficult and expensive to establish a mine, a problem exacerbated by 'political instability and the absence of concession legislation', and 'climatic and health conditions on the West Coast, which took a severe toll of expatriate mining personnel and discouraged experienced engineers from working in the country' (Crisp, 1984:14-15). The problems of transport faced by the mining companies were not insoluble; they had a lot to do with their inability to 'win the cooperation of the Africans who controlled the pre-railroad transportation system' (Rosenblaum, 1977:292). And the role of climate as an inhibiting factor 'has been seriously over-estimated' (Silver, 1981:519).

The European mining companies failed to make much headway in the first three decades of their operations in Ghana largely because they were unable to solve the problem of 'primitive accumulation' and overcome African resistance and competition. They neither had enough capital, nor labour at their disposal. The financial manipulations of 'share-pushers' and 'concession-mongers' made it difficult for these companies to raise sufficient seed-capital to commence production. Poor managerial and technological capacities only made matters worse. Many of the mine managers were ex-government officials or merchants with little knowledge of mining. 'But even more important than their managerial failings was the rudimentary level of the technical knowledge possessed by the European mining companies, especially with respect to the nature of the geological formation with which they were dealing, and the process by which the gold could be extracted from the ore' (Silver, 1981:520). Indeed, 'despite claims of European technological superiority it was some thirty years after the gold rush had begun before European prospectors were able to find a gold deposit not already known to, and worked by, African diggers' (Silver, 1981:521).

These managerial and technological weaknesses were exacerbated by the inability and reluctance of the colonial state to promote the interests of the European mining companies through the provision of public expenditures for the industry, and the imposition of direct taxation and land alienation on Africans, as in South Africa, to force them into working for the mining companies. The colonial state feared that such measures would provoke African resistance which it could not contain, and destroy peasant export production upon which the state itself and merchant capital depended for their viability. Moreover, the state also needed labour to build the colonial infrastructure. It, too, faced labour shortages, to which it responded by using compulsory and imported labour. The state's 'use of forced labour not only depleted the reservoir of potential workers available to the mines, but also made the inhabitants of the mining areas extremely wary of volunteering for work with other expatriate employers' (Crisp, 1984:16). Without state support the mining companies found it extremely difficult to secure labour that was regular and adequate, efficient and reliable, and cheap.

The labour question bedeviled the mining companies and significantly contributed to their failure in the nineteenth century. Lack of state support was only part of the problem. Working conditions in the mines themselves were not attractive. Wages were low. Many peasant commodity producers and independent African gold diggers earned far more than the workers employed by the European companies (Silver, 1981:527). The tasks and pace of work assigned to the workers were also arduous and the methods of supervision harsh. These tasks were assigned to both men and women. Women were mainly employed as carriers, rock sorters and washers. Beatings and other forms of physical coercion were regularly used as a disciplinary measure. Not surprisingly, the mining companies found it difficult to recruit locally. Out of the 17,000 workers in 1903, 43% came from outside the gold-producing areas, some, about 14%, from as far as Liberia (Crisp, 1984:19). Thus, like in South Africa, the mining industry in Ghana became increasingly dependent on migrant labour. Also, as in South Africa, local chiefs, many of whom had leased their land to the mining companies, played an important role in securing labour, for which they received 'costly presents'.

The parallels with South Africa became concretized at the turn of the century with the influx of South African mining capital and personnel, prompted in part by the closure of mines in South Africa due to the Anglo-Boer War. This helped fuel a minor gold rush, which was partly inspired by the construction of the Sekondi-Kumasi railway, and the crushing of the Ashanti uprising of 1900. The South Africans found a mining industry that was keen to improve its labour productivity. Using the new railway, heavier and more efficient machinery was installed, and experiments undertaken with new forms of work organization, through sub-contracting of tasks and payment by task. The South Africans brought to the new labour regime their well-honed punitive and coercive managerial and supervisory techniques. Even the government complained. More importantly for the mining companies, these measures backfired, for they encouraged many workers to leave and discouraged others from coming (Crisp, 1984:22-23).

Another method adopted by the mining companies to increase labour supply was the policy of labour stabilization. Attempts were made to improve the living conditions in the mining towns by building new and attractive villages. But these villages were run, and were perceived by the workers, as replicas of the work place; company supervision was intrusive and coercive. In fact, the settlements were built to maximize company control over the workers' lives. After 1900 they were fenced in ostensibly to curb the problem of gold theft. The mining companies even sought to extend their social control to all the inhabitants living in the concession areas by, for example, establishing village councils to hear petty criminal cases and trying to prohibit drinking. When this failed 'the mines opened their own spirit shops and were given the power to veto all applications for spirit licences from native traders in the area' (Crisp, 1984:26). By South African standards this regime of social control was benign; but by the standards of Ghana it was brutal and harsh and served to worsen the problem of labour shortage.

The mining companies also failed in their bid for monopsony. An attempt in 1901 to form a West Coast African Labour Bureau, which would recruit and distribute labour among the mining companies, was turned down both by the colonial government and the Colonial Office in London. A similar fate met the proposal of the Gold Coast Agency, a subsidiary of the Consolidated Gold Fields of South Africa. In the following year the mining companies formed the Mine Mangers' Association, a forerunner of the West African Chamber of Mines formed three years later, which was clearly modeled on the South African Chamber of Mines. It sought to reduce and standardize wage rates and working conditions in the industry. If its more powerful South African counterpart found it difficult to achieve monopsony, the Ghanaian chamber had little hope. The mining companies were not united. Nor did the state support them. On the contrary, the state itself sought to establish a monopsonistic labour market. More importantly, perhaps, the workers resistance ensured the failure of the project.

Unlike in South Africa, the colonial state in Ghana, as was mentioned earlier, neither had the capacity nor the interest to 'destroy' African peasant agriculture, which was the mainstay of the colonial economy. Mining wage employment, therefore, had to compete with peasant production. The former fared badly because of its low wages and poor working conditions. Moreover, also unlike South Africa, local gold mining in Ghana was not only an ancient industry, but was still being done. Up to the beginning of the twentieth century the mining companies were unable to compete effectively with the African producers who outproduced them. It is, indeed, telling that 'the most successful of the European mining companies not only was managed by Africans rather than Europeans, but also, and more importantly, organized on a pre-capitalist rather than a capitalist basis' (Silver, 1981:524).

No wonder many Africans tried to resist attempts to turn them into workers for the European mining companies. Resistance at the workplace took several forms. Employers commonly complained that workers refused to perform certain tasks or worked at their own rate. This was an attempt by the workers to control or manipulate the pace of work. Moreover, workers refused to sign long contracts of six and nine months favoured by the companies. They also resorted to theft to supplement their low wages. They expressed their discontent by using abusive language against their employers or feigning misunderstanding of instructions. Occasionally physical violence was employed against particularly notorious employers. One of the most popular forms of resistance was desertion. In addition, there were Ludittist forms of resistance in which machinery was destroyed. Finally, there were collective modes of resistance involving strikes. There were a series of strikes in the 1890s and early 1900s, including a general strike at the Ashanti Gold Fields, the colony's largest and most profitable mine, over wages and conditions of work (Crisp, 1984:17-19, 29-32; Silver, 1981:524-8). These struggles circumscribed the development of the mining industry, but they did not stop its growth in the twentieth century.

In Ghana European companies sought to take over the ancient indigenous gold industry. In Northern Nigeria they went after the tin industry. It was probably the West Africa Company, a British merchant firm, which first became aware of the existence of tin in Northern Nigeria in the 1870s. But it was its successor, the Royal Niger Company, which from the 1880s sought to exploit it for export. The market for tin in the rapidly industrializing countries of continental Europe and North America was growing rapidly. The RNC was largely responsible for the conquest of Nigeria and so it saw itself as the proprietor of the country's mineral resources, a fact that was accepted by the British government when it sought to take over the company's administrative responsibilities. In 1899 a royalty deal was reached according to which the RNC would receive half of all government revenues from mineral exploitation in most parts of Northern Nigeria for 99 years. The company also acquired its own prospecting licences over vast areas of the Jos Plateau where the tin fields were located.

The RNC was, however, not keen to transform itself from a merchant firm into a mining company. At first it neither had mineral expertise, nor sufficient capital to exploit the tin mines by itself, so it embarked on selling or leasing its properties to others (Freund, 1981:29-36). The role played by the RNC in the development of the tin industry cannot be overemphasized. It provided transport services, and later provided loan guarantees for the construction of a railway from Lagos to the north. Eventually it began to dispense all sorts of supplies to the mines, and offered them engineering services, cash advances and acted as a financier. The RNC found the provision of these services far more profitable than actually running the mining operations (Freund, 1981:39-40).

British mining companies began flocking to the Plateau in the 1900s. There was an investment fever, so that by 1911 '£E3 million had been placed in Nigerian tin stocks in London, and by the beginning of the New Year, Nigerian tin shares were the most actively traded stocks in London' (Freund, 1981:37). But before the war these companies hardly produced any tin. They merely exported tin ore produced by the Africans using their age-old techniques. In other words, the first stage of the European take over of the Nigerian tin industry was in the sphere of circulation. The European companies bought tin and redirected it from the local into the export market. The result was that 'by 1911, tin was reported to be unavailable in Kano market due to purchases by Europeans, and two years later, Northern Nigeria was already importing substantial tinware from Britain' (Freund, 1981:47). This in itself would not have destroyed the indigenous tin industry. More important than purchase was the expropriation of tin produced by Africans on land now claimed by the European companies.

Thus land appropriation was central to the European takeover of the Nigerian tin industry. The violent conquest of the Plateau, which was met with spirited African resistance, set the basis for the dispossession of the African tin producers of their land and the reorganization of the industry. Following conquest Africans lost the right to work the lands where tin ore was located. There is little evidence that they were ever compensated, although Lugard, the administrator, once proposed that African miners be compensated for their lost land rights. The mining companies were given exclusive licences over the minefields. In order to ensure that Africans did not lease the land, the lease fees were set at a level too high for many Africans, and it was also decreed that all engineers and agents for lessees had to be European. This removed any possibility that Africans would operate in the tin industry in any role other than as labourers.

The seizure of land was accompanied by the prohibition of African mining and smelting (Newbury, 1984:217). The mining companies railed against the smelters because they posed a commercial challenge, contested the companies control of the land, and provided outlets for local miners to sell tin ore, which undermined the companies efforts to recruit labour and appropriate tin ore. By 1913 all the smelters had been closed (Freund, 1981:45-47). This was one more nail in the coffin of the Nigerian tin industry. The colonial mining pattern was established, whereby the Jos Plateau no longer processed tin, but merely exported unsmelted tin ore, 'which British smelters used to *sweeten* less pure ores, notably from Bolivia' (Freund, 1981:36). Dispossessed African producers who had now been turned into reluctant workers for the mining companies responded through theft and social protest (Freund, 1986).

The appropriation of land and the closure of the smelters was largely intended to transform independent local miners into wage labourers for the mining companies. However, the dispossessed local labour force, upon whose mining skills the companies depended, was rather small. The companies had to look further afield for additional labour. Like their counterparts in South Africa and Ghana these companies faced severe labour shortages. They had to compete for labour with other sectors of the economy, including peasant agriculture, which was experiencing something of a boom, as well as the state itself which was constructing the colonial infrastructure. As in Ghana, recourse to forced labour by the state simply aggravated the problems of labour supply for the mining companies (Newbury, 1984:215-6).

The colonial state in Northern Nigeria was probably more wary of provoking resistance from the Muslim emirates than was the case in Ghana, so it was careful not to extend land dispossession beyond the mining areas of the Plateau. But like colonial states everywhere, the government in Northern Nigeria imposed colonial taxes both as a means of raising revenue and as an instrument of labour mobilization. Moreover, conquest led to 'the dislocation of the old bureaucracies and soldieries', from which emerged a reserve army of labour (Freund, 1981:51). The abolition of slavery augmented the reserve army. As in South Africa and Ghana, the Nigerian tin mining companies formed a Chamber of Mines which tried to lower and standardize the industry's wages and centralize labour recruitment. The chamber was unsuccessful on both counts. It was a labour seller's market, so wages did not fall. On the contrary, 'the labour demands of the minefield had the effect... of raising the average Northern wage by 50% from 6d to 9d' (Freund, 1981:53-54). These wages were of course not high by any standard. An attempt to lower them in 1909 provoked the first known strike on the mines. A second attempt a few years later was met by workers' withdrawal from the mines, which caused a labour shortage.

The chamber also failed to rationalize and control labour recruitment. The government rejected the chamber's call to form a state run bureau to be given monopoly over labour recruitment. The companies remained dependent on headmen and labour contractors. Labour contracting 'remained one of the few outlets for African mining enterprise' (Newbury, 1984:217). The labour recruited was mostly migratory. This was not only convenient for the mining companies but also for the workers themselves. The wages were too low to sustain a stable labour force and the mines had difficulty in getting sufficient food for the workers, a problem that culminated in virtual famine between 1911 and 1913, and led to the temporary closure of the mines (Freund, 1981:56-57). For their part, most of the workers still had one leg in the peasant economy.

By 1909 the mining companies employed about 9,000 workers, mostly from Northern Nigeria. The construction of the Lagos-Kano railroad with branches to the Plateau facilitated the flow of labour to the north from Southern Nigeria. Some skilled workers also came from as far as Ghana and Sierra Leone, and there were a few Europeans. Although the ratio of Europeans to Africans on the Nigerian tin mines was very low compared to South Africa, the income gap between the two groups was just as skewed in Nigeria as it was in South Africa. In the early days of the mining industry European salaries 'ran to several hundred pounds per annum, roughly fifty times the wage of a Nigerian labourer' (Freund, 1981:52). Given their high costs, and the fact that local mining skills were highly developed, and there was no supportive settler population, the number of European employees in the tin mines remained small.

Colonial Manufacturing

The development of European manufacturing industries in Africa is largely a phenomenon of the twentieth century. The reasons for this are rather obvious. For the most part, the European colonial empires in Africa were established in the last quarter of the nineteenth century. The first years of colonial rule were taken up with wars of conquest and 'pacification'. Moreover, the early colonial period, an era of primitive colonial accumulation, was not propitious for the establishment of manufacturing industries. At any rate, the colonial powers had no intention of setting up industries in the colonies. The colonies had been acquired primarily to provide markets for manufactured goods and sources of raw materials for the industries of the imperial nations.

Before 1870 European colonialism in Africa was largely confined to Portuguese coastal enclaves in Angola and Mozambique, the British and Boer colonies in South Africa and the French colony of Algeria. The Portuguese enclaves were among the oldest in the continent, stretching back to the sixteenth century. Their fragile economies, which relied mostly on the slave trade, hardly boasted of manufacturing industries (Hammond, 1966; Bender, 1978; Clarence-Smith, 1979b; Vail and White, 1980; Newitt, 1981; Seleti, 1990). Whatever consumer goods the Portuguese settlers needed, and traded with the local communities, were imported, as will be demonstrated in Chapter 15.

By the mid-nineteenth century the British and Boer colonies in South Africa, especially the latter, were quite impoverished and modern manufacturing industries barely existed (De Kiewet, 1957; Marks and Atmore, 1980; Marks and Rathbone, 1982; Elhpick and Giliomee, 1989). Most settler manufacturing was undertaken in households using age-old technologies. Only a few products were manufactured in relatively large enterprises in the fledgling colonial towns of the Cape Colony. Among them were textile, leather and soap-making industries, and steam-powered sugar, corn and saw mills, breweries and wineries, iron foundries, printing presses, and brick and wagon-making establishments (Houghton and Dagut, 1972:73-102).

As pointed out earlier, South Africa's political economy was profoundly transformed by the mineral revolution, which laid the basis for the country's eventual industrialization. From the 1890s the large mining companies began investing in industries supportive of their activities. De Beers, for example, 'invested in collieries to provide the industry with cheap fuel; in railways and telegraphs to build up necessary infrastructure; and in explosives to circumvent the high cost of explosives which arose out of the dynamite monopoly' (Innes, 1984:42). Another mining company, Lewis and Marks, was involved in distilleries, collieries, and making jam, candles, glasses and bottles, leather, bricks and pottery (Innes, 1984:138). In the early 1900s, De Beers spread its investments to other enterprises, including those making bricks and tiles, wine and jam. Thus the mining industry directly contributed to the development of the South African manufacturing sector. Indirectly, it promoted urbanization, which together with its large workforce created new markets for manufactured goods.

It cannot be overemphasized that mining's contributions to industrialization in South Africa remained relatively insignificant until the twentieth century. The mining companies imported most of their supplies from abroad. Indeed, Marks and Rathbone (1982:11) maintain, until the 1920s 'monopoly capital generally had no need for an internal market nor any real interest in the growth of local manufacturing so long as machinery and stores could be obtained more cheaply from abroad'. Moreover, in the late nineteenth century mining developments virtually absorbed 'all available capital, skilled manpower and entrepreneurship leaving little for manufacturing' (Houghton and Dagut, 1972:114). It could even be argued that the mineral revenue probably undermined local craft industries because increased revenues from mineral exports gave rise to increased imports of consumer goods. In short, by 1900 the country's manufacturing sector remained poorly developed.

In the twentieth century South Africa was destined to be one of the most industrialized countries in Africa. The mining companies played a crucial role. The big ones among them ploughed a lot of capital into manufacturing industries. The giant Anglo-American corporation, for example, which started off as a mining company, eventually established a vast manufacturing empire (Lanning with Mueller, 1979; Seidman and Makgetla, 1980; Innes, 1984). Also, the state transferred large surpluses from the mining industry, appropriated through taxation, and used some of it to build the industrial infrastructure and set up state-owned heavy industries.

This process began in earnest only in the 1920s, for reasons that are not agreed among scholars. One group argues that it was the product of the emergence of a new constellation of class forces within South Africa which favoured local industrialization (Davies, et.al., 1976). Another attributes it to the shifts in British imperial strategy spawned by the restructuring of British capital (Innes, 1984:120-7). This debate lies beyond the scope of this chapter. It belongs to the second volume of the study. The point that needs to be made here is that the mineral revolution, begun in the late nineteenth century, was the motor that drove South African industrialization in the twentieth century.

While industrialization was beginning to take place in South Africa in the late nineteenth century, Algeria, colonized by France in 1830, was undergoing what Issawi (1982:150-4) has called 'deindustrialization', that is, the decline of its handicrafts. 'Reindustrialization', the rise of modern factories, had barely started by 1900. The explanation for this must be sought in the motives and policies of French imperialism, the character of the Algerian colonial state, and the nature of the country's class structure and its resource endowment.

The motives and processes behind the French conquest of Algeria are discussed in Chapter 13. At this point suffice it to say that French imperialism in Algeria was largely motivated by economic considerations. It was believed that the occupation of Algeria would enable France to prosper. As Jules Ferry, a keen advocate of colonialism, put it, 'colonial policy is the offspring of industrialization... we must cause fresh categories of consumers to appear in other parts of the world, for, if we fail to do so, modern society will go bankrupt'. Moreover, Algeria would provide an outlet 'to alleviate', in the words of the Africa Commission sent to Algeria in 1833, 'demographic pressures exerted on big cities and the use of capital that has been concentrated there' (quoted in Bennoune, 1988:35). Thus neither the French state nor industry, had any intentions of exporting industrialization to Algeria. On the contrary, Algeria was to be a protected market for French manufactured goods and an outlet for 'surplus' population settlement (Abun-Nasr, 1987).

Industrialization was also not on the agenda of the colonial state or the French settlers. The colonial state was constructed through the violent overthrow of the decadent Turkish state. The process of colonial state construction was a protracted one because of stiff Algerian resistance. It took over half a century before the whole country was conquered militarily. Thus it was not until the 1870s that 'the objective material conditions for accumulation' had been fully laid (Tlemcani, 1986:33). The intensity of Algerian resistance heightened the subsumption of the colonial state by the imperial state, a process consummated by the integration of Algeria with France. The Algerian colonial state, therefore, was more than a dependent appendage of the imperial French state, as most colonial states were (Young, 1988; Berman, 1990). Its territoriality, sovereignty, institutions of rule, legitimacy, legal order and ideological representation were all derived from the imperial state.

The colonial state's exceptionally narrow autonomy was reinforced by the influx of settlers who saw Algeria, located just across the Mediterranean from France, literally as an extension of their motherland. The settlers constituted the dominant power bloc in the colonial social formation. Their material base, as we saw in Chapter 5, was in agriculture. Thus neither the state nor the settlers had the capacity or interest to promote industrialization. It can be seen that the colonial state in Algeria had far less autonomy from the imperial state than the colonial states in South Africa. Also, the Algerian settlers, unlike their South African counterparts, did not construct an autonomous nationality from that of the metropole. And no less important was the fact that at this time Algeria's natural resources lay in the land and agriculture. There was no sudden discovery of huge mineral resources that could have provided the capital and created the social conditions for industrialization as was the case in South Africa.

Thus, compared to South Africa, Algeria had hardly made any industrial progress by 1900. In fact, Algeria suffered considerable 'de-industrialization'. In its efforts to mobilize labour for the settler farmers and a market for French imports the Algerian colonial state introduced restrictive administrative measures against urban craft corporations. The first measures were instituted in 1838, then extended in 1851, and finally in 1868 the corporations were abolished altogether. The number of Algerian artisans fell sharply, from 100,000 in the mid-nineteenth century to only 3,500 a century later. Not surprisingly, 'Algerian handicrafts industries almost disappeared... ousted by French industrial products' (Bennoune, 1988:66-67). The destruction of Algerian manufacturing was reinforced by the decline of traditional education, which had given Algeria a relatively high level of literacy, and had been used to pass on industrial skills. During the period of conquest mosques and koranic schools were confiscated or abandoned. 'On the ashes of the Algerian traditional system of education the authorities laid the foundations of a colonial education destined for the children of the «notables»' (Bennoune, 1988:67).

This does not mean that industries were completely absent. It is merely to point out that the efforts made were quite feeble. Industrialization in Algeria only began in earnest from the Second World War. Between 1880 and 1910 the industrial sector broadly defined received a mere 5% of total investments made in the country. Manufacturing capital was confined to small industries in food processing, such as wineries, flour mills, tobacco factories and fish canneries. In 1901 there were reportedly 11,887 industrial units in the country, but the vast majority of these 'were operated by self-employed individuals without any additional hired labour' (Bennoune, 1988:74). Altogether, they employed 51,502 workers , including Europeans, who constituted over half the workforce. More than half the Algerian workers were unskilled. Women constituted about 37% of the Algerian urban proletariat in 1911. Generally the Algerian workers received half the wages paid to the Europeans performing the same tasks.

Conclusion

It is quite apparent that the beginning of colonial industrialization, like the establishment of colonial agriculture, was steeped in blood and violence. In South Africa the Africans were dispossessed of their lands, in West Africa their mines, and in Algeria their craft industries. In all these cases the role of the colonial state was pivotal.

By the end of the century South Africa had established the largest mining industry in Africa, and one of the largest in the world. The evolution of the industry's monopoly structures and coercive labour system has been charted in this chapter and the point has been made that the industry's development was conditioned by a complex series of struggles between labour and capital. In other words, the industry's structure was not the predictable outcome of some arcane capital 'logic' as some studies tend to portray it. By the same token, migrant labour was also not simply a functionalist product of capitalist manipulation. It was spawned by the conflicting demands of both labour and capital, and remained a contradictory process, although the benefits of the system increasingly lay with capital. Thus while South African labour may have been severely exploited, it was not passive. This chapter has further explained that the mining industry not only revolutionized the South African economy and social structure, as well as the economies and societies of the surrounding countries from which it increasingly drew its labour, it also had a major impact on the epidemiology of disease.

The failure, at least up to 1900, of the various attempts to set up a European-owned mining industry in West Africa is a salutary reminder of the weaknesses of European ventures in early colonial Africa and the continued strength of African enterprise. It has been argued that the colonial states in Ghana and Nigeria lacked the requisite ruthlessness, compared to the South African state, to promote the process of 'primitive accumulation', partly because the settler population was negligible, so that peasant production was the basis of the colonial economy and the key source of state revenues. Moreover, the European mining companies were bedeviled by serious managerial and technological weaknesses and shortages of labour. No less important was the fact that, unlike the mining industry in South Africa which was based on new 'discoveries', in West Africa the aspiring European mining magnates had to compete with a vibrant indigenous mining industry. They could not compete and consequently, sought to take it over. Thus there were two types of struggles in the burgeoning mining industry of West Africa: by the proprietors fighting against the dispossession of their mining enterprises, and by the mine workers seeking better wages and working conditions.

Finally, this chapter has argued that by 1900 there was little colonial manufacturing, even in South Africa where industrialization did not start in earnest until the 1920s, thanks to the base established and capital generated by the mining industry, the recomposition of social forces and reconstitution of the class basis of the neo-colonial state, as well as conjunctural factors in the world economy. But this lay in the future. By 1900 South Africa was still a typical colonial economy dependent for its exports on primary, mainly mineral, products, and for the bulk of its manufactures on imports. The case of Algeria shows that colonial states were not only uninterested in promoting industrialization in their colonies, they sometimes actively sought to destroy any existing industries. A deliberate programme of 'deindustrialization' was launched, which resulted, as we saw, in the abolition of craft corporations and the deskilling and gradual elimination of the Algerian artisan class.

Part IV

Domestic and Regional Trade

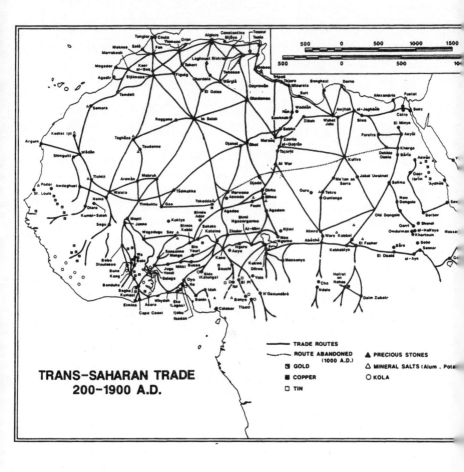

TRANS-SAHARAN TRADE
200-1900 A.D.

9. Trade in North Africa

The Monopoly System

Trade in North Africa has ancient origins. In Egypt for example, recorded trade goes back to pre-dynastic times, that is, before 3000 BC. Thus by the beginning of the nineteenth century North African trade had a long and complex history. In examining the development of the region's trade in this period many studies have tended to concentrate on these countries' integration into the world capitalist system which indeed accelerated in the nineteenth century, and had profound consequences for the region. But the fact still remains that for the greater part of the century domestic trade in North Africa far outstripped international trade with Europe (Shroeter, 1988:1-6).

Domestic trade was conducted in rural and urban markets and at annual fairs which, since the introduction of Islam, coincided with annual religious festivals. Rural trade was sustained by several factors. To begin with, peasant households and village communities were not self-sufficient. The degree of local specialization, with particular villages in a district or households in a village producing special kinds of food or craft manufactures, was quite considerable. Moreover, the peasants were enmeshed in relations of dependence and subordination to powerful outside forces upon whom they sometimes depended for working capital and extra resources to finance the extravagant celebrations of rural life, such as feasts and weddings. Above all, they needed to pay taxes and dues to the state and local notables. So peasants traded their surpluses to meet their needs and obligations.

It would appear that rural markets were periodic and subject to the nature of rural demand. The location of markets differed according to the patterns of population distribution and state policy. In some parts of Morocco the rural markets resembled Polanyi's (1957, 1968) 'ports of trade', for they were located 'on an unclaimed portion of land between two territories, or on holy land attached to a shrine' (Ponasik, 1977:200). Each market was held weekly. Every day of the week had a market or suq, called by the name of the day (Shroeter, 1988:86-90). In effect, Morocco's rural markets constituted cycles of rotating markets. In the more densely populated and centralized Egypt, markets were located both between and within villages depending on the local circumstances.

In the first half of the nineteenth century there was marked state intervention in rural trade as North African governments sought to increase their revenues in order to expand their armies to wrest independence from the

Ottomans, or to meet the growing European challenge, and to embark on programs of modernization. Government monopolies were set up for the sale of agricultural and other produce. These monopolies allowed the government to make large profits by paying peasants low prices for their produce and reselling them to consumers at higher prices. This system allowed the state to appropriate the bulk of rural surplus.

The monopoly system was implemented ruthlessly by Muhammad Ali's regime, which was bent on modernization of the Egyptian army and economy. Between 1811 and 1816 prohibitions were decreed against private trade in cereals, sugar, cotton, indigo, sesame, and beans, among other crops. Fixed prices were set up for each crop. Since the government controlled the supply it could 'dictate the terms on which the harvest was sold to the merchants' (Owen, 1981:66). The differentials between the fixed prices paid to the producers and the resale prices in the domestic and export markets were quite substantial. For example, in 1833 the producers were paid the equivalent of 3.34 francs per hectolitre of wheat, 1.80 francs for maize and 2.00 francs for beans. These products were then sold in the country for 6.40 francs, 3.34 francs, and 3.60 francs, and on the export market for 7.00 francs, 6.60 francs, and 5.00 francs, respectively. Cotton, which became Egypt's main export crop, was bought for 120 francs per metric quintal and resold for export at 250 francs (Issawi, 1982:20).

In Morocco and Algeria commodities were sold to the highest bidder. Indeed, in Morocco the movement of traders was highly restricted, so that:

> there were few non-local traders at many of the rural markets. In addition to limiting the travel of traders, high taxes were charged on the transport of local goods from one area to another, and some items were not allowed to be transported at all (Ponasik, 1977:201).

It has been argued that these controls were aimed at segmenting Moroccan society in order to ensure the hegemony of the Sultan, who had weak military and administrative control over the rural hinterlands. This system differed somewhat from modern forms of commercial nationalization, for:

> commercial activities - strictly defined - that is, the purchasing, packing and transporting of goods to ports of embarkation - were strictly carried out by private individuals who had acquired temporary and revocable monopoly trade rights (Pascon, 1986:47).

The monopoly system was not confined to rural or domestic trade. One of its primary aims, in fact, was to control foreign trade. It served the interests of the military chieftains and oligarchies that dominated the state, but was resented by the hapless peasants, the indigenous merchants and the foreign merchants. Their combined opposition succeeded in loosening the grip of state control. In Algeria the system was dismantled following the French colonization of the country in 1830. After the conquest of Algeria European pressure on Morocco to open its domestic market increased, buttressed by a series of military defeats and treaties of 'recapitulation'. Egypt was also forced to abandon the monopoly system by foreign pressure. By the late 1840s the system of agricultural monopolies had broken down, along with the ambitious industrialization drive, and the policy of state ownership of land. 'From then on the country's peasants were drawn into more and more intimate contact with the merchants, usurers, ginners and others who were intermediaries between them and the world market' (Owen, 1981:74-5).

Urban-based interests increasingly began to finance the peasant producers or to buy directly from them. This practice spread to Tunisia and Morocco as these countries became more integrated into the world capitalist system as exporters of a narrow range of primary products (Valensi, 1985:226-8; Doumou, 1990:17-18). This process not only led to increased merchants' and foreigners' control of rural production, it also profoundly transformed rural social structure and ecology. While it operated the monopoly system had enriched the state, but it also impoverished the peasants and weakened the indigenous merchants, who were therefore in no position to compete against the foreign merchants when the system was later dismantled.

Bazaars and Merchant Guilds

Trade in the towns and cities did not escape the long interventionist hand of the state. But urban markets were not organized in the same way as the rural markets. To begin with, urban markets tended to be more elaborate in their physical construction and were held continuously, usually on a daily basis, because of the concentrated and more effective demand of urban populations. We noted in Chapter 2 that bazaars were at the core of North African cities. The bazaar consisted of quarters for different groups of merchants, as well as markets and squares for specialized crafts and retail trades. The bazaar was a beehive of activity, full of hustle and bustle. In addition to the stationary retail traders and their numerous customers, the bazaar was often swarmed with pedlars and porters.

The organization of the bazaar changed in the course of the nineteenth century, especially as the use of carriages increased and more roads were built. There ensued, as Toledano (1990:169) poignantly puts it in reference to Egypt, 'a quite struggle for space in the cities, especially but not only in Cairo and Alexandria. Wheeled vehicles pushed aside not only pedestrians or those using riding animals, but also artisans and shopkeepers, who used street space as an extension of their working area'. Horse-drawn carriages became for the Ottoman-Egyptian elite a symbol of status, reinforcing the other markers of their social distance, namely, the use of the Turkish language, elegant and official dress, the right to carry guns, and privileges before the law (Toledano, 1990:155-180).

The bazaar was subject to control and regulation by two agencies, merchants guilds and state officials. Virtually all urban trades and services in North Africa were organized in occupational corporations known as hirfa or ta'ifa, (translated as guilds for lack of a better term). New occupations which emerged in the course of the nineteenth century were incorporated into the guild system. In Egypt more than half the guilds, with about two-thirds of total guild membership, were merchant and service guilds, and the remaining one-third were artisan guilds.

The guilds performed many functions arising out of their dual responsibility to the state and to their members. They were expected to ensure that laws and regulations, including those relating to their various trades, were carried out and to assist the authorities in bringing any of their members who had violated the law to justice. They also had the duty to collect tax on behalf of their members, and to supply labour to the government and private employers. As for their members the guilds were expected to defend them whenever their customary or legal rights were infringed upon, and to protect the trade and prices of the goods sold (Baer, 1964; 1969:149-160; Shroeter, 1988:75-77; Toledano, 1990:225-30).

The chief state officials responsible for the fiscal administration of the town in general and the bazaar in particular was known as muhtasib. He was expected to work closely with the guild heads, called shaykh in Egypt and amin in the Maghreb. Among his responsibilities were the jobs of maintaining law and order in the markets, and to control weights, measures and the prices of goods. The muhtasib was quite powerful. It was relatively common for them to use their power to exploit the merchants, who in turn would pass on the costs to the city dwellers. Their power gradually weakened as the state bureaucracy overseeing trade expanded. In Morocco, for example, the muhtasib came to share his powers with other key officials, the governor, the qadi, the religious authority, and the umama, in charge of the fiscal administration of the town. All these officials were appointed directly by the Sultan.

From the 1870s the functions of these officials were streamlined as a result of foreign pressure and in order to curb corruption. Among the administrative reforms introduced were salaries for the officials and prohibitions against them engaging in commerce, and improvements in book-keeping (Shroeter, 1988:135-42). In Libya, the muhtasib 'served the sanjak bey [governor] as his representative in the market-place, although he was responsible in turn to the kadi for carrying his duties in the markets of the city. The office was usually farmed out to one or two individuals for limited periods (up to one year)... the muhtasib was paid both in kind and in specie by the salesmen, shopkeepers, and merchants and by wholesalers at the city gates' (Abou-El-Haj, 1983:309-310).

The guilds began to decline towards the end of the nineteenth century mainly as a result of European pressures. The influx of European goods weakened the craft guilds, while the influx of European merchants undermined the merchant guilds. The latter were also hit by the spread of retail trade and the rapid growth of the cities, for large numbers of the people flocking to the towns did not join or need guilds. The hegemony that guilds previously enjoyed in urban life was further eroded as many of their administrative, fiscal and economic functions were taken over by government departments (Baer, 1969:153-7).

The Merchant Classes

At the beginning of the nineteenth century the indigenous merchant classes in North Africa faced little foreign competition over domestic trade for, as was mentioned above, foreigners were prohibited from engaging in domestic commercial activities. Statistical data on the size of this class or the financial resources of its members is hard to come by, except for Egypt. According to estimates made by members of the French expedition that invaded Egypt in 1798, Cairo had a population of between 250,000 and 300,000 inhabitants. About a quarter of the economically active population were craftsmen and a tenth or so were merchants and retailers. The majority of the merchants were small with limited amounts of stock. An analysis of the wills of 205 small merchants has shown that they left behind an average of 32,924 paras, while the big merchants who were mostly engaged in the international trade in coffee and textiles left several times this amount (Owen, 1981:49-50).

The merchant classes in North Africa developed along different lines depending on each country's social and state structures and the patterns of accumulation. Two examples will suffice. One is the case of Morocco where the fortunes of the merchant class were closely tied to the interests of the state. The other is Egypt where the merchant class played a more marginal role. Shroeter's (1988) detailed study on the merchants of Essaouira, Morocco's principal port in the nineteenth century, amply demonstrates the interdependence of the merchants and the state.

The big merchants in Morocco, both Muslim and Jewish, were almost invariably tujjar sultan, meaning the 'king's traders'. The Sultan provided them with special permits to trade as wholesalers, interest-free loans to finance their activities and houses to live in. The tujjar paid rent for the houses and repaid the loans in monthly instalments. They made annual trips to Marrakesh to pay tribute to the Sultan. They were beholden to him and could not move to another town without his permission and without having a guarantor and depositing money or property as collateral.

Thus the merchants were tied to the Sultan as clients, debtors and tenants. This prevented them from becoming an independent social class and hindered their accumulation. The areas they could invest in were restricted to real estate and tax-farming. Many wealthy merchants, particularly the Jews, found it much safer to export their capital by depositing their money in foreign banks or buying shares in foreign enterprises. And many a fortune was frittered away in the conspicuous consumption of the day: lavish dress and housing, and visiting and sending children to school in Europe (Shroeter, 1988:21-60).

As appendages of the state, the merchants were very vulnerable to any crisis that hit the state. And the Moroccan state was afflicted by intermittent crises from the mid-nineteenth century, fuelled by the interventions of European powers. The state became financially strained by costly military reforms and expenditures. The various European powers against whom Morocco fought, first France and later Spain, imposed heavy reparations and indemnities which depleted the treasury. Morocco also signed commercial treaties, such as the treaty of 1856 with Britain, which abolished the monopoly system and removed restrictions against foreign merchants, so that their numbers increased.

In short, the Moroccan state found itself in dire financial straits. Its capacity to finance and support the merchant class was drastically reduced. Indeed, the imposition of new taxes, such as gate tolls for merchants and pack animals, threatened the interests of the merchant class. Many of them sought a new protective umbrella, which they found among the foreign traders. Local merchants increasingly became proteges or compradors because foreign capital gave them security and opportunities for accumulation under the new dispensation. The commercial treaties offered them 'all sorts of legal and tax privileges, which exempted them from the country's laws, tax liabilities and such other obligations as military duty in the King's expeditionary forces, compulsory for other Moroccan subjects' (Doumou, 1990:16). Thus the Moroccan merchant class exchanged dependence on the state for dependence on foreign capital. In neither case were the merchants able to develop into an independent class capable of dynamic capitalist accumulation.

The Egyptian merchant class enjoyed a slightly different fate. Despite some similarities there were considerable differences in the positions of the merchant class in Egypt and Morocco, particularly in their relations with the state. Egyptian merchants were not patronized as assiduously by the state as their Moroccan counterparts, for they were neither part of, nor critical to, the ruling elite.

The Ottoman-Egyptian elite primarily consisted of the ruling family and top civil and military officials. Altogether, the elite was very small, numbering several thousand. It was a tightly knit group, regimented and conformist, despite its internal rivalries. Its members were bound together by their loyalty to the ruling dynasty, service in Egypt, their Ottoman and Muslim heritage and their honours, titles, privileges, and wealth. Apart from their relatively high salaries, they derived most of their income from land granted to them by the khedive (Toledano, 1990:68-109).

For the elite, wealth and status not only became increasingly intertwined, it also became inseparable from landed property, thanks to the cotton revolution. Land gave the elite its material base. The articulation of landed property and the elite meant that state officials saw themselves as part of an agrarian bourgeoisie, hence the pronounced agrarian bias of the Egyptian state. Hunter (1984) has argued that three kinds of interests were represented at the highest levels of the administration. The officials sought to promote their own goals, as well as rural interests and European interests. They worked to realize local or rural interests not only because they had landed property and the rural areas constituted their power base, but also because the patrimonialization of power at the centre by the khedive excluded any politics other than local. European interests were promoted by the programmes and ideology of reform and westernization championed most vigorously under the reigns of Muhammad Ali and Ismail. Some elites in their struggle for power with other members of the elite relied upon the assistance of European consular missions. Through them 'the seeds of collaboration were being sown, and Europe was establishing a base of support at the highest level of the Egyptian state and administration' (Hunter, 1984:117). The bitter fruits were harvested in the 1870s and 1880s when the power of the khedive was weakened and the Ottoman-Egyptian state was supplanted by the colonial state imposed by Britain.

The establishment of a centralized household government, based on a strong army and bureaucratic elite, by Muhammad Ali and its consolidation by his successors, is what marginalized the role of Egyptian merchants in the nineteenth century (Hourani, 1968). The merchants hardly constituted a corporate body or a socio-political group (Toledano, 1990:71). It can be argued that in Egypt, unlike Morocco, the merchant class was courted neither by the state, whose functionaries' social base was increasingly agrarian, nor by European capital, which had direct access to a growing number of state functionaries themselves. The end result was, however, not much different.

The Egyptian merchant class remained as weak and incapable of sustained capitalist accumulation as their Moroccan counterparts.

Money and Finance

The commodities traded in both the rural and urban markets in nineteenth century North Africa included agricultural and forestry products, manufactured goods, minerals and metals, and slaves. The composition of trade changed gradually over the years. For example, trade in slaves declined sharply in the second half of the century. In the meantime, the distribution of mass consumer goods such as tea and sugar, increased. As a general rule, the range of supplies was greater in the urban than in the rural areas, for urban markets were enmeshed in domestic and foreign trade networks in a way that the rural markets were not.

Trade was conducted through the use of credit and money or barter, with barter the least important of the three methods. The use of credit and money was widespread. It was quite common for wholesale merchants to obtain goods on credit and, in turn, transfer them on credit to shopkeepers and retailers. These credit arrangements were based on personal bonds as well as legally-binding Islamic principles of credit. Two types of credit associations were recognized: the qirad, or commenda, and sharika, or partnership. Both involved the investment of capital by one party in another and the sharing of profits. The difference was that if the capital was lost, the risks were borne only by the supplier in the case of qirad, or they were shared by both parties in the case of sharika (Shroeter, 1988:109-113; Udovitch, 1970). This legal structure facilitated the development of trade and trading networks or diasporas in North Africa. The use of credit was particularly essential for long-distance trade. Many merchants travelling from the coastal cities to the markets of the southern hinterlands traded goods acquired on credit or given on commission.

At the beginning of the nineteenth century the region's currency consisted mainly of silver and copper coins, supplemented by various European and Asian coins, mostly silver. The existence of so many currencies in one country caused considerable confusion and complicated monetary exchanges. There are many indications that in the eighteenth and nineteenth centuries the value of the domestic coins depreciated. Issawi (1982:185) believes that this was 'partly because of the influx of bullion from the New World but mainly because of steady debasement'. The problems involved more than the depreciation in these coins' intrinsic value as the case of the Tunisian piaster shows.

Tunisian piasters decreased in weight, size and silver content. The same happened to the copper coins. The process began in the second half of the eighteenth century and accelerated in the early nineteenth. By 1829, for example, the Tunisian piaster weighed 11.0 grams, down from 22.2 grams in 1735, and its silver content fell from 440 to 286 during the same period. In addition to losing its intrinsic value, the piaster also lost its exchange value as trade with Europe increased. Currency speculation and the violent fluctuations in Tunisia's import-export trade wrecked havoc on the Tunisian currency. Increasingly, Tunisia:

> *became the prisoner of a market it could no longer control. Even its monetary policies lost all independence. No reform could be undertaken without foreign merchants first being informed. In 1847, when the bey decided to open a bank, issue notes, and mint new money, the announcement of these measures provoked a meeting of foreign merchants and a protest by the French* (Valensi, 1985:218-9).

Foreign trade also spelled disaster for the Moroccan currency. The country's bi-metallic system of bronze and silver was disrupted as foreign trade grew, for only silver coins qualified as foreign exchange. Indeed, the repatriation of silver coins to finance trade and pay debts and indemnities led to a situation whereby the Spanish piaster established itself as the silver standard in the country. The uqiya, Morocco's currency, began to inflate against the Spanish piaster. This triggered the counterfeiting of the copper coins, known as flus, which formed small denominations of the uqiya. This reduced the uqiya's value further. The Sultan's attempts to set up fixed exchange rates between the Spanish and French silver coins and the uqiya were to no avail. The depreciation of the uqiya accelerated. Between 1848 and 1858 it fell by over 25% and in the 1870s it tumbled by 100%, and another 100% in the 1880s. In the end two currency systems were allowed to operate. The foreign currency was used for international exchange, and local currency for the domestic market (Shroeter, 1988:63,142-52).

The Egyptian currency also began to depreciate rapidly in the second half of the nineteenth century, thanks to the country's growing unfavourable trade balance with Europe and its rising indebtedness. Attempts to stem the tide by introducing the Egyptian pound did not go far. Since 'few Egyptian gold pounds were actually issued, the least undervalued foreign currency, the pound sterling, came to account for practically the whole of monetary policy' (Issawi, 1982:187). With the British occupation of Egypt in 1882 European merchants came to dominate Egypt's domestic and foreign trade. Their position was strengthened by the expansion of European banks which came to cast a heavy shadow over the Egyptian economy. The banking industry was dominated either by Egyptian-based European money-lenders or by international banks founded in Europe in the mid-nineteenth century (Landes, 1958; Tignor, 1981).

Development of Transport

Transport is an important feature of trade. We mentioned earlier the growing use of carriages by members of the Ottoman-Egyptian elite. Carriages played a negligible role in the transportation of cargo or trade commodities in North Africa during the nineteenth century. Goods were carried either on foot by porters, or on the backs of pack animals, principally mules, donkeys and camels. For waterborne transport canoes, boats and ships were used. Waterborne transport was not used much in domestic trade, except in Egypt where the Nile River was a major trade route for the country's domestic and foreign trade. Sailing ships were important in the sea-borne trade but from the mid-nineteenth century sailing ships were rapidly replaced by steamboats, which helped regularize shipping and expand trade between North Africa and Europe, for they provided a much more reliable mode of transport. But none of the North African countries had a significant merchant marine, so their sea-borne trade was monopolized by foreign, mostly European, shippers (Valensi, 1985:219; Shroeter, 1988:106-9).

In the first half of the nineteenth century overland transport relied mostly on porterage. Porterage was important in both cities and the countryside and porters were indispensable for the transport of goods to, from and within the bazaars. They carried goods for the merchants and traders, and sometimes hawked their own goods as well. Thus porters and pedlars could be distinct people, or both functions could be performed by the same person. Porters, pedlars and auctioneers were hired, but we have little information concerning their wages. Porters and pedlars also plied the trade routes between city and countryside. In addition to porters carrying goods, merchants also employed special couriers for the rapid despatch of commercial information (Shroeter, 1988:74-5, 114).

Caravans of pack animals provided the main means of overland transport across great distances. The largest caravans, particularly those involved in the trans-Saharan trade, could have up to 20,000 camels or more. The norm was probably 1,500 camels with an equal number of travellers, although smaller caravans of 100 to 200 camels were quite common. The camels were often hired.

The caravans were organized as frequently as the markets and security would allow. Protection along the trade routes was provided by the state itself, which set up stations along the major routes, as well as secured through the payment of taxes or tribute to the local rulers. The large caravans moved slowly, for they could rarely manage more than 25 miles a day even in good conditions since they had to stop at provincial markets to replenish food supplies and at customhouses. The distance between Fazzan and Cairo could be covered in 50 days while the segment between Murzuq and Katsina or Timbuktu required 90 days (Walz, 1978).

In the second half of the nineteenth century modes of overland transport began to change with the increasing use of carriages by the elite. Except for the towns and cities the road network linking the rural and urban areas was underdeveloped. 'Only in Algeria [and] Tunisia... were roads significant before the First World War' (Issawi, 1982:53). By 1860, for example, Algeria had a road network of 3,000 kilometres which served economic as well as military functions. The network was greatly extended in the next few decades. 'In Tunisia the French had built 600 kilometres by 1892 and 4,000 by 1914... In Egypt, the building of rural roads started in 1890, and by 1907 there were 2,646 kilometres, mainly in lower Egypt' (Issawi, 1982:53).

One of the most important developments in the overland transport of North Africa was the construction of railways from the 1850s. In this, Egypt led the way. The railway from Alexandria started in 1851 and reached Cairo in 1856 and Suez in 1858. 'By 1869, Egypt had 1,338 kilometres of railway, and by 1905 the state railways aggregated 3,000 kilometres, at an estimated cost of £E25 million. In addition, 1,400 kilometres of narrow-gauge railways had been built by private companies, with an aggregate capital of just over £E3 million, and there were also some suburban lines... Relative to its inhabited area and population, Egypt was remarkably well provided with railways, and railways were carrying the bulk of the internal goods traffic' (Issawi, 1982:54).

In Algeria railway construction started in 1858. Total railway mileage reached 1,100 kilometres by 1880, belonging to six private companies. By 1890 there were 3,056 kilometres of railways. In Tunisia a small line was built in 1876 and by 1890 416 kilometres had been built. In Morocco and Libya railway building started at the beginning of the twentieth century (Issawi, 1982:54-5).

It stands to reason that these changes in the structure of the transport system contributed to the expansion of domestic trade by stimulating production and facilitating the formation of integrated national markets. Both transport costs and travel time were reduced quite considerably. But there were costs as well. Building the transport network was quite expensive. Egypt, for example, incurred heavy debts locally and abroad to construct and subsidize the railways. As it will be demonstrated in Chapter 13, the government's growing indebtedness facilitated Egypt's eventual colonization. In Algeria the transport network built by the French from 1830 was intended more to assist military operations and control and promote the export economy than to develop Algeria for its own sake. Indeed, the expansion of the transport system in North Africa was both a product of, and a precondition for, the region's fuller incorporation into the world capitalist system.

Regional Trade

The foreign trade of the North African countries can conveniently be divided into three types: trade among these countries themselves, trade with other African countries, and trade with the outside world, particularly Europe and Asia. Trade with Europe will be considered systematically in Chapter 13. In this section we will consider intra-North African trade and trade between North Africa and other parts of Africa, especially the Sudan and West Africa.

Data for intra-North African trade is rather poor, particularly for trade between the Maghreb countries. We do have some figures for trade between the Maghreb region as a whole and Egypt, however. According to one estimate, in 1793 this trade amounted to 62.8 million paras, of which 21.7 million paras were Egyptian exports to the Maghreb and 41.1 million paras were Maghreb exports to Egypt (Walz, 1978:62). This apparently constituted 3.9% of Egypt's total foreign trade. From the Maghreb, Egypt imported woollen cloth, coral, hides, Moroccan slippers, honey, oil and butter, salted fish, tarbushes and slaves, in return for manufactures of glass and metal, linen, silk and cotton textiles, spices, coffee and wheat. Some of these products were re-exports, in the case of the Maghreb of goods from the western Sudan or West Africa, and in the case of Egypt from the eastern Sudan, Arabia and India.

Egypt's major trading partner in Africa apart from the Maghreb were the Sudanese kingdoms of Darfur and Sennar . Again using the estimates of 1793, Egypt's trade with these kingdom's was worth 51.1 million paras, or 3.1% of its total foreign trade. Egyptian exports to Darfur and Sennar consisted of textiles, metals and hardware, scents, medicinal herbs and spices, beads and semi-precious materials, and firearms and military supplies, in that order. In exchange, Egypt imported slaves, camels, sism, water-skins, rhinoceros horn, whips, natron and alum, which were consumed domestically, and tamarind, ivory, gum and feathers, which were primarily trans-shipped abroad. Egypt had a trade deficit with the Sudan, amounting to 38.7 million paras in 1793. In reality only 6.2 million paras 'was actually held payable while the remaining balance, some 32 million, was liquidated by means of ordinary market transactions and various fees, customs tolls, exactions and living expenses' (Walz, 1978:60).

Egyptian trade with the Sudan increased in the nineteenth century. Muhammad Ali turned to the Sudan as a source of slave soldiers , gold and agricultural products. The Egyptian conquest of the Sudan in 1821 boosted trade between the two countries, and the number of Egyptian and Sudanese merchants plying the route between Cairo and Khartoum, the new Sudanese capital, increased. While there was little gold, Darfur became Egypt's largest supplier of slaves (Rue, 1983:636-43). The Sudan also became a large supplier of gum: 'as early as 1827-8 about 1,270 metric tons were exported. Cattle for Egyptian agriculture and industry, and animal by-products were important exports: in 1836-7 some 25,000 cowhides, 6,400 goatskins, and 19,600 sheepskins were sent to Egypt, and the camel market was always strong. New crops were grown commercially, some, like sugar and indigo, with success; others, like opium and coffee, failed' (Daly, 1988:193). This trade benefited the state rather than private traders, for Muhammad Ali extended the monopolistic trading system he had imposed on Egypt on the Sudanese trade. Prices were fixed and custom rates adjusted. Private traders found themselves being squeezed out and 'soon came to deal exclusively in slaves' (Walz, 1978:236).

The trade between Egypt and the Sudan had its ups and downs. The volume of trade between Darfur and Egypt diminished quite considerably between 1830 and 1850 as relations between the two became strained (Rue, 1983:644-6). Trade began booming again from 1850 as political tensions between Darfur and Egypt eased and following the withdrawal of monopolies on Sudanese staples in the 1840s. The terms of trade for Darfur merchants gradually improved. The composition of trade changed as trade in slaves declined following the decision by Said to abolish the slave trade. Slave trading at Wakalat al-Gallaba, the square for Sudanese merchants in Cairo was banned. By 1863, for example, slaves exports constituted only 2.3% of the total value of Darfur exports to Egypt; tamarind took 2%, camels 10%, feathers 30%, and ivory 50% (Rue, 1983:664).

In the third quarter of the nineteenth century the Sudan trade 'became big business, flourishing on a scale it had never reached in the eighteenth century' (Walz, 1978:247-8). Chambers of commerce were set up in different centres of the Sudan, including Khartoum where one was established in 1862. A Banque du Soudan was founded in Egypt to finance trade in the Sudan, but it failed in 1873. Egyptian attempts to build railways in the Sudan also failed for lack of capital. More successful was the introduction of steamers on the Nile. 'By 1879 annual exports from Suakin had a declared value of £E254,000, and in 1880 some 758 vessels were said to have called' (Daly, 1988:193). This trade was increasingly dominated by northern Sudanese merchants, 'a few of whom rose from the humblest beginnings to become rulers of vast territories in the Southern Sudan' (Daly, 1988:193).

Direct trade between Egypt and West Africa does not seem to have flourished in the nineteenth century. On the contrary, it appears to have gone into decline by the end of the eighteenth century. A century or so earlier it had been quite vibrant, with Egypt reportedly importing from West Africa between 1,000 and 1,200 kantars, approximately 10,000 and 12,000 lbs, of gold annually, as well as ivory and other staples, in return for textiles and cowrie shells and other items (Walz, 1978).

West Africa was the Maghreb's most important trading partner in Africa. For centuries the trans-Saharan trade had enriched Maghribi states and societies. Lacoste (1974) has gone so far as to argue that the great commercial cities of the Maghreb in the middle ages were nothing but termini for the trans-Saharan trade. Abun-Nasr (1987:19) agrees that this trade was the most important element 'in an extended web of trade relations with which the major Maghribi towns were connected'. Indeed, he believes that 'the Maghribi countryside did not have the economic resources which alone would have made the appearance of large towns possible, nor did the rulers have sufficient control over the country-side to be able to tap the available resources effectively. Hence the importance of trade for the economic well-being of the towns and for the maintenance of the rulers' authority'.

Maghribi-West African trade was still flourishing by the beginning of the nineteenth century. The most valuable commodities imported by the Maghreb states from West Africa were gold and slaves, followed by textiles, leather goods, ivory, gum arabic, wax, kola nuts and spices, in return for textiles, glassware, jewellery, copper, salt, cowries and weapons. There are currently no reliable statistics on the exact volume or value of this trade in 1800. The previous assumption that the trans-Saharan trade had declined from the late sixteenth century following the Moroccan invasion of Songhai in 1591, has been abandoned as a result of new research (Hopkins, 1973:80-7; Austen, 1987:29-31). In fact this trade expanded in the nineteenth century and only went into decline at the turn of the twentieth century.

The Maghreb served as a trans-shipment base for some of West Africa's exports, especially gold and leather, to Europe, and of European exports, particularly textiles and weapons, to West Africa. As is well known, West Africa was the main source of gold for medieval Europe and western Asia, apart from North Africa itself. Thus West African gold sustained these countries' domestic economies and helped maintain their balance of payments with each other and with other regions.

Up to the mid-nineteenth century the trans-Saharan trade was far more important for Morocco than its sea-borne trade. A contemporary estimate in the 1840s put it at 60 million francs, compared to 23 million for the seaborne trade. The latter did not overtake the trans-Saharan trade until the 1870s. The decline of Morocco's Saharan trade in the closing decades of the nineteenth century has been attributed to the diversion of West African commodities to the south, from where they were exported directly to Europe. From the mid-1870s Morocco's sea-borne trade assumed prominence, despite fluctuations. It averaged 75 million francs by the early 1890s and reached 85 million francs in 1900 (Issawi, 1982:24). The decline of the trans-Saharan trade between Morocco and the Western Sudan led some historians to conclude that the trans-Saharan trade as a whole entered a period of rapid and permanent decline (Newbury, 1966; Hopkins, 1973:80, 131). This interpretation has recently been revised by Johnson (1976), Baer (1977), and Lovejoy (1984), among others. According to Baer (1977:41):

> *trade on the far western routes began its final decline in 1875 and was at a standstill by 1900. In contrast, the Tripoli-Kano route declined later. Further east, the Benghazi-Wadai route lasted longer still, with trade continuing strong up to 1913, when the French attacked and captured the Sanusi capital at Ain-Galaka.*

The expansion of trade between West Africa and the Maghreb as a whole during the last quarter of the nineteenth century has been attributed to the dramatic rise in West African exports of ostrich feathers and ivory (both of which were at the time in great demand in Europe) and tanned skins. According to estimates provided by Lovejoy (1984:103), the annual value of the trans-Saharan trade in ivory, ostrich feathers, tanned skins, and slaves, whose exports declined sharply, rose from £E93,000-158,000 in 1862-71 to £E201,000-221,000 in 1872-81. By 1892-1901 the trade was worth £E123,000-132,000, still higher than in the 1860s. Lovejoy (1984:100) emphasizes that these estimates show that the: 'conclusion that the trans-Saharan trade declined after 1875... simply is not true. Furthermore this synthesis points out even more dramatically how serious the decline was when it did come after 1901'.

Recent research has also shown that the trade was not confined to luxury goods as was once postulated by Boahen (1964) and repeated by Hopkins (1973). After 1870 North African slave imports from West Africa were insignificant. In the 1880s and 1890s the average annual flow of slaves had been cut to between 500 and 1,000, about one-eighth of the volume during the period 1830-70 (Lovejoy, 1984:94). The shift to a broader social base is reflected by the fact that between 1860 and 1900 over 70% of West Africa's imports by value through the trans-Saharan trade consisted of cotton textiles and yarns, mostly manufactured in England, which were destined for mass consumption. Moreover, North African merchants 'moved away from the capitals of the Sudanic states and took up residence in small villages' (Baer, 1977:45). A comparison of the value of Tripoli's exports to Kano for the years 1874-1880 and 1894-1900 shows minor variation from £E3.11 million to £E2.73 million. In contrast, Tripoli imported twice as much from Kano in 1874-1880 as it did in 1894-1900 - £E1.60 million as compared to £E0.83 million (Johnson, 1976b:105).

Available evidence indicates that on the whole, relatively few North African merchants actually went to West Africa or the Sudan. Trade between Egypt and the Sudan was monopolized by Sudanese merchants, known as gallaba, while that between the Maghreb and West Africa was largely controlled by several groups of merchants from West Africa and the Sahara. West African merchants dominated the trade from the interior of West Africa to the famous cities on the edges of the Sahel, such as Kumbi, Timbuktu, Jenne, Gao, Kano and Kukawa, which formed the southern termini of the trans-Saharan trade, while merchants from the Sahel and Sahara dominated the portion of the trade across the Sahara, through the numerous towns and market centres dotted over this vast region, to the great northern termini of Marrakech, Fez, Algiers, Tunis, Tripoli and Cairo (Boahen, 1964; Hopkins, 1973; Walz, 1978; Austen, 1987). In the course of time some of the Saharan merchant communities dispersed to the north where they established them-selves as successful traders in the major cities of North Africa. One example is that of the Mizabis whose dispersion to the northern cities of Algeria, including Algiers, was accelerated in the eighteenth and nineteenth centuries by environmental pressures, especially drought. The Mizabis quickly rose to prominence in the commercial world of Algiers (Holsinger, 1980).

The foreign merchants in North African cities were allocated special quarters, where they resided and conducted their trade. This restriction of foreign traders to specific quarters facilitated government control of and collection of taxes from them. In Cairo, the gallaba of the Sudan were located in Wakala al-Gallaba, while merchants from the Maghreb were located in the Fahhamin quarter of the city. These merchants were organized in their own guilds which served to regulate their activities and to mediate between them and the state authorities (Walz, 1978:Chapter 3). Some of these foreigners' guilds became quite wealthy. In Algiers, for example, the Mizabi corporation was at the end of the eighteenth century listed as the richest in Algiers, 'even loaning funds to the Pasha on occasion' (Holsinger, 1980:68). The leader of the corporation, the amin, was chosen from the wealthiest and most influential members of the corporation. He was paid an annual salary, and had the power to levy taxes on establishments belonging to corporation members, and impose fines on his subordinates who had breached the corporation's rules. This potentially lucrative position carried costs and responsibilities as well. The amin 'was responsible for the support of new arrivals in the city and was expected to pay out considerable sums to administrative officials upon assuming office' (Holsinger, 1980:69).

The foreign merchants usually relied on their trading diasporas. Those that did not have such networks, or where the networks did not provide all the necessary services, had to use local intermediaries. Using these intermediaries had several advantages, especially in the light of the restriction on the foreigners' freedom to move and trade locally. Moreover, the local traders and brokers were more likely to be better informed about local consumption trends and tastes. Egyptian merchants, for example, often assisted the Sudanese gallaba, providing them with credit facilities and acting as their agents. Sometimes the two groups formed partnerships and companies. It appears that the Sudanese trade was far more profitable for Egyptian middlemen than the European trade. Some of Egypt's richest merchants were associated with this trade and invested most of their fortunes in agricultural holdings (Walz, 1978:Chapter 3). But both the gallaba and their Egyptian brokers lost control over the Sudan trade towards the end of the nineteenth century. This trade, as much else in Egypt at the time, fell under the control of European merchants in the country and merchants from Ayut who had more resources, contacts and expertise to cope with the rapidly changing colonial economy.

North Africa's trade with West Africa and the Sudan was largely conducted with fellow Muslim societies. The extent to which Islam provided the basis for commercial organization is of course debatable. But it is possible that being Muslim made it a lot easier for the merchants to relate with each other. Indeed, a lot of the foreign trade was conducted or commissioned by the states themselves, whose relations were guided to some extent by Islamic codes. For example, trade between Egypt and the Sudan during the time of the monopoly system was:

> *conducted on a state level and high ranking personages from the Sudan were selected to carry diplomatic messages to and royal business in Egypt... The bestowal of ceremonial gowns by Egyptian authorities represented an official recognition of their status* (Walz, 1978:75).

There can be little doubt that North Africa's domestic and foreign trade grew considerably in the nineteenth century. Certainly trade expanded faster in the nineteenth century than it had in the eighteenth. The growth rate of the region's trade was about the same as the world average; it boomed when the world economy prospered, and it slumped during global recessions (Issawi, 1982:24). This is as good a testimony as any that North Africa was becoming incorporated more deeply into the world economy.

North Africa entered the nineteenth century largely in control of its trade, and with its domestic and regional African trade playing a far more important role than trade with Europe. By the end of the century the situation had almost been reversed: the region was firmly integrated into the European-based world capitalist economy as a dependent periphery. This trajectory was neither unique nor fortuitous. It was a fate that struck the whole continent and the rest of the so-called Third World, thanks in large measure to the emergence of the 'new imperialism' (see Chapter 13).

Conclusion

This chapter has examined the development of North Africa's domestic and regional trade. It looked at the structure of rural and urban markets, and how the organization of bazaars and merchant guilds changed; the growth of the merchant classes and their varied patterns of accumulation in the region; the methods of trade and the ebbs and flows in the monetary system; the transformation of the transport system from one dependent largely on porterage and caravans, to one where railways played an increasingly important role, and the impact that this had on trade itself as well as on the debt structure; and finally, the development of intra- and extra-regional trade.

It has been argued that the monopoly system not only exploited and impoverished the peasants, it also weakened the indigenous merchants vis-a-vis foreign merchants. Apart from foreign merchants and competition, there were, of course, other factors which made it difficult for the indigenous merchant classes to achieve sustained and vigorous capital accumulation even after the monopoly system had been abolished. In Morocco commercial accumulation was circumscribed by the merchants' dependence on the Sultan. The fiscal crisis of the state from the mid-nineteenth century had an immediate and devastating impact on the merchants, who traded their dependence on the state for dependence on foreign capital, which only reinforced their marginalization. In Egypt, the merchant class faced difficulties not because it was incorporated into the ruling elite, but because it was not, so that their interests were not protected or promoted, especially as Egypt became more integrated into the world economy and the ranks of European merchants swelled.

The scale of Egypt's trade with the Sudan and the Maghreb's with West Africa demonstrates quite convincingly that the Sahara was not the great divide it is purported to be between North Africa and that strange concoction of imperial historiography known as sub-Saharan Africa. Certainly the trade links between North Africa and West Africa were far more intense than those between, say, West Africa and Central Africa, or East Africa, fellow 'sub-Saharan' regions. Thus talk of 'sub-Saharan' Africa as if it were an integrated historical unit is meaningless, at least as far as trade is concerned.

As it has been pointed out, the trans-Saharan trade was far more important for the Maghreb countries like Morocco and Libya than their seaborne trade with Europe until the last quarter of the nineteenth century. Research done in the last two decades has cast doubt on earlier assertions that this trade was in decline in the nineteenth century. On the contrary, all indications are that it expanded. Important segments of the trans-Saharan trade, such as the Kano-Tripoli route, did not decline until the beginning of this century. It has also become increasingly clear that this trade was not confined to luxury commodities, as once thought.

10. Trade in West Africa

Organization of Markets

The organization and development of trade in West Africa shared many similarities with North Africa. West African trade was also of considerable antiquity. The periodicity, spatial location and control of markets in West Africa was quite complex. There were periodic, rotational and daily markets. The range of periodicity varied from one place to another and periodic markets were held at intervals of between two and eight days. Various attempts have been made to map out market periodicities in the region (Smith, 1971; Fagerhund and Smith, 1970; Hodder, 1971; Murdock, 1959; Hill, 1966, 1971). Unfortunately many of these maps are based on twentieth century evidence, so it is difficult to tell whether their periodicities correspond to those prevailing in the nineteenth century. It would appear that rotational markets operated in places where the periodic markets were formed into rings or cycles. In a locality having, say, two markets, each would open on alternate days. The temporal and locational spacing of rotating markets varied according to the number of markets in a particular cycle.

Periodic markets were generally concentrated in rural areas where settlements were dispersed and effective demand was rather weak. It has been suggested that except for foodstuffs 'periodic markets were certainly bulking markets', where traders came to purchase local products for 'resell to other traders or consumers' (Hodder, 1971:350). As population and its density grew and the people's purchasing power rose marketing frequency increased until daily or continuous markets developed. The transition from periodic to daily markets was usually gradual. Periodic markets would acquire daily sectors for certain commodities before the entire market became a daily one. The bulk of daily markets were found in the towns and cities. These operated primarily as retail distribution centres, although in the major cities wholesale markets also operated.

Apart from their periodicity, West African markets have also been distinguished by their locality and clientele. According to Arhin (1979:6-7) in Asante there were what he calls 'local', 'district' and 'regional' markets. Arhin emphasizes that these designations are not used in the sense of a hierarchy of markets but in the sense that a local market was meant for the 'local' people, whereas 'district' and 'regional' markets were meant to serve more than the district and one region. In Asante, examples of local markets include the two daily markets of Kumasi, the capital, which served the inhabitants of the town and those from nearby villages. There were numerous district markets located in boundary and industrial towns or at military depots. Finally, regional markets were located on the outskirts of Asante and brought together traders from all over West Africa. Among the most famous of these were Salaga, Bonduku, Atebubu and Kintampo. A similar trade regime can be seen in many other West African states in the nineteenth century.

In many parts of West Africa a clear distinction was made between domestic and foreign trade. In Asante domestic or internal trading was known as dwadi, and its traders as dwadifo, while foreign trade was batadi and the traders batadifo. The two trades were organizationally different. Certainly batadi required far more capital, security, skill and transport services than dwadi.

Trade between different countries and regions in West Africa was well developed by the beginning of the nineteenth century and it expanded in the course of the century.

Inter-regional Trade

The regional trading networks that developed in nineteenth century West Africa were complex and involved many staples. The literature on them is particularly rich on the salt and kola trades (Lovejoy, 1980, 1985). One of the most vibrant trading relations was between Asante and the Sokoto Caliphate. This trade was mainly conducted through the cities of Salaga and Kano , each of which had a population of approximately 40 - 50,000 by the mid-nineteenth century.

The two cities 'fulfilled complementary functions: Salaga served as the bulking point and transit terminus for kola exports and northern imports, while Kano acted as the wholesale centre for kola distribution in the central Sudan' (Lovejoy, 1980:113). Asante expanded its kola exports to Sokoto as the slave trade declined, while Sokoto increased its kola imports because the people of the Caliphate 'were increasingly denied the resort to alcoholic stimulants' by the new Muslim government (Wilks, 1971:130). Lovejoy (1980) estimates that Sokoto's annual imports of kola from Asante by the overland route averaged between 70 and 140 metric tons at the beginning of the nineteenth century, rising to 250 - 350 metric tons towards the end of the century.

There can be little doubt that the kola trade was very profitable. According to figures for 1891 the price mark-up in kola between Salaga and Kano was between 1,700 and 2,800%, or to put it differently, 'prices increased approximately 570 - 680 cowries per mile for each donkey load between Salaga and Kano' (Lovejoy, 1980:122). After covering transport costs, the merchants were left with enough profits to purchase more donkeys if they wanted to and load them with natron on the journey back. From the available data it would appear that kola prices adjusted for inflation remained relatively stable during the nineteenth century in both Asante and Sokoto despite yearly fluctuations .

Asante-Sokoto trade was of course not confined to kola and natron. Asante exports to Sokoto also included gold and, in the course of the century, an assortment of European manufactures acquired from the coast, especially guns, gunpowder and metal ware. Additional Sokoto exports to Asante consisted of animals, such as horses, asses, donkeys, bullocks, sheep and goats, textile and leather goods, dried onion leaves, and some North African re-exports, particularly silk. Slaves constituted another item in both directions (Arhin, 1979:52; Lovejoy, 1980:119-26).

Most studies on long-distance trade in nineteenth century West Africa have tended to ignore trade in grain and other foodstuffs on the assumption that it was confined to 'luxury goods', or that the grain and food trade was limited to local trade only. It cannot be overemphasized that there were many areas that did not, or could not, produce enough grain for themselves, and so depended on imports to satisfy their needs. For example, the Tuaregs of the southern Sahara relied on the Central Sudan for their grain supplies. By the end of the nineteenth century, the estimated 50,000 Tuaregs of Air Massif and Azawak bought up to 7,500 metric tons of grain annually from the Central Sudan (Lovejoy and Baier, 1975:555). In addition to grain, they also bought textiles, swords, tobacco and cola, in exchange for animals, salt and dates.

The Moors of the western Sahara bought their grain from the Maraka in the Middle Niger valley. The Maraka grain markets, especially at Bamako, grew rapidly from the 1880s following the French occupation of Bamako in 1883. The expansion of the Bamako grain market led to increased plantation production and changes in the structure of distribution, whereby farmers began, unlike before, to sell surplus grain from the previous year before the new harvest was safely stored. The farmers became more vulnerable to famine when their crops failed due to drought or insect plagues, as happened in Kita in 1899-1900, when over 1800 people died. But the grain trade was very profitable to the merchants involved. Indeed, 'in many cases, profits from participating in the grain trade were more substantial than those from more exotic products' (Roberts, 1980a:48).

The size of the food trade was quite substantial when it includes the provisioning of long-distance trade caravans and the Atlantic slave trading ships. Northrup (1978: 180) has estimated that by the end of the eighteenth century 1,200,000 yams per annum were sold to slave trading ships at the Bight of Biafra alone. He believes that:

the actual trade from the hinterland to the coast would have been several times this amount since slaves and crew also had to be fed during the many months spent in port assembling a cargo and the coastal inhabitants themselves consumed vast amounts. Moreover, yams were but one of the items supplied from the hinterland. The livestock trade must also have been substantial..

Trade was of great interest to West African states. However, the policies of these states towards trade and traders cannot easily be generalized. That all states sought to derive benefits from trade there can be little doubt. But their ability to control it has often been exaggerated. The thesis that West African states, particularly the coastal ones involved in the Atlantic trade, dominated or monopolized external commerce, has rested largely on the royal monopoly that the kings of Dahomey supposedly enjoyed. Law (1977a:556) has convincingly demonstrated that 'this Dahomian royal commercial monopoly is, for all its influence on the thinking of historians and anthropologists of Africa, essentially a myth'. Thus in West Africa, nothing approaching the North African monopoly system was established. It does not mean, of course, that West African states did not seek to control trade at all. They could intervene in the organization of trade in several ways, for example, by imposing taxes and tolls, sponsoring state traders and restricting the activities of private traders.

Toll fees and taxes on trade and traders offered states an important means of raising revenue. In the Yoruba towns the charges collected from toll gates 'were part of the revenues relied upon by the political elite' (Falola, 1989:69). In the Senegambian region 'the state was entitled to about one-tenth of all passing merchandise, just as it was entitled to about one-tenth of the agricultural produce' (Curtin, 1975:286). In addition, the merchants were expected to give the political authorities 'gifts'. Gift-giving was meant to be mutual and intended to forge cordial social relations between merchants and rulers, but in many instances it lapsed into invisible taxation of the former by the latter. Of course traders could try to avoid routes passing through areas with heavy tolls and taxes. This was easier for those on overland caravans than on canoes. It has in fact been suggested that the predominance of river travel in Senegambian trade facilitated the development and enforcement of a high tax structure (Roberts, 1980b:183).

Elsewhere, it appears, the tax structure on trade caravans was progressive, that is, the larger traders were expected to pay more than the smaller ones. In Asante, Daaku (1971:176) tells us that: 'the only places where regular tolls were known to have been paid by travellers were at ferrying points across rivers'. Those using trade paths were not required to pay tolls. This policy was intended to encourage trade, which the state believed offered more benefits than direct taxation. The more traders there were, for example, the more opportunities women had to sell cooked meals and landlords to rent accommodation.

Among the states which appointed their own traders to compete with private traders were Dahomey and Asante. In the eighteenth century the Dahomian 'king's traders', called akhigan, were stationed at Whydah, where they were responsible for conducting trade on the monarch's behalf as well as collecting customs duties. In the nineteenth century they were replaced by the chacha who were given additional powers, including administrative authority over the European merchants resident at Whydah. These powers were later reduced. Competition from private merchants intensified as palm oil supplanted the trade in slaves (Law, 1977). In Asante the oman or state merchants enjoyed a temporary monopoly in the kola trade. For about 20 days when they were disposing of the state kola the trade routes were temporarily closed to the private traders. Moreover, the latter, unlike the oman traders, paid tolls of 25 nuts on each load. The oman traders could also ply both the northern and coastal markets. They resold ivory and slaves acquired from the north on the coast in exchange for arms and ammunition and other European goods. Some of the slaves were retained in Asante itself and used in collecting kola and on farms near Kumasi. The profits they made were added to the *fotoo* or state treasury (Arhin, 1979).

Private traders could be controlled in a number of different ways. In Dahomey private traders at Whydah could only trade under licence from the king. Apparently 'negotiations between the Europeans and Dahomian traders had also to be conducted through official intermediaries appointed by the Yevogan, the royal governor of Whydah' (Law, 1977:565). Traders from the hinterland were not allowed to trade directly at Whydah. They were expected to sell their commodities, including slaves, to Dahomian traders, who then resold them to the Europeans at the coast.

The Asante state did not worry much about the so-called target traders, whose trade was irregular and confined to selling goods that they had themselves produced in exchange for a specific commodity. It was more concerned about the professional traders, whom it feared might challenge the hegemony of the ruling class if they became too wealthy and powerful. The fact that these traders were mostly Muslims in a largely non-Muslim society reinforced these fears. So their movements in metropolitan Asante were restricted (Wilks, 1971:132-138). Indeed, the external markets were located on the outskirts of Asante, away from its major towns.

The Asante policy of restricting foreign traders to frontier towns such as Salaga and Bonduku was motivated as much by political considerations as economic ones. It allowed the state to control them more effectively and contain any possible disruption from them. Also:

> *by confining the merchants to one market, Asante producers and traders received higher prices. The policy erased the natural advantage that savanna traders possessed through their monopoly of transport livestock and their knowledge of northern markets* (Lovejoy, 1980:19).

But the policy was not without its advantages for the traders themselves. It helped strengthen their corporate identity and relations with other commercial diasporas in the region. Asante suzerainty over these market towns ended when its forces were defeated by the British in 1874. The market of Salaga went into decline. But new market towns emerged, such as Atebubu and Kintampo, both of which owed their growth to their favourable geographical and political positions (Arhin, 1971, 1979).

As in the case of North Africa, West African market towns also had separate quarters for traders from different parts of the region. Each quarter contained a market place and a residential compound where some members of that particular commercial diaspora were permanently settled. These proprietors, known as mai gida in Hausa, provided accommodation to the visiting traders, served as their trading agents and brokers, provided them with short-term credit and packing and storage facilities, and acted as translators. The mai gida were therefore absolutely essential to the smooth operations of the markets. Many of them became wealthy, and profited from juggling the asking and selling prices. Moreover, these proprietors were often substantial traders in their own right. Disputes and problems that might arise among the different groups of traders, and between them and the local state, were usually resolved by informal councils made up of the various community leaders (Lovejoy, 1980:127-31). In Ilorin, where 'political clientage and commercial brokerage were interconnected' (O'Hear, 1986:69), it was virtually impossible for foreigners to conduct trade without making use of local commercial landlord/brokers.

Trading Diasporas

Many of the merchants who dominated trade in the Central Sudan were called Hausa, while those in the Western Sudan were known as Juula. The terms Hausa and Juula were as much ethnic appellations as they were occupational designations. Not all those who were called Hausa were ethnic Hausa, but entrepreneurs who had been integrated into the commercial network radiating from Sokoto. For example, the merchant groups that dominated Asante-Sokoto trade, namely, the Agalawa, Tokarawa and Kambarin Beriberi, were originally immigrants who arrived and were incorporated into Hausa society only in the early nineteenth century. These groups benefited from the disruptions caused by the jihad, or holy wars, which destroyed many of the Hausa commercial communities. They quickly established their own commercial networks which soon transformed them from poor immigrants into some of the wealthiest Hausa communities. The richest among them maintained residences in several cities and supported scores of dependents. They also invested in large plantations employing hundreds of workers, including slaves (Lovejoy, 1973; 1980:Chapter 5).

The occupational origins of the Juula is even clearer. Juula simply meant merchant in Malinke. The Juula were merchants of diverse ethnic origins, bound together by common commercial interests, religion and language. Over the centuries the Juula came to perceive themselves, and to be perceived by others, as a distinct group, with specialized clans, which in reality represented different spatial segments in the commercial complex of the Western Sudan. As early as the seventeenth century several Juula communities had emerged in the Senegambian region. They included the Gajaaga, whose trade network emanated from the upper Senegal and extended eastward to the southern Sahara and the Niger bend; the Jahaanke, who dominated the region between the Gambia in the west and the Niger in the east; the Malinke Mori to the south of Jahaanke, and the Darbo who dominate the lower Gambian region (Curtin, 1975; Wright, 1977). The prosperity and strength of these trading communities and networks shifted with the changing political and economic conditions. The position of the Jahaanke, for example, weakened in the course of the nineteenth century as a result of the destruction of some of Jahaanke settlements by Kaarta at the beginning of the century and later by the end of the slave trade (Curtin, 1975:232).

The Juula and Hausa constituted what Cohen (1971:267) has called a trading diaspora, 'a nation of socially interdependent, but spatially dispersed, communities', developed to overcome the many problems inherent in long-distance trade, such as the exchange of information, the speedy despatch of goods, especially perishable ones, provision of credit, and the adjudication and maintenance of authority structures. The two commercial diasporas were held together by common material interests and the ideological pulls of shared language, the invented tradition of ethnic homogeneity, and adherence to one religion, Islam.

Islam offered the merchants a uniform legal structure and a moral code which regulated and facilitated relations over vast distances within different political, economic and social systems. It also furnished them with literacy an indispensable tool for business. Islam, moreover, gave the traders considerable prestige and protection, given the non-Muslims' respect for the Muslims' spiritual powers. Indeed, it reinforced their exclusivity as an occupational class. Thus Islam amounted to a passport for the traders: it gave them both identification and mobility (Lovejoy, 1971; Curtin, 1975; Cohen, 1971). Its spread in the nineteenth century following the jihads consolidated both the community of believers and the community of traders.

Not all West African trading communities were incorporated into the Hausa or Juula commercial diasporas, or established their own diasporas (Sundstrom, 1974). Traders from communities without diasporas used brokerage facilities of local brokers and agents. The Maraka merchants, for example, who did not have a distinct and coordinated diaspora, relied on local jaatigiw, who housed them and their goods, and located sellers for them, in exchange for a commission. The Maraka merchants made no attempts to solidify 'relations with jaatigiw through marriage ties. This was strictly an economic relationship' (Roberts, 1980b:180).

Women Traders

It is often assumed that the ranks of professional merchants were confined to men, and that women were not involved in trade beyond their localities because they were shackled by domestic chores, and lacked the time, capital and skills to rise above petty trade (Hopkins, 1973:56). Recent research shows that this picture is not entirely correct. Yoruba women, for example, actively participated in trade, including trade organized over long distances. Indeed, as towns and cities grew, and domestic slaves became more available, free Yoruba women in the nineteenth century left food production to concentrate on trade (Agiri, 1980:134; Afonja, 1981:308-9). Law (1977b:231) has shown that the King's wives were particularly active as traders and provided the main source of his wealth. Writing about Dahomey, Law (1977a:565-6) also notes that towards the end of the eighteenth century one of the principal traders at Whydah, owning property to the value of seventy slaves, was a women, called 'Paussie'. Coastal women traders played an important role as economic and cultural brokers in African-European trade. One example is that of the signares of Senegambia who became quite wealthy and powerful (Brooks, 1976; Mahoney, 1965).

More recently, White (1981, 1987) has produced a fascinating and detailed portrait of Krio women traders in nineteenth century Sierra Leone. She has shown how the Krio women manipulated their diverse cultural backgrounds and the colonial situation to advance their interests as traders. Against great odds, including the sexist attitudes of the colonial officials and of the European and African merchants, and the dangers of looting, kidnapping and enslavement in the interior, the Krio women traders made their mark, not only as petty traders, but as professional traders as well. They competed successfully, for example, in the Freetown meat trade, and they were instrumental in the establishment of Freetown's Big Market, which was constructed in 1860 and became a central market in Sierra Leone connecting the local, national and international economies. The Krio women were in fact heavily involved in the kola trade from Sierra Leone to Senegambia and Lagos. In order to facilitate this trade they formed a trading diaspora. These dynamic women were to lose their fortunes and become marginalized in the twentieth century.

Monetary and Credit Systems

Trade within West Africa brought together countries and regions using different currencies. For example, gold was standard in Asante and cowries in Sokoto. Asante's gold currency was used in the form of coins and gold-dust. The latter was more common. Traders would normally carry balances (nsania) and weights (abrammoo) for measuring quantities of gold-dust. One ounce of gold was worth £E4; it was subdivided into sixteen ackies which amounted to 5s each. This was further subdivided into 12 takus of 5d each (Reynolds, 1974:33-34; Arhin, 1979:16; Gerrard, 1980). In the frontier market towns cowries were the main currency used as a medium of exchange, or as units of account. Two thousand cowries were equivalent to one ackey of gold. Needless to say, the monetary transactions in these towns were quite complex (Lovejoy, 1980:126-7).

The subject of West Africa's currencies has received considerable attention from economic historians. There was a time when the substantivist model held that West Africa's 'traditional' currencies represented 'primitive' money. Marion Johnson's studies have done much to debunk this myth. She has demonstrated that gold was widely used as currency in West Africa (Johnson, 1966, 1968, 1970). By the nineteenth century there were many other metals that were used as currency apart from gold. Copper and brass rods and wire were used in the Cross River of modern-day Nigeria (Latham, 1971). Iron currencies were particularly widespread and came in several forms, as coins, manillas, and bars. Examples of iron coins are the sompe or kissi penny used in the northern Ivory Coast and Liberia and north-eastern Guinea. Iron bars were used quite extensively in Senegambian internal and international trade (Curtin, 1975:234, 240-53), and in parts of present-day southern Nigeria (Northrup, 1978:167-64).

Large areas of West Africa used cowries. 'The cowrie currency', Hogendorn and Johnson (1986:1-2) have written in their authoritative study on cowrie money, 'was exceptionally «modern» in a manner not even equalled by the great international currencies of the twentieth century. During the heyday of the pound sterling before World War One, or the US dollar after that time, neither circulated very widely in the market places of other countries. Yet the «primitive» cowrie crossed dozens of frontiers... spent as money in coastal Burma or Timbuktu, in Benin or Bengal, on long stretches of the Ganges or the Niger'. Indeed, it is not far-fetched to say that cowries 'have circulated as currency in more places in the world than any coin' (Safer and Gill, 1982:38).

Cowries had several attributes which made them popular as money: they were relatively scarce, durable, easy and aesthetically satisfying to handle, nearly indestructible, almost impossible to counterfeit, convenient to count, and had little leakage into commodity use. There are about two hundred species of cowrie, but only two, Cypraea moneta and Cypraea annulus, have been widely used as money.

Moneta was the only cowrie money used in West Africa until the mid-nineteenth century when imports of annulus started. By the beginning of the nineteenth century, moneta had been in use in parts of the region from perhaps as early as the eleventh century. The source of moneta for West Africa, as well as India, were the Maldive islands, where the cowrie trade was held by royal monopoly. Moneta imports at first came through North Africa, and later through the European coastal trade, which was dominated by the Portuguese in the sixteenth century, followed by the Dutch and British in the seventeenth. By '1800 the British had achieved almost complete ascendancy' and in the first eight years of the century they brought 'an annual average of over 68 tons compared to 24-ton average for the eight years 1791-1798' (Hogendorn and Johnson, 1986:64). Thus there were two cowrie zones in West Africa, one along the coastal belt, and the other in the savannah interior.

Cowries were 'originally used as «small change» for a gold currency. Gold cannot be subdivided beyond a certain point, and very small purchases such as the day's needs of vegetables had to be made in a different medium' (Hogendorn and Johnson, 1986:114). In the northern zone cowries were counted individually in groups of five, while along the coast they were counted in 'strings' of 40s, 100s or whatever number was the local convention. Until the 1820s cowries were on a gold standard, after which they were on a dollar standard as the use of silver dollars in the region spread. The exchange rate between cowries, gold and silver dollars was sometimes fixed and at other times left to float. Over the centuries the exchange rate between cowries and gold depreciated. In the northern zone, cowrie values fell from about 8,000 shells to an ounce of gold in the fourteenth century to 20,000 by about 1780 and 25,000 around 1850, while in the coastal zone the exchange rate was 32,000 in 1780 and 38,000 in 1850 (Hogendorn and Johnson, 1986:132). There can be little doubt that cowries facilitated the development of an integrated regional market in large parts of West Africa.

The use of cowries began to decline from the mid-nineteenth century for a number of reasons. There was rapid economic growth in West Africa following the abolition of the slave trade, so demand for cowries increased. A new and much nearer source of supply for cowries, of the annulus variety, was found in Zanzibar. At the same time, competing European firms imported large quantities of cowries to purchase palm oil or for speculative purposes (Lovejoy, 1974:575). The result was that between 1851 and 1869 West Africa imported well over 35,000 tons of annulus cowries from East Africa (Johnson, 1970:24). This upset monetary stability in the region. To make matters worse the British, who occupied Lagos in 1861 introduced currency reforms whose effects extended beyond Lagos. These reforms included 'the demonetization of the dollar and the introduction of the British silver coin, both of which had adverse effects on the value of the already depreciated cowrie currency' (Hopkins, 1966:25). The impact was most pronounced along the coast, where between 1850 and 1895 the decline in the value of cowries to the shilling ranged from about 420% in Accra to over 500% in Whydah and 800% in Lagos (Johnson, 1970:340). The inflation gradually spread into the interior to as far as Sokoto where cowries lost 250% of their value between the mid-1840s and the mid-1860s (Lovejoy, 1980:120).

The effects of the inflation were contradictory. On the one hand, it undermined those who held large amounts of cowries, mostly large merchants, aristocrats, and governments. In response, governments, such as the emirates in the Sokoto Caliphate, raised the fixed tax rates. On the other hand, the exchange rates were much lower in the north than in the south, so that 'inflation may have been an important stimulant in the north-south trade at the middle of the century. Hausa traders... arrived in (the south) in ever larger numbers. By the 1880s and 1890s they swelled Lagos by the thousands' (Lovejoy, 1974:579). Hogendorn and Johnson (1986:150) have argued that 'the great nineteenth century inflation that depreciated the cowrie so badly ended its efficacy for large transactions. But it would not have been a sufficiently strong cause to end its usefulness for the smaller everyday purchases in the market place'. The coup de grace was delivered by colonial hostility to the cowrie and inflation of colonial coinage. During the colonial period the cowrie was demonetized without compensation. The last cowrie holders not only lost their personal fortunes, demonetization led to an incalculable loss 'for the economy as a whole, in that centuries' worth of export value sold in exchange for cowries was now gone completely', for cowries, like, ironically, the colonial currencies themselves, 'were full-bloodied in the sense that they had to be acquired by exporting' (Hogendorn and Johnson, 1986:154; Ofonagoro, 1979; Webb, 1982; Hogendorn and Gemery, 1988).

In parts where the cowrie-gold currency system did not penetrate, other currencies were used. Cloth money was used in some parts of the northern savanna. The units were based on the length of the cloth. Combinations of strips formed larger monetary units. Among the Tiv, for example, there were three main units. The smallest was the strip, tsar, which was equivalent to approximately two pence at the beginning of the colonial era. Then came the ten-strip piece, puikonodo, valued at two shillings, and the twenty-strip ikundu, valued at four shillings. There was also the thirty-piece ikundu-berave (Dorward, 1976:582-3). It was normally cheap, undyed cloth that was used for currency. If more expensive cloth was used it was reckoned as multiples of common cloth. Cloth currency rarely circulated alone. A number of ancillary currencies were used alongside the cloth currency. That included grain or beads that could be used for small change in petty transactions, or metal currencies for larger units. In the Senegambian region, for example, one strip, called tama, was equated to five mud of millet. A mud was approximately 2.25 kgs (Curtin, 1975:239). Among the Tiv two atsar were equivalent to one brass rod. The ancillary currencies provided the cloth currencies with greater flexibility and helped moderate any temporary shortages or glut of cloth currency.

The stability of the cloth currencies varied from one place to another depending on the internal strength of a particular economy and the patterns of its integration into the regional and the European-dominated world economy. Among the Tiv the cloth currency appears to have been remarkably stable during the nineteenth century. Indeed, it survived well into the twentieth century. Its decline only came in the 1920s as a result of the massive infusion of colonial money to Tiv labourers involved in the construction of the Eastern Nigerian Railway and the expansion of banniseed production for the colonial market (Dorward, 1976:591; 1975).

The story was quite different in the Chad region. There the cloth currency was based on the copper currency, rotl, that had been dominant until the mid-eighteenth century when the rise in copper value drove out the use of copper as a currency. One rotl was equivalent to four gabaga, or cloth units. The exchange rate of the rotl to the silver dollar fell sharply from the 1820s. In the 1820s 10 rotl were exchanged for 1 silver dollar. In the 1860s the rate was 120 to 1, and it reached 150 to 1 by the end of the century, despite the depreciation of the silver dollar itself against gold. Attempts were made to stabilize the currency in the 1840s.

> *The value of the dollar was known to fluctuate with the arrival of the Saharan caravans, so cowries were introduced at a fixed rate of 32 to the rotl, 8 to the gabaga. Unfortunately this was on the eve of the great cowrie inflation, and the cowrie proved even less stable than the silver*

dollar... After the 1860s, cloth was no longer officially regarded as money in Bornu, but it continued to be used for making purchases, even as late as 1936 (Johnson, 1980:198).

The Senegambian cloth currencies also experienced fluctuations in the nineteenth century. Cloth currencies had been used in this region for many centuries, but on the Gambia they appear to have fallen into disuse in the eighteenth century. They made a comeback in the nineteenth century in response to the expansion of the groundnut trade. In Senegal the local cloth currency, pagne, made of tama, or strips, was increasingly supplemented by French imported indigo-dyed cloth from India called guinee. The guinee was used as currency in lower Senegal. In upper Senegal it became a larger unit equivalent to a number of pagnes. The exchange rate between guinee, pagnes and francs became more complicated from the 1830s as a result of excessive imports of guinees and francs. The price of guinee cloth fell from 30 francs in the early nineteenth century to six francs which ultimately became the ghost-money value. Attempts were made to adjust the pagne, but were complicated by the pagne's alignments to the silver franc and grain. 'Eventually the position was reached when no amount of adjustment would keep guinee, franc/tama/pagne, and grain in line. In some areas, the guinee survived as a ghost-money equivalent to six francs; in others, the tama and pagne came to represent different quantities of cloth, related to the franc and the measure of grain respectively, until eventually the French metricated the grain measure, and finally ousted the pagne from its place in the currency system' (Johnson, 1980:199).

It can be seen that West African societies not only had complex currency systems, but these systems changed with the passage of time. It is now generally accepted among economic historians that West African currencies had all the functions of modern money: medium of exchange, measure of value, store of wealth, and standard for deferred payment.

Given the existence of such a wide range of currencies and extensive trade within the region it stands to reason that capital markets developed in West Africa. Commercial credit markets facilitated domestic and foreign trade. Traders obtained loans to finance their operations from each other or from specialized bankers and money lenders. Cheques and letters of credit were also used by West African merchants. Security was often provided by depositing bonds supplied by third parties or by pawning dependents and livestock, and mortgaging land and other property. Debt repayment was enforced through legal sanctions and moral persuasion. It was legally accepted in many societies for the creditor to seize and hold hostage the defaulting debtor, or his property, or a member of his family, to serve the creditor until the debt was settled. Moral pressure could sometimes go as far as the creditor going on hunger strike 'in full view of the debtor's community' (Sundtsrom, 1974:41). It would appear that the principle of insolvent debtors declaring legally bankrupt was practised in very few places, such as Monrovia.

The risks involved in lending and the shortage of capital were reflected in the high interest rates that were charged. According to Sundstrom (1974:34-5) 'the collected evidence indicates an annual interest that was rarely lower than 100%'. Such expensive credit could act as a barrier to the growth of trade, but this was not universally the case. In some societies, such as among the Bole and northern Ewe, interest was only charged on loans made in currency, not in kind. There were also Islamic strictures against interest. Sundstrom (1974:36) believes, however, that West African merchants 'paid only lip service to Muslim commercial principles. Examples have been found of bankers investing for their depositors, joint stock loan banks, co-operative savings banks, currency exchange brokers, as well as speculation on the future value of currency and staple commodities, growing crops, import and export goods and purchasing goods, such as cloth, on approval and subsequently letting them out at an interest'.

Transport and Transport Workers

Trade required, and led to, the development of several transport systems in nineteenth century West Africa. Overland transport, as in other parts of Africa, depended largely on caravans, while waterborne transport was provided by canoes and boats. The trade caravans have been characterized as 'armed convoys' and 'slow moving markets' (Hopkins, 1973:63). This was not true of all caravans. Daaku (1971:174-5) has argued, for example, that Asante caravans were usually small and 'were never preceded nor followed by armed bands'. According to Roberts (1980b:177) Maraka caravans were also relatively small and 'did not stop at numerous villages en route buying foodstuffs and selling their goods'. Maraka merchants confined their long-distance excursions to the dry season and so wanted rapid turnaround and carried enough food with them.

Hopkins' characterization, however, holds for the great caravans of the Central and Western Sudan and the trans-Saharan trade. As they moved ponderously from town to town, they bought and sold goods on the way. For the duration of the expedition the caravan functioned as a commercial firm with corporate structure and a workforce. In the caravans of the Central Sudan the management unit consisted of the caravan leader, known as madugu, and a number of assistants. As the administrative and military leader of the expedition the madugu was expected to know the route well, direct defence operations, maintain order and settle disputes within the caravan, and negotiate payment of taxes with local rulers. His staff consisted of professional traders and travellers. The madugu's most important assistants were the jagaba, the guide, the uban dawaki, the organizer of the rest stops, the malamin takardi, the keeper of the accounts, the malamin ayari, the scribe, and the mai gangan madugu, the drummer. The caravan leaders were mostly successful and respected merchants. Some caravans would stretch over several miles. Such caravans were divided into sections, each under an assistant caravan leader (Lovejoy, 1980, 1985).

The caravan workers can be divided into three occupational groups - the porters and teamsters, who loaded, unloaded and looked after the pack animals, and the service workers who looked after the caravan personnel by preparing meals, baths, washing clothes, and so on, and the last group consisting mostly of women. In Malinke caravans the hardest service chores, such as fetching firewood, were performed by slave women. When everybody else was resting the women would spin cotton which they later sold for their own profit. It would appear that the women caravan service workers performed the same tasks they did back in the village. This has led Roberts (1980b:178) to characterize caravans as 'slow-moving villages'.

It was, however, not uncommon for women to be employed as porters. A number of observations have been left behind by European explorers, such as Clapperton in the 1820s and Passarge in the 1890s, of 'great numbers' of women porters in the Sokoto Caliphate (Dufill and Lovejoy, 1985:145-50). Estimates from Abomey at the turn of the twentieth century indicate that one-third of the porters in the caravans passing through the town on their way from Savalon to Cotonou were women (Manning, 1985:56). Relatively rare was the situation among the Bette in Guinea where women were dominant both as merchants and porters (Coquery-Vidrovitch and Lovejoy, 1985:16). Also rare was the other extreme of caravans that had no women, as was the case among the Maraka (Roberts, 1980b:177).

The mobilization, control, and remuneration of the caravan workers varied according to the type of labour used, the organization of trade and the distances travelled. Caravans used three main forms of labour: household, slave and wage labour. 'Target marketeers' almost invariably used their own household labour (Arhin, 1979:12). It was also quite common for professional merchants wishing to organize a caravan to use their household members to prepare and load their merchandise and to employ them as their apprentices and assistants on the caravan. As members of the household, these workers were not paid, but were provided with food, clothing and shelter. Moreover, 'in return for their labour, they gained experience, contacts, and access to credit' (Duffill and Lovejoy, 1985:145). But household labour was not always sufficient or reliable, especially for the big merchants.

These merchants often supplemented their household labour with slave and hired labour.

Some merchants found it convenient to use domestic slaves or slaves intended for sale to carry loads. With domestic slaves there was always the risk of escape, while trade slaves were more valuable if they reached the market in a prime condition, not weak and exhausted from long travel and carrying heavy loads. Moreover, trade slaves were unmotivated and inefficient, for 'fully loaded trade slaves, especially if shackled, slowed the pace of the average caravan' (Dufill and Lovejoy, 1985:159). Not surprisingly, the use of trade slaves in caravans was rather limited. Indeed, Daaku (1971:174) contends that 'most of the people who were described as slaves by the European observers were those who had hired their services to some inland traders'. Labour for official traders was often provided through tributary services (Arhin, 1979:12).

By the nineteenth century workers for hire as porters, teamsters and service labour were readily available in many parts of West Africa. These jobs attracted both the poor who needed extra resources to survive, and the relatively well-off who sought to accumulate sufficient capital and experience to become independent traders. Caravan work offered some people a means of supplementing household income during the slack agricultural season, and others the possibility of escaping from unexpected socioeconomic hardships and political persecution. It also gave the adventurous ones an opportunity to explore new worlds. Despite their divergent social origins, the porters and teamsters constituted a working class bound by common interests. They sought to reduce their workload and increase their incomes, while their employers, whoever they were, wanted the exact opposite. Data on wages is hard to come by. According to reports from the Yoruba/Nupe area, porters' wages in the mid-nineteenth century were 1,200 cowries per day, rising to 1,500 per day by the 1890s. Due to inflation the real wages were lower in the 1890s than they had been in the 1850s, the equivalent of 1s 2.5d to 9d. Workers contracted for a day received about a third of the professional porter's wage (Duffill and Lovejoy, 1985:150).

The use of paid labour in caravan transport became increasingly common in the course of the nineteenth century. But not all the porters and teamsters were entirely dependent on the wage relation. Many of them carried personal items for sale in addition to the trade goods for which they were contracted. Thus, apart from being workers they were also petty entrepreneurs. Indeed, for this reason, some porters and teamsters insisted on being paid in kind, rather than in cash. For them a cash wage would dissolve their dual status and leave them unambiguously as workers. Their mode of struggle often reflected this duality. Their strategies were both individualistic and collective. They resorted to desertions as much as they engaged in theft. The caravan expedition reinforced their class solidarity, while the irregularity of their employment diffused it.

In many parts of West Africa human labour constituted the backbone of caravan transport. Indeed, in parts of the forest region porterage was virtually the only form of transporting commodities over long distances. The use of pack animals in this region 'was restricted by a combination of try-panosomiasis [sleeping sickness] and lack of pasture' (Hopkins, 1973:72). The porters carried heavy loads. For example, porters in the Bight of Benin carried:

> up to 40 to 50 kilograms of salt, and moved their loads for carrying them a distance of some 800 to 1000 meters, after which they rested their burdens against the fork of a tree, assisted in this by a pole that they carried for that purpose... The standard day's journey was roughly 25 kilometres, slightly less for those carrying salt (Manning, 1985:56).

Elsewhere in West Africa porterage was supplemented by pack animals, which included horses, oxen, donkeys and camels. Horses were used in the savanna and Sahel regions of West Africa long before camels became dominant. West Africa relied for its supply of horses on imports from North Africa, local stock, and to a smaller extent from the fifteenth century, Portuguese imports (Law, 1980; Elbl, 1991). In the nineteenth century horses were common in the Sahel and savanna regions. Their most important use was military. In addition, they were used for hunting and slave raiding and in festivals and ceremonies. But, according to Fisher (1973:367-8), horses only 'made a moderate contribution as pack animals'. Oxen were regularly used in the savanna, particularly in Bornu. Camel caravans coming from the north often transferred their goods at entrepots on the edges of the savanna to oxen and donkeys, 'which were better suited to savanna conditions' (Hopkins, 1973:72). Oxen carried heavier loads than donkeys, but they were more costly to buy and feed, and they also moved more slowly.

Donkeys were the chief pack animals in the savanna as camels were in the desert. Both were specially bred for transport purposes. Donkeys could carry up to a quarter the load camels could carry - 50 kgs as compared to 200 kgs. They also moved a bit slower - 30 kms per day as compared to 35 kms per day for camel caravans. Moreover, while three to five camels could be handled by one person, one person could handle three donkeys (Duffill and Lovejoy, 1985:153). All this 'gave camels a carrying capacity of more than double that of donkeys and 50% more than oxen' (McDougall, 1985:102). Thus camels required less labour input than donkeys per ton/kilometre. Camel freight, which was by far the cheapest, has been estimated at £E10 per 1,000 kilometres in the Sahel or across the desert at the end of the nineteenth century (Curtin, 1975:280).

Not surprisingly, the largest trade caravans in nineteenth century West Africa were camel caravans. Some of them could exceed 20,000 camels, although it was more common to have caravans of 3,000. Many large caravans were often associations of separate caravan units, which moved together for reasons of security, and usually broke up into smaller groups as danger passed, or as the expedition progressed. On average an individual caravan unit comprised 200 to 300 camels (McDougall, 1985:101). The caravan merchants sometimes owned the camels or hired them, which became more common as trade expanded and economic specialization in Sahelian and Saharan societies increased. The development of this specialized transport industry not only allowed groups with camels to accumulate, but also reinforced pastoral production, and linked the pastoral economies to the regional commercial system. Most of the camels and transporters that were used in the desert trade were provided by the Tuaregs 'who also controlled a sizeable proportion of desert-edge production destined for trans-Saharan export' (Lovejoy and Baier, 1975:558). Tuareg merchants operated business firms in the major cities of the Central Sudan.

Transport along the sea and the navigable rivers was provided by canoes and boats . They ranged in size 'from small fishing canoes carrying a crew of from one upwards, to canoes over 80 ft. in length and with a compliment of one hundred men or more' (Smith, 1970:518). The canoes used for fishing and in warfare differed from the specialized freight canoes. The latter were not only larger but also made of woods most resistant to water damage, and were sometimes fitted with cooking berths and storage rooms. The canoes were propelled on rivers by paddles and punting, while the sea-going vessels were fitted with sails. Needless to say, the canoe and boat-builders were specialists. The busiest waterways were along the coast and on the great rivers of the Niger, Senegal and Volta. Commercial water transport was also important on Lake Chad and the numerous small rivers that criss-crossed West Africa, especially in the forest region.

The freight canoes were owned by wealthy merchants individually or were organized in corporations. The merchants who had no canoes either rented the canoes or cargo space. We have some estimates of the freight charges made by Roberts (1980b:185) who argues that towards the end of the nineteenth century 'a 100-kilogram load could be sent from Jenne to Timbuktu for about 1,500 cowries. Passage could be had for 1,250 cowries. From Sinsani, a 100-kilogram load sent to Timbuktu cost 1,500 cowries and passage 2,000 cowries'. Boat building and renting became very profitable business. It cost between 200,000 cowries and 300,000 cowries to build a canoe. This capital could be retrieved in one voyage. Calculations based on a voyage in 1889 from Sinsani to Timbuktu show that the canoe owner made a net profit of 437,000 cowries, while the merchants who hired the canoe, netted 4,570,000 cowries in profit (Roberts, 1980b:185-6). The renter of the canoe often provided the sailors and was responsible for their upkeep during the expedition.

The volume of merchandise transported in the canoes and boats was quite substantial. For example, at the end of the nineteenth century in Dahomey, some 40,000 tons of goods were carried annually each way across the surf. The entire Bight of Benin may have employed up to 10,000 canoemen (Manning, 1985:62). It has been suggested that 'the trade canoes moved at a speed of some five kilometres per hour, roughly twice the speed of porters. Freight rates of 0.2 per ton-kilometre were about one-fifth the rate for head porterage' (Manning, 1985:61). Thus canoes could move bulky commodities more quickly and cheaply than other carriers. According to one estimate, 'the average 20 to 30 ton freight canoe on the Niger could transport as much produce as a caravan of 1,000 porters, 200 camels or 300 hundred oxen' (Roberts, 1980b:183). Consequently, merchants using canoes generated a lot more revenue per worker than with the other modes of transport, so that they not only made more profit, but could also afford to pay their workers more than, say, porters.

In Sinsani in the 1880s sailors were paid 30,000 cowries for the round trip, half in advance and the other half upon return. The sailors were generally more skilled than the other transport workers. They also tended to be more proletarianized in that their employment was regular and they were more dependent on cash wages and exhibited greater solidarity in defending their collective interests. Like the caravan workers, the boat workers were drawn from the household, or they were slaves, or 'free' wage labourers.

The transport system was transformed with the construction of railways, which were major instruments of colonization. The first railway in West Africa was built in Senegal in 1879, linking St Louis and Dakar, some 163 miles. The line was extended in later years. Other lines were subsequently built in other parts of French West Africa to secure the hinterland from British encroachment, facilitate military conquest, and tap the economic resources of the colonized regions. Military and economic considerations were also behind the British and German railway building programmes (Latham, 1978a:23-4). The British and Germans began railway construction in West Africa relatively late in the century. For example, the first lines built by the British were only laid down in 1896 in Sierra Leone and 1897 in Nigeria. In Togo, a German colony, the first line was opened in 1905. It is quite clear, therefore, that on the whole, railways and other modern forms

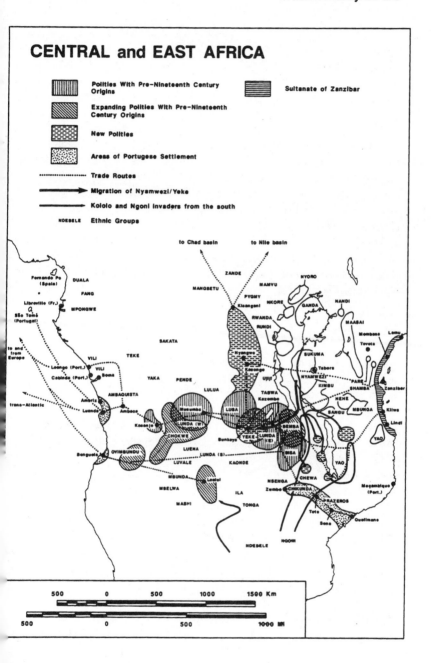

CENTRAL and EAST AFRICA

Polities With Pre–Nineteenth Century Origins

Expanding Polities With Pre–Nineteenth Century Origins

New Polities

Areas of Portugese Settlement

Trade Routes

Migration of Nyamwezi/Yeke

Kololo and Ngoni invaders from the south

NDEBELE   Ethnic Groups

Sultanate of Zanzibar

of transport did not have much impact on West African trade until the twentieth century.

Regional trade in West Africa was complemented by, and connected in complex ways to, trade with North Africa across the Sahara, and Europe across the Atlantic. We have already discussed trans-Saharan trade, and trade with Europe will be analyzed fully in Chapter 14. Our focus on West Africa's regional trade in this chapter has not been based merely on analytical convenience or an attempt to give West Africa 'initiative', but on the simple, if often forgotten, fact that West Africa's internal trade in the nineteenth century vastly exceeded its external trade in both volume and value (Farias, 1974; Austen, 1987:42). It is sobering to note that West Africa's salt trade alone was more valuable than the trans-Saharan trade (Lovejoy, 1984:101-10). There can be little doubt, therefore, that until the end of the nineteenth century regional demands and the regional economy, rather than links with the outside world, were the driving force in West Africa. But the seeds of external dependence had already been sewn, as we shall see in Chapter 14.

Conclusion

West Africa's pre-eminence as a trading region is well-established in African economic historiography. This chapter has recapped many of the well-known features of domestic and regional trade among some of the region's leading states and societies. As the case of Asante shows, the distinction between domestic and foreign trade used in this study is not just an analytical convenience, but was one that was also made at the time. The chapter has also sought to highlight aspects of West African trade that may not be as well known outside the small ranks of specialists on West African economic history. This includes the fact that long-distance trade was not confined to luxuries. Trade in foodstuffs was also quite large, which further undermines the notion of 'subsistence' economies. Moreover, it has become increasingly clear that states in the region did not exercise the amount of control over trade as suggested by some historians. Certainly nothing resembling the monopoly system in North Africa was ever established in West Africa. It is also apparent that women played a far more important role in foreign and inter-regional trade, both as professional traders and transport workers, than was once thought.

It has been argued that the trading diasporas not only facilitated the development of West Africa's intricate commercial networks, but studying them also throws light on some of the processes through which ethnicity was constructed in the precolonial era. In examining the monetary and credit systems , the argument has been made that West Africa currencies in the nineteenth century were as 'modern' as present-day currencies. Runaway inflation is not only a twentieth century invention. More importantly, the devastating impact of the demonetization of West African currencies by colonial governments at the turn of this century has not been adequately appreciated. This is a subject that deserves more research, for it lays bare the fact that the revolutionary impact of colonialism in the commercial sphere may not have been in the introduction of new currencies or methods of trade, for colonialism brought little that was really new, but in the demonetization of African currencies, which led to the loss of wealth accumulated over many centuries and impoverished, overnight, the merchant classes.

This chapter has also tried to unravel the development and organization of the transport industry which serviced West Africa's trade, by looking at the structure of the legendary caravans, and the less well-known waterborne transport system. The picture that is emerging is one of a fairly large and complex industry. Particularly fascinating are accounts of the development of the workforce, focusing on the patterns of skill formation, labour recruitment, remuneration, control and struggle. It is now quite clear that wage labour was more widespread in the precolonial era than was previously realized. Once again, this revises earlier analyses which assumed that before the introduction of colonial capitalism there was little labour differentiation outside of household or slave labour.

11. Trade in East Africa

Trading Centres

Until fairly recently, little was known about the development of trade during the nineteenth century in East Africa. At one time some scholars even believed that trade and markets did not exist in precolonial East Africa (Mair, 1934:130; Bohannan and Dalton, 1962:582; Oliver and Fage, 1962:108-10; Hill, 1963:447). While no reputable historian can now argue that trade in East Africa started as a result of external stimuli, many historians still discuss precolonial East African trade almost exclusively in terms of long-distance trade from the interior to the coast and between the coast and the Indian Ocean commercial world (Iliffe, 1979:40-52; Gray and Birmingham, 1970). For some, East Africa's integration into the Indian Ocean trading system ushered in underdevelopment (Alpers, 1975; Sheriff, 1979), while for others it led to the expansion of trade and production; in a word, development (Roberts, 1970; Austen, 1978, 1987).

As we saw in the case of West and North Africa, the role and impact of international trade during the precolonial era should not be exaggerated. Domestic and regional trade in East Africa was far more important than the region's international trade. Internal East African trade touched on the lives of far more people and involved more traders who carried a greater range and volume of commodities than was the case with overseas commerce. In this chapter, therefore, we will concentrate on analyzing the development of trade within East Africa itself.

The antiquity of trade in East Africa is now well-established. By the beginning of the nineteenth century both domestic and foreign trade in many parts of the region were quite well-developed. The structure and organization of markets in the region bore some similarities to West and North Africa. Markets were organized on a periodic or daily basis depending on the nature of demand, population distribution, and the forms of state intervention. As in the two regions that we have already looked at, periodic markets predominated in the rural areas where demand was relatively low and population dispersed, while daily markets were a feature of urban centres. To date, nobody has attempted to map out market periodicities for the whole of East Africa in the nineteenth century. Indications are that the average market week ranged between three and ten days. For example, the Chagga in present-day Tanzania had a three-day market-week, the Kikuyu in Kenya a four-day week, the Wasambaa also in Tanzania a five-day week, and the Maasai of western Kilimanjaro and Laitokitok had border markets held every ten days (Kjekshus, 1977:115-6). In many parts of Ethiopia markets were held weekly on a particular day which varied from one village to another (Pankhurst, 1968:346). These markets were usually organized in a local circuit so that each day of the week a market would be open in a given area. Among the Chagga each market day was known by the name of the market place.

Nineteenth century East Africa experienced considerable economic growth, characterized by increased specialization among and between communities and the expansion of urban centres. These developments encouraged the growth of daily markets. In Bunyoro-Kitara, Uzoigwe (1979:44) tells us, 'daily marketing seems to have been more widespread in the nineteenth century although such important centres as Katwe and Kibiro seem to have supported daily markets much earlier than that'. The markets were normally opened for several hours either in the morning or in the afternoon. The commodities traded included agricultural products, such as grains, bananas, potatoes, vegetables, coffee and tobacco, dairy products, animals, mineral products, particularly iron goods and salt, and craft manufactures like cloths, pottery, baskets and jewellery. In the second half of the nineteenth century three new commodities assumed greater importance, namely, ivory, arms and slaves. Most of the markets were located at the royal capital, which was moved from time to time, and near the residences of the important county or saza chiefs, and at industrial centres or at strategic sites and along border areas.

Some of the most famous daily markets in nineteenth century East Africa developed at provisioning stations along the major caravan routes. These stations usually developed into towns which depended for their livelihood on the producers and consumers of the surrounding countryside and on the regular visits of caravans engaged in regional and international trade. In Kenya, for instance, Taveta became an important market for caravans going to and coming from the coast. By the 1880s it had a community of some 6,000 people from all over the region (Kjekshus, 1977:115).

In western Tanzania Tabora and Ujiji boasted the largest markets. They grew rapidly in the second half of the nineteenth century. Among the commodities traded in these markets were foodstuffs, including grain crops and dried fish, forest products, livestock, pottery, salt, iron products, and increasingly ivory and slaves. Tabora and Ujiji were dominated by Nyamwezi traders. Other traders came from as far as the east and west coasts (Roberts, 1970).

The coastal belt contained some of East Africa's largest cities, such as Bagamoyo, Kilwa, Zanzibar, Mombasa and Malindi. Zanzibar was the largest. The total population of the island in 1857 was estimated at 300,000 of whom about 200,000 were slaves (Cooper, 1977:56). The markets in these cities served local, regional and international trade and the goods traded and the traders involved were quite varied. The most important commodities geared for local consumption or passed on into the circuits of regional and international trade were grains, especially millet and rice, spices, mainly cloves, fruits, such as coconuts, vegetables, textiles, ivory, slaves, metal and pottery products. The various products were often sold in special quarters or markets. Retail shops became widespread towards the end of the century. The traders included both locals and foreigners. Given the cosmopolitan nature of East African coastal cities, the designations 'local' and 'foreign' cut across various ethnic and racial groups. For example, Arabs who had been settled in Mombasa for centuries were more 'local' than the Akamba who came from the hinterland in nineteenth century caravans, or the Arab traders based in Oman who periodically came to Mombasa. Generally, coastal trade was dominated by Arab and Swahili merchants, who were united by the use of the Swahili language and adherence to Islam (Brown and Brown, 1976; Nicholls, 1971; Chittick, 1974; Freeman-Grenville, 1988).

Further north were the Somali port cities of Mogadishu, Zeila, Berbera and Merka, among others. These cities had vibrant daily markets which not only served the surrounding communities, but also the hinterlands of Somalia, Ethiopia and the Sudan. They were visited by traders from throughout the region. For example, Berbera's annual fair, held during the cool and dry period from October to April was attended, according to several estimates, by between 20,000 and 50,000 people. The growth and scale of these cities can be gauged from their foreign trade figures. For example, Zeila's imports rose from 6.9 million rupees in 1880-1 to 32.9 million rupees in 1890-1, while its exports rose from 7.3 to 30.7 million rupees during the same period. Also during the same period, Berbera's exports more than doubled from about nine to 21.7 million rupees and its imports quadrupled from 7.6 to 28.4 million rupees. Data for Mogadishu and Merka shows that in 1896-7 exports were valued at US$223,492 and US$184,520, respectively, and imports at US$203,824 and US$169,521.

The leading exports from these cities were coffee, ivory, civet, hides and skins, gum, butter, grain, sheep and goats, while the principal imports consisted of textiles, grain, mainly millet and rice, flour, sugar, dates, tobacco, spices, oils and various metals. As on the Swahili coast, Indians played an important role in Somali coastal trade as financiers. Somali and Arab merchants were also active. Many Somalis acted as brokers, or abban, for foreign merchants. In the commercial centres of the interior Somali merchants enjoyed little competition. Each of the different clans had its own networks of abban whose services included supplying pack animals and caravan leaders (Pankhurst, 1968:418-44).

The largest inland cities in East Africa were located in Ethiopia and the Sudan. Gondar was Ethiopia's largest city in the first half of the nineteenth century. Its busiest market days were on Mondays and Thursdays, when thousands of people would attend. In the 1860s, after it had already passed its peak, Gondar's total annual trade was estimated at 166,780 Maria Theresa (MT) dollars. To the North Adowa boasted the largest market, held every Saturday, which in the mid-nineteenth century was normally attended by 5,000 to 6,000 people and towards the end of the century by up to 15,000 to 20,000 people. To the south, large markets were located in Aliu Amba, the nodal point of Shoan trade in the first half of the nineteenth century, and Ankobar, the capital, whose market day attracted as many as 20,000 people. Addis Ababa was founded and made Ethiopia's capital in 1887-91. By the end of the century it had developed the most important market in the country, which was held every day, with the largest attendance on Saturdays, when as many as 30,000 to 50,000 people would attend. Within the market there were specialized markets for various products and shops. Addis Ababa's foreign trade was estimated at 1.6 million MT dollars in 1899-1900.

Trade also flourished in the walled city of Harar, which was occupied and incorporated into Ethiopia by Menelik in 1887. Exports through Harar in 1899-1900 were estimated at 2.7 million MT dollars. Along the coast there were the port cities of Massawa, through which a large share of Ethiopia's foreign trade was conducted, and Assab. A great variety of commodities were bought and sold in these markets, with the most important ones including foodstuffs, coffee, livestock, gold, salt, spices, textiles, leather products, metal ware, ivory, wax and civet (Pankhurst, 1968:355-417).

Ethiopia's markets were linked to each other, and to foreign markets, in a complex web of trade routes and trading diasporas. For example, Gondar was linked to Massawa via Adowa and a host of other towns, while Addis Ababa was linked to the coast via Chercher and Harar to Zeila or Tajura. The journey to Massawa took about five weeks, and that to Zeila or Tajura seven to ten weeks by camel. It can be seen that Ethiopia's domestic trade was conducted over a vast territory, its size amplified by the transport system then in use. The caravan trade between these dispersed regions was monopolized by Muslim Ethiopian merchants, the Jabartis. It is said that Christian Ethiopians generally looked down on commercial activities. Jabarti monopoly was increasingly challenged in the south by an Oromo merchant class, called *Afkala*, who in many cases were ex-slaves or ex-servants of the northern merchants. The *Afkala* established a trading network which greatly assisted them in their activities. In addition to the *Afkala*, Sidama and Somali merchants came to dominate trade in their respective regions in southern Ethiopia (Abir, 1970:126-31).

Sudan's domestic trade was also conducted over vast distances. At the beginning of the nineteenth century the Sudan consisted of a number of states, each with its own towns and cities, linked to one another through the caravan trade. Among the largest trading centres were Kobbei in Darfur, Nimro in Wadai, Sinnar and Shendi. These cities normally consisted of several quarters, divided by public places or markets. The markets contained both open trading places and shops. The Egyptian conquest of the Sudan brought together many formerly separate states and peoples under one administration. In the process, some old market towns went into decline and new ones emerged. Shendi, for example, never fully recovered from its destruction in 1823 during the campaign of conquest. By 1885 it had only 500 people. In the meantime, Khartoum grew from a small village into a large city of between 30,000 and 40,000 people in 1860. It became the major entrepot of domestic and regional trade (Bjorkelo, 1988:114-16). After the establishment of the Madhist state in 1885 the capital was shifted to Omdurman, which became the new centre of domestic trade (Nakash, 1988a:60).

The fact that these cities functioned as entrepots in regional and international trade in addition to serving their local areas, gave them a complex market structure. They served local consumers and producers and were also visited by many caravans that stopped and exchanged their commodities before proceeding or returning. For example, when Shendi was at its peak it received caravans from four main directions: Darfur and Kordofan, Sinnar, Sawakin, and Berber and Dongola.

The caravans from Sinnar brought durra, coffee, gold, ivory, camels, gum, tobacco and an assortment of crafts, while the main imports from Kordofan and Darfur consisted of slaves, natron, leather, ropes and sacks, water skins, wooden dishes and spices, and from Sawakin came beads, Indian goods, cambric Muslin, sandal wood and dhufur (musk). Needless to say, the merchants at Shendi came from different parts of the Sudan, and the neighbouring territories, especially Egypt and Ethiopia. Most of them used Arabic as their lingua franca and were Muslim or familiar with Islamic commercial law (Bjorkelo, 1989:12-27). There was a decrease in Sudan's domestic trade during the early years of the Mahdiyya because of 'the frequent wars until 1895, the decrease in population, the great famine of 1889, and the overall lack of security on the roads' (Nakash, 1988a:60). There was some recovery in the 1890s as conditions improved.

State Participation in Trade

The literature on trade in East Africa has dealt quite extensively on the theme of trade and politics. There are those who believe that trade contributed to state formation, while others contend that states initiated and facilitated trade (Gray and Birmingham, 1970). The reality was far more complex than either assertion makes it out to be. It is certainly futile to assume that the relationship between trade and politics was the same across the region and throughout the nineteenth century. The various states in the region saw trade as an important source of revenue, so they made attempts to control or participate in it. But the methods they used differed, and their efforts were not always successful.

The most common method used by East African states to control or benefit from domestic trade was taxation. As in other parts of Africa, the payment of dues and taxes could assume the guise of gift-exchange. Traders paid taxes on their trade goods, usually in the market place, or on their income, as was the case among the Alur and Baganda and in Tabora. The payment of road tolls was also widespread. The rates were based on the value of the transit goods, the size of the caravan, or the power of the local ruler. Road tolls have been reported from Rwanda, Buganda, Ukambani, Meru, Unyamwezi, Maasailand, and Ethiopia. In many of these places the road tolls were usually levied in one direction. In Ethiopia the eastern ports, known as kellas, were so numerous that they caused great inconvenience and delays for traders. Between Massawa and Gondar, for example, there were 11 kellas. Half-hearted and unsuccessful attempts were made by Emperors Tewodros and Menelik to abolish the internal customs. The central government was too weak to impose its will on the provincial governors for whom the kellas were simply too lucrative as sources of revenue to let go (Pankhurst, 1968:521-26). In most of the centralized states the taxes were passed on from the local chief to the king, with each level of power retaining a portion of the taxes.

In some places the state's power over trade extended beyond taxation. In Bunyoro-Kitara, for example, there were some markets that actually belonged to the King, the omukama. In the reign of Kabalega:

> *four markets are said to have flourished around the neighbourhood of the palace. The Noberemutwe Market operated in front of the palace; the Kibanya Market at the back of it; a third, operated at the east side of it and was controlled by the ekitongole ekihukya of the abarusura (national standing army); and a fourth, called the Kidoka Market operated at the west side* (Uzoigwe, 1979:55).

Foreigners were forbidden from these markets. Trade in ivory and guns throughout the state was strictly controlled by the King.

The most extensive control over local trade was attempted in the Sudan following the Egyptian conquest. Muhammad Ali's regime extended the monopoly system to the Sudan. The free movement, exchange and pricing of commodities became severely restricted. Custom stations were built along the major trade routes and the supervision and control of markets was tightened. The monopoly system had disastrous consequences for Sudanese traders. It:

> forced the jallaba out of various prestigious forms of long-distance trade and into non-monopoly slave trade and short-distance petty trading. The economic power and social standing of the jallaba diminished accordingly and increasing competition both among themselves and with the foreign traders when the monopoly was ended, made it impossible for the majority to rise above the level of small scale trading (Bjorkelo, 1988:118).

As in Egypt the monopoly system was resented by both the local and foreign traders. The restrictions against private trade were gradually eased in the 1840s.

Many East African states regarded foreign trade as a lucrative source of revenue, and so they sought to tax it, or participate directly in it. The most common method of taxing foreign trade was through the imposition of duties on imports or exports or both. In the Madhist state taxes were levied on imported goods. The merchants who traded in such goods had to pay tax in addition to the tithe paid at the custom house. Their total tax came to 22.5% (Nakash, 1988b:372). In Malindi merchants paid an export duty on millet, while in Zanzibar slave exports and cloves were taxed. Initially the export duty on cloves was limited to Pemba, but as state revenues declined due to falling clove prices the export duty was extended to Zanzibar. The tax ranged between 25 and 35% of the export price. The real loser in all this was the grower (Cooper, 1977:86, 115, 138).

In Ethiopia taxes on foreign trade were imposed systematically and became a major source of state revenue from the 1840s. At first only imports were taxed at rather low rates. For example, in the agreement with Britain and France signed in 1841 and 1843, respectively, the rates were set at 5% for British goods and 3% for French goods. The rates were subsequently increased and extended to exports. By 1900 the basic tax:

> was a 10% ad valorem charge on merchandise entering or leaving the empire. This due was collected either in the frontier provinces, with the help of local rulers, or, in the case of caravans following the main trade routes, at the capital itself. The system was, however, often modified (Pankhurst, 1968:527).

Some states sought to actively participate in foreign trade. According to Kapteijns and Spaulding (1982) the states of the eastern Sudan, that is present-day Sudan and Ethiopia , tried to do this in five main ways. First, each state required that taxes be paid in part in locally-available commodities suitable for export. This enabled the state to accumulate commodities which it could trade or redistribute among members of the ruling class. Second, there was the widespread practice of reciprocal gift-giving among the kings, which was intended to promote good political and economic relations among their state. The gifts exchanged could be quite substantial. Third, the kings often despatched royal merchants to trade on their behalf. These merchants usually combined the role of traders and diplomatic emissaries, and they were received as such. Fourth, a kind of royal trading diaspora was established by stationing members of the royal family or trusted agents in the foreign market towns to make royal purchase and to warehouse the king's exports and generally to act as brokers.

Finally, the kings, followed by members of the royal family and state officials, enjoyed the privilege of purchasing goods from foreign merchants before they were offered to the general public. These practices were of course constantly challenged by the subjects themselves, the private merchants, and the subordinate governors through whom the royal caravans passed. Indeed, the conflicts and challenges engendered by this system ensured that royal trade monopoly or royally-administered trade was never really achieved. For example, royal trade had disappeared in Sinnar by the 1820s and it declined in Shilluk from the 1840s. Thus royal merchants in most parts of East Africa were eclipsed in the course of the nineteenth century by private traders.

Regional Trading Networks

Family, clan and ethnic associations, both real and affected, played an important role in the provision of trading skills, capital and credit, and information. Traders formed alliances in foreign countries through marriage and blood-brotherhood . The careers of the famous Swahili and Nyamwezi traders, such as Tippu Tib and Msiri, who created commercial empires in Kasongo and Katanga respectively, were built on shrewd alliances with local rulers or people based on either marriage or fictional kinship ties (Curtin, et.al., 1978:433-37). The technique of forging a blood-brotherhood relationship was peculiar to East and Central Africa. In Bunyoro-Kitara a blood-brother relationship, omukago, 'was considered more important than a clan relationship' (Uzoigwe, 1979:53). This system enabled Baganda traders to trade in Bunyoro-Kitara, despite the general hostility between their two states. Blood-brother alliances have also been reported from Rwanda and among the Kamba and Kikuyu of Kenya and the Nyamwezi of Tanzania (Sundstrom, 1974:14-15; Roberts, 1970:73).

In the eastern Sudan, it was common practice for the court to give each foreign merchant a patron or professional host who provided him 'with lodging and storage facilities, represented his interests at court, supervised his exchange activities and reported any irregular behaviour to the appropriate authorities' (Kapteijns and Spaulding, 1982:36). They were encouraged to marry locally, thus further strengthening their position. They mostly lived in the capital or entrepot where 'they enjoyed both internal self-government under their own community officials and a special socio-legal status superior to that of the commoner class' (Kapteijns and Spaulding, 1982:36).

Thus when foreign merchants arrived in many of the major trading towns they were often welcomed into brokerage networks that facilitated their enterprise. The most active trading groups also established their own diasporas over various parts of the region and sometimes beyond. Among the most notable were the jallaba of the Sudan. The jallaba trading network, mostly composed of the Ja'aliyyin and Danagla from the Nile Valley, extended over large areas of the present-day Sudan. The number of jallaba in the western states of present-day Bahr al-Ghazal province, for example, increased from about 500 in 1796 to 5,000 in 1870. They set up at the Sultan's or provincial capital permanent trade settlements called dehm. In the less accessible areas to the south they established heavily-armed fortified camps called *zariba*. The jallaba diaspora spread to as far as Cairo in Egypt, and by 1850 they had reached the Zande and Mangbetu states of Central Africa (Curtin, et.al., 1978:438-41).

Also remarkable was the coastal Arab-Swahili diaspora which began spreading its tentacles over the East African mainland in the early 1800s and had probably reached as far as Katanga and Buganda by 1852, the year that Tabora in Unyanyembe became their headquarters (Iliffe, 1979:41). From the interior came the trading networks of the Nyamwezi and the Kamba that helped consolidate the links between the Tanzanian and Kenyan interior to the coastal markets (Roberts, 1970; Cummings, 1975).

Foreign trade played an important role in the economic life of both the centralized state societies and the acephalus societies of East Africa. Trade flourished among the states of the interlacustrine region. The main articles of trade among them were salt, iron, cloth, coffee, tobacco, foodstuffs, livestock and pottery products. Bunyoro was a leading exporter of salt and iron products, including hoes, axes, knives and spears. It was also famous for its clay products, particularly pots. Buganda was renowned for its fine backcloths which were exported to Bunyoro, Karagwe, Rwanda and Busoga, none of which produced cloth of comparable quality. Buganda also exported dried bananas and, together with Bunyoro, coffee. Nkole produced the finest tobacco in the region, surpluses of which were exported to Karagwe and Bunyoro. As for food products, Nkole, Tooro and northern Uganda led in the exports of millet, while Rwanda exported sorghum, peas and honey, and Bunyoro exported sweet potatoes and groundnuts (Uzoigwe, 1979:33-36, 49-52; Kamuhangire, 1979:81-82, 87-88).

The trade between these states not only expanded in the nineteenth century, it also became increasingly articulated with other commercial systems in the region, principally the one controlled by coastal Swahili traders, and to a lesser extent the Khartoumers. The coastal traders established their main base in Karagwe. They regularly visited Buganda, which succeeded in preventing them from entering Bunyoro until the 1880s. They brought guns which revolutionized regional warfare, cotton cloths, beads, ordinary brass and copper utensils, expensive cutlery and chinaware, beads and cowrie shells, in exchange for salt and ivory. It would appear that the interlacustrine states did not organize caravans to the coast, for there is only one reported mission sent by Mutesa of Buganda to Zanzibar in 1870 (Zwanenberg and King, 1975:150-2; Tosh, 1970:105-7, 111-17).

Many of Kenya's societies in the nineteenth century were acephalus. But trade among them was no less vibrant (Ambler, 1985). Much of the trade was conducted among adjacent communities. For example, there was regular trade between the Luo and Gusii. The Luo exported such goods as livestock and dairy products, pots, drums, baskets and colourful headdresses, in exchange for Gusii grain, iron implements and jewellery, and soapstone for making vessels and carvings. So important was this trade that it 'continued without interruption - war or no war. It was women and children of both [groups] who largely handled it, especially during periods of hostilities' (Ochieng, 1986:102-3). Muriuki (1986:131) also maintains that trade between the Kikuyu and their neighbours 'continued during periods of tension and even hostilities'. The Kikuyu sold the Maasai grain, gourds of milk, tobacco, ochre and honey, in return for livestock, hides and skins, and leather cloaks. The Kikuyu also traded with the Kamba. The two groups exchanged foodstuffs, livestock, poisons, medicines, tools, cloths, skins, weapons and ritual objects (Jackson, 1986:200, 216-25). These examples of Luo-Gusii and Kikuyu-Maasai-Kamba trade can be replicated for many other societies in nineteenth century Kenya (Wright, 1979).

Trade relations between the Kikuyu, Maasai and Kamba deteriorated towards the end of the century as a result of two developments. First, the ecological disasters that befell the region undermined production and engendered conflicts. Second, the influx of Swahili traders intensified competition over coastal trade. The Kikuyu resented the new foreign traders who, in turn, were also suspicious of the Kikuyu. Both groups were to some extent unfortunate victims of wild stories about each other 'spread by the Kamba in order to keep out competitors, be they coastal or interior people' (Muriuki, 1986:135). By the time the coastal traders started coming only a handful of Kikuyu traders had ventured as far as the coast. That distinction belongs to the Kamba.

The Kamba were Kenya's most dynamic long-distance traders in the nineteenth century. They not only traded with all the Central Kenya peoples - the Embu, Mbeere, Meru and Tharaka, in addition to the Kikuyu - but also with the Gusii further west, the Samburu to the north, and the Mijikenda to the east, and southwards they penetrated north-eastern Tanzania (Lamphear, 1970:80-83). Kamba commercial enterprise culminated in the development of trade with Mombasa. It is not known when exactly the Kamba started trading with Mombasa. There is some evidence, however, that they had been trading with the coastal communities, especially the Mijikenda, long before 1800. In fact, some Kamba communities had been established at the coast by at least 1790.

There has been a vigorous debate among East African historians as to why the Kamba became such active traders. Some have emphasized the fact that Kamba territory was prone to drought and famine, the incidence of which increased between 1790 and 1830, so that trade was essential for Kamba survival (Jackson, 1986:213-14; Low, 1963:307-18). Others have argued that the Kamba propensity for foreign trade was facilitated by their flexible homestead organization which encouraged migration, their prowess as hunters, indispensable for the procurement of ivory, the main trade item to the coast, and their skill in the production of various handicrafts prized in regional commerce (Lamphear, 1970:83-86). Most probably a combination of both sets of factors played a role. Whatever the case, Kamba trade with other societies in the East African interior and the coast increased from the early nineteenth century.

Kamba caravans dominated trade with Mombasa. Indeed, it would be no exaggeration to say that Kamba traders elevated Mombasa into the most prosperous city along the East African coast. The Kamba caravans mainly brought ivory and returned with textiles, metal products and jewellery. The big Kamba merchants organized firms of ivory hunters, porters and traders to conduct the trade on their behalf, while the less prosperous ones were often personally involved in these operations. The names, foibles and activities of some of the big merchants are still remembered today, such as Makuti, Muganya, Kitonga and, the most famous of them all, Kivui. Few women were involved in organizing the coastal caravans, although 'they figured heavily in inter-regional trade' (Jackson, 1986:223). Kivui became so powerful that he could even demand taxes from the Maasai living on his frontiers. In fact it would seem that the Kamba traders were more keen to invest their wealth in political networks and social mobility than in production. Rarely did their trading organizations survive the founders' death. This is to suggest that notwithstanding the impressive achievements of the Kamba traders in creating a commercial empire over much of nineteenth century Kenya, there was little sustained capital accumulation.

Kamba hegemony in the coastal trade was lost from the 1840s. Several factors account for this. By then elephant herds had dwindled in many parts of Ukambani and so ivory supplies declined. Their neighbours were not too keen on allowing the Kamba to hunt for ivory in their territories. In fact, the Kamba were even driven out of some of these territories, such as Mbeere. Relations with the coastal Mijikenda deteriorated so badly that a brief war erupted in 1874. Internal conflicts among different Kamba sections only made matters worse (Lamphear, 1970:98-99). The Kamba failed to develop alternative export commodities valued by the coastal traders. As if that was not enough, Swahili caravans from Mombasa began penetrating the interior and challenged the Kamba monopoly. By the 1860s the Swahili were trading regularly as far as Uganda. Kamba coastal trade became, in Jackson's (1986:230) felicitous phrase, a 'little more than a strained synthesis of archaic economic efforts and piecemeal, haphazard innovation'. Indeed, many of the Kamba traders were reduced into mere agents or middlemen of the new overlords of coastal trade - the Swahili.

The counterparts of the Kamba in Tanzania were the Nyamwezi, who pioneered trading contacts from the interior to the coast, although it is not certain when this trade started. But it is known that coastal caravans had started penetrating the interior by 1811 and by the 1830s most of the caravans involved in this trade still belonged to the Nyamwezi and other inland peoples. There are various estimates of the number of Nyamwezi who visited the coast. Some say that in the 1880s 15,000-20,000 of them did, others put the figure for 1890 as high as 100,000 or up to a third of the Nyamwezi male population. 'If correct, these figures suggest labour migration as widespread as the colonial period' (Iliffe, 1979:45).

At first this trade involved the exchange of ivory from the interior for imports such as textiles and guns from the coast. In the second half of the century the numbers of coastal traders penetrating the interior increased sharply inspired by the rising prices of ivory, falling profits, and growing competition due to the advance of the ivory frontier from Unyamwezi further westwards. Like the Kamba the Nyamwezi increasingly lost their previous dominance. Conflicts between the Nyamwezi and other inland peoples and the coastal traders intensified as the former sought to recoup what they were losing economically by seeking to impose greater political control on the latter. As ivory supplies dwindled further, coastal traders, such as Tippu Tib, sought to establish new commercial empires beyond Unyamwezi and spread their efforts as far as Zaire. Many traders, both from the coast and the interior, turned to the slave trade which quickly expanded. Few of the slaves came from Unyamwezi itself.

East African historians seem to agree that the coastal trade had a far-reaching impact on the societies of the mainland. It is said that it stimulated existing local and regional trade networks; undermined some industries, particularly textiles, and boosted others, such as the salt and iron production, since the two products were widely traded along the caravan routes. Indeed, it is claimed, the caravan trade boosted food production not only because of increased demand, but also through the introduction of new food crops of American origin, especially maize and cassava. The trade also encouraged, it is argued, the growth of economic specialization as new groups of professional traders, ivory hunters and porters, emerged. Moreover, it facilitated cultural intermixture, in particular the spread of Swahili and Islam into the interior.

But the trade, some have pointed out, had its darker side. The slave trade caused havoc in the communities involved and the spread of slavery that it brought about tore the social fabric of many societies. The large-scale import of guns into the interior transformed warfare making it infinitely more violent and devastating in its impact. In fact, the big merchants, both coastal and Nyamwezi, established relatively large standing armies to protect their commercial empires and raid for slaves. The locus of physical power gradually shifted from the old dynastic rulers to the better armed adventurer-traders, such as Tippu Tib, Msiri, Mirambo and Nyungu ya Mawe who carved out their own chiefdoms (Kimambo and Temu, 1969; Roberts, 1970; Webster and Unoma, 1975; Alpers, 1975; Iliffe, 1979).

The temptation to see the coastal trade as the deux ex machina of nineteenth century East African history must be resisted. The impact of the trade was far more limited than it is often suggested. Many of the changes attributed to it were products of complex internal dynamics within the mainland societies themselves. In assessing the economic impact of the coastal trade, the question of accumulation has not been addressed systematically. There is little evidence to show that the traders themselves, whether from the coast or the interior, made any significant productive investment in their respective economies. In this sense, it can be argued, the coastal trade hardly promoted economic development.

Ethiopia's main trading partners in Africa in the nineteenth century were Egypt and the Sudan. At the beginning of the century Egypt was among the country's major suppliers of sugar, tobacco, glassware, soap, olive oil, and

later in the century of textiles, metals and spirits. By the 1880s and 1890s
Ethiopian exports to Egypt consisted of hides and skins, ivory, civet, pearls,
honey, wax, gum and coffee. Most of this trade was handled through
Massawa, and of Ethiopia's trade conducted through Massawa in 1899,
Egypt came sixth as a source of imports and seventh as an export destination.
Throughout the nineteenth century the port was under a succession of foreign
rulers, first the Turks, then from 1868 to 1884 the Egyptians, and after 1885
the Italians (Pankhurst, 1968:357, 377-9, 386-7). To the Sudan Ethiopia
exported some commodities similar to those exported to Egypt, as well as
slaves, durra, iron, livestock, horses and butter, and imported many of the
same items in addition to manufactures, some of which the Sudan itself had
imported from Egypt and the Mediterranean region, including textiles,
carpets and leather, firearms, MT dollars, cutlery, spices and scents
(Pankhurst, 1968:352-3).

A large part of the Ethiopian-Sudanese trade was conducted through
market towns situated along the border areas, such as Bela Shangur, located
west of the Blue Nile, which provided a converging point and exchange area
between Sennar in the Sudan and the Oromo country of western Ethiopia.
Bela Shangur became an important transmission belt for Islam in western
Ethiopia, for many of the traders who came from the Sudanese side were
Egyptian Muslims. The region also became a contested one between the two
countries, particularly following the establishment of Madhist rule in the
Sudan (Triulzi, 1975). As with the East African coastal trade examined
above, some of the writing on Ethiopian foreign trade has concentrated on
the impact of the slave exports, especially from the southern highlands. But
Aregay (1988) has argued that coffee was far more important than slaves in
this region and that it contributed significantly to the rise to power of the
kingdom of Shawa in the nineteenth century.

Egypt and Ethiopia were also the Sudan's major trading partners in Africa.
In fact Egypt had been the Sudan's leading trading partner since time
immemorial (Belshai, 1976:21-25). As we saw in Chapter 9, Egypt's trade
with the Sudan increased rapidly in the nineteenth century. The Sudan also
traded with countries to the west and south. Heavily armed jallaba caravans
penetrated deeply into Central Africa looking for slaves and ivory. They
wreaked havoc on the acephalus societies they came across, some of whom
were wiped out or forced to migrate. The better organized Zande and
Mangbetu managed to contain the exploits of the jallaba bands, but only for
a while, for they were soon confronted by another group of predatory traders
from the Sudan, the so-called Khartoumers. They were slave traders based
in Khartoum, originally European, before Coptic Egyptians took over from
the 1860s and 1870s. The Khartoumers greatly weakened the Zande and

Mangbetu states (Birmingham, 1976:265-6; Curtin et.al., 1978:440-2). The Khartoumers also penetrated the interlacustrine states to the south. Tosh (1970:114) tells us that they 'plundered cattle with which to pay taxes'. However, it would appear that their impact on such states as Buganda and Bunyoro was rather limited, for these states were able to defend themselves. Certainly the number of slaves imported from Buganda and Bunyoro remained rather small.

Sudan's foreign trade declined quite considerably during the Madhist period, continuing a trend that had begun in the 1870s. There were several reasons for this. To begin with, Sudan was embroiled in a war with Ethiopia from 1887 to 1889 in which Ethiopia lost the first round and Sudan the second. The war disrupted trade between the two countries and hampered Sudan's export trade through Massawa. Sudanese foreign trade also suffered from the prohibition declared by the Anglo-Egyptian authorities on trade with the Madhist state in order to starve the revolutionary state of arms and ammunition. Moreover, the new government imposed high taxes on imported goods. The attitude of the new rulers complicated matters further. They sought to insulate their dar al-Islam from the dar al-harb, the countries inhabited by unbelievers, so they put restrictions on trade and traders from regions they considered dar al-harb. Within the country itself the new government also launched a reign of pillage, for booty initially formed its major source of revenue (Nakash, 1988a:62-66; 1988b:37).

Overall, under the Madhiyya the composition of Sudan's foreign trade changed. The import of certain goods, such as tobacco, was prohibited, while the export of slaves fell sharply because 'the Khalifa prohibited the export of males above seven years fearing that they might be recruited into the Egyptian army, and at the same time attempted to increase the jihadiyya force... Also it appears that the Madhist state was unable to obtain new slaves easily', for it was feared that slave raids might lead to rebellions and endanger the regime (Nakash, 1988a:65). Attention was turned to ivory. External markets for ivory were buoyant, but the Madhist state could not get enough of it. In fact, its ivory supplies dwindled as it lost territories in the equatorial regions.

Currencies and Credit

Goods in East Africa exchanged hands either through barter or the use of money. In some parts of the region money had been used since ancient times, while in others its use became widespread only in the nineteenth century. The barter transactions often involved the use of a standard of value or unit of account, which were usually based on cattle, textiles, iron products, or salt. In some societies both barter and money were used in different sectors of the economy or branches of trade. For example, barter would be used in local or rural transactions and money in urban or foreign trade. In many societies it was in fact quite difficult to determine where barter ended and monetary exchange took over. In Bunyoro, for instance, 'trade by barter was carried on alongside trade by ensimbi (cowries)' (Uzoigwe, 1979:54). Cowries were probably introduced in Bunyoro and the other interlacustrine states long before 1800, although their use spread in the nineteenth century. The cowries used in Uganda came from Zanzibar. It has been suggested that the large-scale importation of cowries into Uganda following the development of the coastal caravan trade may have caused a devaluation similar to the one in West Africa, noted in the last chapter (Sundstrom, 1974:95).

Zanzibar itself does not appear to have made much use of cowries in its trade. Instead in the nineteenth century the most widely used money was, first, the MT dollar, and then later rupees (Sundstrom, 1974:97). Coins had been used along the East African coast even before the beginning of the Christian era. Egyptian coins from Alexandrian times have been found in Zanzibar, suggesting that there was some trade between Egypt and the East African coast in ancient times (Freeman-Grenville, 1959:4-6). In later centuries East African coastal cities issued their own coins as their trade expanded. From the twelfth century, for example, 'at least seven rulers of Kilwa, four of Zanzibar, and no less than twenty-four in Mogadishu, issued coins in their names... the genre of eastern African coins is sui generis' (Grenville-Freeman, 1974:75). The coins were chiefly made of copper. Almost 8,000 such coins minted between 1300 and 1700 have been recovered by one collector alone from Mogadishu and the surrounding areas (Grenville-Freeman, 1963). In 1983 ancient Kilwa coins were found as far as Australia, although no one knows how they got there (Grenville-Freeman, 1988). The minting of the Kilwa coins continued, but in small quantities, into the nineteenth century (Grenville-Freeman, 1978:192).

Coins had also been minted in Ethiopia in ancient times, but the most widely used currency at the turn of the nineteenth century was the salt bar, called amole. It continued to be used widely, particularly in the southern regions, but its bulk and difficulty of subdivision made it unsuitable for small or large purchases. In Tigre and the coastal areas cloth served as the main currency. It was easily divisible into halves, quarters and other fractions. Iron bars had been used for centuries, but by the nineteenth century their use as currency had ceased in the northern provinces, although they were used in some parts of central and southern Ethiopia. These currencies were supplemented and later overtaken by the MT or Maria Theresa dollar, the silver coin used in much of North Africa and western Asia. The MT dollar was introduced into Ethiopia at the end of the eighteenth or beginning of the nineteenth century and was accepted slowly and reluctantly. Initially the

Vienna-minted coins were fairly scarce, but their supply gradually increased in the second half of the nineteenth century. The practice was for traders who wanted the dollars to have them specially struck for them. They paid for the metal plus a 10% commission. By 1901 1.5 million dollars were being minted annually.

The MT dollar was bulky, so that its value rose the further one moved from the coast because of transport costs. There were no coins of smaller denominations, so for small change amole, beads, iron bars and cartridges were used. Thus it can be argued that the dollar and the other currencies used in Ethiopia formed a single currency system. The exchange rate between them varied and fluctuated quite considerably throughout the nineteenth century. Added to this complexity was the fact that other foreign currencies, such as Indian rupees and Egyptian coins, were also used in Ethiopia, particularly along the coast and the border with the Sudan. In Harar only the locally produced coin, the maha lek, was allowed. It was later suspended, first by the Egyptians when they occupied Harar in 1875 and then by Menelik who incorporated Harar into Ethiopia in 1887.

The last two decades of the nineteenth century saw the failed attempt by the Italians to introduce a new currency to their colony in Eritrea, and Menelik's more successful effort to establish a national currency both as a symbol of national sovereignty and as a means of stopping the outflow of Ethiopian wealth entailed by the use of foreign currencies. The new currency was issued in 1894. It included a dollar coin, called ber, and six smaller denominations, from the half dollar, alad, to the besa, one sixty-fourth of the dollar. Despite admonitions from the emperor himself, the new currency did not oust the MT dollar and the other currencies until well into the twentieth century. The smaller coins, however, proved far more popular and were quickly adopted (Pankhurst, 1968:460-94).

Currencies used in the Sudan were no less diverse. At the beginning of the nineteenth century they ranged from units of durra or cloth, to beads, iron pieces and various Egyptian and Turkish currencies which were introduced following the Egyptian conquest in 1821. The new currencies became popular only gradually. The Turkish currency was later withdrawn when Muhammad Ali's regime forbade its use in Egypt at the end of the 1830s. So the Egyptian currency became dominant. The new state played a contradictory role in the process of monetization in the Sudan. On the one hand, by demanding that taxes be paid in cash it encouraged monetization, but by transferring large sums of money as tribute to Cairo, it deprived the domestic economy of money. This enabled salaried state officials, who had regular access to money, to become moneylenders. The scarcity of money, particularly outside the main market towns and in the south, allowed the use of barter and local currencies to persist. On the whole, however, the process of monetization accelerated, accompanied by the spread of market relations, which led to the commercialization of an ever expanding web of economic, social and personal relations, including labour services and even marriage alliances (Bjorkelo, 1989: 107-13).

Egypt's hold over the Sudan began to decline sharply from the late 1870s. The Egyptian regime was overthrown in 1885 by the Madhists. As part of their drive to transform the economy and society and to consolidate their power the new Madhist rulers sought to establish a new fiscal and monetary system. In order to weaken the old merchant elite and strengthen the new power elite the capital was moved from Khartoum to Omdurman where a central treasury was established which assumed responsibility for all fiscal matters in the Madhist state. Later five new specialized treasuries were established in order to ensure that the technocrats entrusted with running the central treasury did not become too powerful. The Madhist state also started minting its own coins from coins, precious metals and jewels seized in Khartoum. The new money consisted of a gold pound, a silver rial and a silver half-rial. Unfortunately:

> *the Madhi's coins were made from a superior grade of gold and silver, which led to their gradual disappearance - many goldsmiths would simply melt them down into gold or silver bars which were then exported, mainly to Egypt. Moreover, the absence of suitable machinery for the minting of coins adversely affected their durability, and coins could be broken by hand* (Nakash, 1988b:376).

As the gold reserves dwindled, minting was suspended for almost a year, until the end of 1886. A new mint was established, and the coins were debased and smaller denominations than the half-rial were produced. The regime sought to turn the system into a profitable source of income. The policy of currency debasement was accompanied by the Khalifa's attempt to control the exchange rate. In fact foreign coins were hoarded by the Khalifa and disappeared from circulation. The monetary policies of the early years of Madhist rule triggered inflationary pressures, while those of the latter years created deflationary pressures. But this exercise in fiscal and monetary autonomy was prematurely halted in 1898 when the country was colonized by Britain.

Given the extensive use of money and the development of intricate regional trading networks, there can be little doubt that capital markets and a variety of credit institutions existed in East Africa, although compared to North and West Africa little is known about them. It would appear that private merchants engaged in foreign or long-distance trade either financed themselves, borrowed from moneylenders, started off as agents of other merchants, or raised credit from their relatives and associates. As we saw in the case of West Africa, some merchants were essentially target traders who periodically sold goods that they themselves had produced. It was not uncommon for small traders sometimes to accumulate enough and graduate into the ranks of professional traders. And credit was available, although at high cost. In early nineteenth century Gondar, for example, interest rates could be as high as 120%. Interest rates in Ethiopia 'subsequently fell as a result of more settled conditions and a greater availability of cash' (Pankhurst, 1968:494).

It was not until the early twentieth century that modern banks were set up in Ethiopia, or for that matter, in most of East Africa. In the Sudan 'the lending of money was lucrative business, with interest rates of 4 to 5% and up to 15% per month' (Bjorkelo, 1988:110). The money lenders included the big merchants and state officials. In Zanzibar and along the Swahili and Somali coasts the role of banker was played by Indians. They financed Arab, Swahili and Somali caravan traders penetrating into the interior and handled a large share of the export trade. Despite Islamic prohibition against the transfer of credit to a third party:

> *the great usefulness of cheques and letters of credit in a country noted for long distances and slow communications was generally realized by the merchants trading in the Sudan and East Africa. The rate of discount on such cheques in some instances was 200%, which considering the risks involved, was not unreasonable, although it caused the objections of the more orthodox believers* (Sundstrom, 1974:36).

From Porterage to Railways

The use of pack animals in the transportation of goods over long distances was restricted to the northern countries of East Africa: the Sudan, Ethiopia and Somalia. In the southern countries, namely, Uganda, Tanzania and most parts of Kenya, porterage was virtually the sole mode of transport. In the highlands of Ethiopia they used mules, horses, camels and donkeys depending on the wealth of the wealthy merchant, type of goods being carried, and the terrain being traversed. Camels were far more expensive than mules or donkeys and they also carried more loads, so they tended to be used by the merchants. Human porterage was also used but it was very expensive, particularly in the case of slaves who cost 'two or three times as much as a mule and (carried) only half of its load. This factor, plus the steady rise in the cost of slaves in the nineteenth century, may well have contributed to the gradual disappearance of porters' (Pankhurst, 1968:283).

The porters used in the long-distance trade caravans of the southern countries were largely hired workers. Cummings (1975, 1985) has given us a detailed account of the social origins, recruitment procedures, conditions of work and wages of Kamba porters. They were mostly recruited from the poorer strata of society, especially those vulnerable to famine during the periodic droughts. A few of course joined for the adventure of travel or to acquire skills and capital for their own enterprise. The recruitment process was blended with ritual; the porters received protective medicines and took oaths of unity before departure. During the journey the porters specialized in different tasks: there were carriers, cooks, personal servants, tent makers, and trained fighters to protect the caravan. They were paid in kind, which made them into potential entrepreneurs. When the Swahili traders tried to introduce cash wages in the latter part of the nineteenth century, many Kamba porters resisted the measure, for that threatened to dissolve their dual role as workers and traders. The resistance succeeded for the Swahili traders were forced to pay the porters in kind as before. But it was a temporary victory. Colonialism was just around the corner. In contrast, in Tanzania porters readily accepted cash wages and earned about 13 shillings a month, almost the same as they did in 1935 (Iliffe, 1979:45). The porters were East Africa's first migrant workers.

The rivers and lakes of the region were also used for transportation. For example, boats made of reeds and trunks were used on Lake Tana and other lakes and on sections of the Blue Nile in Ethiopia (Pankhurst, 1968:302-3). The Shilluk in the Upper Nile region relied on canoes on the White Nile for both short and long-distance trading and also for conducting raids (Mercer, 1971:412-3). Lake Victoria, Africa's largest lake, played a major role as a trade route linking the states of the interlacustrine region. Local canoes were used long before sailing boats were introduced by coastal traders in the last quarter of the nineteenth century (Hartwig, 1970). Canoe transport was of crucial importance in the development of trade in the salt and iron producing lake region of southern Uganda. Numerous lakeshore markets grew around Lake George and Lake Edward (Kamuhangire, 1979:77-80).

Some of the earliest attempts to build a modern transport system were made in Ethiopia, where modern road building began in the 1850s during the reign of Tewodros. The roads were initially constructed for military purposes to facilitate the movement of troops. The road building programme accelerated under Emperor Menelik (Pankhurst, 1968:284-9). It was also during Menelik's reign that the installation of a modern postal, telephone and telegraph system and the construction of railways began.

Menelik wanted to link the capital with the coast for both economic and military reasons. He had been interested in the idea of building a railway for a long time, but he waited until after his coronation in 1889 to grant a concession to the Imperial Railway Company of Ethiopia. However, construction work did not begin at Djibuti until 1897. The company had to overcome opposition from the French in Djibuti, the Italians who claimed many parts of Ethiopia, and the British who feared it would destroy the trade of Zeila. Many local people, especially traders and chiefs who feared losing control over the caravan trade and the relative autonomy that poor communications provided them, also opposed the railway. Moreover, it proved harder to raise the capital in Europe than had originally been anticipated. In fact, the original company was restructured and its ownership changed a few times. The line reached Dire Dawa in 1902 and Addis Ababa in 1917; totalling 785 kilometres. The railway had an immediate and significant impact on trade. One of the first results was a rapid increase in the imports and exports of bulky commodities. Passenger traffic also grew rapidly (Pankhurst, 1968:304-41).

Ethiopia was the only country in eastern Africa, indeed one of the only two in Africa, to escape colonization. So the railway system, like that of Egypt began decades earlier, was built as a result of local initiative. Elsewhere, as was noted for West Africa, railways were built as part of the drive for colonization. This was true for the Sudan (Hill, 1965) and the southern territories, Kenya (Hill, 1961), Uganda (O'Connor, 1965) and Tanzania (Hill, 1962). 'The Sudan's railway system', Daly (1988:201) writes, 'began as a strategic lifeline during Kitchener's advance against the Madhist state; it was not designed for civilian transport or to assist in the economic development of the country'.

Strategic and political considerations also weighed heavily in the construction of the Kenya-Uganda Railway by Britain and the Tanganyika Railways by Germany. Railway construction in Kenya began in Mombasa in 1895. The line reached Nairobi in 1899, and Kisumu on Lake Victoria in 1902, from where it was extended into Uganda. In Tanzania construction began from Dar-es-Salaam. By 1896 the first 25 miles of line had been opened from the city, 'the intention being to build two branches of penetration, one to Lake Victoria, the other to Lake Tanganyika' (Latham, 1978a:24).

The impact of the railways cannot be overemphasized. They facilitated colonization and incorporated these countries into the world capitalist economy, altered patterns of trade, reduced transport costs, and rendered human porterage obsolete. The Kenya-Uganda Railway went further. It turned Mombasa into the chief commercial centre of East Africa, and brought large numbers of Indian merchants and European settlers to Kenya (Janmohammed, 1977, 1983; Uzoigwe, 1976; Lonsdale, 1989b; Zeleza, 1989).

Conclusion

One of the major problems in African historiography has been the question of defining regions as historical units. All too often, regional designations are based on colonial divisions, so that East Africa is normally confined to the former British-ruled territories of Kenya, Tanzania and Uganda (Zeleza, 1984, 1985a, 1990). In this chapter, East Africa has been extended to include present-day Somalia, Ethiopia, and the Sudan.

This chapter has shown that there were extensive interlapping trading networks which linked these countries in the nineteenth century. These networks can be divided into three major groups: first, the interlacustrine region; second, the coastal zone; and third, the eastern Sudan, understood here to mean the region extending from modern Chad to the Red Sea (Kapteijns and Spaulding, 1982:29). Each of these networks and the linkages between them became more intricate in the course of the nineteenth century. As in West and North Africa, these networks were sustained by trading diasporas. The most celebrated ones include those created by the Swahili, Nyamwezi, Kamba, and the infamous Sudanese jallaba bands and Khartoumers. The chapter has also shown how the unique institution of blood-brotherhood oiled the wheels of inter-regional trade.

It can no longer be doubted, therefore, that trade in East Africa was no less developed than in West or North Africa. The antiquity, organization and structure of markets, currency and credit systems, and transport in this region bear some important similarities to the other two regions. For example, there was, on the one hand, Ethiopia which, like Egypt, took the initiative to modernize its communications and transport system by constructing, among other things, a railway system, while in the rest of East Africa, as in West Africa and much of North Africa, railway construction was part and parcel of the European drive for colonization.

Historians continue to debate the role of the state, or the connection between 'trade and politics', and the developmental impact of long-distance trade. This chapter has argued that while states in the region made various attempts to reap benefits from trade through taxation and tolls, or by sponsoring official traders and establishing official trading diasporas, private traders remained predominant, and the level of state control was fairly limited, except perhaps in the northern Sudan where Egypt temporarily extended its monopoly system from 1821. Posing the question in the exclusive terms of development or underdevelopment, as many historians tend to do when assessing the impact of coastal trade, is quite unsatisfactory, for it overstates the relative importance of this trade in the economic lives of the vast majority of people in this region.

It cannot be overemphasized that local, internal, or domestic trade was far larger and more important than long-distance trade. Having said that, it can still be argued that trade in agricultural and manufactured products did contribute to increased production, while trade in slaves had a detrimental impact on the economies of the slave exporting societies.

12. Trade in Central and Southern Africa

Organization of Trade

Compared to the three regions already examined, research on the development of trade in Central and Southern Africa has been rather limited, except for the subject of the slave trade. In the available general surveys on African economic history, for example, there is hardly any discussion of the two regions' internal, as distinct from their external, trade (Wickins, 1981; Austen, 1987). Research on Central Africa in particular has prominently featured the Atlantic slave trade and the role of the Portuguese (Birmingham, 1966; Vansina, 1966; Gray and Birmingham, 1970; Broadhead, 1971; Martin, 1972; Miller, 1988). There was, of course, much more to trade in the two regions in the nineteenth century than the Atlantic slave trade or international commerce.

As in other parts of Africa by the beginning of the nineteenth century, local trade had existed for centuries in most parts of Central and Southern Africa, necessitated by the diversity of ecological systems and the uneven distribution of resources, social differentiation and divisions of labour among households, and the pecuniary demands of the state. Trade was conducted in markets or through pedlars. With a few exceptions, we still know little about the spatial and temporal organization of markets in either Central and Southern Africa at the turn of the new century. In the Zaire basin, on which considerably more research has been done, Vansina (1983:87) tells us that a regular four-day market week had developed well before 1500. By the nineteenth century markets were held more frequently, although among the Tio and Tiene the most important markets were still held on the fourth day of the week called mpika, a day that was regarded as sacred. It has been suggested that holding the market on such a day helped to minimize conflict. In terms of practical control markets were under the chief upon whose land they were held. The chief was responsible for settling quarrels and removing troublemakers, in return for which he had the right to tax all goods brought to the market (Harms, 1981:72-73).

The largest markets were often located in the capital, where the concentration of security and consumers offered favourable conditions for trade. Among the most famous in the early nineteenth century were the markets of Buah, the Loango capital (Martin, 1970:141), and of Kazembe's capital on the Luapula (Roberts, 1976:109). In the late nineteenth century major markets grew at Kalamba's capital, ruler of the Ben Lulua (Miller, 1970:183) and at Bukenya, Msiri's capital in Katanga (Roberts, 1976:122). Important markets also developed along the major trade routes, such as Pupanganda on the Tanganyika-Nyasa corridor that linked the state of Kazembe and the east African coast (St. John, 1970:209). Finally, there were the great markets along the major rivers, particularly Zumbo, at the confluence of the Zambezi and Luangwa, and at Malebo Pool in the Zaire basin. Zumbo was founded in the eighteenth century and its trading frontier grew to encompass many parts of present-day Zambia, Zimbabwe and Mozambique (Sutherland-Harris, 1970a). In the second half of the nineteenth century Zumbo fell under the Portuguese and became a notorious slave trading port (Roberts, 1976:123-5).

Malebo Pool was where all the trade circuits of the vast Zaire basin flowed. There were numerous trade settlements along the Zaire river. According to Vansina (1983:114-5), 'by the 1850s places such as Bolobo, Mushie, Bonga, Irebu, Makandza, Upoto and Bosoko each had populations of more than 10,000 people grouped in ten or twelve firms. Several smaller towns had more than 5,000 people'. Given the region's low population density these trading towns were, comparatively speaking, large agglomerations. The Pool itself had about 15,000 people. There were several markets - Ntamo, Kinshasa, Mpila and Mfwa, each of which was open almost daily (Vansina, 1973:255-6). Some of these markets, such as Upoto, had 'two parts: a women's market, where foodstuffs were traded, and a men's market for other products' (Harms, 1981:73). These towns were controlled by the leaders of the firm that founded them, rather than by political authorities of the more traditional kind.

There were several integrated regional economies in Central and Southern Africa, each with a hub that linked numerous local trade circuits and which was, in turn, linked to the expanding world economy. These circuits expanded and intensified during the nineteenth century in response to the growth of regional commercial centres and international trade. For example, both the Pool and Zumbo were linked to international trade along the Atlantic Ocean and the Indian Ocean, respectively. The regional commercial centres in the hinterland of central and southern Africa increasingly became connected to the international trading systems along both coasts. This was particularly so with the Katanga region, which from the mid-nineteenth century was drawn into the orbit of traders from both East Africa and Angola (Katzenellenbogen, 1983).

Needless to say, the commodity composition of trade varied according to the market. Among the Shona, for example, their internal trade was dominated by grain, salt and iron implements, while their external trade revolved around gold, copper and ivory exports, and imports of textiles, crockery, guns and other luxury goods (Beach, 1977:47-55; 1983:258-264). This pattern, whereby foodstuffs and essential goods dominated local or domestic trade and wasting assets and luxury products dominated foreign trade, was replicated in many other societies in Central and Southern Africa. The commodities circulating in the many regional trading networks were of course quite varied. In the Zaire basin the foodstuffs traded included maize, cassava, bananas, groundnuts, palm oil, fish and livestock. The other commodities were metalware, especially iron implements and iron, copper and brass objects, textiles, beads and shells, crockery and pottery, salt, canoes and fishing gear, tobacco, wood products, alcoholic beverages, such as maize beer and sugar, cane wine, ivory, slaves and guns. The greatest concentration of goods could be found in the Pool markets (Vansina, 1973:265-74).

Many of the commodities entering the regional trade networks reached the final consumer after passing through a relay of sales and resales. For example, in the extensive network developed and controlled by the Ovimbundu of the Angolan central highlands, 'cloth, beads, salt, and guns were sold to the Chokwe for ivory and wax, while slaves, ivory, and wax came from the Luba. Viye traders then took these back to the highlands and traded them to the Bailundu who carried those goods and agricultural produce to the coast. Viye traders in turn took slaves onto the Lozi, who sold them for cattle, which were sent to the coast through Portuguese traders' (Heywood, 1985:252-3). In the absence of statistical data it is virtually impossible to determine the terms and balance of trade between different areas and states in the various regional trading networks.

The little evidence that is available would seem to indicate that regional trade was profitable indeed for the traders involved. In the Zambezi valley, for example, 'profits from the ivory trade were estimated at 500%' (Isaacman and Mandala, 1985:216). The mark up on goods between the Pool and the upper river in the Zaire basin is said to have been as high as 500%. After subtracting the transport and transaction costs involved in hiring a canoe, feeding and paying the crew and providing gifts to hosts and ensuring defence for the caravan in case of attack, the traders remained with handsome profits. 'If a trader made one trip per year', writes Harms (1981:105), 'he could recover his original investment in two years... he still had an average of three years to make large profits before new investments would be necessary'.

Patterns of Merchant Accumulation

The present state of our knowledge on how traders in Central and Southern Africa financed their activities and invested their profits is rather limited. It is most likely that petty traders involved in local commerce marketed domestic surpluses. As for the professional traders involved in long-distance or external trade, some were state-sponsored, but the majority, however, were self-financed or raised capital from the existing credit institutions. State-sponsored traders participated with varying degrees of intensity in the trade of lucrative commodities, such as gold and ivory. According to Sundstrom (1974:61-65), there were at least a dozen societies in Central Africa where chiefs or kings monopolized or dominated external trade and royal merchants were central to the conduct of trade. Among them were Loango, Kongo, Bemba, Kazembe, Kuba, Katanga and Chewa.

'Monopoly' is a much abused term in African commercial history. As we saw with Dahomey's famous 'royal monopoly', historians have sometimes been too eager to see monopoly where none actually existed. It is quite likely that many of the 'royal monopolies' of Central and Southern Africa are equally contrived. Mudenge (1974, 1988:Chapter 5) for one, has convincingly demonstrated that the Rozwi Mambo did not monopolize the gold trade, let alone all external trade, as has been postulated by many historians. This is not to say the state did not regulate trade in these societies or that there were no state-sponsored merchants. It is merely to emphasize that most external trade was in the hands of private merchants.

The private merchants relied on their own accumulated resources or they used the available credit institutions. Central and Southern Africa is full of stories of communities which rose from hardship and insignificance to commercial prominence and political power. Particularly fascinating is the story of the Chikunda and Kololo, who, in the course of the nineteenth century, were transformed 'from socially oppressed workers to labour extractors' (Isaacman and Mandala, 1985:209). In the eighteenth century the Chikunda had been slaves of Portuguese and Asian estate holders, the prazeros, in the Zambezi valley, for whom they served as porters, traders and hunters. As the pressure put on them increased and their conditions deteriorated, in the early nineteenth century large groups of Chikunda rebelled and escaped and established themselves as independent operators among the people of the Zambezi and Tchiri valleys. The Chikunda diaspora used their previous experiences to set up their commercial enterprises based on the ivory trade, for which they employed slave labour for porterage. It was not until the 1880s that 'the depletion of the elephant herds and intensified efforts by the newly-installed British and Portuguese colonial regimes to restrict trade across the Zambezi-Tchiri frontier signalled the demise of the Chikunda as entrepreneurs' (Isaacman and Mandala, 1985:224-5).

The Kololo, who established themselves as a major economic and political force in the Tchiri valley, started out as tributary labourers bound to the Sotho-Sokoto aristocracy in Bulozi before they were pressed in the 1850s into the service of Dr Livingstone, the Scottish missionary, as porters, who brought them to the Zambezi valley. When Livingstone left, many of his surviving Kololo porters became canoemen and because of their high demand they commanded relatively high wages. Upon Livingstone's return, some went back to work for him, but their relationship had changed, for the Kololo had become more conscious of themselves as workers. In 1860 they revolted and parted company with Livingstone. They used the guns at their disposal to impose order and provide security to the decentralized societies of the Tchiri valley which were vulnerable to the ravages of slave raiders. The ranks of the Kololo swelled as people seeking refuge were incorporated. A decade later the Kololo had succeeded in setting up six small states in the region which depended for their foreign trade on ivory exports. The newly established Kololo ruling class used their acquired state power to mobilize tributary and slave labour for ivory production and trade (Mandala, 1977, 1983).

It is evident from the case of the Chikunda and Kololo that the processes of commercial accumulation evolved in the context of specific historical circumstances, and that they spawned new ethnic and class interpellations. Another illuminating example is that of the Bobangi, a group originally composed of people in small fishing villages along the Zaire river. As trade along the river expanded in the eighteenth and nineteenth centuries Bobangi dominance increased because they controlled a critical stretch of the river between Tchumbiri and Missongo. The Bobangi villages and towns were increasingly organized as trading corporations. As the Bobangi diaspora extended its trading network over the 'great Congo commerce', alien groups were incorporated and the Bobangi ethnic agglomeration expanded. Bobangi traders played a crucial role in the development and spread of a common trade language in the region, Lingala, which is today one of the major languages in Central Africa. Ties between individual traders and the trading alliances that controlled different stretches of the river trade were often maintained through the institutions of blood brotherhood and marriage. The partnerships thus established could last several generations and cemented links between different villages and towns (Harms, 1981:72-81; Vansina, 1973:247-65).

Bobangi traders wishing to start or expand their businesses mostly relied on wages or profits earned from established firms. The study by Harms (1981) is one of the few that deals with the question of investment strategies of nineteenth century Central African traders in some detail. He shows that

as regional trade expanded, the insurance and social investments of reciprocal assistance which had previously been dominant among the early fishing
communities declined in importance. Indeed, they became indistinguishable
from capital investments aimed at promoting business enterprises. Many
traders invested their money in trade itself: buying or renting canoes, and
acquiring trade goods and labour. Few invested in craft manufacturing,
agriculture or fishing. Prestige investments, which mainly went into the
acquisition of luxury cloths and metals and, most importantly, the titles of
political office and ritual position, also increased in importance. Through
them the traders displayed and consumed their wealth. And they further
buttressed their status and power, thereby safeguarding their future accumulation (Harms, 1981:163-96).

Credit Institutions and Money

There is evidence that credit institutions existed in many societies in Central
and Southern Africa through which traders could avail themselves of loans
to set up or expand their businesses. Sundstrom (1974:34-44) mentions a
number of these societies and notes that in some cases loans involved
interest, while in others they did not. 'On the Lower Congo', he tells us,
'there was a certain amount of native banking and investment. The Vili had
a money-lenders guild, one of whose functions was to enforce payment of
debts' (Sundstrom, 1974:36). Also, letters of credit, known as mukanda,
were used on the Lower Congo, issued by European traders and 'drawn on
factories in various parts of the Guinea coast to pay for goods and services.
The cheques were honoured in import goods by the factories. Recipients of
such cheques might store them for months or pass them on to a third party
before the cheque was finally presented at the factory' (Sundstrom,
1974:36). In some societies debtors pawned their dependents or livestock as
collateral.

Legal and moral pressures were used against defaulting debtors. In many
societies, such as the Vili, Mbundu, Chewa, Kuba, Luba, and those of the
Lower Congo, the defaulting debtors were seized and put to work until the
debt had been repaid. Alternatively, the debtor's property was seized. 'In
order to apply sufficient social pressure on a defaulting debtor, the creditor
might seize a member of the debtor's family, his village, or his nation', or
their property (Sundstrom, 1974:42). This was based on the principle of
collective responsibility, that the community was obliged to protect the
interests of its members in all situations. Upon the defaulter's death his estate
was still expected to pay. Failure to do so could result in the collective
humiliation of his family and community. Sundstrom (1974:43) reports the
practice from Loango and the Lower Congo whereby:

on the demise of a defaulting debtor, unless all outstanding debts were paid by the estate, the creditors suspended the corpse between two poles within view of some frequented road. By this act they forfeited all claims on the estate. Once the dependents and relatives of the deceased had buried him, all debts were legally void. In practice the custom was rarely observed, as the odium attached to it forced the estate to pay.

Not only did many traders rely on credit to raise capital, sometimes commercial operations were also carried on credit, that is, one group of traders would pass their goods to another group on credit, and would receive their proceeds only after the latter had sold the goods. This was the way, for example, that Bobangi merchants conducted some of their trade with Tio merchants who controlled trade at Malebo Pool. This form of commercial credit appears to have been widely practised in the other bustling commercial zones of the region.

In addition to these credit systems, trade was facilitated by the development of all-purpose currencies. The monetary history of Central and Southern Africa still awaits detailed study but there can be little doubt that the structure of exchanges was complex. In some societies barter still predominated. Barter exchanges were in themselves quite complicated for they were often conducted according to established rates, and not merely on the basis of on-the-spot bargaining. Moreover, in order to make profit, merchants had to have a good working knowledge of various markets, their assets and deficiencies, and establish numerous commercial triangles (Sundstrom, 1974:66-73). As for money, it is evident that numerous currencies were in use. Indeed, metal, cloth and shell currencies had been used among many societies in the two regions for a very long time. The most important metal used as currency was copper. It was used in the form of bars, ingots or bracelets of various sizes in many parts of present-day Zaire, Zambia and Zimbabwe (Fagan, 1970:31-34; Sutherland-Harris, 1970b:251; Birmingham, 1983:21, 26; Sundstrom, 1974:240-6). Brass was also widely used, followed by iron monies which came in the form of bars, ingots and plates (Sundstrom, 1974:200-10). The use of gold was restricted, it would appear, to the people of Zimbabwe, who used it to pay for their imports.

Cloth currencies were also of considerable antiquity. They were used quite extensively in the Zambezi valley, the Zimbabwe plateau, the Kongo kingdom, Loango and among the Chokwe and Mbundu of Angola. In some of these places cloth was regarded as being above all other currencies and the proper medium for loans (Martin, 1970:141-3, 1986; Birmingham, 1970:170-1, 1983:27-28; Miller, 1970:183, 1983:146-8; Beach, 1983:263; Sundstrom, 1974:161-9). Loango raphia cloth currency had become 'hard currency' of west-central Africa as early as the seventeenth century. It remained in circulation until the eighteenth century, although 'a method of reckoning tied to cloth and cloth terminology continued in use on the Loango coast and throughout the lower Zaire region in the period of commodity trade during the nineteenth century' (Martin, 1986:8).

The shell used in Central Africa as currency was the nzimbu shell, whose scientific name is olivancillaria nana. During its heyday the Kongo kingdom, for example, had operated a well-established currency system with standardized units based on the nzimbu shell (Birmingham, 1983:27; Miller, 1983:128). In both 'the Kongo kingdom and Angola cowries were counted by units of 40, 100, 250, 400, 500, and by volume measures corresponding to 1,000 (funda), 10,000 (lufuka), 20,000 (cofo), and 100,000 cowries (bondo), while 2,000 shells were termed makuta, equated to the unit of value of the same name' (Sundstrom, 1974:99). The makuta became an abstract unit of account in which other currencies were reckoned.

Another commodity that doubled up as a currency in parts of Central and Southern Africa was salt. Kisama salt had been used widely in some areas of Angola in the fifteenth and sixteenth centuries (Birmingham, 1970:165). Salt blocks served as common units of exchange in parts of Malawi (Reefe, 1983:172). According to Sundstrom (1974:130), 'in Central Africa the majority of salt units varied between 0.25 and 5 kg', and they were used both as 'small change' and as 'big money' depending on the value of the commodity being purchased.

The use of currencies increased in the nineteenth century as the volume of trade expanded and regional markets became more integrated. With this came the universal acceptance of one or two currencies in a particular region. The best example comes from the Zaire basin. For centuries a wide variety of cloth, salt, metal, and shell currencies had been used in different parts of the basin. With the development of an integrated regional economy in the early nineteenth century, copper currency gained universal acceptance. In the second half of the century copper was gradually replaced by currency made of imported brass, known as mitako. The mitako was used side-by-side with the old cloth currency, ibuunu, and the shell currency, nji. But the latter often functioned as small change for the mitako, although the three currencies were strictly not just multiples one of the other since their spheres of exchange differed slightly (Vansina, 1973:282-96).

Porters and Canoemen

Unlike the other regions we have looked at, pack animals hardly played any role in the provision of transport for long-distance trade in Central and Southern Africa. Overland transport was almost entirely provided by porters, while canoes were used along the major navigable rivers. Animal transport was hampered by the existence of tsetse fly belts and other constraints. For example, it has been argued that the use of bullocks in Madagascar was inhibited by the fact that the bullock was considered a sacred animal. Although the traditional prohibition on the commercial utilization of the bullock was gradually relaxed in the first decades of the nineteenth century, transport still relied mainly on human labour because the Merina feared that the improvement and modernization of transport would facilitate European military conquest. In the 1820s Radama I had launched 'a series of road and transport improvement projects... The French naval bombardment of 1829 strengthened this fear and put an end to the short-lived transport experiments' (Campbell, 1980:343). In addition to the strategic considerations, porterage was relatively cheap for the Merina political and commercial elite, for it was based on forced state labour, or fanompoano, which was both servile and unpaid (Campbell, 1980:344-6).

Some historians have argued that porterage was inefficient. The question of efficiency is of course a relative one. Judged against other forms of transport then available in the two regions human porterage was, in fact, quite efficient . Heywood (1985) has demonstrated, for example, that the ox-wagon proved commercially uncompetitive in the central highlands of Angola. Porters, she contends, could carry as much as 35 kgs each, travel under practically all conditions and take any route available, while wagons had to pass through areas with sufficient grazing land and water supplies for their oxen. While it took porters about 25 days to cover a 550 kilometre trip, wagons made the same trip in two months. Heywood (1985:246) concludes that 'porters were the most reliable, fastest, and cheapest form of transport for goods on the long-distance trade routes that linked the heart of Central Africa with the Atlantic ports on the Angolan coast'. The porters included slaves, dependents and hired labourers, although their relative share in the total labour-force varied from employer to employer and changed over time.

It would seem that slaves and dependents dominated in the first half of the nineteenth century, after which hired labour became increasingly critical as commodity production and trade expanded following the eclipse of the slave trade. At first the 'free' wage labourers were recruited through their village heads, who were paid a commission, and from the 1850s it was arranged through a local entrepreneur, known as ocimbalo, who supplied porters for caravans in return for a fee. Finally, people could join caravans on their own. The biggest caravans, which could have as many as 5,000 people, including women and youths who served as attendants, were organized by members of the Ovimbundu ruling class. Caravans going to the coast were apparently more strictly controlled than those going into the interior. Porters in the latter caravans were therefore able to exercise their entrepreneurial flair and convert their wages into commercial profit.

Indeed, increasingly, particularly during the years of the rubber boom, the division between hired porter and petty trader became blurred. It became more difficult to recruit porters. The combination of porterage services and trading activities was manifested in the splintered organization of caravans, particularly those involved in the rubber trade. 'During the period of the rubber boom', Heywood (1985:253) observes, the 'caravans, often comprising over 1,000 people, entered the rubber producing areas and split up, so that porters bartered on a one to one basis with the individual producers right on the banks of rivers where the rubber was gathered and processed. A similar arrangement worked in the wax trade as well, individual deals often being completed at the hive'. So intense was the competition for lucrative commodities, specially rubber, that there developed 'the institution of cambalucao, whereby large firms outbid each other by offering gifts of various sorts to the caravan leaders in the hope of persuading them to trade with this or that firm... such trading techniques tended to expand the market to include even the lowest porter who exhibited more of a preference for transporting and marketing his own products than for working on behalf of someone else' (Heywood, 1985:253).

The competitive pressures enabled many porters to accumulate enough to become independent traders, which helped weaken the ties of dependency within Ovimbundu society that bound the lower to the upper classes. These changes in class relations brought about by the reorganization of porterage and trade were halted in their tracks with the imposition of Portuguese colonial rule towards the end of the century, particularly following the establishment of a railway system, which required the systematic elimination of porters for its profitability. By 1914 Ovimbundu porterage had largely ended and with it 'the era of social mobility that might see a humble man rise to a minor official and village ruler in his lifetime was over' (Heywood, 1985:264).

If porterage produced merchants in Ovimbundu, it spawned slaves in Madagascar. Unlike their Ovimbundu counterparts, the majority of porters in Madagascar were either forced labourers or slaves. The state used fanom-poana labour for porterage, while private merchants depended on slaves, who 'were often hired out, or permitted to hire themselves out. In some instances they never again saw their owners, who simply drew a percentage of the slave's earnings' (Campbell, 1980:346). The system of contracting slaves for porterage grew rapidly in the course of the nineteenth century. A powerful syndicate of slave proprietors, with close ties to the state, and based in Antanarivo, emerged. The porters, known as maromita or borizano, fell into two groups - those that specialized in carrying goods, the mpaka or mpitondra entana, and those involved in bearing travellers, the mpilanja. By the end of the century the porterage system employed an estimated 50,000 to 60,000 men, which represented about a fifth of all slaves in Imerina.

The growth of the porterage system was accompanied by the development of collective organization among the porters. They created their own culture, articulated in songs and a mutual-aid system, and cemented by blood brotherhood, the fatidra, out of which emerged a sort of proto-trade union movement. The porters waged intermittent struggles for higher wages and better working conditions. Partly as a result of these struggles the wage between Toamasina and Antanarivo rose from 2 dollars in 1866 to 5 dollars in 1888 and 8 dollars in 1894. These wages were still very low. But their rise was in itself a tribute to the organizational muscle of the porters. The power of the porters ultimately rested on the absence of an alternative transport system. The French colonization of Madagascar and the subsequent construction of a modern road and rail transport system spelled the end of the porterage system (Campbell, 1980:350-6).

What porterage was to the central Angolan highlands and Madagascar, canoeing was to the Zaire river basin. To make a trading trip in the basin, Harms (1981:93) states, 'a trader needed a canoe, paddlers, trade goods, and contacts. The large trading canoes were enormous by the standards of the canoes seen on the river today'. On average they were 15 metres long, but the largest could be over 20 metres long with a crew of 60 to 70 paddlers. The crews were mostly owned by the rich traders, some of whom had fleets of four or more. Merchants who did not have their own canoes hired them or rented space in the canoes. The paddlers were usually members of the merchant's family, both relatives and slaves, hired labourers, or petty traders who were going to sell their own merchandise and volunteered to paddle in exchange for free transport. Normally canoes would form a fleet, for travelling alone was almost certain to invite attack. The trading trips 'were long, hard and dangerous... A trip took not only the time to paddle to the destination and back, but also time for fishing, resting, bargaining at the destination, or possibly waiting for goods with which to fill the canoe before coming back' (Harms, 1981:95). A trip from Bobangi Esanga to Tchumbiri and back could take an average three to four months. The greatest dangers were posed by the weather, with its unpredictable tropical storms, and pirates. Sometimes in order to avoid the pirates the canoes would travel at night. Otherwise in the evening the crew would land on a sandbank or on the bank and organize camp.

The river transport system was intricately connected with overland caravans using porters. The average caravan consisted of between 100 and

500 people. The caravans travelled during day time and camped at night in temporary shelters. They bought most of their food along the way. Caravans were expected to pay tolls to the chief of every territory they passed. 'Once the toll had been paid the chief had a man escort the traders with his bell through his dominion' (Vansina, 1973:61). The caravan team, as with caravans elsewhere, had an occupational hierarchy, including a leader who was responsible for maintaining internal discipline and making all the necessary negotiations during the trip. The overland caravans carried goods to and from the market villages and towns dotted all along the Zaire river and its major tributaries. Thus the two forms of transport were part of an integrated transport system that facilitated and sustained trade in the Zaire basin.

Canoeing and porterage also formed part of one transport system in the commercial networks developed along the Zambezi and Tchiri rivers. Indeed, here the same group of people, the Chikunda and Kololo, served both as porters and canoe crews. Overland they were porters, and when crossing or travelling along the Zambezi and Tchiri rivers they became canoemen. The Chikunda caravans, often containing 200 people, went as far as the Lunda state of Kazembe in Katanga, and as far south as the Shona states of Manyika and Mwenemutapa, carrying a wide assortment of goods. The caravan leader, known as musambadzi, was responsible for the caravan's success, so he settled disputes, negotiated with rulers through whose territory the caravan passed, selected camp sites where temporary settlements for overnight rest, called misasa, were established, and conducted trade bargains. The commercial acumen of the musambadzi was of course not enough by itself to ensure the success of the enterprise. As Isaacman and Mandala (1985:214-5) argue, 'it also depended on the brawn of the porters and the skill of canoemen' who had to carry heavy loads over long distances and negotiate treacherous rivers.

When the Chikunda diaspora later established their own trading enterprises, they found it difficult to draw on their own labour for transport because of their small numbers, or to recruit tributary and corvee labour since they lacked political power. For their part the indigenous people, 'fearful of travelling through unknown and dangerous regions, refused to serve as porters... As a result, the Chikunda, like their former prazero owners, came to rely on slave labour' (Isaacman and Mandala, 1985:222).

Unlike the Chikunda porters who had started out as slaves, Kololo porters began as tributary labourers. While working for Livingstone, they often supplemented their meagre food supplies by dancing and entertaining villagers along the route and through hunting and gathering. When Livingstone left, they contracted themselves as canoemen and shipping crew to other employers. Their fortunes began to improve. No wonder they could not accept the old arrangement with Livingstone when he returned. After the Kololo had transformed themselves into a ruling aristocracy in the Tchiri valley through the manipulation of local politics, they organized their own caravans based on tributary and corvee labour extracted from their subjects. They also profited from renting canoes and paddlers to caravans crossing the Tchiri river. In order to maintain their monopoly over the river trade the local people, the Mang'anja, were prohibited from owning canoes.

As the numbers of European merchants and colonists in the Tchiri highlands increased from the 1860s, the Kololo used their power to provide porters and appropriate a portion of the porters' wages. Local chiefs who did not provide enough porters were often deposed and replaced with more pliant ones. Since they profited directly from the porters' wages, 'the Kololo supported the wage demands of their labourers as a means of raising their own share. When the Europeans refused to raise wages, the Kololo did not hesitate to withhold their labourers' services' (Isaacman and Mandala, 1985:236).

For their part, the porters engaged in their own struggles against exploitation by refusing to carry oversized packages and by pilfering. 'Loads weighing over fifty pounds', to quote Isaacman and Mandala (1985:257) again, 'were continually left at the chiefs' courts. So successful were Mang'anja porters in this respect, that fifty pound became the standard weight of all loads passing through the Tchiri valley in the 1880s and 1890s'. Through pilfering the porters were not only striking a blow against their employers, but also trying to limit Kololo claims to a portion of their wages.

The cases of the Chikunda and Kololo porters and canoemen demonstrates the complex patterns of working class formation in nineteenth century Southern Africa, and the struggles waged by transport workers to improve their wages and conditions of work. These struggles partly succeeded in transforming the Chikunda and Kololo porters themselves into independent traders who came to employ others as porters and canoemen, from whom emerged new forms of struggle. As in the central Angolan highlands, the curtains were drawn on this unfolding socioeconomic drama with the imposition of Portuguese and British colonial rule in the region, and the introduction of the railway system at the turn of the twentieth century.

Colonial Commerce

Long before the European scramble for Africa in the last quarter of the nineteenth century, there were several colonial enclaves in Central and Southern Africa, principally in present-day Angola and South Africa. These enclaves depended for their viability to a very large extent on trade with, and labour from, the neighbouring African communities. The Portuguese were the first to attempt to establish a colonial empire in these regions, but by 1800 there was little to show for three centuries of effort. Luanda, the capital of the Portuguese colonial enclave in Angola, was a decrepit town with little to offer. 'Luanda's decadence', writes Bender (1978:66), 'noted in the early 1800s, turned to decay by the middle of the nineteenth century... Gambling, drinking, and debauchery were the Europeans' major preoccupations and many fortunes, wives, and lives were won and lost'.

The fledgling colonial economy in Angola, with its fragile plantation and fishing industries, offered few employment opportunities to Portuguese settlers, most of whom were degredados, convicts shipped by the government to spearhead the Portuguese colonization and occupation of Central Africa. Many of the settlers therefore turned to trade. As was shown in Chapter 2, Angola became a major centre of the Atlantic slave trade, but with the end of the slave trade in the second half of the nineteenth century, many Portuguese traders were forced out of the interior, 'thereby eliminating almost the only tokens of Portuguese sovereignty in the hinterland' (Bender, 1978:66). In southern Angola many Portuguese became wandering or itinerant traders known as funantes. The funantes usually sold their goods to African chiefs and merchants in the interior on credit. They themselves 'were also advanced trade goods on credit by the coastal merchants, who in turn were sometimes indebted to Lisbon capitalists' (Clarence-Smith, 1979b:66). They were quite vulnerable, for they were bound to their coastal creditors, but had no effective means to enforce debt repayment from independent African chiefs and merchants.

But the vulnerability of the funantes was more than compensated by the difference between the price paid for certain staple commodities in the interior and the price they fetched on the coast. For example, 'in 1896, an ox could be bought in the Huila highlands for between £E1 and £E1.50 and sold on the coast for about £E3.25. In 1900, a pound of rubber fetched about 3p in eastern Angola and 15p on the coast' (Clarence-Smith, 1979b:66). Not surprisingly, there was intense competition among Portuguese traders attached to different colonial ports and between them and African merchants, for African caravans from the interior visited the coast as well. The Portuguese formed their own caravans of hired porters or slaves, although they failed to compete effectively with the African caravans. A new mode of transport was introduced in southern Angola with the arrival of Boer immigrants from South Africa. Boer ox-wagons, although more expensive and slower than head porterage, became indispensable in the 1890s and 1900s, thanks to the rubber boom and the acute shortage of porters (Clarence-Smith, 1979b:66).

The colonial economy, or rather economies, of South Africa were much more dynamic than those of Angola. At the beginning of the nineteenth century colonial settlement in South Africa was confined to the Cape Colony, which had been a colony of the Dutch East India Company (VOC) since the mid-seventeenth century until 1795. Between 1795 and 1814 the Cape was alternately ruled by British and Batavian 'transitional governments' as Freund (1989) calls them. The Cape was founded as a trading station, and trade remained central to its development. There were four types of trade: trade conducted within the colonial frontiers; trade carried out between the colonies and the neighbouring African communities; trade among the colonies themselves; and trade with the international economy. In this chapter we are mainly concerned with the first three, partly because this chapter is on internal trade, and partly because as Ross (1989:254) has argued, 'exports never played the predominant role that they did in the frequently export-led economies of the New World. With the exception of elephant hunting... there was no sector which produced exclusively, or even predominantly, for the overseas market'.

During the days of company rule, the VOC had the legal right to impose monopolies over the Cape's internal and external trade. In reality, its efforts to control the marketing of the colony's main products - wine, wheat and meat - fell far short of monopoly (Ross, 1989:246-8). From 1795 the British began to free internal trade, although 'all the transitional governments continued to set the prices of staples and to tax produce entering Cape Town' (Freund, 1989:329). Cape Town was the commercial centre of the colony, but in the first decades of the nineteenth century the position of the town's 'merchant community remained parlous. There were numerous bankruptcies among the British settlers' (Ross, 1989:266).

It was only from the 1820s that matters began to improve and Cape Town's major merchants and mercantile houses started getting stabilized. This was accompanied by changes in the retail and distribution system. Unlike before, when almost every household was involved in trade, and general merchants predominated, from the 1820s there was a trend towards specialization. Increasingly, business was conducted in definite shops, away from private houses as had been the case before. The marketing of wine and meat was controlled by the big merchants, while the retailing of cakes, biscuits, fish, fruits and vegetables was largely in the hands of slaves, some of whom managed to accumulate enough capital to purchase their own emancipation. Many freed slaves turned to, and flourished in, Cape Town's small-scale trades and crafts partly because they had limited access to land and other productive opportunities (Elphick and Shell, 1989:214-24; Armstrong and Worden, 1989).

In the Cape Colony's country districts trade was mainly conducted by travelling merchants, the smousen. 'Often Dutch, and later, British young men made a number of trips as smousen in the hope, often illusory, or building up the capital they required for more permanent and settled business. To do this, they began with funds borrowed from major Cape Town or Grahamstown merchants' (Ross, 1989:267). The position of the travelling smousen became increasingly fragile as larger merchant houses and settled traders were established in a growing number of small towns outside Cape Town.

The frontiers of the Cape colony were constantly expanding, so that the spatial context of the Cape's 'internal' trade was always in a state of flux. The first indigenous people with whom the colonists established trading relations were the Khoisan. By 1800 Cape-Khoisan trade had long since paled into insignificance, for Khoisan society had irretrievably broken down due to Boer 'frontier' wars, diseases and miscegenation. Since the mid-seventeenth century the Khoisan had steadily lost their lands, cattle and economic independence, which undermined their capacity to reproduce themselves. Those that survived were incorporated into the Cape economy as a pool of cheap, coerced labour (Elphick, 1977, 1989).

From their base at the Cape, the settlers extended their trade, agrarian and political frontiers in the early nineteenth century northwards and eastwards. The main vehicle used by the settlers for trading on the frontier zone was the commando-like band, which was also employed for raiding and hunting. Not surprisingly, frontier trade between them and the indigenous people often 'shaded into patently unequal barter, unequal barter into theft, and theft into the organized raiding by commandos which characterized the first «frontier wars»... trade and war, therefore, were but two sides of the same coin' (Legassick, 1980:65). On the northern frontier trade was carried out with the Griqua and the Sotho-Tswana (Legassick, 1989), while on the eastern frontier it was with the Xhosa (Giliomee, 1989). The most important products that the colonial traders sought from African communities were cattle to develop their pastoral farming, grains to feed themselves and their workers, and ivory for export. In return, the latter bought mostly tobacco and metal products.

Pondoland, for example, became a major supplier of all the colonial traders' commodities. By the 1830s, regular settler 'trading expeditions geared largely to the ivory trade passed through Pondoland on their way between the eastern Cape and Port Natal'. By the 1850s most of the elephants in Pondoland had been exterminated. Subsequent generations of settler traders that flocked to Pondoland were attracted by the country's cattle which they bought to sell in the colonial markets. It is difficult to estimate the number of cattle leaving Pondoland annually, but Beinart (1980b:137) indicates that 'in the decade before rinderpest, one large trading concern in eastern Pondoland usually sent between 500 and 1,000 head to Pieter-maritzburg every year. Others may have rivalled them, and there were a number of smaller operators'. In addition, Pondoland exported large quan-tities of hides. The trade in hides increased rapidly from the 1860s, due to the spread of lungsickness and drought and declining local demand for hides to make shields and clothing, thanks to the increased availability of cotton textiles and blankets. Indeed, by the 1870s blankets were the major imports into Pondoland. Livestock diseases in Natal encouraged cattle imports from abroad, especially Madagascar, which provided no less than 80% of all Natal cattle imports between 1875 and 1909 (Campbell, 1990-91:116).

By 1870 the European merchants dominated Cape trade. In Natal the Europeans began to face competition from Asian merchants who had just begun arriving due to 'narrowing or limited economic opportunities in India, East Africa and Mauritius, [their] long history of overseas links in trade, credit extension and finance and the attraction of business prospects in Natal' (Padayachee and Morrell, 1991:76). There were two groups of traders, the big merchants who came as passenger Indians, and the petty traders, the dukawallahs, many of whom originally came as indentured labourers. These traders played an important role in extending the colony's commercial network. They penetrated into the hinterland, trading with African com-munities. The small European shopkeepers found it increasingly difficult to compete, so they became resentful. The Indians' success was a tribute to their trading skills, and the vibrancy of their informal credit and lending systems, for they had limited access to the European-controlled banking and credit institutions, which excluded them, or which they avoided for economic and religious reasons. By the end of the century, they were becoming marginalized, thanks to the institutionalization of racial dis-crimination and legal harassment against them, coupled with Natal's economic depression, the loosening of extended family business ties as Indian businesses expanded from Natal to the Transvaal, and the growing dominance of finance capital in South African economic life (Padayachee and Morrell, 1991:77-93).

By the mid-nineteenth century, apart the British colonies of the Cape and Natal, two Boer colonies, the Orange Free State and the Transvaal, had been established in present-day South Africa. This led to the development of a third type of trade, that between the colonies themselves. We noted, in Chapter 5, for example, that the Cape was a major market for Natal sugar. In 1865 the total import and export trade between the two British colonies amounted to about £E 102,000, two-thirds of which represented Cape exports to Natal. Altogether, the Cape's trade with Natal represented less than 2% of its total external trade (Houghton and Dagut, 1972:133). In the early 1860s there were attempts to establish what was called a 'free reciprocal coasting trade' between the two colonies, which was turned down by the Cape (Houghton and Dagut, 1972:130-2). The volume and value of inter-colonial trade expanded greatly with the development of the mining industry in the 1870s and 1880s. As we saw in Chapter 8, the mineral revolution accelerated the processes of urbanization and laid the basis for industrialization, all of which led to the rapid growth of internal markets.

As trade expanded in South Africa the need for money, credit and banking institutions increased. At the beginning of the nineteenth century, the currency of the Cape, in de Kiewet's (1957:36) phrase, 'gave the impression of a numistical collection. There were gold mohurs and rupees from India, pagodas from Madras, johannas, doubloons, and dollars from Spain and her empire, sequins from Venice, and guineas and shillings from England. Most of the currency was in paper Rix dollars, wretchedly printed on poor paper, which was easily defaced and outrageously counterfeited'. The new British administration tried to finance its public expenditures by printing more Rix dollars. The result was soaring inflation and the steady collapse of the Rix dollar. In 1825 it was replaced with British coinage and promissory notes. This move was greeted by vigorous protests in the Cape Colony, for they lost money because of the low rate of conversion from Rix dollars into sterling imposed by British Treasury. In 1841 the Rix dollar ceased to be legal tender and with this the Cape was integrated more firmly into the British empire. British coinage extended to Natal when the new colony was established.

But these moves did not resolve the colonies' monetary problems. For one thing, there was never enough money. For example, in the Cape Colony, the amount of coin in circulation in 1855 was between £E600,000 and £E800,000, rising to £E2.1 million in 1865, while the bank paper currency in Natal amounted to between £E8,000 and £E10,000 (Houghton and Dagut, 1972:148). The shortage of money and credit led to high interest rates which dampened trade, investment and economic growth. If shortage of money was the problem in the British colonies, excessive money supply was the problem in the Boer colonies. In the Transvaal, in 1865, five years after the formation of its so-called South African Republic, the state began issuing paper money secured by government farms. Landlords also issued their own bills. In addition, as Trapido (1980:352-3) observes, 'clergymen, traders, and private individuals issued credit notes which became known as good-furs because of the monetary chaos. It is hardly surprising that the Republic's currency was unacceptable in most commercial transactions and there were occasions when even government departments refused to accept currency which was supposedly legal tender'. It was not until the development of the mining industry that the Transvaal's economy and financial system was put on a more secure footing.

As might be expected, credit and banking services were more developed in the British than the Boer colonies. At the beginning of the nineteenth century most of the credit arrangements were informal. Before banks were set up, rich Cape merchants acted as financiers and bankers. They provided credit to their clients, especially the wool farmers. 'Their notes began to circulate, drawn on their Cape Town offices. When the practice was discontinued, they became representatives on the boards of banks' (Kirk, 1980:231). The largest sources of institutional credit were the church and the Orphan Chamber, which administered the estates of company officials who had died without heirs in the Cape Colony. Both were involved in financing long-term mortgages. Short-term commercial credit was normally obtained from private lenders and the licensed auctioneers. Later banks became an important source of commercial credit.

The first bank in the Cape Colony was the Loan Bank, established in 1793. It initially 'functioned as a combination of mortgage institution and pawn-broker, lending money against the security of fixed property and valuables, such as precious metal and jewellery' (Ross, 1989:261). It only began accepting deposits in 1822. Another bank, the Discount Bank, which provided short-term loans and also elicited deposits from Cape Town's inhabitants, was established in 1808. The two banks were state-owned.

The government blocked any attempts to form private banks until the 1830s. The first private bank in the Cape, the joint stock Cape of Good Hope Bank, was founded in 1837. It was quickly followed by others , especially in the 1850s and 1860s. For example, between 1859 and 1862 alone the number of banks in the Cape increased from 16, with a combined capital of £E2.3 million, to 29, with a combined capital of £E3.4 million (Amphlett, 1914:9). The two Boer colonies relied on banks in the Cape Colony and Natal. Attempts by the Transvaal to establish a bank in the 1860s and 1870s failed. One of the largest and most famous banks established in Cape Colony in the 1860s was the Standard Bank, formed in 1862 with a capital of £E1 million, which was increased to £E2 million in the following year. The bank quickly became the largest in South Africa with branches all over the country. Indeed, by the 1900s it had established branches in Lesotho, Zimbabwe, Zambia, Mozambique, Malawi, and as far as Zaire, Zanzibar and Kenya. Altogether, by 1913 the bank had 215 branches, up from 99 in 1900 and 18 in 1863 (Amphlett, 1914:199).

The development of the banking industry in South Africa underscores the fact that from the mid-nineteenth century capitalism within the country, and the country's integration into the world capitalist system, was accelerating faster than anywhere else in Southern Africa. The spreading tentacles of South African banks in Southern, Central and Eastern Africa at the turn of the twentieth century demonstrates the gradual emergence of South Africa as a sub-regional metropole, a process that was buttressed by the development of a regional transport and communications infrastructure centred on South Africa.

Transport

Until the construction of railways from the 1870s, traders in South Africa relied on wagons to transport their goods. Up to 1870 there were less than 70 miles of railway in the country. By 1886 the Cape had built 1,000 miles, at a cost of £E14 million, most of it from public funds. Thus railways did not have much impact until the 1880s and 1890s. The ox-wagon ruled, plying along the muddy roads, across unbridged gullies, over steep hills, and through rugged valleys. But wagons were expensive and slow. In the mid-1850s a wagon cost £E50 or more, which was a considerable sum of money (Beinart, 1980b:141). The journey between Port Elizabeth and Bloemfontein, for example, not only 'took three months... each wagon required about fifty draught animals' (Houghton and Dagut, 1972:110. italics original). This partly reflected the poor state of most of the long-distance roads. The speed at which wagons moved also depended on the state of the grass. As de Kiewet (1957:98) puts it: 'poor grass weakened the draught animals; good grass gave them strength. That was why ox-wagon loads cost £E15 a ton when the roads were fair and animals well nourished, and £E30 a ton when the roads were wretched and the animals emaciated'.

The ox-wagon has come to be seen as a quintessential symbol of Boer rusticity. But the Boers were not the only transport riders. There were many African entrepreneurs who took to transport riding as well, beginning with the Khoisan (Elphick and Malherbe, 1989:29). They often invested money made in transport riding in land, stock and improvements of their enterprises. The link between transport riding and farming was indeed a close one. In the 1870s, at the height of peasant prosperity, 'many peasants resorted to transport riding once their own crops were harvested' and transported their crops to the markets; 'transport riding was also a convenient means of earning enough money to obtain land' (Bundy, 1979:77).

The expansion of the railway network in the last quarter of the nineteenth century spelled disaster for the transport riders, both African and European. The former suffered a worse fate, because this coincided with the intensification of pressures against African farming, which was aimed at eliminating the competition African farmers posed to the settler farmers, and forcing them into becoming workers for the latter as well as the mining industry. Thus the demise of the African transport riders with their wagons and carts represented the narrowing opportunities for African accumulation in South Africa's rapidly expanding and industrializing racial capitalism.

Conclusion

It is quite evident that a lot more research needs to be done on Central and Southern Africa before more definite conclusions can be drawn as to the structure and organization of markets, the development of the various regional trading systems, and the evolution of money and credit institutions. The available evidence points to the fact that trade in the two regions was no less extensive than in the three regions considered in the previous chapters, and that as the nineteenth century progressed the trading networks expanded and became more intertwined, which facilitated the growth of more integrated regional economies.

The river basins, especially of the Zaire and Zambezi rivers, appear to have been major trading routes along which some of the leading regional trading centres grew and flourished. Not surprisingly, porterage and canoeing were closely connected. As we saw, some groups such as the Chikunda and Kololo served both as porters and canoemen. It would appear that porterage and canoeing were sufficiently developed to offset any disadvantages that the absence of pack animals might have entailed. There are a number of studies which clearly indicate that porterage, for example, was more 'efficient' than ox-wagon transportation.

The studies on the two regions have also raised some interesting questions concerning, for example, the patterns of merchant accumulation. As this chapter has shown, there were those who used existing credit institutions and social support networks to raise capital for trading ventures. Others rose from grinding poverty, using their wages as porters, or prowess as hunters, to establish themselves as traders. In some cases the merchants converted their new found wealth into political power, which they, in turn, used to further their trading interests. Findings from the Zaire basin give a fascinating portrait of the ways in which traders invested their profits. The Central African data as a whole provides valuable insights into the moral economy of the credit system, which reveals that the system was undergirded by moral and social sanctions, not just economic and legal pressures.

In addition, the two regions offer important material on the development of trade in the European colonial enclaves and economies. Once again, the Portuguese seem to have been as poor at establishing viable trading ventures as they were at agriculture. Trade in the South African colonies, especially the Cape, was more vibrant, despite the severe teething problems of poor transportation, unreliable currencies, and fickle markets. It grew steadily before the mineral revolution and exploded afterwards as new cities and towns mushroomed. But, as with settler agriculture and the mining industry itself, this was no simple triumph of economics. Its foundations were rooted in the dynamics of 'primitive accumulation'. Trading relations between the colonists and the indigenous communities were often indistinguishable from robbery and warfare. While the settlers used the commando-like bands as instruments of trade with Africans, they applied legal and political harassment to muscle out and marginalize the Indian merchants.

Part V

International Trade and Imperialism

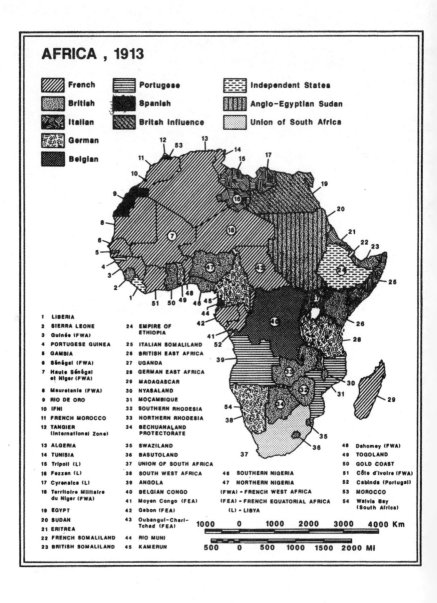

AFRICA , 1913

French	Portugese
British	Spanish
Italian	British Influence
German	
Belgian	

Independent States
Anglo-Egyptian Sudan
Union of South Africa

1 LIBERIA
2 SIERRA LEONE
3 Guinée (FWA)
4 PORTUGESE GUINEA
5 GAMBIA
6 Sénégal (FWA)
7 Haute Sénégal et Niger (FWA)
8 Mauretanie (FWA)
9 RIO DE ORO
10 IFNI
11 FRENCH MOROCCO
12 TANGIER (International Zone)
13 ALGERIA
14 TUNISIA
15 Tripoli (L)
16 Fezzan (L)
17 Cyrenaica (L)
18 Territoire Militaire du Niger (FWA)
19 EGYPT
20 SUDAN
21 ERITREA
22 FRENCH SOMALILAND
23 BRITISH SOMALILAND
24 EMPIRE OF ETHIOPIA
25 ITALIAN SOMALILAND
26 BRITISH EAST AFRICA
27 UGANDA
28 GERMAN EAST AFRICA
29 MADAGASCAR
30 NYASALAND
31 MOÇAMBIQUE
32 SOUTHERN RHODESIA
33 NORTHERN RHODESIA
34 BECHUANALAND PROTECTORATE
35 SWAZILAND
36 BASUTOLAND
37 UNION OF SOUTH AFRICA
38 SOUTH WEST AFRICA
39 ANGOLA
40 BELGIAN CONGO
41 Moyen Congo (FEA)
42 Gabon (FEA)
43 Oubangui-Chari-Tchad (FEA)
44 RIO MUNI
45 KAMERUN
46 SOUTHERN NIGERIA
47 NORTHERN NIGERIA
(FWA) = FRENCH WEST AFRICA
(FEA) = FRENCH EQUATORIAL AFRICA
(L) = LIBYA
48 Dahomey (FWA)
49 TOGOLAND
50 GOLD COAST
51 Côte d'Ivoire (FWA)
52 Cabinda (Portugal)
53 MOROCCO
54 Walvis Bay (South Africa)

1000 0 1000 2000 3000 4000 Km
500 0 500 1000 1500 2000 MI

13. North Africa: Debt Imperialism

Growth of Trade with Europe

By the end of the eighteenth century North African countries had developed an extensive network of international trade with various countries in Africa, Asia and Europe. This chapter examines the trade between the countries of North Africa and those of western Europe, which gradually became dominant.

There is some evidence to show that this trade was a new development. Egyptian trade figures for 1783, for example, show that 44.4% of Egypt's foreign trade was conducted with the Ottoman Empire, including Syria, and 34.5% relationship with Jedda. Europe came far behind with 14.2% (Walz, 1978:62; Owen, 1981:52). There are no comparable figures for the Maghreb, but it would appear that the Maghreb's trade with Europe was relatively more significant than it was for Egypt.

The inadequacy and inaccuracy of the data make it difficult to discuss North Africa's balance of trade and balance of payments with Asia and Europe at the end of the eighteenth century. Figures for Egypt's foreign trade in 1783 indicate that Egypt had a favourable trade balance with the Ottoman empire of 125.5 million paras, and a negative balance of 191.2 million paras with Jedda and 13.4 million paras with Europe. A lot more is known about the composition of trade. The major exports from the Maghreb countries to Europe consisted of olive oil, cereals, especially wheat, hides and leather, raw wool and woollen manufactures (Issawi, 1982:34). The grain exports were quite substantial. Until the 1790s, for example, 'Tunisia continued to serve in good years and bad, as one of Europe's granaries' (Valensi, 1985:221-2).

The European merchants resident in North Africa were restricted to their own quarters. They were often representatives of trading companies and enjoyed relatively more privileges than other foreign merchants, thanks to the protection provided by the treaties of capitulations signed between the Ottoman Empire and several European countries, and the presence of European consuls representing their governments. The capitulations exempted the foreign traders from local laws and set limits on import and export duties.

But these privileges were not cast in stone. As local currencies depreciated in the eighteenth century, North African governments responded to their declining incomes from customs duties by imposing additional duties, monopolies, and prohibitions, particularly on exports, for at this time 'in

North Africa and probably elsewhere, there was a belief that exports impoverished the country and sales to infidels were immoral' (Issawi, 1982:18). Issawi thinks that the basic reason for this anti-mercantilist policy lay 'in the balance of social forces in these countries. The dominant elements were bureaucrats and soldiers, whose interest in economic matters was limited to taxation and provisioning' (Issawi, 1982:17). The struggle between the European merchants and the North African governments was one of the mainstreams from which the forces of European imperialism and colonization in the nineteenth century sprang (Deeb, 1978).

In the nineteenth century western Europe gradually became the main trading partner of North Africa. Western Europe was then industrializing and looking for sources of raw materials, markets for its manufactured goods, and outlets for investment and population settlement. For its part, North Africa was struggling to wrest its independence from the Ottomans and protect itself from European encroachment, presaged by Napoleon's invasion of Egypt in 1798. This required the North African countries to enlarge and modernize their armies and economies, which entailed more trade with that very Europe that threatened their autonomy. Thus, European industrialization and North African modernization were locked in a fateful embrace whose offspring was ultimately colonization.

Three main factors facilitated the expansion of European commerce with North Africa. First, there was a big increase in the numbers of European merchants resident in the region. Second, the introduction of steamships in the mid-nineteenth century, which were faster than the sailing ships and less affected by the hazards of the weather, quickened the tempo of trade and helped reduce ocean rates so that more merchants were able to join the trade. Third, European governments began to play a more active role in seeking to protect the commercial interests of their merchants. They exerted great pressure on North African governments to abolish their trade monopoly policies and practices and open up their economies to the European merchants (Owen, 1981:88-91).

As we saw in Chapter 7, the monopoly system was widely used in domestic trade. The system served the interests of military chieftains and oligarchies which dominated the state, but was resented by the hapless peasants, the indigenous merchants and the foreign merchants. Their combined opposition eventually succeeded in loosening the grip of state control. Many historians have argued that while the monopoly system enriched the state, it impoverished the peasants and weakened the indigenous merchants, who were therefore in no position to compete against foreign merchants when the system was later dismantled.

In fact, the monopoly system favoured European merchants while it operated. In Algeria, for example, 'despite the tight control of these monopolies, the French companies often complained of Algerian merchants who managed to deal excessively with Marseilles themselves, and the state clamped down on them' (Bennoune, 1988:30). The system not only succeeded in eliminating North African merchants from international trade, it also encouraged many of them to become dependent proteges of European merchants, who were restricted to the ports. In Morocco the proteges were exempted from Moroccan authority, including the payment of taxes. This encouraged many wealthy Moroccans to become proteges, thus depriving the state of their taxes, and forcing taxes to be raised for the rest of the population (Ponasik, 1977:204-5). Finally, by stifling local commercial activity the system paved the way for the domination of the domestic market by the Europeans as these countries became firmly integrated into the world capitalist economy in the course of the nineteenth century.

The system was abolished at different times in the various North African countries. Generally by the mid-nineteenth century the system had either been abandoned or had broken down. Trade with Europe soared. Available figures indicate that the region's international trade expanded at an unprecedented rate. The average regional growth rate was about the same as the world average, booming when the world economy was expanding, and slumping during the intermittent recessions of 1873-95. The greatest increase took place in Egypt whose foreign trade increased in value from £E1.5 million in 1810 to £E5 million in 1870-73 and £E36 million in 1900. Algeria's trade rose from £E0.8 million in 1835 to £E21 million in 1891-1900, Morocco's from £E1 million in the 1830s to £E3.5 million in 1900, and Tunisia's from £E0.5 million in 1837-39 to £E1.1 million in 1875-78 (Issawi, 1982:24). It is no wonder that Egypt was coveted by the major West European powers.

Egypt and the Bondholders

Egypt entered the new century under French occupation, having been invaded by Napoleon and his armies in 1798 for economic, political and other reasons. Britain saw the French occupation of Egypt as a direct threat to its interests in India and the adjacent regions, so it forced France to leave the country in 1801. This was the first step in the long struggle between the two powers over Egypt which culminated in the British colonization of the country in 1882. In the next four decades after the ousting of France, Egypt under Muhammad Ali embarked on an ambitious programme of modernizing its economy and army in order to excise the pretensions of Turkish suzerainty and thwart the ambitions of the European powers. The monopoly system became an important anchor in this process of state construction and modernization.

In the 1840s both the monopoly system and the industrialization drive collapsed. With this Egypt could now be integrated more firmly into the expanding world capitalist system as a primary commodity-exporting country. The export revolution was based on cotton whose production, as noted in Chapters 3 and 4, reinforced the process of land privatization and the expansion of irrigated land, all of which had a marked effect on the development of both the state and social classes.

For most of the nineteenth century cotton accounted for between two-thirds and three-quarters of total Egyptian exports. The export of cotton increased by ten and a half times in volume and 21 and a half times in value between 1838 and 1865. The year 1865 marked the last of the cotton boom, caused by the American civil war. By 1875-9, cotton exports had declined to an annual average of 2,229,800 cantars from 2,507,000 cantars in 1865 in volume and from £E15,443,200 in value to £E8,421,633. Thus the value of cotton exports fell more sharply than the volume, indicating a decline in the terms of trade for Egyptian cotton on the world market. By 1900-4 Egypt exported an average 5,941,000 cantars per annum, more than twice its 1865 exports, but earned only £E15,817,000, almost the same as it did in 1865 with half the exports (Owen, 1969:73,90,161,166,198). The major importer of Egyptian cotton in the early 1820s and from the 1840s until the end of the century was Britain. By 1889 Britain took 65% of the Egyptian crop, a figure that rose to over 75% in 1869 (Owen, 1969:161-2). The leading Egyptian imports were textile manufactures, copper, timber, and machinery, followed by an assortment of luxury foodstuffs and beverages. On average, between 1830 and 1880 textile manufactures accounted for about a third of total Egyptian imports (Owen, 1969:172-3).

The expansion of Egypt's trade with Europe was accompanied by an increased influx of European merchants into the country, improvements in transport infrastructure and growing Egyptian financial dependence on Europe. According to Owen (1972:203), 'the number of Europeans in Egypt rose from approximately 8,000 to 10,000 in 1838 to over 90,000 in 1881. The majority were concerned with the production and export of cotton or with banking and finance'. Thanks to the capitulation treaties that governed the status of foreigners within the Ottoman empire, the Europeans in Egypt were a privileged lot, for they 'were virtually beyond the scope of the Egyptian law until the introduction of the mixed courts in 1876. They imported goods at their own valuation. They could only be taxed with the greatest difficulty' (Owen, 1972:203). In short, the European community in

Egypt became more numerous and increasingly assertive as Egypt's integration into the European-based world capitalist system deepened.

In order to service its rapidly growing import-export trade, Egypt built a relatively extensive transport and communications system. Railways, telegraphs, and port facilities were built and repeatedly enlarged and improved in the second half of the nineteenth century. The first railway in Egypt was built in 1853 linking Cairo to Alexandria. By 1890 there were 1,797 kilometres of railways (Issawi, 1982:54). The port of Alexandria was greatly widened and improved so that the approximate tonnage of shipping entering it rose from 140,000 in 1830 to 1.3 million in 1860 and 1.5 million in 1890 (Issawi, 1982:48). It became one of the largest ports along the Mediterranean. In addition, in the 1860s the new ports of Suez and Port Said were built on the Suez Canal which was opened in 1869. And nearly 9,500 miles of telegraph lines were laid.

Egypt not only became deeply immersed in trade with Europe, but also, through the Suez Canal, an indispensable link in world trade. The Canal cut the transport costs between western Europe and Asia by more than half. By the 1880s canal traffic exceeded that around the Cape by value and volume. Travelling time between Egypt itself and western Europe was greatly reduced, while regularity was increased. 'By 1870', Issawi (1982:46) quotes Crouchley (1938:142), 'there were 3 Egyptian, 3 British, 5 French, 4 Austrian, 2 Italian, 1 Russian, and 1 Turkish «lines of steamships maintaining regular services across the Mediterranean to Egypt, as well as a great number of merchant vessels, chiefly English, coming at irregular intervals»'. Improvements in sea transport, indeed, in the transport and communications system as a whole, succeeded in promoting both Egypt's trade with Europe and European dominance over Egypt.

Building this transport and communications network was very costly and government revenues were not sufficient to finance it. Expenditure in Egypt always outran revenue. In the 1860s and 1870s, for example, expenditures outstripped revenues two to one, and in some years three to one. The government revenues came mostly from the land tax and duties from customs and the railways. The tax system was onerous on the poor, for the rich were under-taxed. The rich property owners of ushuriya land, which tended to be the most fertile and represented a quarter of the total cultivated area, paid a tax of £E0.30 per feddan, as compared to the owners of the less fertile kharajiya land who paid £E1.2 per feddan. As for efforts to collect taxes from the European residents they:

> *continued to be thwarted by the invocation of Capitulatory privileges. Foreigners could only with difficulty be persuaded to pay on land they owned while various attempts to impose a house tax on those who lived*

in Cairo and Alexandria were regularly prevented by Consular opposition (Owen, 1981:130).

Thus in order to finance its public works program, as well as to meet the accumulative interests of the corrupt monarchy and ruling class, the state was forced to borrow. This public borrowing brought its own financial pressures, for the debts needed to be serviced and repaid. So before long, as in much of Africa in the 1980s, money was increasingly borrowed - not to add to productive capacity but to repay previous loans. The debt crisis began to unravel under the reign of Said (1854-62). It was under him that the Suez Canal was built, under a bad deal negotiated between the Egyptian government and French business interests led by Ferdinand De Lesseps, who set up a company to build the canal. Said ceded territory around the canal to the company, and agreed to provide it with corvee labour, in addition to purchasing shares at inflated prices. Altogether, hundreds of thousands of Egyptians were mobilized to build the canal, of whom over 120,000 died during its construction. In terms of actual financial outlay the Egyptian government spent £E16 million. It was money the government did not have. So most of it was borrowed from European bankers (Marlowe, 1964; Kinross, 1968; Pudney, 1968). By the time Said died his regime had borrowed £E14 million from foreign bankers (Ayandele, 1986:143).

Egypt's debt load mounted under Said's successor, Ismail (1863-1879). Ismail was an ambitious modernizer in the mould of Muhammad Ali, his grandfather, if only a little more brazen and gullible. In the words of Ayandele (1986:144-5), Ismail 'tried to do everything too quickly and on too big a scale for the economy of the country. He was too easily tricked by the money lenders and their agents who flocked around him. In the attempt to modernize Egypt overnight he built over 13,000 kilometres of irrigation canals, almost 1500 kilometres of railway, 8000 kilometres of telegraph lines, 450 bridges, 4,500 elementary schools and a modern port of Alexandria. Enormous sums were also spent on personal and prestige affairs. He spent £E1 million on entertaining guests at the formal opening of the Suez Canal in 1869. He built luxurious hotels and patronized art on a lavish scale.'

Inexorably, the debts soared. Between 1862 and 1873 Egypt borrowed £E68.5 million from local banks, mostly branches of European banks, and in treasury bonds. The terms for debt servicing became increasingly harsh, with real interest rates rising from 9% in 1862 to 11% in 1873. By 1872/3 £E7.3 million, representing about 70% of the estimated revenue, was needed to service the external and internal debt (Owen, 1981:127).

Egypt found itself in dire financial straits. Indeed, the government became bankrupt. It was unable even to pay interest on the outstanding loans, which in 1875 amounted to a nominal sum of £E100 million, although the country had actually received only £E68 million (Owen, 1972:201). The rest had, Ayandele (1986:145-6) avers, gone to swindlers. In desperation the government, in a move foreshadowing the debt-equity swaps of the 1980s, decided in 1875 to sell its shares in the Suez Canal Company to Britain for £E4 million, which was a small fraction of what Egypt had actually spent on the project. This deal not only gave Britain, which had originally opposed the canal, an economic windfall, but also a political and strategic foothold in Egypt. After the purchase Britain came to hold 44% of the Canal stock, while accounting for over 80% of the traffic (Issawi, 1982:51).

Selling the canal shares was not enough to save Egypt from financial and political disaster and its precarious position soon became abundantly clear. The foreign creditors devised a number of schemes to ensure that the government honoured its debts. These schemes entailed increased European control of Egyptian finances and ultimately the country as a whole. By 1878 the Egyptian government was no longer in control of its financial affairs. The creditors, with the support of their governments, imposed a Briton as a Minister of Finance and a Frenchman as a Minister of Public Works. Debt service payments left the government too broke to even pay its civil servants, many of whom went without salaries. Ismail's attempts in 1879 to re-establish his control by dismissing the British and French ministers in his cabinet led to his own deposition and the consolidation of Anglo-French supervision over all aspects of the Egyptian economy. The Law of Liquidation was passed setting out exactly what the Egyptian government could and could not do in financial matters. Completing this pattern of foreign control was the employment of increasing numbers of Europeans in the civil service. In 1878 over 1,300 of them were brought into the administration (Owen, 1972:203).

These developments provoked growing nationalist discontent and protest. The nationalist movement was an amalgam of different groups who saw their interests undermined by the financial regime imposed by the creditors. These groups included the landowners, worried about increased taxes, army officers, disturbed by early retirement, religious leaders annoyed at the sight of infidels in control, and the long suffering peasants grown tired and weary of the exactions of foreign ruling classes. The nationalists denounced British and French interference in their country's affairs and increasingly expressed dissatisfaction with the corrupt monarchy, whose removal they also demanded. The nationalist movement crystallized around a group of army officers led by Colonel Arabi. In September 1881 Arabi and his troops seized power in Cairo. The new government was widely popular, and it introduced reforms aimed at curbing corruption, misuse of resources, and foreign exploitation. This alarmed the European community in Egypt and the French and British governments. When riots erupted in June 1882 the British saw it as an opportunity to invade.

The role of instability and disorder in Egypt as a catalyst of the British invasion has become one of the stylized facts of imperialist historiography. It is argued that the disorder, supposedly provoked by the nationalist movement, forced reluctant Britain to intervene and colonize Egypt in 1882, partly to bring order to the country, but primarily to protect the Suez Canal and the route to India. Britain's occupation of Egypt inadvertently triggered, the story continues, the partition of Africa, in that France, which was resentful of Britain's single-handed intervention in a country that had previously been under their dual control, decided to compensate for its loss in Egypt by trying to carve up an empire for itself in West Africa. This thesis, which seeks to demonstrate that the causes of the partition lay in the periphery, in this case the instability in Egypt, and that they were decidedly strategic rather than economic, is associated with Robinson and Gallagher's (1961) influential and copious tome, Africa and the Victorians.

But the thesis has a much older pedigree. As Hopkins (1986) has demonstrated in his insightful critique of Africa and the Victorians, this thesis was first advanced by prominent British government officials in the 1880s and 1890s who were anxious to dispel the widely held notion that the British occupation of Egypt was prompted by the need to protect the interests of bondholders, who not only had a large financial stake in Egypt, but also enjoyed considerable political influence with members of the British government. Over half a century later, Robinson and Gallagher resurrected and repackaged the old self-serving imperialist thesis and generalized it to explain the partition of Africa as a whole. They argued that Britain occupied Egypt because of French assertiveness and the political instability in the country, both of which threatened the canal and Britain's sea route to India. Thus the British government, or the 'official mind' in their parlance, did not seek to occupy Egypt for any sordid economic gain, but for strategic reasons. Out of this localized Egyptian crisis and Britain's reluctant, if magnanimous response, sprang the scramble for Africa, for resentful France and Germany now sought to carve up their own colonial empires in West and East Africa. Britain could not stand idly by without losing face internationally, and in the case of East Africa, there was the need to safeguard the sources of the Nile, Egypt's life line, from possible German control.

The Robinson and Gallagher thesis has provoked a lot of debate (Owen and Sutcliffe, 1972; Louis, 1976). Critics have pointed out that Africa and the Victorians suffers from glaring methodological and empirical weaknesses. Their strict separation of economic, political, and strategic factors is analytically untenable, for they are all interconnected (Kiernan, 1974:74-80). And it is fallacious to assume that the reasons for British actions deciphered from the writings of government officials contain all the available reasons. Indeed, the two authors cannot claim, as Hopkins (1986:373) aptly puts it, to 'have presented all the opinions of those who played a part in the decision to invade Egypt, even within official circles; nor is it reasonable to suppose that they could possibly have done so'. Shepperson (1976) has perceptively noted that Robinson and Gallagher's model was as mechanical and unconvincing as many of the simplistic models they sought to overturn. Their work ignored the fact that the 'agents of imperialism believed sincerely that they were working for economic ends' (Shepperson, 1976:165). Uzoigwe, (1974), in fact, looking at the same documents as Robinson and Gallagher found that commercial, rather than political or strategic, considerations were uppermost in the minds of the leaders. Empirically, the critics have also pointed out, the Robinson and Gallagher account despite the density of its detail, plays loose with chronology. For example, French imperial expansion in West Africa and Anglo-French rivalry in the region antedated the Egyptian crisis (Newbury, 1962; Newbury and Kanya-Forstner, 1969; Stokes, 1976).

As for the Egyptian crisis itself, research done in the last two decades has shown that the nature of the crisis was misrepresented at the time, as well as by Robinson and Gallagher (Owen, 1976). To be sure, the Egyptian state was under intense pressure, the legacy of, it cannot be overemphasized, decades of rapacious exploits by foreigners and the corrupt monarchy, but it was not on the verge of collapse (Scholch, 1981; Hunter, 1984). Indeed, the much-touted military protests of February 1879 and February 1881 and the Alexandria riots of June 1882 were far less serious than has commonly been assumed. It no longer appears that the riots, which provided Britain with the pretext to invade, were fomented by Arabi Pasha, who, in any case, was in Cairo, not Alexandria, and only 'got word of the riots several hours later in the afternoon and immediately called out troops to quell the riots' (Galbraith and al-Sayyid-Marsot, 1978:483). The riots themselves were, in fact, provoked by the arrival of British and French fleets, and it was the bombardment of Alexandria by the British fleet in July that aggravated the situation.

Moreover, it is now quite clear that the canal was never in any danger from the nationalists. Certainly neither the Admiralty nor the shipping lobby thought it was. Farnie (1969:294) states in his authoritative study that 'there was no imminent danger to the waterway in any form when the (British) Cabinet sanctioned the invasion'. 'The «security of the canal» argument', Galbraith and al-Sayyid-Marsot (1978:473) state, 'as justification of the occupation of Egypt was put forward ... because it provided the most palatable explanation to the Liberal Party and the general public'.

There is also ample evidence that at the time of the British invasion, Egypt was not sliding into anarchy. On the contrary, the new government established by Arabi Pasha was popular and stable. But that is not what the Europeans wanted. Their dilemma was that a popular and stable government, such as Arabi's, threatened their interests since it was less likely to be pliable to foreign interests. But a more pliable government, as Ismail's had been, tended to be unpopular and unstable. This is the context in which the question of disorder was perceived. 'Since disorder was defined', to quote Hopkins (1986:376), 'as allowing Egyptians a greater say in the running of their own country, it was not surprising that scare stories multiplied in number and intensity' following the establishment of Arabi Pasha's government. 'It was not anarchy', he continues, 'that drew the Europeans into Egypt, but the European presence which made the formula for maintaining stability increasingly complex and represented opposition as anarchy.'

The argument that French ambitions in Egypt spurred Britain to intervene can also be dismissed. The assertiveness of French policy 'was more pronounced at the outset of the crisis than in its crucial final stages, when France opposed intervention' (Hopkins, 1986:378). The decision to occupy Tunisia in 1881 proved costly for France and tied its troops. This helped moderate French imperial ambitions as signified by the collapse of Gambetta's short-lived pro-interventionist regime (Hyam, 1975; Parsons, 1976). It is important to note that the French fleet withdrew from Alexandria on the eve of the bombardment and that Freycinet, Gambetta's more cautious successor, 'was defeated in parliament when finally he asked for funds to mount a joint expedition with Britain' (Hopkins, 1986:378).

It is quite evident, therefore, that Britain's invasion of Egypt was no more provoked by French ambitions than it was a fortuitous or reluctant foray into an African country wrecked by disorder, which supposedly threatened the security of the Suez Canal. It was the product of a conscious and deliberate policy aimed at expanding and defending British economic interests in Egypt. By 1880 Britain had become Egypt's largest trading partner, taking 80% of the country's exports and providing 44% of its imports. And British investment was predominant. The links between the British investors and the policy makers were quite close, and the Egyptian question featured prominently in British government circles many years before the seemingly fortuitous crisis of 1882. In fact, in 1877 'senior ministers considered occupying Egypt ... in anticipation of the collapse of the Ottoman empire, then bending under the strain of war with Russia', and again in 1879 'the government considered military occupation and might have moved ... had troops not been tied down in South Africa by the Zulu war' (Hopkins, 1986:381).

From 1882 Egypt became a fully-fledged British colony in all but name. The trade regime of the primary commodity exports and manufactures imports was consolidated. Cotton's dominant position in the export economy was strengthened. The land devoted to cotton cultivation increased by a little over 50% between 1886 and 1903 (Owen, 1981:218). Whereas in 1878-82 cotton accounted for about 77% of exports in value, the figure rose to 80% in 1898-1902 and nearly 90% a decade later. The actual volume of cotton exports more than doubled between 1878-82 and 1898-1902 from an annual average 2.5 million cantars to 5.9 million cantars. Cotton's spectacular growth is borne out when we consider that in 1848-52 only 0.4 million cantars had been exported annually (Issawi, 1963:28). Egypt became one of the leading suppliers of cotton to Britain.

While cotton clearly dominated exports, the composition of imports was clearly more varied. The leading imports were textiles and food products, such as cereals, vegetables, sugar and coffee. In the 1880s and 1890s these products combined comprised almost half of Egypt's imports. The rest of the imports consisted of goods imported for investment in agriculture and industry. It appears that Egypt's imports of foodstuffs between 1885-9 and 1900-4 increased faster than the total imports, by 132% as compared to 105% (Owen, 1981:241). This demonstrates that following the incorporation into the British Empire, the structures of agrarian underdevelopment in Egypt deepened.

The massive increase in cotton production and exports gave Egypt a healthy trade surplus and favourable terms of trade. However, this was more than offset by the outflow of interest payments on the public debts and dividends to private foreign investors. The overall balance of payments for Egypt deteriorated from - £E419,000 in 1884-92 to - £E2,723,000 in 1900-4 (Owen, 1981:242). The colonial government spent 40% of government revenue on debt servicing, and the rest on defence, administration and pensions. Industry was largely ignored, by both the public and private sectors. Private capital was more interested in financing the cotton industry. Health and education combined accounted for a miserable 1.5% of total expenditure (Issawi, 1982:179).

These processes of external dependence and internal underdevelopment were undergirded by the banking system. Under British rule the banking industry expanded as British, French, Italian and Greek financiers established new, or expanded old, banks. The most important of these new banks was the National Bank of Egypt, founded in 1898 by British financiers. The bank had close ties to the Bank of England and was intended to operate as a central bank (Crouchley, 1936; Landes, 1958; Tignor, 1981). These banks were primarily involved in financing the production, transportation and marketing of cotton. Thus the banks played a crucial role in the integration of Egypt into the world economy as a primary commodity exporting country. Their loans to Egyptian farmers amounted to £E7 million in 1882. The banks did not only finance local producers, they also facilitated the growth of foreign land ownership in the country. By 1887 foreigners owned 225,000 feddans, most of it devoted to 'King Cotton' (Owen, 1981:139).

Thus, from 1882 to 1918 'foreign domination of finance, banking, trade and various joint-stock companies was almost complete' (Deeb, 1978:16). This shows, contrary to the analysis of Robinson and Gallagher and their followers, that Egypt was invaded for its own sake, for the economic opportunities it offered, rather than merely as an inconvenient but strategic appendage to India. The colonization of Egypt constituted a particular configuration of imperialism that was sweeping across Africa. It marked a critical moment in the long process of Egypt's incorporation into the world capitalist system, a process that involved the transformation of the Egyptian economy, society and state. In the course of the nineteenth century Egypt had progressively become enmeshed in the world capitalist economy as an exporter of raw materials, primarily cotton, and an importer of manufactured goods and capital. In the process many local political and social institutions broke down, which served only to reinforce the growing foreign domination of the economy. By 1875 Egypt was virtually bankrupt, perilously indebted to the Anglo-French bondholders. The crisis engendered culminated in the British invasion of 1882. Thus 1882 was neither fortuitous nor spontaneous. Nor was it an isolated event.

Algeria and Settler Colonization

Egypt was not the first country in Africa to be colonized during the imperial 'scramble' of the 1880s and 1890s. As mentioned above, France invaded Tunisia in 1881. This apparently helped seal the fate of Egypt for it encouraged senior British officials to plan for its invasion as a compensation (Hopkins, 1986:382; Johns, 1982:301-2). Tunisia itself was not the first country in North Africa to fall under the colonial yoke. That dubious distinction belonged to Algeria, which was invaded by France in 1830.

By the end of the eighteenth century commercial relations between Algeria and France were already significant. Between 1762 and 1772, for example, France exported goods worth 23 million francs to Algeria, of which 36.5% consisted of woollen cloth (Bennoune, 1988:29). In Algiers there was a sizeable community of French merchants who owned trading shops and factories. The largest French commercial establishment was the Compagnie d'Afrique, established in 1741. The company 'bought wheat, wool, wax and hides. In order to export these goods it had to engage in constant intrigue at the Regency of Algiers, which levied taxes for the authorization of the company to trade there, and even for the provision of the factories' (Bennoune, 1988:30). Although the monopoly system favoured the European trading companies at the expense of Algerian merchants in Algeria's international trade, the latter were not entirely eliminated. French merchants resented the few Algerian merchants who still managed to deal directly with France by themselves.

French merchants in Algeria also complained about the monopoly system. In the early nineteenth century they began exerting more pressure to open up Algerian commerce. This was resisted by the Algerian government, which derived benefits from the monopoly system. The French government then began exploring the possibility of occupying the trading ports along the Algerian coast. Ostensibly to stop piracy, France was motivated by another factor in this move. French merchants did not want to pay back to Algeria debts incurred during the Napoleonic wars, which the merchants had contracted buying wheat and horses for the embattled revolutionary government. Moreover, in 1793 and 1796 Algeria had given the revolutionary government a combined interest free loan of 1.25 million francs. After Napoleon's downfall, 'the French government of the restored monarchy refused to honour the debt or to force her merchants to pay for it' (Bennoune, 1988:31). Grounds were set for confrontation.

Matters reached a head in 1827. At a fateful meeting on 27 April between the dey of Algiers and the French consul, Pierre Deval, the Turkish dey told Deval that in future, French merchants would be treated like all other merchants and that French military forces would not be allowed on Algerian soil. The dey was reacting to the activities of French merchants, including the vice-consul and Deval's nephew 'who had French fortifications in Annaba and al-Qala (La Calle) fortified and provided with cannons' (Abun-Nasr, 1987:249). Deval objected noting that under a 1535 treaty between France and the Ottoman empire, of which Algeria was nominally a part, France had been granted commercial privileges within the empire. This ignored the fact that the North African regencies had been independent from the Porte's suzerainty since 1719. France was of course not interested in such niceties. If its merchants were not granted trading privileges, then the country would be invaded. An excuse, a bizarre one even by the abysmal standards of imperialist rationalizations, was concocted. After the meeting Deval claimed that the dey had struck him with a fly whisk. This was, he proclaimed, an insult to France. The French government accordingly demanded an apology and reparations from the dey. When none was offered, diplomatic relations were broken and France declared a general blockade of the Algerian sea coast in June.

The blockade did not force the dey into submission, for it had little practical effect on the activities of Algerian corsairs. Moreover, the blockade was unpopular with the French merchants of Marseilles who suffered most from it. France sought a way out by sending an envoy in August 1829 to conclude an armistice with the dey. The latter snubbed the envoy, which served to intensify French disaffection for him. In order to control the recalcitrant regime the French Prime Minister began planning for the annexation of the Maghribi regencies to Muhammad Ali's Egypt, with whom France had friendly relations. In this way France hoped to dominate the Maghreb without bearing the costs of conquest and administration and accelerate the disintegration of the Ottoman empire which Britain was working hard to preserve. Hardly had Muhammad Ali accepted the plan than internal pressures mounted for France to undertake the conquest of Algiers by itself. The monarchists wanted glory for the royal army, while the Marseilles merchants believed their fortunes would improve if France controlled Algiers. The King, Charles X, whose power was increasingly opposed by liberal deputies, saw in the invasion of Algeria a means of reinforcing his prestige and that of the royal army. He ordered the invasion on March 2 when opening the new session of the Chamber of Deputies (Abun-Nasr, 1987:250-1).

The French invaders claimed, facetiously, that their mission was not directed at the people of Algeria, but against their Turkish overlords. Nobody of course believed them. The dey capitulated in early July and fled to exile in Naples. The invaders looted over 100 million francs from Algeria, half of which reached the French treasury. The immediate success of the invasion failed to save Charles X, who was forced to abdicate in August. The political turmoil in France gave the army in Algeria a free hand, which pursued policies of colonization without restraint. Army officers engaged in land speculation and encouraged the settlement of colonists. Until 1840 France described its official policy in Algeria as one of limited occupation, meaning that it would only occupy the major towns and rule the rest of the country through native or Turkish rulers. Events on the ground made a mockery of this policy. First, the numbers of settlers were increasing and they wanted more land and power. Second, Algerians offered stiff resistance. In fact, until 1871 Algeria was rocked by a wave of rebellions and wars of national resistance. Altogether, the conquest of Algeria claimed the lives of about half a million Algerians, over 150,000 French soldiers and thousands of colonists (Bennoune, 1988:42; Ayandele, 1986:184-91; Tlemcani, 1986:Chapter 3).

On the ashes of Algeria's ravaged socio-economic and political order was erected a ruthless settler colonial regime. As was demonstrated in Chapter 5, Algerian peasants not only lost large tracts of some of their most fertile land to the settlers, but many of them were turned into a propertyless and cheap labour force for the colonial economy. Unlike other French colonies, Algeria was turned into an administrative part of France in the constitution of 1848. By law and in practice the settlers constituted a privileged minority, while the Algerians themselves languished as an oppressed majority. French rule was consolidated after the suppression of the great rebellion of 1871. Vengeful settlers and a ruthless government demanded an indemnity of 36.5 million from Kabylia, the region where the rebellion had taken place, and the sequestration of all the land of the people who had taken part in the rebellion. As a result of these measures the people of this region lost an estimated 70% of their total capital (Abun-Nasr, 1987:268). This was primitive colonial accumulation, a vicious process that would become all too familiar at the beginning of the colonial era in much of the continent at the turn of the twentieth century.

Following the establishment of French colonial rule the old monopoly system was dismantled and new tariff structures were erected. Duties on French goods exported to Algeria were progressively removed. Algerian produce was also exempted from French duties, beginning with wheat in 1851 and wine in 1867. In 1884 French tariffs were applied to Algeria, and the country was included in France's new protectionist tariff imposed in 1892. Algeria became an appendage of the French economy, and France grew into Algeria's main trading partner, accounting for 82% of the country's trade by 1860, a figure that was maintained for the next hundred years (Issawi, 1982:33, 37). Algeria, like all colonies, developed into an exporter of primary commodities, principally wheat and wine, and a captive market for French manufactures. By 1890 wine accounted for one-third of Algeria's exports.

Thus colonial Algeria's export trade was confined to two agricultural products. This reflected the growing specialization of the country's agriculture. As we saw in Chapter 5, the settlers seized some of the country's best land and turned it into cereal and wine production. Many Algerian producers and merchants were expropriated of their land without compensation. 'Those who were spared were eventually ruined by inflation, which was aggravated by the introduction of French currency' (Bennoune, 1988:36). The old currency was simply 'declared not exchangeable,' with the result that many Algerian merchants lost their wealth and were forced to become colonial workers. This underscores a point made by Webb (1982:465-6), that the demonetization of African currencies and their substitution by European currencies impoverished African merchants and entrepreneurs. In short, in colonial Algeria it was mostly the French who benefited from the expanding domestic and foreign trade.

According to calculations made by Issawi (1982:24), Algeria's foreign trade grew at an average annual rate of 8.6% between the 1830s and the early 1870s, then dropped to 2.4% between the 1870s and 1900. The overall rate of growth between 1830 and 1900 matched that of world trade. In value Algeria's foreign trade grew from £E1.8 million in the 1830s to an average £E9.6 million in 1870-73 and £E21 million in 1900. Despite this expansion, Algeria no longer enjoyed, as in the pre-colonial period, trade surpluses in its trade with France. 'Algerian statistics show a persistent trade deficit until 1913, presumably covered by capital inflow' (Issawi, 1982:28). Foreign capital, both private and public, was used mostly to finance the settler sector, which was predominantly export-oriented, both directly and indirectly, through the provision of infrastructure. The sums involved were quite substantial, given, for example, the fact that by 1913 Algeria's public debt stood at about 750 million francs or £E30 million (Issawi, 1982:68).

A sizeable portion of this foreign investment went into the construction of railways, roads and ports, all of which were indispensable both for the military and administrative control of the colony and the development of its dependent capitalist economy. By 1890 Algeria boasted of 3,056 kilometres of railways, which was 58% of total railway mileage in North Africa, although the lines used at least five different gauges and belonged to six different companies. Algeria also developed a fairly extensive road system, which by the 1860s totalled 3,000 kilometres. And 21 ports were improved, among them Algiers and Oran, which became the second and fourth largest ports of France for shipping. By 1913 the shipping entering Algiers had an approximate tonnage of 9,700, up from 1,400 in 1890 and 20 in 1830 (Issawi, 1982:48-9, 53-4).

No African country in the nineteenth century was as deeply integrated into the economy of a European country as Algeria. Unlike that of Egypt which was firmly tied to the depredations and ambitions of bondholders, Algeria's colonization was inspired by the old imperial search for markets, sources of raw materials, and havens to settle 'surplus' population. In this sense, Algeria's colonization represented another configuration of imperialism in nineteenth century Africa. While Egypt crumbled after foreign capital had already dissolved the old order, Algeria was conquered before foreign capital had much impact. In Egypt foreign capital wanted to consolidate its hegemony, while in Algeria it sought to establish it. If Egypt's colonization was a harbinger of the 'new imperialism', Algeria's was the epitome of the old. Better still, Algeria's colonization represented a transitional form, one that evoked the entrenched settler colonialisms of seventeenth and eighteenth century America, Australia, and New Zealand, and presaged the ultimately untenable settler colonialisms of twentieth century Africa, from Angola and Mozambique, to Kenya, Zimbabwe and South Africa.

Tunisia: Another Bondholders' Domain

The colonization of Tunisia resembled more that of Egypt than Algeria's in that it came in the midst of a severe economic and political crisis, a product of decades of foreign intervention and internal oppression and corruption. The Tunisian case also displays the intensity of European rivalries in bold relief.

After the conquest of Algeria, France was keen to extend its commercial and imperial tentacles to Tunisia. But France was not alone. Tunisia was also coveted by Britain and Italy. Merchants from the three countries competed for control of Tunisia's lucrative olive oil trade. Oil exports rose from over 10,000 hectolitres in 1781 to over 50,000 in 1817 and over 76,000 hectolitres in 1827 (Valensi, 1985:224-7). Like the other North African leaders, the bey of Tunis wanted to monopolize Tunisia's foreign trade partly in order to prevent the county's annexation by the European powers. His fears were increased by the French conquest of Algeria in 1830. The French did not waste time, for in the same year they forced the bey to accept the Capitulation treaties that governed relations between the European countries and the Ottoman empire and enabled European consuls to establish around them autonomous enclaves of European residents and dependents. At the same time, Ottoman pressure in Tunisia, triggered by the growth of European influence in the country, to accept some form of Ottoman sovereignty, increased as well.

Ahmad Bey (1837-55) tried to resist all these pressures. To the Ottomans he only conceded religious ties. In order to strengthen Tunisia's position he greatly expanded the army. To pay for it his government increased taxes and consolidated the monopoly system. However, this only succeeded in enraging both the country's peasants, whose resistance led to the decline of agriculture, and the foreign merchants, who vociferously called on their governments for support. The pressures on Tunisia increased under Ahmed Bey's successor, Muhammad Bey (1855-9). The latter abolished some of the taxes, which, however, reduced state revenues.

Attempts to control the activities of the foreign merchants proved extremely difficult as these merchants had established a firm hold on Tunisia's international trade. They usually bought the oil in advance of the harvests. When the harvests were low, or oil prices fell, the Tunisian government and the peasants bore the costs. Those who failed to pay back their debts had their property confiscated. Muhammad Bey soon discovered how strong the foreign merchants were. When he tried to bring them to heel in 1858, gold and silver coins, the only currencies accepted by foreign merchants in exchange for their goods, disappeared from circulation. In order to keep enough money in circulation the government struck large amounts of copper coins. The merchants refused to accept them, except at half their value in addition to treasury bills for the other half redeemable in four years. In effect Tunisia was providing the merchants with interest free loans. A year before that the government had reluctantly issued what is known as the Fundamental Law which, among other things, allowed foreigners to acquire property, including land, in Tunisia (Abun-Nasr, 1987:272-77).

These developments served to deepen the European penetration of the Tunisian economy. In fact, the European merchants increasingly intervened in the country's political affairs. For example, they were instrumental, together with the religious leaders, in the suspension of the reformist constitution of 1860 only four years after it was promulgated. The constitution had sought to turn Tunisia into a limited monarchy ruled by a council. The European community was alarmed because 'the existence of the supreme council hindered the consuls from obtaining concessions from the bey through the traditional methods of bribing high officials and threatening the bey with the use of force' (Abun-Nasr, 1987:279). The European merchants also derived some of their power from the fact that they lent government officials considerable sums of money. By 1862, for example, the government had borrowed 28 million francs locally.

By the 1860s the Tunisian state was in serious financial difficulties because of its growing internal debt and large expenditure on the military, public projects, and the private projects of the corrupt leaders. As a result, the bey began looking abroad for loans. The first one was negotiated in 1863, but this turned into a yoke around Tunisia's neck. 'The terms of the loan', writes Abun-Nasr (1987:280), 'were very stringent: out of a nominal value of 65,100,000 francs repayable in five years the bey received after various deductions only 37,772,160 francs. In addition, fraudulent transactions carried out by Erlanger (a Parisian banking house) with Khaznadar's (the Tunisian Prime Minister) concurrence included the imaginary sale of the loan bonds and their imaginary repurchase for the Tunisian government by Erlanger at a lower price. The result was the reduction of the loan's real value by a quarter in one year. Henceforth the bey had not only to abandon the public works he in the first place could not afford, but also to borrow locally and abroad to meet the obligations of the first debt'.

The slide to bankruptcy and colonization had began. The decision to raise the poll tax in 1864, in order to increase government revenues, provoked a widespread rebellion in the country which, in turn, prompted British, French and Italian governments to send squadrons to protect their subjects and interests, deepening the economic crisis as agricultural production fell sharply. The government was then forced to borrow more money locally and abroad to meet its previous loan obligations, as local taxes had been reduced in order to put down the rebellion. In 1865 the government incurred its second foreign loan and by 1866 it owed the local creditors 50 million francs. Government officials made a killing. For example, a certain al-Dahdah, an 'official on a salary of 600 francs a month, amassed eight million francs in the three years between 1863 and 1866' (Abun-Nasr, 1987:281). But the state itself was virtually bankrupt. In 1867 alarmed French bondholders formed a committee to protect their interests. In the next few years the committee was replaced by an International Financial Commission which was given power to control Tunisia's finances and ensure debt repayment.

The formation of the commission sounded the death knell on Tunisian economic and political independence. The commission consolidated the outstanding debt claims totalling 275 million francs to 125 million francs at 5% interest. In return, the bey was forced to reduce the size of his army by two-thirds and to lower the poll tax in order to revive agricultural production. The French played the leading role in the commission. The French position in Tunisia weakened in the early 1870s following France's humiliating defeat by Germany in 1870. The Italians and British sought to take advantage and extend their interests and activities. A concerned bey tried to cultivate the goodwill of the Sultan by agreeing, in 1871, to some aspects of Ottoman sovereignty over Tunisia, a proposition opportunistically supported by Britain which, in return, obtained several concessions for its businessmen. But by 1873 the British projects, including the railways and a bank, proved unprofitable. The bank was closed and the railway concessions were taken over by the Italians. And France had recovered its nerve.

In the meantime, a new government led by Khayr al-Din was set up in Tunisia in October 1873. It introduced economic reforms and tried to end corruption and pay its debts on time. It looked like the country was on the road to economic recovery. Some European merchants were obviously pleased, if we are to judge by the popular demonstration they made in April 1875 in support of the Tunisian Prime Minister. But there were many others who were alarmed by the reforms, including the bey and his corrupt cronies, and the European consuls, all of whom engineered Khayr al-Din's ousting in 1877, after which: 'Tunisia reverted to her past tyranny and extortion with the authority of the Prime Minister. While the tax-collectors enriched themselves ... the country's economy was ruined. By the end of 1878 the government was once more unable to meet its obligations to the Financial Commission' (Abun-Nasr, 1987:288).

As Tunisia slid into economic chaos, European rivalry over the country intensified. Italy and France were the chief protagonists following Britain's acceptance of the paramount interests of the French in Tunisia in return for the latter's similar acceptance of British interests in Cyprus. Italy thought its claims over Tunisia were stronger than those of France given the fact that Italians in Tunisia far outnumbered the French. By 1880, for example, there were 20,000 Italians as compared to a mere 200 Frenchmen (Ayandele, 1986:20). The French ignored such awkward realities for their economic stake in Tunisia was large and rapidly growing. As the Italians intensified their campaign to control Tunisia in 1879 the French tried unsuccessfully to convince the bey to accept a French protectorate. They then began looking for an excuse to invade which was not difficult to find. France seized on a customary raid by the Khrumirs into Algeria in March 1881 as a pretext for invasion, despite the bey's willingness to pay compensation and punish the marauding Khrumirs. The invading French forces arrived in Tunis towards the end of April and the bey surrendered the next month. Tunisia then became a French protectorate.

France's share of Tunisia's foreign trade rose rapidly after colonization, although it did not reach Algeria's level. This was partly because it took time to reform Tunisia's tariff system. Tunisia had made treaties with Britain and Italy which would have allowed the two countries to export their goods to France through the latter's new colony. It was not until the early twentieth century that these treaties were renegotiated and Tunisia could be fully incorporated into the French customs zone. Besides, Tunisia never attracted as many settlers as Algeria, for, unlike Algeria where the settlers were granted land, in Tunisia they had to buy it. So only relatively wealthy settlers came to Tunisia. By 1901 there were only 24,000 French settlers, far less than the 71,000 Italians (Abun-Nasr, 1987:294). The development of transport and communications in Tunisia also lagged behind Algeria's. For example, by 1892 only 600 kilometres of roads and 416 kilometres of railways had been built (Issawi, 1982:53-4). But like Algeria, the range of Tunisia's exports narrowed. As Issawi (1982:34) tells us:

> *until the second half of the nineteenth century Tunisia had five main export items: olive oil, ... woollen fezzes and cloth; raw wool; wheat; and hides. Wool and woollen manufactures were gradually eliminated by foreign competition, but olive oil exports increased with the spread of groves, and, as in Algeria, exports of wheat and wine to France grew rapidly after the French occupation.*

Late Colonization: Morocco and Libya

French ambitions in North Africa also extended to Morocco. Again, as in Tunisia, France was not the only European country interested in Morocco. In fact, from the 1830s to the 1870s Britain

Up to the beginning of the 1830s Moroccan trade with Europe was quite insignificant because, as Abun-Nasr (1987:297) tells us, 'the Moroccans objected on religious grounds to exporting the products of their country to Europeans, and whenever exports were allowed some religious justification had to be found', while imports were discouraged 'by imposing fifty percent duty on them'. By 1832 there were only 248 Europeans in the country who were restricted to the ports of Tangier, Rabat, Tatuan and al-Sanira. The European merchants tended to use native Jews, rather than Muslims, as intermediaries, which served to reduce 'ideological conflicts between foreign Christians and the inland area of Morocco, which was strictly Muslim' (Ponasik, 1977:199).

The French invasion of Algeria in 1830 ended Morocco's relative isolation. Morocco tried to come to the aid of Algeria and in the next 15 years Moroccan and French forces clashed several times along the western Algerian border. In 1844 Morocco suffered a crushing defeat, which weakened the Sultan's position both internally and externally. The defeat sparked off rebellions in several parts of the country and encouraged France and other European nations to expand their activities. Moroccan hostility to the Europeans intensified as the numbers of European merchants increased. Taking advantage of this in the mid-1840s the Sultan extended government monopolies to bring about total government control on foreign trade. This provoked concerted European pressure spearheaded by Britain for Morocco to open up her trade which the Sultan found hard to resist. In 1856 the Anglo-Moroccan commercial treaty was signed. It abolished most of the monopolies, reduced import duties to 10%, and allowed British subjects to own property in Morocco.

Except for France and Spain, all European countries represented in Morocco approved the treaty. France hoped it could dominate Moroccan trade by diverting it to Algeria, while Spain saw Morocco as its backyard. Spanish claims were buttressed by force. An attack on newly constructed fortifications in Sabta gave Spain an excuse to occupy Tatuan in 1860. This defeat provoked another wave of rebellions in Morocco which further weakened the Sultan's hand and strengthened the position of European merchants. In its 1860 peace treaty and 1861 commercial treaty with Spain Morocco was forced to cede Malila, pay an indemnity of £E4 million, and grant Spaniards the rights of anchorage in Moroccan ports and fishing off the coasts. The indemnity clauses allowed Spain to control a part of Morocco's customs revenues (Owen, 1981; Abun-Nasr, 1987:302).

By 1867 it became increasingly evident that the Sultan was losing power to local leaders and foreigners. The size of the European community had increased to 1,500 and the numbers of Moroccans enjoying European consular protection had grown quite substantially. The Europeans established their own postal systems and health services, a sign of their growing influence and autonomy. Some of the Europeans took to farming, but the majority were merchants. They created purchasing networks of local intermediaries to whom they advanced working capital to buy the export products, principally olive oil, wool and skins. These merchants:

> then selected intermediaries at a higher level and progressively created alongside the trade administered by the Makhzen a private network that was strongly linked to foreign companies. Within 20 years, from 1880 and 1900, the bulk of trade passed into the hands of private foreign businessmen (Pascon, 1986:48).

Popular resentment against dealings with the Europeans remained as strong as ever. Sultan Mawley Hassan (1873-94) was determined to contain both Europeans and the local overlords. He introduced military, administrative and fiscal reforms. He hoped to create a modern army by imposing a fixed levy of recruits from each major city and bringing European instructors. He tried to strengthen the central government by breaking up the country's 18 provinces into 330 small administrative units. Hassan expected to raise more revenue by devising a uniform system of taxation for both Moroccans and foreigners. In 1869 he set a fixed rate of exchange in an attempt to stabilize the value of the Moroccan currency. None of these reforms really worked. It proved too costly to modernize the army, and the Europeans defied both the taxes and fixed exchange rate (Abun-Nasr, 1987:304-6).

In the meantime, European rivalries and ambitions were intensifying. The French became particularly aggressive. They worked hard 'to prevent the reformation of the Moroccan government while at the same time drawing it towards greater recognition of France's special interests in Morocco by continually raising problems connected with incidents on the frontier with Algeria' (Abun-Nasr, 1987:306). This reflected France's growing economic stake in Morocco. France increased its share of Moroccan trade from the 1880s, particularly following Britain's occupation of Egypt, when Britain, keen to placate France for its occupation of Egypt agreed to Morocco becoming a French sphere of influence. But, as in Tunisia, French ambitions in Morocco did not go unchallenged by other European powers. The number of German firms doing business in Morocco increased and by the murky rules of late nineteenth century imperialism this raised Germany's stake in it.

Morocco in fact became indebted to several European countries. Most of the debts were incurred at the turn of the twentieth century under the reign of Mawley Abdul (1894-1908), a young, inexperienced, impetuous and extravagant ruler, to meet the needs of the corrupt ruling clique and for modernization, particularly of the military. In 1903 and 1904 Morocco borrowed a total of 85 million francs, of which only 61.5 million came, and in 1910 the country borrowed a further 101 million francs at 8% interest to pay off indemnities of 135 million francs to Spain and France (Issawi, 1982:68). The terms of the loans were crippling, for the European creditors were given control of customs as security in addition to generous concessions, some of which bordered on the cessation of sovereignty over portions of Morocco.

The Moroccan question became part of the diplomatic chess game in Europe. France managed to get most of the interested European countries to acquiesce to her imperial claims over Morocco. We have already mentioned Britain, which accepted French claims to Morocco in return for a free hand in Egypt. Italy gave her agreement in 1900 in return for French recognition of her interests in Libya. Spain acquiesced in 1904 after its zone of influence was recognized by France. The major exception was Germany, which succeeded in internationalizing the Moroccan question. In March 1905 there was Kaiser William II's famous visit to Tangier and in July 1911 the German gunboat Panther visited Agadir. The Kaiser's visit was followed by the Algeciras Conference of 1906, which divided the control of Morocco's finances, administration and police between France and Spain.

These activities provoked Moroccan resistance, which periodically erupted in attacks on Europeans in the country. The attacks, in turn, provided France and Spain with excuses for military intervention. Embittered Moroccans also turned their rage on the Sultan, who was defeated in battle by forces led by his brother Abdul-Hafiz. But the new Sultan was unable to contain the French. In March 1912 he surrendered and signed a treaty making Morocco a French protectorate. However, Morocco did not become another Algeria or Tunisia, for France never managed to incorporate it into its customs zone or to completely dominate the country's trade. The conquest and colonization of Morocco had come rather late for such imperial exclusivity.

Libya was also one of the last African countries to be colonized. Its occupation by Italy only came in 1911.

Italian ambitions in Libya had gathered momentum from the 1880s. At the time Libya was an Ottoman province. The Ottomans had assumed direct control of Libya in 1835. The country had been independent from Ottoman rule under the Qaramanli dynasty since the early nineteenth century. Thus at the beginning of the nineteenth century Libya was an independent state. It was ruled by Yusuf Pasha.

The pasha derived most of his revenue from both trade and piracy. By 1805 Libya had a fleet of 24 warships and many other commercial vessels and its leading trading partner was Britain. Most of their trade was conducted through Malta. Exports consisted mainly of livestock and dates and as elsewhere in North Africa, the export trade was a state monopoly.

From about 1810, however, the pasha's income from the trade monopolies and piracy started to decline. The British forced him to surrender his monopoly over the trade in livestock for the British fleet to Maltese traders, and ... piracy ceased altogether in 1818 after a resolution was adopted at the Congress of Aix-la-Chapelle in 1818 calling upon European countries to exert pressure on the Maghribi rulers to abandon piracy, and the French fleet joined the British in awing them into acquiescence (Abun-Nasr, 1987:199).

The number of European merchants in Tripoli increased following the end of monopoly and piracy. Yusuf Qaramanli was concerned lest these traders and their consuls became too powerful. So, like other North African rulers, he sought to curtail their influence and strengthen his country's position by modernizing the military. From the mid-1820s he began enlarging his army and navy, but these reforms only made him indebted to those very Europeans. By the beginning of the 1830s the pasha found himself at the mercy of British and French consuls who demanded that he repay the debts owed their nationals. To reinforce their demands the British and French brought warships to Tripoli. In order to repay his creditors the pasha raised taxes, debased the currency, and even confiscated some people's property. Predictably, these measures provoked widespread rebellion both in the rural and urban centres.

The threat to Libya increased following the French occupation of Algeria. In fact, France lost no time in imposing a treaty on Yusuf Qaramanli that required him to, among other things, abolish the remaining trade monopolies, cease holding Christians captive, pay French nationals in Tripoli war indemnities of 80,000 francs, reduce the size of the navy, and apologize to the French consul for past humiliations (Ayandele, 1986:204). Yusuf's position became so weak that he abdicated in 1832. A succession dispute ensued, largely fuelled by the British and French who supported rival candidates. In the midst of this confusion, the Ottomans decided to flex their muscles and reimpose their lost power on Libya. In May 1835 they sent a fleet to Tripoli. It met little resistance. The Qaramanli dynasty was abolished.

But Ottoman power was compromised by the influential European consuls in Tripoli and, more seriously, by widespread Libyan opposition. To the Libyans the Ottoman Turks were nothing but imperialist conquerors so, not surprisingly, Ottoman rule was ineffective outside the coastal areas. In the 76 years that they ruled the country, there were 33 Ottoman governors. In effect, power in Libya, especially in the interior, was exercised by the Sanusiyya brotherhood (Ayandele, 1986:205-10). Under Ottoman rule 'Libya's exports were always very small and limited to livestock products, cereals, and olive oil. At the end of the nineteenth century esparto grass, used for paper, assumed significance' (Issawi, 1982:34). Hardly any modern transport and communications infrastructure was built.

Italy had set its eyes on Libya for quite some time, but it did not become very assertive until the colonization of Tunisia and Egypt by France and Britain, respectively. The Italians in Tripolitania increasingly challenged Ottoman officials and Britain and France dropped their objections to Italy's occupation of Libya in 1902. Germany, which saw itself as a protector of the Ottoman empire from British and French designs, remained the only major outside obstacle.

As the Italians waited for the opportune moment to send troops to Libya, they pursued a programme of systematic economic penetration. After 1902 an Italian post office and medical services were established in Tripolitania. The Banco di Roma started to sponsor Italian economic enterprises in Libya, which included the foundation of an esparto grass mill in Tripoli, a flour mill in Benghazi, and the purchase of lands for agricultural settlement (Abun-Nasr, 1987:319).

By 1911 Italy could wait no more. It informed the major European powers of its intention to invade Libya and none objected. An excuse was concocted. Italy claimed that its nationals in Libya were in danger and needed protection. An ultimatum to that effect was sent to the Porte. The Italians were not satisfied with the latter's reply, despite guarantees that Italian nationals would be protected. Of course Italy did not want guarantees, it wanted a colony. War was declared at the end of September. But the Italians had not bargained for a long war of resistance from the Libyans themselves. Despite sending 60,000 troops, they had yet to conquer the Libyan interior when the First World War broke out in 1914.

Conclusion

The European colonization of North Africa brings into sharp relief the operations of finance capital in the late nineteenth century. There can be little doubt that the bondholders and creditors were the leading instigators behind the colonial conquest and occupation of countries in the region. Colonization was the culmination of processes set in train by the region's steady integration into the world economy.

This chapter has traced the rapid expansion of North African trade with Europe, especially following the abolition of the monopoly system. It has been argued that this was propelled, on the one hand, by the desire of North African countries to modernize their armies and economies in order to safeguard their political autonomy, and the needs of the industrializing western European countries for markets, sources of raw materials, and outlets for investment and population settlement, on the other.

The pressures exerted by the bondholders were most intense in Egypt and Tunisia. As the export economy in these countries grew, there was an influx of European merchants and creditors, to whom the corrupt monarchies, unwilling to tax the wealthy and unable to tax the foreigners because of the capitulation agreements, increasingly turned for loans to finance their costly military programmes and the construction of the infrastructure to service the export economy. As the debts mounted, the governments intensified their exploitation of their long-suffering peasants and other working people, which only served to deepen popular opposition.

In due course broad-based nationalist movements emerged, which sought to overthrow their incompetent and oppressive governments, and halt their countries' exploitation by the foreign capitalists. They managed to set up reform governments, which, however, did not last long, for they were vigorously opposed by the degenerate local ruling classes and the avaricious foreign merchants and creditors whose interests they threatened. Out of these struggles for hegemony emerged colonization. In Algeria, debt also played a role, but it was a different kind of debt. In this case it was the French merchants who owed Algerians. Colonization offered the former a means of killing two birds with one stone: to default on their debts and corner Algerian trade for themselves.

The debt situation and its repercussions in late nineteenth century North Africa, bear uncanny resemblance to the debt crisis in contemporary Africa. In both cases foreign control was tightened over the financial sector, a crippling share of export revenues went into debt servicing, and debt equity swaps were promoted as the solution. Also, in the Egypt and Tunisia of the 1870s and 1880s as in many highly indebted African countries in the 1970s and 1980s, the retrenchment that followed the debt crisis and the imposition of draconian structural adjustment programmes fell primarily on the shoulders of working people, who saw their incomes fall sharply. And in response, popular opposition movements grew.

Apart from the machinations of the grasping European financiers and corrupt North African rulers, four other salient features stand out in the colonization of North Africa, many of which were replayed elsewhere on the continent. First, in virtually every case, an outlandish excuse was concocted to justify invasion. Much of the imperialist historiography on the partition, has essentially consisted of repackaged contemporary official propaganda. Second, there were intense European rivalries, which reflected not only each country's relative stake in a particular territory, but also wider diplomatic alliances and conflicts. Third, colonial conquest in North Africa was, invariably, fiercely resisted. Finally, once colonialism was in place the export economy was further strengthened and foreign domination con-solidated. In all cases the range of each country's exports narrowed to one or two commodities.

14. West Africa:
The Imperialism of Trade

Growth of Trade with Europe

Research carried out in recent years has made it possible for us to know more accurately the scale, development, composition and impact of West Africa's international trade in the nineteenth century. According to estimates worked out by Inikori (1983:59,62), at the beginning of the nineteenth century the average annual value of West Africa's seaborne exports was £E2,264,860 as compared to imports of £E2,244,695. If these estimates are correct, it would seem that West Africa enjoyed a small trade surplus.

Latham (1978a:66) provides estimates of West Africa's export trade towards the end of the century. In 1883 West African exports were worth £E17 million, rising to £E29.1 million by 1899, an increase of 71.2% in sixteen years, or about 4.5% per annum. The expansion of the export trade by volume was probably greater than this, given the fact that during this period international prices for most of West Africa's exports were unusually low. Latham does not provide comparable data for West African imports, so that it is difficult to determine the region's balance of trade in 1883 and 1899. Frankel's (1938:194-5) import and export data for 1907 shows that imports outstripped exports by a small margin, £E10.9 million as compared to £E10.7 million. This data is too limited to allow for generalizations on West Africa's balance of trade in the late nineteenth century.

West Africa's international trade in the nineteenth century can be divided into two broad periods: the first half of the century during which slaves constituted the leading export, and the second half, when vegetable oils became pre-eminent. Relations among and between African and European merchants varied quite considerably during these two periods. In the second half of the century, the number of merchants engaged in West Africa's international trade and the competition between them rose sharply. Trade rivalries intensified as the economic situation became depressed and West Africa's terms of trade plummeted in the last quarter of the century, thereby cutting into the merchants' profit margins. Out of these rivalries sprang the drive towards partition and colonization. Thus if rising indebtedness paved the way for the colonization of North Africa, falling profits did the same for West Africa. In North Africa the European bondholders sought colonial protection from populist local governments, while in West Africa the European merchants sought protection from competitive local entrepreneurs. Both the bondholders and merchants had been bred in the womb of competitive capitalism. But in Africa they suddenly discovered the virtues of monopoly capitalism.

This periodization is far better than the one that invokes the magic date of 1807, the year Britain finally abolished the slave trade, which was purportedly followed by the dawn of an enlightened era of 'legitimate commerce'. Deprived of trade in slaves, the arguments goes, coastal merchants looked for an alternative export, which they found in palm oil. In short, it is said, the British abolition marked a watershed in the economic history of West Africa (Dike, 1956:67-9; Hopkins, 1973:124-8, 138-41; Fyfe, 1974:46; Flint, 1974a:392; Reynolds, 1974:Chapter 2; Munro, 1976:42-48). This argument is singularly Anglocentric and ignores the fact that other traders from Europe and the Americas continued the notorious trade long after Britain had declared its abolition. In constantly referring to the era of 'legitimate commerce' historians have endowed Britain with a humanitarianism that is clearly at odds with the country's previous massive involvement in the slave trade and its imperial ambitions in nineteenth century Africa. Also, the term assumes a sharp break in economic structures and activities, when in fact there was only gradual change. Finally, the argument gives a cloak of moral rectitude to a trade regime that was increasingly exploitative and took West Africa on the slippery path to colonization.

Structure of Exports to 1850

There was little temporal or causal connection between the decline of the slave trade and the growth of the palm oil trade. As Latham (1983:268) poignantly observes: 'the palm oil trade originally was part of the slave trade'. In discussing Calabar he notes that, 'there is nothing to support [the] suggestion that Calabar turned to oil so early because she had lost her trade in slaves... She remained an important slave port long after the development of the oil trade' (Latham, 1971:55-56).

Northrup (1976, 1978) has made a similar argument with reference to the Bight of Biafra: 'Contrary to opinions common since the early nineteenth century, the rise of the palm oil trade, at least in south-eastern Nigeria, was not dependent upon the decline of the overseas slave trade. In fact the trade in both items expanded during the first decades of the nineteenth century' (Northrup, 1978:227-8). He believes that the two trades were able to coexist because their supply networks in the interior were different (Northrup, 1976:361). Latham (1978b:216-7) disputes this last point, arguing that the trading networks and sources of slaves and palm oil were interlinked.

If the supposed link between the fall of the slave trade and the rise of the palm oil trade is indeed fanciful, then the question that ought to exercise the minds of African economic historians is not why Britain declared its abolition in 1807, but why the nightmare of the slave trade and slavery persisted for millions of Africans well into the mid-nineteenth century. The short answer is that demand for slaves persisted in the Americas and grew in Africa itself as production for export increased. Thus the term: 'legitimate commerce has little analytical value. It is a relic of the moralistic posturing of British abolitionists and industrialists who sought to turn West Africa from an exporter of slave labour into an exporter of vegetable oils then rising in demand 'for industrial lubrication and the «new vogues» of washing with soap and lighting with candles' (Northrup, 1976:359).

And West Africa had the densest concentration of palm trees in the continent, age-old techniques of extracting oil from the palm fruit, and the entrepreneurial skills and commercial organization to process, transport and market huge quantities of palm oil and other products, in addition to slaves. Palm oil did not overtake slaves as the leading export from West Africa until the mid-nineteenth century. As late as the 1830s slave exports accounted for about half of West Africa's total exports (Inikori, 1983:60).

The growth of palm oil exports in the first half of the nineteenth century was quite spectacular, although it must be emphasized that exports of palm oil started long before the nineteenth century. Palm oil had been sold to Europeans as early as 1522. The volume of exports increased in the last quarter of the eighteenth century to reach an average 146.4 tons in the 1790s (Latham, 1971:55-57). At the beginning of the nineteenth century palm oil accounted for a meagre 2.5% of non-slave exports from West Africa to Britain, as compared to 14% for ivory, 15.4% redwood, 16.5% gold, and 21.2% gum. Slaves accounted for 45% of all exports. The share of palm oil among non-slave exports rose to 44.5% between 1827 and 1850 (Inikori, 1983:54,58).

In 1800 Britain's palm oil imports from West Africa were only 223 tons, rising to 1,288 tons in 1810, 10,673 tons in 1830, 25,042 tons in 1845, and 31,457 tons in 1853 (Latham, 1971:57). The number and size of British ships going to West Africa to collect the palm oil increased accordingly. In 1830, 52 palm oil shipping voyages were made, as compared to 112 in 1845 and 137 in 1855. In 1830 the largest ship used in this trade had a registered tonnage of 455, while in 1855 it had 1,240 (Lynn, 1981:334-6). The palm oil trade was initially centred around the Niger Delta region, then from the 1840s areas like Whydah and Badagry were developed, followed in the 1850s by the region running from the Cameroons to Angola. On the other end in Britain, the leading port for palm imports was Liverpool, the old slave trading port. While Liverpool retained its pre-eminence, its share of the palm oil trade declined from 96% in 1830 and 71% in 1855, as compared to the shares of London and Bristol which rose from 2% to 14% and 2% to 15%, respectively, during the same period (Lynn, 1981:336-42).

While Britain dominated the palm oil trade, France came to dominate trade in peanuts or groundnuts, which were used mainly to make cooking oil and soap. Peanuts became a major export from the 1830s on the Upper Guinea coast. The leading exporters were Gambia and Senegal. Gambia's peanut exports rose by over 26.5 times between 1835 and 1851, from 67 tons to 11,095 tons. In 1835 peanuts exports were worth only £E200, a negligible 0.2% of Gambia's total exports. By 1851 their value had risen to £E133,133 and 71% of Gambia's exports. Until 1842 the bulk of the exports were exported to Britain and the USA. Between 1834 and 1842 Britain accounted for 43% of the trade and the USA 42%. The rest was bought by Senegalese and French traders. The trend was reversed from 1843. In the period 1843-51 the share of Senegalese and French traders rose to 80%, while that of British and American traders dropped to 10% and 9%, respectively (Brooks, 1975:34).

The French also came to dominate the peanut export trade from Senegal. By 1853 French merchants shipped 3,000 tons from Rufisque, up from 266 tons in 1843. Exports from the Cayor and Senegal River increased from about 167 tons in 1845 to 1,700 tons in 1849. In the next decade the Casamance had become another major area of peanut production (Brooks, 1975:44-6). French traders also became dominant in the peanut trade of Sierra Leone and Portuguese Guinea (Bowman, 1987:98-100). All this was made possible partly by the fact that these traders were actively supported by French naval officers who made treaties or intervened on their behalf, and partly as a result of the French import tariff of 1845 'which discriminated against colonial produce imported in foreign vessels and thus virtually ensured that West African peanuts would be transported by the French merchant marine' (Brooks, 1975:52).

The two vegetable oil trades - palm oil concentrated around the Niger, and peanuts on the Upper Guinea coast - set the broad contours of British and French commercial hegemony in West Africa which, in the second half of the century, were transformed into colonial empires. In addition to these products, West Africa exported many other commodities, both old and new. Of the old ones the most important were gold, ivory and gum.

Gold had been a major export from West Africa since time immemorial. It continued to be a leading export even during the era of the slave trade. Bean (1974) in fact believes that the export of gold may have been far more important than the export of slaves at certain times, at least for the Gold Coast region, which, as the name implies, supplied most of West Africa's gold. According to some estimates, the average annual exports of gold between

1800 and 1850 reached 40,000 ounces, four times the volume of exports in the 1750-1800 period, but the same as the 1471-1750 period (Reynolds, 1974:8). At the coast gold was sold at £E13 per ounce, so the volume of the gold exports was on average £E120,000 per annum (Inikori, 1983:56).

Ivory was another well-established export commodity. Like gold, ivory had been a major West African export even at the height of the slave trade. Feinberg and Johnson (1982:451) estimates that: 'a minimum of five million English pounds of ivory left West Africa between 1699 and 1725. The cost to the elephant population can only be guessed'. The ivory was imported into Europe mostly by Dutch and British merchants, where it was used to make a wide range of products, from artistic objects, to decorative fixtures on furniture, and carvings of such things as toilet articles, especially combs, cutlery handles, chess pieces and boards, spindles and shuttles, hunting horns, billiard balls and keys for musical instruments.

At the beginning of the nineteenth century West Africa was still the major exporter of ivory to England. In fact, it accounted for virtually all of Africa's ivory exports to England. For example, 99.9% of the 37,679 cwt of African ivory exported to England between 1800 and 1820 came from West Africa. And West Africa provided the bulk of English ivory imports, which in 1800 amounted to 1,930 cwt, or 81% of England's total ivory imports. By 1820 the West African share had fallen to 71%, although the volume of exports had increased to 2,181 cwt. In 1830 West African ivory exports to England rose to 3,071 cwt, but West Africa's share of the English ivory market dropped to 56%.

The decline in West Africa's share of both total African ivory exports and total English ivory imports accelerated in the next few decades. By 1840 West Africa's share of African ivory exports had declined to 84% as exports from other parts of the continent increased, and West Africa's share of English ivory imports had fallen to 36%, as compared to 49% for Indian ivory. By 1860 only 15% of the 10,520 cwt of ivory imported into England came from West Africa, as compared to 63% from the Indian Ocean region. The latter most likely included re-exports from East Africa, for India was the main market for East African ivory (Alpers, 1975).

Out of the 16,416 cwt of ivory exported from Africa between 1841 and 1860 West Africa's share was only 40%, the same as North Africa's, while that of South Africa was 19% and East Africa 1% (Johnson, 1983b:113-131). The picture may be deceptive in that some of what passed as North African ivory was in fact West African in origin. What happened, as Johnson (1978b) has demonstrated in the case of the Cameroons, is that by the mid-nineteenth century the ivory trade had, in some parts of West Africa, been diverted from the coast to the trans-Saharan trade and North Africa, from where the ivory was often re-exported to Europe. Within West Africa itself shifts also occurred in the sources of ivory supply. From the mid-1820s to the mid-1840s Sierra Leone and the Gold Coast provided about half of West Africa's exports. After that their combined share declined quite sharply. By 1860 it was down to 10% as the region further east of the Volta assumed greater importance (Johnson, 1983:93-106).

British hegemony over the ivory trade in Sierra Leone and the Gold Coast was almost matched by French hegemony over gum arabic in Senegal and Mauritania, although non-French ships, especially British, carried a large portion of the gum trade. Ivory and gum shared another similarity: by the 1870s both had been eclipsed in their respective regions by the rapid expansion of the trade in palm oil and peanuts. Gum exports from Senegal and Mauritania, the only sources of supply in West Africa, began in the sixteenth century. By the eighteenth century West Africa had become the sole supplier of gum arabic to Europe, where it was used 'as a stiffener in making paint, paper, glue and ink, and in preparing foodstuffs and cosmetics, and in sizing cloth' (Webb, 1985:149). Industrialization in Europe, particularly the expansion of textile production, increased the demand for West African gum arabic. By the 1830s gum exports from Mauritania and Senegal had apparently reached 2,000 tons per year, double the volume recorded in the 1790s, and almost quadruple that of the early seventeenth century. At a price of £E70 per ton, gum exports were worth at least £E140,000 per annum (Curtin, 1975:215-18; Webb, 1985:152). Thus the gum trade was quite lucrative. In fact, gum was the leading export from Senegambia between 1790 and 1870, as it had been before 1718 when slave exports temporarily took over.

By the mid-nineteenth century palm oil, peanuts, gold, ivory and gum were the leading non-slave exports from West Africa. In addition, there were some new commodities, such as coffee and cocoa, which came to dominate the region's trade in later years. The Gold Coast exported a considerable amount of coffee in the 1820s and 1830s, reaching 15,581 lbs in 1827 and 130,949 lbs in 1837. Thereafter the exports dropped sharply to 2,994 lbs in 1839 and 58 lbs in 1840, and disappeared altogether in 1841 (Reynolds, 1974:94). Another product that enjoyed a spectacular, but short-lived, export boom was guano, a fertilizer. The first exports of guano from West Africa to Britain were apparently made in 1843. In 1844 they reached 76,898 tons, valued at £E768,979, and almost trebled to 206,629 tons, valued at £E2,066,293 in 1843. After that there was a sudden decline. By 1850 guano exports were worth only £E29,529 (Inikori, 1983:58). Wood exports also rose sharply, trebling from 1.7 thousand tons between 1817 and 1837 (Newbury, 1971:92).

Imports and their Impact

As in North Africa, West Africa's imports consisted primarily of manufactured goods. The detailed statistical data provided by Inikori (1983:76-88) on West African-British trade between 1751 and 1850 enables us to map out the main trends in the development of West Africa's import trade up to the mid-nineteenth century. This data shows that in the period 1750-1807 four commodities; textiles, metals, spirits and arms and ammunition; made up 92% of West Africa's imports. The remaining 8% consisted of such items as salt, sugar, tobacco, hats, beads and cowries. Textiles accounted for about 66% of the total, metals about 11%, arms and ammunition 9%, and spirits 7%. It can be seen that textiles enjoyed an overwhelming dominance among West African imports. The textiles consisted of a wide range of cotton and woollen goods. Woollen textiles made up, by value, about 17% of the total, Indian cottons 40%, and British cottons 34%. Altogether during this period, West Africa imported over 266 million square yards of cotton textiles from India and Britain. About a quarter of the imports were made in the first eight years of the nineteenth century, thus presaging the rapid growth West Africa experienced in its overseas trade. Between 1800 and 1807 the average annual imports of textiles reached about seven million square yards, double the 3.5 million square yards imported during the 1750-1799 period.

Textiles continued to be the leading import in the coming decades. In fact, four times more cotton textiles were imported between 1827 and 1850, as during the comparable period from 1751 to 1774. In the latter period an average 2.1 million square yards were imported per annum as compared to 8.6 million yards in the period 1827 to 1850. But there was one major change. Unlike before, Indian cottons accounted for a small percentage of the imports. Out of the 198.4 million yards imported between 1827 and 1850, the share of Indian cottons was only 6.5%. Care must be taken in interpreting this data. What appears to have happened is that only the Indian share of 'British' textiles to West Africa declined, for other European merchants continued to import large amounts of Indian cottons to West Africa. For example, the thriving gum trade in Senegal and Mauritania depended on large imports of Indian guinee cloths. Between 1837 and 1840 French merchants imported 526,000 pieces, which, using Inikori's tabulation would yield 6.3 million square yards (Webb, 1985:164). During the same period Indian cottons imported into West Africa through Britain amounted to 1.9 million square yards.

Thus the imports of Indian cottons at this time may have declined only in relation to trade originating in Britain, then the most advanced industrial nation. By the mid-nineteenth century Britain produced textiles more massively and cheaply than any other nation. Not surprisingly, it dominated the

West African textile market, increasing its share from 34% during the 1780-1807 period to 84% in the 1827-50 period. As textile prices dropped, the share of textiles in the value of West African imports from Britain declined from about 66% in 1750 to about 38% in 1807, although the volume increased substantially.

The relative share of the other major imports also changed. For example, the share of metals declined from about 10.7% during the 1750-1807 period to about 4.4% in the second quarter of the nineteenth century, although the actual volume of imports increased. In 1850 3,691 tons of iron were imported compared to 656 tons in 1827 (Newbury, 1971:93). In contrast to the metals, the share of spirits and firearms rose from 6.9% to 14.6% and 9.1% to 15.5%, respectively, between 1827 and 1850. On average 3.1 million gallons of spirits were imported into West Africa from Britain during this period, and nearly 92,000 guns and three million pounds of gunpowder. If these figures are correct, it would seem that the volume, not value, of gun imports had declined from their levels in the 1750-1807 period when English merchants reportedly imported between 150,000 and 200,000 guns annually to West Africa, out of a total figure of 283,000 to 394,000 (Inikori, 1977:349). The bulk of the spirits and guns, about 61% and 57%, respectively, were imported into the Nigeria-Gabon region, then came the region between Morocco and Cape Apollonia with 22% and 25%, and finally the Gold Coast with 17% and 18%, respectively.

The combined share of the four leading imports declined to 72% in the period 1827-50 from 92% in the earlier period 1750-1807. Of the remaining 28% the leading imports consisted of tobacco with 5%, cowries 2.4% and beads 2.3%. Almost two-thirds of the tobacco was imported in the Nigeria-Gabon region, while nearly three-quarters of the cowries went to the Gold Coast. The import of beads was more evenly spread among the three regions. The quantities of tobacco and cowries were huge. Over 15 million kilograms of tobacco were imported between 1827 and 1850, of which two-thirds came in the 1840s. As for cowries, which, as noted in Chapter 10, were used as currency, their import increased sharply as trade expanded. Between 1791 and 1860 British cowrie exports to West Africa alone amounted to 6,610 tons, or approximately six billion shells. About four-fifths of the cowrie shells were imported between 1834 and 1850 (Hogendorn and Johnson, 1983:160). This triggered monetary inflation in the region's cowrie currency zones. The data provided by Inikori contains no entry for salt, but from all accounts salt was an important import item. Salt imports from Britain rose from 151,418 bushels in 1827 to 469,207 bushels in 1850 (Newbury, 1971:93).

Historians are not agreed on the impact of the seaborne trade on West Africa. Some say it was negative, others believe it was positive, or negligible. To the first school, West Africa exchanged valuable products for worthless trinkets, destructive spirits and armaments, and shoddy manufactures which undermined African industries (Rodney, 1982:Chapter 4; Davidson, 1966:293-5). Proponents of the second approach argue that the import of cheap, mass-produced goods helped improve living standards and the export trade overall stimulated internal trade and the industries servicing this trade, especially canoe manufacturing and food provisioning (Hopkins, 1973:126; Northrup, 1978:208-23). Finally, there are those who believe that imports and this trade in general did little to stimulate the economies of West Africa for they were peripheral to the region's main economic activities of domestic agriculture and craft work (Flint, 1974:397-9; Latham, 1978b:217-9).

Some of these claims are easier to dispel than others. On the question of trinkets, few of the imports listed above can be called that. It is also a gross exaggeration to say that the imports consisted of 'shoddy' goods, for it is unlikely that African merchants and consumers would have put up with them for long if they were. There can be little doubt that African preferences helped shape the goods exported to the various parts of West Africa. Recent research has shown that even the guns were not as poor in quality as suggested by contemporary observers and later historians (Inikori, 1977:359-61; Richards, 1980:52-7). But that does not mean their impact was benign as some would have us believe. Certainly tens of thousands of guns were not imported each year as ceremonial toys for African chiefs, or to scare birds away from fields (White, 1971:173-81; Fage, 1989:107), or to be used for protection in travel and game hunting (Northrup, 1978:166).

The guns were primarily imported to hunt for slaves. There was a correlation in time and place between the increase in the slave trade and the increase in the gun trade (Inikori, 1977; Richards, 1980). It is difficult to see how the slave-gun cycle could have had positive effects. The effects of import of alcohol may be more nebulous to decipher depending on one's predilection for sobriety or inebriation. But it is fatuous to dismiss the potential hazards of a high level of spirits imports by claiming that: 'in African societies [more] than European ones ... alcohol can play useful roles as a social solvent and as a currency' (Fage, 1989:107), or that 'Livingstone discounted the belief that Africans suffered from drinking imported liquor' (Latham, 1971:76), or indeed by repositing that the impression that one gets from the 'sources is that of more alcoholic beverages sold by Africans to European seamen and with more harmful results than the reverse' (Northrup, 1978:166-7).

Thus while it is incorrect to say that African imports consisted of trinkets and shoddy goods, the negative impact of guns and spirits cannot be

dismissed so lightly. It is hard to argue that the imports had much development potential when 35% consisted of such non-productive goods as guns,
gunpowder, spirits and tobacco, and another 40% was made up of two
consumer goods, textiles and beads, while the share of such important raw
materials or capital goods as metals was only 4%. In other words, more
tobacco was imported than metals. The preponderance of the unproductive
and consumer goods is a testimony to the distorted consumption habits,
investment strategies and economic policies of West African ruling classes
and merchants. Of course it could be argued that the imports stimulated the
development of export production and auxiliary industries and services. The
growth in export volumes was truly impressive as we have seen. But it would
be an exaggeration to conclude that this revolutionized the structure of West
African economies, for it should not be forgotten that only a small part of
the gross domestic product of West African societies entered the seaborne
trade.

Determining the impact of the imports on West African industries is
fraught with difficulties. Little research has been done on the impact of
specific imports on the affected industries in particular areas and over a
period of time to warrant the generalizations that are often made. Assertions
that the large volume of imports of, say, textiles led to the de-industrialization of textile manufacturing (Inikori, 1983:70-1), remain just that, assertions. It is possible to argue that the rise in textile imports may not have
signalled declining local production, but rising consumption. Until we know
more about the growth and distribution of incomes in the region, however,
it would be too rash to conclude that standards of living for ordinary people
were rising and that West Africa was undergoing a revolution of rising
expectations (Hopkins, 1973:126). Despite their apparent abundance, textile
imports could hardly have been sufficient to displace local textiles, especially in the interior where the imports were both rare and relatively expensive.

As we argued in Chapters 6 and 7, the ability of industries in West Africa
to supply local needs and to withstand foreign competition should not be
underestimated. This does not mean the impact of European imports and
European trade was everywhere negligible. It is merely to underline the fact
that it varied from place to place and changed over time, as was demonstrated
in Chapter 6 with reference to the iron industry, depending on the organization of both the trade itself and the affected industry, as well as the nature of
the society concerned. What seems certain is that the ultimate impact of the
international economy on West Africa was the colonization of the region.

Terms of Trade

It is often stated that the terms of trade were, on the whole, favourable for
West Africa during the first half of the nineteenth century. Despite periodic

fluctuations, prices of West African exports generally showed an upward trend, while those of the imports fell. Calculations made by Curtin (1975:336) for Senegambia show that the region's net barter terms of trade increased by more than a factor of two between the 1780s and the 1830s. Gum prices, Senegambia's major export after the demise of slaves and before the rise of peanuts, rose by a factor of nearly two and a half. Volumes rose even faster, by a factor of nearly ten and a half, so that the income terms improved sharply as well (Curtin, 1975:331). Peanut prices on the Marseilles market rose from 35 francs per quintal in 1847 to 43 francs in 1865 (Newbury, 1971:93). Palm oil in Liverpool varied between £E40 and £E60 in the 1810s and for most of the 1830s, 1840s and 1850s (Latham, 1978b:213-15). Finally, ivory 'increased four-fold over eighteenth century prices, but fluctuated erratically after 1830' (Newbury, 1971:93).

In the meantime, the prices of imports from Britain and France fell. For example, the prices of British textile imports dropped from 10.5d per yard in 1817 to 3.5d in 1850; salt from 6d per bushel to 3.5d during the same period; gun powder 8.5d per lb in 11817 to 5d in 1825; and iron and steel from £E8 per ton in 1830 to £E7 12s in 1850. 'In French trade prime costs fell for cottons, pottery, woollens, bafts; they remained stable for brandies, corals, powder, and arms' (Newbury, 1971:94).

The fact that the terms of trade moved in favour of West Africa does not mean West Africans were the main beneficiaries. The export prices quoted above were those obtained on the European, and not West African, markets. For example, in the early 1800s gum arabic was purchased in Saint Louis for about £E70 per ton and sold in France or London at between £E160 and £E180 (Webb, 1985:152). In the 1840s peanuts purchased in the Gambia for 20 francs per 100 kilograms sold in France for 37 to 38 francs (Brooks, 1975:41), while peanuts bought in Sierra Leone at between £E3 8s and £E6 3s per ton were sold in England at a price of £E10 to £E14. Timber costing £E2 10s in Sierra Leone fetched £E11 in Europe (Newbury, 1971:100). And palm oil bought in Calabar in 1855 at £E25 per ton sold in London at between £E38 10s and £E50 10s (Latham, 1971:71-2). Thus traders involved in West African produce in Europe easily enjoyed a turnover of profit of 100% and over, even after deducting transport and other costs. The main beneficiaries were the merchant houses or firms based in the leading commercial ports of Britain and France, such as Liverpool and Marseilles. Many of the European traders operating in West Africa were commissioned agents or correspondents. 'By having many correspondents on the coast, great profits accrued to the merchant houses; yet at the same time the correspondents often suffered losses when there were accidents or misfortunes' (Reynolds, 1974:55).

Barring accidents or misfortunes, European merchants operating along the West African coast often fared quite well, for so long as they dominated the external trade they could sell dear and buy cheap. Newbury (1971:100) has noted, for example, that cottons 'cost only 1 franc 49 cents each at Bordeaux and were sold by St. Louis merchants at the rate of 13 francs ... a net profit of 11 francs 26 cents, after deduction of transport and duty'. But the European merchants had very limited control over the supply of African exports from the interior, for they were largely restricted to their ships. So they depended on African brokers and merchants. Thus the latter had considerable power, which they used to maximize their profits. They routinely marked up coast prices for imported goods by 50% to 60% (Newbury, 1971:99,101). But the price differential between the coastal and inland markets were not entirely pocketed by the coastal brokers and merchants. They were shared by the small traders along the trade circuits. However, there can be little doubt that the multitude of local traders upon whom the entire structure rested made the lowest profits. Thus there was a progressive rise in the profits appropriated by each merchant group along the marketing chain that linked the interior to the coast to Europe.

The complexity of some of these chains can be seen in the case of the gum trade along the Senegal River. The harvesting and sale of gum in the interior was done by zawaya herding groups and their clients. Then 'during the season of the gum trade, zawaya caravans transported these stocks west to the Atlantic or south to the river markets' (Webb, 1985:155). The gum markets along the river were seasonal, so they were called in French escales, instead of marché. The zawaya caravans were met by the river traders, who acted as hosts, 'providing food and gifts to the caravaners and brokers and to the emirs and their representatives and their entourages' (Webb, 1985:158).

The river traders, or traitants as they were called, owned their own boats and had workers who transported the gum along the river to St. Louis, which had its own commercial hierarchy. On top were the negociants, a 'small group of French traders who either represented mainland French commercial houses or were themselves the owners of Saint-Louisian import-export houses or both' (Webb, 1985:156). They monopolized the import of guinee cloth, the main import along the river trade network. Below them were the licensees, mostly small shop-keepers and owners of commercial stalls. All these groups sought their piece of the gum profits. When prices were too low, they were passed down the chain to the zawaya who could send their gum to other markets or suspend supplies. It was a very competitive business.

Relations between the different trading groups were complex and became more so as time passed. That these traders were mutually dependent cannot be denied. The absence of a commonly accepted currency and the segmentation of the markets necessitated the development of a series of credit systems. African and European merchants on the coast developed indispensable credit relations, despite holding mutual misgivings. There were two main types of credit. One involved the advance by one coastal trader to another of trade goods on credit. On the Gold Coast 'Africans frequently offered the European trader staple exports on credit when the goods he wanted were not immediately on hand. The European trader likewise offered the African trader goods on credit to be paid for with the produce of the country when it was available' (Reynolds, 1974:150).

Thus the picture that is often painted of the rich European lender and the poor African borrower is grossly oversimplified (Curtin, 1973:303). The sums involved could be large. By 1855, for example, Efik traders in Old Calabar held over £E250,000 in credit (Latham, 1971:80). The second system became more common from the 1840s, and particularly following the development of steamship services between West Africa and Europe. It involved 'direct purchase by African and European merchants from commission houses in England in return for consignments of produce' (Newbury, 1972:85). Some Sierra Leone merchants started doing this as early as 1818. The system spread to the Gold Coast in the 1840s and Lagos in the 1860s, but did not catch on in Senegambia where the first system prevailed (Newbury, 1972:86-88).

The credit system involved great risk, for it was not unusual for the debtors to default on payment. Thus it was a source of perennial conflict between African and European merchants. Tension between them was exacerbated as each group sought to cross the other's traditional trade boundaries. Both groups thought they could make more profits by bypassing the other. Some European merchants tried to trade directly with the producers in the interior, while some African merchants tried to do the same with Europe. In Senegal, for example, the negociants employed 'several thousand agents and carriers of their own. By 1841 their seasonal debt was calculated at about £E100,000' (Newbury, 1972:88). These agents 'had a clear commercial advantage over the traditional traitants. The employee with secured wages could undersell the independent trader without personal risk' (Webb, 1985:164). For their part, there were some African traders who could effectively compete with European traders in the external markets. In the Gold Coast, for example, by the 1840s there were some who could import 'goods from England to the amount of £E20,000 to £E30,000 annually on their own credit' (Reynolds, 1974:95). These rivalries intensified in the second half of the nineteenth century with tragic consequences not only for the African merchant class, but for their societies as well.

Rise of Trade Rivalries

Trade rivalries were not confined to conflicts between African and European merchants. They also existed within each group. The numerous studies on the Niger Delta (Dike, 1956; Jones, 1963; Ikime, 1968; Latham, 1971; Northrup, 1978) and those on the Gold Coast (Priestley, 1969; Reynolds, 1974; Kaplow, 1977, 1978) have amply demonstrated the rise of a new African merchant class composed primarily of ex-slaves, liberated Africans, and the mission-educated elite who began to challenge the commercial and political hegemony of the old ruling classes.

The rise of the new merchant class changed the old order, even where the integrative social mechanisms were strong. This was of course not the first time in West African history that the emergence of a new class challenged the existing ones. But now the struggle between the old and new commercial classes was taking place in the context of growing rivalries between African merchants as a whole and European merchants. The new class consolidated itself in the third quarter of the nineteenth century. It was to offer fierce competition to both the old African merchant class and the European merchants. Its ascendancy over the former exacerbated the disintegration of coastal societies, while its effective challenge against the latter ensured that European commercial hegemony could only be attained through colonization.

The conflicts among European merchants occurred both between and among traders of different European nations. The main contenders in West Africa were British and French traders. During the Napoleonic wars in Europe Britain blockaded and then occupied Saint Louis, the French colonial enclave in Senegal. It was returned to France in 1817. For their part, the French sought to have their share of the Niger Delta palm oil trade. By the mid-nineteenth century the British had managed to eliminate Danish and Dutch competition from the Gold Coast after years of conflict. The Danes sold their forts to Britain in 1850 after all efforts to make them profitable had proved futile. The Dutch sold their forts to Britain in 1871. However, by then a new competitor for Britain and France was beginning to make its presence felt. That was Germany. Between 1845 and 1850 direct exports from West Africa to Hamburg totalled five million marks (Harding, 1983:378-9).

One of the little known aspects of the European trade rivalries was the competition between merchants from the same country. Lynn (1981, 1989) has shown how new small-scale traders in Bristol and London sought to challenge the big established Liverpool traders in the 1830s, 1840s and 1850s for the palm oil trade of the Niger Delta. The increased competitive tension among them helped alter the organization of 'a trade originally noted for its reliance on personal contacts, understandings and informal agreements amongst a small group of merchants' (Lynn, 1981:348). The newcomers were not committed to the earlier practices. The intra-English trade rivalries 'spilled over into assaults on African middle men'. It was, therefore, 'incidents between English traders as much as between English and African traders that led to the appointment of John Beecroft as the first British consul in the Delta area in 1849 and thus began the move to British political control' (Lynn, 1981:348).

Among the French there was competition between merchants from Bordeaux and those from Marseilles for the control of the Senegal River gum trade. The two groups operated in different ways. The Marseilles merchants operated as transients, unlike the Bordeaux merchants who had been long resident in St. Louis where they enjoyed close relations with Senegalese merchants. In the early nineteenth century the latter dominated the slave trade while the former controlled the secondary gum trade. When the slave trade declined, the Marseilles merchants sought to enter the gum trade, which the Bordeaux merchants wanted to monopolize. Excessive competition between them wreaked havoc on the gum trade. The Senegalese middlemen were the first to suffer the consequences. Many operated at a loss and became:

> *increasingly indebted to the resident Frenchmen who had extended them credit. By 1841, their aggregate indebtedness had reached proportions that also touched the solvency of the French merchants to whom they were indebted. Under these conditions, using the economic crisis as justification, the Bordeaux merchants were able to persuade the colonial administration to intervene to their competitive advantage* (McLane, 1986:46).

Thus was promulgated the Ordinance of 1842 which banned Europeans from the river markets, ostensibly to protect the interests of the Senegalese merchants.

The 1842 ordinance was beneficial to the Bordeaux merchants and other Frenchmen resident in St. Louis, for it 'recreated the traditional pattern of trade through Senegalese middlemen which the resident merchants utilized. Entry into this closed system by newcomers was difficult' (McLane, 1986:48). But the struggle was far from over. The Marseilles merchants continued campaigning for 'free trade' and the French government appointed an inter-ministerial commission, on which the Bordeaux interests were poorly represented. A new ordinance was passed in 1842 which had:

> *the effect of severing the bonds between the Senegalese middlemen and the old-timer French merchant houses at Saint Louis. Even more to the*

*point, captains and merchants could sail to the escales in their own ships
to 'supervise' the transactions, legalizing a practice which had become
common since the opening of the escales to former slaves in 1849'*
(McLane, 1986:50).

The Marseilles traders hired the ex-slaves as their agents. By 1853 the
number of ships visiting Saint Louis from Marseilles had increased to 20
from 12 in 1849, reflecting the new competitive trade regime.

As the Bordeaux merchants saw their predominance erode, they resolved
to fight back and eliminate the competition posed by the Marseilles merchants. In 1851 they petitioned the governor and publicized their case in
France for land grants in the interior to establish permanent protected posts
from which to spread French commerce and 'civilization'. They had a
sympathetic hearing from the new minister of colonies, himself a merchant-
shipper from Bordeaux and a former member of its chamber of commerce
and their demands were accepted. A fort was constructed in the teeth of
African resistance. When the governor began to temporize, the Bordeaux
merchants engineered his ousting and had Louis Faidherbe, a young, ener-
getic director of the Engineer Corps of Senegal, appointed in his place.
Faidherbe did not waste time in getting the land grants demanded by the
Bordeaux merchants and changing the location of the gum trade to their
posts. Thus the Bordeaux merchants were well on their way to controlling
the gum trade. The formation of the French empire in West Africa had begun.

By the mid-nineteenth century the extent of European colonial expansion
in West Africa was confined to a few coastal 'finger-heads', as Freund
(1984b:74) calls them. British colonial power was restricted to Sierra Leone,
founded in 1787 as a haven for freed slaves, and Bathurst, founded in the
Gambia in 1816, in addition to a growing, but precarious, consular presence
on the Gold Coast and the Niger Delta. In 1851 they occupied Lagos. The
French were established in Saint Louis along the Senegalese coast and Grand
Bassam and Assinie on the Ivory Coast. Dakar, the future capital of Senegal,
was seized in 1857. From these coastal enclaves the British and French were
poised to move inland and extend their colonial empires in the coming
decades.

The colonial drive was fuelled by developments taking place both in West
Africa itself and in Europe. Needless to say, these developments were
interconnected and reinforced each other. Within West Africa the trade
rivalries and tensions noted above between African and European merchants, and between European merchants of different nations as well as
among those from the same nation, became so intense that the trading system
built over the past half century began to crumble. At the heart of the
deepening crisis was the fact that the numbers of traders increased, while the

prices of West African export products fell. This meant more traders than ever were competing for a shrinking pie of profits. It was a fine recipe for converting fierce commercial rivalries into deadly political struggles, which culminated in the scramble and partition of the region among European powers.

The most important European newcomer was Germany. German trade with West Africa grew steadily in the 1850s and 1860s, and exploded from 1870. Germany's leading imports were palm oil, palm kernels, camwood, ebony, ivory, rubber, coffee, cocoa and peanuts. The total value of West African products exported directly to Hamburg rose from 1.1 million marks in 1860 to five million marks in 1875, 22.5 million marks in 1890 and 51.3 million marks in 1900. Until 1860 palm oil was the main export, accounting for 88.6% of the total value of exports in that year, followed by camwood with 6.7%, and ivory 4.6%. By 1875 palm kernels, whose exports were first recorded in 1861, was in first place with 45.8%, followed by palm oil with 35.9%, ivory 8.3%, rubber 6.6% and camwood 1.6%, and the rest was coffee and ebony. By 1890 the share of palm kernels had risen to 60%, and that of palm oil had dropped to 12.6%. Rubber was now in second place with 18.2%, and coffee had increased its share to 4.7%, and cocoa took 0.5%. The major change by 1900 was that cocoa's share had jumped to 33% and peanuts took 5.2%. Germany's main exports were spirits and wine, guns and gunpowder, cotton textiles and salt, in that order. In 1890 the relative share of the four groups of products was 47.1%, 11.3%, 8.5% and 0.9%, respectively (Harding, 1983:377-91).

The growth of German trade and competition latched onto the age-old Anglo-French rivalries. German merchants began challenging British and French merchants all along the West African coast. They imported palm oil and palm kernels from Lagos and Cameroon, ebony from Cameroon, Gabon and Old Calabar, ivory from Lagos, Gabon and Monrovia, and cocoa from Sao Tome. In 1880 the Germans even established coffee plantations in Liberia and Gabon (Harding, 1983:366-71). The Hamburg shipping line, Woermann, became the most serious competitor of British shipping in West Africa.

In the meantime, the deep-seated antagonism between French and British merchants intensified. The French sought to increase their stake in the rich Niger Delta trade dominated by the British traders. The Compagnie Française de L'Afrique and the Compagnie du Senegal, formed in 1880 and 1881 respectively, established branches all over the delta. British merchants were given cause for concern. In 1884 the British National African Company, the predecessor of the Royal Niger Company, bought out the French firms. 'This episode', Hopkins (1973:160) believes, 'demonstrated that

British supremacy could not be challenged successfully by purely commercial means, at least by France'. The French drive for a protected colonial empire was given added impetus.

At the same time that rivalries among and between the European merchants were intensifying, the new class of African merchants, referred to earlier, grew in size, power, confidence and wealth. They clearly constituted an emergent bourgeois class, who were quite conscious of themselves as 'new men', distinct from the old mercantile classes. Many of them converted to Christianity, received European education, took European names, and betrayed a preference for Victorian dress, values and ambivalence towards some prevailing African social practices and traditions. Their ranks included both independent operators, and agents of European merchants. The two were not mutually exclusive. Some started as agents and ended up as independent traders, and vice-versa.

One example is that of Bishop Crowther's sons. The Bishop invested church funds in shares of Holland Jacques and Company, a major trading company on the Niger in the 1860s. 'During the next decade, Bishop Crowther's son, Josiah, was put in charge of Holland Jacques' trade on the Niger. Josiah Crowther [replaced] all the Europeans on the company's ships with African staff, except for engineers and ships' captains. Another son, Joseph, became the general agent for the West Africa Company, another major trading company. Yet another son, Samuel, was appointed trading master of WAC. Bishop Crowther's daughter, Mrs Macaulay, was active in commerce between Lagos and the kingdom of Nupe... In 1880, the Crowther Brothers went one step further and placed their own steamer on the Niger' (Ehrensaft, 1972:480-1).

Many of West Africa's wealthiest traders were to be found in the towns of Monrovia, Freetown and Lagos, and on the Niger Delta. Among them was Richard Blaize, who was born in Freetown but moved to Lagos in 1862 where he made his money. By the mid-1890s he was estimated to be worth £E150,000, 'which is', as Hopkins (1975:153) says, 'a large sum even today, when the value of the pound sterling is far less than it was in the nineteenth century'. The Niger Delta had the most celebrated 'merchant princes' of nineteenth century West African historiography, such as Jaja of Opobo and Nana of Itsekeri. Jaja rose from humble origins as a slave to become an important merchant in Bonny. However, his social origins prevented him from taking political office. So he left Bonny and established his own state at Opobo, 'carefully placed so as to cut off Bonny from its trading empire on the river', from which position he rose to become 'the greatest king of the Delta' (Webster and Boahen, 1967:201). Nana was also of humble origins, not as a slave, but as a commoner. In 1884 prominent Itsekeri traders appointed him Governor of the Benue River in recognition of his wealth and power (Ikime, 1968:50).

On the Gold Coast there were merchants like James Bannerman, educated in England, who as early as 1828 was trading goods worth well over £E7,000; George Blankson, who had factories all along the Gold Coast; Robert Ghartey, renowned for his diversified interests in the timber, gold mining and palm kernel trades, and as King of Winneba; Francis Grant, a celebrated 'native gentleman' and reportedly 'equal to any European on the coast in commercial standing'; Thomas Hughes, a wealthy merchant and pioneer in the modern mining industry in Ghana; John Sarbah and his son John Mensah Sarbah, famous for their extensive networks of stores and trading stations in the region.

There were also some remarkable women traders, such as Mrs Swanzy and Mrs Barnes, who was apparently one of the richest African merchants on the Cape Coast (Reynolds, 1974:107-14). In Liberia there was Stephen Benson, a future president of the country, whose coasting trade in the early 1840s was worth £E14,000; James McGill whose trade was worth £E15,000; and the partnership of Payne and Yates that was worth £E34,000 (Syfert, 1977:227). The Liberian 'merchant princes' became the country's social and political elite and were behind the proclamation of Liberia's independence, which they saw as a means of promoting their interests against British merchants who challenged the legality, under international law, of tariffs, commissioning requirements, and port of entry legislation imposed by the Liberian colony.

The rise of the new African merchant class owed a lot to their very marginality. As ex-slaves, liberated Africans and mission-educated elements, they did not have the traditional opportunities for accumulation. But by the same token, they were not constrained by the dead hand of tradition from exploiting the arising new trading opportunities. They were products of a changing old world and a struggling new one. They had ties to both the traditional kin networks and European merchant houses. The kin connections furnished them with such key resources as lands and residences which could be converted into commercial premises, and low cost household labour, as well as providing some protection against bankruptcy for, as Kaplow (1978:27) states in the case of the Gold Coast, 'the African merchants kept certain assets from their overseas creditors by claiming them as family property'. From the Europeans they got credit, either as commissioned agents or as independent operators.

In short, families, households, or the contiguous house system that developed in the Niger Delta facilitated the financing, organization and development of African merchants' activities. In return, the merchants were expected to spend a considerable part of their income on meeting the needs of their supportive or sponsoring unit for property, labour, education and consumer goods, as Dumett (1973) has shown in his case study of John Sarbah. Sarbah, together with several associates, tried to invest in mining by floating a mining company in 1882 with a nominal capital of £E25,000. But the company folded after a year. African merchants did try to invest in industry and agriculture, but the bulk of their wealth was either invested in trade or providing the needs of their families and households. Such expenditures were not 'unproductive' as such, but they did not encourage a process of sustained accumulation either. Indeed, when a merchant died, his or her assets were often divided up and redistributed. It would appear, therefore, that there was little inter-generational accumulation. As Hopkins (1973:153) observes with reference to Richard Blaize, his 'business, like that of most of his contemporaries, died with him'. This weakened the position of the new African merchant classes and generally undermined their capacity to fight effectively against their European competitors.

The rapid expansion of this class from the 1850s was greatly helped by the transition from sail to steam navigation. The steamers moved faster than sail, had larger cargo-carrying capacities and provisions for transporting cargoes for African traders in small lots. It became easier and cheaper than before for African traders to import goods directly from Europe, either on their own or as agents of European manufacturing firms. But the steamer proved to be a mixed blessing. In Liberia, steamers plying along its ports, together with the fluctuation and decline of overseas market prices for Liberian produce, spelled disaster for the coasting trade. Between 1847 and 1871 the Liberians owned and operated at least 139 vessels. In 1872 there were 29 vessels in operation. 'After 1883 the existence of no more than three Liberian vessels can be documented in any given year until the end of the century' (Syfert, 1977:233). The steamers did not simply come filled with merchandise. They brought with them an influx of European merchants, for whom trade with West Africa also became easier, faster and cheaper to conduct than in the days when sailing ships ruled the seas.

Steamships were used on a regular basis in West Africa from 1852. The leading lines were British - the African Steam Ships Company and the British and African Steam Navigation Company. From 1870 'the two companies agreed to fix freight rates and sailing dates, and thereafter remained close' (Lynn, 1989:229). From 1891 the two lines were run by Elder Dempster and Company. There were also several French lines which were amalgamated into the Fabre-Frassinet line in 1889. From Germany there was the Woermann Line of Hamburg, which became the main competitor of the British lines. In the mid-1890s, the Elder Dempster and Woermann lines established the West African Shipping Conference, which by using a rebate system virtually forced traders to use Dempster's or Woermann's ships.

The Slide to Colonization

With the arrival of the steamer, both freight rates and travel time between West Africa and Europe fell drastically. The freight rates of palm oil to Britain, for example, fell from £E5 per ton in 1855 to around £E2 per ton in 1907 (Lynn, 1989:229). Steamers, unlike sail, could also travel at any time, and call at several ports along the coast during the voyage, regardless of the weather. And most critically for the competition over West African trade, with the arrival of the steamship traders did not have to own or charter a ship to trade, for they could hire cargo space. Thus the activities of trading and shipping were divorced. The established sailing firms, most of whom failed to convert to steam, lost control of the trade. There was a flood of African and European traders, previously inhibited by the high capital costs involved in owning or chartering a ship.

The consequences were profound. Competition intensified and profits began to fall. In the 1850s and 1860s there was fierce competition between the supercargoes and the steamers, and the trading regimes they represented all over West Africa, particularly in the established centres, such as Old Calabar (Latham, 1971:58-63). The introduction of steamers also helped bring structural changes in the way trade was conducted, 'namely the shift of traders away from using ships as their trading centres on the coast to using «hulks» moored in a river, and then, in the move from «ship to shore» that occurred from the 1860s, developing on-shore «factories»' (Lynn, 1989:230). The ascendancy of the steamer was swift. In 1855 steamships carried 6.5% of the palm oil from West Africa to Britain. This increased to 76.2% in 1875 and 98.8% in 1890 (Lynn, 1989:234).

Two new developments followed in the oil trade. First, Liverpool, which was the home of the steamships, regained its dominance over London and Bristol. Second, since the steamer could call along the entire West African coast, new areas were opened up as suppliers of palm oil and other products. The number of West African ports exporting oil increased from 14 in 1850 to 47 in 1870 and 108 in 1890 (Lynn, 1989:240-1). With these changes the volume of West African exports skyrocketed. In the meantime, their prices fell, thus further fuelling competition. Palm oil prices in Liverpool fell from £E50 a ton in 1854-6 to £E32 in 1862-66 and £E20 in the late 1880s. The prices of palm kernels, exported in large quantities from 1860, fell from £E15 per ton in the 1860s to about £E10 in the late 1880s. Prices of peanuts also fell by over half, from around 27.5 francs in the period 1857-1867 to about 15 francs in the period 1877-1900 (Hopkins, 1973:133). Camwood prices in Liverpool fell from £E26.5s per ton to £E15 in 1874 (Syfert, 1977:232).

The fall in palm oil and peanut prices was directly affected by changes in the structure of supply as a result of the introduction of steamships. In addition, the structure of demand also changed. The West African oils were being squeezed out of the market by the development of gas and electric lighting, the development of new mineral oils in the USA from 1859, the increase in imports of Asian vegetable oils following the opening of the Suez Canal, and the general contraction of the market for raw materials as a result of the intermittent recessions experienced by the major European countries between 1873 and 1896 (Munro, 1976:65-72; Lynn, 1989:228).

Thus the net barter terms of trade moved decisively against West Africa. There was what Austen (1983:10) has called 'differentials in vulnerability' among the various groups involved in West Africa's trade with Europe. The least affected were the firms in Europe and the supplies in the West African hinterland, the former because they effectively set the prices and the latter because they could withdraw from export trade if prices dropped too low. Individual European and African merchants had neither option. Persistently low prices threatened them with bankruptcy, so conflicts among them deepened, as shown by the increased incidents of malpractice and cheating on both sides, and disputes about their respective areas of operations and jurisdiction. They saw each other as parasitic middlemen who had to be bypassed. These disputes were aggravated, according to Hopkins (1973:149-50, 155), by the growing use of European currencies. The group most hurt by this was the old mercantile elite and traders in the interior who found their money quickly losing value. The demonetization of African currencies had began. The impact on many groups of African ruling classes was to prove disastrous (Webb, 1982:465).

As a result of these changes, conflicts and developments, the credit system was put under enormous strain. Europeans' distrust of African merchants led to the introduction of controversial European bankruptcy legislation on the Gold Coast in 1858. The most celebrated bankruptcy case was that of Joseph Smith of Cape Coast, who reportedly owed an English firm, Foster and Smith, £E18,000. In actual fact, it was the firm that owed Smith money. Over a fifteen year period Smith had conducted trade worth £E138,723 2s and paid £E32,000 in freight, interest and sundry. The company had been cheating him by adding 25 to 50%, or more, on the cost of the goods they supplied him. When he discovered this he confronted the company, which admitted to overcharging him, but refused to reduce the money he owed. When Smith tried to sell his oil directly to England, the firm had it confiscated. The matter was taken to court where the case was ruled in Smith's favour; the money the company deceived him, £E28,000, exceeded what he owed. But the company pleaded statute of limitation and Smith's debt was reduced by only £E2,000. Smith was ordered to pay this sum 'in three months and as he was without means to pay, he declared himself bankrupt in 1861' (Reynolds, 1974:154).

This practice of European creditors cheating African debtors, called 'whitewashing' became increasingly common. African merchants and producers responded in various ways, especially by boycotting European merchants and holding up their produce from them, as happened on the Gold Coast from 1858 to 1860, in 1865 and 1872 (Reynolds, 1974:140, 148; Webster and Boahen, 1967:219), in Calabar in 1862 and 1864 (Latham, 1971:62, 71) and in other parts of the Niger Delta in the 1880s, and among the gum producers of Senegal and Mauritania in 1885-6 (Hopkins, 1973:155). The conflict soon turned into a political struggle for supremacy. In 1868 the Gold Coast merchants came together with the traditional rulers and set up the Fante Confederation for the purpose of defending themselves from British imperial ambitions and the threat posed by Asante in the interior. The emphasis on economic matters in the confederation's constitution betrayed its primary objectives (Hayford, 1970; Wilson, 1969). The example spread to Accra where the Accra Confederation was also formed. In Abeokuta, Nigeria, the educated elite formed the Egba United Board of Management, as their vehicle for modernization and state construction. Among the many things they did they 'organized a postal service to Accra, opened a secular school... [and] established a source of revenue for the central government of Abeokuta through the introduction of customs duties on exported produce' (Pallinder-Law, 1974:70).

These experiments in modern state construction proved short-lived. For one thing, they were not welcomed by many members of the traditional ruling elite. More importantly, the British were unremittingly hostile to them. For example, they saw the Fante Confederation as a challenge to their power and jurisdiction in southern Ghana, so they were determined to crush it. First, they played the chiefs against the merchants. Then in December 1871 all members of the Executive were arrested on a fabricated charge of treason. Once the confederation was dead the British decided to colonize southern Ghana. They achieved that in 1874 following the defeat of Asante, the strongest power in the region, against whom they had fought intermittently since 1823 (Fynn, 1978). The annexation of southern Ghana as a British colony was declared in July 1874.

The next major theatre of British operations was the Niger Delta, where British merchants faced very stiff competition from African merchants. In 1879 George Goldie persuaded 'the four main trading firms to amalgamate under his leadership in order to force down produce prices and share profits' (Flint, 1974a:400). Thus was formed the United Africa Company. It quickly moved to monopolize the palm oil trade by trying to get exclusive trade agreements with local rulers and to drive French merchants into bankruptcy by temporarily offering artificially high prices. The company soon discovered that these measures were not enough to eliminate competition. Consequently it sought the protection and power of a royal charter, which it was granted in 1886. The company was renamed the Royal Niger Company. Immediately it set about the destruction of the African merchant class by imposing heavy licences and taxes on them and limiting their freedom of movement. Then it was the turn to get rid of Jaja and Nana. The British demanded that they sign treaties of protection, which should include a free trade clause. Both refused. When British traders at Opobo tried to fix oil prices, Jaja tried to circumvent them by selling directly to England. That sealed his fate. In 1887 he was arrested and deported to the Caribbean where he died four years later. Nana met the same fate in 1894. He was arrested after British forces had bombarded his capital at Ebrohimi.

In the meantime, the French had also become convinced that only direct colonial rule would eliminate their commercial rivals. Their failure to compete with the British on the Delta reinforced the need, in their minds, to consolidate their position in the areas where they already had a bridge-head, principally Senegal. In 1877 France had introduced differential tariffs in Senegal in order to protect her trade there and raise revenue for the colonial administration, a move against which Britain protested. Undeterred two years later the French began advancing from Senegal into the interior of the western Sudan towards the upper and middle basins of the Niger. Numerous wars were fought along the way, most notably with Samori Toure, who was then trying to build a new state bent on modernization in the region (Person, 1978). The French invasion forces also went south into Côte d'Ivoire, Dahomey and Guinea. By the early 1890s France had carved an empire several times its size in West Africa.

These developments made German merchants, whose trade with West Africa was increasing rapidly, fear that they might be excluded from West Africa as France and Britain showed signs of expanding colonial rule over regions where they enjoyed commercial hegemony (Turner, 1967). German merchants had a growing stake in the Cameroons, where British traders were well ensconced, and France exhibited imperial ambitions, for in 1883 it declared a protectorate over Malimba to the south of Doula. Like the other European merchants elsewhere in West Africa the Germans were also experiencing growing competition with African merchants, the Doula. In 1884 Germany annexed the Cameroon. They 'made it clear in their public and confidential statements immediately following annexation that they had every intention of destroying the Duala trade monopoly in order to exploit

Cameroon more effectively' (Austen, 1982:12). The German government initially thought it could turn over the colony to the local trading firms to run. When the firms showed reluctance to carry the financial burdens of colonial administration and African resistance erupted, the government itself assumed the reins colonial rule. Germany also annexed Togo.

Details of the European conquest of West Africa and African resistance to it are too well known to be recounted here any further (Hargreaves, 1974a, 1974b; Crowder, 1981; Ajayi and Crowder, 1974; Boahen, 1987b). From our discussion it is quite clear that economic rivalries played a central role in determining the causes and courses of colonization. We have focused on these rivalries as they unfolded in different parts of West Africa. It cannot be overemphasized, however, that these processes were driven by the motor of capitalist development in Europe. It is often argued that the partition of Africa was an offspring of the European 'Great Depression' of 1873-96, which stoked the fires of international competition and forced business interests to pressurize their governments to secure new and protected colonial markets (Hynes, 1979). Anxious governments abandoned liberal free trade and laisser-faire policies and began erecting protectionist barriers, beginning with Austria in 1875, Spain 1877, Italy 1878, Germany 1879, Switzerland 1884 and France 1881 and 1892. 'State control and regulation', Munro (1976:67) writes, 'of the market became a favoured device both to secure adjustments in existing commercial situations undergoing stress and to forge new links between Africa and the international economy'.

This analysis needs some qualification. There are economic historians who believe that there was not one Great Depression in Europe but a series of cyclical fluctuations in the last quarter of the nineteenth century. Economic expansion was not entirely halted, although many European economies expanded at a slower rate than in the preceding and succeeding boom periods (Saul, 1969). Moreover, it is simplistic to assume that only depressions generate conflict; periods of prosperity can do the same, for both depression and growth are always uneven, and can leave in their trail heightened conflict between classes and countries. It could be argued, therefore, that the European colonization of West Africa in the last quarter of the nineteenth century sprang from, on the one hand, the turbulence of uneven cyclical fluctuations engulfing European countries and economies, and on the other, the economic, social and technological changes in the organization and structure of West African-European trade.

There can be little doubt that the economics of trade conditioned the European colonization of West Africa. Political, diplomatic and military considerations of course influenced the nature and timing of the process, but neither of them constituted the driving force. And, like North Africa, the invasions occurred when new stable regimes bent on modernization were being formed, such as the Fante Confederation, the Delta River states of Opobo and Itsekeri, and Samori's Mandinka empire. Thus as Hargreaves (1974:408) correctly puts it, 'it was the growing strength and confidence of Jaja and Opobo and Lat Dior, not their weakness, which provoked European intervention against them'. But it is futile to 'blame' the beginning of the partition of West Africa on French activities as Hargreaves (1974:405-7, 415-9) and Hopkins (1973:161-2) tend to do. The partition of West Africa did not have a single trigger which was pressed by one country. It was a complex and messy process in which the major European powers, Britain, France and Germany, all had a hand.

Conclusion

If the colonization of North Africa was largely the product of 'finance imperialism', that of West Africa was the outcome of 'trade imperialism'. While North African countries became vulnerable because of rising indebtedness, West Africa fell victim to the steep fall in commodity prices.

In trying to map out the development of commercial relations between West Africa and Europe, this chapter has tried to challenge and qualify some popular interpretations. It has been suggested that the use of the term 'legitimate commerce' to celebrate the dawn of a new era ignores the fact that abolition of the slave trade was a gradual process, and that there was no abrupt change in the structure of West Africa's trade with Europe. Moreover, the fact should not be overlooked that it was, indeed, on the backs of 'legitimate commerce' that West Africa hurtled towards colonization.

Although it is beyond dispute that West Africa's trade with Europe increased phenomenally in the nineteenth century, and that West Africa exported primary products and imported manufactured goods, there is little agreement on the impact of European imports on West African economies. It has been demonstrated that it is spurious to claim that West Africa exchanged valuable products for worthless trinkets or shoddy commodities. But neither were the bulk of the imports productive goods. Certainly the guns and spirits were primarily destructive. The textiles were consumer products, and although imported in large quantities, they were not large enough to satisfy the entire West African market, so that it is more likely that they complemented rather than supplanted local production. Thus the evidence is not compelling that imports either stimulated the economies of West Africa or undermined them. Their impact on production was a lot more limited and differentiated.

It has also been argued that the contention that West Africa's terms of trade in the first half of the nineteenth century were favourable, needs to be qualified by the fact that the main beneficiaries of this were not West African merchants but the merchant firms in Europe. As for the trade rivalries, while the primary conflict was between the African and European merchants, the rivalries within each group also significantly affected the trajectory of imperialism in West Africa. Indeed, it would appear that the move towards political control by Britain in the Niger and France in Senegal in the mid-nineteenth century was fomented as much by intra-British and intra-French trade rivalries as by conflict with African rivals. The arrival of German traders from the second half of the century reinforced intra-European rivalries.

On the African side, the new merchant class did not always get along with the old ruling classes. As their position became stronger, the former gradually began to accumulate political power at the latter's expense. The Europeans were able to use these divisions to weaken efforts by the new African mercantile classes to consolidate themselves by forming 'modern' states and political units.

The crisis in the trading system was largely triggered by two inter-related developments. On the one hand, there was the sharp rise in the number of traders, both European and African, itself a product of the rapid growth of trade in the previous half century, which was further stimulated by the introduction of steamships. On the other hand, the prices of West African commodities on the European markets declined precipitously, thanks to the changing structure of demand and the intermittent recessions of the last quarter of the century. The credit system was put under enormous strain, exacerbated by the progressive demonetization of African currencies. As the crisis deepened, commercial rivalries turned into bitter struggles for political supremacy. The partition of West Africa brings out clearly the complex connections between trade, social transformation, technological change, economic cycles, and colonization.

15. The Imperialisms of the South

Growth of Trade with Europe

Central, Southern and East Africa are vast regions. Despite the obvious differences among and within them, the ways in which their trade with Europe developed and the patterns of their colonization differed quite significantly from North and West Africa. First, unlike North Africa, these regions were not a playground for bondholders. On the whole, finance and commercial capital played a less important role than mining and speculative capital in the establishment of colonial rule in these regions. Second, the slave trade persisted for much longer in parts of Central and East Africa than in West Africa. Third, vegetable oils accounted for a smaller proportion of non-slave exports in the three regions than in West Africa. Instead ivory, rubber, wool, minerals and spices, predominated. These commodities were not as badly affected by the introduction of steamships and the intermittent European recessions of the late nineteenth century. Fourth, long established European settlers, especially in Angola, Mozambique and South Africa, played an active role in the organization of export production and trade.

Thus the three regions were integrated into the world capitalist system and partitioned into colonies quite differently from North and West Africa. The colonization of North Africa came in the midst of a deepening debt crisis, while in West Africa it was facilitated by falling trade profits. In Central Africa speculative capital held sway, while in Southern Africa mining capital was the engine that pulled the locomotive of colonization. East Africa, long an important part of the Indian Ocean trading system, was the last region to be fully integrated into the expanding European-dominated world capitalist system. Here speculative capital also played a role, as did the politics of pre-emptive colonization.

In the first half of the nineteenth century slave exports were dominant in the trading networks centred on the mouth of the Zaire river, and along the Angolan and Mozambican coasts. Zaire and Angola supplied at least two-thirds of all the slaves entering the trans-Atlantic trade in the nineteenth century (Curtin, et.al., 1978:424). Actual figures are in serious dispute. The most recent estimates by Manning (1990:70-1) show that between 1800 and 1860 slaves exports from Loango averaged between 5,000 and 15,000 annually and from Angola they averaged between 15,000 and 25,000. Most of these slaves ended up in Brazil and Cuba where demand for slave labour kept rising. In Mozambique the slave trade lasted longer than almost everywhere else in Africa. It was still the dominant commercial activity by the 1880s, thanks to demand for slaves in the expanding plantation economies of the Indian Ocean islands (Alpers, 1975:216-9). According to data provided by Liesegang (1983:463-4), during the period 1800-1842 slave exports fluctuated between about 4,500 and 30,000. Altogether during this period at least 397,100 slaves were exported. The Portuguese were the leading slave traders both on the Angolan and Mozambican coasts. Portugal's abolition of the slave trade in 1836 had little immediate effect. The Angolan trade only began to die down after the closure of Brazilian ports to slaving vessels after 1850 (Seleti, 1990:34).

Considerable numbers of slaves were also exported from the Tanzanian coast, the Horn and the Eastern Sudan. Annual slave exports from the Tanzanian coast, which drew on the hinterland of modern Tanzania, much of Malawi and north-eastern Zaire, averaged 15,000 between 1820 and 1870. For the Horn they averaged between 4,000 and 5,000 in the period 1805-1880, most of whom came from the Sidama and Oromo regions of modern Ethiopia. Slave exports from the Eastern Sudan, which had remained steady in the eighteenth century at less than 5,000 per annum, shot up in the nineteenth, and fluctuated between 5,000 and 12,500 before the trade began petering out in the late 1870s (Manning, 1990:76-81). Most of the slaves exported from the Tanzanian coast were used on Arab-Swahili plantations along the coast and on European plantations in the Indian Ocean. These plantations produced mainly for the world market. The slaves from the Horn and the Eastern Sudan ended up in North Africa or western Asia. slave trade

Of the major trading networks in Central, Southern and East Africa the only one that was not dependent on slave exports was the Cape. The Cape economy itself relied on slave labour imported largely from Asia. From 1806 the Cape Colony became a British colony, which meant it was affected by the abolition of the slave trade in the British empire in 1807 and of slavery in 1834. For a long time the Cape had little to offer the world market, except provisions to passing ships. Certainly its role was marginal compared to the trading networks of Angola and Zaire, not to mention those of West Africa. By 1807 Cape exports amounted to only £E30,000, of which £E9,000 were re-exports, rising to £E103,000 in 1810, half of which were re-exports. In the next 30 years the exports of Cape products increased by four and half times, while the total value of all exports, including re-exports, grew by over ten and half times. It can be seen that re-exports played a critical role in the international trade of the Cape colony (Ross, 1983:254-5).

The Cape's exports were principally wine, wool, grain, hides and skins, and ivory. As the value of grain exports declined that of ivory increased. By 1840-44, for example, only £E13,000 worth of grain was exported, compared to £E129,000 in 1775-9 (Ross, 1983:257). In the latter period the grain had largely been sent to the Dutch stations in Java and India. The decline in grain exports reflected the growth of the internal market, rather than a fall in production. In contrast, ivory had a limited internal market, so that it was primarily produced for export. South African ivory exports to Britain rose steadily from an average 47.9 cwt per annum in the 1800s to 279.5 cwt in the 1820s and about 1,000 cwt in the 1850s (Johnson, 1983b:122).

Wine products were by far the most important exports in the first four decades of the nineteenth century. Cape wine production and export was boosted by the preferential tariff arrangements it enjoyed within the British empire following the British occupation of the Cape in 1806. The bulk of the wine was exported to Britain, with smaller amounts to Australia. Between 1806 and 1839 the Cape generally exported between 34 and 50% of its total wine production (Ross, 1983:256).

Despite the apparent rapid growth of exports, the Cape suffered from persistent trade deficits. During the period from 1807 to 1855 imports exceeded exports in all but three years. The trade imbalance averaged £E268,500 per annum. Ross (1983:24) believes that 'it was the presence of a large establishment of British troops that allowed the Cape's imports to exceed its exports to such an extent'. The deficit was covered by money transfers to the Cape for the payment and provisioning of the troops. The imports consisted mostly of consumer goods and armaments. The main beneficiaries of this trade were the large Cape Town merchants and the agricultural producers, particularly the wine growers. The Cape export economy was revolutionized from the 1840s when wool assumed pre-eminence. Ross's (1983:258) data shows that wool exports increased from 297,562 kilograms in 1840-4 to 5,450,458 kilograms in 1855, an increase of 115% per annum. Also 'in terms of value wool exports increased by 18 percent per annum over the period 1840-4 to 1855-9' (Ross, 1983:243). Until the discovery of diamonds and gold, wool became the mainstay of the Cape economy. Natal also exported some wool, but its main export was initially ivory before it was overtaken by sugar.

By 1855 the total value of Cape exports was about £E1.1 million. This was less than the total value of the trade at the mouth of the Zaire River. As the Zairean trade in slaves diminished from the 1850s, ivory and palm oil became increasingly dominant. Ivory had been exported from this region since the sixteenth century, but until the 1860s the ivory trade had been eclipsed by the trade in slaves. The volume of ivory exports rose from a ton and a half in 1832 to over 80 tons in 1859. By the 1880s between 150 and 300 tons arrived annually at Malabo Pool from the upper tributaries of the Zaire (Harms, 1981:40). The size of this ivory trade can be gauged from the fact that Zairean ivory accounted for 'a sixth of all the ivory that was marketed in London' (Curtin, et.al., 1978:425). Large quantities of palm oil and palm kernels were also exported. The palm oil trade was dominated by the Dutch 'for whom the Lower Congo represented a source of palm oil supply outside British control' (Munro, 1976:51). We know far less about the Zaire palm oil trade than the palm oil trade of West Africa. In 1870 the Rotterdam firm of Kerdijk and Pincoffs imported 1.6 million guilders worth of palm oil, and smaller quantities of palm kernels, peanuts and coffee (Wesseling, 1981:497). Besides these products increasing quantities of tobacco were also exported.

The composition of imports did not differ markedly from the West African pattern. Vansina (1973:268-9) distinguishes six major categories of imported goods that were traded at the Pool in the 1880s: metals, cloth, beads and shells, crockery, firearms, and miscellaneous items such as sea salt, candles and mirrors. Harms (1981:44) adds alcoholic beverages and observes that 'goods in a single category often came in a variety of styles, reflecting both the diversity of local preferences and the vicissitudes of fashion. The Bobangi, for example, distinguished seventeen types of cloth, but these represented only a fraction of the total number of the designs that entered the Zaire trade'.

The impact of these imports on local production appears to have been minimal for these goods were largely consumed by 'traders, chiefs and lineage heads, so they did not necessarily compete with local substitutes on the local market' (Harms, 1981:46-7). By the early 1880s, 'the annual value of trade at the Congo mouth was about £E3 million sterling, somewhat more than the value of trade at the mouth of the Niger' (Curtin, et.al., 1978:425). As in West Africa this trade facilitated the rise of new groups of merchants, some of whom converted their wealth into political power. Conflicts between the new merchants and the old ruling classes became more open and intense as time went by. However, it cannot be overemphasized that in comparison to West Africa, the way these processes unfolded in Zaire has been little studied.

While ivory and palm oil were the major exports from Zaire from the 1860s, in Angola it was wax and rubber, although the latter also exported some ivory. Ivory exports at Luanda rose from 1.2 tons in 1832 to about 43 tons in 1844. In the next 15 years they rose another 80% at Luanda as well as Benguela. Wax had been exported from Benguela since the seventeenth century. Wax exports at Luanda increased rapidly in the nineteenth century, rising from 165,890 lbs in 1809 to 452,987 lbs in 1817 and 1,698,248 lbs in 1857 (Miller, 1970:178; 1983b:241). The Ovimbundu and Cokwe dominated both the ivory and wax trades because of their favourable geographical location and prowess as hunters. By the late 1850s the two products accounted for more than 80% of the total value of exports from Angola.

The composition of Angolan exports changed dramatically in the last quarter of the nineteenth century. Ivory diminished as elephant herds became depleted, and rubber entered the scene. The export of rubber began in 1869. A decade and a half later its value had surpassed that of wax and ivory combined. Once again, the Chokwe dominated the new trade, and in their search for rubber-producing trees as those nearest the coast became exhausted, they began migrating northwards together with their families since, unlike elephant hunting which was restricted to men, women and children were also seen as efficient tappers of rubber (Miller, 1971:186-94). By the late 1890s the rubber boom had turned Benguela, its main outlet, into the leading exporting port of Angola, eclipsing Luanda.

Overall, Angola's import and export trade through the ports of Luanda, Benguela, Macamedes and Ambriz grew by about three and a half times between 1869 and 1900, or at an annual rate of 7.6%. Luanda accounted for 52% of the total trade conducted during this period, Benguela 32.4%, Ambriz 10.6%, and Macamedes 5.2%. Generally imports outstripped exports, by an average 253 contos a year (Clarence-Smith, 1983:407-10). The leading imports were textiles, alcohol and weapons. According to data collected by Miller (1983:211-227) on Luanda imports between 1785 and 1823, textiles accounted for more than half the imports, alcohol for one-fifth, and weapons only 5%, almost the same as foodstuffs, made up mostly of rice, wheat flour, olive oil, cheeses and vinegar which was mainly destined for the European residents. One quarter of the textile imports were made up of European woollens and linens, and the rest were Asian cottons. Iron ware and other metals accounted for 0.9%, less than the 1.5% for such items as hats, braid and 'red caps'.

Portugal claimed suzerainty over the Angolan coast, but it did not dominate Angola's trade. Miller's (1983:228-9) data on the distribution of imports by area of origin between 1785 and 1823 shows that Portugal supplied between 12.2% and 30.6% of Angola's imports with supplies consisting mostly of wine, foodstuffs and gunpowder. The leading source of Angola's imports was Asia, which accounted for between 24% and 61.6%, mostly cotton textiles. Next came Brazil with a share ranging from 12.9% to 39.7%, consisting largely of rum, tobacco, sugar, rice and re-exports of European goods. Portugal was in third place. In last place were the northern European countries, whose share ranged between 4.8% and 25.1%, composed of woollen and linen piece goods largely from Britain and to a smaller extent France, the low countries and Germany.

Angola was the jewel of the fledgling Portuguese empire in Africa. Data available for the years 1880 to 1900 shows that Portugal's trade through its colonial enclaves in Africa totalled 159,701 contos. Out of this Angola's share was 64.5%, followed by Sao Tome with 23.5%, Cape Verde 5.4%, Mozambique 5.3%, and finally Guinea 1.3%. Collectively the African territories became increasingly important for Portuguese trade, especially after Brazil gained its independence in 1822. In 1824 they accounted for 1% of Portugal's total foreign trade, as compared to 20% for Brazil. By 1861 the African colonial enclaves had raised their share to 6%, while that of Brazil had dropped to 14%. Thirty years later the former had overtaken the latter with 11% to 10%, respectively. By 1899 the African share had risen to 17%, while Brazil's had dropped to 7%. In terms of value, Portugal's trade with its African colonial enclaves rose from 160 contos in 1824, to 2,593 contos in 1861, 9,108 contos in 1891, and 19,154 contos in 1899, which according to the prevailing exchange rate was equivalent to almost £E3 million (Clarence-Smith, 1983:400-3).

As pointed out earlier, the export trade of Mozambique was dominated by slaves until the 1880s. The export of other commodities was limited. By 1874, for instance, Mozambique exported only 81 tons of ivory, up from 29 tons in 1844. Ivory contributed a third of the country's non-slave exports. Another quarter consisted of new items exported only since the 1840s, such as sesame, peanuts and other agricultural products. The expansion of sesame and peanut exports was quite remarkable. Between 1868 and 1874, for example, sesame exports more than doubled from 787,000 litres to 1.9 million litres, and peanut exports jumped from 47 lbs to 5.4 million litres. Rubber, wax, copal and orchila contributed 13% of the total exports in 1874. The exports of orchila rose from 47 tons in 1868 to 77 tons in 1874, and those of wax from eight tons to 55 tons during the same period. But the exports of copra and coir fell from 83 tons to 52 tons and 25 tons to seven tons, respectively. Of the total exports 16% came from hides and skins, mainly in transit from the Transvaal, and 14% consisted of foreign gold and silver (Liesegang, 1983:469-70).

As in Angola, rubber became the leading export product in Mozambique in the last quarter of the nineteenth century. Rubber exports rose from 42 tons in 1874 to 447 tons in 1887, by which time they contributed 32% of the total value of Mozambique's exports. The importance of the oil seeds, peanuts, sesame, and copra, also increased. In 1884 they contributed 52% of the exports from Quelimane. In some years peanuts alone made up 40% of the value of exports from Mozambique island. By 1901 the country as a whole was exporting 7,488 tons of peanuts worth 403 contos. Copra exports peaked in 1891 when 2,119 tons were exported from Quelimane. Small quantities of sugar were exported from the Zambezi beginning in 1893. In that year 600 tons were exported. By 1900 the figure had risen to 3,400 tons. Sugar was on its way to becoming Mozambique's leading export, accounting for 41% of the country's total exports by 1914 (Liesegang, 1983:480-7).

In terms of imports, in 1874 textiles made up 42%, firearms 9%, foreign gold and silver 8%, alcohol 7%, iron hoes 6%, beads 3%, sugar 2%, and the rest consisted of miscellaneous items. Between a quarter and a third of these imports were consumed within the Portuguese settlements themselves and the rest traded in the interior. The composition of imports changed quite significantly in the last quarter of the century as reflected in the imports into Maputo. Maputo became a leading trading centre in the country, superseding the old capital on the island of Mozambique, as well as Quelimane. This was a product, in part, of the construction of the harbour and railway system aimed at servicing the rapidly expanding South African economy. The rail line between Maputo and Johannesburg was completed in 1894. Maputo became the source of more than half of government revenue, derived mostly from import duties. According to the list of imports into Maputo in 1897 the leading item was foodstuffs taking 16.5% of the total, followed by iron goods with 15%, wine 13%, textiles 11%, Portuguese specie 8%, wood 7%, machines 3%, coal 2%, and so on. For the country as a whole between 1897 and 1900 imports exceeded exports by 3.5:1 (Liesegang, 1983:507-8).

The international trade of Madagascar, located across the Mozambique channel, also grew quite substantially in the course of the nineteenth century. It was centred around the port of Toamasina, which was fully incorporated into the expanding Merina state in the 1820s. According to Campbell (1983:528), 'during the first half of the nineteenth century, foreign trade was restricted by the mercantilist policies of the Merina Court which limited commerce by a series of monopolies involving the Crown and a handful of foreign merchants'. The adoption of more liberal economic policies in the 1860s following the death of the conservative-minded queen, Ranavalona I, led to the rapid expansion of Madagascar's international trade. The leading foreign traders were British, French and American.

Madagascar exported a wide variety of commodities, including rubber, bullocks, hides, raffia, rice, coffee, tobacco, wax and gum. The value of these commodities fluctuated quite considerably. For example, in the period 1885-88 the value of rubber and hides, the leading exports, averaged $300,000 and $437,500, respectively. By 1890 they had fallen to $202,268 and $117,693, respectively. American merchants dominated the trade in rubber and hides, while British traders were prominent in the export of bullocks, rice, raffia, coffee and tobacco. As for imports, cotton goods claimed supremacy, followed by a wide assortment of items such as alcohol, hardware, crockery, glass, furniture and petroleum. Between the mid-1860s and mid-1880s, the bulk of the cotton goods, sometimes up to four-fifths, came from the United States, and the remainder from Britain, and to a very small extent France.

Altogether, between 1864-5 and 1890 the total value of exports and imports through Toamasina grew by one and a half times, from $844,603 to $1,295,002. In most years the value of imports outstripped exports by two to one (Campbell, 1983:541-52). Behind this expansion lay fluctuations and growing trade rivalries. Generally the 1860s and early 1870s were years of economic growth. For the rest of the 1870s there was sustained economic stagnation, thanks in large measure to the world recession. The stagnation fuelled competition among the importers, and between them and the Merina government. 'It was largely due to the intense rivalry in this trade that most foreign firms established agencies in Antanarivo as well as Toamasina in the 1870s' (Campbell, 1983:532). As in West Africa, this rivalry culminated in colonization.

By the beginning of the nineteenth century the East African coast 'remained largely outside the capitalist world economy' (Wallerstein, 1976:36). For centuries its primary external links had been with the countries of western and south-western Asia (Chittick, 1974; Ochieng', 1976; Chaudhuri, 1989; Freeman-Grenville, 1988). This continued to be the case for the greater part of the nineteenth century. The most important exports from East Africa to Asia, especially India, were ivory and cloves. Bombay served as the main trading centre of East African imports. Ivory was used to make bangles, which were regarded as indispensable bridal ornaments for women. The value of East African ivory exports to Bombay averaged 256,000 rupees in the 1800s, 189,000 rupees in the 1810s, 216,000 rupees in the 1820s, 292,000 rupees in the 1830s, 544,000 rupees in the 1840s, 846,000 rupees in the 1850s, 780,000 rupees in the 1860s, 872,000 rupees in the 1870s, 1,149,000 rupees in the 1880s, and 774,000 rupees in the 1890s (Sheriff, 1983:423-6). The value of Bombay clove imports from East Africa rose from 4,000 rupees in 1803 to 27,000 rupees in 1827/8, 291,000 rupees in 1846/7, and 780,000 rupees in 1863/4 (Sheriff, 1983:444-9). Altogether, between 1801 and 1870 Bombay imported goods worth 65.6 million rupees from East Africa, of which about 71% was ivory, 20% cloves, and 6% copal, while the value of its exports was 44.6 million rupees, out of which cotton goods accounted for 63% (Sheriff, 1987:249-52).

Trade with Asia brought East Africa into the orbit of the expanding world capitalist economy, for the Asian markets 'were now themselves being incorporated into the capitalist world-economy' (Wallerstein, 1989:33). In fact, the rise in Indian demand for East African ivory in the course of the nineteenth century was not prompted by the need to satisfy local needs, which remained stagnant, but for re-export to London. Thus India increasingly assumed 'the role of an intermediary in the ivory trade between East Africa and London' (Sheriff, 1983:422). From the 1820s Bombay normally re-exported between a third and four-fifths of its total ivory imports to the United Kingdom (Sheriff, 1983:423-6). Out of the 46.3 million rupees of ivory imported from East Africa between 1801 and 1870, 75.4% was re-exported to London (Sheriff, 1987:249-52).

From the 1820s direct trade between East Africa, Europe and the United States began to expand as well. It was centred on ivory. East Africa produced 'soft' ivory, unlike West Africa which produced the 'hard' variety. Demand for 'soft' ivory increased as new uses were found, such as the manufacture of combs, piano keys and billiard balls. Re-exports of East African ivory from Bombay failed to satisfy the demand, and so from the 1830s British and American merchants involved in the Indian trade entered the East African ivory market. Before long, the Europeans and Americans appointed resident agents in Zanzibar, the leading commercial and political centre along the coast, in order to consolidate their respective commercial positions in the region. By 1859 the United States was the leading trading partner of Zanzibar, followed by India. Together the two countries accounted for nearly two-thirds of the total imports and exports of Zanzibar (Sheriff, 1987:128-9). Next came France and Germany, who between them took 30% of Zanzibar's total trade. Britain's share was less than 1% (Sheriff, 1987:135).

France and Germany dominated trade in the new commodities, such as coconuts, sesame and orchilla weed, which was used in the dyeing process. For example:

> *export of coconut products to France rose from Maria Theresa dollars 96,000 (MT$) in 1859 to about MT$169,000 annually during the early 1860s. Large quantities of sesame began to be produced along the northern coast of Kenya for export, rising from about MT$100,000 in 1859 to an annual average of MT$150,000 in the 1860s. More than half of this went to France and about a third to Germany* (Sheriff, 1987:134).

German firms also controlled the short-lived lucrative trade in cowrie exports from East to West Africa in the 1850s where cowries were in short supply. In 1859 the value of East African cowrie exports reached MT$244,000. But the boom quickly petered out. In the 1860s cowrie exports were worth only an average MT$60,000.

The American presence declined sharply following the outbreak of the American Civil War. By 1864-5 the American share of Zanzibar's external trade had declined to 8% from 24% in 1859. India shot to first place with

40%. The respective shares of Germany, France, and Britain rose to 14%, 12%, and 7% (Sheriff, 1987:135). The latter became an important market for East African ivory. By the 1880s Britain was importing an average 82 tons of ivory from East Africa, up from 29 tons in the 1860s and eight tons in the 1930s. This rose to 109 tons in the 1890s, by which time East Africa had become the leading exporter of ivory to Britain, eclipsing both West Africa and India (Sheriff, 1983:428-32).

Terms of trade remained generally favourable for East Africa in the first three quarters of the nineteenth century. Ivory prices maintained an upward spiral in all the major ivory markets because demand outstripped supply. For example, 'at Zanzibar the price rose from $22 per frasila (35 lb.) in 1823 to $89 in 1873, a threefold increase within half a century, or an average increase of about 6% p.a.' (Sheriff, 1983:433). Similarly, 'the price of gum copal rose from MT$3 in 1823 to MT$8 in 1853' (Sheriff, 1987:102). In the meantime, the price of the chief import, cotton goods, declined. For example, the price of American unbleached cotton sheeting, known as merikani, fell from MT$3 in 1827-8 to MT$1.95 in 1852-3. The price remained below three dollars until the early 1870s (Sheriff, 1987:253-6).

The favourable terms of trade made East African commerce very profitable. This, in turn, attracted more foreign merchants to East Africa, facilitated the growth of the local merchant class, and stimulated the expansion of the ivory frontier and the extension of Zanzibar's commercial network deep into the East African interior. Competition among the Europeans grew and each group sought to sign what Sheriff (1987:127) calls 'most favoured-nation' commercial treaties with the Zanzibari state. These treaties suppressed export duties and reduced import duties to 5%, except specie, which entered duty free. What the state lost in customs duties on external trade it more than made up in internal customs revenue.

The local merchant class was heterogeneous, consisting of the ruling dynasty, including the Sultan himself, Seyyid Said, the local Arabs and Swahili, and the Indians. The latter became dominant, despite the fact that many of them had come to East Africa as poor migrants. Their rise to a position of commercial preeminence has been attributed to their parsimony and links to both India and the foreign merchants. The richest among them included men like Jairam Sewji, whose firm had assets of MT$5.5 million by 1846. These merchants financed much of the caravan trade into the East African interior and many of the coastal plantations. In addition, they became important money lenders to the Sultan as well as some European merchants.

As trade expanded the sources of supply for ivory, copal and other commodities extended deeper into the East African hinterland. By the 1870s the ivory frontier had reached as far as eastern Zaire. Sheriff (1987:155-200) has divided the commercial hinterland of Zanzibar into three sectors. The core was the hinterland behind the Mrima coast, which during 1848 and 1874 supplied between 40% and 82% of Zanzibar's ivory, and 42% and 96% of the gum copal. Altogether, by the early 1870s this region provided 57% of Zanzibar's total imports. The ivory and copal trade of Mrima was a state monopoly.

Next in importance was the southern hinterland, extending from Kilwa to Tungi near Cape Delgado, which enjoyed varying degrees of political and economic independence from Zanzibar. It accounted for 21% of Zanzibar's imports by 1874. The share of the northern hinterland extending from Mombasa and Lamu to Benadir, a region that developed its own independent trading links with the interior and the outside world, especially Arabia and India, was 15%.

The Mombasa commercial network encompassed the coastal Mijikenda people of modern Kenya and the Kamba in the interior, whose trade activities were examined in Chapter 11. Mombasa ivory exports peaked in the late 1840s. In 1849, for example, an estimated 2,500-3,000 frasilas of ivory were exported. This dropped to 1,250 frasilas in 1872 and 500 frasilas in 1887 (Sheriff, 1987:171). A remarkable feature of Mombasa's export trade from the mid-nineteenth century was the growing importance of food exports, principally to Arabia. In 1884, for example, Mombasa exported 336,000 frasilas of millet, maize, beans, sesame and copra, and 100,000 coconuts, all of which was worth MT$95,500, as compared to the MT$92,150 for non-agricultural items, such as ivory (Cooper, 1977:101). The agricultural exports of Malindi were even larger. For example, in 1884 alone 500,000 frasilas of millet, 120,000 frasilas of sesame and 120,000 frasilas of beans were exported. Three years later the volumes for sesame and beans had risen to 250,000 and 200,000 frasilas, respectively. In terms of value Malindi's exports were worth MT$275,000 in 1884 and MT$381,800 in 1887 (Cooper, 1977:85). At the turn of the century Mombasa was poised to become the chief commercial centre of East Africa, eclipsing Zanzibar, thanks to the construction of the Kenya-Uganda Railway, the locomotive of East African colonization (Janmohamed, 1983).

Ethiopia's trade with the international economy expanded throughout much of the nineteenth century, although there were considerable fluctuations due to external and internal wars. A large proportion of the country's trade was handled through the port of Massawa, which was under foreign control, first by the Turks, followed by the Egyptians from 1868 to 1884, and after 1885 by the Italians. Trade in Massawa was dominated by Indian merchants 'who were supported by merchant houses in Aden and Bombay' (Pankhurst, 1968:359). Available estimates indicate that in the first two-thirds of the century trade remained fairly constant. The total value of Massawa's exports and imports averaged over MT$500,000. Rapid expansion followed in the last quarter of the century. For example, in 1879 the total value of Massawa's foreign trade reached MT$2.1 million, of which 60% were exports. By 1900 the figure had risen to MT$4.3 million. In that year the ports of Eritrea as a whole exported and imported goods worth MT$12.1 million (Pankhurst, 1968:361-2). In addition to Massawa, Ethiopia's international trade was conducted through other cities and ports such as Addis Ababa and Harar, Zeila and Berbera. Estimates for 1899-1900 show that Addis Ababa handled exports and imports valued at MT$1.6 million and MT$3 million, respectively. The equivalent figures for Harar were MT$2.7 million and MT$3.8 million. Zeila's and Berbera's import and export trade added about a couple million dollars more (Pankhurst, 1968:396-426).

In the first half of the nineteenth century Ethiopia's leading exports were slaves, gold, ivory, civet, butter, pearls, cereals, wax, hides and skins, mules, coffee, and gum, in that order. In the second half of the century the export of slaves was greatly reduced. By the turn of the 1880s the leading exports were, excluding gold, hides and skins, butter, ivory, civet, pearls, coffee, honey and wax. These exports went mostly to Arabia and southern Europe, and to a smaller extent, western Europe and India. As for imports, the leading items were textiles, followed by metals, luxury goods, from mirrors to spices and perfumes, other manufactured goods such as cutlery and tools, and finally, weapons and munitions of war. While there was hardly any change in the composition of imports, there were some changes in their place of origin. At the beginning of the century Ethiopia's imports mainly came from India, England, Italy, and Turkey. By the end of the century India's position was being challenged by Italy, followed by Britain, Turkey, Austria-Hungary, France, the United States and Russia (Pankhurst, 1968:371-88).

In contrast to the countries considered above, Sudan's international trade seems to have declined in the last quarter of the nineteenth century. Sudan's direct trade with Europe had been increasing steadily since from the 1840s following the abolition of the state monopolies. The size of the European merchant community in the country grew and steamers were introduced on the Nile, all of which encouraged exports. 'By 1879 annual exports from Suakin had a declared value of £E254,000, and in 1880 some 758 vessels were said to have called. A large part of that trade was in gum: in 1881 Britain alone imported some 3,620 tons, valued at £E180,084' (Daly, 1988:193). The ivory trade also expanded, and with it the trade in slaves, for slaves were used as hunters and porters. Sudan's ivory was in great demand because of its high quality: 'it was soft, opaque, easily worked and climate resistant'

(Beshai, 1976:25). As elsewhere in Eastern Africa as demand for ivory increased, its availability became more scarce, and the ivory frontier was extended to encompass regions previously untouched.

In return, the Sudan imported manufactured products, principally cotton textiles. In 1879, for example, 24,784 pieces of clothing were imported, together with 8,578 tons of cotton goods, 67 tons of sewing cottons, 19 tons of shoes, 589 tons of sandalwood and 205 tons of soap (Nakash, 1988:57).

The establishment of the Madhist state in 1881 severely disrupted Sudan's international trade. Several factors accounted for this. In 1885-86 Suakin, the Sudan's major coastal town, was under siege. Then from early 1887 to early 1889 the Sudan was at war with Ethiopia, which hampered trade between Kassala and Massawa. And in August 1889 war broke out with Egypt which blocked the northern routes from Berber and Dongola to Wadi Halfa and Aswan. For their part, the British authorities in Egypt prohibited trade with the Sudan in an effort to prevent the smuggling of arms and ammunition into the Sudan. The new government itself was antagonistic to trade with 'unbelievers' and was unwelcoming to foreigners. It also occasionally levied high taxes on imported goods (Nakash, 1988:62-3).

Gum exports fell sharply during the Mahdiyya, from an estimated 7,543 tons in 1881 to 1,146 tons in 1885, and a mere 7 tons in 1890, and 160 tons in 1895 (Daly, 1988.217). Trade began to recover from 1890 following the relaxation of the wars, and a change in government policy towards foreign trade prompted in part by the famine of 1889. Between 1892 and 1898 goods worth £E875,320 were exported from and imported into the Sudan via Suakin and Aswan, of which 55% constituted exports and 45% imports (Nakash, 1988:66). In 1898 the Madhist state fell to Anglo-Egyptian forces and a new colonial government, the so-called Anglo-Egyptian Condominium, was imposed. The recovery in the export trade accelerated. By 1901 gum exports had 'regained pre-Madhiyya levels (7,695 tons). Gum rapidly became the country's chief export, and remained so, with few annual exceptions, until overtaken by cotton in the late 1920s' (Daly, 1988:216).

Central Africa and Speculative Capital

As noted above, Central Africa's commodities were not as badly affected by the slump of the late nineteenth century as the commodities from West Africa. Thus, unlike the latter region, trade rivalries between European and African merchants were not as critical in fomenting pressures for colonization as were inter-European rivalries. Also, contrary to the situation in West and North Africa, it was not the colonial super-powers, Britain and France, who eventually held sway, but the weaker nations, Portugal and Belgium, the latter through the machinations of its ambitious monarch, Leopold II

(Vail, 1976; Martin, 1983). This was to have a profound impact on the subsequent patterns of colonial capitalist construction in the region.

Portuguese claims over Angola were centuries old, although the Portuguese presence on the ground was confined to a tiny coastal enclave. Many scholars, both on the right and left of the historiographical spectrum have viewed Portuguese imperialism as peculiar because, it is said, Portugal was itself backward and underdeveloped. The thesis first formulated by Hammond (1961, 1966) has been echoed, reformulated and restated in the works of writers as diverse as Anderson (1962) who found Portuguese colonialism so peculiar that he thought it constituted a separate genre, that of 'ultra-colonialism'. For some scholars, the Portuguese case provides a refutation of all Marxist theories of imperialism, while for others it is an exception that proves the Marxist rule on imperialism.

The works of Clarence-Smith (1979a, 1979b, 1983, 1985), Vail and White (1980), Vail (1983) and Seleti (1990) have done much to debunk the thesis and to show that Portuguese colonialism was no less a product of economic forces than the colonialisms of the other European powers. The Portuguese bourgeoisie was, indeed, in the words of Clarence-Smith (1979a:173), 'the most economically motivated of all European bourgeoisies during the «Scramble for Africa»... Whereas colonies could be considered an ideological and political luxury for the rich bourgeoisies, they were seen as a matter of life and death by their Portuguese poor relations. As a weak and insecure class, the Portuguese bourgeoisie was more in need of protectionism than any of its counterparts'.

These arguments are persuasive. But the fact still remains that the Portuguese bourgeoisie not only invested little in its putative colonies, such as Angola, they did not even dominate their trade. To be sure, Angola was the jewel of the Portuguese empire in Africa, accounting for two-thirds of its African trade in the 1880s and nearly 8% of its total foreign trade. Notwithstanding this, it needs to be pointed out that the expansion and consolidation of the Portuguese empire in Angola, and especially Mozambique, was facilitated less by the 'effective occupation' of Portuguese capital, than the speculative exploits of foreign capital. It is not enough to say, as Clarence-Smith (1979a:173) does, that the compradors among the Portuguese bourgeoisie facilitated the penetration of foreign capital into the Portuguese empire because they 'were only interested in asserting Portuguese sovereignty over as large an area of Africa as much as possible in order to maximize their role as intermediaries'. This is a convoluted way of saying Portuguese capital was weak. Accepting this fact does not mean economic motives were peripheral to Portuguese colonization or that Portuguese colonialism was 'peculiar'. Far from it. It only serves to explain the process by which the empire was established and the form it took.

The loss of the Zairean basin to Leopold II of Belgium in the early 1880s, and subsequently of the swathe of territory lying between Angola and Mozambique to British interests, out of which were forged Zambia, Zimbabwe and Malawi, frustrated Portuguese hopes of creating a 'New Brazil' and threatened to rob Portugal of its colonial claims in Angola and Mozambique. After the Berlin Conference it became imperative to demonstrate 'effective occupation' before one's imperial claims could be accepted and respected by the other colonial powers. This came home dramatically to Portugal in 1890 when Britain issued an ultimatum demanding Portuguese withdrawal from the lower Tchiri valley of present-day Malawi, as well as from parts of present-day Zimbabwe, 'on pain of a break in diplomatic relations' (Vail and White, 1980:106).

The ultimatum threw Portugal into turmoil. The country felt humiliated. The government was swept away, the monarchy lost some of its clout for accepting the ultimatum, while the political stock of the young and untried Republican leaders rose. Matters were exacerbated by the fact that the economy was in a perilous condition. It was the economic crisis, in fact, which prevented Portugal from mounting an effective response to the British diktat, while at the same time reinforcing the need for empire. The Portuguese firmly believed that colonies paid, if not immediately, then in the longer run.

Portugal was faced with a dilemma. Its need for colonies had never been greater, but its capacity to acquire them had never been weaker, for unlike before, now there were other richer and more powerful countries swimming in the same pond of empire building. The solution was to grant concessions to foreign-owned chartered companies. With this, Portugal hoped to kill two birds with one stone. First, these companies would encourage investment and stimulate economic growth in the colonies which would be of great benefit to Portugal itself. Second, the companies would secure effective occupation for Portugal, for not only would their operation depend on accepting Portuguese sovereignty, but their charters would require them to set up administrative systems and provide the transport and communication infrastructure in the areas under their control. In return, the companies would make their profits by taxing the inhabitants in their areas, control their trade in peasant-grown produce, and establish plantations for which the state would ensure regular and adequate labour supply.

Mozambique was the haven of the concession companies. This was because it was in this region that Portugal faced its greatest challenge, the forces of British imperialism personified in Cecil Rhodes, the English mining magnate and imperialist. In 1891 and 1892 Portugal gave charters to a number of concession companies which were controlled by British, South African, and German capital to administer Mozambique. Britain recognized Portuguese claims in Angola when the French frantically began signing treaties in the Congo, for Portugal was regarded as a friendly power and easier to manipulate. But when the Germans in Namibia began threatening Portuguese interests in Southern Angola, Portugal turned to France and granted a vast concession to a French company. During the partition alliances shifted with the ease of sand in the desert.

Like the Portuguese colonial empire, Leopold's vast colonial estate in Zaire was the creation of speculative capitalist enterprise. The commercial vitality of the 'Great Congo' commerce, which was in volume and value only second to that of the Niger Delta, whetted the appetite of Leopold II, an unabashed imperialist, who fervently believed that colonies would bring profit and glory to small Belgium (Stengers, 1972:259-265). Leopold was an interloper in Zaire, for Belgium hardly had a foothold in the region's trade. Dutch merchants had the largest sales volume of Zairean trade, while Britain had the greatest economic interests in the region, and Portugal the loudest colonial pretensions. In the late 1870s, Portugal tried unsuccessfully to get Britain's agreement over their respective areas of economic interest in the Zaire basin but the agreement floundered because of opposition from the other European powers as well as from within Portugal and Britain. The Portuguese government was widely seen as corrupt and protectionist. Therefore, the other European nations, especially the Netherlands, France and Britain itself, were intent on resisting Portuguese claims in order to protect the interests of their merchants. Meanwhile, France began claiming parts of the region on the strength of treaties made by the explorer, Brazza.

Into this turmoil stepped Leopold. As a constitutional monarch he found it difficult to impose his imperial ambitions on a sceptical Belgian government so he resorted to the formation of a private organization, the International African Association, which, he maintained, was geared to scientific research and philanthropy. His real motivation soon became clear, for when Britain, France, Portugal and the Netherlands 'began to quarrel about their claims to the mouth of the Congo, Leopold suggested that it be given to his organization, so that the river would be neutral. He promised that he would impose low duties on exports from the area and thus satisfy the traders of all nations' (Gavin, 1986:333).

Germany supported the idea, more to thwart the ambitions of its rival powers than to accede to the King's ambitions. The crisis over Zaire threatened to get out of hand. Bismarck, the shrewd German chancellor, invited representatives of 14 European governments and the United States to come to Berlin to discuss, first, freedom of trade in the region of the Congo river; second, freedom of navigation on the Congo and Niger rivers; and third, the establishment of regulations concerning the further expansion of territory along the African coasts by European powers. It can be seen that rivalry over the Zaire commerce was central to the convening of the Berlin Conference and the conduct of its deliberations. In fact, the question of the Niger was quickly settled for Britain insisted that the region fell exclusively within its sphere of influence and no one raised any serious objections. Thus the Berlin Conference, contrary to conventional wisdom, was not called to 'partition Africa', but to regulate relations between the major European powers over the trade of the Zaire basin.

While nobody opposed the principle of a free trade zone in the Zaire basin, there was considerable dispute over what 'free trade' in this case actually implied. It was agreed that the zone should be as large as possible. But the Dutch feared for the extension of the principle to the Netherlands Indies (Wesseling, 1981:502-7). The French and Portuguese opposed an American plan proposing the neutrality of the Zaire basin. And everybody opposed a British plan to have a general embargo declared on slave traffic, for they felt that was extending the scope of the conference beyond its original agenda. In the end they settled for the recognition of Leopold's nominal suzerainty over the Zaire basin as the lesser of all evils.

The faith displayed at the Berlin Conference in free trade and Leopold's intentions and promises may appear naive and misplaced in hindsight. But it in fact reflected two entirely different realities at the time. First, Britain and the Netherlands, the leading trading powers in the Zaire basin, believed that their economic interests would be better served by the establishment of a free trade regime rather than by the formation of a costly colonial empire, which was bound to be resisted by the other European powers. Coupled with this was the fact that neither Britain nor the Netherlands had the political will to carve an empire in the region at this time. The Netherlands, which was then the second largest colonial power in the world was, to use Wesseling's (1981:508) phrase, a 'saturated power' as far as the colonies were concerned. Britain, the colonial super-power, was, on the other hand, too embroiled in other far more significant regions, namely the Niger basin and Egypt, to move decisively in the Zaire basin.

Seen in this way, Leopold II offered British and Dutch merchants the freedom of action they wanted, and their governments were saved the costs of colonial conquest and administration. Leopold of course was destined to frustrate the British and Dutch faith in the spoils of 'informal empire', as he consolidated his grip on the territory and established one of the most brutal and exploitative regimes in colonial Africa, equalled only by the Portuguese.

In both cases what had started as speculative ventures, thanks to the economic and political weaknesses of the aspiring imperialists, matured into ruthless neo-mercantilist enterprises.

Southern Africa and the Randlords

The construction and incorporation of South Africa into the world capitalist system has been at the centre of the debates about the 'new imperialism'. In fact, Hobson (1965, 1969), the English liberal economist, who coined the term, was greatly influenced by the South African experience in his writings on the 'new imperialism'. To many Marxists and neo-Marxist scholars, the development of a monopolistic structure in the South African mining industry, and the pivotal role that the industry played in the country's political economy in the last quarter of the nineteenth century, confirms the Leninist thesis that imperialism was identifiable with monopoly capitalism (Lenin, 1978; Marks and Atmore, 1974; Innes, 1984).

South Africa has also attracted scholars anxious to rebut the theories of Hobson, Lenin and their followers. The South African case constitutes the second leg of Robinson and Gallagher's (1974) thesis that local crises, in this case Boer nationalism, threatened Britain's sea-route to India, and therefore forced imperial intervention, which subsequently triggered the partition of the subcontinent. This thesis has been restated and reformulated by a number of historians. Newitt (1984:35) contends that local political crises 'continually forced European and colonial authorities to make decisions and to adopt, often reluctantly, a «trouble-shooting» or «crisis management» role'. Schreuder (1980) argues that 'the politics of the periphery were crucial in shaping the partition' and concludes that South Africa offers a 'revealing narrative of how the New Imperialism worked in actuality: not so much the consequence of a «stage of capitalism» as of historical development arising out of the state of the overseas periphery' (Schreuder, 1980:3, 317-8). In Schreuder's account the South Africa War of 1899-1902 is nothing more than a local skirmish by competitive local states. To Porter (1980) it was the product of misguided 'public opinion' in England, which was created by, and later entrapped, Milner the Cape governor and Chamberlain the Colonial Secretary. O'Brien (1979) simply blames the war and British intervention in South Africa on Milner, who we are told, had little interest in economic matters.

Blaming such tumultuous events as the construction of South Africa and the South African War on individuals is simply bad history. Attributing it to 'public opinion' merely scratches the surface and does not get to the substance of the matter. And divorcing the 'local events' from their 'global context' is too contrived. Like Robinson and Gallagher, whose periodization for the partition 'South of the Sahara' tends to ignore imperial interventions in West Africa before the Egyptian occupation in 1882, Schreuder's periodization of 1877-1895, disregards the British occupation of Griqualand West in 1871, and the various confederation schemes hatched in the 1870s, all of which were largely inspired by the discovery of diamonds. By stopping in 1895 he avoids examining the role of monopoly mining capital in generating the South African War and facilitating the eventual unification of the country.

The attempt by Kubicek (1979) to argue that the mining magnates were not responsible for the war, indeed that they opposed it, is based almost entirely on the correspondence of one Randlord. Readings of the correspondence of other Randlords demonstrates quite convincingly that not only was the relationship between the Randlords and the state close, despite periodic conflicts of interest, but also the fact that the Randlords, in spite of important differences among them, shared a number of overriding interests. Above all, they wanted to reduce their production costs. Consequently, they demanded concessions from Kruger's government in the Transvaal, which the latter was not prepared to give. Moreover, they also wanted the supply of regular, abundant and cheap African labour. The first fostered conflict with the Transvaal, which culminated in the South African War, and the second encouraged the conquest of the remaining independent African states (Simons and Simons, 1969; Duminy and Guest, 1976; Fraser and Jeeves, 1977; Pakenham, 1979; Noer, 1979; Marks, 1982; Innes, 1984; Wheatcroft, 1985).

As was demonstrated above, before the mineral revolution, South Africa's trade with Europe could hardly match that of either West or Central Africa, let alone North Africa. The Boer Republics were especially impoverished. As late as 'April 1877, the cash in the Transvaal Treasury amounted to twelve shillings and sixpence' (Keppel-Jones, 1975:96). A decade later, following the discovery of gold, the sudden transformation of the Transvaal into the industrial heartland of South Africa began. The economic balance of power among the settler colonies was profoundly altered. Rivalry and conflict between the English and Boer colonies intensified.

Diamonds were first discovered in 1867. The discoveries were located in the Griqualand, then ruled by the Griquas. Immediately conflicting claims arose over the area between the Cape Colony, the Orange Free State and the South African Republic, as the Transvaal was then known. In 1871 the Cape annexed the diamond fields and nine years later incorporated the whole of Griqualand into the Cape Colony. The discovery of gold in the poor but fiercely independent Transvaal fuelled the dreams of Cape and British imperialists for confederation of the settler colonies. Mining capital and settler immigrants flocked to the Rand. Kruger's government treated the uitlanders, as the English and other foreigners were called, with suspicion. Conflict developed between the Boers and the uitlanders over the government's policies concerning dynamite monopolies, high and discriminatory taxation, lack of state support for English-medium schools, strict citizenship and franchise laws, and other matters.

In the mid-1890s the mining companies, distressed about high working costs and market fluctuations, colluded with the uitlanders and the Cape government, then ruled by Rhodes, the leading mining magnate, to overthrow the Transvaal government. The Jameson Raid was launched from Rhodes' colony of Southern Rhodesia between December 1895 and January 1896. The uitlander uprising that the plotters had hoped to ignite did not occur.

The Raid resulted in disaster. Relations between the British colonies and the Boer Republics worsened. The British imperial government adopted an increasingly belligerent line against the republics, demanding that the uitlanders be granted political rights. Kruger refused and demanded the removal of British troops on the border. Both sides began preparing for war. It broke out in October 1899 and lasted two and half years. Britain mobilized 448,000 troops from Britain itself, the Cape and the empire, and the Boers mobilized a fifth of that. In the aftermath of the war the Union of South Africa was formed (Holt, 1958; Thompson, 1960; Marais, 1961; Le May, 1965; Pakenham, 1966; Goodfellow, 1967; Davenport, 1978).

The mineral revolution not only gave the fractious settler colonies more than ample reason to fight and unify, but also provided them 'with the money, the technology, and the resources required to conquer the African states; and it transformed many African societies from independence and self-sufficiency into a rural reservoir of industrial labour' (Denoon and Nyeko, 1982:76). Thus the remaining independent African states, such as the Zulu, were finally conquered and incorporated into South Africa's emerging racial capitalism. The destruction of African power was not only seen as a prerequisite for the unification of South Africa under the hegemony of mining capital, but it also provided the settlers with large resources of cheap labour with which to exploit the newly discovered minerals. As demonstrated in Chapter 8, the mining industry played a major role in the development of all the critical structures of the settler state and economy, from the African loss of land and political rights, to the institutionalization of migrant labour.

The mineral revolution firmly integrated South Africa into the world capitalist system. The country attracted the bulk of foreign investment in Africa. Of the £E1.2 billion invested in sub-Saharan Africa between 1870 and 1936, about 43% went to South Africa (Lanning with Mueller, 1979:72).

The South African mining industry, as shown in Chapter 8, spawned some of the continent's largest companies and some of the world's monopolies, including Rhodes' De Beers, which by 1890 had achieved control of the world diamond trade, and Anglo-American, the South African-owned mining giant formed by Ernest Oppenheimer at the beginning of the twentieth century. South Africa became a major supplier of mineral products to the world economy, especially gold, a money commodity, which was then indispensable for the liquidity of the world economy.

South Africa also became a sub-imperial metropole in the Southern African region. Its capital, especially mining capital, penetrated the subcontinent, and extended its tentacles to the mining, infrastructural and industrial enterprises of the countries in the region, from Zimbabwe to Zambia, Namibia to Angola, Mozambique to Malawi, not to mention the 'hostage' states of Lesotho, Swaziland, and Botswana. Many of these countries became labour reservoirs for South Africa. Indeed, capital generated from the South African mining industry played a direct role in the colonization of some of these countries, especially Zimbabwe, Zambia, and to a lesser extent, Malawi. This was done through the auspices of the British South African Company.

The BSA Company was formed by Cecil Rhodes and granted a Royal Charter in October 1889. Rhodes sought to use it as an instrument for his colonization of the lands north of the Limpopo, where he expected to find a new Rand. The company did not plan to be involved in actual mining, but to provide an administrative and transport infrastructure. It also hoped to make profits through shareholding in mining companies. In June 1890 the so-called 'pioneer column' of about 200 settlers, escorted by 500 police was despatched. A speculative boom ensued, accompanied by the dispossession of some of the indigenous people of their land and livestock, especially following the War of 1893 and the Rebellions of 1896-7. By 1900 the 'Second Rand' had failed to materialize and the speculative bubble had burst. But a modest mining industry had been established, settler farming had started, and both peasant commodity production for the new colonial markets and wage employment on the mines and settler farms were expanding. In short, the structures of settler colonialism and the new bases of struggle between Africans and the settlers had been laid (Ranger, 1967; Palmer, 1977; Phimister, 1988).

Colonial pressures in Zambia and Malawi antedated the formation of the BSA Company. But the latter turned the inchoate imperial ambitions of missionaries and traders into the iron grip of colonial rule. At the same time that the 'pioneer column' was edging its way to Zimbabwe, envoys from Rhodes were making treaties with Lewanika, the Barotse king, in western

Zambia. The British government recognized the BSA Company's 'protectorate' over Barotseland in 1891. The rest of the country was conquered by 1899 (Roberts, 1968, 1976; Indakwa, 1977). The BSA Company was excluded from Malawi through the combined opposition of traders, missionaries and planters already established in the country. However, the company subsidized the new colonial administration set up in 1891, and the British government appointed one of Rhodes' proteges as its commissioner (McCracken, 1968; Pachai, 1973; Indakwa, 1977).

Eastern Africa: Delayed Incorporation

Eastern Africa was the last region in Africa to be partitioned by the European powers. This is because 'its primary links had been across the Indian Ocean' (Wallerstein, 1989:33). In this region Britain squared off with the new nations of Germany and Italy, rather than its traditional imperial rival, France. Although Britain established a consular presence on the island of Zanzibar as early as 1840, it was not until the 1870s that British imperialist ambitions became marked. From 1873 Britain launched 'anti-slave trade campaigns as a means of establishing British economic and political hegemony in the area' (Wolff, 1974:333). The anti-slave trade crusade not only provided an ideological cover for Britain's imperialist offensive, but the suppression of the slave trade seriously weakened the economic base of the ruling Omani sultanate, both of which facilitated British colonization (Cooper, 1977:122-49). By the early 1890s Britain had declared itself a 'protecting power' over Zanzibar (Flint, 1965:641-6).

In the meantime, Germany had already established its colonial hold over the mainland. Germany was not only a new colonial power, but also a new nation-state, having been formed in 1871. The reasons for German interest in colonization have been widely debated. Some have argued that a reluctant Bismarck was goaded into imperialism by public opinion, or by the diplomatic objective of winning French friendship by adopting an anti-British policy. As Henderson (1965:125) stated some time ago, 'none of these explanations is very convincing... Germany was rapidly becoming a highly industrialized state, and it seemed prudent to secure territories which might in future provide her with additional raw materials and new markets for manufactured goods'. Germany had to act fast because the opportunities of acquiring a colonial empire were rapidly disappearing. By April 1883, Illife (1979:89) states, Bismarck 'began to suspect that Britain and France were conspiring to discriminate against German trade in West Africa.'

Thus unification and industrialization laid the basis for Germany's drive to acquire a colonial empire, to establish its 'place in the sun' (Turner, 1967). Imperialism provided, Wehler (1972:84-85) has argued, an outlet for the social crises generated by Germany's transformation into an industrial society, and became 'an integrative force in a recently founded state which lacked stabilizing historical traditions and which was unable to conceal its sharp class divisions'. At first the German government hoped to establish its colonial empire in Africa, including East Africa, through a chartered company. As was shown in the last chapter, the German trading firms in the Cameroon were reluctant to undertake the risks and financial burden of administration.

In East Africa, where German merchants were not as well established, Tanganyika was acquired by the Society for German Colonization, which set up the German East African Company to administer the territory. The company was granted imperial protection on 27 February 1885, a day after the Berlin Conference had ended. But in 1890 the company gave up its administrative functions to the Reich and concentrated entirely on its commercial interests. As elsewhere in Africa, claiming possession did not immediately translate into effective control. Fierce and protracted African resistance saw to that (Kimambo and Temu, 1969; Jackson, 1970; Kieran, 1970; Illife, 1979:Chapter 4).

Following the German colonization of Tanganyika, 'British policy began an intensive search for ways to acquire a non-negotiable sphere in East Africa' (Wolff, 1974:39). Until the mid-1880s Britain's hegemony in the region had 'rested on the shaky fiction of the mainland sovereignty of her protected creature the Sultan of Zanzibar and, more securely but at unwelcome expense, on the Royal Naval squadron which scoured the Indian Ocean coast for Arab slavers' (Lonsdale, 1989b:8). This was clearly no longer enough. Britain intensified its anti-slave trade crusade and for the first time offered support to British commercial interests seeking to establish commercial hegemony in the area. Mackinnon and his business associates who had shipping and commercial interests throughout the Indian Ocean trading zone sought to consolidate their position by gaining a foothold along the East African coast, for which they hoped to get shipping and railway guarantees from the British government (Munro, 1987). In 1887-8 Mackinnon's Imperial British East Africa Company was given a royal charter, conferring upon it exclusive economic privileges, as well as the power to colonize and administer from the Kenyan coast to Uganda. The company believed both objectives could best be achieved through the construction of a railway from Mombasa to Uganda. While construction began in 1895, by then the company had slid into bankruptcy and Britain was forced to annex the East African Protectorate, as Kenya was then called. The rest of the decade was marked by widespread wars of conquest and resistance (Low, 1965b; Mungeam, 1966; Zeleza, 1982; Lonsdale, 1989b).

For a few years the new protectorate was administered from Zanzibar. To the British government, according to Ogot (1974:249), the East African Protectorate 'appeared in itself to be of little economic or strategic significance. But since Zanzibar and the coast formed a necessary base for British operations in East Africa and in the Indian Ocean complex, the protectorate, a kind of Zanzibar backyard, had to be made safe'. Zanzibar formed the eastern flank of British interests in East Africa, Uganda the western one.

Uganda's first direct contacts with Europe were not established until the 1860s and were initially through missionaries, whose activities fuelled factional politics at the Buganda court (Nabudere, 1980:20-28). The missionaries and traders who visited Buganda were impressed by the country's high degree of political centralization and its economic potential. However, at the time of Uganda's colonization, it was 'the logic of intra-imperialist rivalry and not the lure of existing products' that played the fundamental role (Mamdani, 1976:40). The British colonization of Uganda came 'by the stroke of the pen which signed the Anglo-German agreement,' which declared 'the area north of Lake Victoria... a British sphere of influence' (Kiwanuka 1974:314). The IBEAC was empowered by its royal charter to trade and administer the country. Once the company had done its job of preparing the ground for the imperial government to take over, it was replaced in April 1893. Uganda was officially declared a British protectorate in June 1894.

In the meantime, Italy was flexing its muscles in north-eastern Africa. In the early 1880s the Italians occupied Assab and Massawa, from where they sought to advance to the Ethiopian heartland. But the Ethiopians were more than ready for them. Emperors Tewodros and Menelik were determined to meet the European challenge by modernizing the army. The results were seen at Adowa in March 1896 where the Italians suffered a humiliating defeat. Ethiopia remained the only African state during the partition to score a decisive military victory against the European invaders and to retain its sovereignty (Marcus, 1975; July, 1992).

The Italians had better luck in southern Somalia. Northern Somaliland went to the British and the French, who took the enclave of Djibouti. By then the French already occupied some Indian Ocean islands, such as Reunion and Comoros, and in 1895 they finally conquered Madagascar, their appetites whetted by expectations of massive profits from gold production (Campbell, 1988c:116-126; Mutibwa, 1974). Meanwhile, in early 1896 Britain launched campaigns to conquer the Sudan. The British invaders had two problems, one military, to conquer the Mahdiyya on the ground, and the other diplomatic, to forestall Egyptian opposition to, and European criticism of, their expansion into the Sudan, which had been an Egyptian dependency between 1821 and 1885. Thus the fiction of the condominium was concocted. In 1898 Omdurman, the Mahdiyya capital, was sacked by British forces, and the British flag was hoisted, followed by the Egyptian flag. In January 1899, the Condominium Agreement was signed between Britain and the Pasha of Egypt. The reality was that 'Britain had gained control of the Sudan, and while her policies and plans there would often have to take account of Egypt, that control was maintained by force, not by the Condominium Agreement' (Daly, 1988:18). After all, Egypt itself was a British colony.

Conclusion

It can be seen that in Central, Southern and East Africa, trade with Europe expanded as rapidly as it did in West and North Africa, although there were considerable differences in the composition of exports. For example, slave exports lasted longer in West-central and Eastern Africa than in West Africa. This chapter has examined several networks, from the one concentrated in the Zaire basin, which was, for decades, the leading trading zone, to Angola and Mozambique, long craved by the Portuguese, down to the Cape, a relatively impoverished provisioning station until the expansion of wool exports in the 1840s, and across the Indian Ocean to the island of Madagascar, ruled at the beginning of the century by a mercantilist state, to the vigorous Swahili trading coast, then north to the ancient state of Ethiopia, and the Egyptian-controlled and later revolutionary Sudan. There were many similarities as well as some differences in the way international trade developed in each of these networks. Along the East African coast trade with Asia remained important, while the southern and central African regions looked westwards to the Atlantic.

It can plausibly be argued that there were three patterns of colonization which roughly corresponded with the three regions. In Central Africa, primarily Zaire and Angola, and Mozambique in the south-east, colonization was largely the product of speculative capital. Neither King Leopold II, nor Portugal, invested much in the territories which they ended up occupying. But lack of capital does not mean they were not determined imperialists or that they had no economic motives. It simply meant they employed new methods to achieve their goals. The Portuguese resorted to the use of neo-mercantilist concession companies to 'effectively occupy' the territories they claimed, while Leopold formed his speculative association, which managed, with the connivance of the major commercial powers in the Zaire basin, Britain and the Netherlands, to seize control of a vast chunk of territory.

If Central Africa was colonized by the 'feeble', Southern Africa attracted the mightiest of them all, Britain. It has been noted that the case of South Africa has featured extensively in the debates on the nature and dynamics of the 'new imperialism' ever since that term was coined by Hobson. It was argued that the struggle for South Africa in the last three decades of the century was largely fuelled by the mineral revolution. So coveted were the mineral resources that a fierce inter-imperialist war was fought, the only country where such a war was fought during the scramble for Africa. Mineral resources and the demands of the mining economy also facilitated and necessitated the conquest of the remaining independent African states in what is today South Africa. Moreover, the mineral revolution turned South Africa into a sub-imperial metropole in the region, which was partly concretized in the fact that mining capital, in the form of the BSA Company was instrumental in the colonization of Zimbabwe, Zambia, and to a lesser extent, Malawi.

Chartered companies were also used in parts of East Africa, for example, in the German colonization of Tanzania, and the British colonization of Kenya and Uganda. But unlike the BSA Company, the East African chartered companies were undercapitalized, speculative ventures, which quickly surrendered their administrative privileges to their respective governments. These companies embarked on colonization not because of existing trade links, but as vehicles for pre-emptive colonization in the face of intensifying inter-imperialist rivalries. Thus the incorporation of East Africa was not only relatively 'late', it could also be characterized as pre-emptive. Imperial rivalries in the region were acute, involving the colonial superpowers, Britain and France, as well as the colonial newcomers, Germany and Italy.

Conclusion:
Expanding the Horizons of
African Economic History

'It is not what we don't know that's dangerous,
it's what we do know that's not true.'
An old aphorism

This study was inspired by the need to strip the thick layers of myth from the complex maze that is African economic history. If by the end of reading this book the reader feels that she or he has not learnt anything new, but questions some of the things they thought they knew, then writing it was well worth the effort. All too often, African societies and economies have been described for what they were not, rather than what they were.

The existing literature is filled with false comparisons with developments elsewhere, especially in Europe. A lot of scholarly energy has been wasted searching for external stimuli behind any 'growth', 'innovation', 'change', or 'development' that occurred in African economies. This is not to deny the important role that external forces have played in African history. It is merely to underscore the fact that internal developments constituted the motor that pushed African history forward. The study has interrogated many of the standard characterizations and interpretations on a whole range of issues, from the nature of the African environment, demography, agriculture, mining, manufacturing and trade, to specific questions such as the impact of environmental change, new diseases, the slave trade and European imports, and the patterns of urbanization, gender divisions of labour, market organization, primitive settler accumulation, and colonization.

As the book's key arguments and contents are summarized in the introduction and the conclusions at the end of each chapter, it would be superfluous to present another detailed set of conclusions at this point. It will suffice to outline briefly some of the study's premises and findings. Specifically, the study intended, first, to cover the economic history of the whole continent; second, to analyze both the processes of production and exchange as broadly as possible; and third, to provide a long-term historical perspective.

I believe that the continent as a whole must be the basis of generalizations that purport to talk of 'Africa'. Divisions based on the Sahara or skin pigmentation, as in the designations 'sub-Saharan Africa' and 'Black Africa', tell us very little about the dynamics of historical change within the continent. In examining the different topics, the study has, therefore, tried to cover all the major regions within the continent. One conclusion that can be drawn is that there was great diversity among African economies. Moreover, levels of development were extremely uneven. There were the relatively simple societies for whom the highest and most effective form of economic and political organization was the village community. At other extreme, there were the more advanced societies with complex economic and political systems extending over vast areas.

This study has placed considerably more weight on production processes than on exchange systems, as is customarily the case. Not only was the range of productive activities examined quite extensive, from agriculture and mining, to manufacturing and construction, an attempt was made to link the economic processes to physical processes. It has been argued that the ecosystem must not be treated merely as a backdrop to historical events. It needs to be adequately integrated into analyses of economic change. The organization of agricultural production, for example, was intimately bound up with things like soil types, rainfall patterns, crop diseases, and other ecological variables and environmental changes. Thus 'forces of production' must be explored as seriously and dynamically as the 'relations of production' often are. Such comprehensive inquiries would give us more realistic views of production processes, and enable us to assess their full costs and benefits. The calculus of 'efficiency' or 'productivity' has to incorporate the equation of nature, for it is nature that furnishes the very materials for human survival. Indeed, humanity is a part of nature. It can be seen from the study that the patterns of adaptation to the ecosystem varied enormously across the continent and changed in the course of the century.

Throughout the study there was continuous focus on the changing relations of production in different societies and contexts. Whether the subject was agriculture, mining, manufacturing, or trade, an attempt was made to analyze the labour process: how work was organized, controlled and contested, along the divisions of gender, age and skill, as well as how surplus was appropriated and distributed. A number of conclusions can be drawn. First, the gender divisions of labour were extremely varied, so that it is wrong to assume either generalized patriarchal oppression or gender equality across the length and breadth of Africa. Relations between men and women were far more dynamic and ambiguous than it is sometimes realized.

Second, the labour process encompassed a wide range of forms, from household, to bonded (slave, indentured, and sharecropping labour), and free wage labour. Third, it is quite clear that most African societies were not collections of homogeneous masses of people who basked in the simple joys of 'communal' and 'egalitarian' life. Social differentiation existed and it

became more pronounced as the century progressed. In many of the centralized states peasants were exploited with varying degrees of severity by the
ruling classes. The responses of peasants, and other groups of working
people, veered between the dialectical poles of accommodation and resistance.

By looking at the nineteenth century as a whole, it becomes possible to
trace long-term economic and social changes and unravel the structural
continuities and discontinuities. The overriding impression is that this was
a period of tumultuous change in virtually all spheres, from the environment
and demography, to agriculture, industry, and trade. The designation by
political historians of the nineteenth century as a 'revolutionary' period in
modern African history is apt. Environmental conditions fluctuated violently
between the prolonged dry spells at the beginning and end of the century and
the wetter conditions in between. The demographic structure was transformed by the staggered abolition of the slave trade, the ravages of new
diseases and spreading old ones, mass regional migrations and the immigration of European and Asian settlers, the expansion of urbanization, especially in North and West Africa and the new mining centres of South Africa,
and the depredations of colonial conquest.

During the century African agriculture became more diversified than ever
before. In many societies new methods of cultivation and animal husbandry,
crops and tools were adopted as a result of the environmental and
demographic challenges, or arising economic opportunities. The available
evidence seems to indicate that there was a remarkable increase in agricultural production, including production for export. However, for some
societies and vulnerable social classes the problems of hunger persisted and
even deepened as a result of the very transformations taking place, as well
as the periodic outbreaks of environmental crisis and political conflicts.
Moreover, as production for export increased there was a tendency, especially among the burgeoning colonies and other countries that were becoming deeply incorporated into the world economy, towards monoculture and
the decapitalization of the food sector - developments that would intensify
and come to haunt twentieth century Africa.

It is more difficult to assess the trends in the mining and manufacturing
industries across Africa. The contention that these industries declined as a
result of imports from Europe has been questioned. African industries had
more resilience than they have been given credit for. While the skills of
African artisans cannot be doubted, there is little evidence that the age-old
technologies of mining and manufacturing were revolutionized during the
nineteenth century, outside the ultimately unsuccessful industrialization
drives in such countries as Egypt and Madagascar, and South Africa follow-

426 A Modern Economic History of Africa

ing the mineral revolution. This, however, does not mean that the organization of mineral and craft production remained static. In the major production centres there were important changes in the labour processes, which research is only beginning to unravel.

As for trade, which is perhaps the best researched aspect of precolonial economic history, all the evidence indicates that each of the various forms of trade - domestic, regional, and international - grew rapidly in the nineteenth century. Intra- and inter-regional commercial networks expanded, and merchant classes swelled. In the meantime, monetization spread, new credit institutions developed, and transport systems were extended and reorganized. In short, many of the features commonly associated with colonial capitalism were already well-developed in the great commercial centres of nineteenth century Africa. It is important, therefore, to be more discerning when discussing capitalist penetration in Africa. Often the term capitalism is used as a synonym for European colonization. All the characteristics of capitalism, from the private ownership of the means of production, production for the market, the sale of labour power as a commodity, to class struggle, the pursuit of profit, company formation, and the possession of that enigmatic of capitalist qualities, the entrepreneurial spirit, already existed in various forms and combinations in the continent's leading economies. These economies may not have been, in the Marxian sense, capitalist social formations, but they were not 'pre-capitalist' either.

European colonization was the second major external intrusion in modern African history which had a significant impact on the continent's societies and economies, the first being the slave trade. The two were sequentially and structurally linked. The slave trade weakened the African societies which were involved in various ways - demographically, economically, socially, and politically - while at the same time it strengthened, in the same measure, the countries of western Europe which organized the trade, so that the latter gradually accumulated the military power, economic voracity, and racial arrogance to colonize the entire continent towards the end of the nineteenth century. Thus the slave trade set the basis for colonization.

This study has critiqued some of the interpretations which seek to absolve Europe of the ultimate responsibility for both the slave trade and colonization. It is well to remember, that while there were many Africans who actively participated in the slave trade, and others who 'collaborated' during the partition, or 'made alliances' as Boahen (1987b) prefers to call it, neither the hapless slaves not the vanquished Africans had marched to Europe begging to be enslaved or colonized. It was the Europeans who came, launched the Atlantic slave trade and established the colonial empires. It was they who controlled and benefited most from the trade in human cargo and the seizure of other peoples lands. Both the slave trade and colonial conquest were accompanied by incredible violence. The institution of the colonial economy, as we saw in the case of the Portuguese colonies in Angola and Mozambique, the British and Boer colonies in South Africa, and the French colony in Algeria, were truly processes of 'primitive accumulation' written, to echo Marx (1978:875-6), 'in letters of blood and fire.'

The rest of the continent experienced this baptism of blood and fire at the turn of the twentieth century. And the continent is still reckoning with the consequences.

References

Abel, W, *Agricultural Fluctuations in Europe From the Thirteenth to the Twentieth Centuries.* New York: St. Martin's Press, 1980.

Aberibigbe, A B *Lagos: The Development of an African City.* London: Longman, 1975.

Abir, M, 'Southern Ethiopia'. In Gray, R and Birmingham, D, eds, 1970.

Abou-El-Haj, R, 'An Agenda for Research in History: The History of Libya Between the Sixteenth and Nineteenth Centuries'. *International Journal of Middle East Studies,* 15:305-319, 1983.

Abrams, P and Wrigley, E A, eds. *Towns in Societies: Essays in Economic History and Historical Sociology.* Cambridge: Cambridge University Press, 1978.

Abu-Lughod, J, *Cairo: 1001 Years of the City Victorious.* Princeton, N J, Princeton University Press, 1961.

Abun-Nasr, J M, *A History of the Maghreb in the Islamic Period.* Cambridge: Cambridge University Press, 1987.

Afigbo, A E, et.al., eds. *The Making of Modern Africa.* Vol.1: *The Nineteenth Century.* London: Longman.

Afonja, S, 'Changing Modes of Production and the Sexual Division of Labour Among the Yoruba'. *Signs,* 7:299-313, 1981.

Agiri, B, 'Slavery in Yoruba Society in the Nineteenth Century'. In Lovejoy, P E, ed., 1981.

Agiri, B, 'The Introduction of Nitida Kola into Nigerian Agriculture, 1880-1920'. *African Economic History,* 3:1-14, 1977.

Ahn, P M, *West African Soils.* Oxford: Oxford University Press, 1970.

Ajaegbu, H I, 'The Demographic Situations in Pre-colonial and Early Colonial Periods in West Africa: An Assessment of the Usefulness of Non-conventional Data Sources.' In Fyfe, C and McMaster, D, eds., 1977.

Ajayi, J F A, ed., *Africa in the Nineteenth Century Until the 1880s.* Vol. 6 of *Unesco General History of Africa.* 8 Vols. Oxford: Heinemann, 1989.

Ajayi, J F A and Crowder, M, eds. *History of West Africa.* Vol.2, 1974.

Ajayi, J F A and Crowder, M, eds., 'Africa at the Beginning of the Nineteenth Century'. In Ajayi, J F A, ed., 1989.

al-Sayyid-Marsot, A L, 'Religion or Opposition? Urban Protest Movements in Egypt.' *International Journal Middle East Studies,* 16:541-552, 1984.

Allen, J de V and Wilson, T H, eds., *Swahili Houses and Tombs on the Coast of Kenya.* London: Art and Archaeology Research Papers,. 1979.

Allen, J de V, 'The Swahili House: Cultural and Ritual Concepts Underlying its Plan and Structure'. In Allen, J de V and Wilson, T H, eds., 1979.

Alpers, E A, 'Rethinking African Economic History'. *Ufahamu,* 3:97-129, 1973.

Alpers, E A, *Ivory and Slaves in East and Central Africa to the Later Nineteenth Century.* London: Heinemann, 1975.

Alpers, E A, 'State, Merchant Capital, and Gender Relations in southern Mozambique to the end of the Nineteenth Century: Some Tentative Hypotheses'. *African Economic History,* 13:25--55, 1984a.

Alpers, E A, '"Ordinary Household Chores": Ritual Power in a Nineteenth Century Swahili Women's Spirit Possession Cult'. *International Journal of African Historical Studies,* 17:677-702, 1984b.

Ambler, C H, 'Population Movement, Social Formation and Exchange: Central Kenya in the Nineteenth Century'. *International Journal of African Historical Studies*, 18:201-222, 1985.

Amin, S, *Accumulation on a World Scale*. 2 Vols. New York: Monthly Review Press, 1974.

Amin, S, ed., *Modern Migrations in West Africa*. London: Oxford University Press, 1974.

Amin, S, *Unequal Development*. New York: Monthly Review Press, 1976.

Amin, S, *Imperialism and Unequal Development*. New York: Monthly Review Press, 1977.

Amin, S, *The Law of Value and Historical Materialism*. New York: Monthly Review Press, 1978.

Amin, S, *Class and Nation*. New York: Monthly Review Press, 1980.

Amin, S, *Delinking: Towards a Polycentric World*. London: Zed Books, 1990.

Amphlett, G T, *History of the Standard Bank of South Africa Ltd. 1862-1913*. Glasgow: Glasgow University Press, 1914.

Andah, B, 'Iron Age Beginnings in West Africa: Reflections and Suggestions'. *West African Journal of Archaeology*, 9:135- 150, 1983.

Anderson, P, 'Portugal and the End of Ultra Colonialism'. *New Left Review*, 15:83-102, 16:88-123, 1962.

Anderson, L, 'Nineteenth-Century Reform in Ottoman Libya'. *International Journal of Middle East Studies*, 16:325-348, 1984.

Anderson, D and Grove, R, eds., *Conservation in Africa. People, Policies and Practice*. Cambridge:Cambridge University Press, 1987.

Anderson, D. and Grove, R, 'Introduction: The Scramble for Eden: Past, Present and Future in African Conservation'. In Anderson, D and Grove, R, eds., 1987.

Andrews, P A, 'Tents of the Tekna, Southwest Morocco'. In Oliver, P, ed., 1971.

Anstey, R, *The Atlantic Slave Trade and British Abolition 1760-1810*. Cambridge: Cambridge University Press, 1975.

Anthony, K R M , et.al., *Agricultural Change in Tropical Africa*. Ithaca and London: Cornell University Press, 1979.

Archer, 1, 'Nardam Compounds, Northern Ghana'. In Oliver, P, ed., 1971.

Aregay, M W, 'The Early History of Ethiopia's Coffee Trade and Rise of Shawa'. *Journal of African History*, 29:19-25, 1988.

Arens, W, ed., *A Century of Change in Eastern Africa*. The Hague: Mouton, 1976.

Arhin, K, 'Atebubu Markets: ca.1884-1930.' In C. Meillassoux, ed., 1971.

Arhin, K, *West African Traders in Ghana in the Nineteenth and Twentieth Centuries*. London:Longman, 1979.

Armstrong, J C and Worden, N A, 'The Slaves, 1652-1834.' In Elphick, R and Giliomee, H, eds., 1989.

Arnold, D, 'Introduction: Disease, Medicine and Empire'. In Arnold, D, ed., 1988.

Arnold, D, ed., *Imperial Medicine and Indigenous Societies*. Manchester: Manchester University Press, 1988.

Aronson, L, 'History of Cloth Trade in the Niger Delta: A Study of Diffusion'. *Textile History*, 11:899-107, 1980.

Arrighi, G, *The Geometry of Imperialism: The Limits of Hobson's Paradigm*. London: Verso, 1983.

Asad, T and Wolpe, H, 'Concepts of Modes of Production.' *Economy and Society*, 5:197-240, 1976.

Atieno-Odhiambo, E S, 'The Rise and Decline of the Kenyan Peasant - 1881-1922', in *The Paradox of Collaboration and Other Essays*. Nairobi: East African Publishing House, 1974.

Atkins, K E, '«Kaffir Time»: Preindustrial Temporal Concepts and Labour Discipline in Nineteenth Century Colonial Natal'. *Journal of African History*, 29:229-244, 1988.

Austen, R A, 'Economic History'. *African Studies Review*, 14:425-438, 1971.

Austen, R A, 'African Commerce Without Europeans: The Development of International Trade in the Pre-Modern Era'. *Kenya Historical Review*, 6:1-21, 1978.

Austen, R A, 'The Trans-Saharan Slave Trade. A Tentative Census'. In Gemery, H A and Hogendorn, J S, eds., 1979.

Austen, R A and Headrick, D, 'The Role of Technology in the African Past.' *African Studies Review*, 26:163-184,. 1983.

Austen, R A, 'The Metamorphoses of Middlemen: The Duala, Europeans and the Cameroon Hinterland, Ca.1800 - Ca.1960.' *International Journal of African Historical Studies*, 16:1-37, 1983.

Austen, R A, 'African Economies in Historical Perspective'. *Business History Review*, 59:101-113, 1985.

Austen, R A, *African Economic History*. London: James Currey, 1987.

Austen, R A, 'On Comparing Pre-Industrial African and European Economies.' *African Economic History*, 19:21-24, 1990-91.

Awad, M H, 'The Evolution of Landownership in the Sudan.' *The Middle East Journal*, 25:212-228, 1971.

Ayandele, E A, 'Northern Africa'. In Afigbo, A E, et.al., 1986.

Ayrout, H H, *The Egyptian Peasant*. London:Beacon Books, 1963.

Azarya, V, 'State and Economic Enterprise in Massina'. *Asian and African Studies*, 13:157-190, 1979.

Azevedo, M J, 'Epidemic Disease Among the Sara of Southern Chad, 1890-1940'. In Patterson, K D and Hartwig, G W, eds., 1978.

Badri, H K, *Women's Movement in the Sudan*. New Delhi: Asia News Agency, 1986.

Baier, G, *A History of Land Ownership in Modern Egypt, 1800-1850*. London: Oxford University Press, 1962.

Baier, G, *Egyptian Guilds in Modern Times*. Jerusalem, 1964.

Baier, G, *Studies in the Social History of Modern Egypt*. Chicago: University of Chicago Press, 1969.

Baier, S, 'Trans-Saharan Trade and the Sahel: Damergu, 1830-1970.' *Journal of African History*, 18:37-60, 1977.

Ballard, C, '«A Year of Scarcity»: The 1896 Locust Plague in Natal and Zululand'. *South African Historical Journal*, 15:34-52, 1983.

Ballard, C, 'Drought and Economic Distress: South Africa in the 1880s'. *Journal of Interdisciplinary History*, 27:359-78, 1986.

Barbour, K M, *The Growth, Location and Structure of Industry in Egypt*. New York: Praeger, 1972.

Bates, R H, *Essays on the Political Economy of Rural Africa*. Berkeley: University of California Press, 1983.

Bates, R H, 'Some Contemporary Orthodoxies in the Study of Agrarian Change', In Kohil, A, ed., 1986.

Bates, R H, *Towards a Political Economy of Development: A Rational Choice Perspective*. Berkeley: University of California Press, 1988.

Bay, E G, ed., *Women and Work in Africa*. Boulder, Colo.: Westview Press, 1982.

Beach, D, 'The Shona Economy: Branches of Production.' In Palmer and Parsons, eds., 1977.

Beach, D N, *The Shona and Zimbabwe 900-1850: An Outline of Shona History.* New York: Africana Publishing Co., 1980.

Beach, D N, 'The Zimbabwe Plateau and its Peoples.' In D. Birmingham and P. Martin, eds., 1983.

Bean, R, 'A Note on the Relative Importance of Slaves and Gold in West African Exports'. *Journal of African History,* 15:351-356, 1974.

Bean, R N and Thomas, R P, 'The Adoption of Slave Labour in British America'. In A. Gemery and J.S. Hogendorn, eds., 1979.

Beck, l and Keddie, N, eds., *Women in the Muslim World.* Cambridge: Harvard University Press, 1978.

Beckford, G L, *Persistent Poverty: Underdevelopment in Plantation Economies of the Third World.* New York: Oxford University Press, 1972.

Beinart, W, 'Labour Migrancy and Rural Production: Pondoland c.1900-1950'. In Mayer, P, ed., 1980a.

Beinart, W, 'Production and the Material Basis of Chieftainship: Pondoland, c. 1830-1880.' In Marks, S and Atmore, A, eds., 1980b.

Beinart, W, *The Political Economy of Pondoland.* Cambridge: Cambridge University Press, 1982.

Beinart, W, 'Settler Accumulation in East Griqualand from the Demise of the Griqua to the Native Lands Act'. In Beinart, W, Delius, P and Trapido, S, eds., 1986.

Beinart, W, Delius, P and Trapido, S, eds., *Putting a Plough to the Ground: Accumulation and Dispossession in Rural South Africa, 1850-1930.* Johannesburg: Ravan Press, 1986.

Beinart, W and Delius, P, 'Introduction. Approaches to South African Agrarian History'. In Beinart, W, Delius, P and Trapido, S, eds., 1986.

Beinart, W and Bundy, C, *Hidden Struggles in Rural South Africa: Politics and Popular Movements in the Transkei and Eastern Cape 1890-1930.* London: James Currey, 1987.

Beinart, W, 'Introduction: The Politics of Colonial Conservation'. *Journal of Southern African Studies,* 15:143-162, 1989.

Bell, C, 'Alternative Theories of Sharecropping: Some Tests Using Evidence From Northeast India.' *Journal of Development Studies,* 13:317-346, 1977.

Bell, R H V, 'Conservation with a Human Face: Conflict and Reconciliation in African Land Use Planning.' In Anderson, D and Grove, R, eds., 1987.

Belshaw, D, 'Taking Indigenous Technology Seriously: The Case of Inter-cropping Techniques in East Africa.' *IDS Bulletin,* 10:24-27, 1979.

Ben-Amos, P D, *Social Change in the Organisation of Wood Carving in Benin City, Nigeria.* Ph.D. dissertation, Indiana University, 1971.

Bender, G J, *Angola Under the Portuguese: The Myth and the Reality.* Los Angeles: University of California Press, 1978.

Bennoune, M, *The Making of Contemporary Algeria, 1830-1987,* Cambridge: Cambridge University Press, 1988.

Benoit, D, and Lacombe, B, 'Towards Getting Precise Data in Contemporary Africa for the Years 1920-30.' In C. Fyfe and D. McMaster, eds., 1977.

Benoit, D, and Lacombe, B, 'Main Results of a Survey Based on Parish Registers of Kongoussi-Tikare, 1978.' In Fyfe, C and McMaster, D, eds., 1981.

Berg, G M, 'Riziculture and the Founding of Monarchy in Imerina.' *Journal of African History,* 22:289-308, 1981.

Berg, J V D, 'A Peasant Form of Production: Wage-Dependent Agriculture in southern Mozambique'. *Canadian Journal of African Studies*, 21:375-389, 1987.

Berger, M T, 'Imperialism and Sexual Exploitation: A Response to Ronald Hyam's «Empire and Sexual Opportunity».' *Journal of Imperial and Commonwealth History*, 17:83-89, 1988.

Berman, B, *Control and Crisis in Colonial Kenya: The Dialectic of Domination.* London:James Currey, 1990.

Bernal, M, *Black Athena.* Vol.1. London: Free Association Books, 1987.

Bernal, M, *Black Athena.* Vol.2. London: Free Association Books, 1991.

Bernstein, H and Pitt, M, 'Plantations and Modes of Exploitation.' *Journal of Peasant Studies*, 1:514-526, 1974.

Bernstein, H, 'Notes on Capital and Peasantry'. *Review of African Political Economy*, 10:60-73, 1977.

Bernstein, H and Depelchin, J, 'The Object of African History: A Materialist Perspective', In *History in Africa*, 5:1- 19, 1978.

Bernstein, H and Depelchin, J, The Object of African History: A Materialist Perspective', In *History in Africa*, 6:17-43, 1979.

Berry, S S, 'The Concept of Innovation and the History of Cocoa Farming in Western Nigeria.' *Journal of African History*, 15:83-95, 1974.

Berry, S S, *Cocoa, Custom and Socio-Economic Change in Rural Western Nigeria.* London: Oxford University Press, 1975.

Berry, S S, 'The Food Crisis and Agrarian Change in Africa'. *African Studies Review*, 27:59-112, 1984.

Beshai, A A, *Export Performance and Economic Development in Sudan, 1900-1967.* London: Ithaca Press, 1976.

Bhaduri, A, 'A Study of Agricultural Backwardness under Semi-Feudalism.' *Economic Journal*, 83:120-137, 1973.

Bharat, A, *The Asians in East Africa.* Chicago: Nelson Hall, 1972.

Biermann, B, 'Indlu: The Domed Dwelling of the Zulu.' In Oliver, P, ed., 1971.

Birmingham, D, *Trade and Politics in Angola.* Oxford: Clarendon Press, 1966.

Birmingham, D, 'Early Trade in Angola and its Hinterland.' In Gray, R and Birmingham, D, eds., 1970.

Birmingham, D, *Trade and Politics in Angola.* Oxford: Clarendon Press, 1971.

Birmingham, D, 'The Forest and Savanna of Central Africa'. In Flint, J E, ed., *From c. 1790 to c. 1870.* Vol.5 of *The Cambridge History of Africa.* 8 Vols. Cambridge: Cambridge University Press, 1976.

Birmingham, D, 'The Coffee Barons of Cazengo.' *Journal of African History*, 19:523-538, 1978.

Birmingham, D and Martin, P, eds., *History of Central Africa*, 2 Vols. London and New York: Longman, 1983.

Birmingham, D, 'Society and Economy Before A.D. 1400.' In Birmingham, D and Martin, P, eds., 1983.

Bjorkelo, A, *Prelude to the Madhiyya: Peasants and Traders in the Shendi Region, 1821-1885.* Cambridge: Cambridge University Press, 1989.

Bloch, M, ed., *Marxist Analyses and Social Anthropology.* London: Malaby, 1975.

Bloch, M, 'Modes of Production and slavery in Madagascar.' In Watson, J L, ed., 1980.

Blomstrom, M and Hettne, B, *Development Theory in Transition. The Dependency Debate and Beyond: Third World Responses.* London: Zed Books, 1988.

Bloomhill, G, 'The Ancient Copper Miners of Africa: Lemba Tribe's Secret «Mutsuku' Rites»'. *Africa World*, 6, 1963.

Boahen, A, *Britain, the Sahara and the Western Sudan, 1788-1861*. Oxford: Clarendon Press, 1964.

Boahen, A, *African Perspectives on Colonialism*. Baltimore: The Johns Hopkins University Press, 1987a.

Boahen, A, ed., *General History of Africa*. Vol.7: *Africa Under Colonial Rule*, 8 Vols. Berkeley and London: California University Press and Heinemann, 1987b.

Boahen, A A, 'New Trends and Processes in Africa in the Nineteenth Century'. In Ajayi, J F A, ed., 1989.

Boesen, J, 'On Peasantry and the Modes of production Debate'. *Review of African Political Economy*, 15/16:154-161, 1979.

Bohannan, P, 'Some Principles of Exchange and Investment Among the Tiv'. *American Anthropologist*, 57:60-70, 1955.

Bohannan, P and Dalton, G, eds., *Markets in Africa*. New York: Anchor Books, 1962.

Bohannan, P and Bohannan, L, *Tiv Economy*, London: Longman, 1968.

Bohannan, P, 'The Impact of Money on an African Subsistence Economy'. *Journal of Economic History*, 19:491-503, 1969.

Bohannan, P and Curtin, P D, *Africa and Africans*, 3rd ed. Prospect Heights, Ill: Waveland Press, 1988.

Bonte, P, 'Ecological and Economic Factors in the Determination of Pastoral Specialisation.' *Journal of Asian and African Studies*, 16:33-49, 1981.

Boserup, E, *The Conditions of Economic Agricultural Growth: The Economics of Agrarian Change Under Population Pressure*. London: Allen and Unwin, 1965.

Bourliere, F, ed., *Ecosystems of the World .13. Tropical Savannas*. Amsterdam: Elsevier Scientific Publishing Co., 1983.

Bower, J G, 'Native Smelting in Equatorial Africa.' *The Mining Magazine*, 37:137-147, 1927.

Bowman, J L, 'Legitimate Commerce and Peanut Production in Portuguese Guinea, 1840s-80s.' *Journal of African History*, 28:87-106, 1987.

Bozzoli, B, *The Political Nature of a Ruling Class: Capital and Ideology in South Africa 1890-1933*. London: Routledge and Kegan Paul, 1981.

Bradford, H, *A Taste of Freedom: The ICU in Rural South Africa 1924-1930*. New Haven: Yale University Press, 1987.

Brandstrom, P, et.al., *Aspects of Agro-Pastoralism in East Africa*. Uppsala: Scandinavian Institute of African Studies, 1979.

Braverman, A and Srinivasan, T N, 'Credit and Sharecropping and Interlocking of Agrarian Markets.' *Journal of Development Economics*, 9:289-312, 1981.

Brenner, R, 'The Origins of Capitalist Development: A Critique of Neo-Smithian Marxism.' *New Left Review*, 104:25-92, 1977.

Brett, M, 'Continuity and Change: Egypt and North Africa in the Nineteenth Century'. *Journal of African History*, 27:149-162, 1986.

Brewer, A, *Marxist Theories of Imperialism: A Critical Survey*. London: Routledge and Kegan Paul, 1980.

Briggs, A, 'Cholera and Society in the Nineteenth Century.' *Past and Present*, 29:76-96, 1961.

Broadhead, S H, *Trade and Politics on the Congo Coast, 1770-1870*. Ph.D. Dissertation, Boston University, 1971.

Brooks, G E, 'Peanuts and Colonialism: Consequences of the Commercialisation of Peanuts in West Africa, 1830-1870.' *Journal of African History*, 16:29-54, 1975.

Brooks, G E, 'The Signares of Saint-Louis and Goree: Women Entrepreneurs in Eighteenth-Century Senegal'. In Hafkin, N and Bay, E, eds., 1976.

Brooks, H C and El-Ayouby, Y, *Refugees South of the Sahara: An African Dilemma*. Westport, Conn: Negro University Press, 1976.

Brothwell, D R, 'Bio-Archaeological Evidence for Morbidity in Earlier African Populations.' In Fyfe, C and McMaster, D, eds., 1981.

Brown, L C, *The Tunisia of Ahmed Bey*. Princeton, N.J.: Princeton University Press, 1974.

Brown, B and Brown, W T, 'East African Towns: A Shared Growth.' In Arens, W, ed., 1976.

Brown, M B, *The Economics of Imperialism*. Harmondsworth: Penguin, 1978.

Brown, B, 'Facing the Black Peril: The Politics of Population Control in South Africa.' *Journal of Southern African Studies*, 13:256-273, 1987.

Bruce-Chwatt, L J and J M, 'Malaria and Yellow Fever'. In Saben-Clare, E E et.al., eds., 1980.

Bryant, A T, *Olden Times in Zululand and Natal*. Cape Town: Struik, C, 1965.

Bundy, C, *The Rise and Fall of the South African Peasantry*. London: Heinemann, 1979.

Bundy, C, 'Vagabond Hollanders and Runaway Englishmen: White Poverty in the Cape Before Poor Whiteism.' In Beinart, W, Delius, P and Trapido, S, eds., 1986.

Burke, K and Durutoye, A B, 'A Dry Phase South of the Sahara 20,000 years ago.' *West African Journal of Archaeology*, 1:1-8, 1971.

Burke, G and Richardson, P, 'The Profits of Death: A Comparative Study of Miners' Phthisis in Cornwall and the Transvaal, 1876-1918'. *Journal of Southern African Studies*, 5:147-171, 1978.

Burridge, R M and Kallen, E, eds., *Problems and Prospects in Long and Medium Range Weather Forecasting*. London: Springer-Verlag, 1984.

Butzer, K W, Isaac, G L and Richardson, J L, 'Radiocarbon Dating of East African Lake Levels.' *Science*, 1069-1076, 1972.

Cain, P J and Hopkins, A G, 'Gentlemanly Capitalism and British Expansion Overseas I: The Old Colonial System, 1688-1850.' *Economic History Review*, 39:501-525, 1986.

Cain, P J and Hopkins, A G, 'Gentlemanly Capitalism and British Expansion Overseas II: New Imperialism, 1850-1945'. *Economic History Review*, 40:1-26, 1987.

Caldwell, J C, 'Major Questions in African Demographic History.' In Fyfe, C and McMaster, D, eds., 1977.

Calvocoressi, D and David, N, 'A New Survey of Radio Carbon and Thermoluminescence Dates for West Africa.' *Journal of African History*, 20:1-29, 1979.

Camaroff, J L, 'Dialectical Systems, History and Anthropology: Units of Study and Question of Theory.' *Journal of Southern African Studies*, 8:143-172, 1982.

Campbell, D J, *Strategies for Coping with Drought in the Sahel: A Study of recent Population Movements in the Department of Maradi, Niger*. Ph.D. thesis, Clark University, 1977.

Campbell, G, 'Labour and the Transport Problem in Imperial Madagascar, 1810-1895.' *Journal of African History*, 21:341-356, 1980.

Campbell, G, 'Madagascar and the Slave Trade, 1810-1895.' *Journal of African History*, 22:203-227, 1981.

Campbell, G, 'Toamasina (Tamatave) and the Growth of Foreign Trade in Imperial Madagascar, 1862-1895.' In Liesegang, G, Pasch, H and Jones, A, eds., 1983.

Campbell, G, 'The Monetary and Financial Crisis of the Merina Empire, 1810-1835.' *South African Journal of Economic History*, 11:99-118, 1986.

Campbell, G, 'The Adoption of Autarchy in Imperial Madagascar, 1820-1835.' *Journal of African History*, 28:395-409, 1987.

Campbell, G, 'Slavery and Fanompoana: The Structure of Forced Labour in Imerina.' *Journal of African History*, 29:463-486, 1988a.

Campbell, G, 'Missionaries, Fanompoana and the Menalamba in late Nineteenth Century Madagascar.' *Journal of Southern African Studies*, 15:54-73, 1988b.

Campbell, G, 'Gold Mining and the French Takeover of Madagascar, 1883-1914'. *African Economic History*, 17:99-126, 1988c.

Campbell, G, 'The East African Slave Trade, 1861-1895: The Southern Complex.' *International Journal of African Historical Studies*, 22:1-26, 1989.

Campbell, G, 'An Industrial Experiment in Pre-colonial Africa: The Case of Imperial Madagascar, 1825-1861', *Journal of Southern African Studies*, 17:525-559, 1991.

Campbell, G, 'Disease, Cattle, and Slaves: The Development of Trade Between Natal and Madagascar'. *African Economic History*, 19:105-133, 1990-91.

Cannon, B D, 'Nineteenth-Century Arabic Writings on Women and Society: The Interim Role of the Masonic Press in Cairo - (Al-Latif, 1865-1895).' *International Journal of Middle East Studies*, 17:463-484), 1985.

Carney, J and Watts, M, 'Disciplining Women? Rice, Mechanization and the Evolution of Mandinka Gender Relations in Senegambia', *Signs: Journal of Women in Culture and Society*, 16:651-681, 1991.

Carr-Saunders, A M, *World Population: Past Growth and Present Trends.* Oxford: Clarendon Press, 1936.

Carruthers, 'Creating a National Park, 1910 to 1926'. *Journal of Southern African Studies*, 15:188-216, 1989.

Caulk, R A, 'Armies as Predators: Soldiers and Peasants in Ethiopia, c. 1850-1935.' *International Journal of African Historical Studies*, 11:457-493, 1978.

Chaichian, M A, 'The Effects of World Capitalist Economy on Urbanization in Egypt.' *International Journal of Middle East Studies*, 20:23-43, 1988.

Chandler, T and Fox, G, *3000 Years of Urban Growth.* New York: Academic Press, 1974.

Chanock, M, 'Agricultural Change and Continuity in Malawi.' In R. Palmer and N. Parsons, eds., 1977.

Chaudhuri, K N, *Trade and Civilization in the Indian Ocean.* Cambridge: Cambridge University Press, 1989.

Childe, V G, 'Civilization, Cities and Towns.' *Antiquity*, 31:36-38, 1958.

Childs, S T and Schmidt, P R, 'Experimental Iron Smelting: The Genesis of a Hypothesis with Implications of African Prehistory and History.' In Haaland, H and Shinnie, P, eds., 1985.

Chittick, N, *Kilwa: An Islamic Trading City on the East African Coast.* Nairobi: British Institute of Eastern Africa, 1974.

Clarence-Smith, W G and Moorsom, R, 'Underdevelopment and Class Formation in Ovamboland, 1845-1915.' *Journal of African History*, 16:365-381, 1975.

Clarence-Smith, W G, 'Slaves, Commoners and Landlords in Bulozi.' *Journal of African History*, 20:219-234, 1979a.

Clarence-Smith, W G, *Slaves, Peasants and Capitalists in Southern Angola, 1840-1926.* Cambridge: Cambridge University Press, 1979b.

Clarence-Smith, W G, 'The Myth of Uneconomic Imperialism: The Portuguese in Angola, 1836-1926.' *Journal of Southern African Studies*, 5:165-181, 1979c.

Clarence-Smith, W G, 'Portuguese Trade with Africa in the 19th Century: An Economic Imperialism with a note on the trade of Angola.' In Liesegang, G, Pasch, H and Jones, A, eds., 1983.

Clarence-Smith, W G, *The Third Portuguese Empire, 1825- 1975: A Study in Economic Imperialism.* Manchester: Manchester University Press, 1985.

Clark, J D, 'Pre-European Copper Working in South Central Africa'. *Roan Antelope*, May, 1957.

Clark, J D, 'Prehistoric Populations and Pressures Favouring Plant Domestication in Africa.' In Harlan, et.al., eds., 1976.

Clark, W C, 'Scales of Climate Impacts.' *Climatic Change*, 7:5-27, 1985.

Cleveland, W L, 'The Municipal Council of Tunis, 1858- 1870: A Study in Urban Institutional Change.' *International Journal Middle East Studies*, 9:33-61, 1978.

Cline, W, *Mining and Metallurgy in Negro Africa.* Menasha, Wisconsin, George Banta, 1937.

Cloudsley-Thompson, J L, *Insects and History.* London: Weidenfeld and Nicholson, 1976.

Cobbing, J, 'Mfecane as Alibi: Thoughts on Dithakong and Mbolompo'. *Journal of African History*, 29:487-519, 1988.

Cobbing, J, 'The «Mfecane» Aftermath: Towards a New Paradigm'. University of the Witwatersrand, 1991.

Coghlan, H H, *Notes on the Prehistoric Metallurgy of Copper and Bronze in the Old World.* Oxford: Oxford University Press, 1956.

Cohen, A, 'Cultural strategies in the organization of trading diasporas.' In Meillassoux, C, ed., 1971.

Cohen, J M and Weintraub, D, *Land and Peasants in Imperial Ethiopia:The Social Background to a Revolution.* Asse, Netherlands: Van Gocum, 1975.

Cohen, D and Atieno-Odhiambo, E S, *Siaya: The Historical Anthropology of an African Landscape.* London: James Currey, 1989.

Cole, J R, 'Feminism, Class, and Islam in Turn-of-the Century Egypt.' *International Journal of Middle East Studies*, 13:387-407, 1981.

Coleman, D C, 'Proto-Industrialisation: A Concept Too Many.' *Economic History Review*, 36:435-448, 1983.

Conah, G, *African Civilizations. Precolonial Cities and States in Tropical Africa: An Archaeological Perspective.* Cambridge: Cambridge University Press, 1987.

Cooper, F, *Plantation Slavery on the East African Coast.* New Haven: Yale University Press, 1977.

Cooper, F, 'The Problem of Slavery in African Studies.' *Journal of African History*, 20:103-125, 1979.

Cooper, F, *From Slaves to Squatters: Plantation Labour and Agriculture in Zanzibar and Coastal Kenya, 1890-1925.* New Haven: Yale University Press, 1980.

Cooper, F, 'Peasants, Capitalists and Historians: A Review Article.' *Journal of Southern African Studies*, 7:284-314, 1980.

Cooper, F, 'Africa and the World Economy.' *African Studies Review*, 24:1-86, 1981.

Coquery-Vidrovitch, C, 'Research on an African Mode of Production.' In Gutkind, P and Waterman, P, eds., 1977.

Coquery-Vidrovitch, C, 'Towards an African Mode of Production.' In Seddon, D, ed., 1978.

Coquery-Vidrovitch, C and Lovejoy, P E, 'The Workers of African Trade in Precolonial Africa.' In Coquery-Vidrovitch, C and Lovejoy, P E, eds., 1985.

Coquery-Vidrovitch, C and Lovejoy, P E, eds. *The Workers of African Trade.* Beverly Hills: Sage Publications, 1985.

Coquery-Vidrovitch, C, *Africa: Endurance and Change South of the Sahara.* Berkeley: University of California Press, 1988.

Cordell, D D and Gregory, J W, 'Historical Demography and Demographic History in Africa: Theoretical and Methodological Considerations.' *Canadian Journal of African Studies*, 14:389- 416, 1980.

Cordell, D D, 'The Savanna Belt of North-Central Africa.' In Birmingham, D and Martin, P, 1983.

Cordell, D D, *Dar al Kuti and the Last Years of the Trans-Saharan Slave Trade*. Madison: Wisconsin University Press, 1985.

Cordell, D D et.al., eds., *African Population and Capitalism*. Boulder, Col.: Westview Press, 1987.

Cordell, D D and Gregory, J W, 'Earlier African Historical Demographies.' *Canadian Journal of African Studies*, 23:5-27, 1989.

Coupland, R, *The British Anti-Slavery Movement*. London: Butterworth, T, 1933.

Coursey, D G, 'The Origins and Domestication of Yams in Africa'. In Harlan, et.al., 1976.

Crisp, J, *The Story of An African Working Class: Ghanaian Miners' Struggles 1870-1980*. London: Zed Books, 1984.

Crosby, A W, 'Ecological Imperialism: The Overseas Migration of Western Europeans as a Biological Phenomenon.' In Worster, D, ed., 1988.

Crosby, A W, *Ecological Imperialism: The Biological Expansion of Europe, 900-1900*. Cambridge: Cambridge University Press, 1989.

Crouchley, A E, *The Economic Development of Modern Egypt*, London: Longmans, 1938.

Crowder, M, ed., *West African Resistance: The Military Response to Colonial Occupation*. London: Hutchinson, 1978.

Crowder, M, *West Africa Under Colonial Rule*. London: Hutchinson, 1981.

Crummey, D, 'Society and Ethnicity in the Politics of Christian Ethiopia During the Zamana Masfet.' *International Journal of African Historical Studies*, 1975.

Crummey, D, 'Abyssinian Feudalism.' *Past and Present*, 89: 115-138, 1979.

Crummey, D and Stewart, C C, eds., *Modes of Production in Africa: The Precolonial Era*. Beverly Hills: Sage Publications, 1981.

Crummey, D, 'State and Society: Nineteenth Century Ethiopia.' In D. Crummey and C.C. Stewart, eds., 1981a.

Crummey, D, 'Women and Landed Property in Gondarine Ethiopia.' *International Journal of African Historical Studies*, 14:444-465, 1981b.

Crummey. D, ed., *Banditry and Rebellion and Social Protest in Africa*. London: James Currey, 1986.

Crummey, D, 'Banditry and Resistance: Noble and Peasant in Nineteenth Century Ethiopia.' In D. Crummey, ed., 1986a.

Crush, J, *The Struggle For Swazi Labour*. Kingston and Montreal: McGill-Queen's University Press, 1987.

Cummings, R J, *Aspects of Human Porterage with Special Reference to the Akamba of Kenya: Towards an Economic History, 1820-1920*. Ph.D. Dissertation, University of California, Los Angeles, 1975.

Cummings, R J, 'Wage Labour in Kenya in the Nineteenth Century.' In Coquery-Vidrovitch and Lovejoy, P E, eds., 1985.

Cuno, K M, 'The Origins of Private Ownership of Land in Egypt: A Reappraisal.' *International Journal Middle East Studies*, 12:245-275, 1980.

Curtin, P D, *The Image of Africa: British Ideas and Action, 1780-1840*. Madison: University of Wisconsin Press, 1964.

Curtin, P D, *The Atlantic Slave Trade: A Census*. Madison: University of Wisconsin Press, 1969.

Curtin, P D, 'The Lure of Bambuk Gold.' *Journal of African History*, 14:623-631, 1973.

Curtin, P D, *Economic Change in Precolonial Africa: Senegambia in the Era of the Slave Trade*, 2 Vols. Madison: University of Wisconsin Press, 1975.

Curtin, P D, et. al., *African History*. Boston: Little Brown, 1978.

Curtin, P D, 'Nutrition in African History'. *Journal of Interdisciplinary History*, 14:371-382, 1983.

Curtin, P D, *Cross-Cultural Trade in World History*. Cambridge: Cambridge University Press, 1984.

D'Hoote, J L, *Soil Map of Africa*. Lagos: Commission de Co-Operation Technique en Afrique au Sud du Sahara, 1964.

Daaku, K Y, 'Trade and trading patterns of the Akan in the seventeenth and eighteenth centuries.' In Meillassoux, C, ed., 1971.

Daaku, K Y, *Trade and Politics on the Gold Coast 600- 1700*. Oxford: Oxford University Press, 1970.

Dalby, D, et.al., eds., *Drought in Africa*. London: International African Institute, 1977.

Dalton, G, ed., *Tribal and Peasant Economies: Readings in Economic Anthropology*, New York: Natural History Press, 1967.

Dalton, G, 'Comment: What Kinds of Trade and Markets?'. *African Economic History*, 6:134-138, 1978.

Daly, M W, *Empire on the Sudan: The Anglo-Egyptian Sudan 1898-1934*. Cambridge: Cambridge University Press, 1988.

Danby, M, 'Ganvie, Dahomey'. In Oliver, P, ed., 1971.

Darish, P, 'Dressing for the Next Life: Raffia Textile Production and Use Among the Kuba of Zaire.' In Schneider, J and Weiner, A B, eds., 1989.

Darkoh, M B K, *Combating Desertification in the Southern African Region: An Updated Regional Assessment*. Nairobi: UNEP, 1989.

Daumas, E M, *Women of North Africa or «The Arab Women»*. San Diego, Cal., 1943.

Davenport, T R H, *South Africa: A Modern History*, 2nd ed. Toronto: University of Toronto Press, 1978.

David, N, 'The Ethnography of Pottery: A Fulani Case Seen in Archaeological Perspective.' *Module*, 21:1-29, 1972.

David, N, 'Prehistory and Historical Linguistics in Central Africa: Points of Contact.' In Ehret, C and Posnansky, M, eds., 1982.

Davidson, B, *Black Mother: The Years of the African Slave Trade*. Boston: Little Brown, 1961.

Davidson, B, *A History of West Africa to the Nineteenth Century*. Garden City, N.Y: Doubleday, 1966.

Davis, D B, *The Problem of Slavery in the Age of Revolution, 1770-1823*. Ithaca, N.Y.: Cornell University Press, 1975.

Davies, R, et.al., 'Class Struggle and the Periodisation of the State in South Africa.' *Review of African Political Economy*, 7:4-30, 1976.

Davies, J N P, *Pestilence and Disease in the History of Africa*. Johannesburg: Witwatersrand University Press, 1979.

Davies, R H, *Capital, State and White Labour in South Africa 1900-1960*. Brighton: Harvester, 1979.

Davison, P and Harries, P, 'Cotton Weaving in South-East Africa: Its History and Technology.' *Textile History*, 11:175- 192, 1980.

Dawson, M H, 'Smallpox in Kenya, 1880-1920.' *Social Science and Medicine*, 13:245-250, 1979.

Dawson, M H, 'Disease and Population Decline of the Kikuyu of Kenya, 1890-1925.' In Fyfe, C and McMaster, D, eds., 1981.

De Kiewet, C W, *British Colonial Policy and the South African Republics*, 1929.

De Kiewet, C W, *A History of South Africa: Social and Economic*. London: Oxford University Press, 1957.

De Vries, J, 'Measuring the Impact of Climate on History: The Search for Appropriate Methodologies.' In Rotberg, R I and Rabb, T K, eds., 1981.

Dean, P, *The Evolution of Economic Ideas*. Cambridge: Cambridge University Press, 1978.

Deeb, M, 'The Socioeconomic Role of the Local Foreign Minorities in Modern Egypt, 1805-1961'. *International Journal of Middle East Studies*, 9:11-22, 1978.

Delegorgue, A, *Travels in Southern Africa*, Vol. 1. Durban: University of Natal Press, 1990.

Denoon, D and Nyeko, B, *Southern Africa Since 1800*. London: Longman, 1982.

Denoon, D, *Settler Capitalism: The Dynamics of Dependent Development in the Southern Hemisphere*. Oxford: Clarendon Press, 1983.

Denoon, D, 'The Political Economy of Labour Migration to Settler Societies: Australia, Southern Africa, and Southern South America, between 1890 and 1914.' In Marks, S and Richardson, P, eds., 1984.

Derricourt, R, 'Invasion Models and Zonal Exploitation in Later South African Prehistory.' In Fyfe and McMaster, eds., 1977.

Dewey, C and Hopkins, A G, eds., *The Imperial Impact: Studies in the Economic History of Africa and India*. London: Athlone Press, 1978.

Dias, J R, 'Famine and Disease in the History of Angola c. 1830-1930.' *Journal of African History*, 22:349-378, 1981.

Dike, K O, *Trade and Politics in the Niger Delta 1830-1885*. Oxford: Clarendon Press, 1956.

Diop, L M, 'Metallurgie et l'age de fer en Afrique.' BIFAN, 30:10-38, 1968.

Dorward, D C, 'An Unknown Nigerian Export: Tiv Benniseed Production, 1900-1960.' *Journal of African History*, 16:431-459, 1975.

Dorward, D C, and Payne, A I, 'Deforestation, the Decline of the Horse, and the Spread of the Tsetse Fly and Trypanosomiasis Nagana in the Nineteenth Century Sierra Leone.' *Journal of African History*, 16:239-256, 1975.

Dorward, D C, 'Pre-Colonial Tiv Trade and Cloth Currency.' *International Journal of African Historical Studies*, 9:576-591, 1976.

Douglas, M, 'The Lele Resistance to Change'. In Bohannan, P and Dalton, G, eds., 1965.

Douglas, M, 'Raffia Cloth Distribution in the Lele Economy.' In Dalton, G, ed., 1967.

Doumou, A, ed., *The Moroccan State in Historical Perspective 1850-1985*, Dakar: Codesria Book Series, 1990.

Doxey, G V, *The Industrial Colour Bar in South Africa*. London: Oxford University Press, 1961.

Drescher, S, *Econocide: British Slavery in the Era of Abolition*. Pittsburg: University of Pittsburg Press, 1977.

Drescher, S, *Capitalism and Anti-Slavery: British Popular Mobilization in Comparative Perspective*. New York: Oxford University Press, 1987.

Dubos, R, *Mirage of Health*. New York: Harper and Row, 1959.

Dubos, R, *Man, Medicine, and Environment*. Harmondsworth: Penguin Books, 1968.

Duffill, M B and Lovejoy, P E, 'Merchants, Porters, and Teamsters in the Nineteenth Century Central Sudan.' In Coquery Vidrovitch, C and Lovejoy, P E, eds.

Duly, C, *The Houses of Mankind*. London: Thames Hudson, 1979.

Dumett, R, 'The Rubber Trade of the Gold Coast and Asante in the Nineteenth Century. African Innovation and Market Responsiveness.' *Journal of African History*, 12:79-101, 1971.

Dumett, R, 'John Sarbah, the Elder, and African Mercantile Entrepreneurship in the Gold Coast in the Late Nineteenth Century.' *Journal of African History*, 14:663-679, 1973.

Duminy, A H and Guest, W R, eds., *Fitzpatrick, South African Politician: Selected Papers, 1888-1906*. Johannesburg and New York: McGraw-Hill, 1976.

Dumont, R, *Types of Rural Economy: Studies in World Agriculture*. London: Methuen, 1957.

Dupire, M, 'The Position of Women in a Pastoral Society The Fulani WoDaaBe, Nomads of the Niger'. In Paulme, D, ed., 1963.

Dupre, G, and Rey, P, 'Reflections on the Relevance of a Theory of the History of Exchange.' In D. Seddon, ed., 1978.

Durand, J D, «The Modern Expansion of World Population». *Population Problems, Proceedings of the American Philosophical Society*, 3, 1967.

Dyer, M, 'Export Production in Western Libya, 1750-93.' *African Economic History*, :117-136, 1984.

Dyson-Hudson, R and McCabe, J T, *South Turkana Nomadism: Coping with Unpredictably Varying Environment*. 2 Vols. New Haven: Human Relations Area Files, 1985.

Ehrensaft, P, 'The Political Economy of Informal Empire in Pre-colonial Nigeria, 1807-1884.' *Canadian Journal of African Studies*, 6:451-490, 1972.

Ehret, C, 'The Demographic Implications of Linguistic Change and Language Shift.' In Fyfe, C and McMaster, D, eds., 1981.

Ehret, C and Posnansky, M, eds., *The Archaeological and Linguistic Reconstruction of African History*. Los Angeles: University of California Press, 1982.

Ehret. C, «Linguistic Inference About Early Bantu History». In Ehret, C and Posnansky, M, eds., 1982.

Ehret, C, 'East African Words and Things: Agricultural Aspects of Economic Transformation in the Nineteenth Century.' In Ogot, B A, ed., 1985.

Elbl, I, 'The Horse in Fifteenth-Century'. *International Journal of African Historical Studies*, 24:85-109, 1991.

Eldridge, E A, 'Drought, Famine and Disease in Nineteenth- Century Lesotho.' *African Economic History*, 16:61-93, 1987.

Eldridge, E, 'Women in Production: The Economic Role of Women in Nineteenth Century Lesotho', *Signs: Journal of Women in Culture and Society*, 16:707-731, 1991.

Elphick, R, *Kraal and Castle: Khoikhoi and the Founding of White South Africa*. New Haven: Yale University Press, 1977.

Elphick, R and Shell, R, 'Intergroup Relations: Khoikhoi, Settlers, Slaves and Free Blacks, 1652-1795.' In Elphick, R and Giliomee, H, eds., 1989.

Elphick, R and Giliomee, H, eds., *The Shaping of South African Society*, 2nd ed. Cape Town: Longman, 1989.

Elphick, R and Malherbe, M C, 'The Khoisan to 1828.' In Elphick, R and Giliomee, H, 1989.

Eltis, D, 'Trade Between Western Africa and the Atlantic World Before 1870: Estimates of Trends in Value, Composition and Direction.' *Research in Economic History*, 12:151-196, 1989.

Emmanuel, A, *Unequal Exchange: A Study of the Imperialism of Trade*. New York: Monthly Review Press, 1974.

Erskine, J M, *Ecology and Land Usage in Southern Africa*. Pretoria: Africa Institute of South Africa, 1987.

Etherington, N, 'African Economic Experiments in Colonial Natal 1845-1880.' *African Economic History*, 5:1-15, 1978.

Etherton, D, 'Algerian Oases.' In Oliver, P, ed., 1971.

Evans-Pritchard, E E, *The Sanusi of Cyrenaica*. Oxford: Clarendon Press, 1949.

Faegre, T, *Tent: Architecture of the Nomads*. New York: Anchor Books, 1979.

Fagan, B M, 'Early Trade and Raw Materials in South Central Africa.' In Gray, R and Birmingham, D, eds., 1970.

Fage, J D, *An Introduction to the History of West Africa.* Cambridge: Cambridge University Press, 1955.

Fage, J D, 'Slavery and the Slave Trade in the Context of West African History.' *Journal of African History*, 10:393-404, 1969.

Fage, J D, 'The Effects of the Export Slave Trade on African Populations.' In R.P. Moss and R.J. Rathbone, eds., 1975.

Fage, J D, *History of Africa.* London: Hutchinson, 1978.

Fage, J D, 'Slaves and Society in Western Africa, c.1445 - c.1700.' *Journal of African History*, 21:289-310, 1980.

Fage, J D, 'African Societies and the Atlantic Slave Trade.' *Past and Present*, 125:97-115, 1989.

Fagerhund, V G, and Smith, H T, 'A Preliminary Map of Market Periodicities in Ghana.' *Journal of Developing Areas*, 4, 1970.

Fagg, B, 'Recent Work in West Africa: New Work on Nok Culture.' *World Archaeology*, 1:41-50, 1969.

Fagg, W, and Picton, J, *The Porters' Art in Africa.* London: British Museum, 1970.

Fagg, W, *Miniature Wood Carvings of Africa.* New York: Graphics Society, 1970.

Falola, T, ' Power Relations and Social Interactions Among Ibadan Slaves, 1850-1900.' *African Economic History*, 16:95-114, 1987.

Falola, T, 'The Yoruba Toll System: Its Operation and Abolition'. *Journal of African History*, 30:69-88, 1989.

Farias, P F de M, 'Silent Trade: Myth and Historical Evidence.' *History in Africa*, 7:9-24, 1974.

Farnie, D A, *East and West of Suez: The Suez Canal in History, 1854-1956.* Oxford: Clarendon Press, 1969.

Farnsworth, N R, et.al., 'Potential Value of Plants as Sources of New Anti-fertility Agents.' *Journal of Pharmaceutical Sciences*, Part I 64/4:535-598, Part II 64/5:717-754, 1975.

Feeley-Harnik, G, 'Cloth and the Creation of Ancestors in Madagascar.' In Schneider, A and Weimer, A B, eds., 1989.

Feierman, S, *Health and Society in Africa: A Working Bibliography.* Waltham, Mass, 1979.

Feierman, S, 'Struggles for Control: The Social Roots of Health and Healing in Modern Africa.' *African Studies Review*, 28:73-147, 1985.

Feierman, S, *Peasant Intellectuals: Anthropology and History in Tanzania,* Madison: University of Wisconsin Press, 1990.

Feinberg, H M, and Johnson, M, 'The West African Ivory Trade During the Eighteenth Century: The «...and Ivory» Complex.' *International Journal of African Historical Studies*, 15:435-453, 1982.

Fieldhouse, D K, *The Theory of Capitalist Imperialism.* London: Longman, 1967.

Fieldhouse, D K, *Economics and Empire, 1830-1914.* London: Wedenfeld and Nicholson, 1973.

Fika, A, *The Kano Civil War and British Over-Rule, 1882-1940.* Ibadan: Oxford University Press, 1978.

Filipowiak, W, 'Iron Working in the Old Kingdom of Mali.' In Haaland, R, et.al., 1985.

Fisher, A G B and Fisher, H J, *Slavery and Muslim Society in Africa.* London: G. Hurst, 1970.

Fisher, H J, 'He Swalloweth the Ground with Fierceness and Rage: The Horse in the Central Sudan: Its Introduction.' *Journal of African History*, 13:369-388, 1972.

Fisher, H J, 'The Horse in the Central Sudan II: Its Use.' *Journal of African History*, 14:355-379, 1973.

Flint, J E, 'Zanzibar 1890-1950'. In V. Harlow and E.M. Chilver, eds., 1965.

Flint, J E, 'Economic Change in West Africa in the Nineteenth Century.' In J.F.A Ajayi and M. Crowder, eds., 1974a.

Flint, J E, *Cecil Rhodes*. Boston: Little Brown, 1974b.

Flint, J E, ed., *The Cambridge History of Africa*. Vol. 5. *From c.1790 to c. 1870*, 8 Vols., Cambridge: Cambridge University Press, 1975.

Ford, J, *The Role of the Trypanosomiases in African Ecology: A Study of the Tsetsefly Problem.* Oxford: Clarendon Press, 1971.

Foster, G M, *Traditional Societies and Technological Change*. New York: Harper and Row, 1973.

Foster-Carter, A, 'The Modes of Production Controversy'. *New Left Review*, 107:47-77, 1978.

Frank, G, *Capitalism and Underdevelopment in Latin America*. New York: Monthly Review Press, 1967.

Frank, G, *Latin America: Underdevelopment or Revolution*. New York: Monthly Review Press, 1969.

Frank, G, *World Accumulation 1492-1789*. London: Macmillan, 1978a.

Frank, G, *Dependent Capitalism and Development*. New York: Monthly Review Press, 1978b.

Frank, A G, *Crisis: In the World Economy*. London: Heinemann, 1980.

Frank, A G, *Crisis: In the Third World*. London: Heinemann, 1981.

Frankel, S H, *Capital Investment in Africa*. Oxford: Oxford University Press, 1938.

Frantz, C, 'Fulbe Continuity and Change under Five Flags Atop West Africa.' *Journal of Asian and African Studies*, 16:89- 114, 1981.

Fraser, M and Jeeves, A, *All That Glittered: Selected Correspondence of Lionel Phillips, 1890-1924*. Cape Town: Oxford University Press, 1977.

Freeman-Grenville, G S P, 'The Times of Ignorance: A Review of Pre-Islamic Settlement on the East African Coast.' *Uganda Museum Occasional Papers*, 4:4-17, 1959.

Freeman-Grenville, G S P, 'The Coast, 1498-1840.' In Oliver, R and Mathews, G, eds., 1963.

Freeman-Grenville, G S P, 'Some Aspects of the External Relations of the East African Coast: Before 1800.' In Ingham, K, ed., 1974.

Freeman-Grenville, G S P, 'Numistic Evidence for Chronology at Kilwa.' *Numismatic Chronicle*, 28:191-196, 1978.

Freeman-Grenville, G S P, *The Swahili Coast, 2nd to 19th Centuries: Islam, Christianity and Commerce in Eastern Africa*. London: Variorum Reprints, 1988.

Freund, B, *Capital and Labour in the Nigerian Tin Mines*. Harlow: Longman, 1981.

Freund, B, 'Labour and Labour History in Africa: A Review of the Literature.' *African Studies Review*, 27:1-58, 1984a.

Freund, B, *The Making of Contemporary Africa: The Development of African Society Since 1800*. London: Macmillan, 1984b.

Freund, B, 'Theft and Social Protest among the tin miners of Northern Nigeria'. In Crummey, D, ed., 1986.

Freund, B, *The African Worker*. Cambridge: Cambridge University Press, 1988.

Freund, B, 'The Cape Under the Transitional Governments, 1795-1814.' In Elphick, R and Giliomee, H, 1989.

Friede, H, 'Notes on the Composition of Pre-European Copper and Copper-Alloy Artefacts from the Transvaal.' JSAIMM, 75, 1975.

Frishman, A, 'The Population Growth of Kano, Nigeria.' In Fyfe, C and McMaster, D, eds., 1977.

Fyfe, C, 'Reform in West Africa: The Abolition of the Slave Trade.' In Ajayi, J F A and Crowder, M, eds., 1974.

Fyfe, C, ed., *African Studies Since 1945*. London: Longman, 1976.

Fyfe, C and McMaster, D, eds., *African Historical Demography*, Vol.1. Edinburgh: University of Edinburgh, Centre for African Studies, 1977.

Fyfe, C and McMaster, D, eds., *African Historical Demography*, Vol.2. Edinburgh: University of Edinburgh, Centre for African Studies, 1981.

Fyle, C M, 'Northeast Sierra Leone in the Nineteenth and Twentieth Centuries: Reconstruction and Population Distribution in a Devastated Area.' In Fyfe, C and McMaster, D, eds., 1981.

Fynn, J K, 'Ghana-Asante Ashanti'. In Crowder, M, ed., 1978.

Gabel, C, 'Demographic Perspectives on the African Pleistocene.' In Fyfe, C and McMaster, D, eds., 1977.

Galaty, J G, 'Land and Livestock among Kenyan Maasai.' *Journal of Asian and African Studies*, 16:68-88, 1981.

Galbraith, J S and al-Sayyid-Marsot, A A, 'The British Occupation of Egypt: Another View.' *International Journal of Middle East Studies*, 9:471-488, 1978.

Galletti, R, Baldwin, K D S and Dina, I O, 'Clothing of Nigerian Cocoa Farmers' Families.' In Roach, M and Eicher, J B, eds., 1965.

Garlake, P S, *The Early Islamic Architecture of the East African Coast*. Nairobi and London: Oxford University Press, 1966.

Garlake, P S, 'Pastoralism and Zimbabwe.' *Journal of African History*, 19:479-493, 1978.

Gavin, R J, 'The European Conquest of Africa'. In Afigbo, E A, et.al., 1986.

Gebremedhin, N, 'Some Traditional Types of Housing in Ethiopia.' In Oliver, P, ed., 1971.

Geiger, S, 'Women and Class in Africa: A Review.' *African Economic History*, 16:115-122, 1987.

Gemery, H A and Hogendorn, J S, 'The Atlantic Slave Trade: A Tentative Economic Model.' *Journal of African History*, 15:233-246, 1974.

Gemery, H A and Hogendorn, J S, 'Technological Change, Slavery, and the Slave Trade.' In Dewey, C and Hopkins, A G, eds., 1978.

Gemery, A and Hogendorn, J S, eds., *The Uncommon Market: Essays in the Economic History of the Atlantic Slave Trade*. New York: Academic Press, 1979.

Genovese, E D, *From Rebellion to revolution: Afro-American Slave Revolts in the Making of the Modern World*. Baton Rouge: Louisiana State University, 1979.

Gerrard, T F, *Akan Weights and the Gold Trade*. London: Longman, 1980.

Ghai, Y P and Ghai, D P, *Portrait of a Minority: Asians in East Africa*. Nairobi: Oxford University Press, 1970.

Giblin, J, 'Famine and Social Change During the Transition to Colonial Rule in Northeastern Tanzania.' *African Economic History*, 15:85-105, 1986.

Gifford, P and Louis, W R, eds., *Britain and Germany in Africa*. New Haven: Yale University Press, 1967.

Gifford, P and Louis, W R, eds., *France and Britain in Africa*. New Haven: Yale University Press, 1971.

Gifford, P and Louis, W R, eds., *Decolonization and African Independence: The Transfers of Power, 1960-1980*. New Haven: Yale University Press, 1988.

Giliomee, H, 'The Eastern Frontier, 1770-1812.' In Elphick, R and Giliomee, H, eds., 1989.

Gislain, J J, 'On the Relations of State and Market.' *Telos*, 73:147-152, 1987.

Glantz, M H, ed., *Drought and Hunger in Africa: Denying Famine a Future.* Cambridge: Cambridge University Press, 1987a.

Glantz, M H, 'Drought and Economic Development in Sub- Saharan Africa.' In Glantz, ed., 1987b.

Glass, D V and Eversley, D E C, *Population in History.* Chicago: Aldine Publishing Co., 1965.

Glass, D V and Revelle, R, *Population and Social Change.* London: Edward Arnold, 1972.

Gleave, M B and Prothero, R M, 'Population Density and Slave Raiding - A Comment'. *Journal of African History*, 12:319-327, 1971.

Gluckman, M, 'Land Tenure: Group and Individual Rights.' In Z A and J M Konczacki, eds., 1977.

Gold, A E, 'Women in Agricultural Change: The Nandi in the 19th Century'. In Ogot, B A, ed., 1985.

Golledge, R, ed., *A Ground for a Common Search.* Santa Barbara: University of Santa Barbara Press, 1988.

Good, C M, 'Man, Milieu, and the Disease Factor: Tick- borne Relapsing Fever in East Africa.' In Patterson, K D and Hartwig, G W eds., 1978.

Goodfellow, C F, *Great Britain and South African Confederation, 1870-1881.* New York: Oxford University Press, 1967.

Goody, J, *Technology, Tradition and the State in Africa.* London: Oxford University Press, 1971.

Goody, J, *Production and Reproduction: A Comparative Study of the Domestic Domain.* Cambridge: Cambridge University Press, 1976.

Goody, E N, 'Daboya Weavers: Relations of Production, Dependence and Reciprocity.' In E.N. Goody, ed., 1982.

Goody, E N, ed., *From Craft to Industry: The Ethnography of Proto-Industrial Cloth Production.* Cambridge: Cambridge University Press, 1982.

Goucher, C L, 'Iron is Iron 'Til it is Rust: Trade and Ecology in the Decline of West African Iron-Smelting.' *Journal of African History*, 22:179-189, 1981.

Grace, J, *Domestic Slavery in West Africa with Particular Reference to the Sierra Leone Protectorate, 1896-1927.* London: Frederick Muller, 1975.

Gran, P, *Islamic Roots of Capitalism in Egypt, 1760-1840.* Austin: University of Texas Press, 1979.

Graves, A and Richardson, P, 'Plantations in the Political Economy of Colonial Sugar Production: Natal and Queensland, 1860-1914.' *Journal of South African Studies*, 6:214-229, 1980.

Gray, R F, *The Sonjo of Tanganyika: An Anthropological Study of an Irrigation-Based Society.* London: Oxford University Press, 1963.

Gray, R and Birmingham, D, eds., *Precolonial African Trade.* Oxford: Oxford University Press, 1970.

Greenland, D J and Lal, R, eds., *Soil Conservation and Management in the Humid Tropics.* Chichester: John Wiley, 1977.

Gregory, J W et.al., *African Historical Demography: A Multidisciplinary Bibliography.* Los Angeles: Crossroads, 1984.

Grove, A T, 'Desertification in the African Environment.' In Dalby, D, et.al., eds., 1977.

Grove, R, 'Early Themes in African Conservation.' In Anderson and Grove, eds., 1987.

Grove, R, 'Scottish Missionaries Evangelical Discourses and the Origins of Conservation Thinking in Southern Africa, 1820-1900.' *Journal of Southern African Studies,* 15:163-187, 1989.

Guelke, L, 'Freehold Farmers and Frontier Settlers, 1657- 1780.' In Elphick, R and Giliomee, H, eds., 1989.

Gugler, J and Flanagan, W G, *Urbanization and Social Change in West* Africa. Cambridge: Cambridge University Press, 1978.

Gump, J, 'Ecological Change and Pre-Shakan State formation'. *African Economic History,* 18:57-71, 1989.

Gutkind, P C W and Wallerstein, I, eds., *The Political Economy of Contemporary Africa.* Beverly Hills: Sage, 1976.

Gutkind, P C W and Waterman, P, eds., *African Social Studies: A Radical Reader.* London: Heinemann, 1977.

Gutkind, P C W, Cohen, R and Copans, J, eds., *African Labour History.* Beverly Hills: Sage, 1978.

Guy, J, *The Destruction of the Zulu Kingdom.* London: Longman 1979.

Guy, J, 'Ecological Factors in the Rise of Shaka and the Zulu Kingdom.' In Marks, S and Atmore, A, eds., 1980.

Guy, J, 'The Destruction and Reconstruction of Zulu Society.' In Marks, S and Rathbone, R, 1982.

Guy, J, 'Analysing Pre-Capitalist Societies in Southern Africa.' *Journal of Southern African Studies,* 14:18-37, 1987.

Guyer, J I, 'Household and Community in African Studies.' *African Studies Review,* 24:87-137, 1981.

Haaland, R and Shinnie, P, eds., *African Iron Working - Ancient and Traditional.* Oslo: Norwegian University Press, 1985.

Haaland, R, 'Iron Production, Its Socio-Cultural Context and Ecological Implications.' In Haaland, R and Shinnie, P, eds., 1985.

Hafkin, N J and Bay, E S, eds., *Women in Africa: Studies in Social and Economic Change.* Stanford: Stanford University Press, 1976.

Hair, P E H, 'From Language to Culture: Some Problems in the Systemic Analysis of the Ethno-Historical Records of the Sierra Leone Region.' In Moss, R P and Rathbone, R J, eds., 1975.

Hakem, A A, and Hrbek, I, 'The Civilization of Napata and Meroe.' In Mokhtar, G, ed., 1981.

Hall, M and Vogel, J C, 'Some Recent Radiocarbon Dates from Southern Africa'. *Journal of African History,* 21:431-455, 1980.

Hall, M, 'Archaeology and Modes of Production in Pre- Colonial Southern Africa.' *Journal of Southern African Studies,* 14:1-17, 1987.

Hamdan, G, 'Evolution of Irrigation Agriculture in Egypt.' In Stamp, L D, ed., 1961.

Hammond, R J, 'Economic Imperialism, Side-lights on a Stereotype'. *Journal of Economic History,* 21:582-598, 1961.

Hammond, R J, *Portugal and Africa 1815-1910.* Stanford: Stanford University Press, 1966.

Hance, W A, *The Geography of Modern Africa.* New York: Columbia University Press, 1975.

Hansen, B, 'Income and Consumption in Egypt, 1886/1887 to 1937.' *International Journal of Middle East Studies,* 10:27-47, 1979.

Hansen, W and Schulz, B, 'Imperialism, Dependency and Social Class.' *Africa Today,* 1981:5-36, 1981.

Harding, L, 'Hamburg's West Africa Trade in the 19th Century.' In G. Liesegang, H. Pasch and A. Jones, eds., 1983.

Hargreaves, J D, 'The European Partition of West Africa'. In Ajayi, J F A and Crowder, M, eds., 1974a.

Hargreaves, J D, *West Africa Partitioned: The Loaded Pause*. Madison: University of Wisconsin Press, 1974b.

Harlan, J R, et.al., 'Plant Domestication and Indigenous African Agriculture.' In Harlan et.al., eds, 1976a.

Harlan, J R, et.al., eds., *Origins of African Plant Domestication*. Mouton: The Hague, 1976b.

Harlow, V and Chilver, E M, eds., *History of East Africa.* Vol.2. Oxford: Clarendon Press, 1965.

Harms, R, 'Slave Systems in Africa.' *History in Africa*, 5:327-335, 1978.

Harms, R W, *River of Wealth, River of Sorrow: The Central Zaire Basin in the Era of the Slave and Ivory Trade, 1500-1891*. New Haven: Yale University Press, 1981.

Harms, R, 'Sustaining the System: Trading Towns Along the Middle Zaire.' In Robertson, C C and Klein, M A, eds., 1983.

Harrell-Bond, B E, *Imposing Aid Emergency Assistance to Refugees*. Oxford: Oxford University Press, 1986.

Harries, P, 'Slavery, Social Incorporation and Surplus Extraction; The Nature of Free and Unfree Labour in Southern Africa.' *Journal of African History*, 22:309-330, 1981.

Harries, P, 'Kinship, Ideology and the Nature of Pre- Colonial Labour Migration.' In Marks, S and Rathbone, R, eds., 1982.

Harries, P, 'Plantations, Passes and Proletarians: Labour and the Colonial State in Nineteenth Century Natal.' *Journal of Southern African Studies*, 13:372-399, 1987.

Harris, D R, 'Traditional Systems of Plant Food Production and the Origins of Agriculture in West Africa.' In Harlan, J R, et.al., 1976.

Harris, N, *The End of the Third World.* Harmondsworth: Penguin, 1986.

Hart, K, *The Political Economy of West African Agriculture*. Cambridge: Cambridge University Press, 1982.

Hartwig, G W, 'Economic Consequences of Long-Distance Trade in East Africa: The Disease Factor.' *African Studies Review*, 18:63-73, 1975.

Hartwig, G W, 'Social Consequences of Epidemic Diseases: The Nineteenth Century in Eastern Africa.' In Patterson, K D and Hartwig, G W eds., 1978.

Hartwig, G W, 'Demographic Considerations in East Africa During the Nineteenth Century.' *The International Journal of African Historical Studies*, 12:653-672, 1979.

Hartwig, G W, 'Smallpox in the Sudan.' *African Studies Review-*, 24: 5-33, 1981.

Harvey, T J, *The Paleolimnology of Lake Mobutu Sese-Seko, Uganda - Zaire: The Last 28,000 years*. Ph.D. Dissertation, Duke University, 1976.

Hay, M J, and Stichter, S, eds., *African Women South of the Sahara*. Harlow: Longman, 1984.

Hay, M J, 'Queens, Prostitutes and Peasants: Historical Perspectives on African Women, 1971-1986.' *Canadian Journal of African Studies*, 22:431-447, 1988.

Hayes, C J H, *A Generation of Materialism, 1871-1900*. New York: Harper and Row, 1941.

Hayford, J E C, *Gold Coast Native Institutions*, new ed. London: Frank Cass, 1970.

Headrick, D, *Tools of Empire: Technology and European Imperialism in the Nineteenth Century*. New York: Oxford University Press, 1981.

Headrick, D, *The Tentacles of Progress: Technology in the Age of Imperialism 1850-1940*. New York: Oxford University Press, 1988.

Hedlund, H, 'Contradictions in the Peripheralization of a Pastoral Society: The Maasai.' *Review of African Political Economy*, 15/16:15-34, 1979.

Henderson, W O, 'German East Africa 1884-1918.' In Harlow, V and Chilver, E M, eds., 1965.

Henige, D, 'Measuring the Immeasurable: The Atlantic Slave Trade, West African Population and the Pyrrhonian Critic.' *Journal of African History*, 27:295-313, 1986.

Henn, J K, 'Women in the Rural Economy: Past, Present, and Future.' In Hay, M J and Stichter, S, eds., 1984.

Herbert, E W, 'Aspects of the Use of Copper in Pre- colonial West Africa.' *Journal of African History*, 14:179-194, 1973.

Herbert, E W, 'Smallpox Inoculation in Africa.' *Journal of African History*, 16:539-559, 1975.

Herbert, E W, *Red Gold of Africa: Copper in Precolonial History and Culture*. Madison: University of Wisconsin Press, 1984.

Hermassi, E, *Leadership and National Development in North Africa*. Berkeley: University of California Press, 1972.

Herskovits, M J, 'The Cattle Complex in East Africa.' *American Anthropologist*, 28:230-72, 361-80, 494-528, 633-664, 1926.

Hesselberg, J, *The Third World in Transition: The Case of the Peasantry in Botswana*. Uppsala: Scandinavian Institute of African Studies, 1985.

Heywood, L, 'Porters, Trade and Power: The Politics of Labour in the Central Highlands of Angola, 1850-1914.' In Coquery-Vidrovitch, C and Lovejoy, P E, eds., 1985.

Heywood, L M, 'The Growth and Decline of African Agriculture in Central Angola, 1890-1950.' *Journal of Southern African Studies*, 13:355-371, 1987.

Heywood, L and Thornton, J, 'African Fiscal Systems as Sources for Demographic History: The Case of Central Angola, 1799-1920.' *Journal of African History*, 29:213-228, 1988.

Hill, P, *The Gold Coast Cocoa Farmer: A Preliminary Survey*. London: Oxford University Press, 1956.

Hill, M F, *Permanent Way*. Vol.1. *The Story of the Kenya and Uganda Railway*, 2nd ed. Nairobi: East African Railways and Harbours, 1961.

Hill, M F, *Permanent Way*. Vol.2. *The Story of the Tanganyika Railways*. Nairobi: East African Railways and Harbours, 1962.

Hill, P, 'Markets in Africa.' *Journal of Modern African Studies*, 1:441-453, 1963.

Hill, P, 'Notes on Traditional Market Authority and Market Periodicity in West Africa.' *Journal of African History*, 7:295- 311, 1966.

Hill, R, *Sudan Transport*. London, 1965.

Hill, P, 'Two Types of West African House Trade.' In Meillassoux, C, ed., 1971.

Hill, P, 'Problems with A.G. Hopkins' Economic History of West Africa'. *African Economic History*, 6:127-133, 1978.

Hill, M and Vogel, J C, 'Some Recent Radio Carbon Dates from Southern Africa.' *Journal of African History*, 21:431-455, 1980.

Hindess, B and Hirst, P Q, *Pre-Capitalist Modes of Production*. London: Routledge and Kegan Paul, 1975.

Hindess, B and Hirst, P Q, *Mode of Production and Social Formation: An Auto-Critique of 'Pre-capitalist Modes of Production*. London: Macmillan, 1977.

Hitchcock, R R and Smith, M R, eds., *Proceedings of the Symposium on Botswana: The Historical Development of a Human Landscape*. Marshalltown, S.A.: Heinemann Educational Books, 1982.

Hoben, A, *Land Tenure Among the Amhara of Ethiopia*. Chicago: The University of Chicago Press, 1973.

Hobsbawm, E and Ranger, T, eds., *The Invention of Tradition*. Cambridge: Cambridge University Press, 1989.

Hobson, J A, *Imperialism: A Study*. Ann Arbor: University of Michigan Press, 1965.

Hobson, J A, *The War in South Africa*. New York: Fertig, 1969.

Hodder, B W, 'Periodic and Daily Markets in West Africa.' In Meillassoux, C, ed., 1971.

Hogendorn, J, 'The Economics of Slave Use on two 'Plantations' in the Zaria Emirate of the Sokoto Caliphate.' *The International Journal of African Historical Studies*, 10:369- 383, 1977.

Hogendorn, J S, *Nigerian Groundnut Exports: Origins and Early Development*. Zaria and Ibadan: Amadhu Bello University Press and Oxford University Press, 1978.

Hogendorn, J S and Johnson, M, 'The Cowrie Trade to West Africa from the Maldives in the Nineteenth Century.' In Liesegang, G, Pasch, H and Jones, A, eds., 1983.

Hogendorn, J S and Johnson, M, *The Shell Money of the Slave Trade*. Cambridge: Cambridge University Press, 1986.

Hogendorn, J S and Gemery, H A, 'Continuity in West African Monetary History? An Outline of Monetary Development'. *African Economic History*, 17:127-146, 1988.

Hogendorn, J S and Gemery, H A, 'Assessing Productivity in Precolonial African Agriculture and Industry 1500-1800.' *African Economic History*, 19:31-35, 1990-91.

Hollingsworth, T H, *Historical Demography*. New York: Ithaca, 1969.

Holsinger, D C, 'Migration, Commerce and Community: The Mizabis in Eighteenth and Nineteenth Century Algeria.' *Journal of African History*, 21:61-74, 1980.

Holt, E, *The Boer War*. Putman: London, 1958.

Holt, P M and Daly, M W, *The History of the Sudan*. London: Weidenfeld and Nicholson, 1979.

Homewood, K and Rodgers, W A, 'Pastoralism, Conservation and the Overgrazing Controversy'. In Anderson, D and Grove, R, eds., 1987.

Hopkins, A G, 'The Currency Revolution in South West Africa.' *Journal of the Historical Society of Nigeria*, 3:471- 483, 1966.

Hopkins, A G, *An Economic History of West Africa*. London: Longman, 1973.

Hopkins, B, *Forest and Savanna*, 2nd ed. London: Heinemann, 1974.

Hopkins, A G, 'Imperial Connections.' In Dewey, C and Hopkins, A G, eds., 1978a.

Hopkins, A G, 'Innovation in a Colonial Context: African Origins of the Nigerian Cocoa-Farming Industry, 1880-1920.' In Dewey, C and Hopkins, A G, eds., 1978b.

Hopkins, A G, 'Africa's Age of Improvement.' *History in Africa*, 7:141-160, 1980.

Hopkins, A G, 'The Victorians and Africa: A Reconsideration of the Occupation of Egypt, 1982.' *Journal of African History*, 27:363-391, 1986.

Hopkins, A G, 'African Entrepreneurship: An Essay on the Relevance of History to Development Economics.' *Geneve-Afrique*, 26:8-28, 1988.

Hopkins, A G, 'African Economic History: The First Twenty- Five Years'. *Journal of African History*, 30:157-163, 1989.

Horn, L V, 'The Agricultural History of Barotseland, 1840-1964.' In Palmer and Parsons, eds., 1977.

Horowitz, R, *The Political Economy of South Africa*. London: Weidenfeld and Nicholson, 1967.

Horowitz, M and Little, P D, 'African Pastoralism and Poverty: Some Implications for Drought and Famine.' In Glantz, M H, ed., 1987.

Horton, R, *Kalabari Sculpture*. Apapa, Nigeria: Department of Antiquities, 1965.

Houghton, D H, *The South African Economy*, 2nd ed. Cape Town: Oxford University Press, 1967.

Houghton, D H and Dagut, J, *Source Material on the South African Economy, 1860-1970*. Vol.1: *1860-1899*. Cape Town: Oxford University Press, 1972.

Hourani, A, 'Ottoman Reform and the Politics of Notables.' In Polk, W and Chambers, R, eds., 1968.

Hourani, A H and Stern, S M, eds., *The Islamic City*. Berkeley and Los Angeles: University of California Press, 1970.

Howard, A M, 'The Relevance of Spatial Analysis for African Economic History: The Sierra Leone-Guinea System'. *Journal of African History*, 17:365-388, 1976.

Hsiao, J C, 'The Theory of Share Tenancy Revisited.' *Journal of Political Economy*, 18:1023-1032, 1975.

Hull, R W, *African Cities and Towns Before the European Conquest*. New York: Norton, 1976.

Hunt, K S, *The 1820 Settlers*. Cape Town, 1984.

Hunter, F R, *Egypt Under the Khedives 1805-1879*. Pittsburg: University of Pittsburg Press, 1984.

Hyam, R and Martin, G, *Reappraisals in British Imperial History*. London, 1975.

Hyam, R, *Britain's Imperial Century, 1815-1914: A Study of Empire and Expansion*. London: B.T. Batsford, 1976.

Hyam, R, 'Empire and Sexual Opportunity.' *Journal of Imperial and Commonwealth History*, 14:34-89, 1986.

Hyam, R, '"Imperialism and Sexual Exploitation": A Reply.' *Journal of Imperial and Commonwealth History*, 17:90-98, 1988.

Hyden, G, *Beyond Ujamaa in Tanzania*. London: Heinemann, 1980.

Hyden, G, *No Shortcuts to Progress*. London: Heinemann, 1983.

Hynes, W G, *The Economics of Empire: Britain, Africa and the New Imperialism*. London: Longman, 1979.

Idiens, D, 'An Introduction to Traditional African Weaving and Textiles.' *Textile History*, 11:5-21, 1980.

Igbafe, P A, 'Slavery and Emancipation in Benin, 1897-1945.' *Journal of African History*, 16:409-429, 1975.

Igbozurike, U M, *Agriculture at the Crossroads: A Comment on Agricultural Ecology*. Ile-Ife: University of Ife Press, 1977.

Ikime, O, *Merchant Prince of the Niger Delta: The Rise and Fall of Nana Olomu Last Governor of the Benin River*. Ibadan: Heinemann, 1968.

Illife, J, *A Modern History of Tanganyika*. Cambridge: Cambridge University Press, 1979.

Illife, J, *The African Poor: A History*. Cambridge: Cambridge University Press, 1987.

Imperato, P J, *African Folk Medicine: Practices and Beliefs of the Bambara and Other Peoples*. Baltimore: York Press, 1977.

Indakwa, J, *Expansion of British Rule in the Interior of Central Africa, 1890-1924: A Study of British Imperial Expansion into Zambia, Zimbabwe and Malawi*. Washington: University of America Press, 1977.

Ingham, K, ed., *Foreign Relations of African States*, London: Butterworths, 1974.

Inikori, J E, 'Introduction.' In Inikori, J E, ed., 1982.

Inikori, J E, 'Measuring the Atlantic Slave Trade on Africa: A Review of the Literature.' *Journal of African History*, 17:197-223, 1976.

Inikori, J E, 'The Import of Firearms into West Africa, 1750-1807.' *Journal of African History*, 18:339-368, 1977.

Inikori, J E, 'Under-Population in Nineteenth Century West Africa: The Role of the Export Slave Trade.' In Fyfe, C and McMaster, D, eds., 1981.

Inikori, J E, ed., *Forced Migration: The Impact of the Export Slave Trade on West African Societies.* New York: Africana Publishing Co., 1982.

Inikori, J E, 'West Africa's Seaborne Trade, 1750-1850.' In Liesegang, H, Pasch, and Jones, A, eds., 1983.

Innes, D, *Anglo-American and the Rise of Modern South Africa.* New York: Monthly Review Press, 1984.

Irvine, F R, *West African Crops.* London: Oxford University Press, 1969.

Isaacman, A, *Mozambique: The Africanization of a European Institution. The Zambezi Prazos, 1750-1902.* Madison: University of Wisconsin Press, 1972.

Isaacman, A and Isaacman, B, 'The Prazeros as Transfrontiersmen: A Study in Social and Cultural Change.' *International Journal of African Historical Studies*, 8:1-12, 1975.

Isaacman, A, *The Tradition of Resistance in Mozambique: Anti-Colonial Activity in the Zambezi Valley, 1850-1921.* London: Heinemann, 1976.

Isaacman, A, 'Social Banditry in Zimbabwe Rhodesia and Mozambique, 1894-1907: An Expression of Early Peasant Protest.' *Journal of Southern African Studies*, 4:1-30, 1977.

Isaacman, A and Mandala, E, 'From Porters to Labour Extractors: The Chikunda and Kololo in the Lake Malawi and Tchiri River Area.' In Coquery-Vidrovitch, C and Lovejoy, P E, eds., 1985.

Isaacman, A, 'Ex-Slaves, Transfrontiersmen and the Slave Trade: The Chikunda of the Zambezi Valley, 1850-1900.' In Lovejoy, ed., 1986.

Isaacman, A, 'Peasants and Rural Social Protest in Africa.' *African Studies Review*, 33:1-120, 1990.

Issawi, C, *Egypt in Revolution: An Economic Analysis.* London: Oxford University Press, 1963.

Issawi, C, 'De-Industrialization and Re-Industrialization in the Middle East.' *International Journal of Middle East Studies*, 12:469-479, 1980.

Issawi, C, *An Economic History of the Middle East and North Africa.* New York: Columbia University Press, 1982.

Jackson, D, 'Resistance to the German Invasion of the Tanganyikan Coast, 188-1891.' In Rotberg, R I and Mazrui, A A, eds., 1970.

Jackson, M, 'The Dimensions of Kamba Pre-colonial History.' In Ogot, B A, ed., 1986.

Jacoby, E H, *Man and Land: The Fundamental Issue in Development.* London: Andre Deutsch, 1971.

Jagger, P, 'Kano City Blacksmiths: Precolonial Distribution, Structure and Organisation.' *Savanna*, 2:11-25, 1973.

James, C L R, *The Black Jacobins.* New York: Vintage Books, 1963.

Janmohammed, K, *A History of Mombasa: Some Aspects of Economic and Social Life in an East African Port Town During Colonial Rule.* Ph.D. Dissertation, Northwestern University, 1977.

Janmohammed, K, 'The Emergence of Mombasa as the Chief Commercial Centre of East Africa:1895-1914.' In Liesegang, G, Pasch, H and Jones, A, eds., 1983.

Jeeves, A H, *Migrant Labour in South Africa's Mining Economy: The Struggle for the Gold Mines' Labour Supply 1890-1920.* Kingston and Montreal: McGill-Queen's University Press, 1985.

Jeng, A A O, *The Export Economy of the Gambia: Production, Marketing and International Trade: A Study in Dependency and Underdevelopment.* Ph.D. dissertation, University of Birmingham, 1978.

Jewsiewicki, B and Letourneau, J, eds., *Modes of Production: The Challenge of Africa.* Ste-Foy: SAFI, 1985.

Jewsiewicki, B and Newbury, D, eds., *African Historiographies: What History for Which Africa.* Beverly Hills: Sage, 1986.

Jewsiewicki, B, 'Toward a Historical Sociology of Population in Zaire: Proposals for the Analysis of the Demographic Regime.' In Cordell, J et. al., eds., 1987.

Johns, B R, *Business Investment and Imperialism: The Relationship Between Economic Interests and the Growth of British Intervention in Egypt, 1838-82.* Ph.D. thesis, Exeter University, 1982.

Johnson, D G, 'Resource allocation under share contracts. *Journal of Political Economy,* 58:111-123, 1950.

Johnson, D H and Anderson, D M, eds., *The Ecology of Survival: Case Studies From Northeastern African History.* Boulder, Col.: Westview,. 1988.

Johnson, M, 'The Ounce in Eighteenth Century West African Trade.' *Journal of African History,* 7:197-214, 1966.

Johnson, M, 'The Nineteenth Century Gold 'Mithqal' in West Africa and North Africa.' *Journal of African History,* 9:547-569, 1968.

Johnson, M, 'The Cowrie Currencies of West Africa.' *Journal of African History,* 3:17-49 Part 1, 331-353 Part 2, 1970.

Johnson, M, 'The Economic Foundations of an Islamic Theocracy - The Case of Masina', *Journal of African History,* 17:481-495, 1976a.

Johnson, M, 'Calico-Caravans: The Tripoli-Kano Trade After 1880.' *Journal of African History,* 17:95-117, 1976b.

Johnson, M, 'Technology, Competition, and African Crafts.' In C. Dewey and A.G. Hopkins, eds., 1978a.

Johnson, M, 'By Ship or by Camel: The Struggle for the Cameroons Ivory Trade in the Nineteenth Century.' *Journal of African History,* 19:539-549, 1978b.

Johnson, M, 'Cloth as Money: The Strip Cloth Currencies of Africa. *Textile History,* 11:193-202, 1980.

Johnson, M, 'On Computerising Trade Statistics.' In G. Liesegang, H. Pasch and A. Jones, eds., 1983a.

Johnson, M, 'Ivory and the Nineteenth Century Transformation in West Africa.' In Liesegang, G, Pasch, H and Jones, A, eds., 1983b.

Johnson-Odim, C and Strobel, M, eds., *Restoring Women to History.* Bloomington: Organization of American Historians, 1988.

Johnston, B F, *The Staple Food Economies of Western Africa.* Stanford: Stanford University Press, 1963.

Johnstone, F, *Class, Race and Gold: A Study of Class Relations and Racial Discrimination in South Africa.* London: Routledge Keegan Paul, 1976.

Jones, W O, *Manioc in Africa.* Stanford: Stanford University Press, 1959.

Jones, G I, *The Trading States of the Oil Rivers.* London: Oxford University Press, 1963.

July, R W, *A History of the African People,* 4th ed. Prospect Heights, Ill.: Waveland Press, 1992.

Kader, S A, *Egyptian Women in a Changing Society, 1896-1987.* Boulder and London: Lynne Rienner, 1987.

Kahn, J S and Llobera, J R, eds., *The Anthropology of Pre-capitalist Societies.* London: Macmillan, 1981.

Kallaway, F, 'Preliminary Notes Toward a Study of Labour on the Diamond Fields of Griqualand West.' Paper delivered at the Workshop on the Social and Economic History of South Africa, Oxford University, 1974.

Kamuhangire, E R, 'The Precolonial Economic and Social History of East Africa.' In Ogot, B A, eds., 1979.

Kaplow, S, 'The Mudfish and the Crocodile: Underdevelopment of a West African Bourgeoisie.' *Science and Society*, 41:317-33, 1977.

Kaplow, S B, 'Primitive Accumulation and Traditional Social Relations on the Nineteenth Century Gold Coast.' *Canadian Journal of African Studies*, 12:19-36, 1978.

Kapteijns, L and Spaulding, J, 'Precolonial Trade Between States in the Eastern Sudan, ca. 1700 - ca. 1900.' *African Economic History*, 11:29-57, 1982.

Katzenellenbogen, S E, 'Katanga's Trade in the Pre- Colonial Period and its Collapse on the Eve of the Belgian Penetration.' In Liesegang, G, Pasch, H and Jones, A, eds., 1983.

Kay, G, *Development and Underdevelopment: A Marxist Analysis*. London: Macmillan, 1975.

Kea, R, *Settlements Trade and Politics in the Seventeenth- Century Gold Coast*. Baltimore: Johns Hopkins University Press, 1982.

Keddie, N R, 'Problems in the Study of Middle Eastern Women.' *International Journal of Middle East Studies*, 10:225- 240, 1979.

Kedourie, E and Hain, S G, eds., *Economic History of the Middle East*, London: Frank Cass, 1988.

Keegan, T, 'The Share Cropping Economy, African Class Formation and the Natives' Land Act in the Highveld Maize Belt.' In Marks, S and Rathbone, R, eds., 1982.

Keegan, T, 'The Sharecropping Economy on the South African Highveld in the Early Twentieth Century.' *Journal of Peasant Studies*, 10:201-226, 1983.

Keegan, T, 'Trade, Accumulation and Impoverishment: Mercantile Capital and the Economic Transformation of Lesotho and the Conquered Territory, 1870-1920.' *Journal of Southern African Studies*, 12:196-216, 1986a.

Keegan, T, 'White Settlement and Black Subjugation on the South African Highveld: The Tlokoa Heartland in the North Eastern Orange Free State, ca. 1850-1914'. In Beinart,W, Delius, P and Trapido, S, eds., 1986b.

Keegan, T, *Rural Transformations in Industrialising South Africa: The Southern Highveld to 1914*. London: Macmillan, 1987.

Keegan, T, *Facing the Storm: Portraits of Black Lives in Rural South Africa*. Athens: Ohio State University, 1988.

Keegan, T, 'The Origins of Agrarian Capitalism in South Africa: A Reply.' *Journal of Southern African Studies*, 15:666- 683, 1989.

Keenan, J, 'The Concept of the mode of production in hunter-gatherer societies.' In Kahn, J S and Llobera, J R, eds., 1981.

Kehoe, D P, *The Economics of Agriculture on Roman Imperial Estates in North Africa*. Gottingen: Vandenhoeck and Ruprecht, 1988.

Kendall, R L, 'An Ecological History of the Lake Victoria Basin.' *Ecological Monograph*, 39:121-176, 1969.

Kense, F J, *Daboya: A Gonja Frontier*. Ph.D. Dissertation, University of Calgary, 1981.

Kense, F J, *Traditional African Iron-Working*. Calgary: University of Calgary, African Occasional Papers, 1, 1983.

Kense, F J, 'The Initial Diffusion of Iron to Africa.' In Haaland, R and Shinnie, P, eds., 1985.

Keppel-Jones, A, *South Africa: A Short History*. London: Hutchinson, 1975.

Kerridge, E, *The Agricultural Revolution*. New York: M. Kelley, 1968.

Keteku, E, *The Iron Age in Ghana*. M.A. thesis, University of Calgary, 1975.

Kibrieab, G, *Some Reflections of the African Refugee Problem: A Critical Analysis of Some Basic Assumptions*. Uppsala: Institute of the African Studies, 1983.

Kieran, J A, 'Abushiri and the Germans.' In Ogot, B A, ed., 1970.

Kiernan, V G, *Marxism and Imperialism*. London: Edward Arnold, 1974.

Kimambo, I N and Temu, A J, eds. *A History of Tanzania*. Nairobi: East African Publishing House, 1969,

Kimble, J, 'Labour Migration in Basutoland c. 1870-1885.' In Marks, S and Rathbone, R, eds., 1982.

King, A D, ed., *Buildings and Society: Essays on the Social Development of the Built Environment*. London: Routledge and Kegan Paul, 1980.

Kinross, Lord, *Between Two Seas: The Creation of the Suez Canal*. London: The Camelot Press, 1968.

Kinsman, M, '"Beasts of Burden": The Subordination of Southern Tswana, ca. 1800-1840.' *Journal of Southern African Studies*, 10:39-54, 1983.

Kirk, T, 'The Cape Economy and the Expropriation of the Kat River Settlement, 1846-1853.' In Marks, S and Atmore, A, eds., 1980.

Kiwanuka, M S M, 'Uganda Under the British.' In Ogot, B A, ed., 1974.

Kjekshus, H, 'The Population Trends of East African History: A Critical Review.' In Fyfe, C and McMaster, D, eds., 1977b.

Kjekshus, H, *Ecology Control and Economic Development in East African History*. London: Heinemann, 1977a.

Klein, M A, 'African Social History'. *African Studies Review*, 15:97-112, 1972.

Klein, M, 'Servitude Among the Wolof and Serer of Senegambia.' In Miers, S and Kopytoff, I, eds., 1977.

Klein, M A, 'The Study of Slavery in Africa: A Review Article.' *Journal of African History*, 19:599-609, 1978.

Klein, M A and Lovejoy, P E, 'Slavery in West Africa.' In Gemery, H and Hogendorn, J, eds., 1979.

Klein, M A, 'Women Slavery in the Western Sudan.' In Robertson, C and Klein, M A, eds., 1983.

Klein, M A, 'The Demography of Slavery in Western Sudan: The Late Nineteenth Century.' In Cordell, D D and Gregory, J W, eds., 1987.

Klingshirn, A, *The Changing Position of Women in Ghana*. Ph.D. dissertation, Philipps University, Marburg/Lahn, 1971.

Knuffel, W E, *The Construction of the Bantu Grass Hut*. Graz, Austria: Akademische Druck, 1973.

Koebner, R and Schmidt, H D, *Imperialism: The Story of a Political Word, 1840-1960*. Cambridge: Cambridge University Press, 1964.

Kohil, A, ed., *The State and Development in the Third World*. Princeton, N.J: Princeton University Press, 1986.

Konczacki, Z A and J M, eds., *An Economic History of Tropical Africa*. 2 Vols. London: Frank Cass, 1977.

Konczacki, Z A, Parpart, J L and Shaw, T M, eds., *Studies in the Economic History of Southern Africa*. London: Frank Cass, 1990.

Koponen, J, 'War, Famine, and Pestilence in Late Precolonial Tanzania: A Case for a Heightened Mortality.' *International Journal of African Historical Studies*, 21:637-676, 1988.

Kopytoff, I and Miers, S, 'African "Slavery" as an Institution of Marginality'. In Miers, S and Kopytoff, I, eds., 1977.

Krapf-Askari, E, *Yoruba Towns and Cities*. Oxford: Clarendon, 1969.

Kriedte, P, et.al., *Industrialisation Before Industrialisation.* Cambridge: Cambridge University Press, 1981.

Kubicek, R V, *Economic Imperialism in Theory and Practice: The Case of South African Gold Mining Finance, 1886-1914.* Durham, N.C: Duke University Press, 1979.

Kutzbach, J E, 'Estimates of Past Climate at Paleolake Chad, North Africa Based on a Hydrological and Energy-balance Model.' *Quaternary Research*, 14:210-223, 1980.

Lacey, M, *Working for Boroko: The Origins of a Coercive Labour System in South Africa.* Johannesburg: Ravan Press, 1981.

Lacoste, Y, 'General Characteristics and Fundamental Structures of Medieval North African Society.' *Economy and Society*, 3:1-17, 1974.

Lado, C, 'Agricultural and Environmental Knowledge: A Case Study of Peasant Farming in Maridi District, Southern Sudan.' *Malaysian Journal of Tropical Geography*, 13:7-36, 1986.

Lal, R and Greenland, D J, eds., *Soil Physical Properties and Crop Production in the Tropics.* Chichester: Wiley, 1979.

Lamb, V, *West African Weaving.* London: Duckworth, 1975.

Lamb, H H, *Climate: Present, Past and Future.* Vol.2. *Climatic History and the Future.* London: Methuen, 1977.

Lamb, V and Lamb, A, 'The Classification of Horizontal Treadle Looms in Sub-Saharan Africa.' *Textile History*, 11:22- 62, 1980.

Lamb, H H, *Climate, History and the Modern World.* London and New York: Methuen, 1982.

Lamphear, J, 'The Kamba and the Northern Mrima Coast.' In Gray, R and Birmingham, D, eds., 1970.

Lamprey, H F, 'Pastoralism Yesterday and today: The Overgrazing Problem.' In Bourliere, F, ed., 1983.

Landes, D, *Bankers and Pashas: International Finance and Economic Imperialism in Egypt.* Cambridge, Mass.: Harvard University Press, 1958.

Lane, E W, *Manners and Customs of Modern Egyptians.* The Hague and London: East-West Publications, 1978.

Lanning, G with Mueller, M, *Africa Undermined: A History of the Mining Companies and the Underdevelopment of Africa.* Harmondsworth: Penguin, 1979.

Last, M, *The Sokoto Caliphate.* London: Longman, 1977.

Latham, A J H, 'Currency, Credit and Capitalism on the Cross River in the Pre-Colonial Era.' *Journal of African History*, 12:599-605, 1971.

Latham, A J H, *Old Calabar 1600-1891: The Impact of the International Economy Upon a Traditional Society.* Oxford: Clarendon, 1973.

Latham, A J H, *The International Economy and the Underdeveloped World.* London: Croom Helm, 1978a.

Latham, A J H, 'Price Fluctuations in the Early Palm Oil Trade.' *Journal of African History*, 19:213-218, 1978b.

Latham, A J H, 'Palm Oil Exports from Calabar 1812-1887 With a note on Price Formation.' In Liesegang, G, Pasch, H and A. Jones, A, eds., 1983.

Law, R, *The Oyo Empire, c.1600-c.1836: A West African Imperialism in the Era of the Atlantic Slave Trade.* Oxford: Clarendon Press, 1976.

Law, R, 'Towards a History of Urbanisation in Pre- colonial Yorubaland.' In C. Fyfe and D. McMaster, eds., 1977a.

Law, R, 'Royal Monopoly and Private Enterprise in the Atlantic Trade: The Case of Dahomey.' *Journal of African History*, 18:555-577, 1977b.

Law, R, 'In Search of a Marxist Perspective on Pre- Colonial Tropical Africa'. *Journal of African History*, 19:441-452, 1978.

Law, R, *The Horse in West African History: The Role of the Horse in the Societies of Pre-Colonial West Africa.* London, 1980.

Law, R, 'For Marx, But with Reservations about Althusser: A Comment on Bernstein and Depelchin.' *History in Africa*, 8:247-251, 1981.

Law, R, 'Technology and Imperialism.' *Journal of African History*, 23:271-272, 1982.

Lawson, F H, 'Rural Revolt and Provincial Society in Egypt, 1820-1824.' *International Journal of the Middle East Studies*, 13:131-153, 1981.

Le May, G H L, *British Supremacy in South Africa, 1899-1907.* London: Clarendon Press, 1965.

Le Veen, E P, *British Slave Trade Suppression Policies, 1821-1865.* New York: Arno Press, 1977.

Legassick, M, 'South Africa: Capital Accumulation and Violence.' *Economy and Society*, 3:253-291, 1974.

Legassick, M, 'Perspectives on African 'Underdevelopment'. *Journal of African History*, 17:435-440, 1976.

Legassick, M, 'Gold, Agriculture, and Secondary Industry in South Africa, 1885-1970: From Periphery to Sub-Metropole as a Forced Labour System.' In Palmer, R and Parsons, N, eds., 1977.

Legassick, M, 'The Frontier Tradition in South African Historiography.' In Marks, S and Atmore, A, eds., 1980.

Legassick, M and F de Clercq, 'Capitalism and Migrant Labour in Southern Africa: The Origins and Nature of the System.' In Marks, S and Richardson, P, eds., 1984.

Legassick, M, 'The Northern Frontier to c. 1840: The Rise and Decline of the Griqua People.' In Elphick, R and Giliomee, H, eds., 1989.

Lehane, B, *The Compleat Flea.* London: Murray, 1969.

Lemarchand, R, 'African Peasantries, Reciprocity and the Market.' *Cahiers d' Etudes Africaines*, 113:33-67, 1989.

Lenin, V I, *Imperialism: The Highest Stage of Capitalism.* Moscow: Progress Publishers, 1978.

Lenzen, G, *The History of Diamond Production and the Diamond Trade.* London: Barrie and Jenkins, 1970.

Levin, M D, 'House Form and Social Structure in Bakosi.' In Oliver, P, ed., 1971.

Lewcock, R, 'Zanj, the East African Coast.' In Oliver, P, ed., 1971.

Lewis, M, *The Myth of the Machine and Human Development.* New York: Brace and World, 1967.

Lewis, J, 'The Rise and Fall of the South African Peasantry: A Critique and Reassessment.' *Journal of South African Studies*, 11:1-24, 1984.

Lewis, L A and Berry, L, *African Environments and Resources.* Boston: Unwin Hyman, 1988.

Liesegang, G, 'A First Look at the Import and Export Trade of Mozambique 1800-1914.' In Liesegang, G, Pasch, H and Jones, A, eds., 1983.

Liesegang, H, Pasch, H and Jones, A, eds., 1983. *Figuring African Trade: Proceedings of the symposium on the Quantification and Structure of the Import and Export and Long Distance Trade in Africa 1800-1912.* Sankt Augustin. Berlin: D.Reinner, 1986.

Lindahl, B, 'Architecture and Art During the Gondar Period.' College of Architecture, University of Addis Ababa, 1969.

Livingstone, D A, 'Environmental Changes in the Nile Headquarters.' In Williams, M A J and Faure, H, eds., 1979.

Lockhart, J G, *Rhodes*. London: Hodder and Stoughton, 1963.

Lomax, A and Arensberg, C M, 'A World Wide Evolutionary Classification of Culture by Subsistence Systems.' *Current Anthropology*, 18:659-701, 1977.

Lonsdale, J, 'States and Social Processes in Africa: A Historiographical Survey.' *Africa Studies Review*, 2/3:139-225, 1981.

Lonsdale, J, 'African Pasts in Africa's Future'. *Canadian Journal of African Studies*, 23:126-146, 1989a.

Lonsdale, J, 'The Conquest State, 1895-104.' In Ochieng', W R, ed., 1989b.

Lopez, R, *The Birth of Europe*. New York: Phoenix House, 1966.

Louis, W R, 'The Berlin Congo Conference.' In Gifford, P and Louis, W R, eds., 1971.

Louis, W R, ed., *Imperialism: The Robinson and Gallagher Controversy*. New York: New Viewpoints, 1976.

Lovejoy, P E, 'Long-Distance Trade and Islam: The Case of the Nineteenth Century Hausa Kola Trade.' *Journal of the Historical Society of Nigeria*, 5:537-547, 1971.

Lovejoy, P E, 'The Kambarin Beriberi: The Formation of a Specialised Group of Hausa Kola Traders in the Nineteenth Century.' *Journal of African History*, 14:633-651, 1973.

Lovejoy, P E, 'Interregional Monetary Flows in the Precolonial Trade of Nigeria.' *Journal of African History*, 15:563-585, 1974.

Lovejoy, P E and Baier, S, 'The Desert-Side Economy of the Central Sudan.' *International Journal of African Historical Studies*, 8:551-581, 1975.

Lovejoy, P E, 'Plantations in the Economy of the Sokoto Caliphate.' *Journal of African History*, 19:341-368, 1978a.

Lovejoy, P E, 'The Borno Salt Industry.' *International Journal of African Historical Studies*, 11:629-668, 1978b.

Lovejoy, P E, 'The Characteristics of Plantations in the Nineteenth Century Sokoto Caliphate Islamic West Africa.' *American Historical Review*, 84:1267-1292, 1979.

Lovejoy, P E, *Caravans of Kola, The Hausa Kola Trade: 1700-1900*. Zaria: Ahmadu Bello University Press, 1980.

Lovejoy, P E, 'Slavery in the Sokoto Caliphate.' In Lovejoy, P E, ed., 1981.

Lovejoy, P E, ed., *The Ideology of Slavery in Africa*. Sage: Beverly Hills, 1981.

Lovejoy, P E, 'The Volume of the Atlantic Slave Trade in Africa: A Review of the Literature.' *Journal of African History*, 23:473-501, 1982.

Lovejoy, P E, *Transformations in Slavery: A History of Slavery in Africa*. Cambridge: Cambridge University Press, 1983.

Lovejoy, P E, 'Commercial Sectors in the Economy of the Nineteenth-Century Central Sudan: The Trans-Saharan Trade and Desert-Side Salt Trade.' *African Economic History*, 13:85-116, 1984.

Lovejoy, P E, *Salt of the Desert Sun: A History of Salt Production and Trade in the Central Sudan*. Cambridge: Cambridge University Press, 1985.

Lovejoy, P E, 'Fugitive Slaves: Resistance to Slavery in the Sokoto Caliphate.' In Okihiro, G, ed., 1986a.

Lovejoy, P E, 'Problems of Slave Control in the Sokoto Caliphate.' in Lovejoy, P E, ed., 1986b.

Lovejoy, P E, ed., *Africans in Bondage: Studies in Slavery and the Slave Trade*. Madison: Wisconsin University Press, 1986c.

Lovejoy, P E, 'The Impact of the Slave Trade on Africa: A Review of the Literature.' *Journal of African History*, 30:365-394, 1989.

Low, D A, 'British East Africa: The Establishment of British Rule, 1895-1912.' In Harlow, V and Chilver, E M, eds., 1965a.

Low, D A, 'The Northern Interior: 1840-1844.' In Oliver, R and Mathews, G, eds., 1963.

Low, D A, 'Uganda: The Establishment of a Protectorate.' In Harlow, V and Chilver, E M, eds., 1965b.

Lucas, A and Harris, J R, *Ancient Egyptian Materials and Industries*. London: Edward Arnold, 1962.

Luxembourg, R, *The Accumulation of Capital*. London: Routledge and Kegan Paul, 1941.

Lynn, M, 'Change and Continuity in the British Palm Oil Trade with West Africa, 1830-1855.' *Journal of African History*, 22:331-348, 1981.

Lynn, M, 'From Sail to Steam: The Impact of the Steamship Services on the British Palm Oil Trade with West Africa, 1850- 1890.' *Journal of African History*, 30:227-245, 1989.

Mabogunje, A L, *Urbanization in Nigeria*. London: University of London Press, 1968.

Mabro, T and Radwan, S, *The Industrialization of Egypt, 1939-1973: Policy and Performance*. Oxford: Clarendon, 1976.

Mack, J, 'Bakuba Embroidery Patterns: A Commentary on their Social and Political Implications.' *Textile History*, 11:163-174, 1980.

Mackenzie, J H, 'Chivalry, Social Darwinism and Ritualised Killing: The Hunting Ethos in Central Africa up to 1914.' In Anderson, D and Grove, R, eds., 1987.

Mafeje, A, 'The Problem of Anthropology in Historical Perspective: An Inquiry into the Growth of the Social Sciences.' *Canadian Journal of African Studies*, 10:307-333, 1976.

Mafeje, A, 'On the Articulation of Modes of Production: Review Article.' *Journal of Southern African Studies*, 8:123- 138, 1981.

Mafeje, A, *African Households and Prospects for Agricultural Revival in Sub-Saharan Africa*. Dakar: Codesria, 1991.

Maggs, T, 'Some Recent Radiocarbon Dates From Eastern and Southern Africa.' *Journal of African History*, 18:161-191, 1977.

Maggs, T, 'The Iron Age Sequence South of the Vaal and Pengola Rivers: Some Historical Implications.' *Journal of African History*, 21:1-15, 1980.

Mahadi, A and Inikori, J E, 'Population and Precapitalist Development in Precolonial West Africa: Kasar Kano in the Nineteenth Century.' In Cordell, D D and Gregory, J W, eds., 1987.

Maher, V, *Women and Property in Morocco: Their Changing Relation to the Process of Social Stratification in the Middle Atlas*. Cambridge: Cambridge University Press, 1974.

Mahoney, F, 'Notes on Mulattoes of the Gambia Before the Mid-Nineteenth Century'. *Transactions of the Historical Society of Ghana*, 8, 1965.

Mair, L P, *An African People in the Twentieth Century*. London: Routledge and Kegan Paul, 1934.

Maley, J, 'Paleoclimates of Central Sahara During Early Holocene.' *Nature*, 269:573-577, 1977.

Mama, A and Imam, A, 'The Role of Academics in Limiting and Expanding Academic Freedom.' Codesria Symposium on Academic Freedom, Research and the Social Responsibility of the Intellectual in Africa, Kampala, Uganda, 1990.

Mamdani, M, *Politics and Class Formation in Uganda*. New York and London: Monthly Review Press, 1976.

Mamdani, M, 'A Great Leap Backward: A Review of Goran Hyden's No Shortcut to Progress.' *Ufahamu*, 14:178-194, 1985.

Manchuelle, F, 'The «Patriarchal Ideal» of Soninke Labour Migrants: From Slave Owners to Employers of Labour.' *Canadian Journal of African Studies*, 23:106-125, 1989.

Mandala, E, *The Kololo Interlude in Southern Malawi, 1861-1895.* M.A. Thesis, University of Malawi, 1977.

Mandala, E, *Capitalism, Ecology and Society: The Lower Tchiri Shire Valley of Malawi, 1860-1960.* Ph.D. Dissertation, University of Minnesota, 1983.

Mandala, E, 'Capitalism, Kinship and Gender in the Lower Tchiri Shire Valley of Malawi, 1860-1960: An Alternative Theoretical Framework.' *African Economic History,* 13:137-169, 1984.

Mandala, E, *Work and Control in a Peasant Economy: A History of the Lower Tchiri Valley in Malawi 1895-1960.* Wisconsin: University of Wisconsin Press, 1990.

Mangat, J S, *A History of the Asians in East Africa, 1886-1945.* London: Oxford University Press, 1969.

Manning, P, 'The Enslavement of Africans: A Demographic Model.' *Canadian Journal of African Studies,* 15:499-526, 1981.

Manning, P, 'Contours of Slavery and Social Change in Africa.' *American Historical Review,* 88:835-857, 1983.

Manning, P, 'Merchants, Porters and Canoemen in the Bight of Benin: Links in the West African Trade Network.' In Coquery-Vidrovitch, C and Lovejoy, P E, eds., 1985.

Manning, P, 'Local Versus Regional Impact of Slave Exports on Africa'. In Cordell, D D, et al. eds., 1987.

Manning, P, 'Social Versus Regional Impact of Slave Exports on Africa.' In Cordell, D D et. al., eds., 1988a.

Manning, P, 'Divining the Unprovable: Simulating the Demography of African Slavery.' *Journal of Interdisciplinary History,* 19:177-201, 1988b.

Manning, P, 'The Prospects for African Economic History: Is Today Included in the Long Run?' *African Studies Review,* 32:49-62, 1989.

Manning, P, *Slavery and African Life: Occidental, Oriental, and African Slave Trades.* Cambridge: Cambridge University Press, 1990.

Manning, P, 'The Warp and Woof of Precolonial African Industry.' *African Economic History,* 19:25-30, 1990-91.

Mannix, D P and Cowley, M, *Black Cargoes: A History of the Atlantic Slave Trade, 1518-1865.* New York: Viking, 1962.

Maquet, J and Naigiziki, S, 'Land Tenure Rights in Ancient Rwanda'. In Z A and J M Konczacki, eds., 1977.

Marais, J S, *The Fall of Kruger's Republic.* Oxford: Clarendon Press, 1961.

Marcus, H G, *The Life and Times of Menelik II.* Oxford: Clarendon, 1975.

Maret, P de and Nsuka, F, 'History of Bantu Metallurgy: Some Linguistic Aspects.' *History in Africa,* 4:43-65, 1977.

Maret, P de, D Van Noten and Cohen, D, 'Radio Carbon Dates for West Central Africa.' *Journal of African History,* 18:481-505, 1977.

Maret, P de, 'New Survey of Archaeological Research and Dates for West Central Africa.' *Journal of African History,* 23:1-15, 1982.

Maret, P de, 'The Smith's Myth and the Origin of Leadership in Central Africa.' In Haaland, R, et.al. eds., 1985.

Marks, S and Richardson, P, eds., *International Labour Migration: Historical Perspectives.* London: Institute of Commonwealth Studies, 1984.

Marks, S and Atmore, A, 'The Imperial Factor in South Africa: Towards a Reassessment.' *Journal of Imperial and Commonwealth History,* 3:105-139, 1974.

Marks, S and Atmore, A, eds., *Economy and Society in Pre-Industrial South Africa.* London: Longman, 1980.

Marks, S and Rathbone, R, 'Introduction.' In Marks, S and Rathbone, R, eds., 1982.

Marks, S and Rathbone, R, eds., *Industrialization and Social Change in South Africa: African Class Formation, Culture and Consciousness, 1870-1930*. London: Longman, 1982.

Marks, S, 'Scrambling For South Africa.' *Journal of African History*, 23:97-113, 1982.

Mark, P, 'Quantification of Rubber and Palm Kernel Exports from the Casamance and the Gambia, 1884-1914.' In Liesegang, G Pasch, H and Jones, A, eds., 1983.

Marks, S, 'Class, Ideology and the Bambata Rebellion.' In Crummey, D, ed., 1986.

Marlowe, J, *The Making of the Suez Canal*. London: The Crescent Press, 1964.

Marsot, A A al-Sayyid, 'The Revolutionary Gentlewoman in Egypt.' In Keddie, N and Beck, L, eds., 1978.

Marsot, A A al-Sayyid, *Egypt in the Reign of Muhammad Ali*. Cambridge: Cambridge University Press, 1984.

Martin, P, 'The Trade of Loango in the Seventeenth and Eighteenth Centuries.' In Gray, R and Birmingham, D, eds., 1970.

Martin, P, *The External Trade of the Loango Coast, 1576-1870*. Oxford: Oxford University Press, 1972.

Martin, P, 'The Violence of Empire'. In Birmingham, D and Martin, P, eds., 1983.

Martin, S, 'Gender and Innovation: Farming, Cooking, and Palm Processing in the Ngwa Region, South-Eastern Nigeria, 1900-1930.' *Journal of African History*, 25:411-427, 1984.

Martin, P, 'Power, Cloth and Currency on the Loango Coast.' *African Economic History*, 15:1-12, 1986.

Marx, K, *Capital*. Vol.1. Harmondsworth: Penguin, 1978.

Mason, M, 'Population Density and "Slave Raiding": The Case of the Middle Belt of Nigeria.' *Journal of African History*, 10:555-564, 1969.

Mason, M, 'Captive and Client Labour and the Economy of the Bida Emirate: 1857-1901.' *Journal of African History*, 14:453-471, 1973.

Mason, M, 'Production, Penetration and Political Formation, 1857-1901'. In Crummey, D and Stewart, C C, eds., 1981.

Mason, R J, 'Early Iron Age Settlement at Broederstroom 24/73, Transvaal.' *SAJS*, 77:401-416, 1981.

Mathieson, W L, *British Slavery and Its Abolition, 1823-1838*. London: New York: Octagon Books, 1926.

Matsetela, T, 'The Life Story of Nkomo Mma-Pooe: Aspects of Sharecropping and Proletarianization in northern Orange Free State, 1890-1930.' In Marks, S and Rathbone, R, eds., 1982.

Mayer, P, 'The Origin and Decline of Two Rural Resistance Ideologies.' In Mayer, P, ed., 1980.

Mayer, P, ed., *Black Villages in an Industrial Society: Anthropological Perspectives on Labour Migration in South Africa*. Cape Town: Oxford University Press, 1980.

Mazrui, A A, *The Africans: A Triple Heritage*. Boston: Little Brown, 1987.

McCarthy, J A, 'Nineteenth Century Egyptian Population.' *Middle Eastern Studies*, 12:1-39, 1976.

McClellan, C W, 'Land, Labour, and Coffee: The South's Role in Ethiopian Self-Reliance, 1899-1935.' *African Economic History*, 9:69-83, 1980.

McCracken, J, 'The Nineteenth Century in Malawi.' In Ranger, T O, ed., 1968.

McCracken, J, 'Colonialism, Capitalism and Ecological Crisis in Malawi: A Reassessment.' In Anderson, D and Grove, R, eds., 1987.

McDougall, E A, 'Camel Caravans of the Saharan Salt Trade. Traders and Transporters in the Nineteenth Century.' In Coquery-Vidrovitch, C and Lovejoy, P E, eds., 1985.

McDougall, E A, 'Production in Precolonial Africa.' *African Economic History*, 19:37-43, 1990.

McEachem, D, Archer, J W and Richard, D, *Households and Communities*. University of Calgary, Archaeological Association, 1989.

McLane, M O, 'Commercial Rivalries and French Policy on the Senegal River, 1831-1858'. *African Economic History*, 15:39- 67, 1986.

McLoughlin, P F M, 'Introduction.' In McLoughlin, P F M, ed., 1970.

McLoughlin, P F M, ed., *African Food Production Systems: Cases and Theory*. Baltimore: The Johns Hopkins Press, 1970.

McMaster, D N, 'Speculation on the Coming of Banana to Uganda.' In Z A and J M Konczacki, eds., 1977.

McNeil, W H, *Plagues and Peoples*. New York: Anchor Press, 1976.

Meier, G M and Seers, D, eds., *Pioneers in Development*. New York: Oxford University Press, 1984.

Meillassoux, C, ed., *The Development of Indigenous Trade and Markets in West Africa*. London: Oxford University Press, 1971.

Meillassoux, C, '"The Economy" in Agricultural Self- Sustaining Societies: A Preliminary Analysis.' In Seddon, D, ed., 1978.

Meillassoux, C, *Maidens, Meal and Money: Capitalism and the Domestic Community*. Cambridge: Cambridge University Press, 1981.

Meillassoux, C, 'Female Slavery.' In Robertson, C C and Klein, M A, eds., 1983.

Melotti, U, *Marx and the Third World*. London: Macmillan, 1981.

Mendels, F F, 'Proto-Industrialisation. The First Phase of the Industrialisation Process.' *Journal of Economic History*, 32:241-261, 1972.

Menne, F R, 'Production and Export of Cloves towards the end of the 19th Century and Cultivation Attempts in German East Africa.' In Liesegang, G, Pasch, H and Jones, A, eds., 1983.

Mercer, P, 'Shilluk Trade and Politics From the Mid-Seventeenth Century to 1861.' *Journal of African History*, 12:407-426, 1971.

Michael, P, Petras, J and Rhodes, R, 'Imperialism and the Contradictions of Imperialism.' *New Left Review*, 85:83-104, 1974.

Michell, G, *Architecture of the Islamic World, Its History and Social Meaning*. London: Thames Hudson, 1978.

Middleton, J, *The Effects of Economic Development on Traditional Political Systems in Africa South of the Sahara*, Surveys of Research in the Social Sciences, Vol.VI., The Hague, 14, 1966.

Miers, S and Kopytoff, I, eds., *Slavery in Africa: Historical and Anthropological Perspectives*. Madison: University of Wisconsin Press, 1977.

Miers, S and Roberts, R, eds., *The End of Slavery in Africa*. Madison: University of Wisconsin Press, 1988.

Miller, J C, 'Chokwe Trade and Conquest in the Nineteenth Century.' In Gray, R and Birmingham, D, eds., 1970.

Miller, J C, 'The Significance of Drought, Disease and Famine in the Agriculturally Marginal Zones of West Central Africa.' *Journal of African History*, 23:17-61, 1982.

Miller, J C, 'The Paradoxes of Impoverishment in the Atlantic Zone.' In Birmingham, D and Martin, P, eds., 1983a.

Miller, J, 'Imports at Luanda, Angola, 1785-1823.' In Liesegang, H. Pasch and A. Jones, eds, 1983b.

Miller, J C, 'Demographic History Revisited.' *Journal of African History*, 25:93-96, 1984.

Miller, J C, *Way Of Death: Merchant Capitalism and the Angolan Slave Trade, 1730-1830*. Madison: University of Wisconsin Press, 1988.

Mintz, S W and Wolf, E R, 'Haciendas and Plantations in Middle America and the Antilles.' *Economy and Society*, 6:380-412, 1977.

Miracle, M P, *Maize in Tropical Africa*. Madison: University of Wisconsin Press, 1966.

Miracle, M P, *Agriculture in the Congo Basin: Tradition and Change in African Rural Economies*. Madison: University of Wisconsin Press, 1967.

Mkandawire, T and Bourenane, N, eds., *The State and Agriculture in Africa*. Dakar: Codesria Book Series, 1987.

Mkandawire, T, 'The State and Agriculture in Africa: Introductory Remarks', In Mkandawire, T and Bourenane, N, eds., 1987.

Mokhtar, G, ed., *General History of Africa*. Vol.2: *Ancient Civilizations of Africa*. London and Berkeley: Heinemann and University of California Press, 1981.

Monsted, M and Walji, P, *A Demographic Analysis of East Africa*. Uppsala: Scandinavian Institute of African Studies, 1978.

Moock, J L, ed., *Understanding Africa's Rural Households and Farming Systems*. Boulder and London: Westview Press, 1986.

Moran, E F, *Changing Agricultural Systems in Africa*. Wiilliamsburg, VA: Department of Anthropology, College of William and Mary, 1979.

Morojole, C M H, *The 1960 Agricultural Census of Basutoland*. Maseru: Government of Basutoland, 1963.

Morris, M, *The State and Development of Capitalist Social Relations in the South African Countryside: A Process of Class Struggle*. Ph.D. dissertation, University of Sussex, 1981.

Morris, P, ed., *Africa, America and Central Asia: Formal and Informal Empire in the Nineteenth Century*. Exeter: University of Exeter, 1984.

Mortimer, M, *Adapting to Drought: Farmers, Famine and Desertification in West Africa*. Cambridge: Cambridge University Press, 1988.

Moss, R P and Rathbone, R J A R, eds., *The Population Factor in African Studies*. London: University of London Press, 1975.

Moss, R P, ed., *The Soil Resources of Tropical Africa*. London: Cambridge University Press, 1968.

Mudenge, S I, 'The Role of Foreign Trade in the Rozwi Empire: A Reappraisal.' *Journal of African History*, 3:373-391, 1974.

Mudenge, S I, *A Political History of Muhnumutapa c.1400-1902*. Harare: Zimbabwe Publishing House, 1988.

Mudimbe, V Y, *The Invention of Africa*. Bloomington, Ind: Indiana University Press, 1987.

Muhly, J D, *Copper and Tin*. Hamden, Conn: Anchor Books, 1973.

Mungeam, G H, *British Rule in Kenya, 1895-1912*. London: Oxford University Press, 1966.

Munro, J F, *Africa and the International Economy, 1800-1960*. London: J.M. Dent, 1976.

Munro, J F, 'Shipping and Railway Gurantees: William Mackinnon, Eastern Africa and the Indian Ocean, 1860-93'. *Journal of African History*, 28:209-230, 1987.

Murdock, G P, *Africa, Its Peoples and Their Culture History*. New York: McGraw-Hill, 1959.

Muriuki, G, *A History of the Kikuyu, 1500-1900*. Nairobi: Oxford University Press, 1974.

Muriuki, G, 'The Kikuyu in the Pre-Colonial Period.' In Ogot, B A, ed., 1986.

Murmann, C, *Change and Development in East African Cattle Husbandry*. Copenhagen: Akademisk Forlag, 1974.

Murray, C, 'Review Article: Landlords, Tenants and Share-Croppers - Agrarian Change in Regional Perspective.' *Journal of Southern African Studies*, 14:153-159, 1987.

Murray, M J, 'The Origins of Agrarian Capitalism in South Africa: A Critique of the Social History Perspective.' *Journal of Southern African Studies*, 15:645-665, 1989.

Mutibwa, P, *Malagasy and the Europeans: Madagascar's Foreign Relations, 1861-1895*. London: Longman, 1974.

Mutwira, 'A Question of Condoning Game Slaughter: Southern Rhodesian Wild Life Policy 1890-1953'. *Journal of Southern African Studies*, 15:250-262, 1989.

Nabi, I, *Contracts, Resource use and Productivity in Sharecropping*. Department of Economics, Quaid-e-Azam University, Islamabad, 1984.

Nabudere, D W, *Imperialism and Revolution in Uganda*. London: Onyx Press, 1984.

Nakash, Y, 'Fiscal and Monetary Systems in the Madhist Sudan, 1881-1898.' *International Journal of Middle East Studies*, 20:365-385.

Nakash, Y, 'Reflections on a Subsistence Economy: Production and Trade of the Madhist Sudan, 1881-1898.' In Kedourie, E and Hain, S G, eds., 1988a.

Nelson, C, 'Women and Power in Nomadic Societies of the Middle East.' In Nelson, C, ed., 1973.

Nelson, C, ed., *The Desert and the Sown: Nomads in the Wider Society*. Berkeley: Institute of International Studies, University of California, 1973.

Nelson, C, 'Public and Private Politics: Women in the Middle Eastern World.' *American Ethnologist*, 1, 1974.

Netting, R, et.al. 'Introduction.' In Netting, R, et.al. eds.

Netting, R, et.al., eds., *Households: Comparative and Historical Studies of the Domestic Group*. Berkeley: University of California Press, 1984.

Newbury, C W, 'Victorians, Republicans, and the Partition of West Africa.' *Journal of African History*, 3:493-501, 1962.

Newbury, C W, 'North African and Western Sudan Trade in the Nineteenth Century: A Reevaluation.' *Journal of African History*, 7:233-246, 1966.

Newbury, C W and Kanya-Forstner, A S, 'French Policy and the Origins of the Scramble for West Africa'. *Journal of African History*, 10:253-276, 1969.

Newbury, C W, 'Prices and Stability in Early Nineteenth Century West African Trade.' In Meillassoux, C ed., 1971.

Newbury, C W, 'Credit in Early Nineteenth Century West African Trade.' *Journal of African History*, 13:81-95, 1972.

Newbury, C W, 'The Imperial Workplace: Competitive and Coerced Labour Systems in New Zealand, Northern Nigeria and Australia New Guinea.' In Marks, S and Richardson, P, eds., 1984.

Newitt, M, *Portugal in Africa: The Last One Hundred Years*. London: Longman, 1981.

Newitt, M, 'Economic Penetration and the Scramble for Southern Africa'. In Morris, P, ed., 1984.

Newitt, M D D, 'Drought in Mozambique 1823-1831'. *Journal of Southern African Studies*, 15:15-35, 1988.

Newton-King, S, 'The Labour Market of the Cape Colony, 1807-28'. In Marks, S and Atmore, A, eds., 1980.

Nicholls, C S, *The Swahili Coast: Politics, Diplomacy and Trade on the East African Littoral, 1798-1856*. London: Allen and Unwin, 1971.

Nicholson, S E, 'Climatic Variations in the Sahel and Other African Regions During the Past Five Centuries.' *Journal of Arid Environments*, 1:3-24, 1978.

Nicholson, S E, 'The Methodology of Historical Climate Reconstruction and its Application to Africa.' *Journal of African History*, 20:31-49, 1979.

Nicholson, S E and Flohn, H, 'African Environmental Changes and the General Atmospheric Circulation in late Pleistocene and Holocene.' *Climatic Change*, 2:313-348, 1980.

Nicholson, S E, 'The Nature of Rainfall Fluctuations in Subtropical West Africa.' *Monthly Weather Review*, 108:473-487, 1980.

Nicholson, S E, 'The Historical Climatology of Africa.' In Wigley, T M L, et.al. eds., 1981.

Nicholson, S E, and Entekhabi, D, 'The Quasi Periodic Behaviour of Rainfall Variability in Africa and Its Relationship to the Southern Oscillation.' *Meteorology and Atmospheric Physics*, 34:311-348, 1986.

Nicklin, K, 'Annang Ibibio Raphia Weaving.' *Textile History*, 11:142-162, 1980.

Nindi, B C, 'African Refugee Crisis in a Historical Perspective.' *TransAfrican Journal of History*, 15:96-107, 1986.

Noer, T J, *Britain, Boer and Yankee: The United States and South Africa, 1870-1914*. Kent, Ohio: Kent University Press, 1979.

Northrup, D, 'The Compatibility of the Slave and Palm Oil Trades in the Bight of Biafra.' *Journal of African History*, 17:353-364, 1976.

Northrup, D, *Trade Without Rulers: Precolonial Economic Development in South-Eastern Nigeria*. Oxford: Clarendon Press, 1978.

Northrup, D, 'Nineteenth Century Patterns of Slavery and Economic Growth in Southeastern Nigeria.' *International Journal of African Historical Studies*, 12:1-16, 1979.

Noten, F V, 'Ancient and Modern Iron Smelting in Central Africa: Zaire, Rwanda and Burundi.' In Haaland, R, et.al. eds., 1985.

O'Brien, P, *The Revolution in Egypt's Economic System: From Private Revolution to Socialism, 1952-1965*. London: Oxford University Press, 1966.

O'Brien, T H, *Milner*. London: Constable, 1979.

O'Connor, A M, *Railway Development in Uganda: A Study in Economic Geography*. Nairobi: Oxford University Press, 1965.

O'Connor, A, *The African City*. London: Hutchinson, 1983.

O'Fahey, R S, 'Slavery and the Slave Trade in Dar Fur.' *Journal of African History*, 14:29-43, 1973.

O'Hear, A, 'Political and Commercial Clientage in Nineteenth-Century Ilorin'. *African Economic History*, 15:69-83, 1986.

O'Sullivan, J M, 'Slavery in the Malinke of Kabadougou Ivory Coast.' *International Journal of African Historical Studies*, 13:633-650, 1980.

Ochieng', W R, *Kenya and Its Invaders*. Nairobi: Kenya Literature Bureau, 1976.

Ochieng', W R, 'The Gusii Before 1900'. In Ogot, B A, ed., 1986.

Ochieng', W R, ed., *A Modern History of Kenya: 1895-1980*. London and Nairobi: Evans Brothers, 1989.

Ofonagoro, W I, 'From Traditional to British Currency in Southern Nigeria: Analysis of a Currency Revolution, 1880-1948'. *Journal of Economic History*, 39:623-654, 1979.

Ogot, B A, 'Kenya Under the British, 1895-1963.' In Ogot, B A, ed., 1974.

Ogot, B A, ed.; *Zamani: A Survey of East African History*. Nairobi: Longman/East African Publishing House, 1974.

Ogot, B A, ed., *Economic and Social History of East Africa*. Nairobi: East African Literature Bureau, 1975.

Ogot, B A, 'African Ecology in Historical Perspective: Problems and Prospects.' In Ogot, B A, ed., 1979.

Ogot, B A, ed., *Ecology and History in East Africa.* Nairobi: Kenya Literature Bureau, 1979.

Ogot, B A, ed., *Economic and Social History of East Africa.* Nairobi: Kenya Literature Bureau, 1979.

Ogot, B A, ed., *Kenya in the Nineteenth Century.* Nairobi: Bookwise and Anyange Press, 1985.

Ogot, B A, ed., *Kenya Before 1900.* Nairobi: East African Publishing House, 1986.

Okeke, C S, 'Uses of Traditional Textiles Among the Anioch Igbo of Mid-Western Nigeria'. *Textile History,* 10:108-118, 1979.

Okeke, C S, 'Factors which Influenced Igbo Traditional Woven Designs for Apparel Fabrics'. *Textile History,* 11:116- 130, 1980.

Okigbo, B and Greenland, D J, 'Intercropping Systems in Tropical Africa.' In Papendiek, R J, et.al., eds., 1977.

Okihiro, G Y, 'Precolonial Economic Change Among the Thlaping c. 1795-1817.' *International Journal of African Historical Studies,* 17:59-79, 1984.

Okihiro, G Y, ed., *In Resistance: Studies in African, Afro-American and Caribbean History.* Amherst, Mass.: University of Massachussets Press, 1986.

Okyar, O, 'The Role of the State in the Economic Life of the Nineteenth-Century Ottoman Empire'. *Asian and African Studies,* 14:143-164, 1980.

Oliver, P, ed., *Shelter in Africa.* New York: Praeger, 1971.

Oliver, P, ed., *Shelter, Sign and Symbol.* London: Barrie Jenkins, 1975.

Oliver, R and Fagan, B M, *Africa in the Iron Age.* Cambridge: Cambridge University Press, 1975.

Oliver, R and Fage, J D, *A Short History of Africa.* Harmondsworth: Penguin, 1962.

Oliver, R and Mathews, G, eds., *History of East Africa.* Vol.1. Oxford: Oxford University Press, 1963.

Oliver, P, *Dwelling: The House Across the World.* Austin: University of Texas Press, 1987.

Omer-Cooper, J D, *The Zulu Aftermath: A Nineteenth-Century Revolution in Bantu Africa.* London: Longman, 1978.

Onimode, B, *An Introduction to Marxist Political Economy.* London: Zed Books, 1985.

Onyango-Abuje, J C and Wandibba, S, 'The Paleoenvironment and its Influence on Man's Activities in East Africa During the Latter Part of Upper Pleistocene and Holocene.' In Ogot, B A, ed., 1979.

Oppong, C, 'A Note on Some Aspects of Anthropological Contributions to the Study of Fertility.' Paper on Population and Demography, National Research Council, 1981.

Oroge, E A, 'Iwofa: An Historical Survey of the Yoruba Institution of Indenture.' *African Economic History,* 14:75-106, 1985.

Owen, E R J, *Cotton and the Egyptian Economy, 1820-1914.* Oxford: Oxford University Press, 1969.

Owen, R and Sutcliffe, B, eds., *Studies in the Theory of Imperialism.* London: Longman, 1972.

Owen, R, 'Egypt and Europe: From French Expedition to British Occupation.' In Owen, R and Sutcliffe, B, eds., 1972.

Owen, R, 'Robinson and Gallagher and Middle Eastern Nationalism'. In Louis, W R, ed., 1976.

Owen, E R J, *The Middle East in the World Economy, 1800-1914.* London and New York: Methuen, 1981.

Pachai, B, *Malawi: The History of the Nation.* London: Longman, 1973.

Pachai, B, *The International Aspects of the South African Indian Question, 1860-1971.* Cape Town: C Struik, 1971.

Packard, R M, *White Plague, Black Labour: Tuberculosis and the Political Economy of Health and Disease in South Africa*. Pietermaritzburg: University of Natal Press, 1989.

Padayachee, V and Morrell, P, 'Indian Merchants and Dukawallahs in the Natal Economy, c.1875-1914.' *Journal of Southern African Studies*, 17:71-103, 1991.

Pakenham, E, *Jameson's Raid*. London: 1966.

Pakenham, T, *The Boer War*. New York: Random House, 1979.

Pallinder-Law, A, 'Aborted Modernization in West Africa? The Case of Abeokuta'. *Journal of African History*, 15:65-82, 1974.

Palma, R, 'Dependency: A Formal Theory of Underdevelopment or a Methodology for the Analysis of Concrete Situation of Underdevelopment?' *World Development*, 6:881-924, 1978.

Palmer, R and Parsons, N, eds., *The Roots of Rural Poverty in Central and Southern Africa*. London: Heinemann, 1977.

Palmer, R, *Land and Racial Discrimination in Rhodesia*. London: Heinemann, 1977.

Pankhurst, R, 'The History and Traditional Treatment of Smallpox in Ethiopia.' *Medical History*, 9:344-356, 1965.

Pankhurst, R, 'The Great Ethiopian Famine of 1888-1892: A New Assessment.' *Journal of the History of Medicine*. Part 1, April 1966:95-124; Part 2, July 1966:271-294, 1966.

Pankhurst, R, *Economic History of Ethiopia*. Addis Ababa: Haile Sellassie University Press, 1968.

Panzac, D, 'The Population of Egypt in the Nineteenth Century.' *Asian and African Studies*, 21:11-32, 1987.

Parpart, J L and Staudt, K, eds., *Women and the State in Africa*. Boulder and London: Lynne Rienner, 1989.

Parsons, J W, *France and the Egyptian Question, 1875-1894*. Ph.D. thesis, Cambridge University, 1976.

Parvin, M and Putterman, L, 'Population and Food Dynamics: A Caloric Measure in Egypt.' *International Journal of Middle East Studies*, 12:81-100, 1980.

Pascon, P, *Capitalism and Agriculture in the Haouz of Marrakesh*. London: Routledge and Kegan Paul, 1986.

Patterson, K D, 'Disease and Medicine in African History: A Bibliographical Essay.' *History in Africa*, 1:141-148, 1974.

Patterson, K D, 'The Vanishing Mpongwe: European Contact and Demographic Change in the Gabon River.' *Journal of African History*, 16:217-238, 1975.

Patterson, K D and Hartwig, G W, 'The Disease Factor: An Introductory Overview.' In Patterson, K W and Hartwig, G W, eds., 1978.

Patterson, K D and Hartwig, G W, eds., *Disease in African History*. Durham: Duke University Press, 1978.

Patterson, K D, 'Bibliographical Essay.' In Patterson, K D and Hartwig, G W, eds., 1978.

Patterson, K D, *Infectious Diseases in Twentieth-Century Africa: A Bibliography of their Distribution and Consequences*. Waltham, Mass:Crossroads Press, 1979.

Patterson, O, *Slavery and Social Death: A Comparative Study*. Cambridge: Harvard University Press, 1982.

Paulme, D, ed., *Women of Tropical Africa*. Berkeley and Los Angeles: University of California Press, 1963.

Pearce, R, 'Sharecropping: Towards a Marxist View'. *Journal of Peasant Studies*, 10:42-70, 1983.

Peel, J D Y, 'Urbanization and Urban History in West Africa.' *Journal of African History*, 21:269-277, 1980.

Peires, J B, 'The British and the Cape 1814-1834.' In Elphick, R and Giliomee, H, eds., 1989a.

Peires, J B, *The Dead Will Arise: Nongqaawusa and the Great Xhosa Cattle-Killing of 1856-7.* Johannesburg and London: Ravan Press, James Currey, 1989b.

Pellow, D, 'Recent Studies on African Women.' *African Studies Review*, 20:117-126, 1977.

Penrose, E F, ed., *European Imperialism and the Partition of Africa.* London: Frank Cass, 1974.

Perinbam, B M, 'The Political Organization of Traditional Gold Mining: The Western Lobi c.1850-c.1910.' *Journal of African History*, 29:437-462, 1988.

Person, Y, 'Guinea-Samori'. In Crowder, M, ed., 1978.

Peters, P, 'Gender, Developmental Cycles and Historical Process: A Critique of Recent Research on Botswana.' *Journal of Southern African Studies*, 9:100-122, 1983.

Phillips, J, *The Development of Agriculture and Forestry in the Tropics.* London: Faber and Faber, 1966.

Phillipson, D W, 'Population Movement and Interaction in African Pre-history: Some Examples from the Last 2000 Years in Eastern Zambia.' In Fyfe, C and McMaster, D, eds., 1977a.

Phillipson, D W, *The Later Prehistory of Eastern and Southern Africa.* London: Heinemann, 1977b.

Phillipson, D W, 'Early Food Producing Communities in East Africa: Problems of Recognition.' In Fyfe, C and McMaster, D, eds., 1981.

Phillipson, D W, *African Archaeology.* Cambridge: Cambridge University Press, 1985.

Phimister, I R, 'Alluvial Gold Mining and Trade in Nineteenth Century South Central Africa.' *Journal of African History*, 15:445-456, 1974.

Phimister, I R, *An Economic and Social History of Zimbabwe, 1890-1948: Capital Accumulation and Class Struggle.* London: Longman, 1988.

Picton, J and Mack, J, *African Textiles: Weaving and Design.* London: British Museums Publications, 1979.

Picton, J, 'Women's Weaving: the Manufacture and use of Textiles Among the Igbirra People of Nigeria.' *Textile History*, 11:63-88, 1980.

Pitcher, M A, 'Sowing the Seeds of Failure: Early Portuguese Cotton Cultivation in Angola and Mozambique, 1820-1926.' *Journal of Southern African Studies*, 17:43-70, 1991.

Pittock, A B, et.al., *Climatic Change and Variability: A Southern Perspective.* Cambridge: Cambridge University Press, 1978.

Pokrant, R J, 'The Tailors of Kano City.' In Goody, E N, ed., 1982.

Polanyi, K, et.al., eds., *Trade and Markets in Early Empires.* New York: Free Press, 1957.

Polanyi, K, *Primitive, Archaic and Modern Economies: Essays of K. Polanyi.* Ed. Dalton, G, Garden City, N.Y.: Double Day, 1968.

Pole, L M, 'Decline or Survival? Iron Production in West Africa from the Seventeenth Century to the Twentieth Centuries.' *Journal of African History*, 23:503-513, 1982.

Polk, W and Chambers, R, eds., *The Beginnings of Modernization in the Middle East.* Chicago: Chicago University Press, 1968.

Polychroniou, C, *Marxist Perspectives on Imperialism: A Theoretical Analysis.* New York: Praeger, 1991.

Ponasik, D S, 'The System of Administered Trade as a Defence Mechanism in Protectorate Morocco.' *International Journal of Middle East Studies*, 8:195-207, 1977.

Pool, D I, A Framework for the Analysis of West African Historical Demography.' In Fyfe, C and McMaster, D, eds., 1977.

Porter, A N, *The Origins of the South African War: Joseph Chamberlain and the Diplomacy of Imperialism, 1895-1899*. Manchester: Manchester University Press, 1980.

Posnansky, M. 1977. 'Brass Casting and its Antecedents in West Africa.' *Journal of African History*, 18:287-300.

Post, J D, *The Last Great Subsistence Crisis in the Western World*. Baltimore: Johns Hopkins University Press, 1977.

Post, J D, *Food Shortage, Climatic Variability and Epidemic Disease in Pre-industrial Europe*. Ithaca and London: Cornell University Press, 1985.

Post, K, '«Peasantization» and Rural Political Movements in Western Africa'. *European Journal of Sociology*, 13:223-254, 1972.

Priestly, M, *West African Trade and Coast Society: A Family Study*. London: Oxford University Press, 1969.

Prussin, L, *Architecture in Northern Ghana: A Study of Form and Functions*. Berkeley: University of California Press, 1969.

Pudney, J, *Suez: De Lesseps' Canal*. London: J.M. Dent and Sons, 1968.

Purseglove, J W, 'The Origins and Migrations of Crops in Tropical Africa.' In Harlan, J, et.al., eds., 1976.

Qunta, C, ed. 1987. *Women in Southern Africa*. London: Allison and Busby.

Raikes, P, *Modernising Hunger*. London: CIIR, 1988.

Ranger, T O, *Revolt in Southern Rhodesia, 1896-7: A Study in African Resistance*. London: Heinemann, 1967.

Ranger, T O, ed., *Aspects of Central African History*. London: Heinemann, 1968.

Ranger, T O, 'Resistance in Africa: From Nationalist Revolt to Agrarian Protest.' In Okihiro, G, ed., 1986.

Ranger, T O, 'The Invention of Tradition in Colonial Africa.' In Hobsbawm, E and Ranger, T, eds., 1989.

Rapoport, A, *House Form and Culture*. Englewood: Prentice Hall, 1969.

Rapoport, A, 'Vernacular Architecture and the Cultural Determinants of Form.' In King, A D, ed., 1980.

Rasmusson, E M, 'Global Climate Change and Variability: Effects on Drought and Desertification in Africa.' In M.H. Glantz, ed., 1987.

Rassam, A, 'Introduction: Arab Women: The Status of Research in the Social Sciences and the Status of Women in the Arab World.' In Unesco, ed., 1984a.

Rassam, A, 'Towards a Theoretical Framework for the Study of Women in the Arab World.' In Unesco, ed., 1984b.

Ratcliffe, B M, 'The Economics of the Partition of Africa: Methods and Recent Research Trends.' *Canadian Journal of African Studies*, 15:3-31, 1981.

Rawley, J, *The Transatlantic Slave Trade: A History*. New York: Norton, 1981.

Raymond, A, *The Great Arab Cities in the Sixteenth and Eighteenth Centuries: An Introduction*. New York: New York University Press, 1984.

Reefe, T Q, 'The Societies of the Eastern Savanna.' In Birmingham D and Martin, P, eds., 1983.

Reining, P, 'Social Factors and Food Production in an East African Peasant Society: The Haya.' In P.F.M. McCloughlin, ed., 1970.

Reynolds, E, 'Trade and Economic Change on the Gold Coast, 1807-1874. Harlow: Longman, 1974.

Reynolds, E, *Trade and Economic Change on the Gold Coast, 1807-1874*. Harlow: Longman, 1978.

Reynolds, C, *Modes of Imperialism*. Oxford: Martin Robertson, 1981.

Rice, C D, *The Rise and Fall of Black Slavery*, New York: Harper and Row, 1975.

Richards, A, ed., *Subsistence to Commercial Farming in Present-day Buganda.* Cambridge: Cambridge University Press, 1973.

Richards, A, 'Growth and Technical Change: 'Internal' and 'External' Sources of Egyptian Underdevelopment.' *Asian and African Studies*, 15:45-67, 1981.

Richards, A, *Egypt's Agricultural Development: Technical and Social Change.* Boulder, Colo: Westview Press, 1982.

Richards, P, 'Ecological Change and the Politics of African Land Use.' *African Studies Review*, 26:1-71, 1983.

Richards, P, *Indigenous Agricultural Revolution: Ecology and Food Production in West Africa.* London: Hutchinson, 1985.

Richards, W A, 'The Import of Firearms into West Africa in the Eighteenth Century.' *Journal of African History*, 21:43-59, 1980.

Richardson, D, 'The Eighteenth Century British Slave Trade: New Estimates of its Volume and Distribution.' *Research in Economic History*, 12:197-239, 1988a.

Richardson, D, 'Slave Exports from West and West-Central Africa, 1700-1810: New Estimates of Volume and Distribution.' *Journal of African*, 30:1-22, 1989b.

Richardson, P, 'The Recruitment of Indentured Labour for the South African Gold Mines, 1903-1908, 18, 1977.

Richardson, P and Van Helten, J J, 'Labour in the South African Gold Mining Industry, 1886-1914.' In Marks, S and Rathbone, R, eds., 1982.

Richardson, P and Van-Helten, J J, 'The Natal Sugar Industry, 1849-1905: An Interpretive Essay.' *Journal of African History*, 23:515-527, 1982.

Richardson, P, 'The Natal Sugar Industry in the Nineteenth Century.' In W. Beinart, P. Delius, and S. Trapido, eds., 1986.

Rigby, P, *Persistent Pastoralists: Nomadic Societies in Transition.* London: Zed Books, 1985.

Rivlin, H A B, *The Agricultural Policy of Muhammad Ali in Egypt.* Cambridge, MA: Harvard University Press, 1961.

Roach, M E and Eicher, J B, eds., *Dress, Adornment and the Social Order.* New York: John Wiley, 1965.

Roberts, A D, 'The Nineteenth Century in Zambia.' In T.O. Ranger, ed., 1968.

Roberts, A D, *A History of Zambia.* London: Heinemann, 1976.

Roberts, A, 'Nyamwezi Trade.' In Gray, R and Birmingham, D, eds., 1970.

Roberts, R and Klein, M, 'The Banamba Slave Exodus of 1905 and the Decline of Slavery in the Western Sudan.' *Journal of African History*, 21:375-94.

Roberts, R L, 'The Emergence of a Grain Market in Bamako, 1883-1980.' *Canadian Journal of African Studies*, 14:37-54, 1980a.

Roberts, R L, *Warriors, Merchants and Slaves: The State and the Economy in Middle Niger Valley, 1700-1914.* Stanford: Stanford University Press, 1987.

Roberts, R, 'Long Distance Trade and Production: Sinsani in the Nineteenth Century.' *Journal of African History*, 21:169-188, 1980b.

Robertson, A F, *The Dynamics of Productive Relationships: African Share Contracts in Comparative Perspective.* Cambridge: Cambridge University Press, 1987.

Robertson, C and Berger, I, eds., *Women and Class in Africa.* New York: Holmes and Meier, 1986.

Robertson, C C and Klein, M A, eds., *Women and Slavery in Africa.* Madison: University of Wisconsin Press, 1983.

Robertson, C, *Sharing the Same Bowl: A Socioeconomic History of Women and Class in Accra, Ghana.* Bloomington: Indiana University Press, 1984.

Robinson, R J and Gallagher, *Africa and the Victorians: The Official Mind of Imperialism*. London: Macmillan, 1974.

Rodney, W, 'African Slavery and Other Forms of Oppression on the Upper Guinea Coast in the Context of the Atlantic Slave Trade.' *Journal of African History*, 7:431-443, 1966.

Rodney, W, *How Europe Underdeveloped Africa*. Washington: Howard University Press, 1982.

Roe, E M, 'Lantern on the Stern: Policy Analysis, Historical Research, and Pax Britannica in Africa'. *African Studies Review*, 30:45-62, 1987.

Romero, P W, '"Where Have All the Slaves Gone?" Emancipation and Post-Emancipation in Lamu, Kenya.' *Journal of African History*, 27:497-512, 1986.

Rosenblaum, P, *Gold Mining in Ghana, 1894-1900*. Ph.D. Dissertation, Columbia University, 1977.

Ross, R, 'Smallpox at the Cape of Good Hope in the Eighteenth Century.' In Fyfe, C and McMaster, D, eds., 1977.

Ross, R, 'The Relative Importance of Exports and the Internal Market for the Agriculture of the Cape Colony.' In Liesegang, G, Pasch, H and Jones, A, eds., 1983.

Ross, R, 'The Origins of Capitalist Agriculture in the Cape Colony: A Survey'. In Beinart, W, Delius, P and Trapido, S, eds., 1986.

Ross, R, 'The Cape of Good Hope and the World Economy, 1652-1835.' In Elphick, R and Giliomee, H, eds., 1989.

Rotberg, R I and Mazrui, A A, eds., *Protest and Power in Black Africa*. New York: Oxford University Press, 1970.

Rotberg, R I and Rabb, T K, eds., *Climate and History*. Princeton: Princeton University Press, 1981.

Roth, H L, *Studies in Primitive Looms*, 3rd ed. Halifax: Bankfield Museum, 1950.

Rue, G M La, 'The Export Trade of Darfur, c. 1785 to 1875.' In Liesegang, G, Pasch, H and Jones, A, eds., 1950., 1983.

Ruedy, J, *Land Policy in Colonial Algeria: The Origins of the Rural Public Domain*. Berkeley and Los Angeles: University of California Press, 1967.

Ruthenberg, H, *Farming Systems in the Tropics*, 3rd ed. London: Oxford University Press, 1980.

Rutter, A F, 'Ashanti Vernacular Architecture.' In Oliver, P, ed., 1971.

Saadawi, N el, *The Hidden face of Eve*. Boston: Beacon Press, 1980.

Saben-Clare, E E, et.al., eds., *Health in Tropical Africa During the Colonial Period*. Oxford: Clarendon Press, 1980.

Safer, J F and Gill, F M, *Spirits from the Sea: An Anthropological Look at Shells*. New York, 1982.

Saha, S C, 'Agriculture in Liberia During the Nineteenth Century: Americo-Liberians' Contribution.' *Canadian Journal of African Studies*, 22:224-239, 1988.

Said, E, *Orientalism*. New York: Vantage Books, 1979.

Salmons, J, 'Funerary Shrine Cloths of the Annang Ibibio, South-east Nigeria.' *Textile History*, 11:120-141, 1980.

Sandbrook, R and Cohen, R, eds., *The Development of an African Working Class*. London: Longman, 1975.

Sanders, J, 'Palm Oil Production on the Gold Coast in the Aftermath of the Slave Trade: A Case Study of the Fante.' *International Journal of African Historical Studies*, 15:49-63, 1982.

Saul, J S and Woods, R, 'African Peasantries'. In Shanin, T, ed., 1979.

Saul, S B, *Myth of the Great Depression, 1873-1896*. London: Macmillan, 1969.

Schlippe, P de, *Shifting Cultivation in Africa: The Azande System of Agriculture*. London: Routledge and Kegan Paul, 1956.

Schmidt, P R, 'A New Look at Interpretation of the Early Iron Age in East Africa.' *History in Africa*, 2:127-136, 1975.

Schmidt, P R and Avery, D H, 'Complex Iron Smelting and Prehistoric Culture in Tanzania.' *Science*, 201:4361 1085- 1089, 1978.

Schmidt, P R, *Historical Archaeology: A Structural Approach in an African Culture*. Westport: Greenwood Press, 1978.

Schmidt, P R, 'Steel production in Prehistoric Africa: Insights from Ethno Archaeology in West Lake, Tanzania.' *Proceedings of the Eighth Pan-African Congress of Prehistoric and Quaternary Studies*. Nairobi:335-340, 1980.

Schmidt, P R, 'The Origins of Iron Smelting in Africa: Complex Technology in Tanzania.' *Research Papers in Anthropology*, 1, Brown University, 1981.

Schneider, H K, 'The Pastoralist Development Problem.' *Journal of Asian and African Studies*, 16:27-32, 1981.

Schneider, J and Weimer, A B, eds., *Cloth and Human Experience*. Washington: Smithsonian Institution, 1989.

Scholch, A, *Egypt for the Egyptians: The Socio-Political Crisis in Egypt, 1878-1882*. London: Middle East Centre, St. Anthony's College Oxford, 1981.

Schove, D J, 'African Droughts and the Spectrum of Time.' In Dalby, D, et.al., eds.,1977.

Schreuder, D M, *The Scramble for Southern Africa, 1877- 1895: The Politics of Partition Reappraised*. Cambridge: Cambridge University Press, 1980.

Schumpeter, J A, *Imperialism and Social Classes*. New York: Augustus M. Kelley, 1951.

Schwerdtfeger, F, 'Zanj, the East African Coast.' In Oliver, P, ed., 1971.

Scott, J C, 'Everyday Forms of Peasant Resistance.' *Journal of Political Science*, 13:5-35, 1985.

Scott, J C, *Weapons of the Weak: Everyday Forms of Peasant Resistance*. New Haven: Yale University Press, 1985.

Searing, J F, 'Aristocrats, Slaves and Peasants: Power and Dependency in the Wolof States, 1700-1850.' *International Journal of African Historical Studies*, 21:475-503, 1988.

Seddon, D, ed., *Relations of Production: Marxist Approaches to Economic Anthropology*. London: Frank Cass, 1978.

Seidenberg, D A, *Uhuru and the Kenya Indians*. New Delhi: Vikas Publishing House, 1983.

Seidman, A and Makgetla, A S, *Outposts of Monopoly Capitalism: Southern Africa in the Changing Global Economy*. London: Zed Press, 1980.

Seleti, Y, 'The Development of Dependent Capitalism in Portuguese Africa'. In Konczacki, J L Parpart, and Shaw, T M, eds., 1990.

Sen, A K, 'Peasants and dualism with or without surplus.' *Journal of Political Economy*, 74:425-450, 1966.

Sen, A K, *Poverty and Famines*. Oxford: Clarendon Press, 1981.

Shanin, T, ed., *Peasants and Peasant Societies*. Harmondsworth: Penguin, 1979.

Shaw, T, 'Early Crops in Africa: A Review of the Evidence.' In Harlan, J R, et.al., eds., 1976.

Shaw, T, 'Questions in the Holocene Demography of West Africa.' In Fyfe, C and McMaster, D, eds., 1977.

Shaw, T, 'Towards a Prehistoric Demography of Africa.' In Fyfe, C and McMaster, D, eds., 1981.

Shea, P, *The Development of an Export Oriented Dyed Cloth Industry in Kano*. Ph.D. Dissertation, University of Wisconsin, 1975.

Shenton, B and Watts, M, 'Capitalism and Hunger in Northern Nigeria.' *Review of African Political Economy*, 15/16:53-62, 1979.

Sheriff, A M H, 'Trade and Under-development.' In Ogot, B A, ed., 1979.

Sheriff, A M H, 'Ivory and Economic Expansion in East Africa in the Nineteenth Century.' In Liesegang, G, Pasch, H and Jones, A, eds., 1983.

Sheriff, A M H, 'Social Formations in Precolonial Kenya.' In Ogot, B A, ed., 1985.

Sheriff, A M H, *Slaves, Spices and Ivory in Zanzibar*. London: James Currey, 1987.

Shinnie, P L, *The African Iron Age*. Oxford: Oxford University Press, 1971.

Shinnie, P L and Kense, F J, 'Meroitic Iron Working.' *Meroitic Studies Meroitica*, 6:17-28, 43-49, 1982.

Shinnie, P, 'Iron Working at Meroe.' In Haaland, R and Shinnie, P, eds., 1985.

Shipton, P, 'African Famines and Food Security: Anthropological Perspectives'. *Annual Review of Anthropology*, 19:353-394, 1990.

Showers, K B, 'Soil Erosion in the Kingdom of Lesotho: Origins and Colonial Response, 1830s - 1950s.' *Journal of Southern African Studies*, 15:263-286, 1989.

Shroeter, D J, *Merchants of Essaouira: Urban Society and Imperialism in Southwestern Morocco, 1844-1886*. Cambridge: Cambridge University Press, 1988.

Shukla, J, 'Predictability of time Averages.' Part II: 'The Influence of the Boundary Forcing.' In Burridge, R M and Kallen, E, eds., 1984.

Sieber, R, *African Furniture and Household Objects*. Bloomington: Indiana University Press, 1980.

Silberfein, M, 'The African Cultivator: A Geographic Overview'. *African Studies Review*, 20:7-23, 1977.

Silver, J, 'The Failure of European Mining Companies in the Nineteenth Century Gold Coast.' *Journal of African History*, 22:511-529, 1981.

Simmons, H J, and R E, *Class and Colour in South Africa 1850-1950*. Harmondsworth: Penguin, 1969.

Sindiga, I, 'The Use of Geography in Recent Historical Research in East Africa.' *TransAfrican Journal of History*, 14:124-138, 1985.

Sivers, P von, 'Insurrection and Accommodation: Indigenous Leadership in Eastern Algeria, 1840-1900'. *International Journal of Middle Eastern Studies*, 6:259-275, 1975.

Sivers, P von, 'Algerian Landownership and Rural Leadership, 1860-1940: A Quantitative Approach'. *The Maghreb Review*, 4:58-62, 1979.

Sjoberg, G, *The Preindustrial City: Past and Present*. Glencoe, Ill.: Free Press, 1960.

Smaldone, J P, *Warfare in the Sokoto Caliphate: Historical and Sociological Perspectives*. Cambridge: Cambridge University Press, 1977.

Smith, E B, *Egyptian Architecture as Cultural Expression*. New York: American Life Foundation, 1968.

Smith, J, et.al., eds., *Households and the World Economy*. Beverly Hills: Sage, 1984.

Smith, M G, *Baba of Kano*. London: Oxford University Press, 1954.

Smith, R H T, 'West African Market Places: Temporal Periodicity and Locational Spacing.' In C. Meillassoux, ed., 1971.

Smith, R, 'The Canoe in West African History.' *Journal of African History*, 11:515-533, 1970.

Smith, W S, *The Art and Architecture of Ancient Egypt*. Harmondsworth: Penguin, 1958.

Smith, P E L, 'Early Food Production in Northern Africa as seen From South-Western Asia.' In J.R. Harlan, et.al., eds., 1976.

Soejarto, D D, et.al., 'Fertility Regulating Agents from Plants.' *Bulletin of the World Health Organisation*, 56:343-352, 1978.

Solway, B L and Engelman, S L, eds., *British Capitalism and Caribbean Slavery: The Legacy of Eric Williams.* Cambridge: Cambridge University Press, 1987.

Spaulding, J, 'Slavery, Land Tenure and Social Class in the Northern Turkish Sudan.' *International Journal of African Historical Studies,* 15:1-20, 1982.

St. Croix, F W de, *The Fulani of Northern Nigeria: Some General Notes.* Lagos: Government Printer, 1944.

St. John, C, 'Kazembe and the Tanganyika-Nyasa Corridor, 1800-1890.' In Gray, R and Birmingham, D, eds., 1970.

Steel, R H, 'Iron Age Mining and Metallurgy in South Africa'. In Hitchcock, R R and Smith, M R, eds., 1982.

Steiner, K G, *Intercropping in Tropical Smallholder Agriculture with Special Reference to West Africa.* Eschborn: GTZ, 1982.

Stengers, J, 'King Leopold's Imperialism'. In Owen, R and Sutcliffe, B, eds., 1972.

Stern, P, *Small-Scale Irrigation: A Manual of Low-Cost Water Technology.* London: Intermediate Technology of Publications, 1980.

Stevenson, R F, *Population and Political Systems in Tropical Africa.* New York: Columbia University Press, 1968.

Stichter, S, *Migrant Labourers.* Cambridge: Cambridge University Press, 1985.

Stichter, S B and Parpart, J L, eds., *Patriarchy and Class: African Women in the Home and the Workforce.* Boulder and London: Westview Press, 1988.

Stokes, E, 'Imperialism and the Scramble for Africa: The New View.' In Louis, W R, ed., 1976.

Stone, L, *The Family, Sex and Marriage in England 1500-1800.* New York: Harper, 1979.

Street, F A and Grove, A T, 'Environmental and Climatic Implications of late Quaternary lake-level Fluctuations in Africa.' *Nature,* 261:385-390, 1976.

Streeten, P P, 'Development Dichotomies.' In G.M. Meier and D. Seers, eds., 1984.

Strobel, M, 'From Lelemama to Lobbying: Women's Associations.' In Hafkin, N and Bay, E G, eds., 1976.

Strobel, M, 'Slavery and Reproductive Labour in Mombasa.' In Robertson, C C and Klein, M A, eds., 1983.

Strobel, M, *Muslim Women in Mombasa, 1890-1975.* New Haven: Yale University Press, 1979.

Sud, C and Fennessey, M J, 'Influence of Evaporation in Semi-Arid Regions on the July Circulation: A Numerical Study'. *Journal of Climatology,* 4:383- 398, 1984.

Summers, R, *Ancient Mining in Rhodesia.* Salisbury: National Museums of Rhodesia, 1969.

Sundstrom, L, *The Exchange Economy of Precolonial Africa.* New York: St. Martin's Press, 1974.

Suret-Canale, J, *Essays on African History: From the Slave Trade to Neocolonialism.* Trenton, N.J.: Africa World Press, 1988.

Sutherland-Harris, N, 'Zambian Trade with Zumbo in the Eighteenth Century.' In Gray, R and Birmingham, D, eds., 1970a.

Sutherland-Harris, N, 'Trade and the Rozwi Mambo.' In Gray, R and Birmingham, D, eds., 1970b.

Sutton, I, 'The Volta River Salt Trade: The Survival of an Indigenous Industry.' *Journal of African History,* 22:43-61, 1981.

Sutton, I, 'Labour in Commercial Agriculture in Ghana in the late Nineteenth Century and Early Twentieth Century.' *Journal of African History,* 24:4671-483, 1983.

Sutton, J E G and Roberts, A D, 'Uvinza Salt Industry.' *Azania,* 3:45-86, 1968.

Sutton, J E G, 'Population Estimates From Selected African Iron Age Sites.' In Fyfe, C and McMaster, D, eds., 1981.

Sutton, J E G, 'Archaeology in West Africa: A Review of Recent Work and a Further List of Radio Carbon Dates.' *Journal of African History*, 23:291-313, 1982.

Sutton, J E G, 'Irrigation and Soil Conservation in African Agricultural History.' *Journal of African History*, 25:25-41, 1984.

Sutton, J E G, 'Temporal and Spatial Variability in African Iron Furnaces.' In Haaland, R, et.al., eds., 1985.

Swindell, K, 'Serawoollies, Tillimbukas and Strange Farmers: The Development of Migrant Groundnut Farming Along the Gambia River, 1848-1895.' *Journal of African History*, 21:93- 104, 1980.

Swindell, K, *The Strange Farmers of The Gambia: A Study in the Redistribution of Population*. Centre for Development Studies, Monograph Series no.15, University College of Swansea, Geo Books, Norwich, 1981.

Syfert, D N, 'The Liberian Coasting Trade, 1822-1900.' *Journal of African History*, 17:217-235, 1977.

Tahir, I, 'Scholars, Sufis, Saints and Capitalists in Kano: 1904-74.' Ph.D Thesis, University of Cambridge, Cambridge, 1975.

Talle, A, *Women at a Loss: Changes in Maasai Pastoralism and their Effects on Gender Relations*. Stockholm: University of Stockholm, 1988.

Tambo, D C, 'The Sokoto Caliphate Slave Trade in the Nineteenth.' *International Journal of Africa Historical Studies*, 9:167-217, 1976.

Taylor, A J P, *Germany's First Bid for Colonies, 1884-5*. London: Macmillan, 1938.

Temu, A and Swai, B, *Historians and Africanist History: A Critique*. London: Zed Press, 1981.

Terray, E, *Marxism and 'Primitive' Societies: Two Studies*. New York: Monthly Review Press, 1972.

Terray, E, 'Classes ad Class Consciousness in the Abron Kingdom of Gyman.' In Bloch, M, ed., 1975.

Thomas, D B, *Importing Technology into Africa*. New York: Praeger.

Thomas, M F and Whittington, G W, eds., *Environment and Land Use in Africa*. London: Methuen, 1969.

Thompson, B W, *Africa: The Climatic Background*. London: Oxford University Press, 1975.

Thompson, L M, *The Unification of South Africa, 1902-1910*. Oxford: Clarendon, 1960.

Thornton, J, 'Demography and History in the Kingdom of Kongo, 1550-1750.' *Journal of African History*, 28:507-530, 1977a.

Thornton, J, 'An Eighteenth Century Baptismal Register and the Demographic History of Manguenzo.' In Fyfe, C and McMaster, D, eds., 1977b.

Thornton, J, 'The Slave Trade in Eighteenth Century Angola: Effects on Demographic Structures.' *Canadian Journal of African Studies*, 14:417-427, 1980.

Thornton, J, *The Kingdom of Kongo: Civil War and Transition, 1641-1718*. Madison: University of Wisconsin Press, 1983a.

Thornton, J, 'Sexual demography: The Impact of the Slave Trade on Family Structure.' In Robertson, C C and Klein, M A, eds., 1983b.

Thornton, J, 'The Historian and the Precolonial African Economy.' *African Economic History*, 19:45-54, 1990-91a.

Thornton, J, 'Precolonial African Industry and the Atlantic Trade, 1500-1800.' *African Economic History*, 19:1-19, 1990-91b.

Tickwell, C, *Climatic Change and World Affairs*. Cambridge, MA: Harvard University Press, 1977.

Tignor, R L, 'The Introduction of Modern Banking into Egypt, 1855-1920'. *Asian and African Studies*, 15:103-122, 1981.

Timberlake, L, *Africa In Crisis: The Causes, the Cures of Environmental Bankruptcy*. London: Earthscan, 1988.

Tlemcani, R, *State and Revolution in Algeria*. Boulder, Colo: Westview Press, 1986.

Todd, J A, 'Iron Production by the Dimi of Ethiopia.' In Haaland, R and Shinnie, P, eds., 1985.

Toledano, E R, *State and Society in Mid-Nineteenth Century Egypt*. Cambridge: Cambridge University Press, 1990.

Torry, W I, 'Natural Disasters, Social Structure and Change in Traditional Societies.' *Journal of Asian and African Studies*, 13:167-183, 1978.

Tosh, J, 'The Northern Interlacustrine Region.' In Gray, R and Birmingham, D, eds., 1970.

Trapido, S, 'The Friends of the Natives: Merchants, Peasants and the Political and Ideological Structure of Liberalism in the Cape, 1854-1910.' In Marks, S and Atmore, A, eds., 1980.

Trapido, S, 'Putting a Plough to the Ground: A History of Tenant Production on the Vereening Estates, 1896-1920.' In Beinart, W Delius P, and Trapido, S, eds., 1986.

Trevor, T G, 'Some Observations on the Relics of Pre-European Culture in Rhodesia and South Africa.' *JRAI*, 60:389-99, 1930.

Trigger, B G, 'The Myth of Meroe and the African Iron Age.' *International Journal of African Historical Studies*, 2:23-50, 1969.

Triulzi, A, 'Trade, Islam, and the Madhia in Northwestern Wallaga, Ethiopia.' *Journal of African History*, 16:55-71, 1975.

Tucker, J E, 'Problems in the Historiography of Women in the Middle East: The Case of Nineteenth Century Egypt.' *International Journal of Middle East Studies*, 15:321-336, 1983.

Tucker, J E, *Women in Nineteenth Century Egypt*. Cambridge: Cambridge University Press, 1985.

Turner, H A, 'Bismarck's Imperialist Venture.' In Gifford, P and Louis, W R, eds., 1967.

Turrell, R, 'Kimberley: Labour and Compounds, 1871-1888.' In Marks S and Rathbone, R, eds., 1982.

Turshen, M, *The Political Ecology of Disease in Tanzania*. New Brunswick, N.J: Rutgers University Press, 1984.

Tylecote, R F, 'The Origins of Iron Smelting in Africa.' *West African Journal of Archaeology*, 5:1-9, 1975.

Tylecote, R F, 'Early Copper Slags and Copper Base Metal From the Agades region of Niger.' *Journal of the Historical Metallurgy Society*, 16:58-64, 1982.

Tyson, P D, 'Temporal and Spatial Variation of Rainfall Anomalies in Africa South of Latitude 22 During the Period of Meteorological Record.' *Climatic Change*, 2:363-371, 1980.

Udovitch, A L, *Partnership and Profit in Medieval Islam*. Princeton: Princeton University Press, 1970.

UNESCO, *Social Science Research and Women in the Arab World*. London and Dover, N.H: Francis Pinter, 1984.

United Nations, *Determinants and Consequences of International Demographic, Economic and Social Factors*. New York: United Nations, 1973.

Usoro, E J, 'Notes on Quantitative Approaches to Research on West African Economic History.' In Dewey, C and Hopkins, A G, eds., 1978.

Uzoigwe, G N, *Britain and the Conquest of Africa*. Ann Arbor: University of Michigan Press, 1974.

Uzoigwe, G N, 'The Mombasa Victoria Railway, 1890-1902: Imperial Necessity, Humanitarian Venture, or Economic Imperialism.' *Kenya Historical Review*, 4:11-34, 1976.

Uzoigwe, G N, 'Precolonial Markets in Bunyoro-Kitara.' In Ogot, B A, ed., 1979.

Vail, L, 'Mozambique's Chartered Companies: The Rule of the Feeble'. *Journal of African History*, 17:389-416, 1976.

Vail, L, 'Ecology and History: The Example of Eastern Zambia.' *Journal of Southern African Studies*, 3:129-155, 1977.

Vail, L, 'The Political Economy of East-Central Africa.' In Birmingham, D and Martin, P, eds., 1983.

Vail, L and White,L, *Capitalism and Colonialism in Mozambique*. London: Heinemann, 1980.

Valensi, L, *Tunisian Peasants in the Eighteenth and Nineteenth Centuries*. Cambridge: Cambridge University Press, 1985.

Van Bath, B H S, *The Agrarian History of Western Europe*, A.D. 500-1850. London: Arnold, 1963.

Van Onselen, C, 'Reactions to Rinderpest in Southern Africa.' *Journal of African History*, 13:473-488, 1972.

Van Onselen, C, *Chibaro: African Mine Labour in Southern Rhodesia*. Nottingham: Pluto, 1976.

Van Onselen, C, *New Babylon*, Vol.1 of *Studies in the Social and Economic History of the Witwatersrand*, 1886-1914. 2 Vols. London: Longmans, 1982a.

Van Onselen, C, *New Nineveh*, Vol.2 of *Studies in the Social and Economic History of the Witwatersrand*, 1886-1914. 2 Vols. London: Longmans, 1982b.

Van Onselen, C, 'Race and Class in the South African Countryside: Cultural Osmosis and Social Relations in the Share- Cropping Economy of the South-Western Transvaal, 1900-1950.' *American Historical Review*, 95:99-123, 1990.

Vansina, J, *The Tio Kingdom of the Middle Congo, 1880-1892*. London: Oxford University Press, 1973.

Vansina, J, *Kingdoms of the Savanna*. Madison: University of Wisconsin Press, 1975.

Vansina, J, 'Finding Food and the History of Precolonial Equatorial Africa: A Plea.' *African Economic History*, 7:9-20, 1979.

Vansina, J, 'The Peoples of the Forest.' In Birmingham, D and Martin, P, eds., 1983.

Verity, P, 'The Kababish Nomads of Northern Sudan.' In Oliver, P, ed., 1971.

Walker, C, 'Review Article: Women's Studies on the Move'. *Journal of Southern African Studies*, 13:433-438, 1987.

Waller, R, 'Economic and Social Relations in the Central Rift Valley: The Maa-Speakers and their Neighbours in the Nineteenth Century.' In Ogot, B A, ed., 1985.

Wallerstein, I, *The Modern World System*. New York: Academic Press, 1974.

Wallerstein, I, 'The Three Stages of African Involvement in the World Economy.' In Gutkind, P C W, et.al., eds., 1976.

Wallerstein, I, *The Capitalist World Economy*. Cambridge: Cambridge University Press, 1979.

Wallerstein, I, *The Modern World System*. Vol.2. New York: Academic Press, 1980.

Wallerstein, I, *Historical Capitalism*. London: Verso, 1983.

Wallerstein, I, *The Politics of the World Economy*. Cambridge: Cambridge University Press, 1984.

Wallerstein, I, 'Africa and the World Economy.' In Ajayi, J F A, ed., 1989.

Walz, T, *Trade Between Egypt and Bilad As-Sudan, 1700- 1820*. Cairo: Institute Francais D'Archaeologie Oriental, 1978.

Wamba-dia-Wamba, E, 'How is Historical Knowledge Recognized?' *History in Africa*, 13:331-344, 1986.

Wamba-dia-Wamba, E, *History of Neo-Colonialism? Self-Determination and History in Africa*. Africa Research and Publications Project, Working Paper, No.5, 1987.

Warburg, G, 'Slavery and Labour in the Anglo-Egyptian Sudan.' *Asian and African Studies*, 12:221-245, 1978.

Warren, B, 'Imperialism and Capitalist Industrialization.' *New Left Review*, 81:3-44, 1973.

Warren, B, *Imperialism: Pioneer of Capitalism*. London: New Left Books and Verso, 1980.

Warriner, D, *Land Reform and Development in the Middle East: A Study of Egypt, Syria, and Iraq*. London: Oxford University Press, 1962.

Washburne, C, *Primitive Drinking: A Study of the Uses and Functions of Alcohol in Preliterate Societies*. New York: University Publishers, 1961.

Waterbury, J, *Hydropolitics of the Nile Valley*. New York: Syracuse, 1979.

Watson, J L, ed., *Asian and African Systems of Slavery*. Berkeley: University of California Press, 1980.

Watts, M, *Silent Violence: Food, Famine and Peasantry in Northern Nigeria*. Berkeley: University of California Press, 1983.

Watts, M, 'Drought, Environment and Food Security: Some Reflections on Peasants, Pastoralists and Commoditization in Dryland West Africa.' In M.H. Glantz, ed., 1987.

Watts, M, 'Struggles Over Land, Struggles Over Meaning.' In Golledge, R, ed., 1988.

Webb, J L A, 'Toward the Comparative Study of Money: A Reconsideration of West African Currencies and Neoclassical Monetary Concepts.' *International Journal of African Historical Studies*, 15:455-465, 1982.

Webb, J L A, 'The Trade in Gum Arabic: Prelude to French Conquest in Senegal.' *Journal of African History*, 26:149-168, 1985.

Webster, J B and Boahen, A A, *The Growth of African Civilisation: The Revolutionary Years. West Africa Since 1800*. London: Longman, 1974.

Webster, J B and Unoma, A C, 'East Africa: The Expansion of Commerce.' In Flint, J E, ed., 1975.

Webster, J B, ed., *Chronology, Migration and Drought in Interlacustrine Africa*. New York: Africana Publishing, Dalhousie University Press, 1979.

Webster, J B, 'Drought, Migration and Chronology in the Lake Malawi Littoral.' *Trans-African Journal of History*, 9:70- 90, 1980.

Webster, J B, 'Periodization in African History c.1050- 1840.' *Journal of General Studies*, 4:5-23, 1983.

Webster, D J, 'The Political Economy of Food Production and Nutrition in Southern Africa in Historical Perspective.' *Journal of Modern African Studies*, 24:447-463, 1986.

Wehler, H U, 'Industrial Growth and early German Imperialism.' In Owen, R and Sutcliffe, B, eds., 1972.

Welch, C E, 'Peasants as a Focus in African Studies'. *African Studies Review*, 20:1-5, 1977.

Wembah-Rashid, J A R, 'Iron Workers of Ufipa.' International Committee of Urgent Anthropological and *Ethnological Research Bulletin*, 11:65-72, 1969.

Wesseling, H L, 'The Netherlands and the Partition of Africa.' *Journal of African History*, 22:495-509, 1981.

Wheatcroft, G, *The Randlords*. London: Weidenfeld and Nicholson, 1985.

White, E F, 'Creole Women Traders in the Nineteenth Century.' *International Journal of African Historical Studies*, 14:626-642, 1981.

White, E F, *Sierra Leone's Settler Women Traders: Women on the Afro-European Frontier.* Ann Arbor, Mich.: University of Michigan Press, 1987.

White, G, 'Firearms in Africa: An Introduction'. *Journal of African History*, 7:173-181, 1971.

White, Landeg, *Magomero: Portrait of an African Village.* Cambridge: Cambridge University Press, 1987.

White, Louise, 'Women in the Changing African Family.' In Hay, J and Stichter, S, eds., 1984.

Wickins, P L, *An Economic History of Africa From the Earliest Times to the Partition.* Cape Town: Oxford University Press, 1981.

Wigley, T M L, et.al., eds., *Climate and History.* Cambridge: Cambridge University Press, 1981.

Wilcox, W F, 'Increase in the Population of the Earth and of the Continents Since 1650.' *International Migrations.* Vol.2: *Interpretations.* New York: National Bureau of Economic Research, 1931.

Wilhite, D A and Glantz, M H, 'Understanding the Drought Phenomenon: The Role of Definitions.' *Water International*, 10:111-120, 1985.

Wilks, I, 'Asante policy towards the Hausa trade in the nineteenth century.' In Meillassoux, C, ed., 1971.

Williams, D, *Icon and Image.* London: Allen Lane, 1974.

Williams, E, *Capitalism and Slavery.* London: Andre Deutsch, 1981.

Williams, M A J and Faure, H, eds., *The Sahara and the Nile.* Rotterdam: A A Balkema, 1979.

Willis, J R, *Slaves and Slavery in Muslim Africa.* 2 Vols. London: Frank Cass, 1985.

Willoughby, J, *Capitalist Imperialism, Crisis and the State.* New York: Harwood Academic Publishers, 1986.

Wilson, F, *Labour in the South African Gold Mines, 1911-1969.* Cambridge: Cambridge University Press, 1972.

Wilson, H S, ed., *Origins of West African Nationalism.* London: Macmillan, 1969.

Wilson, K B, 'Trees in Fields in Southeastern Zimbabwe.' *Journal of Southern African Studies*, 15:369-383, 1989.

Wilson, T H, 'Swahili Funerary Architecture of the North Kenya Coast.' In J de V Allen and Wilson, T H, eds., 1979.

Wipper, A, 'Reflections on the Past Sixteen Years, 1972-1988, and Future Challenges'. *Canadian Journal of African Studies*, 22:409-421, 1988.

Wolf, E, *Peasant Wars of the Twentieth Century.* New York: Harper and Row, 1969.

Wolff, E R, *Peasants*, Englewood Cliffs: Prentice Hall, 1966.

Wolff, R D, *The Economics of Colonialism: Britain and Kenya, 1870-1930.* New Haven: Yale University Press, 1974.

Wolpe, H, 'Capitalism and Cheap Labour-Power in South Africa: From Segregation to Apartheid.' *Economy and Society*, 1:425-456, 1972.

Wolpe, H, *Race, Class and the Apartheid State.* Trenton, N.J: Africa World Press, 1990.

Wood, C A, 'A Preliminary Chronology of Ethiopian Droughts.' In Dalby, D, et.al., eds., 1977.

Worden, N, *Slavery in South Africa.* Cambridge: Cambridge University Press, 1985.

Worster, D, *The Ends of the Earth: Perspectives on Modern Environmental History.* Cambridge: Cambridge University Press, 1988.

Wright, D R, 'Darbo Jula: The Role of a Mandinka Jula Clan in the Long Distance Trade of the Gambia River and Its Hinterland.' *African Economic History*, 3:33-45, 1977.

Wright, M, 'Societies and Economies in Kenya, 1870-1902.' In Ogot, B A, ed., 1979.

Wright, M, 'Iron and Regional History: Report on a Research Project in South Western Tanzania.' *African Economic History*, 14:147-165, 1985.

Wright, M, 'Towards a Critical History of Iron Makers in Sumbamanga District, Tanzania.' Mimeo, n.d.

Wrigley, C C, 'Neo-Mercantile Policies and the New Imperialism.' In Dewey, C and Hopkins, A G, eds., 1978.

Wrigley, C, 'Population and History: Some Innumerable Reflections.' In Fyfe, C and McMaster, D, eds., 1981.

Wrigley, C C, 'Population in African History.' *Journal of African History*, 25:93-96, 1984.

Wylie, D, 'The Changing Face of Hunger in Southern African History, 1890-1980.' *Past and Present*, 122:159-199, 1989.

Wyndham, H A, *The Atlantic and Slavery.* London, 1935.

Young, M C, 'Nationalism, Ethnicity and Class in Africa: A Retrospective.' *Cahiers d'Etudes Africaines*, 103:421-495, 1986.

Young, C, 'The Colonial State and Post-Colonial Crisis.' In Gifford, P and Louis, W R, eds., 1988.

Zaalouk, M, *Power, Class and Foreign Capital in Egypt: The Rise of the New Bourgeoisie.* London: Zed Books, 1989.

Zeleza, P T, *Dependent Capitalism and the Making of the Kenyan Working Class During the Colonial Period.* Ph.D. Dissertation, Dalhousie University, 1982.

Zeleza, T, 'African History: The Rise and Decline of Academic Tourism.' *Ufahamu*, 13:9-43, 1983.

Zeleza, T, *Record of Minutes of UNESCO-Sponsored Consultative Meeting on the Revision of History Textbooks in East and Central Africa.* Nairobi: UNESCO, 1984.

Zeleza, T, *Record of Minutes of UNESCO-Sponsored Consultative Meeting on the Revision of History Textbooks in East and Central Africa.* Nairobi: UNESCO, 1985a.

Zeleza, T, 'The Problems of Teaching African Economic History,' paper Presented to UNESCO Conference on Revision of History Textbooks in East and Central Africa, Nairobi, UNESCO, 1985b.

Zeleza, T, 'The Problems of Writing History Textbooks: The Case of East Africa,' paper presented to the Meeting of Experts on History Teaching and Textbooks in African Schools, Nairobi, UNESCO, 1989b.

Zeleza, T, 'The Current Agrarian Crisis in Africa: Its History and Future.' *Journal of Eastern African Research and Development*, 16:151-186, 1986.

Zeleza, T, 'African Sugar in the World Market.' *Journal of Eastern African Research and Development*, 18:1-23, 1988.

Zeleza, T, 'The Establishment of Colonial Rule.' In Ochieng', W R, ed., 1989.

Zeleza, T, 'The Production of Historical Knowledge for Schools'. *Transafrican Journal of History*, 19:1-23, 1990.

Zeleza, T, 'African Social Scientists and the Struggle for Academic Freedom', *Journal of Eastern African Research and Development*, 22:11-32, 1992.

Zwanenberg, R M A and King, A, *An Economic History of Kenya and Uganda, 1800-1970.* London: Macmillan, 1975.

Zwanenberg, R M A, 'Dorobo Hunting and Gathering: A Way of Life or a Mode of Production?' *African Economic History*, 2:12-24, 1976.

Index

A

Abeokuta
  nationalism 392
  population 76-77
Accra Confederation 392
Accra, nationalism 392
Ada, salt production 194
Addis Ababa
  markets 299
  population 78
  trade 408
adoption, Maasai 139
Adowa
  markets 299
  textiles 209
Adulis, urbanization 76
Afkala, trade 299
Afrikaners 74-75, 162
Agadez, copper production 183, 185
Agalawa, trade 279
agriculture 6-11, 115-116, 425
  and colonialism 156-172
  and imperialism 145
  labour 160-161, 165-166, 169
  labour, gender division 93
  and mining 161
  mixed farming 110-111
  productivity 7-8
  and slavery 133-145, 154
  tools 92-95, 115
agro-forestry 88
Air Massif, salt production 196, 198
Akamba, trade 298
Akjoujt, copper production 183
al-Masallamiyya, growth of 78
al-Matamma, growth of 78
Alamaya, agriculture 91
Albert, Lake 28
alcohol 237-238, 403
Alexandria 347

population 77, 81
rainfall 30
settlers 81
Algeria
  agriculture 91, 93, 98-99, 143, 357
  architecture 213
  colonization 167-170, 354-359, 368
  crafts 250
  currency 357
  economy 358
  education 251
  exports 357-358
  and France 167-170, 354-359
  imports 357
  industrialization 249-252
  labour 251
  land ownership 167-170
  population 58
  railways 358
  rainfall 30
  settlers 73, 169-170, 250, 357
  trade 256-257, 270, 345, 357-358
  transport 265, 358
  urbanization 77
Algiers
  population 76-77
  port 358
  trade 270
Alima, agriculture 103
Aliu Amba, markets 299
Alur, taxation 301
Ambriz, trade 401
Anglo-American Corporation 249, 417
Anglo-Turkish Treaty 220
Angola
  agriculture 103-104, 156-157
  colonialism 332
  colonization 410-411, 421
  currency 325-326

G

Gabon
  disease 66
  exports 386
  plantations 386
  salt production 195
Gajaaga, trade 280
Gambia
  agriculture 99
  colonization 385
  currency 286
  exports 373, 380
Ganvie, architecture 215
Gao
  trade 270
  urbanization 76
Gaza Nguni, and slavery 135
Gedi, urbanization 76
gender
  and agricultural labour 93
  analysis 11-12
  and architecture 215-216
  and division of labour 145, 147-155,
207-209, 424
General Mining 232
German East Africa Company 419
Germany
  in East Africa 418-419
  and Libya 367
  and Morocco 364-365
  and West Africa 386, 393
Gezira, agriculture 109
Ghadmes, agriculture 97
Ghana
  agriculture 100-101, 129
  architecture 213
  colonization 392
  construction 216
  gold production 240-244, 396
  iron production 175, 179
  labour, agricultural 137
  land ownership 128-129
  migrants 72
  mining 240-244, 252
  salt production 194-195

textiles 208
Ghartey, Robert 388
gold
  currency 282
  exports 268, 372-373
  production 188-194, 227, 230-233,
240-244
Gold Coast
  bankruptcy case 391
  colonization 385
  credit systems 382
  exports 375
  merchants 388
  nationalism 392
  trade 392
Goldie, George 392
Gondar
  credit systems 314
  markets 299
  population 78
grain, exports 398, 407
Grand Bassam, colonization 385
Grant, Francis 388
Griqua, trade 334
Griqualand 415
groundnuts 99, 129-130
guano, exports 375
guilds 258-259, 270
Guinea
  agriculture 99
  caravans 288
  climate 30
  currency 282
  exports 373
  population 66
  trade 402
Guinea-Bissau
  agriculture 130
  land ownership 130
gum 381-382, 384-385
  exports 372, 375, 408
  prices 380, 406
Gusii, trade 305-306
Gwandu, agriculture 140

H

Hamama, textiles 207
Harar
  agriculture 108
  currency 312
  markets 299
  population 78
  trade 408
Hausa
  agriculture 36-37
  architecture 214
  food shortages 36-37
  households 127
  labour distribution 127
  pottery 211
  textiles 202, 207-208
  trade 279-280
healing, organization of 49
health
  and migrant labour 240
  mineworkers 235
  mining communities 231, 236
hides, exports 403
hoes 95, 180, 403
Holland Jacques and Company 387
households 12, 126-128, 138-140
  and textile production 209-210
housing 213-216
Hughes, Thomas 388
Hutu, agricultural labour 137

I

Ibadan, population 77
Ibibia, textiles 203
Ibibio, textiles 208
Ife
  brass production 186
  pottery 212
Igbirra, textiles 207
Igbo Ukwu, brass and bronze production 186
Ikelemba, agriculture 103
Ilorin
  population 76-77

trade 279
Imerina
  agriculture 91
  population 225
immigration 70, 74-75, 83
Imperial British East Africa Company 419-420
Imperial Railway Company 316
imperialism 16-22
  and agriculture 145
  and disease 41
imports, effects of 378-379
Indians, in East Africa 406
indigo 100, 109, 202
industrialization 216-221, 223-226, 251-252
inflation 284-285
influenza 41
inoculation 49
intercropping 87-88
International African Association 412
Inyanga, agriculture 89, 92
Irebu, population 320
iron production 174-176, 178-183
  imports 181-182, 377
  labour 178-180, 182
  prices 380
  smelting 176
  and social status 180
  trade 180-183
irrigation 89-92
Islam, and trade 271, 280, 298
Ismailia, population 77
Italy
  in East Africa 420-421
  and Libya 365, 367
  and Morocco 365
  and Tunisia 362
ivory
  exports 267, 372, 374-375, 386, 399-400, 402, 404, 407
  prices 380, 406
  trade 404-406
Ivory Coast
  colonization 385
  currency 282

ERRATA

We would like to call the attention of readers to the following errors. Please note that unless otherwise specified the lines are counted from the top to the bottom, excluding the page number and book or chapter title. We apologise for the inconvenience.

Currency Notation:

All references to '£E' should read '£' denoting British pound sterling, except for the following pages, where '£E' denotes Egyptian pound - 221; 267; 353; 408; 409.

Page 90 line 24	'12.6 million' should read '£12.6 million'
" 97 line 18	'9,073;655' should read '£9,073,655'
" 97 line 19	'1,037,046' and '82,130' should read '£1,037,046' and '£82,130'
" 298 lines 32-3	currency is 'MT$' not 'US$'.

Other Changes:

Page 221 lines 31-4	delete quotation marks.
" 232 line 32	'Rhodeshodes, Cecil' should read 'Rhodes'.
" 314 line 8	Delete 'wealthy' between 'the' and 'merchants'.
" 323 line 3	'Sotho-Sokoto' should read 'Sotho-Kololo'.
" 338 line 22	Italicized words in the preceding quote are 'three' and 'draught'.
" 363 line 4	After 'Britain' add the following: 'accounted for between three-quarters and two-thirds of Morocco's international trade'.
" 398 line 23	After 'Asia' delete words 'slave trade'.
" 406 line 5	'1930s' should read '1830s'.